LIFE

Letters Home from Lt. William R. Larson, USNR, a Beloved Son, Brother, and WWII Torpedo Bomber Fighter Pilot — Squadron VC 38

December 1, 1915 to December 27, 1943

Don J. Larson

Family Edition — June 2016

Contents

Preface

When I was a young boy of roughly seven or eight years of age, I richly remember climbing up the narrow, wooden staircase to the second floor of my grandparent's farmhouse in Sioux Trail Township, Divide County, North Dakota. At the top of the stairs, to the left, was an old steamer trunk with leather straps and metal buckles to safely secure the contents within. As the lid was opened, along with the creak of the hinge, an overwhelming scent of moth balls and old clothing filled the air. The trunk was stuffed full of olive-green and white uniforms, along with leather lambskin flight pants and jackets, an officer naval hat, dress shoes, naval grooming kit, and a yellow lifejacket. A pinewood naval trunk in the second-story bedroom just off to the south also contained a treasure-trove of items that were a wonderment to a young boy who grew up on the wind swept prairies of North Dakota—black and white photographs of planes and people, multi-colored postcards from New York, Alaska, Florida, and the Hawaiian Islands, a smoking pipe, and paper matchbooks from night clubs in Bermuda, Cuba, San Francisco, Hollywood, and New York.

As I dug deeper into the wooden trunk, there were stacks of letters with airmail postage marks, mostly from a naval address, and additional flight gear—goggles and aviation sunglasses. I remember clutching some of these items, running down the steps, and out of the house through the front porch screen door, and over to the nearest field, where my father was driving a tractor while summer fallowing. "*Dad, look what I found! Can I keep it?*" These were items that had been untouched for years and years, as my grandparents had carefully placed these items in William's old bedroom and never touched them again — until my two older brothers and I discovered them and started asking questions.

That naval trunk was eventually moved to Williston, North Dakota when my grandmother, Mary, moved into our old house on 909 Main Street. After her passing, the trunk ended up at our family home in Williston. The trunk, pictures, and letters were then all kept by my mother, Mary Ann, in an upstairs closet until we had to sell the family home in Williston for health reasons, and my mother moved out to an assisted living facility in Vancouver, Washington to be closer to me. Mary Ann had devotedly assembled a chronology of these letters and had presented us three boys with a copy in 2011. Not until this past winter, did I read the letters.

This is the story and history of my uncle William Rudolf Larson, nicknamed "Lucky." It is just one of about 300,000 stories that occurred in World War II. What makes this a unique story is that the story is in his own words. The letters in the pinewood trunk were Lieutenant William's letters home to his proud parents, Olaf and Mary Larson, and his kid-brother, Lloyd (my father).

After reading these letters, I began a journey researching William's naval voyages and the history of his fellow air squadron members. By chance luck in September 2013, I stumbled upon Walt Wagner, the son of William's radioman, Richard Wagner, who flew with William on bombing missions over the Solomon Islands. Walt's information on his father, Richard, was instrumental in filling in the canvas of Lucky's Life. At the same time, classified and top secret intelligence reports (declassified in

December 31, 2012) of William's squadron during the Bougainville Campaign of World War II, were discovered, and added tremendously to this story. This journey started off as a family history, but has now ended with a book on Lucky's life and a tribute to the airmen of Squadron VC 38 of World War II. I sincerely hope you enjoy the flight.

Donald James Larson
Portland Oregon
Winter 2013

Close Family of William Rudolf Larson

Martin Larson
Birth: Jan 20 1847, Norway
Death: Aug 19 1933, Farm, Todd County Minnesota

Olena Larson (Holmlie)
Birth: Jul 10 1847, Verdalen, Norway
Death: Apr 1 1941, Farm, Todd County Minnesota

Robert Johnson
Birth: Apr 30 1851, Hojet, Denmark
Death: Aug 24 1929, Hirsch, Saskatchewan Canada

Ellen Christine Johnson (Villads)
Birth: Aug 9 1868, Sondersted, Denmark
Death: Sep 22 1937, Bienfait, Saskatchewan Canada

Olaf M Larson
Birth: Jul 20 1885, Family Farm, Todd County Minnesota
Death: May 24 1964, Williston, North Dakota

Mary Larson (Johnson)
Birth: Dec 2 1891, La Moure, North Dakota
Death: Mar 7 1982, Williston, North Dakota

William Rudolf Larson
Birth: Dec 1 1915, Osakis, Minnesota
Death: Dec 27 1943, Pacific Ocean near New Caledonia

Lloyd Jerome Larson
Birth: Aug 20 1920, Family Farm, Sioux Trail Township, North Dakota
Death: May 15 1995, Williston, North Dakota

Mary Ann Larson (Valentine)
Birth: Nov 30 1935, Hope, North Dakota
Death: Jan 13 2016, Vancouver, Washington

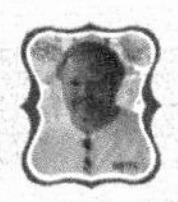

William Lloyd Larson
Birth: May 2 1962, Williston, North Dakota

David Jeffrey Larson
Birth: Jan 15 1964, Williston, North Dakota

Donald James Larson
Birth: Jun 28 1967, Williston, North Dakota

MyHeritage

Acknowledgments

For inspiring me to start this journey on my uncle's story, I thank my mother, Mary Ann V. Larson, for keeping safe William's naval trunk. For priceless help on researching the records of Air Group 38, I thank my neighbor and friend, Rick Bryant. For completing the final brushes on the canvas of Lucky's Life, I also thank Walt Wagner, whose father's war diary and photographs filled in the war story of 1943. Additional thanks goes to Daniel Leary, whose dad's photographs and maps of VC 38's WWII activities greatly contributed to the tribute to those brave men. Thanks also to my two brothers and friends for encouraging me along the way.

In memoriam to Lt. William Rudolf Larson (VC 38), Lt. Cmd. (USNR) John Risse Little (Bombing Squadron 98), Lt. (USNR) Kenneth Robert Speer, Lt. (jg-USNR) August George Kafer, Lt. (jg-USNR) Norman William Mackie, Lt. (jg-USNR) Donald Everett Winters, Lt. (jg-USNR) Glenn Guy Parker, the twelve gunners of Bombing Squadron 98 (VB-98), and the pilot, Captain Reynolds Hill Knotts (USMCR VMJ 153), and crew; 2nd Lt. John Thomas Jr. Felts (USMCR VMJ 153), Sgt. James C. Duignan (USMCR VMJ 153), Master Sargent (Mt Sgt.) Opal C. Hughes (USMCR VMJ 153), Mt Sgt. Louise White McCay (USMRC VMJ 153) of the R4D-5 transport plane which crashed near the Loyalty Islands on December 27th 1943, my grandparents Olaf and Mary Larson, and my beloved father, Lloyd Jerome Larson.

In grateful memory of William Rudolf Larson, who died in the service to his country at Sea, Pacific Area, Composite Squadron 38, 27 December 1943. He stands in the unbroken line of patriots who have dared to die that freedom might live, and grow, and increase its blessings. Freedom lives, and through it, he lives — in a way that humbles the undertakings of most men.

— Franklin D. Roosevelt

Guide to Abbreviations and Acronyms

Breton	USS Breton (CVE-23) was a Bogue class escort carrier of the United States Navy
Buttons	Code name of Espiritu Santo Airfield — New Hebrides
Cactus	Code name of Henderson Airfield — Guadalcanal
COMAIRSOLS	Commander Aircraft Solomons — AirSols units came from elements of the: United States Navy (USN), United States Marine Corps (USMC), the Royal New Zealand Air Force (RNZAF) and the Thirteenth Air Force, United States Army Air Forces (USAAF).
Copahee	USS Copahee (CVE-12) was a Bogue class escort carrier of the United States Navy
Dauntless	U.S. Navy/ Marine Douglas SBD dive-bomber
D.F.C.	Distinguished Flying Cross
Duck	Grumman J2F single engine amphibious biplane
F4F	U.S. Navy/Marine Grumman Wildcat fighter
F4U	Vought "Corsair" fighter

F6F	U.S. Navy Grumman Hellcat fighter
Glamour Ship	crew nickname of the USS Nashville Cruiser (CL-43)
Hellcat	U.S. Navy Grumman F6F carrier based fighter
J2F	J2F Duck — Grumman single engine amphibious biplane
Lucky	William's nickname from the USS Nashville
NAS	U.S. Naval Air Station
NAAS	U.S. Naval Auxiliary Air Station
P39	Bell Aircraft P39 Airacobra fighter
P40	Royal New Zealand Air Force Curtiss "Warhawk" fighter
R4D-5	Navy Transport Aircraft built by Douglas Aircraft company (C-47 Skytrain — the military version of the DC-3)
Saratoga	USS Saratoga (CV-3) was a Lexington-class aircraft carrier built for the United States Navy during the 1920s
SCAT	South Pacific Air Transport
SBD	U.S. Navy/Marine Douglas Dauntless dive-bomber
SHAG	Code name of Munda Airfield
SNJ	North American T-6 Texan Plane (trainer) — Naval designation
SOC	U.S. Navy Scout Observation Plane (Seagull) — seaplane

TBF	U.S. Navy/Marine Grumman Avenger carrier torpedo/light bomber
USNR	United States Naval Reserve
USS	United States Ship (in a ship name)
VB	U.S. Navy dive bomber squadron
VC	U.S. Navy combined squadron; fighters, dive bombers, torpedo bombers
VF	U.S. Navy fighter squadron
VGS	U.S. Navy escort scouting squadron
VMF	U.S. Marine fighter squadron
VMJ	U.S. Marine utility squadron
VMSB	U.S. Marine scout-bombing squadron
VMTB	US Marine torpedo squadron
VT	U. S. Navy Torpedo bombing squadron
Wildcat	U.S. Navy/Marine F4F Wildcat fighter
Zero	Imperial Navy Mitsubishi A6M fighter

INTRODUCTION

The Early Years & Family Background

My uncle, William Rudolf Larson, was born at Osakis, Minnesota, on December 1st, 1915, to Olaf and Mary Larson. He grew up on the family farm in Sioux Trail Township, Divide County, North Dakota, where his father homesteaded in 1909. He had one kid-brother, Lloyd (my father), who was five years younger. William attended the local rural school in Sioux Trail and graduated May 29, 1929. He entered high school at Sioux Trail, and then spent his senior year at Grenora High School, Grenora, North Dakota, graduating on June 1, 1933.

William then studied at Concordia College in Moorhead, Minnesota, graduating June 7th, 1937, with a Bachelor of Arts

Concordia Graduation — 1937 (21 yrs old)

degree. While William was attending Concordia College he wrote, "Study Myself" in November 1934. It is a self-reflective study on his heritage, education and present self. It provides a tremendous background on William's family and his experiences growing up in Sioux County Township, Divide County, North Dakota. The following 9 pages are excerpts of that study.

"I have written this, the story of my life, in order that I might become better acquainted with myself and my ancestors. In the light of my heritage, environment, and training, I can more readily understand my present traits. The story is divided into three main divisions: (1) my heredity; (2) my education; and (3) my present and future self. My family tree will be found in the rear of the book. With references to the key, the family tree will be easily understood. The few pictures in the book will give the reader a better understanding of the author's physical development. A picture of my home and family is also contained in this book.

I wish to thank my parents, Mr. and Mrs. Olaf M. Larson, Hanks, North Dakota, for so kindly giving me the necessary information on my heritage."

November 1934 William Larson — To My Loving Parents

MY HERITAGE

Just a few months ago I stood within an old dilapidated farm home near Osakis, Minnesota. I felt a sort of reverence and respect for that house, because it was here that I was born on December 1, 1915. Shortly after my arrival, my mother took me out to the rugged prairies of northwestern North Dakota where my father had taken a homestead. I grew up on those prairies and learned to love them.

My great-grand parents on my father's side were all hardy, hard working Norsemen. They were carpenters and farmers. They were pious people and lived to be very old. Family ties were strong. All of them died in Norway.

My grandfather on my father's side came to America and homesteaded near Osakis, Minnesota. He was a successful farmer and carpenter. He was very healthy and a hard worker throughout his life. My grandfather, Martin Larson, died at the age of eighty-seven.

Christian Holmlie, my great-grandfather on my father's mother's side, was also a farmer. He and his wife died at an old age in Norway.

Jorgen Jorgenson, my great-grandfather on my mother's father's side, was a tailor and small farmer. He and his wife died at the age of eighty in Denmark. His wife, Maren, wrote beautiful letters and poems. They were pious, joyful, and contented people. They had seven children: (1) Fred Johnson, as Jorgenson was changed to Johnson after coming to America, was the oldest child. He was a strong, healthy farmer. He died a wealthy retired farmer, in Los Angeles, at the age of eighty-two. (2) Peter Johnson was a tailor at Paris, Missouri. He had two children who are now instructors in high-school. He died at about eighty years of age. (3) Robert Johnson, my grandfather, was once a cook on a steamboat. He liked to eat and was fat ever since I can remember him. He took a homestead at La Moure, North Dakota and died a farmer. He did not believe in an education. If his children knew how to cook and work, he thought that was all that was necessary. He was in comfortable circumstances as long as he lived. He died at the age of seventy-two at Hirsch, Saskatchewan, Canada. (4) Nels Johnson died a prosperous farmer at the age of seventy at Osakis, Minnesota. (5) Christine Frederickson is a store keeper's wife in Copenhagen, Denmark. (6) Christian Johnson is a sergeant in the army at Copenhagen; (7) Mary Low is a retired farmer's wife and lives in comfortable circumstances at Oakes, North Dakota.

William, Mother Mary & Grandmother Ellen March 18 1916

Marie Villads[1]*, my great-grandmother on my mother's mother's side, was a poetess. She had dark eyes and black hair. After her husband died, she made her living by selling her books of poems. Some of her poems were written especially for the King of Denmark. She was very healthy, full of fun, and enjoyed living. When about sixty-five years old she came to America. She died at the age of seventy-five at La Moure, North Dakota.*

My father was the fifth child of a family of seven children. The children in order are: Carl Larson, Osakis, Minnesota; Mrs. Anna Johnson, Osakis, Minnesota, Mrs. Julia Johnson,

1 Marie Villads's poetry is on collection at The Royal Library in Copenhagen, Denmark. She visited King Christian IX and met the Czar of Russia at Fredensborg Castle. She was supported by Princess Marie and received a royal wage of 50 kroner a year before she left to America.

William Age of 2 1/2 yrs

Sherwood, North Dakota; Marius Larson, Hanks, North Dakota; Olaf M. Larson, Hanks, North Dakota; Mrs. Lena Brakken, Zahl, North Dakota; and Mrs. Mary Aasboe, deceased. My father has always been a healthy, strong man. He has black hair, brown eyes, high cheek bones, and is quite large. He likes to read the papers and keeps well posted on the affairs of the day. He is a firm believer in a good education and I admire him for trying to give his children an education in spite of present difficulties. He has a keen, alert mind and is very good in mathematics. He does not smoke, drink, or chew, so has been a good example for his two sons, Lloyd, my younger brother, and myself. Although he does not attend church regularly, I am certain that he has firm religious convictions at heart. My father homesteaded in Northwestern North Dakota about 1909. He erected good buildings within a few years, secured good farm equipment, and has lived there ever since. He is now forty-eight years old.

My mother, Mary Larson, was the second child of a family of four. The children in order are: William Johnson, Fargo, North Dakota; Mrs. Mary Larson, Hanks, North Dakota; Eli Johnson, Hirsch, Saskatchewan, Canada; and Mrs. Esther Finstad, Hirsch, Saskatchewan, Canada. My mother is now forty-two years old, has brown hair and blue eyes, is quite stout, and is strong and healthy. As she taught school for five years before marrying my father, she has a good general education. She likes music, is a good singer, and can play the piano. She tries to attend church regularly and wants her children to do so too. My mother enjoys taking part in the social life of our community. She is an active and interested member of several clubs and associations in the community. She, too, believes in a good education and is making great sacrifices in order that her children might have the chance to obtain one.

MY EDUCATION

William's Family (1925) Right-to-Left: Olaf, Lloyd, William, Mary

My parents have always been lenient with me and have let me make decisions and think things out for myself. This gave me a self-reliant quality and a feeling of trustworthiness. It was from my parents that I first learned about God, the difference between right and wrong, and many important facts of life. Going to school taught me how to associate with others. Living in the country taught me to love animals and nature.

As a child, I enjoyed very much to play with mechanical toys. As a youth I enjoyed working with tractors, trucks, cars, and machinery. I started working in the fields with machinery at a very early age. This was not because I had to but because I wanted to, and felt as though I was grown up. I was only thirteen years old when I first hired out to run a Wallace tractor in the harvest fields. How grown up I felt as I was now actually running a tractor! And, incidentally, it was through this experience that I earned my first money, and learned the value of it. Because of this knowledge I have always used considerable judgment in spending money.

The sports I have always enjoyed are skiing, baseball, and basketball. I started boxing when I was in the fifth grade and am indebted to a neighbor boy, Boyd Brakken, for learning the manly art of self-defense. He owned a set of boxing gloves and gave me a bloody nose so many times that I just had to learn to box in order to get even with him. I was extremely thankful for this early training in self-defense, for it came in handy many times throughout grade school and will again, possibly in the future.

I lived three miles from a consolidated country school, Sioux Trail Consolidated. I attended this same school from the time I was in the first grade until I was in the fourth year of high school. I graduated from the Grenora High School, Grenora, North Dakota and am now in my sophomore year at Concordia College, Moorhead, North Dakota. During the summers, I attended Norwegian, or parochial school. After a few summers attendance at this school, I was confirmed by Rev. Dydvik in 1928.

Confirmation Picture
(13 yrs old)

I had an average of ninety-three and a fraction in my four years of high school. I received a Concordia scholarship for maintaining this average. Last year I made seventy-five dollars by maintaining a B average during the first semester of college work.

As the grade teachers provided no special play for the children during recess and noon, the children frequently rid themselves of surplus energy by fighting. There was one boy whom I especially enjoyed fighting with — not because I could handle him but because he enjoyed fighting with me too. He was sort of a sneaky fellow — always trying to get me on the sly. Later on, when games were provided during noon and recess, we quit fighting, but we still had no love for each other.

I had no special dislike for any subjects in high school. This is probably due to the way Mr. and Mrs. Warner Peterson, whom I consider as the best teachers I have ever had, taught them. Mr. and Mrs. Warner Peterson were my high school teachers up to the senior year. It was through them that I learned how to really study. It was they who organized the first basket-ball team at Sioux Trail, started a school paper, organized the P.T.A., organized the young citizens' league, put on plays, and woke Sioux Trail up generally.

William Rudolph Larson
about 2 yrs old.

I remember that I used to swear quite a bit when I was small. I had learned it from various hired men. When I was just beginning to ice skate I use to swear every time I fell down. My aunt, Mrs. Anna Johnson, told me that God makes me fall as a punishment for swearing. I immediately made every effort possible to prevent swearing or cussing. By the time I had learned to skate without falling I had also broken the habit *of cussing. Ever since this experience I have sworn very little.*

I believe I am an honest person. My first experience in honesty came about in the following way: When I was very young, I broke a steel tape-measure which my father had said I should not play with. As soon as I had broken it I became afraid, and hid it. Later, my father, knowing I had broken the tape-measure, asked me if I had broken it. I told him I hadn't. Then he told me it would be better for me to tell the truth than to tell a lie and try to escape punishment. By this time my conscience was bothering me very much. I burst into tears and told him the truth. He did not punish me but said it was always the best policy to tell the truth. This little lesson in honesty stuck with me ever since.

Physically I was a tough, hardy little fellow. I was also stubborn in some ways. I never wanted to put on new clothes and very few old clothes even in the heart of winter. On a very cold day in the middle of a hard winter I walked out of the house without cap or coat, took my toboggan, and struggled through deep snow on my way over to see a neighbor boy who lived one-half mile east of our place. When I finally arrived at his place, my ears were entirely frozen. A blister the size of a hen's egg soon appeared on each ear. If that neighbor boy's mother, Mrs. Holman, had not known just what to do for me I would have had some sorry looking ears today. Although I was in extreme pain, I made the most of it — I wanted to be tough! I have had to be tough, too, to go through some of my experiences such as having my lips and hand cut up by running into a barbed wire fence on a toboggan, being run over by a drill, and falling eighty feet to the plank floor of a grain elevator.

When I was a just old enough to walk, I used to sneak away from the house and walk way over to my cousin's place which was one mile west of my home. The only language that my cousin, Olaf Johnson, could talk and understand

Brother Lloyd and William (Age 16)

was Norwegian; the only language I could handle was English. In spite of this difficulty, we enjoyed frequent playtimes together very much. It was through him that I became familiar with the Norwegian language. It was through me that he became familiar with the English language.

I have had no outstanding fears. However, I was afraid of the dark for several years during my childhood. This was due to a scare I received in the dark from one of our hired men. I believe I have had as much courage, though, as other children of my age.

***Study Myself* by WR Larson is included in Appendix A.**

Following his college graduation from Concordia, William moved back to northwestern North Dakota and taught science and mathematics to freshman students at Arnegard High School, Arnegard, North Dakota, for two years. He then enlisted and trained at the U.S. Naval Reserve Aviation Base at Wold-Chamberlain Airport in Minneapolis, Minnesota from June 15 to July 14, 1939.

This time period is at the end of The Great Depression (1929 — 1939), which caused many farmers to lose their cattle and land. By 1936, almost one-half of North Dakotans were receiving government aid. By 1939, one-third of the state's farmers had lost their lands. My grandparents were not spared these troubles. Family stories include receiving government aid of barrels of molasses that the family poured on bales of thistles to encourage the cattle to feed on what was available — drought had reduced the prairie's ability to sustain cattle. At one time, my grandfather also moved his cattle herd to eastern North Dakota during The Great Depression so the cattle would survive and not starve. Reviewing family land deeds from this time, my grandfather lost some land back to the bank and government due to unpaid taxes. Times were tough in 1939, especially in western North Dakota.

My family has no letters or notes on why William decided to quit teaching and join the peacetime U.S. Naval Reserve in 1939. Those who would have known are gone now. Family speculation is that it was perhaps to aid the family financially. William makes references throughout his story of sending money back to his kid brother for college tuition and to his folks on the family farm. His monthly rate of pay while training at Wold-Chamberlain Airport was $36.

Whatever the reasons were in 1939, it is here where our story begins — the story of Lucky. With his courage, skill, and splendid judgment, he became a great naval aviator flying off the back of a U.S. Naval cruiser in the Bering Sea and eventually flying from aircraft carriers and jungle airfields in the Solomon Islands during World War II. Lucky's story is HIS STORY — his words from letters and postcards written home to the family farm located in Hanks, North Dakota.

U.S.NAVAL RESERVE AVIATION BASE
WOLD-CHAMBERLAIN AIRPORT
MINNEAPOLIS, MINNESOTA.

23 February 1939

Mr. William R. Larson
Arnegard, North Dakota,

Dear Sir:

You are requested to report at this Base for interview and flight physical examination on Saturday March 4th 1939, at 8:30, AM.. Travel will be at your own expense and the examination may take the entire day. It is suggested you bring an inexpensive pair of dark glasses to wear after eye refraction.

Your formal application complete with documentary data must be on file at this Base before completion of physical examination.

Please advise promptly whether you will report at designated time.

Yours very truly

C.S.Smiley
C.S.Smiley
Lieut.Comdr.U.S.Navy
Commanding Officer.

Enlisted as Seaman, second class, V-5, USNR Date 2 June, 1939

At USNRAB, Minneapolis, Minn. for four full years

Born December 1, 1915 at Osakis, Minnesota

Ratings held S2c, V-5, USNR

Special duties for which qualified ---

Trade or Service Schools attended None

Served on active or training duty on the following vessels and stations:

USNRAB, Minneapolis, Minn. 6/15/39 - 7/14/39
" " " 9/21/39 (1 day only)

Total number of drills and equivalent instruction or duty periods performed None

Final average in all marks upon discharge ----

DESCRIPTIVE LIST

Strike out one { Made after careful examination at date of discharge. / ~~[struck out]~~

Height 5 feet 9 inches. Weight 140 lbs.

Eyes Hazel V1 Normal Hair Dk.Brown Complexion Ruddy

Personal marks, etc. Vac. sc. lft. arm, V shaped sc. ¼", upper lip. Lin. sc. back head ½", Mole abv. rt. buttock, Irreg. sc. base rt. ind. fgr.

~~Has~~ / Has not } disqualifying defects (List here defects)

None

L.M.Hammerstad
L.M.Hammerstad, Lieut. (jg) MC-V(G) {U.S.N.R.
(Signature Medical Officer or Commanding Officer)

Monthly rate of pay when discharged $36.00

I hereby certify that William Rudolph LARSON

has been paid One - - - - dollars and nineteen-- cents ($ 1.19--------) in full to date.

OR

~~XXXXXXXXXXX~~

~~XXXXXXXXXXXXXXXXXXXXXXXXXXXXXX~~
(Strike out one)

21 September, 1939 Total net services for pay purposes - years months days.

(Supply or Commanding Officer's Signature) {U.S.N.

U.S. GOVERNMENT PRINTING OFFICE 4—7079

Navy Training Planes (N3N-1) — Chamberlain Airfield
Minneapolis, Minnesota — 1939

William on Left — 1939, Chamberlain Airfield

William trained at Chamberlain Airfield, MN starting in June 1939 and was discharged September 21, 1939 to accept an appointment as an Aviation Cadet at Pensacola, Florida. While at Chamberlain Airfield, William flew N3N-1 planes, recorded 11.7 hours of flying, and was in flight training class with six other pilots. The commanding officer at Chamberlain Airfield was Lt. Commander C.S. Smiley.[2]

N. Nav. 213
(July, 1931)

DEPARTMENT OF THE NAVY
BUREAU OF NAVIGATION

CERTIFICATE OF DISCHARGE

United States Naval Reserve

THIS IS TO CERTIFY that William Rudolph LARSON 410-55-36
(Name in full) (Service Number)

a Seaman, Second Class, V-5, U.S.N.R., has this day been discharged from
(Rating—do not abbreviate)

the U.S.Naval Reserve Aviation Base, Minneapolis, Minnesota, and from the U. S. NAVAL RESERVE
(Ship or organization)

by reason of own request (Special Order of C.O.) to accept appointment as Aviation Cadet
(Enter expiration of enlistment, order Bureau of Navigation (date) or other reason)

with G O O D discharge, this 21st day of September, 1939
(Character of discharge)

Is ---- recommended for reenlistment.

C. S. Smiley, Lieut. Comdr. {U. S. N. / U. S. N. R.
Commanding Officer,
USNRAB, Minneapolis, Minn.

4—7079

2 Curtis Stanton Smiley would later serve as Captain Smiley of the escort carrier USS Rudyerd Bay during World War II

William on Left — 1939, Chamberlain Airfield

The seven members of flight training class at Chamberlain Airfield — William seated on chair — date of completion was 14 July 1939

CHAPTER 1

Time at US NAS Pensacola Florida

Timeline:
Germany Invades Poland on September 1 1939

Off to Pensacola Florida Flight School September 18 1939 — wood plank sidewalk of the Family Farm at Hanks, North Dakota (23 years of age)

"**Dear Folks**, Here's the train a couple of us took from Mpls. to Chicago. Arrived here at 8:30 late last night. Leave for Birmingham at 2:30 this P.M. Stayed with Lloyd in Moorhead and Ole at Mpls, Your Son William."

September 23 1939 Postcard Home

William and a N3N1 Plane at Corry Field

Part of the warm-up line at Corry Field

View of Corry Field Pensacola Florida - November 1939

"***Dear Lloyd,*** I'm skipping ground school this morning so will drop you a line and some cash. Glad to hear that you received high marks in all your subjects and pulled an A in Chem. Too bad Longhammerer isn't there to give you some real chemistry. That beautiful blond seems to attract your attentions every once in a while. Well, I found one down here a couple of weeks ago that's really interesting as well as pleasantly pretty. Eyes of blue, five foot two, shapely, intelligent, and very cautious — a point which I consider as being decidedly in her favor. She works for the G Motors Acceptance Corp. She knows nothing of wild western N. Dak either. A "chippie" might be synonymous with "bag" — everybody's girl, dense, smokes, drinks, and is game for anything. There are plenty of those here — but this blonde isn't one of them.

N3N1 Plane

Finished flying in Squadron three this week and checked in at Squadron one. We were flying nine-plane formations which was fun but hard on nerves. You have to stay in position pretty well or run the risk of getting your tail clipped off. We're scheduled for seven weeks in Sq. 1 and two in Sq. 5 after which we receive the golden wings (on payment of $4.00). I've been assigned to scouting and observation duty which will be on cruisers or battleships — if I finish. Won't get a crack at those big patrol boats in Sq.4 but I'm not too disappointed. They weigh about 8 tons and fly like a freight-train. We get a couple of weeks leave when we finish here so will be home then. Saw F.D.R. come down the gang-plank yesterday. He just returned from that little fishing trip. Didn't see the fish however. Your brother, Bill."

March 2 1940 Letter to Brother Lloyd
— US NAS Pensacola Florida, Flight Log Entry
for March 4 1940: N3N1 plane -1 HR flight

William's aviation training at US NAS Pensacola, Florida, included student ground school and flying school in four squadrons. Ground school included aircraft engines and structures, navigation and tactics, gunnery, communication, and aerology. His flight school included 184.6 hours of solo flying, 71.4 hours of dual flying, and 28 hours as a passenger. William soloed his first plane at Pensacola on Monday, November 6th, 1939.

William completed catapulting training in a seaplane on March 29, 1940 and graduated in flight class 130-C. A Fitness Report, dated January 22, 1940, and signed by instructor William H. Grevemeyer, Captain, USMCR, remarked, *"Cadet Larson has*

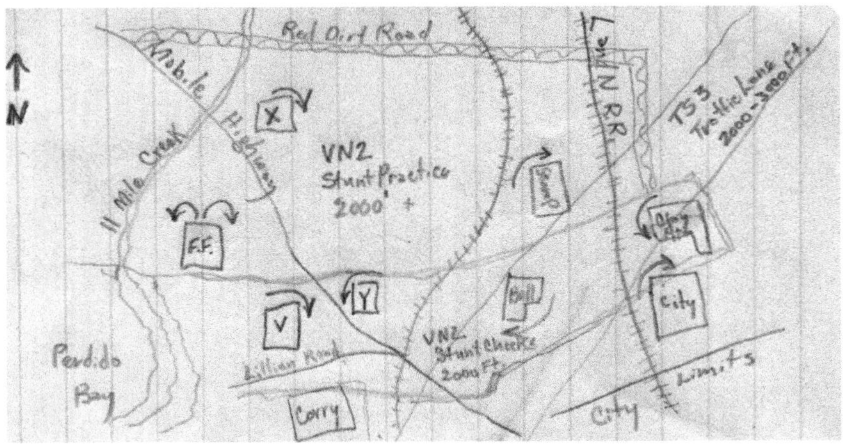

Hand-sketched Map of Corry Field by William

been a hard worker and willing student. He has shown an above average progress in his work. He has a very cheerful disposition and has a good moral character. He has handled his regular and additional duties in an efficient and military manner." William, however, had a few close calls during his flight training at Pensacola. On April 23, 1940, he was warned for dangerous flight conduct. Lieutenant R.J. Greene, USNR of Squadron Four, reported, *"Squadron One plane #56 [flown by William], leader of a 2-plane formation, left the formation in a break up by making a wing-over into a dive headed above my plane #21 from an altitude about 800 feet higher. I was at 1000 feet over the shoreline between Fair Point and Deer Point. Student continued dive until dangerously close, and I nosed plane over to avoid being hit if student continued course. This student apparently saw me when about 300 to 400 feet above me and made an abrupt turn to the left to avoid me. The plane was close enough to make the situation very dangerous."* William's response was, *"I was not intentionally diving on patrol plane as I failed to see it until after I started a shallow dive. On seeing the plane I immediately nosed up."* He was assigned a mark of 1.0 that day in aptitude (scale of 1.0 to 4.0) on his flight instruction record. William's Final Report of Aviation Training from NAS Pensacola, Florida, is included in Appendix B.

Ensign Rank — April 1940

"**Dear Lloyd,** Seems as though these money orders are getting more rare, and smaller, but it's the best I can do. When we start getting that ensign's pay we'll pay the Concordia shylocks[3] off in fine shape. For some unknown reason living expenses

3 William's kid brother, Lloyd, was attending Concordia College in Moorhead, MN at the time.

seem to go up with the advance of spring. Hope you had enough to get away for Easter vacation. We worked as usual here. Went to Lutheran church Sunday morning. All five Concordia students were there. Haven't done much flying the past weeks. Have to wait for the group ahead of us to finish navigation hops. Two students ride together on a nav. hop. One is pilot and the other is radioman. Each hop is 150-200 miles long. The pilot is navigator and the radioman keeps contact with the base. Guess I didn't tell you about catapult shots, a cannon attached to a fifty foot platform gives you a "snappy" take off. The first time I was shot off I didn't know what the score was until we were out in the middle of the bay. Seventeen pounds of gun powder moves you in a hurry.

Mary Glenn Grimmes — Tallahassee, Florida

The cadet glee club took quite a trip to the Florida State College for Women at Tallahassee this weekend. The campus was beautiful — and some of the 2000 girls were likewise. A blonde senior from Tampa helped me enjoy the stay. Some of us had supper at the sorority Sat. night. After the "concert," which was just a minor event, we had a dance. The girls did all the cutting. Yep, it was a great place for a fellow with a uniform and brass buttons. Too bad it's 212 miles away. . . . Hope to see you about the time school is out. Your brother, Bill."

April 1 1940 Letter to Brother Lloyd
— US NAS Pensacola Florida

THE

President of the United States of America.

To all who shall see these presents, greeting:

Know Ye, that reposing special Trust and Confidence in the Patriotism, Valor, Fidelity and Abilities of WILLIAM RUDOLPH LARSON I do appoint him AN ENSIGN in the Naval Reserve of The United States Navy to rank from the FIFTEENTH day of APRIL 1940 He is therefore carefully and diligently to discharge the duties of such office by doing and performing all manner of things thereunto belonging.

And I do strictly charge and require all Officers, Seamen and Marines under his Command to be obedient to his orders. And he is to observe and follow such orders and directions from time to time as he shall receive from me, or the future President of The United States of America, or his Superior Officer set over him, according to the Rules and Discipline of the Navy.

This Commission to continue in force during the pleasure of the President of the United States, for the time being.

Done at the City of Washington this THIRTEENTH day of JUNE in the year of our Lord One Thousand Nine Hundred and FORTY and of the Independence of The United States of America the One Hundred and SIXTY-FOURTH.

By the President:

[signature]
ACTING Secretary of the Navy

1140

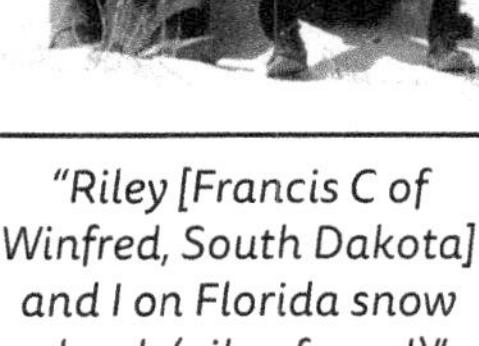

"Riley [Francis C of Winfred, South Dakota] and I on Florida snow bank (pile of sand)" — 1940

NAS Pensacola, FL. — 1939

Ensign Rank – April 1940

N. Nav. 360
(Rev. April 1939)

APPOINTMENT IN NAVAL RESERVE

Nav 1641 CFC
83169-4

June 25, 1940

From: THE CHIEF OF THE BUREAU OF NAVIGATION, NAVY DEPARTMENT.

To: Ensign William Rudolph Larson, A-V(N), USNR,
Naval Air Station, Pensacola, Florida.

Via: Commandant, Naval Air Station, Pensacola, Florida.

Subject: Appointment in United States Naval Reserve.

Inclosure: (A) Commission.

1. Having been appointed an Ensign in the United States Naval Reserve to rank from April 15, 1940, the Bureau takes pleasure in transmitting herewith your commission, dated June 13, 1940. You are hereby assigned to the Volunteer Reserve for Aviation Duties effective on the date you execute acceptance and oath of office under your commission.

C. W. NIMITZ
Chief of Bureau.

J. B. Lynch
(By direction)

ACCEPTANCE AND OATH OF OFFICE

I, William Rudolph Larson, do hereby accept the above appointment, and having been appointed an Ensign in the United States Naval Reserve, do solemnly swear (or affirm) that I will support and defend the Constitution of the United States against all enemies, foreign and domestic; that I will bear true faith and allegiance to the same; that I take this obligation freely, without any mental reservation or purpose of evasion; and that I will well and faithfully discharge the duties of the office on which I am about to enter: So help me God.

U.S. Naval Air Station
Pensacola, Florida } ss: William Rudolph LARSON
(Signature)

Subscribed and sworn to before me this 1st day of July, 1940.

A. C. READ,
(Signature and official title)
Captain, U.S. Navy.

(INSTRUCTIONS ON REVERSE SIDE)

4—6975

United States Naval Air Station

Pensacola, Florida

Know all men by these presents that

Ensign William R. Larson, A V(N) U.S.N.R.

has completed the prescribed course of training as a Student Naval Aviator and, having met successfully all the requirements of the course, has been designated a

Naval Aviator

In Witness Whereof, *this certificate has been signed on this 1st day of July 1940, and the Seal of the Naval Air Station hereunto affixed*

Captain, U.S. Navy
Commandant

Commander, U.S. Navy
Executive Officer

Lieut-Commander U.S. Navy
Superintendent of Aviation Training

Front Row L to R: William R Larson, Charles H. Mester Jr. (Langeloth, PA — later a Rear Admiral and recipient of 2 Navy Crosses), William J Denholm Jr. (Elizabeth, NJ). Back Row: Marion K Smith (Union City, GA), Lief O Johnson (Jamestown, ND), Anthony J Schultheis Jr. (Little Falls, MN — later a Lt. Commander and recipient of the Navy Cross). — April 1940 NAS Pensacola — Naval Aviators

"The Five Flying Cobbers" — Front Row L to R: Delwin A Liane (Lisbon, ND), Leif O Johnson (Jamestown, ND) Back Row: William R Larson, Philmore A Dahlberg (Audubon, MN), Einar R Solo (Nevis, MN) — April 1940 — Naval Aviators

"**Dear Folks**, Expected to be on my way home now but here I sit waiting for orders. Completed instrument flying and check last Friday. Expect my orders tomorrow however so will be home the end of this week or beginning of next. William."

June 25 1940 Postcard Home — Pensacola Florida

"He [William] graduated at Pensacola, Florida in 1940. Came home in a new car. We took him to San Pedro, Calif. after 2 weeks. We all went and visited Medora, Yellowstone Park, Salt Lake City, etc. Drove 4,695 miles. Went thru 10 different states. (Came home along the Pacific for 1200 miles.) Went thru the Redwoods, wonderful!" — Mother Mary Larson's note on back of photo-frame and family pictures.

William and his new 1940 Pontiac sedan — July 1940 at Aunt Esther's (Canada)

1940-FLORIDA AUTOMOBILE REGISTRATION CARD-1940

William Larson

Street Address Naval Air Station

9 D 1949

County Escambia City Pensacola, FLORIDA

Is Owner's Residence Rural ☐, or Within Corporate Limits of City ☐.

Date 6/24/40 Make Pontiac No. Cyls 6 Type Sedan

Eng. No. 6-739086 Pass. Capacity 4 Weight

Kind of Fuel Used (Gasoline, Diesel or Other) gasoline

T. C. No. App new Date Acquired 6/24/40 (Month, Day, Year) Year Make 1940

Model P6HA Serial No. P6HA 67919 '39 Tag No. new

Use private No. Wheels 5

Amt. Sent with App. $ 7.50 Additional Paid $ 1.50

MAIL PLATE TO (Name & Address)

1 D. W. FINLEY, Motor Vehicle Commissioner, Tallahassee, Florida.

25c SERVICE FEE ON EACH APPLICATION

Nav 1641 OFC
83169-5

NAVY DEPARTMENT
BUREAU OF NAVIGATION
WASHINGTON, D. C.
June 25, 1940.

From: The Chief of the Bureau of Navigation.
To: Ensign William R. LARSON, A-V(N), USNR, Naval Air Station, Pensacola, Florida.
Via: Commandant, Naval Air Station, Pensacola, Florida.

Subject: Orders to active duty, and change of duty.

1. When directed by the Commandant, Naval Air Station, Pensacola, Florida, upon completion of active duty undergoing training and acceptance of appointment as Ensign, A-V(N), U. S. Naval Reserve, you will regard yourself detached from your present station; and will proceed to San Pedro, Calif., and report to the Senior Officer Present, Fleet Air Detachment, Naval Air Station, for active duty involving flying in Cruiser Scouting Squadron Eight (U.S.S. Nashville). Report also by letter to the Commanding Officer, U.S.S. Nashville, for this duty.

2. These orders constitute your assignment to duty in a part of the Aeronautic Organization of the Navy, and you are hereby detailed to duty involving flying, effective upon the date of reporting in obedience to these orders.

3. You are authorized to delay for a period of 15 days in reporting in obedience to these orders, such delay to count as leave. Upon the commencement of the leave you will immediately inform this bureau of the exact date, and upon the expiration thereof you will return the attached form, giving dates of commencement and expiration of leave. Keep the Bureau of Navigation and your new station advised of your address.

4. You reported for active duty undergoing training on September 25, 1939. The amount of the monthly premium on your $10,000 government life insurance policy is $6.70.

5. The records of this bureau show that you are not drawing a pension, disability allowance, disability compensation, or retired pay from the Government of the United States.

C. W. NIMITZ.

Copy to: Bu Aero
Comdt NAS Pensacola, Fla.
CO USS Nashville
CO Cruiser Scout Squad 8
ComCruDiv 8
SOP FAD NAS San Pedro, Calif.

Lloyd, William, and Olaf— "On our way to San Pedro CA in William's new Pontiac. In Yellowstone Park" — July 20, 1940 (mother Mary was taking the picture)

William, Olaf, and Lloyd— July 1940, San Pedro California

Buddy Ranch near Medora, N.D. - July 19, 1940, our first night lodging on that big trip (mother Mary's notes) – Lloyd, mother Mary, & William

CHAPTER 2

Days Aboard the USS Nashville (1940 to 1942)

After earning his wings, William was ordered to report to USS Nashville — San Pedro, California, on June 25, 1940, to fly with Cruiser Scouting Squadron Eight. William served on the USS Nashville from approximately July 15, 1940, to September 25, 1942. William and his fellow seamen affectionately referred to the ship as "The Glamour Ship." William flew sea-recovered float planes (SON and SOC planes) that were catapulted off the back of the cruiser and then hoisted out by crane. "*A cannon attached to a fifty foot platform gives you a "snappy" take off. The first time I was shot off I didn't know what the score was until we were out in the middle of the bay. Seventeen pounds of gun powder moves you in a hurry.*" SOC meant that it was a scout/observation (SO) aircraft produced by Curtis -Wright (C). The USS Nashville received 10 Battle Stars by the end of World War II.

"Here's our happy home. The aviation hangar is in the back end where you can see the crane. We have four planes." (Author's Note: This is the St. Johns Bridge of Portland Oregon — just 4 miles from my current home on the Columbia River. USS Nashville visited Portland Oregon during Fleet Week of July 23, 1939.)

(Photo Source: National Archives, photo no. 19-N-28993)

USS Nashville (CL-43), a Brooklyn-class light cruiser, was laid down on 24 January 1935 by New York Shipbuilding Corporation, Camden, New Jersey; launched on 2 October 1937; sponsored by Misses Ann and Mildred Stahlman; and commissioned on 6 June 1938, Captain William W. Wilson in command.

Early service

In the spring of 1939, Nashville carried American representatives to the Pan American Defense Conference in Rio de Janeiro, Brazil, returning them to Annapolis, Maryland on 20 June 1939. On 23 June, she steamed westwards from Norfolk, Virginia for the Pacific via the Panama Canal, arriving at San Pedro, California, on 16

July for two years of operations. In February 1941, she and three other cruisers carried US Marines to Wake Island. On 20 May, she departed Pearl Harbor for the east coast, arriving Boston on 19 June to escort a convoy carrying Marines to Iceland.

World War II

From August–December 1941, Nashville was based at Bermuda for the Neutrality Patrol in the Central Atlantic. With the bombing of Pearl Harbor, Nashville steamed to Casco Bay, Maine, where she joined with a troop and cargo convoy to escort them to Iceland. She continued escort duty to Bermuda and Iceland until February 1942.

"***Dear Folks***, Flew to San Diego today. The old plane had lots of pep with no wheels on. Wish I could be home for turkey tomorrow. Your son, William."

November 20 1940 Postcard Home
— Terminal Island NAS California

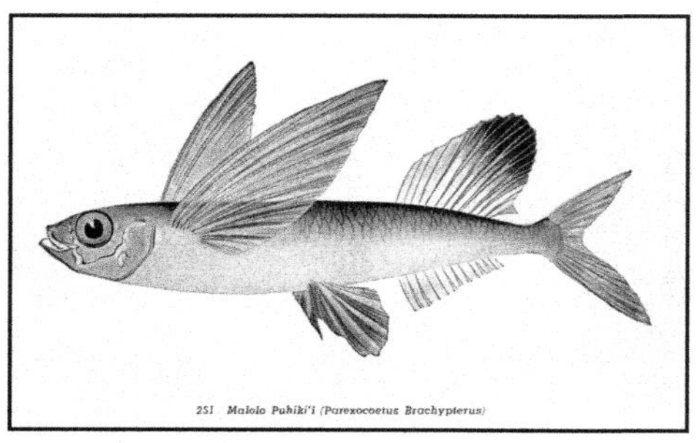

"***Dear Folks***, Thanks a lot for the swell birthday presents and cards. . . . Have been doing plenty of flying this week. Flew to San Diego again today. This is a picture of the fish we saw flying around the ocean. About 12" long. Your son, William."

December 4 1940 Postcard Home — Terminal Island NAS California

William's time on the USS Nashville was filled with challenges and adventures. Prior to the start of WW II, the USS Nashville operated on the west coast based out of San Pedro, California. In February 1941, Lucky and the crew of The Glamour Ship ferried US Marines to Wake Island, returning to Pearl Harbor. On May 20th 1941, the ship set sail for the east coast, via the Panama Canal, to Norfolk, Virginia and landed the first US Marines on Iceland. William's letter home, dated June 17, 1941 presents details of that voyage.

"***Dear Folks***, Was very glad to hear from everybody at home and get all the news. A destroyer met us at sea yesterday and gave us a much welcomed month's accumulation of mail. I received six of your letters — May 26 to June 30. We left Boston — and the States — shortly after I telephoned home. It's been plenty chilly, but a pleasant relief from the sultry climate we were used to. The flying weather is much poorer here however, too much fog, or high winds with a very rough, choppy sea. We put in a considerable amount of flying though. Think I have about 850 hours now. Our new heavy leather jackets have been put to good use.

At sea
June 17, 1941

Dear Folks,

Was very glad to hear from everybody at home and get all the news! A destroyer met us at sea yesterday and gave us a much welcomed month's accumulation of mail. I received six of your letters – May 26 to June 30. We left Boston – and the States – shortly after I telephoned home. It's been plenty chilly, but a pleasant relief from the sultry climate we were used to. The flying weather is much poorer here however. Too much fog, or high winds with a very rough, choppy sea. We put in a considerable amount of flying though, think I have about 850 hours now. Our new heavy leather jackets have been put to good use.

Wonder if you've been up to Canada on a fishing trip yet. Almost every time we anchor a couple of dozen fishermen toss their lines over the side of the ships. Some

Wonder if you've been to Canada on a fishing trip yet. Almost every time we anchor a couple dozen fishermen toss their lines over the side of the ship. Some of the old boatswains have good luck too. Several halibut were caught in Newfoundland. We were anchored in Placentia Bay, Newfoundland for several days. We took some sightseeing hops and several gunnery hops while there. The country was green and covered with innumerable lakes. Looked like a fisherman's paradise. People were scarce. Whenever there were a half-dozen buildings, presumably a town, there was also a fair sized church.

From Placentia Bay we went on up to Reykjavik, Iceland. Reykjavik is a city of about 30,000. The natives are of Scandinavian descent, but most of them could speak some English. They study Danish and English in the grammar schools. I had some fun brushing up on my Americanized Norse. There were plenty of blond gals to kid (that went both ways) and dance with. However the night life wasn't quite what we were accustomed to — probably because there was no night. It was rather difficult to believe that the clocks were correct at 1130 when the sun was still visible. "Night" was no darker than a cloudy day. We had patrol every other day, which was flown in four hour shifts day & "night."

There's a squadron of "Norsky" fliers based at Reykjavik. They had some slick looking American made planes, Northrup Attacks, on twin floats. The bloody Englishman are up there too!

The shores of Iceland are nice and green now it's fairly warm. Temperature night and day is about 40°F. For all practical purposes, I might say there are no trees on the island. I heard rumors to the effect that someone in a neighboring town had been playing nursemaid to a tree for the last twenty years — it has now attained a height of ten feet, and is still growing. Fishing seems to be the main industry, no matter what sort of meal you order in their restaurants, you always get the same thing — fish. I held out for an hour and half one day trying to get an order of steak. Just as I was about to give up in despair and settle for the fish, the waitress brought me an order of mutton. If there's anything that tastes less like steak than fish it's mutton. Hereafter I'll stick to a simple order of well fried fish. The waitress was purely Icelandic and didn't seem to understand a word of my Norse. The merchants up here are what you might call real optimists. They were advertising bathing suits and sun tan lotions in their store windows. There was a swimming pool in

ocal Man In Navy On Icelandic Patrol

illiam Larson Of Hanks Writes Of Midnight Sun On Island

It's hard to believe the clock hen the sun shines at 11:30 p.m. rites one young man from this rritory to his parents, telling of s experiences with the U. S. avy in Iceland, whose protec-on has been taken over by the nited States government.

He is William Larson, son of r. and Mrs. O. M. Larson of anks. A recent letter, writ-n at sea and mailed at first op-ortunity when his ship reached ore, tells of the visit to Iceland. art of the letter follows:

"From Placentia bay (New-oundland) we went on up to eykjavik, Iceland. Reykjavik is city of about 30,000. The natives e of Scandinavian descent but ost of them could speak some nglish. They study Danish and nglish in the grammar schools. had some fun brushing up on y Americanized Norse. There ere plenty of blonde gals to kid hat went both ways) and dance ith.

No Night Life

"However, the night life wasn't uite what we were accustomed —probably because there was o night. It was rather difficult believe that the clocks were rrect at 11:30 when the sun as still visible. "Night" was no arker than a cloudy day.

"We had patrol every other ay, which was flown on four our shifts day and "night." here's a squadron of "Nosrky" ers based at Reykjavik. They ave some slick looking Ameri-an made planes. Northrup at-cks, on twin floats. The bloody Englishmen are up there, too.

"The shores of Iceland are nice and green now and it's fairly warm (the letter was written during the summer). Tempera-ture night and day is 40 degrees. For all practical purposes, I might say there are no trees on the island. I heard rumors to the effect that someone in a neigh-boring town had been playing nursemaid to a tree for the last 20 years—it has not attained a height of 16 feet and is still growing.

Fish and More Fish

"Fishing seems to be the main industry. No matter what sort of meal you order in their restaur-ants, you always get the same thing—fish. I held out for an hour and a half one day trying to get an order of steak. Just as I was about to give up in despair, the waitress brought me an order of mutton. If there's anything that tastes less like steak than fish, it's mutton—hereafter I'll stick to a single order of well fried fish.

"The merchants up there are what you might call real opti-mistic. They were advertising bathing suits and sun tan lotions in their store windows. There was a swimming pool in the town, though, the water coming from a natural hot spring. You could rent bathing suits (1805 model) and take a swim for 1 krona (about $.16)."

For REPAIRING on your RADIO or REFRIGERATOR
Call GAMBLE STORES Williston Phone 20

The navy man wrote of plac as far removed as Newfoundlan from where the trip to Icela started, the Panama Canal, a Cuba, all visited on the same tr which ended back in Unit States ports where their lett written at sea could be mailed.

NEW SECRETARY NAMED FOR K

FARGO, Sept. 8—(AP) — Ral Wilkinson of Minot has be named state secretary of t Knights of Columbus, it was a nounced here Sunday by Fra J. Webb, Grand Forks, state d puty, at a district meeting of t Knights of Columbus here Su day.

Wilkinson succeeds A. Beaudry of Minot, who resign at the time he moved to Ca fornia.

Ben L. Miller of Jamestow district deputy, presided at t district meeting Sunday and re resentatives from councils Fargo, Grand Forks, Wahpet and Jamestown.

Speakers, in addition to We and Miller, were Pat Mulloy Wahpeton; Ed Cosgriff of Far and George Lally, grand knig of Fargo council.

Webb, who was the princip speaker at Sunday's session o

Let Us You

with our new Koch This service no

town though. The water came from a natural hot spring. You could rent bathing suits (1905 models) and take a swim for 1 Krona (about 16¢).

Didn't tell you about our trip through the Panama Canal. Went through at night so didn't see an awful lot. The canal is fifty miles long and we steamed on a Northwest course in passing from the Pacific to the Atlantic. Five sets of locks raise and lower the ship a height of 85 feet.

We stopped a few days at Guantanamo Bay, Cuba — a desolate hell hole. I got a box of Cuban cigars down there that I don't know what to do with. Maybe I should send them home to you so you could give them to Jorgen. Maybe those "el ropos" would do him good — kill or cure. Sorry to hear he and Annie were sick.

Hope to get into New York in a few days so will mail this letter then. Have had only one opportunity to write (in Boston) since leaving Honolulu. Nobody knows where we're going or why, until we get there. Unless we're in a States port we can send no letters or radio messages. Some of the officer's wives who were just getting settled in Honolulu have been in pretty much of a quandary. Our orders for ship's movements are received at sea, so the usual grapevine telegraph of navy wives, is utterly incapacitated — hence the confusion.

In perforce, learned something about Naval Court procedures last week. I was recorder (state's attorney) or sea-lawyer in a summary court martial. One of the gobs[4] "borrowed" another gob's blankets up in Newfoundland and forgot to return them. The second gob got a bit chilly and reported his loss to the master-at-arms, who tracked them down six days later. It was a guilty case, so not much of a job outside of organizing the court and recording the proceedings.

So Lloyd had a little experience teaching? He can be thankful that <u>one</u> out of seven remembered what he'd told them when it came to the test. Perhaps he "cribbed" a bit. Wonder what congress will do about draft age college students. Hope the kid brother can continue with school this fall.

This is getting lengthy. Hope I can get it in the mail shortly. Sorry I can't write more often, but don't worry about us. We hope to be in New York a few days but it's doubtful that any of us get any leave. I'm certainly glad to hear that you're getting plenty of rain and that the crops look fine. Best wishes for your Birthday, Dad! May you enjoy this one and many more to come! Your son, William."

June 17 1941 Letter Home
— At Sea — USS Nashville.
Letter was published in Williston Herald September 19, 1941: Local Man in Navy on Icelandic Patrol; William Larson of Hanks Writes of Midnight Sun on Island.

4 An American sailor or ordinary seaman.

Reykjavík — Tjörnin

Reykjavík — Dómkirkjan og Alþingishúsið

. Islenskur Hestur

(Photo Source: National Archives)

Curtiss SOC "Seagull" Scout-Observation Planes

The biplane SOC was designed mainly as a catapult-launched floatplane, flying from battleships for gunfire observations, and from cruisers as a scout. It was capable of flexible employment, with folding wings allowing more planes to fit in cruisers' small hangars and a float that could be exchanged for wheeled landing gear, facilitating operation from aircraft carriers and shore bases in a utility role. Powered by a Pratt & Whitney R-1340 single-row radial engine and fitted with leading edge slats and flaps on the upper of its two wings, it had good low-speed flight characteristics, well-suiting it for catapult operation and short-distance landings in the relatively smooth-water "slick" that a turning ship could create on the open sea.

Dimensions: Wing Span, 36 feet; Length, 31.1 feet (floatplane—length as a landplane was 26.8 feet); Wing Area, 342 square feet. Weights: Empty, 3633 pounds; Gross, 5306 pounds. Powerplant: One 550 horsepower Pratt & Whitney R-1340-22 radial engine. Crew: Two men—Pilot and Observer/Gunner. Armament: Two .30 caliber machine guns (one firing forward from a fixed mounting in the wing; one on a flexible mounting in the after cockpit); Two small bombs or depth bombs under lower wings (Landplane version could carry a bomb below the fuselage). Performance (at 5188 pounds): Maximum Speed 162 m.p.h. @ sea level.

"***Dear Folks,*** Received another letter from home again today so I'll write right away. Sent you a letter a few days ago. Sorry I couldn't get something in the mail for Dad's Birthday. Hope he had a pleasant day.

Think we'll be pulling out of here sometime next week. Could have had about five days leave, but I'll hold out for a week or two at Christmas- I hope! Have no idea where we'll be going.

Well I've seen quite a bit of New York the last few days. Saw the Yanks beat the Cleveland Indians at the Yankees Stadium. A professional baseball team really works smooth. Seems like they have to knock the ball into the bleachers to get on base. Joe DiMaggio put one in the bleachers (420 feet) for a homer. Saw a very good stage show the other night called "Panama Hattie." Then there are all kinds of night clubs—all expensive. We get from place to place on subways at the cost of 5¢. They're fast but not very scenic. Also saw the statue of liberty as we were coming into port—and, in the distance, Coney Island.

Took a trip through the Bowery and China-town last night. Rode an old bus and had a typical "Wallace Beery"

as a guide. A new aviator just reported aboard. He's moving in with me. If we'd have come in here when you weren't so busy, you could have driven down and we'd have taken in the sights together. Might have a chance some other time. Here's hoping you have a good harvest. Did Paul Rodvold get caught in the draft yet? Will send a picture folder showing some of the sights. Hope you are all well. Return "Tiny's" greetings. Your son, William."

July 25 1941 — Letter Home — Brooklyn Navy Yard

"***Dear Folks***, Well, we're still in the big city but not for long- I hope. We're scheduled to stop at Norfolk for a day or two- where to from there nobody knows. I've seen all I care to see of New York. Haven't done a bit of flying service since we arrived, so I'll be glad to get out and go to work again.

I'm glad to hear the crops look well. Here's hoping nothing happens to them before they're harvested. Dad should be getting a radio one of these days. I had one aboard for awhile but a ship's order came out forbidding use of all radios at sea. It seems they act not only as receivers but, to some extent, as transmitters. Well, it sort of looked like I had a white elephant on my hands so I traded for a battery set. Hope you can use it. I seem to remember you mentioning Rodvold's radio last winter.

Went with another officer to see the stage show "Pal Joey" a few nights ago. His uncle had given him the tickets $9.40 apiece. 44 cents would have been high. Heard Lily Pons and the Philharmonic Symphony Orchestra at the Lewisohn Stadium Tuesday night. This stadium is on the campus of the College of the City of New York. The concert was really good. Heifetz plays there tomorrow night. We have about five new ensigns report aboard. Have about twenty reserve ensigns aboard — all college men. The line of officers spent four years at the naval academy.

Went to Coney Island the other day too, by the way. Not much to see and very filthy. Hope you are all well. See the kid brother was down cultivating Arnegard friends. William."

July 31 1941 — Letter Home — New York City NY

"***Dear Folks***, Looking the city of Norfolk over this evening. Looks like they might as well have rolled up the pedewalks — no activity. Leaving in the morning. William."

August 6 1941 — Post Card Home — Norfolk VA

"Here's the gal I met last time I went to Church — remember?"

Norfolk VA

The USS Nashville left Norfolk, Virginia, and was based out of Hamilton, Bermuda, for Neutrality Patrol in the Central Atlantic area from August-to-December 1941.

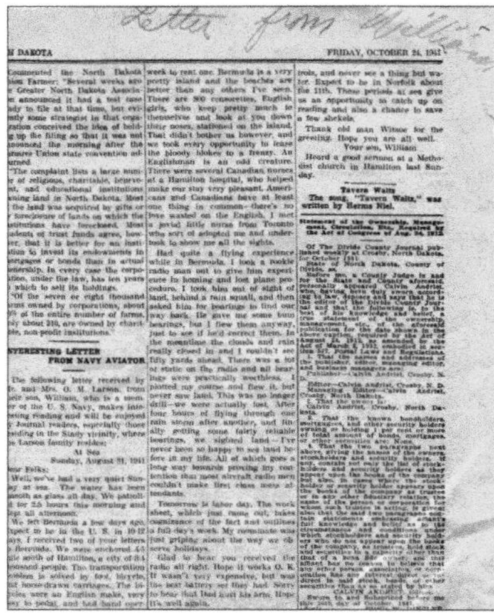

INTERESTING LETTER FROM NAVY AVIATOR

The following letter received by Mr. and Mrs. O. M. Larson, from their son, William, who is a member of the U. S. Navy, makes interesting reading and will be enjoyed by Journal readers, especially those residing in the Sindy vicinity, where the Larson family resides:

At Sea
Sunday, August 31, 1941

Dear Folks:

"***Dear Folks***, Well we've had a very quiet Sunday at sea. The water has been smooth as glass all day. We patrolled for 2.5 hours this morning and slept all afternoon.

We left Bermuda a few days ago. Expect to be in the U.S. in 10-12 days. I received two of your letters in Bermuda. We were anchored 4-5 miles out of Hamilton, a city of 4-5 thousand people. The transportation problem is solved by foot, bicycle, and horse-drawn carriages. (I again got several good whiffs of the familiar old odor of horse manure.) The bicycles were an English make, very easy to pedal, and had hand operated brakes. Cost 1 pound ($4.00) a week to rent one. Bermuda is a very pretty island and the beaches are better than any others I've seen. There are 800 censorettes[5] English girls, who keep pretty much to themselves and look at you down their noses, stationed on the island. That didn't bother us however, and we took every opportunity to tease the bloody blokes to a frenzy. An Englishman is an odd creature. There were

5 It's been said Bermuda was "Britain's number-one listening post" during World War II [1939-1945] –and if that's true, then the Princess Hotel was its headset. "A messages in invisible ink or if an extra period, when magnified, might reveal a hidden message," former hotel manager Ian Powell has said. Ultimately some 1,500 British intelligence officers, academics and code-breakers descended on Bermuda to man the Imperial Censorship station shortly after the outbreak of the war. Many of the censors were attractive young women — largely university students — who became known as the "Censorettes".

several Canadian nurses at a Hamilton Hospital who helped make our stay very pleasant. Americans and Canadians have at least one thing in common — there's no love wasted on the English. I met a jovial little nurse from Toronto who sort of adopted me and undertook to show me all the sights.

Had quite a flying experience while in Bermuda. I took a rookie radio man out to give him experience in homing and lost plane procedure. I took him out of sight of land, behind a rain squall, and then asked him for bearings to find our way back. He gave me some bum bearings, but I flew them anyway, just to see if he'd correct them. In the meantime the clouds and rain really closed in and I couldn't see fifty yards ahead. There was a lot of static on the radio and all bearings were practically worthless. I plotted my course and flew it, but never saw land. This was no longer a drill — we were actually lost. After four hours of flying through one rain storm after another, and finally getting some fairly reliable radio bearings, we sighted land — I've never been so happy to see land before in my life. . . .

Tomorrow is Labor Day. The work sheet, which just came out, takes cognizance of the fact and outlines a full day's work. My roommate was just griping about the way we observe holidays. Glad to hear you received the radio all right. Hope it works out. It wasn't very expensive, but was the best battery set they had. Sorry to hear that Dad hurt his arm. Hope it's well again. We're running on two week patrols. And never see a thing but water. Expect to be in Norfolk about the 11th. These periods at sea give us an opportunity to catch up on reading and also a chance to save a few shekels.

Hope the kid brother had a Happy and pleasant Birthday. When does school open again? Thank old man Witsoe for the greeting. Hope you are all well. Your son, William."

August 31 1941 — At Sea — USS Nashville — Letter was published in Divide County Journal, Crosby ND Friday October 24, 1941: Interesting Letter From Navy Aviator

Rapid Transit, Bermuda 120

171 Twenty-One Club, Bermuda

TOM MOORE HOUSE AND TAVERN, BERMUDA

"***Dear Folks***, Well, we're still hanging around the "Pearl of the Atlantic." In our eyes the luster is fast fading. There's good swimming here, but not much variety in the way of evening entertainment. . . . We're doing quite a bit of flying. Practice gunnery, radio, etc and do lots of scouting. Had three hours of night flying a couple of nights ago. I had a little mishap the last time we were out at sea. Was coming in for a landing when a swell bounced me into the air. The wing dropped suddenly and the second landing was on a

William and Canadian nurse at Grape Bay Bermuda - September 1941

wing tip float. Well, the wing tip float wasn't made to take that sort of landing so it sheared off. My radioman and I got out on the opposite wing in time to keep the plane from rolling over. The plane was recovered without having had a salt water bath, but it was rather an embarrassing recover for me. . . . Radios aboard ship are decommissioned at sea, but my roommate and I have a jook-box we play for a little diversion. Have records by Robeson, Crosby, Eddy Durbin, Crooks, Heifetz Thomas, and several popular orchestras. . . . Don't know from one day to the next where, when, or why we're going. The married men really sing the blues.

Wonder how the crop turned out at home. Hope it was a good one. Will send the kid brother some money the first of next month. Sent him $50 the 20th of August with the hopes that he'd get started in school again. Your son, William."

September 26 1941 Letter Home: Hamilton, Bermuda

"***Dear Folks***, . . . The nurse I knew went to New York to work. Not much to do now except ride bicycles and look at the scenery — which gets rather dull in three or four months. ....Went

to a Presbyterian service in town last night. Heard a real sermon for a change. Gave a pep talk for God and not a "God save Britain" (with America's help) propaganda line. The preacher said God was essential to civilization — not Great Britain. I admired the old boy's spirit. He was an old timer — so he very likely has no political or military ambitions. Prospects for Christmas at home are not very bright, but I still have hope. . . . Am spending part of my spare time making a calf-skin leather bill-fold. Haven't made one since taking the boys scout course in college. . . . Got a complete set of winter flight clothing a while ago, though so we're all set, for any climate. Happy Thanksgiving. Your son, William."

November 17 1941 Letter Home: Hamilton, Bermuda

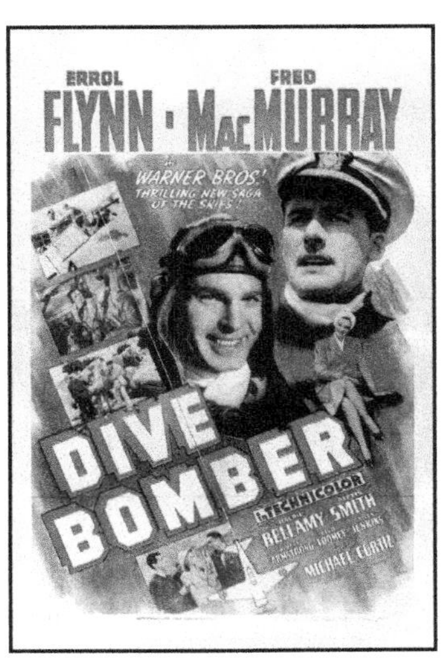

"***Dear Folks***, . . . That confounded accordion next door is going full blast again. And an accordion in the hands of an expert is no sweet music. In the hands of a timeless beginner it's maddening. It has the volume of a merry-go round calliope and is as harmonious as a steel riveting machine. ...Just saw the movie "Dive Bomber" aboard. And was very pleasantly surprised in finding a card from the kid brother, your letter and a box of candy on my desk when I returned to my room. . . . Got a new pilot aboard recently. Think I'll turn over the job of material officer. He's fresh out of Pensacola with 185 hours. Comes from West Virginia. . . . Your son, William."

November 30 1941 Letter Home: USS Nashville (reference to Howard Roy Burkett — later missing at sea)

Timeline:

US Declares War on Japan December 8 1941

Immediately following the bombing of Pearl Harbor, Lucky and crew made another mission from Maine to Iceland to safely escort a troop and cargo convoy. Escort duty aboard the Glamour Ship continued to Bermuda and Iceland until February 1942.

"***Dear Folks***, Just saw a stinkeroo of a movie aboard, "Two Faced Woman." The first we've had in months. . . . Another aviator reported aboard recently. That makes

Shipmates on USS Nashville playing volleyball

Fellow SOC Aviators and Radiomen on the USS Nashville – 1st Row, 2nd from left: Lt. James Holladay, 3rd Row Standing, 5th from left: Lt. David Soper.

seven of us and there's one more coming. Maybe I'll have a chance for a transfer. . . . The crew had several contests on the stern this afternoon. One contest was called "The Smoke Screen." The contest being to determine who could smoke a cigar the fastest—starting from scratch. The winner smoked his in one minute and 35 seconds. The prize—one box of cigars. He didn't look as though he was anxious for a smoke just right away however. Most of the contests were good for a lot of laughs. Received a copy of the Arnegard "Spud[6]" a few days ago. My little freshmen are now sophisticated Seniors. I'm surprised that the "Spud" survived Mittelstadt's departure. Your son, William."

January 25 1942 Letter Home—United States Fleet, Cruisers, Battle Force, Cruiser Division Eight, USS Nashville at sea.

6 "Spud" was the school paper of Arnegard High School, N.D. where William taught freshman classes for 2 years starting in 1937. Ruth Mittelstadt was the High School principal of Arnegard.

SOC Floatplane Taxies to Recovery Mat alongside USS Nashville to be picked up by cruiser's crane

25 March [illegible] Non-Transferable

OFFICER OFFICER

IDENTIFICATION PASS

Navy Yard, Mare Island, California

8492 No. 8492

Expires - - - - - -

RANK and NAME Ens. W.R. Larson A-V(N)USNR

Ship or Station USS NASHVILLE NYMI

E.G. Dailey Lt U.S.N. (Ret)

Pass and Traffic Officer

8395—M.I.N.Y. 2-9-42—1M

USS *Nashville* (CL-43)

Doolittle Raid

On 4 March 1942, she rendezvoused with Hornet off the Virginia Capes, and then escorted the aircraft carrier to the West Coast via the Panama Canal, arriving on 20 March at San Diego. Hornet and Nashville steamed from San Francisco on 2 April, with the carrier laden with 16 Army B-25 Mitchell medium bombers on her flight deck, bombers under the command of Lieutenant Colonel Jimmy Doolittle, USAAF, for the Doolittle Raid on Japan. On 13 April, they rendezvoused with other US Navy warships, under Vice Admiral William F. Halsey, Jr., north of Midway Atoll, and then they set course for Japan. When about 1,000 mi (1,600 km) away from Japan on 17 April, the destroyers of the task force were detached due to lack of fuel, and then Nashville, the other escorting cruisers, and Hornet and Enterprise made a high-speed dash to the air raid launching point 500 mi (800 km) from Japan. The next day, the task force was sighted by a Japanese picket boat, which reported the presence of the carrier task force before being sunk by scout planes from Enterprise. A second picket boat was then sunk by gunfire from Nashville, but the advantage of surprise was lost. The B–25s were launched 150 mi (240 km) short of the intended launching point in heavy seas. Immediately after the launch, the strike force reversed course and steamed eastwards for Honolulu. The "Shangri-La" task force returned to Pearl Harbor on 25 April.

In March 1942, the Glamour Ship rendezvoused with the aircraft carrier USS Hornet off the Virginia Capes, and then escorted the carrier via the Panama Canal, to San Francisco. Leaving San Francisco on April 2, the *Nashville* and *Hornet* had aboard 16 B-25 Mitchell bombers under the command of Lt. Colonel Jimmy Doolitte, USAAF. The *Nashville*, on the "Shangri-La raid" on Tokyo in April 1942, sank her only two ships of the war, when she spotted and destroyed two small Japanese ships on April 18. These Japanese ships had spotted the U.S. task force shortly before James Doolittle launched his famous B-25 raid off the *Hornet's* carrier deck on the way to the Japanese capitol. Immediately after the bomber launch, the strike force headed back to Honolulu.

WAR DIARY—SATURDAY APRIL 18, 1942 SECRET U.S.S. NASHVILLE SECRET TASK FORCE 16[7]

NARRATIVE: At dawn the NASHVILLE was steaming in company with aircraft carriers ENTERPRISE and HORNET and cruisers NORTHAMPTON, SALT LAKE CITY, AND VINCENNES enroute to a point at which the bombers on the HORNET were to be launched. At 0741 an enemy ship was sighted bearing 360 relative at a distance of about 10,000 yards. The following is a chronological record of the engagement:

0748 Enemy ship bore 201 T. at a range of 9,000 yards.

0752 Received order from Admiral Halsey to attack vessel and sink same.

0757 Enemy headed toward the NASHVILLE

7 Secret War Dairy of U.S.S. Nashville, dated April 18, 1942 (declassified December 31, 2012)

0801 Bombing planes made another attack on enemy ship. This fire returned by enemy.

0819 Commenced firing salvo fire.

0821 Steadied course 095 T. Enemy vessel on fire.

0835 Enemy ship sunk

0827 Commenced maneuvering to pick up survivors. Attempts to rescue one man sighted proved unsuccessful.

1153 Resumed station in formation. The ship sunk was a Japanese patrol boat and was equipped with radio and anti-aircraft machine guns. During the encounter with the craft the Army bombers carried on the HORNET were launched to make their attack on Tokyo. During the afternoon the following action took place:

1409 Went to General Quarters, OTC having ordered this ship to sink two Japanese sampans reported by aircraft.

1415 Dive bombers made attack on enemy

1417 Planes made second attack on enemy; their fire was returned by the enemy.

1422 Opened fire with main battery firing salvo fire at range of 4,500 yards.

1440 Ceased fire as vessel was sinking. Prepared to pick up survivors.

1445 Enemy vessel sank. Five survivors were

seen. These men were all picked up by this ship.

1500 Picked up last survivor and began maneuvering to rescue pilot and passenger of ENTERPRISE plane which crashed in water astern of ship.

1517 Rescued two fliers.

1518 Commenced maneuvering to rejoin formation. The second ship sunk was a patrol craft similar to the first. 65 rounds of 5″ ammunition and 102 rounds of main battery ammunition were used in this engagement.

The complete USS Nashville War Diary of April 18, 1942, provides a detailed account of that day and is included in Appendix C.

Next up for William and the crew of the *Nashville*, was Task Force 8 duty in the Bering Sea. On May 26, 1942, they arrived in Kodiak, Alaska, just days before Japanese carrier planes bombed Dutch Harbor on June 3rd. From June to November, *Nashville's* duty was bombarding enemy shore positions and covering operational landings in the land of 50 mph fog. On August 7, the *Nashville* participated in the attack on Kiska which inflicted heavy damage to Japanese shore installations on this Aleutian island. *Nashville* was the first ship to bombard Japanese positions in Alaska during World War II.

USS Nashville (CL-43)

Flagship

Nashville left Hawaii on 14 May 1942 to become the flagship of Task Force 8 (TF 8) defending Alaska and the Aleutians, and arrived at Dutch Harbor, Alaska on 26 May. She steamed for Kodiak, Alaska two days later to join with other units of the task force.

On 3–4 June, Japanese carrier planes struck Dutch Harbor. *Nashville* and her accompanying warships were unable to make contact with the enemy due to heavy fog. Admiral Isoroku Yamamoto withdrew his diversionary force from the Aleutians after his defeat at the Battle of Midway. As the Japanese departed, they left occupying forces behind on Attu and Kiska Islands in the Aleutians. From June–November, *Nashville* patrolled the North Pacific Ocean, and participated in the attack on Kiska on 7 August, in which heavy damage was inflicted on Japanese shore installations.

USS Nashville bombarding Kiska Island, August 7 1942 (Source: S Bustin)

William and his fellow SOC aviators were patrolling the skies above the *Nashville* during all these events, performing scouting and anti-submarine patrols. William, by this time nicknamed, "Lucky", participated in several missions off the back of the cruiser. Two of these missions were chronicled by a roving newspaper reporter, B.J. (Barney) McQuaid, of the Chicago Daily News. One included the story of Lucky's 3,500-foot descent and ocean landing on the Bering Sea under "pea soup" fog conditions at night.[8] The other tale included Lucky's return after two nights alone in his seaplane, riding out a brutal Alaska storm in a bay while his radioman was stranded on the beach. Lucky saved the naval float plane from damage and the lives of his crew. Both of these stories start out the same, Lucky got lost in the impenetrable fog of the Aleutian Islands, but they illustrate his endurance and aviation judgement that he had honed since growing up on the windswept prairies of North Dakota.

THE CHICAGO DAILY NEWS
400 W. MADISON ST.
DEARBORN 1111

Dear Mr. Larson:

At the request of Captain Francis S. Craven, (Navy Yard, Navy #128, % Fleet Post Office, San Francisco, California) I enclose two clippings of dispatches received from our correspondent Mr. McQuaid. Although your son's name is not mentioned I surmise that both stories refer to him. If you are certain that this is the case I should appreciate your verifying my supposition.

The dispatch of July 24th is taken from the files of the Foreign Service as our regular Back Numbers department supply of that date is completely exhausted. We shall probably have no occasion to refer to this dispatch but in the remote possibility that we do, may we be assured that we may recover it from you?

Very sincerely yours,
Marian Avery
Secretary
Chicago Daily News Foreign Service

8 This story was also chronicled in Our Navy, Mid-December, 1943 by Fletcher Pratt in an article titled, "Chit-Chat of the Fighting Fliers."

Chicago Daily News:
July 24, 1942

Pluck and Skill Rescue "Lucky" from Foggy Sea

By B.J. M'Quaid

Kodiak, Alaska, July 24—The pilot was known to his shipmates as "Lucky", which may have had something to do with it. Nevertheless, the operation was at least 90 percent scientific. For that reason, it should, and no doubt will, go into the record books as an object lesson in lost plane procedure in the open sea. "Lucky" got lost through no fault of his, or ours. He'd been up on a routine search flight, from which he'd returned, swift and sure, to his appointed rendezvous with our warship. But when he got there, we were swallowed up in a great bank of fog—the kind of thing that makes the sea and air operations in these northern waters a business of endless hazard and treachery.

We got him back aboard after he'd been lost nearly three hours. We did it at night, under the same zero-zero conditions that led to his getting lost in the first place.

Fog "Settled for Night"

To appreciate this achievement, it is necessary to understand that the Pacific is a large ocean and that a scout seaplane is a small object. When we finally broke radio silence and discovered "Lucky"—"sprung him" in the seagoing airman's idiom—he was a good 20 miles astern. Darkness was gathering and the fog, which had been alternately lifting and lowering had settled down for the night. "Pea soup" gives you no idea. From the bridge, we could barely make out our forward gun turrets. The problem was to bring the plane in on course, guide it down through 3,000 feet of solid overcast and set it on the sea at a point close enough to the ship to make searching for it something more than a gesture. All we had was our radio communication with the plane and certain other apparatus, not primarily intended for such use, which enabled us to give "Lucky" a fairly good notion of the ship's position relative to his own. As for coming down through the soup and landing in the darkness on moderately rough water under zero-zero conditions—that was "Lucky's" personal problem. We could not help him there.

Told to Ride it Out.

But we got him over the ship. (We heard his motor, faintly.) And we sent him on down, an estimated five miles or so ahead. We told him to ride it out, for a bit, and we'd be along and pick him up. Our needle was now out of the haystack. All we had left to do was to thread it. Somewhere out ahead, imprisoned by the alabaster wall of fog, "Lucky" and his radioman sat bobbing on the restless sea. We knew about what their position must have been a few seconds before the landing impact. We knew "Lucky" would head into the wind and rev his motor enough to hold against the drift, though this would be largely guesswork on his part.

The rub was that if he got as much as a couple hundred feet off our course, we might go on past without ever seeing him. Even the powerful beams of our search-lights bounced back off the solid fogbanks a few yards from the ship. We moved on in what we took to be the direction of the plane. So many minutes at such and such a speed, then a drop to four or five knots. We should be on the mark in 20 minutes.

There had been excitement enough on the bridge—of a tense and suppressed kind—during the earlier stages of this operation. As, for example—after we had lifted radio silence and begun communicating to "Lucky," our improvised notions of how to get him back. After each set of instructions "Lucky's" voice would come crackling tersely through the loudspeaker: "Lucky' to Goz, okay" or "Lucky' to Goz, righto," brimming with a staccato confidence that filled us with sudden surprised awareness—this lean and modest young North Dakotan, so casually accepted as the partner of wardroom joys and grievances, was a man of courageous greatness and nobility of spirit. This we should have known already as "Lucky's" fellow pilots knew it. But it is hard for the layman, or nonpilot, to get the flier's point of view. His fellow airmen knew it had cost "Lucky" to maintain radio silence, even after he knew he was hopelessly lost, and before we had decided to "spring him." They knew how he had been tortured as he made his decision to stay at sea and try to get back to the ship rather than head for nearest land. (He might have made it, or he might have fallen into the sea, fuelless, and been lost a mere dozen miles from the beach.)

Suspense for All.

But there was suspense enough for all of us—in the movements and quick voices of those on the bridge, in the quietly relayed orders and messages, the fog-blunted stabs of giant search-lights. All this had been prologue. Now "Lucky" was on the water. He had made his decisions and done his part of the job superbly. It was up to us to find him, and if we were to find him at all it would have to be soon. To miss the plane on our first run up to the estimated position would probably mean missing it forever. To leave it out all night on the sea would probably mean certain destruction for it and its occupants. The fog perhaps would lift before morning, but a few hours in moderately rough water would tear the light machine to fragments. We came up on the end of our planned run. Still no sign of the plane. One's heart sank. What optimistic fools we were. How could we have expected, in all this green-gray vastness of impenetrability, to steer to within a few score feet of the infinitesimally insignificant airplane. At this point one of "Lucky's" fellow pilots had an idea. A fairly obvious idea, you'll say. Indeed it seemed so to us — as soon as we heard it mentioned. It was the kind of thing that should have been thought of at once, should have been down in the black and white in all the elementary procedure manuals.

An Idea Brings Rescue.

"Why not have 'Lucky' fire a few bursts from his machine gun?" We waited anxiously for the instruction to go out: "GOZ to 'Lucky'; this is GOZ to 'Lucky.' Fire a few machine-gun bursts at

The four scout planes of the USS Nashville - Ouzinkie, Alaska (Ouzinkie Packing Corp. cannery in background) - September 1942

30-second intervals. I will repeat. Fire machine gun at intervals 30 seconds. Go ahead." Some of us went aft on the bridge and stood in the glare of the lights, our ears straining. The sound came from off our port bow; faintly, at first and strong by alteration as the wind fell and quickened. And that was the show. Within a few seconds a destroyer to port of us had picked up the plane with her light. Soon we saw the little red and green lamps of its wingtips riding up astern. The floats bounced and slid jauntily and defiantly through the following seas. As a final burst of power brought the plane within hoisting range we could see the flames from its exhaust stacks snorting a challenge to the North Pacific and to all fogbanks since the voyage of Noah.

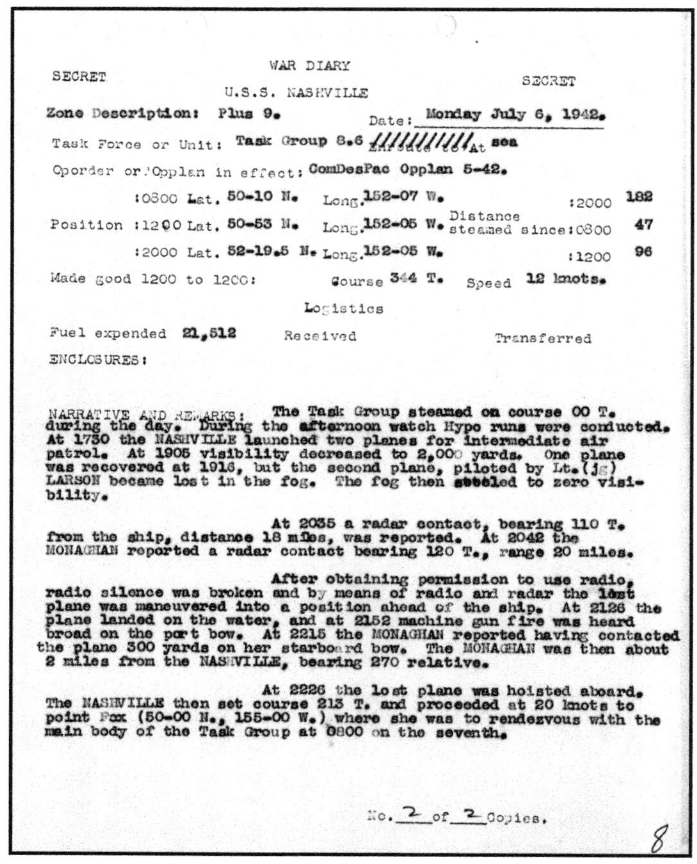

SECRET WAR DIARY SECRET
U.S.S. NASHVILLE

Zone Description: Plus 9. Date: Monday July 6, 1942.

Task Force or Unit: Task Group 8.6 At sea

Oporder or Opplan in effect: ComDesPac Opplan 5-42.

Position
:0800 Lat. 50-10 N. Long. 152-07 W.
:1200 Lat. 50-53 N. Long. 152-05 W.
:2000 Lat. 52-19.5 N. Long. 152-05 W.

Distance steamed since
:2000 182
:0800 47
:1200 96

Made good 1200 to 1200: Course 344 T. Speed 12 knots.

Logistics

Fuel expended 21,512 Received Transferred

ENCLOSURES:

NARRATIVE AND REMARKS: The Task Group steamed on course 00 T. during the day. During the afternoon watch Hypo runs were conducted. At 1730 the NASHVILLE launched two planes for intermediate air patrol. At 1905 visibility decreased to 2,000 yards. One plane was recovered at 1916, but the second plane, piloted by Lt. (jg) LARSON became lost in the fog. The fog then settled to zero visibility.

At 2035 a radar contact, bearing 110 T. from the ship, distance 18 miles, was reported. At 2042 the MONAGHAN reported a radar contact bearing 120 T., range 20 miles.

After obtaining permission to use radio, radio silence was broken and by means of radio and radar the lost plane was maneuvered into a position ahead of the ship. At 2126 the plane landed on the water, and at 2152 machine gun fire was heard broad on the port bow. At 2215 the MONAGHAN reported having contacted the plane 300 yards on her starboard bow. The MONAGHAN was then about 2 miles from the NASHVILLE, bearing 270 relative.

At 2226 the lost plane was hoisted aboard. The NASHVILLE then set course 213 T. and proceeded at 20 knots to point Fox (50-00 N., 155-00 W.) where she was to rendezvous with the main body of the Task Group at 0800 on the seventh.

No. 2 of 2 Copies.

8

Daily Operational Journal of the USS Nashville describing the lost plane event of Lt. (jg) William R. Larson — July 6 1942

Chicago Daily News, September 4, 1942

NAVY SCOUTER MADE POSSIBLE KISKA TRIUMPH

By B.J. M'Quaid.

With a U.S. Task Force in Aleutian Waters. Aug. 17—(Delayed)—So our admiral ordered us to turn back in to the Kiska fogbank, for one more try at what had begun to seem the hopeless proposition of getting enough of a look at the Japs to shoot at them, and the men of these ships cheered him for a stubborn and relentless seadog. The admiral, however, refuses to take credit. He says the praise belongs to a lowly SOC pilot from his own flagship. It was this pilot, we now discover, who first observed that the fogbank was beginning to lift along the whole lee shore of Kiska, from Vega point to South Head. On his own initiative, he broke radio silence and flashed back word to our ships. On the basis of this information, as interpreted by the admiral, the ships which a few minutes earlier had run up to within three miles of the beach without finding a hole, went back to try their luck again.

Humble Plane Comes Through.

This successful surface ship action, in which months of Jap effort may have been undone, considerable shipping damaged or sunk, and shore installations flattened, turns out to have relied for its ultimate success on the humblest airplane in any branch of the national service. The SOC is a scout observation biplane. It is a joke, even to the men who fly it. It has neither the speed nor the guns to deal on equal terms with enemy fighters and patrol planes. Its performance limitations confine its ordinary usefulness to such missions as sweeping for subs in vicinity of its own ships and hauling sleeves for gunnery practices out at sea. In an action such as we performed, it would ordinarily be employed to "spot" gunfire, and relay information to the gun crews to correct for range and deflection errors. On this occasion, however, visibility over our main targets was insufficient to permit spotting.

No Easy Job for Pilots.

SOC's are carried by cruisers, which catapult them into the air when their services are required. SOC pilots are normally a disgruntled but sociable lot who suffer from an excessive desire to be somewhere else- specifically in a super high speed fighter based on a carrier. They regard their present jobs as neither exciting or glamorous. Their casualties, in these waters, have been quite severe. They get wrapped up in fog, the way the ships do, only they don't come unwrapped as easily, or as often.

If they meet Jap fighters, even the floatplane variety, it is likely to be too bad for the SOC's. The lad who turned in this fine piece of weather reporting at Kiska had a tight squeeze. Zeroes chased him and put more than 50 bullets in his airplane.

But he got back, having done a splendid job, and is being recommended for the Navy cross.

Oakland Tribune,
Friday November 6, 1942

No.8: Japs Unlucky if 'Lucky' Lands on Kiska

ABOARD A U.S. WARSHIP IN THE BERING SEA, Sept. 30 –

"Now, once again, Lieut. L------, through excellent judgment, calmness, resourcefulnesss and endurance, has saved his plane and perhaps the lives of himself, and his radioman. The commanding officer believes that these two performances of Lieut. L----- are worthy of a letter of commendation from the commander in chief." — From a memorandum to the "Cincpac" by the skipper of this cruiser.

Lieut. L---- is "Lucky," the young North Dakotan previously celebrated in your correspondent's dispatch for his almost unbelievable feat of getting his plane back to the ship after he had become lost at night, in impenetrable fog.

This story starts out the same way: Lucky got lost. He had been catapulted from the cruiser on a communications mission to the place where U.S. troops, under the protection of this naval task force, are establishing an advanced base to carry the Aluetian war to the Japs. Weather out here where the ships are operating was excellent at the time of the takeoff. At the other end of the mission — only a few miles away — everything was shut in tightly by fog. However, there was no way of checking the weather at the other end, because these ships are under the obligation of maintaining a strict radio silence.

LOW ON GAS

Shortly after launching, Lucky's plane encountered strong beam winds, whose strength he under estimated. These carried him considerably west of his destination. When, finally he sighted a few land elevations muzzling up through the fog, he could recognize none of the contours. "Flew around island," says Lucky's written report. "Was getting low on gasoline. It was also getting dark, and I landed in first bay I could find, with 30 gallons of gasoline." (Enough for about an hour of flight.). "Dropped anchor 100 yards off shore, which was composed of boulders, and breakers were coming in on the beach. Sat in plane all night, getting wet every 15 minutes. In the morning, S. (the radioman) took the life raft and went ashore and investigated trapper's cabin. We found two names written on wall: North End Bay and Hot Springs. I checked all navigation, studied the charts and concluded that this must be Tanaga Island . . . S.'s life raft exploded and he was stranded on the beach. He spent all day building a wooden raft out of driftwood. He launched it that evening, and it sank to the bottom.

BACK TO BASE

"Weather was closed in all day, raining fequently. S. went back to the cabin, built a fire and stayed all night. During the night the weather cleared. He came out early in the morning, inflated his lifebelt and started to swim to the plane. He was exhausted halfway out. I started plane and picked him up. We put on dry clothes immediately. I could not pull up anchor (machine gun), so cut line. Took off immediately on course. Landed at base with 10 gallons of gasoline."

This is Lucky's best laconic style, but manages to convey one or two hints of the hazards and hardships faced by the stranded plane crew. Note that Lucky's anchor was his "free machine gun." Cruiser planes are, of course, equipped with anchors, and Lucky put down his when he first landed, but it proved inadequate to the job of holding the plane against the heavy swell. His unhesitating use of the machine gun may be commentary on the Navy's changing sense of economic values. In former days, Navy emphasis on money values and individual responsibility for material would have caused a pilot to think twice in this situation.

MODESTY

The best bit of understatement is Lucky's description[9] of his rescue of the radioman. "He was exhausted...I started plane and picked him up." Maybe you think that's a simple matter, in a small

9 Lucky's first-hand account of his Flight to Tanaga is included in Appendix D.

biplane tossed about by raging surf and requiring all an ordinary man's efforts just to keep it afloat and in one piece. Lucky, by this time, had sat out in an open cockpit, drenched by rain and spray from the cold Bering sea, for two nights and a day. (More Tomorrow) **B.J. McQuaid accompanied U.S. Occupation Fleet which took over new bases in Aleutian Islands. In a series of articles for The Tribune he tells what happened and forecasts: Barring some incredible and unforeseen upset our forces in the Aleutians stand on the eve of one of this war's most amazing victories."**

OAKLAND TRIBUNE. FRIDAY, NOVEMBER 6, 1942

No. 8: Japs Unlucky if 'Lucky' Lands on Kiska

Special to The Tribune and the Chicago Daily News, Inc.

ABOARD A U.S. WARSHIP IN THE BERING SEA, Sept. 30.—"Now, once again, Lieut. L——, through excellent judgment, calmness, resourcefulness and endurance, has saved his plane and perhaps the lives of himself and his radioman. The commanding officer believes that these two performances of Lieut. L—— are worthy of a letter of commendation from the commander in chief."—From a memorandum to the "Cincpac" by the skipper of this cruiser.

Lieut. L—— is "Lucky," the young North Dakotan previously celebrated in your correspondent's dispatches for his almost unbelievable feat of getting his plane back to the ship after he had become lost, at night, in impenetrable fog.

This story starts out the same way: Lucky got lost. He had been catapulted from the cruiser on a communications mission to the place where U.S. troops, under the protection of this naval task force, are establishing an advanced base to carry the Aleutian war to the Japs.

Weather out here where the ships are operating was excellent at the time of his takeoff. At the other end of the mission—only a few miles away — everything was shut in tightly by fog. However, there was no way of checking the weather at the other end, because these ships are under the obligation of maintaining a strict radio silence.

LOW ON GAS

Shortly after launching, Lucky's plane encountered strong beam winds, whose strength he underestimated. These carried him considerably west of his destination. When, finally, he sighted a few land elevations muzzling up through the fog, he could recognize none of the contours.

"Flew around island," says Lucky's written report. "Was getting low on gasoline. It was also getting dark, and I landed in first bay I could find, with 30 gallons of gasoline." (Enough for about an hour of flight.) "Dropped anchor 100 yards off shore, which was composed of boulders, and breakers were coming in on the beach.

"Sat in plane all night, getting wet every 15 minutes. In the morning, S. (the radioman) took the liferaft and went ashore and investigated trapper's cabin. We found two names written on wall: North End Bay and Hot Springs. I checked all navigation, studied the charts and concluded that this must be Tanaga Island . . . S.'s liferaft exploded and he was stranded on the beach. He spent all day building a wooden raft out of driftwood. He launched it that evening, and it sank to the bottom.

BACK TO BASE

"Weather was closed in all day, raining frequently. S. went back to the cabin, built a fire and stayed all night. During the night the weather cleared. He came out early in the morning, inflated his lifebelt and started to swim to the plane. He was exhausted halfway out. I started plane and picked him up. We put on dry clothes immediately. I could not pull up anchor (machine gun), so cut line. Took off immediately on course. Landed at base with 10 gallons of gasoline."

This is in Lucky's best laconic style, but manages to convey one or two hints of the hazards and hardships faced by the stranded plane crew. Note that Lucky's anchor was his "free machine gun." Cruiser planes are, of course, equipped with anchors, and Lucky put down his when he first landed, but it proved inadequate to the job of holding the plane against the heavy swell. His unhesitating use of the machine gun may be a commentary on the Navy's changing sense of economic values. In former days, Navy emphasis on money values and individual responsibility for material would have caused a pilot to think twice in this situation.

MODESTY

The best bit of understatement is Lucky's description of his rescue of the radioman.

"He was exhausted . . . I started plane and picked him up."

Maybe you think that's a simple matter, in a small biplane tossed about by raging surf and requiring all an ordinary man's efforts just to keep it afloat and in one piece. Lucky, by this time, had sat out in an open cockpit, drenched by rain and spray from the cold Bering sea, for two nights and a day.

(More Tomorrow)

CL43/P20-1/(088) September 5, 1942

CONFIDENTIAL

From: Commanding Officer.
To: Commander in Chief Pacific Fleet.
Via: Commander Task Force EIGHT.

Subject: Report of excellent judgment and performance of duty by Lieut.(jg) W. R. Larson, A-V(N), USNR, during recent flights.

Reference: (a) NASHVILLE letter CL43/A6-2 of 13 July 1942, on Procedure for recovery of a lost plane in a fog.

Enclosures: (A) Copy of report of Lieut. Larson dated 4 Sept. 1942.
(B) Copy of statement by R. J. Schledwitz, ARM2c.
(C) Copy of reference (a).

1. In the reference the Commanding Officer had occasion to report the recovery of a plane under difficult conditions. An important element in the recovery of the plane was the expert airmanship and good judgement displayed by the pilot, Lieutenant (jg) W. R. Larson, A-V(N), USNR.

2. Now, once again, Lieutenant Larson, through excellent judgment, calmness, resourcefulness and endurance, has saved his plane and perhaps the lives of himself and his radioman. The circumstances are best understood from Enclosures (A) and (B).

3. The anchor which Lieutenant Larson used, to keep his plane off a lee shore during two nights and a day of bad weather, was his free machine gun, the plane's regular anchor having proved ineffective. By sacrificing the gun he saved the plane. He evidently made this decision quickly, since there obviously was little time for delay. It obviously was a difficult decision to anyone familiar with the money value of a machine gun and the Navy's peace-time emphasis upon responsibility for material. That it was a correct decision, reflecting excellent judgment under critical conditions, seems unquestionable.

4. The Commanding Officer believes that these two performances of Lieutenant Larson are worthy of a letter of commendation from the Commander in Chief, since they were largely instrumental in saving valuable aircraft and probably also valuable lives. Such a letter would be of great value to Lieutenant Larson in the event that he requests transfer to the regular Navy, as the Commanding Officer has suggested that he do.

F. S. Craven

Captain Craven's request of a letter of commendation for William Larson from the Commander in Chief.

CONFIDENTIAL

4 September, 1942

August 31 - 1630: Catapulted from ship. Enroute to ADAK ISLAND we encountered very heavy fog. First land sighted wasn't ADAK, Mr. Larson figuring the wind drift caused us to miss our destination. We navigated slightly to the west. Shortly thereafter we sighted a large island which we explored thoroughly by flying around it, investigating each cove and harbor. After completing our search around the island we know it was not ADAK so we flew back to a large harbor previously sighted, landed, and immediately anchored the plane. By this time it was quite dark. Both Mr. Larson and I spent first night in plane, Had a lot of trouble with anchor due to rough water and strong winds. At sunrise I inflated life raft and rowed ashore, securing raft far upon the beach and proceeded to a small trappers cabin to investigate for possible clues as to our whereabouts. Found some writing in cabin, much being in Russian. I could make out two names of bays - OLD NORTH BAY and HOT SPRINGS BAY. Relayed this information to Mr. Larson who is still in the plane. Attemtping to return to plane in rubber life raft, it exploded leaving no transportation to plane. I immediately started building a raft and by time I finished, it was dark. I attempted once to launch it but undertow of surf made it impossible. Telling Mr. Larson my predicament he suggested I return to cabin and start a fire to dry my clothing. Also to spend night in cabin and return to beach in morning and make another attempt to launch raft. Next morning I tore one bunk from cabin to enlarge raft and after doing so triedto launch once again and encountered same trouble. The wind still strong and surf was very heavy. Telling Mr. Larson my trouble I asked his permission to swim back to plane as weather was clearing and Mr. Larson wanted to take off as soon as possible. After receiving his consent I took off my heavy clothing and started to swim towards plane which was still anchored. About half way to plane I started getting cramps and hollered to Mr. Larson to turn up plane and come to my assistance. He done so with remarkable speed. As the plane neared he cut the engine, climbed out of cockpit and pulled me aboard the wing. I took off my wet clothing and put on some of Mr. Larson's dry clothes. Mr. Larson attempted to raise anchor but was too weak so he cut the line. Shortly thereafter we took off and followed a hunch of Mr. Larson's. We flew approximately 40 miles and then sighted ADAK ISLAND. We shook hands and then landed by the U.S.S. TEAL. After securing plane we went aboard ship where we were given food, a shower and a bed. "Thank God"

Respectfully,

R. J. Schledwitz, ARM2c

ENCLOSURE (B) TO NASHVILLE SERIAL CL43/P20-1/(OSS) of 5 September, 1942.

Lucky's radioman Raymond John Schledwitz's account of their flight to Tanaga Island

William (on right) — fly fishing in Alaska

Jim Holladay & William at Ouzinkie, Alaska Sept 1942 — Greek Orthodox Church

USS Nashville crew showing their trout catch, William 3rd from right standing

Aboard USS Nashville — August 17 1942

William & Jim Holladay at Ouzinkie, Alaska Sept 1942 — Greek Orthodox Church

Salmon fishing off the stern of the USS Nashville

Following these exploits and a recommendation from his commander, Captain Craven of the *Nashville*, Lucky requested a transfer to carrier operations.

Captain Francis Sanderson Craven — USS Nashville — 1942

Lucky's Travels Aboard the USS Nashville (CL-43)[10]

November — December 1940	Terminal Island, San Pedro, CA
February 1941	Depart Pearl Harbor, HI, to ferry US Marine troops to Wake Island
May 20, 1941	Depart Pearl Harbor, travel via Panama Canal to Norfolk, VA, land US Marine troops on Iceland
June — July 1941	Norfolk, VA
August 1941	Neutrality Patrol in the Central Atlantic. Bermuda to Azores, Portugal
September — October 1941	Hamilton, Bermuda
November 1941	Norfolk, VA
December 7-11, 1941	Portland, ME (Casco Bay)
December 11-15, 1941	Depart to Iceland, land US Marine troops on Iceland, then travel back through Newfoundland and Nova Scotia, Canada
January 1942	Norfolk, VA
February 1942	Boston, MA
March 1942	Depart New York, NY, travel to Puerto Rico and Dominican Republic, travel via Panama Canal, arrive San Diego, CA
March 28, 1942	Mare Island, San Francisco, CA

10 Based on Lucky's Aviators Flight Log Book and the personal WWII diary of Billie Ray Lyerly (CY USN) provided by the Randall Library, University of North Carolina Wilmington.

April 2, 1942	Depart San Francisco, CA to escort the USS Hornet and USS Enterprise on the Doolittle Raid on Japan (April 18th) — return to Pearl Harbor
May 3 -18th, 1942	Depart Pearl Harbor on May 3 for Midway Island. On May 6th, USS Nashville lost contact with one of its SOC plane piloted by Ensign Burkett — later declared Missing in Action. Arrived Midway on the 8th. Following ship fueling, accidental grounding of ship damaged #2 screw and rudder, return to Pearl Harbor for repairs. On May 15th departed Pearl Harbor to Midway and landed US Marines at Midway on May 18th. Departed Midway on May 19th enroute to Kiska Island, AK. *Note: Battle of Midway began 15 days later on June 4th.*
May 25, 1942	Arrived Dutch Harbor, AK
June — July 1942	Patrol in Bering Sea, AK
August 7, 1942	Bombard Kiska Island, AK
September 1942	Landed troops on Adak Island, AK
September 21, 1942	Lucky departed USS Nashville flying SON-1 plane number 1157 to Adak Island, AK and arrived in Dutch Harbor, AK

USS Nashville at Mare Island, California — April 1 1943
(Source: National Archives photo no. 19-LCM-271)

USS Nashville during the Doolittle Raid - April 1943
(Source: National Archives photo no. 19-LCM-271)

CHAPTER 3

VGS-21 Days—West Coast

Lucky requested and received Change-Of-Duty orders on September 25, 1942, to report to Kodiak, Alaska, then fly to Seattle, WA, and report to the Thirteenth Naval District. His wish to transfer to carrier operations was soon approaching. Lucky was granted a 14-day leave between stations, and traveled home to be at the family farm in Hanks, North Dakota between October 6th to October 20th, 1942.

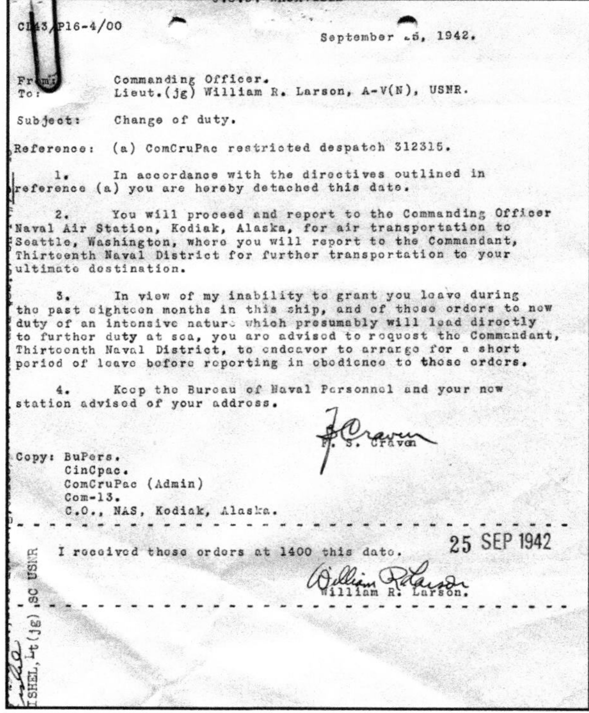

CL43/P16-4/00

September 25, 1942.

From: Commanding Officer.
To: Lieut.(jg) William R. Larson, A-V(N), USNR.

Subject: Change of duty.

Reference: (a) ComCruPac restricted despatch 312315.

1. In accordance with the directives outlined in reference (a) you are hereby detached this date.

2. You will proceed and report to the Commanding Officer Naval Air Station, Kodiak, Alaska, for air transportation to Seattle, Washington, where you will report to the Commandant, Thirteenth Naval District for further transportation to your ultimate destination.

3. In view of my inability to grant you leave during the past eighteen months in this ship, and of these orders to new duty of an intensive nature which presumably will lead directly to further duty at sea, you are advised to request the Commandant, Thirteenth Naval District, to endeavor to arrange for a short period of leave before reporting in obedience to these orders.

4. Keep the Bureau of Naval Personnel and your new station advised of your address.

F. S. Craven

Copy: BuPers.
CinCpac.
ComCruPac (Admin)
Com-13.
C.O., NAS, Kodiak, Alaska.

I received these orders at 1400 this date. 25 SEP 1942

William R. Larson.

ISHEL, Lt(jg) SC USNR

Last Family Photograph in Early October 1942 — (Last Time Home), Father Olaf, William, Brother Lloyd, and Mother Mary

North American SNJ-4 Plane

"***Dear Folks***, Have been running around like wild trying to get checked in here. Will start flying SNJ's when I get squared away. That's a North American advanced training plane. Have flown them before — nice planes. Took a physical exam for promotion to Lt. this morning. Passed ok so will be a full fledged Lieutenant before long. This outfit is just being organized. The officers are a nice lot. Expect to go to Alameda (San Francisco) in ten days. Suppose you're still busy threshing. Hope everything is OK at home. Your son, William."

October 21 1942 Letter Home — NAS Seattle, VGS-21[11]

"***Dear Folks***, Well, I really stuck my foot in it when I volunteered for this duty. I'm third senior officer in this squadron and they've made me "Operations" or "Flight Officer." As near as I can make out, the job corresponds to that of Senior Aviator aboard ship. It's really got me going. Have lot to learn about the administrative duties as well as the flying part of it. At least I'm not going stale for a while. . . . We're going to Alameda (San Francisco) this coming Sunday. Gas rationing is supposed to start Nov 22. I can get along without the Pontiac easier than you, so I wish you'd all take the Chevy to San Francisco & return in the Pontiac. If you think the Chevy can't make it maybe Dad can come out on the train & pick it up. In either case, suppose you'd have to start not later than the 15th of Nov. in order to make the trip before rationing starts. I'll send the money. We may be in

11 VGS stands for Escort-Scouting Squadron

Alameda for several months. Perhaps till February. . . . Hope everything is fine at home. Your son & bro, William."

October 28 1942 Letter Home — NAS Seattle, VGS-21

"***Dear Mom, Dad, & Lloyd,*** Just settled in my new home here. Have a room by myself so not bad. Drove down from Seattle. Started Monday, so you see I've been taking my time. Had a nice trip. Came through the redwoods on highway 101. . . . Have been getting about 21 miles per gallon in the Pontiac. Stopped at Portland over night, by the way. Saw Henry Foss and the Paul Thompson Family. Muriel is quite a charming gal now — married however. Just opened a checking account. Am sending a check for one or all of you to come out to pick up the Pontiac. Might be quicker for Dad or Lloyd to hop the train and come right out. Or if all of you can take the Chevy out — that's ok. Whichever is done though has to be done immediately as gas rationing begins the 22nd. 4 gal per week from then on. .... Please wire me your intentions. We may be here for some months, but everything is so uncertain that I'd feel better if the Pontiac were home. . . . More when I get settled. VGS-21 is auxiliary aircraft carrier scouting squadron #21. Your son & bro, William."

TBF-1 Plane
(Source: National Archives photo no. 80-G-464124)

November 5 1942 Letter Home — Bachelor Office Quarters — Naval Air Station Alameda California

Letter from Olaf Larson to Mrs. Olaf Larson

"***Dear Folks***, Have had a good rest today after a long and tiresome ride got here Sat. noon, tried to phone to William but no luck this here clock-work phones always gave me my nickel instead of connection. About 2 or 3 o'clock I thought I better try to get to the Station. Got on a bus to Oakland, here I was stuck for another 3-4 hours. A bus every 20 m to Alameda — the first 10 or so was so full they did not even stop. Anyhow I go to station gate at 5 pm and the guards to start phoning to the main-office, but said he was not there, well I staid around their waiting and phoning til about 9 when I thought better get up-town while the bus was running, so did not see William til Sunday morning, had a good time with him the rest of the day. Tomorrow I will start for home sweet home, wonder if Lloyd and Eli are back yet. Been raining all afternoon. Good-bye, O.M.

November 16 1942 — Hotel Sir Francis Drake — San Francisco California (Olaf was 57 years old at the time)

"***Dear Mom***, Dad left for home yesterday morning, so I suppose he'll be home before long. Hope he has no troubles on the way. Sorry you couldn't all come out. I was pretty busy, but we had one day together anyway. Had quite a time finding each other to begin with. Guess Dad will tell you all about it. It's been raining here the last three days. Get in an occasional flight. Take up the rest of the time with lectures, reading, mail, and getting organized. . . . Guess Dad will give you all the news if any. Was great to see him again. . . . Your son, William."

November 18 1942 Letter Home — NAS Alameda California — VGS-21

"***Dear Folks***, Thanks Mom, Dad, & Lloyd for the swell birthday gifts and cards. I bought the shoulder marks yesterday and am wearing khakis now. It's a little chilly, but my greens really needed cleaning. The marks cost $4.70 so aren't very cheap either. Got a fighter in the unit today.

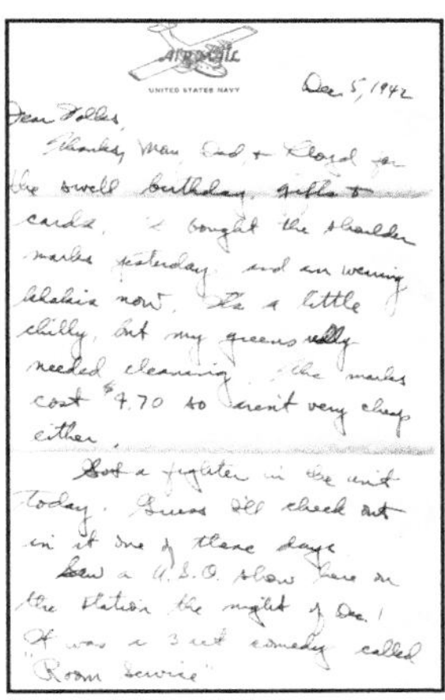

UNITED STATES NAVY

Dec. 5, 1942

Dear Folks,

Thanks Mom, Dad, & Lloyd for the swell birthday gifts & cards. I bought the shoulder marks yesterday and am wearing khakis now. It's a little chilly, but my greens really needed cleaning. The marks cost $4.70 so aren't very cheap either.

Got a fighter in the unit today. Guess I'll check out in it one of these days.

Saw a U.S.O. show here on the station the night of Dec. 1. It was a 3 act comedy called "Room Service"

Guess I'll check out in it one of these days. . . . Flying is pretty much as usual. I'm going to ship & plane recognition school two hours each morning now. Have the final exam next Saturday. I'm going to have to do a lot of cramming. Just like college days. Saw one of the former Nashville officers the other night. Had quite a chat. Guess the glamour ship is now in the last warm port we hit. . . . Your son & bro, William."

December 5 1942 Letter Home —
Naval Air Station Alameda California

"***Dear Mom, Dad, & Lloyd,*** The "soup" has rolled in on us again so no flying. Thought I'd left the fog when I left Alaska but this country is just about as bad. Christmas Day was a beautiful, sunshiny day however. Went to the Lutheran Church in Oakland Christmas morning. The President of the Ladies' Aid took me home for dinner after the services. Had a great big turkey and all the trimmings. It was the biggest dinner I'd had since I was home. There were two boys in the family — one in third grade and the other about a freshman in high school. The third grader was a live-wire. A couple of neighbor gals (university students) came over so the little fellow and I took 'em on for a couple of games of cards. The third grader would alter the rules considerably so we usually won. All in all a good time was had by all. Wish I could have been home, but since I'd just had leave I couldn't get off again. Saw another operetta Saturday night. Everett Marshall in "Blossom Time. . . . Your son & bro, William."

December 28 1942 Letter Home —
Naval Air Station Alameda California

"*We shall continue to take the top part of the Pacific, Mister Tojo—while the bottom is all yours; I'll see to that!*"

MID-DECEMBER, 1942 79

Our Navy cartoon — among the contents of Lucky's trunk

"***Dear Lloyd,*** Thanks for the Christmas gift — it's a handy gadget. I'm chewing on a piece of Mom's delicious candy too. Saw a three act comedy last night — "Arsenic & Old Lace." Hope you're enjoying the holiday season. Your brother, Bill."

December 30 1942 Postcard to Brother Lloyd — Berkeley CA

Interior of TBF Plane Cockpit (Source: Public Domain)

"***Dear Mom, Dad, & Lloyd,*** Another Sunday night has rolled around, which sort of reminds me to drop a line home. Had a family I met at church out here for dinner and the show this evening. We ate at the officer's club. Guess they enjoyed it. I don't believe I got around to taking Dad to the club. It's a fairly nice place. There are two daughters in this family — one, a high school student, the other, a nurse. Weather has been pretty good the past week. Had a ground fog all day today though, so didn't do any flying. I have about eight hours in the torpedo plane now. I believe I'm going to like it. There are an awful lot of gadgets in the plane. Sort of fun experimenting with them. It's the largest stick flying plane[12] out. Really travels too — will run away from our fighters. Powered by a 1700 h.p. 14 cylinder motor. Weighs about seven tons. I think I showed one of them to Dad when he was here. . . . Suppose the holiday celebrating routine is

12 William flew TBF-1 & TBF-1c Avengers

about over now. Wish I could have been in on it — maybe next year. Wonder if the kid brother has been seeing any more of that raven-haired beauty he mentioned. Nothing new. Had a little letter from Mary Albough. I'm in the peak of condition — weigh the same as usual. Hope you are all well. Your son and bro William. P.S. Had to order a new pair of green trousers — just $18 (what a racket!)"

January 10 1943 Letter Home — Alameda California

"***Dear Mom, Dad, and Lloyd,*** Another day of sitting around on our "duffs". Gets pretty monotonous. A ground haze settles in here and doesn't lift for days. We'll probably be here for another couple of months. I glad to hear that Lloyd enjoys his teaching experience. I received a letter from Borghild Larson this week. She had seen my name in the Concordia Directory. She works right here on the station. She graduated from Concordia in '38. Lives with Hazel Danielson, '38, who is married to a 3rd class navy radio-man. I had dinner there one night. Hashed over quite a few memories of Concordia College school days. The U.S.O. gave another show on the station this week. Lots of gags and a chorus of 16 dancing girls. The boys in the outposts of civilization would really appreciate a show like that. I'm receiving the Williston Herald now. Takes four days to get here. Yes, I'd be glad to get some copies of the New Yorker. Wonder if you care for the magazine at all. It's a little different from the usual run of magazines. Took a cute little blonde to a nice dance last night. She's a first grade teacher at one of the schools in Alameda. Quite charming. Suppose Lloyd is getting acquainted with his "fellow" pedagogues in Grenora. Wonder is Dad is doing much trucking now. Hope you are all well. Your son & bro, William."

January 16 1943 Letter Home — Alameda California

TBF Avenger (Source: U.S. Navy)

The Grumman TBF Avenger was a torpedo bomber developed initially for the United States Navy and Marine Corps.

There were three crew members: pilot, turret gunner and radioman/bombardier/ventral gunner. One .30 caliber machine gun was mounted in the nose, a .50 caliber gun was mounted right next to the turret gunner's head in a rear-facing electrically powered turret, and a single .30 caliber hand-fired machine gun mounted ventrally (under the tail), which was used to defend against enemy fighters attacking from below and to the rear. This gun was fired by the radioman/bombardier while standing up and bending over in the belly of the tail section, though he usually sat on a folding bench facing forward to operate the radio and to sight in bombing runs. Later models of the TBF/TBM dispensed with the nose-mounted gun for one .50 caliber gun in each wing per pilots' requests for better forward firepower and increased strafing ability. There was only one set of controls on the aircraft, and no access to the pilot's position from the rest of the aircraft. The radio equipment was massive, especially by today's standards, and filled the whole glass canopy to the rear of the pilot. The radios were accessible for repair through a "tunnel" along the right hand side.

The Avenger had a large bomb bay, allowing for one Bliss-Leavitt Mark 13 torpedo, a single 2,000 pound bomb, up to four 500 pound bombs, or ten 100 pound bombs. Maximum speed was 275 m.p.h. with a 1,000 mile range.

"***Dear Dad***, Received a letter from the Treasury Dept. in regards to that $100.00 check that I lost. Takes almost an act of Congress to get a duplicate. Will you please sign the form I've enclosed and return it? Have to return that and some other papers to the ship. Have been flying quite a bit the last three days. That TBF is a good plane. Expect to go out ice skating with those Concordia friends this evening. That will be the first in years. Hope everything is fine at home. Your son, William."

January 19 1943 Letter Home — Alameda California

"***Dear Mom, Dad, & Lloyd,*** Will write a little before going out on a hop. Have been standing by the last couple of days expecting to go out on search for the Pan American Clipper that was lost, but bad weather has prevented operations. No use searching if you can't see. Was surprised to run into Bob Barstad at the Officers Club in the Leamington Hotel last Saturday night. He's now an Ensign and going to Diesel school at the Univ. of Calif. He and I used to work together at the S&S store in Moorhead. Lloyd probably knows him. Went ice skating with the former Concordia gals I told you about. Had a lot of fun and noticed no ill effects. Some of those girls at the rink were evidently Iona Hein's aspirants. Cut trim figures and you could see a lot of them. Had another dinner with the Pres. Of the Ladies Aid. The neighbor gal came over again and we played several games of carroms. Richard, the little third grader, is quite a live wire. Must be pretty chilly at home. It's not cold here but is usually foggy. If it's not foggy, it's raining. Once in a great while the sun shines. I almost preferred the Aleutian weather. Glad to hear that the kid brother enjoys his teaching experience. Sorry about Dad's two teeth. Hope you are all well. Your son & bro, William.

January 27 1943 Letter Home — Alameda California

"***Dear Mom, Dad, & Lloyd,***
Sorry to hear about the kid brother getting the mumps. Hope he recovers with no ill after-effects. Have been quite busy the last few days. I lead a flight of four planes up to Redding, Calif to search the mountain area there for that missing Clipper plane from Hawaii. We stayed overnight at Redding. Had a big dinner at a private home and then went to the local night club. The country up there is pretty rugged. Must have been ten feet of snow on the mountain tops. I looked at the trees so much that I imagined they were waving at me. Got pretty well acquainted with the area. The plane was found about 80 miles north of Alameda. We were about 200 miles north. Took an altitude hop in a low pressure chamber one day. Showed us how and why to use oxygen on high altitude hops. We went up to 28,000 feet.

Took tests at sea level, 15,000 feet without oxygen, and at 28,000 with oxygen. Results at 15,000 without oxygen were far inferior to the others. I thought it was very interesting and informative. Received Dad's letter today. Also got one from Jack Davis. Took the 1st grade teacher to "Junior Miss" a play in S.F. Sunday night. Thanks for the New Yorkers. Your son & bro, William."

February 2 1943 Letter Home — Alameda California

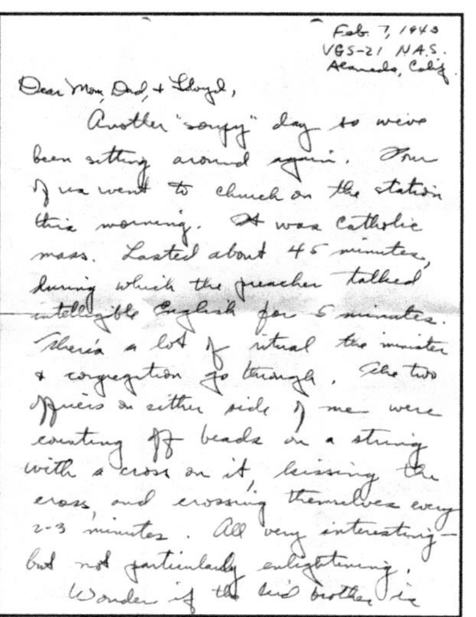

Feb. 7, 1943
VGS-21 N.A.S.
Alameda, Calif.

Dear Mom, Dad, + Lloyd,

Another "soupy" day so we've been sitting around again. Four of us went to church on the station this morning. It was Catholic mass. Lasted about 45 minutes, during which the preacher talked intelligible English for 5 minutes. There's a lot of ritual the minister + congregation go through. The two officers on either side of me were counting off beads on a string with a cross on it, kissing the cross, and crossing themselves every 2-3 minutes. All very interesting— but not particularly enlightening. Wonder if the kid brother is

"***Dear Mom, Dad, and Lloyd,*** Another "soupy" day so we've been sitting around again. Four of us went to church at the station this morning. It was Catholic mass. Lasted about 45 minutes, during which the preacher talked intelligible English for 5 minutes. There's a lot of rituals the minister and congregation go through. The two officers on either side of me were counting off beads on a string with a cross on it, kissing the cross, and crossing themselves every 2-3 minutes. All very interesting — but not particularly enlightening. Wonder if the kid brother is back teaching again. Hope he recovered with no ill effects. I've been fortunate in having no illness other than an occasional slight cold. The 1st grade teacher and I went to hear Richard Crooks, the Metropolitan tenor, at the Oakland Auditorium Friday night. He's a great big bald-headed man. William Primrose, violist, was on the program. They were both very good. . . . Hope it's getting a little warmer around home now. Noticed in the "Believe or Not" section of the Sunday paper that is got so hot at

Colgan, North Dakota, that corn popped on the cob. Your son & bro, William."

February 7 1943 Letter Home — Alameda California

V-Mail from Lt. J.M. Holladay

"***Dear Buddy-Buddy:*** Just a note. Mail is leaving the ship tomorrow, we think. Soper [Lt. David L Soper] was transferred just before we last sailed — with only two hours notice. Then that nite Allison came down with Black Malaria, and has been pretty sick. He is being sent ashore tomorrow, and probably will be sent to the States. Detached from here, anyway. So old Pick [Lt. John Wheeler Pickens] is now Senav [Senior Naval Aviator]. He doesn't want it much for it ruins his chances at transfer. Also he has to set too good an example. We have a new aviator ordered to the ship. Wife is now in Frisco. Don't know her address, except that she was going to stay with Mrs. Burkett at 1105 Bush St. for a while. Look her up. She knows more about you than you think. Soper went to the States, so I guess he is married by now. His home address, in case you don't have it, is 1625 Euclid Ave, San Marion, Calif. We have been busy — I flew 62 hours in January, and Al got in nearly a hundred. Everything is about the same — terrible. The ship is more uncomfortable than it has been since I've been on board. That's all there is — there ain't no more, old yankee."

February 10 1943 — FPO USS Nashville- At Sea
(Lucky's former roommate on the Glamour Ship)

"***Dear Mom, Dad, & Lloyd,*** Have a day off today so am taking it easy this morning. Didn't get up till 10 o'clock. It's a beautiful day, so the airplanes are really buzzing. We've been kept pretty busy lately. Have all our planes and pilots, and the weather has been fine. Did a little glide bombing in the TBF last week. Carry 12 one hundred pound water-filled bombs. It's quite a lot of fun — as long as it's not a real target we're bombing. Saw a comical show on the station a few nights ago — Jack Benny in "George Washington Slept Here." . . . Glad to hear that the kid brother is O.K. and back on the job again. Am enclosing a picture of the first grade teacher I've been seeing quite often. She's not beautiful — but cute as a bug's ear. Gives me ideas I never had before. What do you think? . . . Hope the weather at home is starting to ease up a little and that you're all well. Your son & bro, William."

Ruth Cronkite

February 16 1943 Letter Home — Alameda California

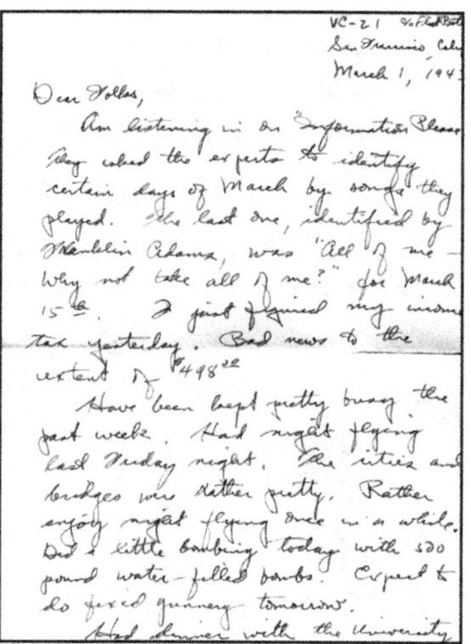

VC-21 c/o Fleet Post
San Francisco, Cal[illegible]
March 1, 194[illegible]

Dear Folks,

Am listening in on "Information Please." They asked the experts to identify certain days of March by songs they played. The last one, identified by Franklin Adams, was "All of me — Why not take all of me?" for March 15th. I just figured my income tax yesterday. Bad news to the extent of $498.22

Have been kept pretty busy the past week. Had night flying last Friday night. The cities and bridges were rather pretty. Rather enjoy night flying once in a while. Did a little bombing today with 500 pound water-filled bombs. Expect to do fixed gunnery tomorrow.

Had dinner with the University

"***Dear Folks***, Am listening in on "Information Please." They asked the experts to identify certain days of March by songs they played. The last one, identified by Franklin Adams, was "All of me — why not take all of me?" for March 15th. I just figured my income tax yesterday. Bad news to the extent of $498. Have been kept pretty busy the past week. Had night flying last Friday night. The cities and bridges were rather pretty. Rather enjoy night flying once in a while. Did a little bombing today with 500 pound water-filled bombs. Expect to do fixed gunnery tomorrow. Had dinner with the University gal and her folks last night. Also took a drive to San Francisco and saw the big food mill fire. It was very picturesque, but cost an estimated 6 million dollars. . . . Yes, I think you're right about forgetting. I probably wouldn't be a very good bet for marriage anyway. Not sure I cherish the freedom especially, but variety is interesting. I'd really like to help put in the crop this spring, but I rather doubt that furlough applies to officers. . . . Hope everything is OK at home, Your son, William."

March 1 1943 Letter Home — Alameda California

William trained with the Grumman TBF Avenger, a torpedo bomber plane, while at NAS Alameda, NAS El Centro, and NAAS Otay Mesa Airfields. The pilot seat in the TBF was accessed from the wing and was separated from the radio compartment and the rest of the crew area. There were three crew members: pilot, radioman/bombardier, and the rear turret gunner. William's plane crew changed almost daily during these training flights. One of the radiomen, Richard Wagner, first flew with William on March 10, 1943. He would later be assigned as William's permanent radioman and go on to log over 150 flight hours seated behind William in the Avenger.

MAR 1943

Date	Type of Machine	Number of Machine	Duration of Flight	Character of Flight	Pilot	Passengers	Remarks
3-1	TBF-1	06085	1.5	G	Larson	Wright Schram	
3-2	"	06145	1.5	K	"		
3-6	"	06082	1.0	K	"	[illegible]	
3-6	"	06113	1.4	K	"	[illegible]	
3-7	"	06082	2.0	K	"	[illegible]	
"	"	"	1.1	K	"	[illegible]	
3-9	"	"	1.0	K	"	[illegible]	
3-9	"	06181	1.0	K	"	Stuart	
3-10	"	06195	1.2	J	"	[illegible]	
"	"	"	1.5	J	"	Wagner	
3-11	"	06113	1.3	K	"	[illegible]	
3-12	"	06082	3.0	E	"	Stuart	
3-13	OS2U	5690	.5	F	"	Lee	
"	"	"	.5	F	"	Lee	
3-14	TBF-1	06082	.7	E	"	Stuart	
3-14	"	"	1.6	J	"	[illegible]	
3-15	"	06080	2.0	J	"	[illegible]	
3-15	"	06082	.5	K	"	Wagner	
"	"	"	1.0	K	"	[illegible]	
3-21	"	06080	.5	O	"	[illegible]	Otay to San Diego
Total time to date,							

Lucky's Aviators Flight Log Book

Character of Flight Codes: E = Familiarization, F = Gunnery, G = Bombing, H = Torpedo Run, J = Scouting/Anti-Sub Patrol, K = Tactical, L = Navigation, N = Ferrying, O = Utility,

"***Dear Folks***, Well we're just getting squared away in our new location. We're at Otay Mesa now — a little field just southeast of San Diego. Have just a short distance to the Mexican border. Facilities aren't too good here, but I like it. Wide open spaces with good fresh air and lots of sunshine. Nights are plenty cool, so there's good sleeping. Can see the mountains in the distance and the skies are very pretty. All in all it looks like a good health resort.

I lead a flight of 9 TBFs down from Alameda. Took just 2 ½ hrs. Followed the airways at 8,000'. We live in barracks here. Two in a room. I'm rooming with a new Lt from North Carolina. He was a Prof at Duke University. Taught the classics. He's the son of a Methodist minister. His name is Jim Truesdale.[13] . . . Can't say I regret having left Alameda particularly, so I guess it was temporary infatuation. Saw a couple of the wives from the glamour ship a few days ago. They seemed to think she was in the South Pacific area at present. Sort of wish I were with her again. Think I'd better send all but one of the pictures back home. Would like a group picture if they're ready. Sent a box with a few things home a couple of days ago.... I want to travel as light as possible from now on. Hope everything is OK at home, Your son, William."

March 22 1943 Letter Home — Otay Mesa California.

---

13 James N. Truesdale was a Duke graduate all the way: AB in 1928, Master's in 1929 and PhD in 1936. Beginning his teaching career in 1930, he gradually gained a long-lived reputation as a conscientious, kindly professor who introduced countless students to "the wonder and glory of Hellenism" as one former student declared. Describing Truesdale as a "marvelous blend of quiet dignity and genuine friendliness in and out of the classroom," this same Duke alumnus who himself became a professor, paid Truesdale the ultimate academic tribute: "You were my finest teacher and the most significant influence upon my academic development. THE LAUNCHING OF DUKE UNIVERSITY, 1924 – 1949 by Robert Franklin Durden.
Lt. James Truesdale was later the Air Combat Intelligence Office (ACIO) of VC 38.

"**_Dear Folks_**, Received your letter a couple of days ago and a bundle of New Yorkers today. The New Yorker is rather a screwy magazine, but it sometimes gets off some pretty good humor — such as it is. Wonder if the snow isn't disappearing around home now. Seems to me it would be spring. Weather here is almost too nice. Fly 4-5 hours per day and sometimes at night. Was out a few nights ago on a night torpedo hop. Used radar to find the target. Radar is quite an aid in several ways. Requires a good operator though. Dropped my first exercise torpedo last week. Was very interesting to watch it enter the water, settle down on its course, and swim along at about 40 kts per. Believe it would have been a hit too. The exercise torpedoes are set to run at a depth of 30 feet, so they pass under the target. After running about 2 miles they come to the surface, and are recovered. A torpedo is really a wonderful machine and cost thousands of dollars. No, Mom, I didn't give the little gal a ring. Guess it's a good thing. It's not a very good bet as a marriage risk. Anyhow the ideal girl doesn't exist — or isnt' it Sylvia? Happened to run into a very charming Irish girl in Coronado. Went to a dance at the Coronado Hotel and had a very pleasant evening. She's an "army brat,", as she expressed it. Her father is a high ranking army officer. Watched the caterpillars pushing the dirt making roads and runways around here. Sometimes I wish I could hop on one and work the levers for a while. Drove old Trehus' cat at Arnegard one afternoon. Great sport. Hope everything is OK at home, Wonder if Dad will be able to get some help for springs work. Your son, William."

April 5 1943 Letter Home — Otay Mesa California.

"***Dear Folks***, Completed another day of flying on the mesa. Has been a beautiful day too. Dropped exercise torpedoes on the last hop this evening. Got 3 hits out of 4 drops. Ruth, the Alameda school teacher, came down here last Friday. Left last night. I got off yesterday, so we took in some of the sights of San Diego. There's an excellent zoo at Balboa Park. Told the little gal to go back and marry the army captain — so I imagine that's what she'll do. Has been sort of wet around here the past week. We've been wading around in the mud up to the ankles. The mud is just like Canadian clay. Have a couple of pool tables set up here in the recreation hall now, so the boys have something to play with. Things are going the same as usual. Had a sore throat a couple days but am OK now. Hope everything is ok at home. Your son, William."

April 12 1943 Letter Home — Otay Mesa California

"***Dear Folks***, Am aboard a converted carrier this evening. Going out for a day or so to qualify in carrier landings. Will be a new experience for me. Had chicken dinner aboard and saw a show, "The Powers Girl." . . . Hope you had a nice Easter. . . . Hope everything is fine at home. Will write more later. Your son, William."

April 25 1943 0925 PM — USS Altamaha [William's Flight Log Entry for April 27 1943: four qualifying carrier landings made aboard USS Altamaha]

"***Dear Folks***, Had a day off today. Just got back from San Diego. Saw a Messerschmitt 109 E there. It's a German fighter plan that had been shot down over England. Looks like a good plane. Imagine Dad is busy with the spring's work now. Wish I could help with it. Was out to sea for a couple days last week. Am a full — fledged carrier pilot now. Made four landing in a row and had no trouble at all. They require 8 landings, as a rule, to qualify you for carrier work the first time. I think carrier landings are as easy, if not easier, than recoveries on a cruiser. . . . Flew around the Palomar observatory yesterday. That's where the big telescope is that we read about some years ago. Took a year or so to cool the glass for it. Hope everything is fine at home. Your son, Willliam."

May 4 1943 Letter Home — Otay Mesa California

"***Dear Folks***, It's a beautiful afternoon and I'm just taking it easy. Soaked up a little sun, but it's too hot to stay out long. This is Mother's Day too, hope you're having a nice day, Mom. The preacher gave a good sermon using mother's love as a theme this morning. Got quite a kick out of Gerald's letter. I'd love to return it for the files. Yep, the glamour ship was evidently in Sydney. Wish I'd been with her on that trip. However, I'm enjoying this work and I'm really glad I had the chance to do some carrier operations. Some of us went to Tijuana last night. Visited with three native sisters that were quite charming. They're from a strict catholic family, have gone through college, and are thoroughly steeped in Mexican (or Spanish) customs and traditions. Six "Limies" are on the station for training now. Two moved in on either side of my room. Seem to be "jolly good fellows," you know. Nothing much new. See no hopes of getting out to sea in the immediate future. Suppose Dad is pretty busy in the fields now days. Guess I'll get a little exercise in the form of a volleyball game. Your son, William.

May 9 1943 Letter Home — Otay Mesa California

"***Dear Folks***, Have high winds tonight so we're not doing any flying. Don't' know whether or not I told you we're flying nights now. We fly from 8

William in a TBF Avenger Plane

o'clock in the evening to 5 o'clock in the morning. This place is hot as Hades in the daytime but our barracks are air conditioned so it's not too hard to sleep. ...We'll probably be flying nights for about a month. Experimenting with illumination, etc. It's really dark here too with no moon. The sky is usually clear though. . . . This is just about fishing time. Wish I could get home for it but it's out of the question. Suppose Lloyd is through teaching now, so you can all run up to Canada for a little fishing. Flew the SNJ over to North Island on my day off. Spent the day (quite pleasantly) with a little beauty operator I know in San Diego. Comes from Missouri. Our fighters came back from Attu. The skipper was lost.[14] Guess they didn't care much for the flying conditions up there. Hope everything is ok at home. Your son, William."

June 1 1943 Letter Home — Marine Air Station El Centro California

14 Lt. Commander Lloyd Keyes Greenamyer was killed over Attu Island, Territory of Alaska, on May 14, 1943 operating off the USS Nassau and flying a F4F-4 fighter plane with VF-21. He was posthumously awarded the US Navy Cross for actions during the seizure and occupation of Attu Island in May of 1943.

CHAPTER 4

VC 38 Days—California, At Sea, Guadalcanal, & Munda Point

TBF-1 Plane with Control Tower at Otay Mesa in Background 6/17/43

"***Dear Folks***, Have no hop this morning so I'll dash off a little letter. Glad to see you got up to Canada for a little fishing. Wish I could have been along. Nope, I'm not a Lt. Cmdr. and don't expect to be for some time. The old squadron was decommissioned yesterday. We're in a new squadron now—Air Group 38 which consists of fighters, dive bombers, and our torpedo-bombers. We're still night flying but expect to quit in a couple of nights. We're getting pretty tired of it. Was plenty dark the first two weeks but the moon is up now, so it's practically the same as flying in the daytime. Heard the glamour ship was in San Francisco getting repairs. Would be great to see some of the fellows aboard her again. How is

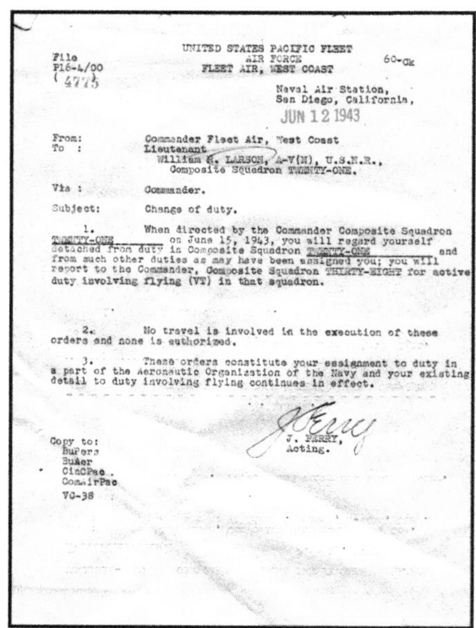

UNITED STATES PACIFIC FLEET
AIR FORCE
FLEET AIR, WEST COAST

File
P16-4/00
(4775)

60-Ck

Naval Air Station,
San Diego, California,
JUN 12 1943

From: Commander Fleet Air, West Coast
To : Lieutenant
William R. LARSON, A-V(N), U.S.N.R.,
Composite Squadron TWENTY-ONE.

Via : Commander.

Subject: Change of duty.

1. When directed by the Commander Composite Squadron TWENTY-ONE on June 15, 1943, you will regard yourself detached from duty in Composite Squadron TWENTY-ONE and from such other duties as may have been assigned you; you will report to the Commander, Composite Squadron THIRTY-EIGHT for active duty involving flying (VT) in that squadron.

2. No travel is involved in the execution of these orders and none is authorized.

3. These orders constitute your assignment to duty in a part of the Aeronautic Organization of the Navy and your existing detail to duty involving flying continues in effect.

J. Perry
J. PERRY,
Acting.

Copy to:
BuPers
BuAer
CinCPac.
ComAirPac
VC-38

the gas rationing situation around home? Can you get enough? Went to El Centro for a swim today. Most exercise I've had in a long time. Have a day off tomorrow so I'll dash off to San Diego in an SNJ to see the bright lights. Wonder when Lloyd will be going to Minneapolis? Am sending a little picture of myself in one of our TBFs. Weighs 7 tons and has 1700 horses in front. Your son, William."

June 17 1943 Letter Home — Otay Mesa California

VC38/P16-4/00 COMPOSITE SQUADRON THRITY EIGHT CEB/jph

June 21, 1943

From: Commander, Composite Squadron Thirty Eight.
To : Lieutenant Commander Charles E. Brunton, U.S.N.

Subject: Change of duty.

1. Upon receipt of these orders you will take charge of the below named officers and proceed immediately and report to the Commander, Composite Squadron Thirty Eight, at the Auxiliary Air Station, Otay Mesa, California.

Lieutenant W.R. LARSON, A-V(N), U.S.N.R.
Lieutenant B.B. ROGERS, A-V(S), U.S.N.R.
Lieutenant J.N. TRUESDALE, A-V(S), U.S.N.R.
Lieutenant (jg) R.B. GIBLIN, A-V(N), U.S.N.R.
Lieutenant (jg) R.F. REGAN, A-V(N), U.S.N.R.
Lieutenant (jg) R.A. MARSHALL, A-V(N), US.N.R.
Lieutenant (jg) J.A. LEARY, A-V(N), U.S.N.R.
Lieutenant (jg) B.C. BISHOP, A-V(N), U.S.N.R.
Lieutenant (jg) H.T. LEAKE, A-V(N), U.S.N.R.
Ensign C. TAHLER, A-V(N), U.S.N.R.
Ensign R.H. BEHN, A-V(N), US.N.R.
Ensign H. WILSON, Jr., A-V(N), U.S.N.R.
Ensign J.P. SCHOLFIELD, A-V(N), U.S.N.R.

C.E. BRUNTON.

VC38/P16-4/00 COMPOSITE SQUADRON THIRTY EIGHT CEB/jph

FIRST ENDORSEMENT June 21, 1943.

From: Commander, Composite Squadron Thirty Eight.
To : Lieutenant Commander, Charles E. Brunton.

1. You and the officers in your charge reported this date.

C.E. BRUNTON.

Wildcat F4F4 Plane, Source: Public Domain

"***Dear Folks***, Well, here I am back at Otay Mesa. Kind of nice to get back too. Got plenty of night flying over at El Centro. Flew all night and slept all day. Temperatures in the day time there ran about 110 to 115F, but all the buildings were air conditioned, so it wasn't bad sleeping in the daytime.

Spent a couple of days fishing at a little lake between here and El Centro this week. Wish I could have gone home but didn't get enough time off. Fishing wasn't so hot. Had one good bite and lost the hook — a 75¢'er too.

Took a fighter up today for the first time. A Grumman Wildcat F4F4. It flies easier than the TBF. Can't say I like it any better though. And it isn't much faster. Has six guns that I'd like to have in the TBF though. Guess I told you VC-21 was de-commissioned. We're in a new squadron now — VC-38 which is composed of fighters, dive bombers, and torpedo planes. **I'm now operations officer**. ....Had a little target practices with a 38 six-shooter today. A Jap would be fairly safe unless I could push the barrel right in his ribs. Am sending a picture of the little beauty operator in San Diego. She's French-English, 24, the right measurements, and lots of fun. Can even cook. Hope you are all well. Your son, William."

William and Bette Burton. Taken at Calexico Calif., June 1943

June 30 1943 Letter Home — Otay Mesa

Left to Right: 3rd seated — Cecelia "CC" Boullie, Lt. Ray A Marshall, Bette Burton, William — June 23, 1943 (During VC 38's 7-day leave — Top's Club, San Diego, CA)

"***Dear Folks***, . . . My roomy, Jim Truesdale, went to San Ysidro to see a little girl. Sure great to have him as a room-mate again. He's the professor I told you about. Was gone for quite awhile during the occupation of Attu. . . . Have been battling poison-oak ever since that little fishing trip in the mountains. It's pretty well under control now, but I certainly looked like an Indian on the war path for days. Had my eyes, nose and ears all painted up with calamine solution — a whitish paste. Have been getting some instrument hops in an SNJ lately. Sit in the rear cock-pit under a hood. Practice take-offs, maneuvers, and recovery from unusual positions. Good stuff but hard on the nerves. Played with a fighter again the other day. Got quite a kick out of doing slow rolls. If Dad wants to use the little money there is in the bank for the first payment on the farm, he's welcome to it. Sorry to hear about Dad being sick. Hope he's well now and that you're all feeling fine. Wish I could accompany the kid brother on his social exploits. By the way, the 1st of July was an important anniversary — many happy returns! Wonder how you spent the fourth. We flew — as usual. Your son, William."

July 8 1943 Letter Home — Otay Mesa

Lucky and a TBF plane — July 16, 1943 (assumed to be NAAS Otay Mesa, CA)

Lucky and a TBF plane — July 16, 1943 (assumed to be NAAS Otay Mesa, CA)

Lucky in pilot seat of F4F Wildcat plane — July 16, 1943
(assumed to be NAAS Otay Mesa, CA)

William's Flight Log Entry for July 24 1943: "Four carrier landings USS Copahee" (Source: National Archives photo no. 19-LCM-271 — May 9 1943)

"***Dear Folks***, Expect to leave tomorrow or next day so I'm sending the safe-keeping receipts I've received home. ....Tried to call you last night and today. Will try again in the morning. Will write more later, Your son, William."

July 31 1943 Letter Home — Otay Mesa

ACCOUNT NO: 17296

WAR SAVINGS BOND SAFEKEEPING RECEIPT
(Nontransferable)
TREASURER OF THE UNITED STATES
WASHINGTON, D. C.

CASE NO: 31670
November 30, 1942

DATE OF BONDS	SERIAL NUMBERS	DENOMINATIONS	MATURITY VALUE
Oct. 1, 1942	C224387862		$100

Received From:
Ensign William Rudolph Larson
U.S.S. Nashville
c/o Postmaster
San Francisco, California

(SIGNED) W.A.JULIAN
TREASURER OF THE U.S.

This receipt is to be surrendered when Bonds are withdrawn from safekeeping.

The squadron's flight training in the TBF-1 planes included torpedo bombing, gunnery, night torpedo tactics, catapult take-offs from carrier decks, carrier landings, anti-sub bombing, and night oxygen flying. The squadron spent over a month training at NAS El Centro practicing night illumination, mine laying, carrier rendezvous, and glide bombing maneuvers, all while flying at night.

Lucky's previous flight experience from the USS Nashville and flying in the hazardous and great fog banks of the Aleutian Islands, and landing in the rough waters of the Bering Sea aided him immensely. *"Made four landings in a row [carrier deck landings] and had no trouble at all. They require 8 landings, as a rule, to qualify you for carrier work the first time. I think carrier landings are as easy, if not easier, than recoveries on a cruiser."*

By the time Lucky — now Senior Operations Officer, and his fellow VC 38 squadron shipped out to their over-seas missions, Lucky had recorded 1726.8 hours of naval flight time since he first trained at Chamberlain Airfield in Minnesota, back in 1939. Of those hours, 280 had been in the new TBF-1 Avenger torpedo bomber plane.

Lucky and his assigned radioman, Richard Wagner, were now ready. As they sailed on a converted escort carrier for 25 days to their unknown destination, Lucky wrote home to the family farm in Hanks, North Dakota, *"Expect the [monotonous] routine [on ship] will be shaken up before too long."* Within 32 days of that statement, Lucky and his crew would be on their first dive bombing mission against the Japanese.

"***Dear Folks***, Well, here we are on the briny deep again. Tried to call you Saturday but I guess you were in Williston as no one answered. Couldn't make connections Sunday. .... Can't quite believe it's true, but ***I gave a diamond to the little girl*** I sent you a snap-shot of. Can't begin to tell you all about her but I'm sure you'll like her as much as I love her. Her name is Bette Burton. She said she'd write home. Jim Truesdale is here beside me writing home too. We had a couple of games of cribbage. We're feeling fine, but some of the boys are a little sea-sick. It's the first time out for many of them. .... Glad to hear the crops are looking good. I've been getting the Williston paper quite regularly. Notice wheat stays around $1.16. Thanks for sending me the New Yorkers. I'll have plenty of time to read them in the next few days. You mentioned the family pictures were ready. I'd like to have one. Took a short hop in a Taylor Cub the other day. Quite a lot of fun but for going places I'll take the TBF. Hope you are all well. Your son, William."

August 2 1943 Letter Home — at sea [USS Long Island][15]

15 [ ] Brackets indicate William's location based on his Flight log and Radioman Wagner's war diary. **The family was unaware of Lucky's true locations throughout 1943 after leaving the West Coast.**

August 8 — 10, 1943 USS Long Island stopped in Hawaii

"***Dear Folks***, Still cruising along, sitting on our duffs, and playing innumerable games of cribbage — getting to be old stuff. Get up at six to eat breakfast, perhaps have an hour's bull session, watch the flying fish play, do a little reading, play some cribbage, sweat through a third rate movie in the wardroom, and so to bed. This routine, for days on end, gets a bit monotonous. Expect the routine will be shaken up before too long though. Glad you had a little trip. Also that the kid brother's back is better. Wanted to contact you on the phone to tell you about Bette and shoving off. Perhaps she's written by this time. Wish I could see the crops at home now. Too bad the Federal Land Bank upped the price. Am trying to get an allotment through to the Williston Bank. If Dad needs what little cash is there, he can use it. . . . Hope you are all well, Your Son, William."

August 14 1943 Letter Home — At Sea [USS Long Island]

USS Long Island: (CVE-1) was lead ship of her class and the first escort carrier of the United States Navy. *Long Island* departed San Diego on 8 July and arrived Pearl Harbor on the 17th. After a training run south to Palmyra Island, she loaded two squadrons of Marine Corps aircraft and got underway for the South Pacific on 2 August. Touching at Fiji on 13 August, she then steamed to a point 200 miles southeast of Guadalcanal and launched her aircraft (19 Grumman F4F Wildcats and 12 Douglas SBD Dauntless dive bombers). These planes, the first to reach Henderson Field, were instrumental in the Guadalcanal campaign and went on to compile a distinguished war record. 13,700 ton displacement. 21 air craft carried. (Photo source: National Archives, photo no. 19-LCM-271, February 14 1945)

"***Dear Lloyd,*** How's the kid brother?... Got ashore for a couple of hours recently. Saw some of the local color — pretty dark. All the men wore skirts (multi-colored and dazzling) and everybody went barefooted. Most of them were flat-footed as ducks. The local siren was at the dock. Wore a black dress with bright yellow trimmings, carried a parasol, wore huge gold earrings and no shoes. She didn't seem to be making much time though. I'm now a member of that venerable organization of the Ancient Order of the Deep — a Shellback. Had an initiation which left its marks on the posterior for several days.

Shellback Initiation: King Neptune & his court — USS Long Island August 14, 1943 crossing of the Equator. (Source: W Wagner)

No college initiation could compare with it. Guess you know by now that I fell completely for a beautiful little charmer in San Diego. Scotch-Irish-English, green eyes speckled with brown, dark hair, about 5-5, and 119 lbs. of loveliness. She's the main reason why I'm not particularly crazy about this cruise. Guess you'll be harvesting about now. Wish I could be in on it. Wishing you a Very Happy Birthday, Your brother, Bill."

August 18 1943 Letter to Brother Lloyd — At Sea [USS Long Island — Stopped in Pago Pago, Samoa]

"***Dear Mom, Dad, & Lloyd,*** Am writing this in a little Quonset hut that passes for an Officer's Club. Have been stuck here for four days. It's about 900 miles from the rest of the gang. Been raining every day — and they tell me the rainy season is due shortly. Sun is shining this morning though, so I hope to get back today. . . . Waded through the streets of a dirty little village the other night. Bought some French pastry — which almost made me sick. . . . Glad to hear the crops are looking good. Wish I could be there to help with the harvest. This Boy Scout Camp life is a bit monotonous as a steady diet. Living conditions aren't bad though. We eat and sleep well. Have outdoor plumbing and do our own washing. Wash in a steel helmet. Don't worry about me if you don't hear for quite a stretch of time. I'm feeling fine and getting along OK in every way. Anxious to get back though. Hope you are all well, Your son & bro, William."

August 31 1943 Letter Home — [Flight Log Entry: Tontouta to Espiritu Santo 2.8 HR duration of flight]

Luganville Airfield, Espiritu Santo Island, New Hebrides: During World War II, particularly after the Japanese attack on Pearl Harbor, the island was used by Allied forces as a military supply and support base, naval harbor, and airfield. In highly fictionalized form, it is the locale of James Michener's *Tales of the South Pacific* and the subsequent Rodgers and Hammerstein musical, *South Pacific*. The presence of the Allies later contributed to the island's diving tourism, as the United States dumped most of their equipment and refuse at what is now known as "Million Dollar Point". (Photo Source: National Archives photo no. 80-G-224013)

"***Dear Folks***, . . . Happy to hear the crop is so good. Only wish I were there to help harvest it. I'm sore at the kid brother though for hopping off the tractor and joining the Navy as a gob. He'd be a lot more valuable on the farm. However, I can appreciate his feeling. Believe he could have volunteered in a more desirable branch of service though. He'll probably find the going rather rough and tough. But he can take it.

Well Mom, Bette is neither Jew nor Catholic. She's Protestant-Baptist I believe. Must confess I never went to church with her. She's a lovely lady and I hope you and Dad can meet her before too long. Heard Italy had dropped out of the war yesterday.

Jim and I went to church last Sunday. The roof had several holes in it. The fruit of one of the trees overhead dropped through the ceiling and bonked one of the enlisted men. The chaplain looked over, after a bit and said, "Did you get hurt, son?" The gob, with a pained-expression, says "No-Sir! — all good things come from above."... Saw a fellow running around with a butterfly net yesterday. Good indicator of what happens when you've been out here too long. I'll probably be going for bats myself. . . . Jim and I intend to find a river tomorrow and fish for trout. It's our day off. What to do on a day off is really a problem. Hope Dad is not working too hard with the harvest. Tell "Shorty" Sandvold "Hello". I'm eating and sleeping well here and not working very hard. Need six weeks harvest labor to put me in good shape. However, I'm feeling well and getting along ok. Hope you are all well, Your son, William."

September 10 1943 Letter Home — [Espiritu Santo Island, New Hebrides — Code named "Buttons"]

SEP 1943

Date	Type of Machine	Number of Machine	Duration of Flight	Character of Flight	Pilot	Passengers	Remarks
1	TBF	23958	1.7	L	Self	Wagner.	
2	TBF	24244	1.0	L	"	Wagner Wright.	
3	TBF	23959	1.0	L	"	Wagner, Wright	
3	TBF	23959	1.1	L	"	Tuck McCarthy.	
6	TBF	24244	1.8	H	"	Wagner Wright	Haggerty
6	TBF	24244	1.5	L	"	SAME	
8	TBF	24244	1.7	L	"	SAME Perkins.	
8	TBF	24182	1.5	F	"	SAME Haggerty	
9	TBF	24244	1.0	G	"	Wagner Perkins. Kemper	
9	TBF	24244	1.0	F	"	Wagner, Sparks, Haggerty	
10	TBF	24244	1.0	F	"	Wagner Perkins.	
13	TBF	24182	4.5	N	"	" Wright	Buttons to Cactus
15	"	24244	4.5	G	"	" "	Attack Ballale
18	"	24182	5.0	N	"	" "	To Buttons.
21	"	24244	1.2	G	"	" "	Buganich
22	"	24244	1.3	F	"	" "	
27	"	24244	2.0	J	"	" "	Anti Sub. 1CL
27	"	24182	4.3	J	"	" "	" " 1CL
28	"	47555	1.0	N	"	" "	To Buttons from Brenton
Total time to date.							

Lucky's Aviators Flight Log Book
Character of Flight Codes: E = Familiarization, F = Gunnery, G = Bombing, H = Torpedo Run, J = Scouting/Anti-Sub Patrol, K = Tactical, L = Navigation, N = Ferrying, O = Utility,

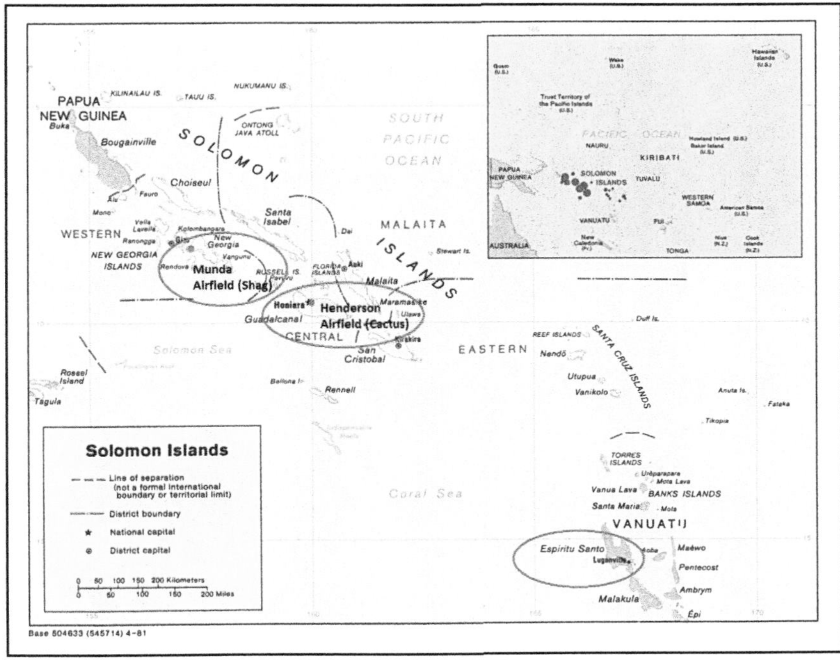

Lucky operated from Espiritu Santo, Guadalcanal & Munda Point airfields

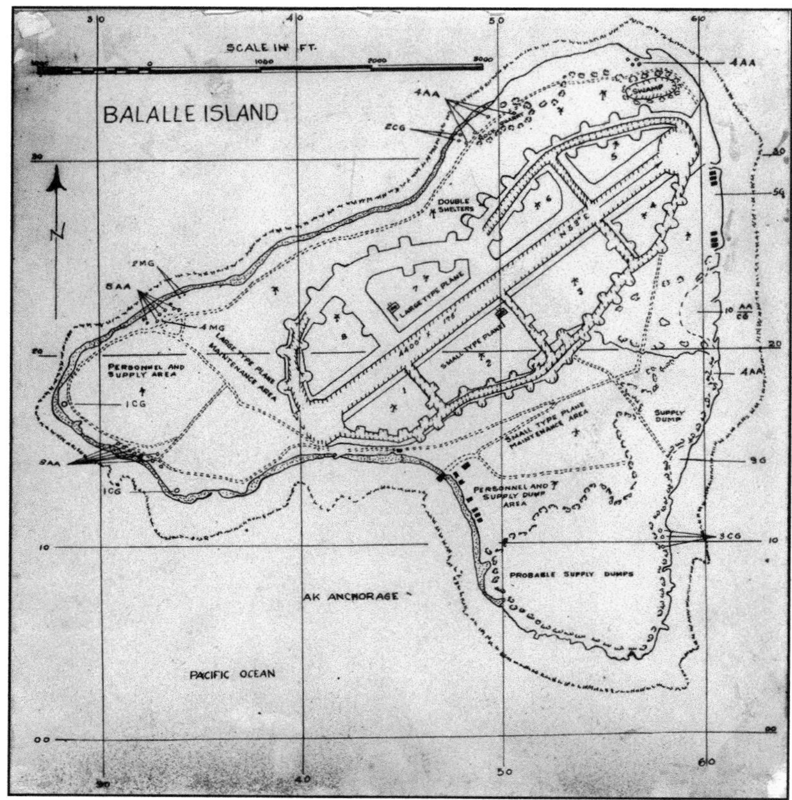

VC 38 Map of Ballale Airfield —
(Source: Lt.(jg) John Leary's Map — the Leary Family Collection)

Lucky's Radioman Richard Wagner's War Diary:

Today I went on my first strike against the Japs. It was the Island of Ballale just a few miles from Bougainville. Ballale is a small island with a bomb strip covering almost the entire island. There was lots of heavy AA[16] and zeros. One Zero started a move on us but a P39 shot him down before he got a good start. During the three day attack on Ballale we lost two TBFs and three F6Fs. Two of the fighter pilots were picked up but the others were not. We [Navy and Marine fighters] **shot down 5 zeros.**[17]

— September 15 1943 entry

16 AA stands for anti-aircraft fire
17 Japanese Navy Mitsubishi A6M fighter plane

INTELLIGENCE REPORT[18]—SEPTEMBER 15, 1943

S E C R E T TBF OPERATIONS—GUADALCANAL

Mission: Strike Ballale

Planes: 24 TBF's (6- VC38, 6-VC 40, 12-VMTB233)
30 SBD's
72 VF

AA: Medium and heavy --- moderate to slight

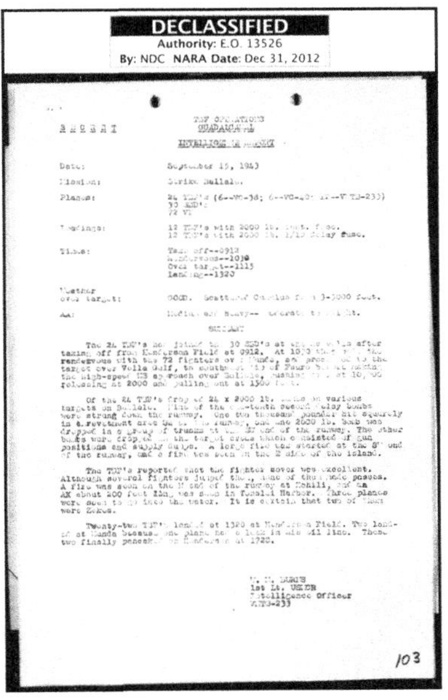

DECLASSIFIED
Authority: E.O. 13526
By: NDC NARA Date: Dec 31, 2012

S E C R E T

TBF OPERATIONS
GUADALCANAL
INTELLIGENCE REPORT

Date: September 15, 1943

Mission: Strike Ballale.

Planes: 24 TBF's (6--VC-38; 6--VC-40; 12--VMTB-233)
30 SBD's
72 VF

Loadings: 12 TBF's with 2000 lb. inst. fuse.
12 TBF's with 2000 lb. 1/10 delay fuse.

Times: Take off--0912
Rendezvous--1030
Over target--1115
Landing--1320

Weather over target: GOOD. Scattered Cumulus [illegible] 3-5000 feet.

AA: Medium and heavy-- moderate to slight.

SUMMARY

The 24 TBF's had joined the 30 SBD's at [illegible] after taking off from Henderson Field at 0912. At 1030 they [illegible] the rendezvous with the 72 fighters over Munda, and proceeded to the target over Vella Gulf, to southwest [illegible] of Faure [illegible] making the high-speed NS approach over Ballale, pushing [illegible] at 10,000 releasing at 2000 and pulling out at 1500 feet.

Of the 24 TBF's dropped 24 x 2000 lb. [illegible] on various targets on Ballale. Nine of the one-tenth second delay bombs were strung down the runway. One two thousand pounder hit squarely in a revetment area [illegible] the runway, and one 2000 lb. bomb was dropped in a group of trucks at the [illegible] end of the runway. The other bombs were dropped [illegible] the target areas which consisted of gun positions and supply dumps. A large fire was started at the S[illegible] end of the runway, and a fire was seen on the E side of the island.

The TBF's reported that the fighter cover was excellent. Although several fighters jumped them, none of them made passes. A fire was seen on the N end of the runway at Kahili, and an AK about 200 feet long was seen in Tonolei Harbor. Three planes were seen to go into the water. It is certain that two of them were Zekes.

Twenty-two TBF's landed at 1320 at Henderson Field. Two landed at Munda because one plane had a leak in his oil line. These two finally [illegible] on Henderson at 1720.

[illegible]
1st Lt. USMCR
Intelligence Officer
VMTB-233

103

SUMMARY

The 24 TBFs had joined the 30 SBDs at the Russells after taking off from Henderson Field at 0912. At 1030 they made the rendezvous with the 72 fighters over Munda, and proceeded to the target over Vella Gulf, to the southwest tip of Faure before making the high-speed NS approach over Ballale, pushing over at 10,000 releasing at 2000 and pulling out at 1500 feet.

Of the 24 TBF's dropped 24 x 2000 lb. bombs on various targets on Ballale. Nine of the one-tenth

18 Available declassified Air Command Solomons Intelligence Reports & War Diary of VC-24, VC-38, VC-40, VMTB-134, VMTB-143, VMTB-232, VMTB-233, VMTB-236, VMSB-235, VMSB-243, and VMF-213 are included in Appendix E. These were all declassified on December 31, 2012.

second delay bombs were strung down the runway. One two thousand pounder hit squarely in a revetment area SE of the runway, and one 2000 lb. bomb was dropped in a group of trucks at the SW end of the runway. The other bombs were dropped in target areas which consisted of gun positions and supply dumps. A large fire was started at the SW end of the runway, and a fire was seen on the E side of the island.

The TBF's reported that the fighter cover[19] was excellent. Although several fighters jumped them, none of them made passes. A fire was seen on the N end of the runway at Kahili, and an AK about 200 feet long was seen in Tonolei Harbor. Three planes were seen to go into the water. It is certain that two of them were Zeros. Twenty-two TBFs landed at 1320 at Henderson Field. Two landed at Munda because one plane had a leak in his oil line. These two finally pancaked on Henderson at 1728. **W.M. Burns, 1st Lt. USMCR, Intelligence Officer, VMTB-233**

PLANE BU.NO.	PILOT	RADIOMAN	TURRET	TAKE OFF	LAND
		VC—38			
24244	Larson	Wagner	Wright	0906	1329
47502	Regan	Misner	Brandt	0906	1325
23959	Leary	Greslie	Dale	0907	1322
47553	Wilson	Haller	Wilson	0907	1323
24182	Bishop	Schramm	Barnes	0908	1323
47504	Behn	Dill	Buis	0909	1324

19 Air Group 38 flew with a team of Hellcat F6F fighters (VF-38 & VF-33) & F4U-1A Corsair fighters (VMF-213), SBDs (VB-38) and TBFs (VC-38).

WEDNESDAY, 15 SEPTEMBER 1943
(another account of same event assembled by www.pacificwrecks.com)

SOUTH PACIFIC (Thirteenth Air Force): B-25's bomb Vila Airfield, Kahili and Kara Airfield. B-24's, with fighter escort, later pound the runway area of Kahili Airfield; others hit Parapatu Point on New Georgia. During the night, B-25's hit Kahili Airfield twice and heavy bombers bomb Buka Airfield and Ballale Airfield. During the day, Ballale Airfield is also hit by USN dive bombers, supported by AAF, USN and US Marine Corps (USMC) fighters; a bivouac area, revetments, supply dumps and gun positions are hit; the runway appears badly damaged by the strikes. Lost are F6F Hellcat 25883 (MIA), F6F Hellcat 26009 (rescued), F4U Corsair 17489 (rescued).

THURSDAY, 16 SEPTEMBER 1943
(account of the 3rd day of attack by www.pacificwrecks.com)

SOLOMONS (13th AF & USMC, USN, RNZAF): US Navy 24 SBD and 31 TBF strike Ballale Airfield, while a multi-service escort, with 13 F6F from VF-38 and 11 F6F from VF-40 (first mission for Hellcats in theater) took off from Fighter One on Guadalcanal. Also, 13th AF and RNZAF P-40s. In addition, 23 F4Us of VMF-214 "The Black Sheep" including Boyington took off from Banika at 1pm and rendezvous over New Georgia with the formation. In total, more than 100 aircraft proceeded to the target. Weather was partly cloudy; the attack began around 14:50. There were a total of 71 escorts in the air. Over the target 40-50 Japanese fighters including Zeros and Tonys[20] and heavy anti-aircraft fire was encountered. The 204th Kokutai launched 26 Zeros. A large, sprawling dog fight ensued over hundreds of miles. Greg Boyington scored victories over several Zeros, he landed at Munda with only 10 gallons of gas, 30 rounds of ammo, and minor damage from flying through the debris of a Zero that exploded in mid-air. After refueling, he returned to Banika. VMF-214 were credited with 11 Zeros and 8 probables. One Hellcat was damaged, landing at Munda Airfield, and then flown back to Fighter One for a week of repairs. Two VMF-214 F4Us were minorly damaged. Lost were: TBF-1 23909 (MIA), TBF-1 06452 (MIA), F4U 17527 (MIA), F6F piloted by Presley(MIA), F6F 25839 (survived), & F6F Lt. Riley (survived).

20 The Kawasaki Ki-61 Hien ("flying swallow") was a Japanese World War II fighter aircraft used by the Imperial Japanese Army Air Force. The first encounter reports claimed Ki-61s were Messerschmitt Bf 109s: further reports claimed that the new aircraft was an Italian design, which led to the Allied reporting name of "Tony", assigned by the United States War Department.

Lucky's Radioman Richard Wagner's War Diary:

Returned to Santos and for the next month we operated off the *USS Breton* — September 17, 1943 entry

USS Breton (CVE-23) was a Bogue class escort carrier of the United States Navy. *Breton* was in service as an escort carrier from 1943 to 1946 and as an aircraft transport from 1958 to 1970. *Breton* launched on 27 June 1942 by Seattle-Tacoma Shipbuilding of Tacoma, Washington. Captain E. C. Ewen in command. Throughout her World War II service, *Breton* operated with the Carrier Transport Squadron, Pacific Fleet. Her sailings carried her throughout the Pacific supplying men, material, and aircraft to units of the fleet engaged in making strikes on the enemy. 7800 tons displacement. 24 aircraft carried. (Photo Source: National Museum of Naval Aviation)

"***Dear Mom & Dad,*** Was happy to receive your letter of Sept 6 yesterday. Mail service this way is pretty good, but seems to be fouled up from here to the states. Betty writes practically every day. She hadn't heard for weeks until just recently. However, as you know, I'm not a prolific letter writer. Must be a wonderful crop this year. Would be great to be in on the harvest. . . . Not much I can tell you except I'm in the best health and getting along o.k. in every way. Hope you're both well and getting along all o.k. . . . Your son, William."

September 22 1943 Letter Home — [Aboard USS Breton]

"***Dear Mom & Dad,*** . . . Have been rather busy the last few days, but that's a lot better than just standing by. Glad to hear the crop turned out so well. Too bad the prices aren't twice as high. Notice the price stays right around $1.15 per bushel (courtesy Williston Daily Herald). I get a bunch of Heralds every few weeks. Sent $400 to the Williston bank a short time ago. You might check to see that they got it next time you're in town. Jim and I just saw a show at a nearby open air theater. Leslie Howard in "Spitfire." All about the designer of the British fighter plane. Yep, Jim is quite a guy. Taught Greek at Duke University for 12 years. He's traveled quite a lot in Europe. He's quite short, has red hair and blue eyes that snap and sparkle as he spins his yarns. Very sincere and eager in everything he does. Son of a Methodist minister. . . . A good dog and a Jeep would be ideal to keep those cattle in line. Get the dog now and I'll see what I can do about a Jeep later. . . . Your son, William."

September 30 1943 Letter Home — [Espiritu Santo Island, New Hebrides (Vanuatu)]

OCT 1943

Date	Type of Machine	Number of Machine	Duration of Flight	Character of Flight	Pilot	Passengers	Remarks
2	TBF	24182	1.7	N	Larson	Wagner Wright	To Breton 1CL
2	"	"	2.0	K	"	" "	Att " 1CL
2	"	"	1.0	N	"	" "	To Buttons. 1CAT.
3	"	24244	1.7	N	"	" "	To Breton 1CL
3	"	23959	1.3	K	"	" "	Att. " 1CL.
3	"	"	.5	N	"	" "	To Buttons.
8	TBF	24182	3.1	N	"	" "	To Saratoga 1CL
8	"	"	.5	N	"	" "	To Breton 1CL
8	"	"	3.4	K	"	" "	Att Force 1CL
9	"	"	2.0	K	"	" "	" " 37 1CL
9	"	"	1.9	K	"	" "	" " 37-2 1CL
10	"	"	4.0	J	"	" "	Anti-Sub Breton 1CL
10	"	"	.7	N	"	" "	To Buttons.
12	"	24244	2.0	K	"	" "	
13	"	24244	1.7	K	"	" "	
19	TBF-1c	24244	1.5	Ferry Bomb	"	Perkins "	Guadal to Munda
19	"	"	1.5	L	"	" "	Return to Guadal.
20	"	"	1.5	O	"	Wagner "	Ferry bombs to Munda
20	"	"	1.5	L	"	" "	Return Guadalcanal
25	TBF-1	24242	1.7	L	"	" "	Cactus to Munda

Total time to date

Lucky's Aviator Flight Log Book

Letter from William's fiancée Bette Burton

Dear Bill, Just Finished my last customer for today and it is now 9:30 and I am really tired we have been so busy business is good. Now to catch myself a car and get home not so tired that a nice hot bath and a good night sleep won't help me and then to do the same thing tomorrow, ha! Darling I received two letters today wasn't the post-man good to me. Anyway I was happy to hear from you that's the one thing I look forward to and when I don't hear from you for days I wonder why, so see you are really spoiling me. However I haven't been doing badly myself. I haven't missed so many days writing to you, surely hope you don't get tired hearing the same thing. So your brother doesn't like what he picked so well maybe he will change after he is in awhile. I certainly hope so. I know your folks miss him. Honey, do write them often and say hello from me. Maybe I will have the pleasure of meeting them soon. Will your kid brother be anywhere on the west coast? If so let me know. Only wish it could be you but then we would have something in common. Honey how are you and is there anything I can do for you? I know you must think that is the broken record but you will never tell me. I think you have a birthday in the very near future so just to be in time I want to wish you a "Happy Birthday" darling and only wish we could be together but maybe we will your next one. How is Jim [Truesdale] and Ray [Marshall]? Give them my best regards and one of these days I will try and write them a few lines. Must close now and comb my lady so bye till next letter. Loving you too much and missing you more. Love Always, Bette "Boop"."

October 5 1943 — San Diego California

"***Dear Mom & Dad***, . . . Been pretty gloomy around here the last couple of days. Continuous down pour. Dug out what I expected to be a pair of dry shoes. They were so green with fungi growth I thought I had an impromptu Victory garden. Must get at least an inch of rain per hour. Wonder if you could send me an exercising gadget. It's made of five elastic cords with a hand grip on either end. Gives the arm and chest muscles a little workout. Jim had one, but so many people used it that all the elasticity was taken out of the cords. Maybe you could get one in Williston or through a mail order catalogue. . . . Your guesses are very nearly correct. I'm in the best of health and getting along OK. Works pretty much in spurts. Not much news and there's quite a bull session on which makes it hard to concentrate. Hope you are both well and not working too hard. Suppose Dad is busy trucking.

Greet the folks up in Canada if you go up. Your son, William."

October 7 1943 Letter Home — [Espiritu Santo]

"***Dear Lloyd,*** ... Mighty hot and damp around here. Dug out a pair of what I expected to be dry shoes last night. They were so green with fungi that they looked like a couple of miniature gardens. It doesn't rain — it pours. And Morton's salt doesn't stand the chance of a snowball in Hades of living up to its advertisement. Have outdoor plumbing here — six holers. Yep, it's a great life. . . . Your brother, Bill."

Where I Wish I Weren't
Oct 7, 1943

Dear Lloyd,

Was pleased to get your letter today kid brother. Was amused at your definition of A.S. Would like to get my hands on the officer that advised you to go into the V-6 program. Have an itchy trigger-finger. What did he tell you — that V-6 was just a grade above V-5? If I were you I'd go see the personnel officer and tell him your situation. You shouldn't have any trouble getting the 90-day course for Officer's training. If the personnel officer is a regular guy — and not some dumb stoop like the guy who got you into V-6 — he'll be able to tell you how to do it. Of course you can work your way up through the ranks, but it's a long tedious process — and absolutely no need of it, with your education. Wish I'd been with you when you took your physical.

October 7 1943 Letter to Brother Lloyd — Where I Wish I Weren't — [Espiritu Santo]

Radioman Richard Wagner's War Diary:

Left Santos for Munda on the Island of New George. We were the first TBF Squadron to be based at Munda -

October 17 1943 entry

October 1943 (cont.)

Date	Type of Machine	Number of Machine	Duration of Flight	Character of Flight	Pilot	Passengers	Remarks
10-26-43	TBF1c	24294	3.0	Attack	Larson	Wagner - Wright	Bomb Kahili - 2000 Y/O
28	TBF-1	06472	3.0	"	"	" "	Bomb Kara "
31	TBF1c	24406	3.3	"	"	" "	Bomb Kara "

Total time to date,

Composite Squadron 38

	Pilot	Pass.	Total
Brt. Fwd.			1768.2
This Month			44.5
Total To Date			1812.7

Lucky's Aviator Flight Log Book

Oct 23, 1943

Dear Mom & Dad,

Have established somewhat of a home for a few days. Am sitting in front of it now and taking things easy. Live in a tent, not infrequently co-inhabited by rats, and there's a nice skull mounted on a pole right in front of the door. At nights our illumination consists of one bright candle. Rains violently - followed by an unmerciful sun which is never in the right part of the sky. Rain sounds good on the canvass roof at night though. Sunsets here are beautiful - but I'd much rather see them on a picture post card - in N. Dak.

A couple of enlisted men who used to be in the aviation unit on the glamour ship looked me up yesterday. They're both Chiefs now. We had quite a chat. I was glad to see them.

"**Dear Mom & Dad,** Have established somewhat of a home for a few days. Am sitting in front of it now and taking it easy. Live in a tent, not infrequently co-inhabited by rats, and there's a nice skull mounted on a pole right in front of the door. At nights our illumination consists of one bright candle. Rains violently followed by an unmerciful sun which is never in the right part of the sky. Rain sounds good on the canvass roof at night though. Sunsets here are beautiful — but I'd much rather see them on a picture post card — in N. Dak. A couple of enlisted men who used to be in the aviation unit on the glamour ship looked me up yesterday. They're both Chiefs now. We had quite a chat. I was glad to see them. . . . Was certainly glad to hear there was such a wonderful crop around home. Only wish I could have been in on the harvest. Could use a little hard work. A doctor, an engineer, and another aviator & I are living in the same tent at present. We eat well, get plenty of sleep as a rule, and are getting along ok. I'm in the best of health. Had another tooth filled not long ago. The dentist was from N. Dak. Sorry to hear you need some new teeth, Mom. Guess Dad is getting used to his by now. Time to start moving. Hope you are all well. Your son, William."

October 23 1943 Letter Home — [Guadalcanal — Code named "Cactus", Flight Log Entry: Guadalcanal]

Radioman Richard Wagner's War Diary:

Attack Kahili on the Island of Bougainville. We encountered a great deal of heavy AA and also light AA. I saw two Jap bombers on the ground. Everyone returned o.k.

- October 26 1943 entry

INTELLIGENCE REPORT—26 OCTOBER 1943

S E C R E T COMMMANDER AIRCRAFT SOLOMONS S E C R E T

STRIKE COMMAND

Squadrons: VMTB-232 (20 planes), VC-38 (7 planes), VC-40 (9 planes)

Type of Mission: Bomb Kahili Airfield

Planes: 36 TBF's

Anti-Aircraft: Intense heavy, moderate light

Damage to Planes: Empennage of one plane damaged by AA; tail of another plane severely damaged by heavy AA; one plane shot down.

Observations: AA guns: 4 heavy guns on Kangu Hill and 4 auto- Southerly edge of Eberly's base: one heavy gun at North side therof. 2 heavy guns in Target #3; 2 guns to East thereof. 2 heavy guns in clearing South west of Malabita Hill. Heavy guns at North end of strip.

Ten barges along beach half way between Kahili and Moila Pt. Four ships off beach at Target #6. Two ships in Tonolei Harbor.

Lost Plane: First Lieutenant Philip

Field, N.A., U.S.M.C., VMTB 232, pilot, Sergeant Edward R. Dzama, U.S.M.C., turret gunner, and Private Joseph D. Miller, U.S.M.C., radio gunner, flying in Plane Bu.No. 06416 were observed to pull out of glide at 1000 ft. The engine was on fire, and, after making a turn to the left, the plane dove into the water at a 20 degrees angle about half way between the beach and Erventa Island. Two men were seen to jump; one chute opened; the other did not and the man was seen to go into the water. No other information was obtainable.

Fredrick Frelinghuyson, Lt. USNR, VC-40, Intelligence Duty Officer.

Plane Bu.No.	Pilot	Radioman	Turret Man	Out	In
		VC-38			
24244	LARSON	Wagner	Wright	0717	1005
23981	GAMMAGE	Morrissey		0717	1005
47494	LEARY	Greslie	Dale	0717	1006
24242	WILSON	Haller	Wilson	0717	1000
24182	REGAN	Misner	Brant	0717	1006
23975	LEAKE	Boyle	O'Daniel	0718	1006
24265	PHILLIPPI	Bond	Tyler	0718	0839 DNA
24194	DRAUGHON	Deal	Paul	0720	1002
		VMTB-232			
06406	Schrader	Seamonds	Jenkins	0729	1002
06422	Goodman	Wood	Cardno	0729	1002
24264	SMITH, Maj.	Waldvegel	Stanner	0721	0955
47504	METZELAARS	Pollow	Eldridge	0721	0955
06411	EVERETT	Ward	Norby	0723	0956
06190	DAUGHERTY	Railey	Donovan	0724	0956
06475	STAMETS	Severson	Brodeski	0722	0959
24268	HUMPHREY	Martin	Adams	0722	0956
47501	WHITE	Crumpton	Moon	0727	0957
06118	McCOLE	Sears	Blackerby	0727	0958
06341	BURRIS	Lossie	Wagner	0727	0958
064714	LAUGHLIN	Akrody	Spychalla	0728	0958
06420	CAREY	Downey	Copeland	0728	0957
06416	FIELD	Miller	Dzama	0728	_____
06432	EVERSON	Pell	Marker	0728	1001
06359	DEXHEIMER	Jackson	Nilsen	0729	0959
06125	SPARKS	Rader	Sauter	0729	1001
06489	THOMAS	Schleeter	Akey	0729	1001
24358	OLSON	Heke	Mitchell	0729	1001
47510	GARILLI	Schafer	Hall	0729	0959

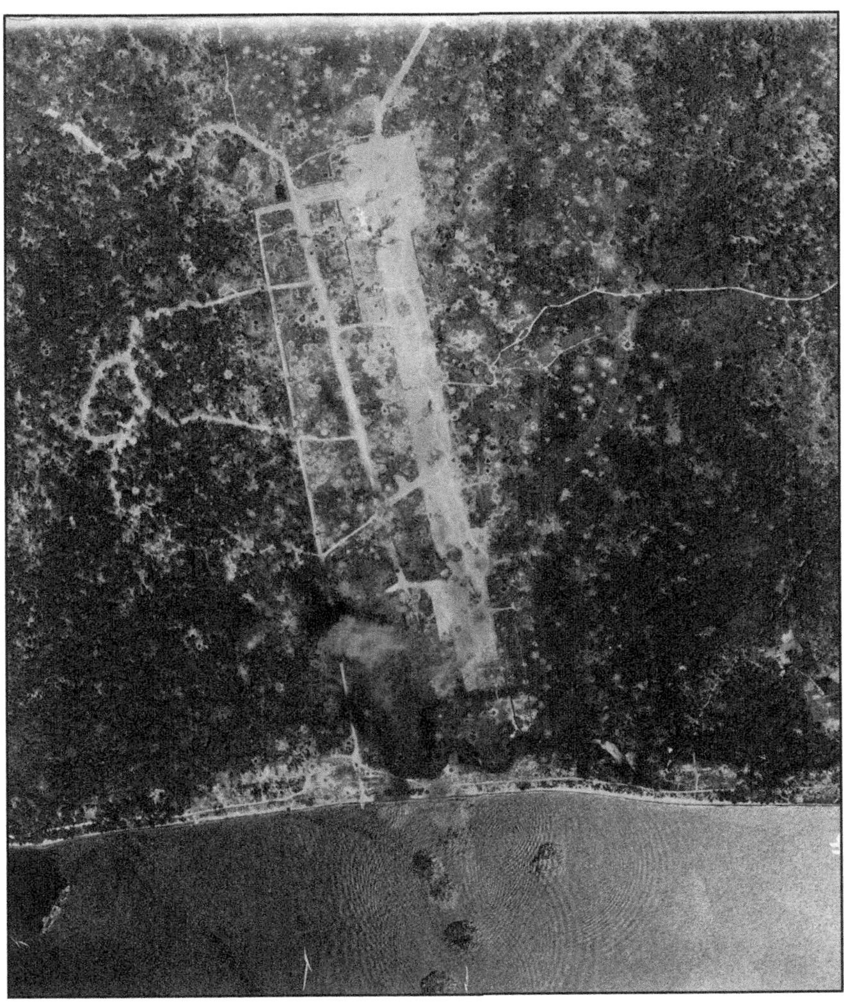

Kahili Airfield Bombing (Source: Lt (jg) John Leary's Photograph provided by the Leary Family Collection)

TBF Formation over Munda after a raid on Kahili Airfield — October 28 1943
(Source: National Archives photo no. 80-G-56483)

INTELLIGENCE REPORT—28 OCTOBER 1943 S E C R E T COMMMANDER AIRCRAFT SOLOMONS S E C R E T STRIKE COMMAND

Squadrons:	VMTB-143 (1 pilot), VC-38 (9 pilots), VC-40 (9 pilots)
Type of Mission:	Bombing and strafing of Kara Airfield and anti-aircraft positions
Planes:	19 TBF's
Anti-Aircraft:	Light automatic AA intense. Automatic AA from known positions (possible 50 caliber and 20MM. New position: NE and NW corners of strip, SE end of strip
Damage to Planes:	4 planes were hit by AA. 1 plane made a forced water landing and 3 are out of commission for an indefinite length of time,
Observations:	1 Corvette at Tonolei. One 10,000 ton ship 600 yards off Kahili (1 pilot's observation).
Note:	1. Plane #118 crashed on take off at 0619 and was damaged beyond repair. Its pilot, Lt. (J.G.) Harry W. Wilson was killed. Minor injuries were sustained by

W.M. Haller, ARMS/c and L.E. Wilson, AOM3/c. This crew was attached to VC-38. The Bureau Number for the aforementioned plane is 06118.

2. Plane #120, Bureau Number 06475—Lt. (J.R.) Douglas B LaPierre A-V (N), pilot, turret gunner R.E. Faust, AMM2/c, J.E. DeVore, ARM2/c—was hit by 40 MM anti-aircraft fire from a gun at the NE or NW corner of the strip immediately after the push over at an altitude of 5000-6000 feet. A piece, 2 feet square, was blown off of the leading edge of the starboard win outward of the fold, and the engine was damaged. The pilot continued in his glide and is believed to have dropped his bombs on the strip. The plane continued on the route home but the engine and tail vibrated increasingly bad. Crash-boat USS C-9495 was observed in Wilson Strait, directly south of Baga Island. The pilot made a water landing; but, due to the hole in the wing the plane stalled and

cartwheeled 180 degrees. The radioman's left leg was broken by gear which broke loose in the cartwheel. The plane floated for two minutes, permitting the pilot and gunner to remove the lift raft and radioman. The pilot and gunner were uninjured. **Myron Sulzberger, Captain U.S.M.C.R., VMTB-143, Intelligence Duty Officer.**

Plane Bu.No.	Pilot	Radioman	Turret Man	Out	In
		VC-38			
24244	BRUNTON	Sunday	Kemper	0618	0847
23981	SCHOLFIELD	Ulrich	Dills	0618	0847
23959	GIBLIN	Lee	Perkins	0622	0848
24265	MARSHALL	Lane	Tye	0618	0848
24194	DRAUGHAN	Deal	Paul	0618	0851
06472	LARSON	Wagner	Wright	0601	0851
06406	PHILLIPPI	Bond	Tyler	0601	0852
24358	BISHOP	Schramm	Barnes	0605	0853
06489	TAHLER	Jeffrey	Brewer	0620	0844

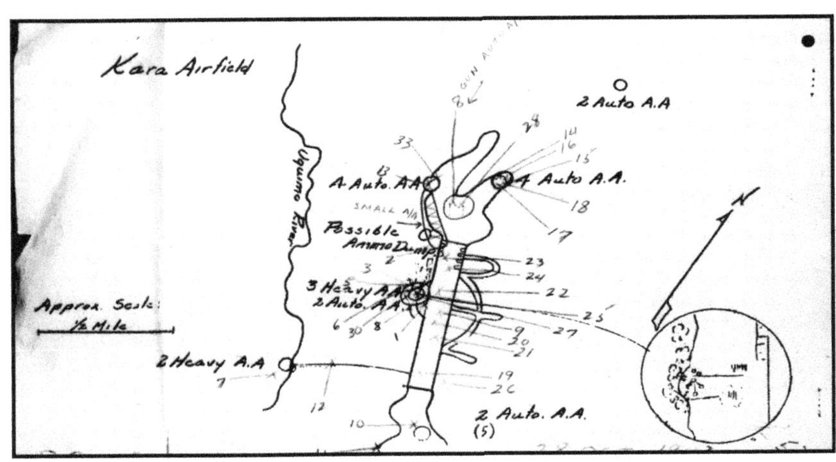

TBF Planes at Munda Airfield, New Georgia — October 26 1943. Plane #108 (circled in red) was flown by William on October 28 1943 (Source: National Archives, photo no. 342-FH-3A44430-A80632AC)

Plane #108 (BuNos 06472) was the actual plane flown by Lucky on October 28, 1943 while VC38, VC40, and VMTB-143 bombed and strafed Kara Airfield. These TBFs were a mix of TBF, TBF-1, and TBF-1c planes. The planes were all interchangeable between Naval and Marine squadrons based on William's Aviators Flight Log Book and the available Mission Reports (Appendix F).

"***Dear Mom & Dad,*** . . . Sure glad to hear you're through threshing and that the crop was so good. Should almost put farming on a paying basis. Wonder if you're getting any rain. We wade around in mud up to our ankles around here. Have to wear high shoes. Uniforms, as a whole, aren't too neat. If you don't get your clothes soaked in rain, they're soaked in perspiration. Haven't had a crease in my trousers since I left the states — not that it matters much. Am with Jim again. We've both been pretty busy though, so we haven't seen much of each other. He and Olav Njus[21] are two friends I'll never forget. . . . We're getting along pretty well here and the work has been interesting. Thanks to the Lord, and your prayers, no uncomfortable experiences. We managed to get several cases of orange and grapefruit juice yesterday. ***Almost drank ourselves sick.*** Yes, I well remember my trip home last October. Seems like an awful long time ago. . . . Saw a couple of my classmates from Pensacola recently. One is a night fighter. Had good hunting. I have over 1800 hrs now. Like our planes. Hope everything is ok at home. Your son, William."

November 3 1943 Letter Home —
[Munda airfield — Code named "Shag", Flight Log Entry November 2, 1943: Chasing Jap fleet with torpedo]

"***Dear Mom & Dad,*** Taking things easy here so will write a little. Suppose the kid brother has been home and gone again. Wonder what sort of assignment he got. Hope he went to some school. Think I'd

21 Olav Njus was an Army Air Force Colonel and weather forecaster during the offensive against Germany and the invasion of France. He met Lucky at Concordia College. Olav passed away in February 2002 at New London, Minnesota and was a former teacher at Gale College.

have gone to work in some aircraft plant before becoming a gob. Good wages — pleasant surroundings. The road was slippery we skid off into the ditch this morning. Now you can't see the road for the fine clay dust over it. The sun really dries things up in the open areas. Saw a fair show last night. Fred Astaire and Joan Leslie in THE SKY's THE LIMIT. Astaire can really tap dance. . . . Feeling fine. Get my vitamin pills every day — and plenty of bread, water, & sunshine. . . . Your son, William."

November 9 1943 Letter Home —
[Munda airfield, New Georgia — Code named "Shag"]

Munda Airfield, October — November 1943
Photos by Lt. (jg) David Bagley, SBD pilot of VC 38
(Source: Gregory Pons Collection)

VC 38's TBF Planes Taxiing on Munda Airfield (Source: Gregory Pons Collection)

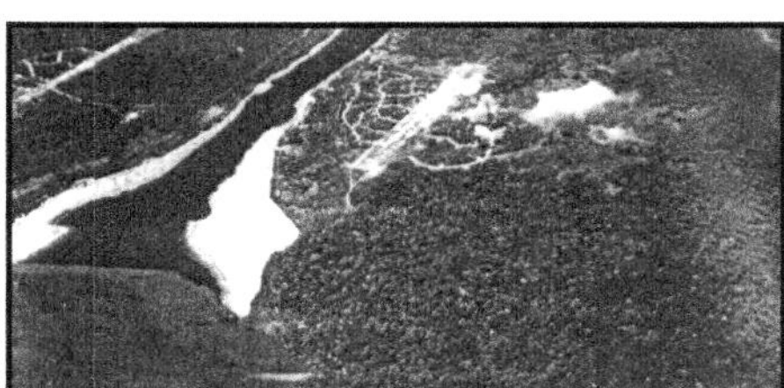

Buka (on right) and Bonis Airfields — Nov. 1943

Radioman Richard Wagner's War Diary:

Attacked Buka Airdrome on the Island of Buka. A great deal of heavy and light AA was encountered. The Marines lost two SBDs. Our attack was very successful due to the fact that it was quite a surprise to them. We dropped our 2000 lb on the runway and I saw two ammunition dumps blow up — November 10 1943 entry (Photo source: www.arrakis-ttm.com)

INTELLIGENCE REPORT—10 NOVEMBER 1943 S E C R E T TBF OPERATIONS MUNDA AIRFIELD S E C R E T

Squadrons: VMTB-233 (5), VC-38 (11), VC-40 (9), VMTB-143 (8)

Mission: Bomb and strafe Buka and Bonis Airfields, Buka Passage area.

Planes: 33 TBF's (18 on Buka) (15 on Bonis)

60 SBD's

AA Fire: Heavy of medium intensity from 5-6 guns on north tip of Sohana Island. Heavy of light intensity from know positions E and N of Bonis strip. Automatic of light intensity from known positions about both strips.

Bomb Hits Buka Airfield

7—Confirmed hits on strip, concentrated on west and center 1/3.

	6- Unconfirmed probable hits thru the length of Airstrip.
Attack:	From 13000′, left turn from N/E to S/W. Bonis Attack made from close over strip, necessitating dives too steep and fast for accuracy.
Route Back:	Rally 3 miles S/W of Madehas Island thence down Southern coast of Bougainville and direct to base.

D.J. Rourke, Lt. USNR, Intelligence O.

SQD. NO.	PLANE BU NO.	PILOT	PASSENGERS	OUT	IN
116	06311	Gammage	Morissel	0612	0950
4	24242	Marshall	Lane, Tye	0612	0936
5	24182	Giblin	Lee, Perkins	0612	0950
6	23975	Tahler	Jeffery, Brewer	0612	0939
7	24265	Larson	Wagner, Wright	0612	0950
22	24490	Bishop	Schramm, Barnes	0622	0950
8	24194	Leary	Greslie, Dale	0613	0940
125	06353	Regan	Misner, Brandt	0613	0944
130	06341	Phillippi	Bond, Tyler	0613	0945

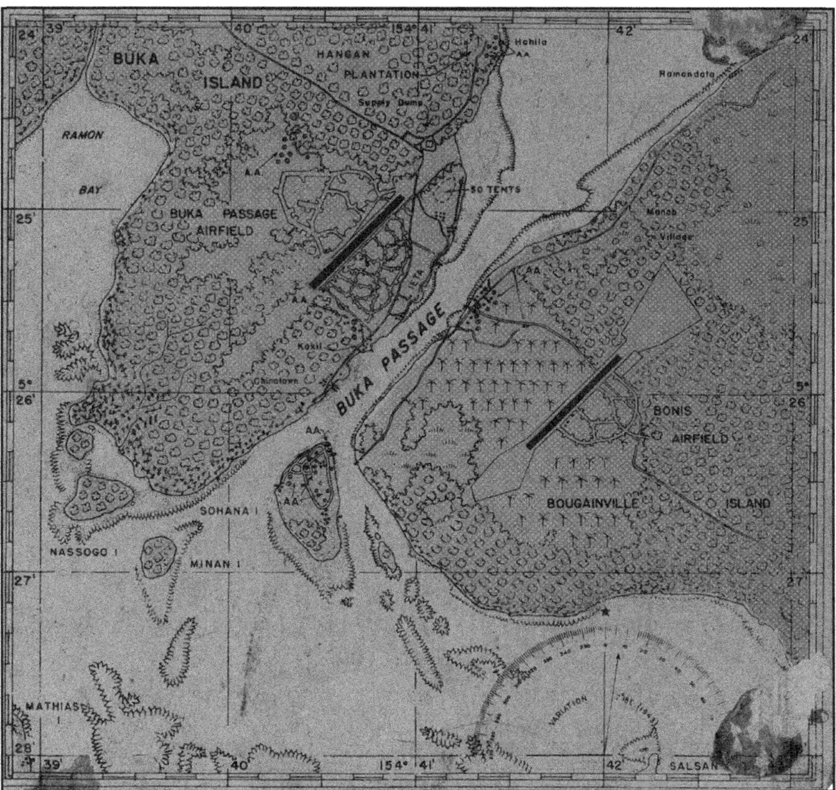

COMSOPAC Map of Buka Passage — The twin Japanese Airfields at Buka and Bonis (Source: Leary Family Collection)

Radioman Richard Wagner's War Diary:

Attack Jap ground troops in the Empress Augusta Bay Region. Our ground troops had too much to handle so we dropped our hundred lbs bombs by their direction. We killed about 300 Japs and those who were still alive were stunned so that our troops just stuck them with a knife

- November 14 1943 [22]

22 November 1943 by Eric Hammel: Solomon Islands (Nov 12 1943): Eighteen USN land-based TBFs from VC-38 and VC-40 responding to an air-support mission request lodged the previous afternoon, drop 100-pound bombs on Imperial Japanese Army (IJA) defensive positions within only 100 yards of friendly troops. As a result of the attack, the IJA force abandons its positions.

INTELLIGENCE REPORT—14 NOVEMBER 1943 S E C R E T TBF OPERATIONS MUNDA AIRFIELD S E C R E T

Squadrons:	VC-38 (12), VC-40 (8)
Type of Mission:	Bombing in support of ground troops.
Planes:	20 TBF's Loadings: 12 x 100# fuse: nose 1/10
Damage to Planes:	Two planes received shrapnel and bullet holes in their tails, believed to be have resulted from our own bombs and strafing ricochetes.
Attack:	Course up direct. Upon arrival, contacted Bomb Base and Aircraft Liaison Party #21. Instructed by radio to orbit until 0830 over Cape Torokina; given coordinates of target area and instructed to bomb triangle area (approximately 500 yards to E side) north of base line upon smoke signals being given. . . . Released bombs at 600-1100 feet. After bombing run, planes circled and made strafing run over target area.

Fredrick Frelinghuysen, Lt. USNR VC-40 Intel O.

NO.	BU.NO.	PILOT	PASSENGERS	OUT	IN
1	24244	Brunton	Sunday, Kemper	0610	1033
2	23981	Scholfield	Ulrich, Dills	0601	1033
3	23959	Giblin	Lee, Perkins	0601	1033
4	24242	Tahler	Jeffery, Brewer	0601	1033
5	24182	Droughon	Deal, Paul	0609	1034
6	23975	Bishop	Schramm, Barnes	0603	1034
7	24265	Larson	Wagner, Wright	0608	1034
8	24194	Phillippi	Bond, Tyler	0608	1034
9	24208	Leake	Boyle, O'Daniel	0603	1035
21	24515	Leary	Greslie, Brandt	0603	1035
22	24490	Regan	Misner, Brandt	0609	1035
19	23970	Marshall	Lane, Tye	0605	1507

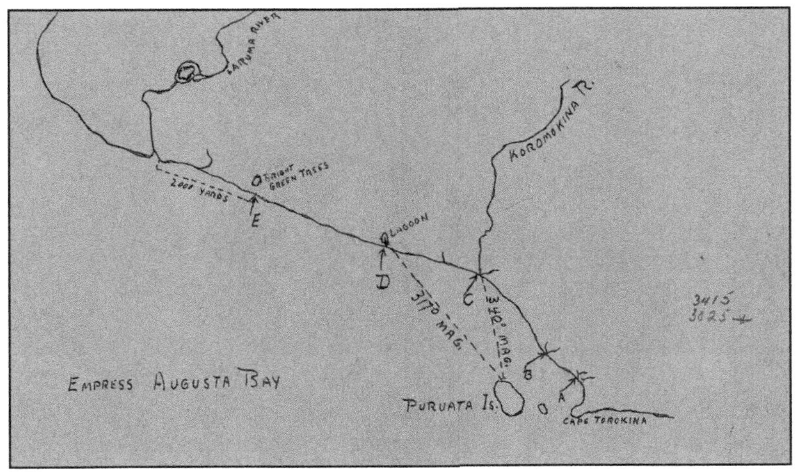

VC 38 Lt.(jg) John Leary's Map provided by the Leary Family Collection

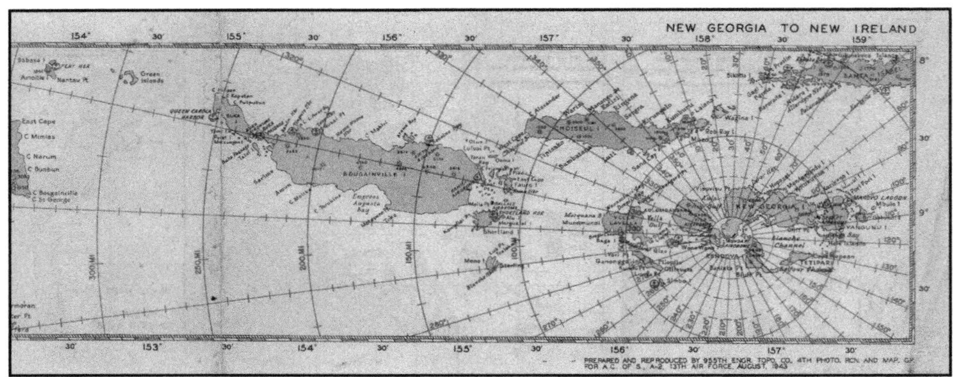

COMSOPAC Strip Map of Bougainville Island — Compass Directions from Munda Airfield on New Georgia (Source: Leary Family Collection)

Munda Airfield (Shag) 1943 (Source: Gregory Pons Collection, photo by Lt. David Bagley — VC 38 SDB pilot October thru November 1943)

Lucky and his VC 38 Squadron were part of the Solomon Air Offensive that began after the Naval Battle of Guadalcanal of November 13, 1942. The VC 38 Squadron flew missions with other Naval squadrons and U.S. Marine Fighting Squadrons and Scout-Bombing Squadrons throughout September, October, November, and December 1943, mercilessly pounding the Japanese airfields of Kahili, Kara, Buka, and Ballale, including Japanese supply areas of Tarlena and Kieta, Bougainville. Initially these bombing missions were large scale assaults including up to 194 aircrafts, consisting of TBFs, SBDs, B-25s, P-39s, Kittyhawks, F4Us (Corsairs) and F6F Hellcat fighter planes in a single attack. The VC 38 Squadron worked off both land-based air fields (Espiritu Santo, Guadalcanal, and Munda) and carrier-based operations (USS Breton and the USS Saratoga). However, the majority of Lucky's time was spent in bombing operations based out of Munda airfield located on New Georgia Island of the Solomon Islands chain.

The invasion of Bougainville (Bougainville Campaign) began on November 1, 1943 when the U.S. Marines (3d Marine Division and two attached Marine Raider battalions) landed on Cape Torokina, in central Bougainville's Empress Augusta Bay. VC 38 actually bombed the Japanese troops fighting the marines on November 14th and 20th, 1943, by dropping 100-pound bombs near the Japanese positions. Success at Bougainville set up the U.S. forces to finally reach the Japanese stronghold of Rabaul on the Island of New Britain.

Rabaul was the Japanese fortress of military power, which included a harbor and five airfields. The march up the Solomons chain, starting at Guadalcanal to now Bougainville airfield (Piva airfield), allowed Allied fighter aircraft to finally reach Rabaul within their operational range. VC 38 Squadron's heroic actions during the Bougainville and the New Britain campaigns from October 1943 to March of 1944 culminated in a Scorecard of 112 aerial missions, 3 night missions, and 37 aerial victories, with over 30 enemy ships sunk or damaged. Appendix F includes a tribute to VC 38, Air Group 38's Scorecard, a list of all personnel, Richard Wagner's war diary, and other information obtained on VC 38. Appendix E includes the available declassified Intelligence Reports and War Diaries of VC 38's activities during the Solomon Air Offense of 1943 and 1944. A map of the Solomon Islands Air Campaign is presented on page 131.

VC 38 – Aboard USS Long Island August 1943 – Lucky, Standing, 13th from left. Radioman Richard Wagner seated –center. Turret Gunner Ben Wright seated – right side. (Source: W. Wagner)

"**Dear Brother Lloyd,** Glad to get another letter from the kid brother. . . . Steer clear of aviation radio if you can. Aviation mechanics would be better. Aviation radiomen have rather a rugged life. I know, because I've had several riding in my rear seat. .....Yes, I'm looking forward to going into partnership with you after this war — farming or some other enterprise which shows promise. If you happen to be stationed in San Diego be sure to look up Bette. Would treasure your frank opinion on her. I know she has her faults — such as a stormy temperament — but I think it's love. . . . Well, kid brother, it's after 12 so I'll have to turn in. 4 o'clock comes pretty early. Let me know how you're doing. Good luck! Your brother, Bill."

November 18 1943 Letter to Kid-Brother Lloyd — [Munda airfield]

November 1943

Date	Type of Machine	Number of Machine	Duration of Flight	Character of Flight	Pilot	Passengers	Remarks
11/2/43	TBF-1	06223	4.5	L	Larson	Wagner - Wright	Chasing Jap fleet with torpedo.
11/10/43	TBF-1c	24265	4.0	Attack G	"	" "	Bomb Buka - 2000 inst
10	TBF-1c	24265	1.5	L	"	" "	Munda to Guadal.
11	TBF-1c	"	1.7	L	"	" "	Guadal to Munda.
14	"	"	4.5	G	"	" "	Bomb Troops Empress Augusta Bay - 12-100#s.
20	TBF-1	23981	3.5	G	"	" "	Troops in Emp. Aug. Bay - Rained out 12-100
22	TBF-1c	24334	3.1	G	"	" "	Bomb Kahili - 2000# 1/10
24	TBF-1	06455	3.8	G	"	" "	Bomb Supply Area, Tarlena, Boug. - 2000 inst

Total time to date

~~USS~~ Composite Squadron 38

	Pilot	Pass.	Total
Brt. Fwd.			1812.7
This Month			26.6
Total To Date			1839.3

Lucky's Aviator Flight Log Book

"***Dear Mom & Dad,*** Guess I haven't written in some time. Have been fairly busy the past few weeks. It's a whole lot better than standing by though. Makes you feel as though it's bringing you closer to getting home again. . . . There's a shirtless sailor in here who has some rather unique tattoos. One nipple is labeled "sweet," the other, "sour." Then, of course, there are the usual grotesque figures. What possesses a sailor to permanently mark up his body is something I haven't been able to fathom. ...No, Ruth Cronkite didn't get married. Had a long letter from her not long ago. She had joined the WAFS, which means Women's Army Ferrying Service. Expects to ferry army planes around the country. Glad to hear the folks in Canada are fine. . . . Hope you are all well. We're getting along OK here and feeling fine. Happy Birthday on the 2nd Mom! Wish I could send something, but can't buy a thing here. How about a new permanent? Your son, William."

November 18 1943 Letter Home — [Munda airfield]

Gunner Wright (age 20) • Pilot Lucky Larson (age 27) • Radioman Wagner (age 25) — Bomber Strip at Munda Airfield, November 12 1943
Note: The muzzle in the TBF wing is covered with tape to protects its machine gun from coral dust

"***Dear Mom & Dad,*** Here it is Thanksgiving — and I have a day off, which is something to be thankful for. Wish we were sitting down to a big meal on the farm. We'll probably get an extra vitamin pill. However I'm truly thankful to the Lord for his many blessings. Among them good health, the best Mom & Dad in the world, the kid brother, and constant protection — plus innumerable others. Heard a little music last night, which was a real treat. ...They set up right next to the outdoor plumbing — an eight holer. So some of the boys had the unprecedented luxury of soothing music for added comfort. I still have the little Marine Band Harmonica. Sometimes play it and Jim tap dances. He certainly kicks up his heels, and has some might tricky steps. .....Our roving photographer took a picture of all plane crews the other day. Am sending a snap of our crew. Wright, the gunner, comes from Florida. Wagner, the radioman is from So. Dakota. Both good men. . . . Your son, William."

November 25 1943 Letter Home — [Munda airfield]

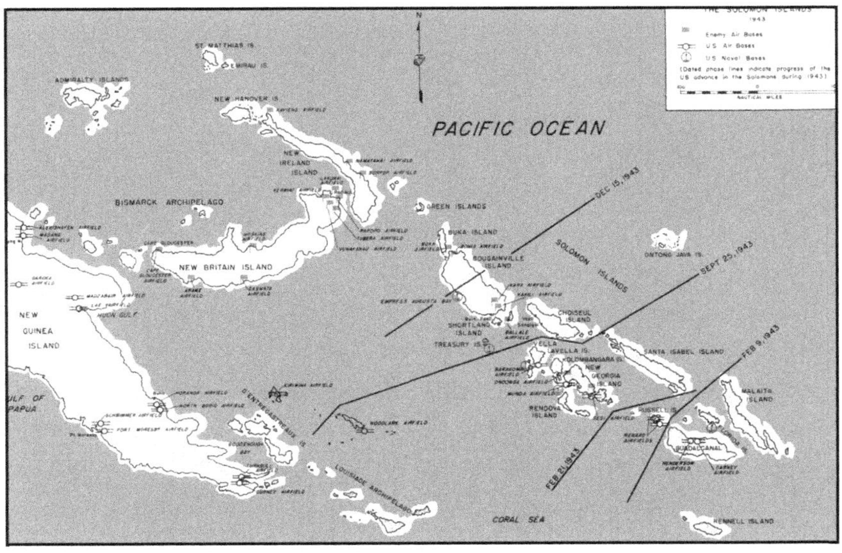

Solomon Islands map

"***Dear Mom & Dad,*** Received your letter dated Nov. 5th yesterday. Mention of snow makes me wish I could see some of it. Here rain will pour down for five minutes, the sun will blaze away for 15, then it will rain again. Finally got some food in here so we had a big Thanksgiving supper — turkey and trimmings. Had a piece of cheese and a slice of bread for dinner, plus a vitamin pill. However we're all feeling fine and should have no complaints. Dispose of the Chevy as you wish. If you can get $150, well and good. If you want to sell or give it to the Canucks, that's OK too. ...Glad to hear that the kid brother is getting officer's training. . . . We're fairly busy here at times but everything is pretty well under control. May get ***a little vacation*** before too long — at least we're all anticipating one. There are some small lizard-like animals running around here catching flies that are really fast. Quickest moving form of life I've seen in these parts. . . . Your son, William."

November 30 1943 Letter Home — [Munda airfield]

"***Dear Mom & Dad,*** Received the can of candy and a letter from home on the 2nd — Mom's Birthday. The candy came through in pretty good shape. It was excellent, as usual, and I enjoyed it a lot. So did several of the other boys who sampled it. Can't keep candy more than a day or two here because of the moisture and numerous small insects — minute ants, lice, etc. Would be O.K. in an airtight container. Candy is hard to get here though, so it's highly appreciated — thanks a lot.

Olaf, Lloyd, & Mary at Williston N.D. train depot — Lloyd returning to training at Great Lakes, IL — Oct 1943

Was glad to receive the snapshot. You're all looking good. Mom & Dad seem to be holding their own in weight. And the kid brother looks like a real sailor. Sure nice to see you all. Well, Dad, I've been on several ships since leaving the cruiser — all small carriers. But never really settled down on any of them. Had my four years service in last September — still looking for the discharge papers. . . . Suppose there's snow on the ground at home now. I'm sitting in an open tent, have no shirt on, and it's still warm. . . . Your son, William."

December 4 1943 Letter Home — [Munda airfield]

"***Dear Lloyd,*** Thanks a million for the Birthday card. 28 years old — getting to be an old stud, but there's still a lot of fight in me. Had a day off today. Thought I'd take a hop in the "Duck" J2F, but found so much red tape connected with it that I gave up. Just thought it would be nice to see the spray on a few water landings and take-offs again. .....Just dug out the old Harmonica. Was plenty rusty but I still managed to blow a few of the old time tunes. . . . As I sit here with no shirt on it's hard to realize that Christmas is just about here. Wish I could send you something, but can't even get a Christmas card. A check is very unsatisfactory, but it's the best I can do. With it goes my heartiest wish for a Merry Christmas and a Good New Year! Wish you'd drop me a line every once in a while to keep me posted of your activities. Will enclose a recent snapshot taken by our roving photographer. I was tickled to get the snap of you, in your sailor's outfit, and Mom & Dad at the Williston depot. Your brother, Bill."

Grumman J2F Duck — Source: Wikipedia

December 6 1943 Letter to Kid-Brother Lloyd — [Munda airfield]

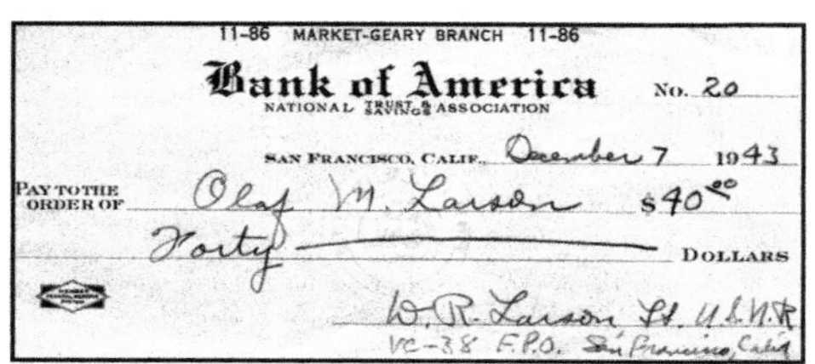

11-86 MARKET-GEARY BRANCH 11-86
Bank of America No. 20
NATIONAL TRUST & SAVINGS ASSOCIATION
SAN FRANCISCO, CALIF., December 7 1943
PAY TO THE ORDER OF Olaf M. Larson $40.00
Forty —— DOLLARS
D. R. Larson Lt. U.S.N.R.
VC-38 F.P.O. San Francisco, Calif.

Un-cashed Christmas Check to Family

"***Dear Mom & Dad,*** Has been a dull, dreary day and not a thing to do. Steady drizzle and no sun. Reminds me of a rainy day during threshing. . . . Things were getting pretty tough there for awhile. Sometimes had three kinds of beans, black coffee and nothing else. Oh yes, bread without butter — not even the 190 ° won't melt bread. ...... Land seems to be plenty cheap. Guess Dad can't go wrong on buying some. What's in the Williston Bank is available. Hard to realize that Christmas is just a short way off. Would like to be tramping around in the snow — at home. Wish I could send something, but can't even get a card. Will have to send a check. With it goes a wish for you Very Merry Christmas and a Prosperous, Happy New Year! Am feeling find and looking forward to receiving the exerciser Dad sent."

December 7 1943 Letter Home — [Munda airfield]

Radioman Richard Wagner's War Diary:

Attack Jakohina, it's a Jap supply base near Kahili. We made a good hit on a house. Some small fire but no heavy A.A.

— December 11 1943 entry

Attack Kieta Airdrome on the east side of Bougainville. No heavy AA but some small guns are firing.

— December 12 1943 entry

Attack Chabai ground and coastal guns. We made a direct hit on a big coastal gun with a 2000# bomb.

- December 13 1943 entry

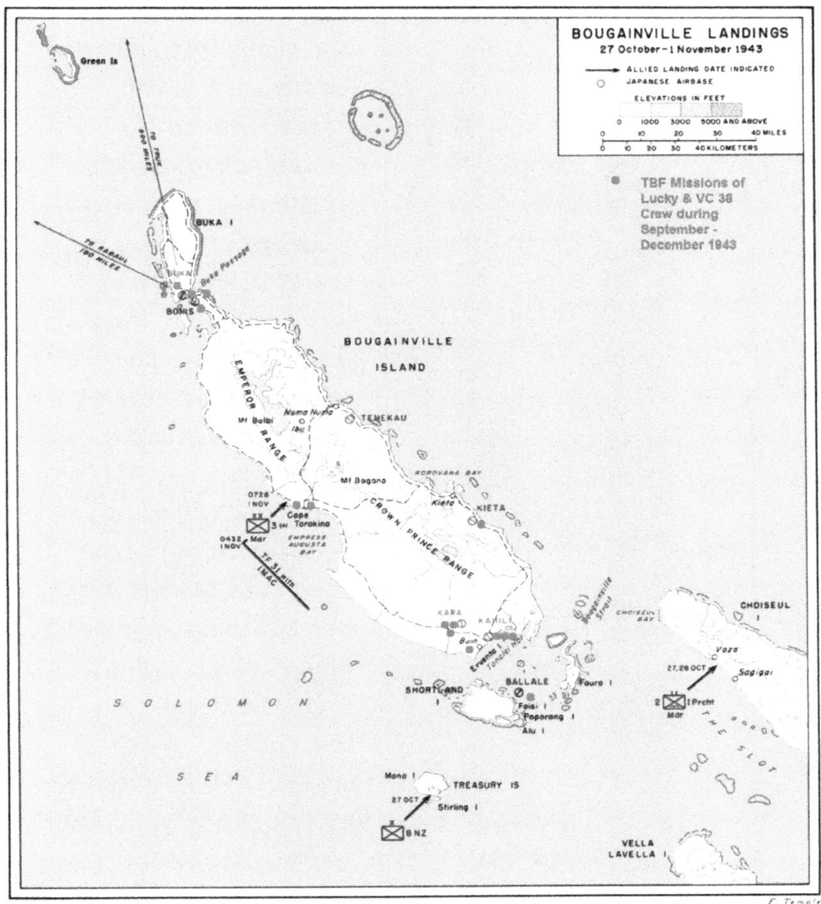

MAP 15

"***Dear Mom & Dad,*** Received the exerciser, stationary, money-belt, and several other things a couple of days ago. Santa Claus really got out this way. Thanks a million. Can't manage more than three springs on that exerciser yet, Dad. Perhaps in a year I'll be able to put on the other two. All the boys in the Unit had to try it out. Jim Truesdale's eyes just about popped out, he was trying so hard — with five springs. This is really a good picture of the kid brother. He sent me a nice hair brush. Wonder how he's doing. Received

Dec. 16, 1943

Dear Mom & Dad,

Received the exerciser, stationery, money-belt, and several other things a couple of days ago. Santa Claus really got out this way. Thanks a million. Can't manage more than three springs on that exerciser yet, Dad. Perhaps in a year I'll be able to put on the other two. All the boys in the hut had to try it out. Jim Truesdale's eyes just about popped out, he was trying so hard - with five springs. This is really a good picture of the kid brother. He sent me a nice hair brush. Wonder how he's doing.

Received the air force stationery and pamphlet from the Luther League. Will have to write to the secretary.

the air force stationery and pamphlet from the Luther League. Will have to write to the secretary. Expect to get a little vacation shortly. Guess we can all use it too. Wish we could all be home for Christmas. A sleigh ride would be great. Dug out some old gear I hadn't seen for some time today. Got the old C.C. [Concordia College] ring out. Looks good. Well, Mom & Dad, here's wishing you a Very Merry Christmas and a Happy New year! Your son, William."

December 16 1943 Letter Home- [Munda airfield] — LAST LETTER FROM WILLIAM

Radioman Richard Wagner's War Diary:

Left Munda for our rehabilitation leave in Sydney Australia

– December 15, 1943 entry (Source of December 16, 1943 Rehabilitation Leave Orders: Leary Family Collection).

COMPOSITE SQUADRON
THIRTY-EIGHT

VC-38/P10/L20/00/MM

16 December 1943.

From: Commanding Officer.
To: Flight Crews, Composite Squadron, THIRTY-EIGHT.

Subject: Rehabilitation Leave.

Reference; (a) ComFair, South's conf. ltr., FF12-5(1)/P10, serial 1280 dated 6 November 1943.
(b) ComFair, South's conf. ltr , FF12-5(1)/P10/00/MM dated 16 December 1943.

1. In compliance with reference (b), you are hereby granted seven (7) days leave in Sydney, Australia.

2. You will report to the Commander Fleet Air, South Pacific, for necessary arrangements prior to 16 December 1943.

FIRST GROUP

SUNDAY, H.W., ACRM.
KEMPER, M.D , ACOM
LANE, L.A., ARM2c
TYE, D., AOM3c
BUIS, R.P., ARM2c
BREWER, E.E., AOM1c.
BOND, A.E., ARM2c
GRESLIE, D.R., ARM2c
DALE, L.E., AOM3c.
WAGNER, R.C., ARM2c
WRIGHT, B.W., AOM2c
THATCHER, P.E., ARM2c
NUMAN, D.W., ARM3c
EMERSON, R.E., ARM3c
METZGAR, W.C., ARM3c
HOLDEN, W.J., ARM3c

SECOND GROUP

LARSON, W.R., Lieut.
WOODMAN, W.E., Lieut.
MARSHALL, R.A., Lieut.(jg).
BISHOP, B.C , Lieut.(jg).
TAHLER, G., Lieut (jg)
LEARY, J.A., Lieut.(jg).
LEAKE, H.T., Lieut.(jg).
REGAN, R.F., Lieut.(jg).
GIBLIN, R.B., Lieut.(jg).
BAGLEY, D., Lieut. (jg)
KNOWLES, C.G., Lieut.(jg).
OLNEY, S., Ens.
CAWLEY, W.P., Ens.
SHIRLEY, J.G., Ens.
SEWELL, R.H., Ens.
BURGETT, A.P., ARM3c

THIRD GROUP

LEE, J.J., ARM3c.
PERKINS, R.L., AOM2c
SCHRAMM, R.E., ARM3c
BARNES, E.C., AOM3c
DILLS, F. J., AOM3c
BOYLE, J.E., ARM2c
O'DANIEL, R.R., AOM3c
DEAL, J.H., ARM3c
MISNER, W.J., ARM3c
BRANDT, C.E., AOM3c
BLANK, W.F., ARM 3c
DURHAM, R., ARM3c
MARTIN, E.T., ARM3c
LANDESS, J.S., ARM2c
BLOCK, A.L., ARM3c
EARNEST, G.C., ARM2c

Radioman Richard Wagner's War Diary:

Mr. Larson was killed returning from Sydney. The DC he was in crashed after leaving New Caledonia

– December 27 1943 entry

December 1943

Date	Type of Machine	Number of Machine	Duration of Flight	Character of Flight	Pilot	Passengers	Remarks
12/1/43	TBF-1	06474	3.8	G	Larson	Wagner - Wright	Bomb Kara via Chabai 4X500#
12/10/43	TBF-1c	24242	2.7	G	"	" "	Jokohinu Supply & Personnel Area 2000#
12/12/43	TBF-1	23972	3.5	G	"	" "	Kieta Village (Pier) 4X500
12/13/43	TBF/c	24489	4.0	G	"	" "	Porton Gun Emplacement (Heavy) 2000#
14	F-6-F		1.2	E	"	——	"Hellcat" Familiarization. Munda Pt.
15	TBF-1	23975	1.4	O	"	Wagner - Wright	Ferry Aerial Mine, Munda to Guadalcanal
15	"	"	4.3	L	"	" "	Guadal to Espiritu Santos (Bomber #5)
			20.9				
Total time to date,							

Lucky's Aviator Flight Log — last entry

CLASS OF SERVICE

This is a full-rate Telegram or Cablegram unless its deferred character is indicated by a suitable symbol above or preceding the address.

WESTERN UNION

A. N. WILLIAMS, PRESIDENT — NEWCOMB CARLTON, CHAIRMAN OF THE BOARD — J. C. WILLEVER, FIRST VICE-PRESIDENT

1204

SYMBOLS
DL=Day Letter
NT=Overnight Telegram
LC=Deferred Cable
NLT=Cable Night Letter
Ship Radiogram

The filing time shown in the date line on telegrams and day letters is STANDARD TIME at point of origin. Time of receipt is STANDARD TIME at point of destination

81 Govt. Washington,DC 649PM 1/3/44

Mr & Mrs Olaf M Larson Hanks

The Navy department deeply regrets to imform you that your Son Lt.Williams Rudolph Larson USNR is missing in the performance of his duty and in the service of his Country following plan crash condition indicate that your Son probably lost his life.But due to in evidences he will be carried in the missing status until further word is received you will be promptly advised of any change in status sincre sympathy is extended to you in your great anxiety.

Rear Admiral Randall Jacobs
Chief of Navy Personnal.

935 dr 4

THE COMPANY WILL APPRECIATE SUGGESTIONS FROM ITS PATRONS CONCERNING ITS SERVICE

Western Union Telegram received by Olaf & Mary January 3 1944

Last Known Photo of William — November 1943

CHAPTER 5

The Aftermath

Weather that day on January 3, 1944, in Sioux Trail Township, North Dakota, was 9°F. I can envision my grandmother Mary washing dishes in the little white kitchen sink of the family farmhouse and looking out north through the lace curtained window into the snow-covered farm yard. When my grandparents opened the door and received and read the Western Union telegram, I'm sure their hearts sank beyond belief. William was only 28 years old, and now was reported missing in a far off land. In fact, my grandparents only knew William was in the South West Pacific theatre somewhere aboard an unnamed carrier, as all of Lucky's letters home were censored.[23] Several unopened letters to William from my grandparents in December 1943 were eventually returned to the Hanks, North Dakota farm address marked — Returned to Sender — Unclaimed.

23 A majority of William's letters were stamped: Passed by Naval Censor, initialized by J.N.T. (Lucky's roommate at Otay Mesa, CA, and friend Jim N. Truesdale).

"**Dear Son William,**

Wonder how you are doing by now, and wonder if you get anything to eat. It can't be very interesting to eat vitamin pills. But suppose they contain the necessary vitamins to sustain life, so better than nothing.

It may be as hot there now as it is cold here. This morning it was 18 below. Radio said 13 below at Fargo. ...This will be the first Christmas we have had the past 28 yrs. that we did not have a kid home for Christmas. Lloyd does not expect to be able to get away. He asked us to come there. Says there is work in Chicago. He goes there 3 or 4 times a week to work at Campbell's.

Just heard a story on the radio — an installment of The Guiding Light. A boy came home with malaria. Was honorably discharged, nothing seemed the same to him but his mother. She was the same, and understood how he felt. She didn't question him, as she knew he did not want to be questioned. Good thing there are some good mothers in the world.

Thanks son, for the compliment to us in your last letter. I know we are just as thankful for having such lovely sons, as you are of having both your parents and a kid brother. Daddy and Sandvold were to Crosby after coal Friday. Sandvold said you boys were the nicest boys in the country. Krogen's picture of you stands in a Williston window with hundreds, I guess, of other boys in the service, and she says you are the most manly looking one in the bunch. Well, we think too you are the very best one there, and the best looking one. Thank you for the picture — was nice to see you even on a picture, and see you are smiling too. Hope you can soon come home with a smile — and be OK in every way. Hear quite a bit about the bombing in the South Pacific. Mother prays that you may be spared.

Boeck was here Tuesday and we butchered a pig. Wed. we took 3 quarters to Williston to be put in the locker. Have another to butcher, but may sell it alive. There has been an embargo on pigs — so the market must be clogged. Daddy was to Grenora yesterday to pay his income tax. It was 3 times as much as last year — but that was not so bad after all. About $36. He didn't give in this year's crop, only what has been sold. $400 worth. If we could get another crop like last year I think we would be all out of debt, and that would be nice. . . . We've had 3 new calves the past week. Every calf makes a little more work. Sold a calf to Nereson for $50 — he likes our white faces. Brakken bought one for $55 but don't come to get it. We have 30 head now and 3 horses. Will sell some more chickens when we go to Williston soon.

Ivan Olsen sat here last night till after 1 o'clock. He just came back from Spokane, so he had much to tell. Spokane is overrun with soldiers. Traffic was a jam morning & evening. He seemed content to come back to the wide open spaces where he isn't crowded.

Got your letter written Nov 30 today after I wrote this letter. Glad you got some food there at last. It may be Christmas when you get this, so I hope you have as good a one as possible, and that the New Year will see an end to this conflict — and peace can reign on earth once again. We sent your exerciser Nov. 1. Also a bit for Christmas. Hope you get it in time. Sure glad you have your harmonica. That's better than nothing. You don't seem very satisfied with the plumbing. Do you still have to do your own washing in your steel helmet? ..."

December 14 1943 Letter from Mary & Olaf to son William — RETURNED

Dear Son William,

Oh how we wonder about you now. What has happened? We had a telegram yesterday from the Navy Dept. that you had crashed and was missing. They would notify us when they knew more about it. Oh, dear, darling William! How we hope you are safe, and not a prisoner or hurt or killed. After we got that horrid message we have been in a sort of daze and pain. How we hope you come back safely to your base then find a letter from mother and others waiting for you, and get the vacation you mentioned, and can come home. We would all be so happy. Wrote to the kid brother today, and told him that message. So he will be worried too now for you. We hope and pray you may be safe — and can come back. We are afraid you crashed in enemy territory, and anything could happen. But Mother can't believe the worst has befallen you, as not one sparrow falls but what God knows about it, and I can't believe he would let you fall. Our dear lovely beautiful son, who has always been so kind, good, thoughtful of his parents and others. Anyone who has helped make a happier nicer place here should not be snatched away. ...Daddy does not break down like Mother does, but he feels just as deeply. I know he did not sleep last night. As long as there was nothing definite stated we will believe you are alive — & will come back. We know you have much endurance, resistance, and you're resourceful and clever. I believe you can come back to your boat, and the Lord will let us get together here on earth again. If it should be his will that we never meet again here on earth — may we by the help of God lead such lives that we may meet and be together in the great beyond — where we all aim to go at the close of our days here. As Jesus died to pay for our sins here, we all have the chance to get in to heaven, as He will forgive us if we only ask Him. . . . This forenoon Grandpa Witsoe[24] was here and wanted to see that telegram. Palmer Solheim also read it. Daddy said, "Put it out of sight. I can't stand the looks of it." ....Oh this war is hell on earth. It brings nothing but heartache and misery, both for the boys and for those at home.

We are OK only very anxious about you now. Mother prays you may be safe and get returned to us. We have no boys to lose or spare. You two are all we have, and all our thoughts and hopes are for you. And what would life be to us without you. I know we may not live long but I sure hope we may leave this world before either of you. Now with much love to you, and may God bless you and be merciful to us all. Your loving Mom & Dad."

January 4 1944 Letter from Mary and Olaf to son William — UNABLE TO DELIVER

24 Rasmus Witsoe was born at Tronhjem, Norway in 1868. His family immigrated to Minnesota in 1887. In 1905, Rasmus homesteaded in Fertile Valley Township, just west of the Larson family farm. Rasmus and his wife, Bertha, had 13 children. Rasmus died in 1948. Two of his daughters, Thelma and Viola, were confirmed with William at Bethany Lutheran Church in 1928. (Source: Divide County History – 1974 and Appendix B)

Condolence letters received by the family are presented in order of written date, as air-mail from the South Pacific was slow.

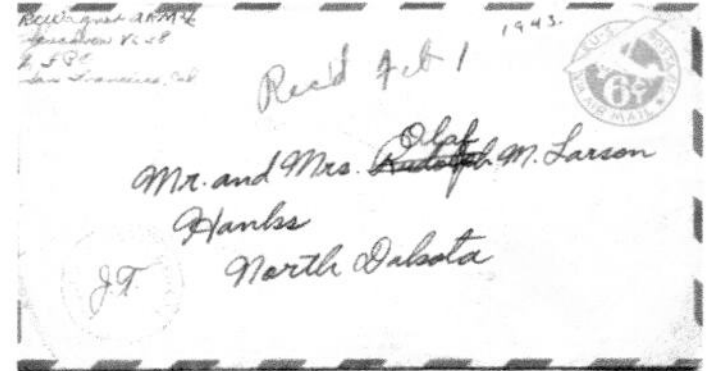

*"**Dear Mr. & Mrs. Larson,** I cannot express in words the deep sympathy that I feel for you by the loss of your son Lt. W.R. Larson. I have been his radioman for the last six months and we have flown over a hundred and fifty hours together, during that time we became very good friends. He was the best pilot I have ever flown with and also the best officer friend an enlisted man could have. If there is anything I could do for you now, or anytime in the future, please do not hesitate to ask. My home is in Watertown, S. Dak. And on my next leave I will make every attempt to pay you a visit. Sincerely yours, Dick Wagner."*

December 31 1943 -Dick Wagner — VC 38

Richard (Wag) Clayton Wagner (5/25/1918 to 9/24/1982): Richard Wagner was Lucky's radioman and was from Watertown, South Dakota. On June 26, 1944, he was awarded the Purple Heart for wounds in combat. Richard served until December 8, 1945. Wag settled in San Diego where he met his wife, graduated from college, and started a photography business. He is buried at the Fort Rosecrans National Cemetery overlooking the Pacific Ocean and the various U.S. Navy bases in San Diego Bay. His son, Walt, lives in Carlsbad, CA, and has been a great source of information on his father and the VC 38 Squadron (Appendix F) for this book. His father's war photographs include two pictures of William Larson from Hanks, North Dakota. (Photo Source: Walt Wagner)

*"**Dear Mary & Olaf,** Dad just came home and told us the sad news. We are terribly sorry Mary and Olaf, but there is still hope. I have read of many who have been reported missing who have been well and safe. Let's hope and pray that the same is true of William. You told me his companions called him "Lucky" Larson. We will hope that name still applies to him. If he had to go, we know he was ready. You could tell where his thoughts were by his letter. Mother has always commented on the nice letters William writes. You have our sincerest sympathy. I'll admit we wept, too, when we heard the news. Our love and sympathy, Lena and Hulda."*

January 4 1944 — William's cousin Hulda and Aunt Lena — Hanks North Dakota

Lena Brakken and Hulda: (11/24/1887 to 1/14/1980): Lena was Lucky's aunt (father Olaf's sister) and was born in Todd County, Minnesota. In 1906 she moved to western North Dakota with her sister. The first summer in North Dakota she herded cattle. She later returned to MN and in 1909 moved back to Divide County and homesteaded in Sioux Trail Township at the age of 22. She married John Brakken in 1913 and lived to be 92. Her daughter, Hulda, is currently living at a nursing home in Fargo, North Dakota. Their family farm is just 1.5 miles south of the Larson farm. Lena was one of the original homesteaders in Sioux Trail Township.

*"**Dear Mr. & Mrs. Larson,** I just want to send you this short note and let you know that you have my sincerest sympathy. Bill was a real friend to all of us, an excellent naval aviator and a real gentleman. There really isn't much I can say to you, except that Lt. Larson and I flew together for almost a full year and he always commanded my full respect. You certainly need hold no reserve in being proud of him. All the boys in the squadron will fully agree that he was one of the best. Sincerely, Jack Scholfield."*

January 6 1944 — Lt. J.P. Scholfield — VC 38

Lt. Jack P. Scholfield: (1/14/1920 to 12/11/2014): Lt. Scholfield was awarded the Distinguished Flying Cross (D.F.C.) for action during a combined Navy and Marine bombing attack against enemy ships in Rabaul Harbor, New Britain, on February 17, 1944. Flying right behind Commander Brunton, Jack targeted and sank a transport ship by flying right down on the water's surface and "skip bombing" a 2,000 pound bomb into the ship's side. Jack later served on the USS Bon Homme Richard with VF(N) 91. Jack moved to Seattle with his wife and graduated from law school in 1948 from the University of Washington, Seattle. Judge Scholfield retired in 1995 from the Washington State Court of Appeals. Jack was born in Kansas. He had two sons, James and Donald. Jack is buried next to his son Donald and his wife Lucille at Sunset Hills Memorial Park in Bellevue, WA. He met Lucky at Marine Air Station El Centro, CA, during experimental night flying training. (Photo Source: VC 38 group picture aboard the Long Island — W. Wagner)

*"**My dear Mr. & Mrs. Larson,** as a fellow squadron member and personal friend of your son, I'd like to extend my deepest sympathy on the tragic accident of Bill's death. It was a most unfortunate and costly accident in that we not only lost one of our best pilots but also the best liked man in the outfit. Bill was loved and respected by all and we all greatly mourn his loss. I've had the pleasure of being associated with Bill (or Willy as I called him) since Jan of 1943 and I've found our friendship and association to be a most pleasant and enjoyable one both socially and officially. I had never seen him when he wasn't the same friendly, smiling friend and advisor — always ready to do a favor and also do his own job to the best of his ability. There isn't much use in my describing the details of his accident. Suffice it to say the Navy, Squadron VC-38 in particular, lost one of its best members, and the world in general lost one of its favorite people. Once again may I extend my condolences. Respectfully, Lt. Graham Tahler."*

January 1944 — Lt. Graham Tahler — VC 38

Lt. Graham "Ham" Tahler: (3/2/1921 to 10/31/1998): Graham Tahler, 77, a Navy aviator and decorated WWII veteran, who retired as a Rear Admiral in 1974, died at Bethesda Naval Medical Command in 1998. Admiral Tahler was awarded a Navy Cross during WWII for actions as a torpedo bomber pilot in Rabaul Harbor in which he sank a Japanese transport ship and severely damaged a Japanese battleship. (Photo source: www.fold3.com memorial page of Graham Tahler)

*"**Dear Mr. & Mrs. Larson,** It is with deepest regrets that I write this letter. There just aren't words to express my sorrow over Bill's loss. I had the privilege of being a close friend of Bill's. To know Bill was to like him and respect him. We all shall miss him, and none will ever forget all he gave us. We share your loss. We lost a real friend, and the Navy has lost a grand officer. With deepest sympathies I remain — very truly yours, John A Leary."*

January 5 1944 — Lt. John A Leary — VC 38

Source: Leary Family Collection

Judge John A Leary: (5/4/1919 to 10/8/2003): Lt. John A Leary was born in Hudson Falls, New York. John was one of the group of VC 38 pilots that attacked Rabaul Harbor. He flew in at masthead level to skip bomb a Japanese cargo ship through a curtain of anti-aircraft machine gun fire on February 17, 1944. He was a recipient of both the D.F.C. and the Navy Cross. After the war, John returned to Hudson Falls, New York, where he practiced law and raised three sons — John, Chris, and Daniel. Judge Leary retired in 1989.

*"**Dear Mr & Mrs Larson,** Just a note to convey my condolences on the loss of your son, Bill. As you know it was a great loss to us boys of the squadron. I want you to know that I consider your son Bill as one of the finest gentlemen I have ever had the pleasure of knowing. Bill is gone in body but in spirit he remains with us, and I know he has a great reward in store for him. I hope someday to meet you. Until then. I remain Sincerely, Ensign T.M. Gammage."*

January 5 1944 — Ens. T.M. Gammage — VC 38

Ens. Thomas Milton Gammage: (2/1/1918 to 12/24/1990): Ens. Gammage later became a Lt. Commander, and was awarded the Navy Cross for extraordinary heroism in operations against the enemy while serving as pilot of carrier based Navy torpedo plane (USS Bataan) and section leader in VT-47, in action at Kure Harbor, Honshu Island, Japan, on July 28, 1945. Thomas is buried in Sumter County, Florida. (Photo Source: VC 38 group picture aboard the Long Island—W. Wagner)

"***Dear Mr. & Mrs. Larson & Family,*** *I am a fellow flyer in Bill's air squadron, and, I wish to extend to you my deepest sympathy. Bill was a wonderful man and a person that everyone found pleasure in calling friend. Many things happen which we are never able to explain. Why did it have to be Bill? Has been the question in our squadron for many days. May God be with you in your grief. My best wishes and sympathy to all, A friend, Grant A Phillippi.*"

January 6 1944—Lt. G.A. Phillippi—VC 38

Source: Lt. Col. Daniel Phillippi

Lt. Grant A Phillippi: (11/16/1914 to 7/30/1996): Lt. Grant Phillippi was born in Ohio and raised in Virginia. He joined the USNR and flew TBF planes in Squadron 38, fighting the Japanese over the Solomon Islands on multiple missions. On February 13, 1944, Grant and his gunner, W.L. Rice, were both injured during an emergency landing at Piva airfield, Bougainville. Lt. Phillippi suffered a broken back upon landing and crashing into a Seabee caterpillar located on the runway. Grant was transferred out of the Pacific theater for recovery at Mare Island, California, and then later transferred to Whidbey Island, Washington. Lt. Phillippi married his wife, Myrtle, whom he met in San Diego prior to shipping out to Espiritu Santo, and moved to Sacramento, California to raise two sons—Robert and Daniel. Grant owned a janitorial supply company in Sacramento, California. (Source: Lt. Col. Daniel Phillippi of Sacramento, CA. His father's WW II photo album contains a picture of Bill Larson from North Dakota [the Krogen Studios portrait]).

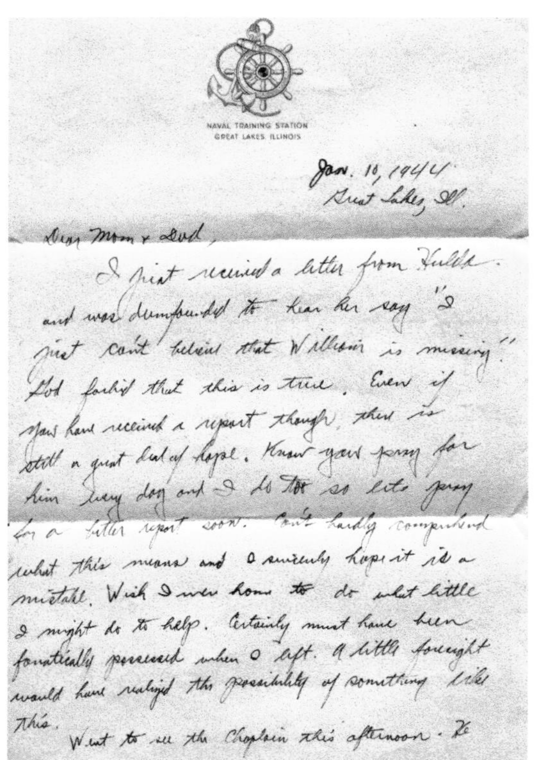

NAVAL TRAINING STATION
GREAT LAKES, ILLINOIS

Jan. 10, 1944
Great Lakes, Ill.

Dear Mom & Dad,

I just received a letter from Hulda and was dumfounded to hear her say "I just can't believe that William is missing". God forbid that this is true. Even if you have received a report though, there is still a great deal of hope. Know you pray for him every day and I do too so lets pray for a better report soon. Can't hardly comprehend what this means and I sincerely hope it is a mistake. Wish I were home to do what little I might do to help. Certainly must have been fanatically possessed when I left. A little foresight would have realized the possibility of something like this.

Went to see the Chaplain this afternoon. He

"Dear Mom & Dad,

I just received a letter from Hulda and was dumbfounded to hear her say "I just can't believe that William is missing." God forbid that this true. Even if you have received a report though, there is still a great deal of hope. Know you pray for him everyday and I do too so let's pray for a better report soon. Can't hardly comprehend what this means and I sincerely hope it is a mistake. Wish I was home to do what little I might do to help. Certainly must have been fanatically possessed when I left. A little foresight would have realized the possibility of something like this. Went to see the Chaplain this afternoon. He said 60% of the men reported missing are found. Surely there is a great deal of hope and I hope that by now you have heard of William's safety.

News like this leaves us cold and so hopelessly helpless to do anything. I know how you must feel but we can hope and pray. Somehow I feel that William is safe and may God speed the day we hear that he is. Can't write much now with this hanging cloud of uncertainty suddenly appearing. May God strengthen you and comfort you until you hear of William's safety again — it must come. Your son, Lloyd."

January 10 1944 — Brother Lloyd —
Naval Training Station, Great Lakes Illinois

"**Dear Mr. and Mrs. Larson,** *You and I have suffered a great loss. We all know how great it is for you. Bill and I had been together since we both reported to our squadron in Seattle at about the same time. Since then he became a very good friend and respected officer. In that time we had many experiences together both in the air and on the ground. I'll never forget the pleasant time we had when he and I drove from Seattle to Alameda together in November 1942. My home is in St. Paul and I graduated from St. Thomas College there. We often talked of our schools and the friendly competition between them. Bill's accident almost happened to many of the rest of us. That is, we were on the plane ahead of the one which was lost. If that had been our fate instead of his, the squadron's loss would have been far less. As you may know, Bill was not flying the plane in which he was lost but a passenger. It would have been an extremely difficult situation in the air which Bill couldn't have flown thru. All of us had the greatest regard for him personally and for his ability and leadership both in the air and on the ground. I also want to assure you that Bill has well done his duty of fighting the enemy and has participated in many aerial actions against the enemy. I am, Very respectfully, Robert B. Giblin. P.S. If there is anything I can do for you, please do not hesitate to write and ask and I'll do anything I can for you.*"

January 11 1944 — Lt. R.B. Giblin — VC 38

"**Dear Mrs. Larson,** *I hardly know how to start this, and it certainly doesn't seem right that is has be done under these circumstances. Words cannot express how I feel. I only wish there was something I could do, I can't lead myself to believe it is true, but just know that he is alive and we will both hear or see him before long. Bill is the grandest person I have ever known and I loved him with all my heart. We had so much fun together and had so many plans for the future and it just can't be that God has shattered them all. I would like so very much to meet* *you and maybe some of these day's I can as I hope to make a trip back there before too long and see my people, and will certainly make every effort to see you. Bill left a few personal things with me and I will send them to you as I think you should have them. I must close for now hoping this finds you well and that we will have good news soon. Please let me hear from you. Very Sincerely, Your friend, Bette Burton."*

January 11 1944 — William's fiancée Bette Burton — San Diego California

Bette Burton: (Date of Birth to Date of Death: Unknown): My grandparents received 9 letters from Bette in 1944 and then no word (last letter dated October 8, 1944). She was born in Missouri. Last known address of Bette was 1015 12th Ave, San Diego, California.

*"**My dear sister Mary and Olaf,** Esther, Knute, and girls were over last nite and brought your letter along — tears flowed from all eyes big and little when the news was received of William's missing. We all hope and pray he will yet be found. He might be a prisoner of war and someday before long you may get a wire he is alive and well. And God we pray that day will come soon and roll this burden on your hearts away. We are all so terribly sorry and sad over this news. God we feel so sorry for you. We are all praying William is safe and will be heard from soon. The kids here are heartbroken about it as are we all. The house shed more tears over this shocking news than was ever shed in all their lives before especially Ronnie & Ralf also Ruby — They have cried themselves to sleep 2 nites now — they pray so earnestly William is safe and that God will keep him from all harm. There isn't much I can say that can help in this strain of anxiety. God is still on the throne. I am certain he will hear your prayers. Poor little Lloyd. I sure feel sorry for him when he heard*

William was missing. But am sure he also shows no doubt about William he will be heard from soon. Hope Lloyd can come home soon and stay home. You need him worse than Uncle Sam's Navy does. . . . Brother Eli & Family."

January 14 1944 — William's Uncle Eli Johnson — Hirsch, Saskatchewan — Canada

*"**Dear Mary & Olaf,** I received your letter today and was so very sorry to hear the sad news about William being missing. I do hope he is alive and safe yet somehow. Our girls went over to Eli's this morning and the place seemed so empty all of sudden without the kids. I suggested we go to town as it was such a nice day — and then I read your letter, I cried all the way home and then we went over to Eli's and everybody cried, so you know we all sympathize with you and Olaf & Lloyd. I know Lloyd feels awful about it too. When we got home from Eli's we went to bed, but I just couldn't sleep so, I got up and thought maybe if I wrote a few lines to you tonight I'd feel better. It's 2 am now. There are no words that help much in time of grief, and the greatest grief is to lose someone we love so dearly. . . . I can't believe that William is not alive. He was too fine a boy to be gone for good. We will all pray for his safe return. I am glad you came up for Xmas, if it meant a less lonely Xmas for you. You brought up so much to make our Xmas happy — In fact 2 sets of Xmas presents that I thought it was a too big expense for you to visit all these Canucks. May God give you strength to be brave and carry on — Your sister, Rose."*

January 13 1944 — William's Aunt Esther — Bienfait, Saskatchewan — Canada

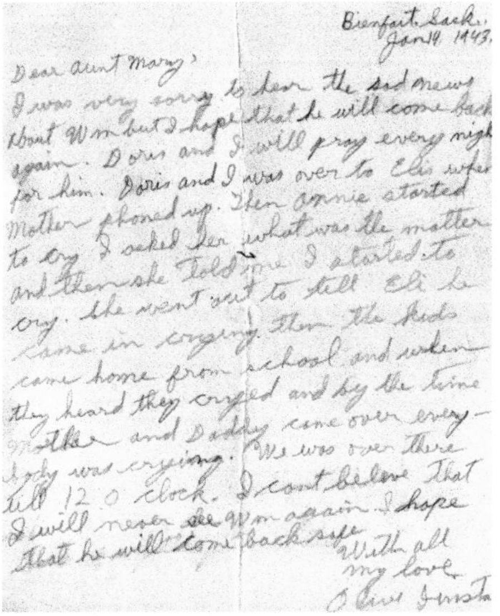

*"**Dear Aunt Mary,** I was very sorry to hear the sad news about Wm but I hope that he will come back again. Doris and I will pray every night for him. Doris and I was over to Eli's when Mother phoned up. Then Annie started to cry I asked her what was the matter and then she told me. I started to cry. She went out to tell Eli he came in crying then the kids came home from school and when they heard they cried and by the time Mother and Daddy came over everybody was crying. We was over there till 12 o'clock. I can't believe that I will never see Wm again. I hope that he will come back safe. With all my love, Olive Finstad."*

January 14 1944 — William's Cousin Olive Finstad — Bienfait, Saskatchewan — Canada (young girl of age 12)

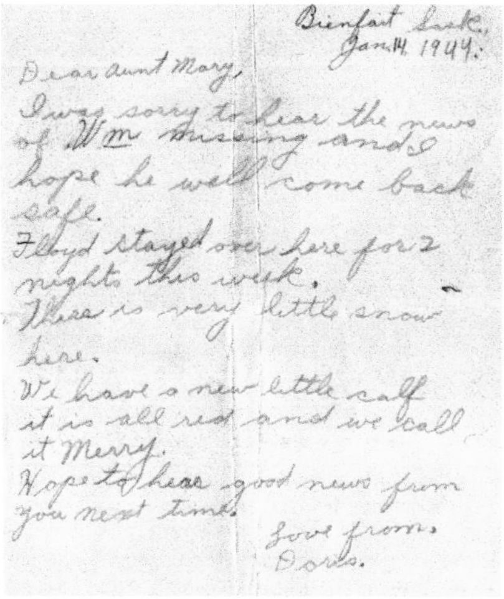

*"**Dear Aunt Mary,** I was sorry to hear the news of Wm missing and I hope he will come back safe. Floyd stayed over here for 2 nights this week. There is very little snow here. We have a new little calf it is all red and we call it Merry. Hope to hear good news from you next time. Love from Doris."*

January 14 1944 — William's Cousin Doris Finstad — Bienfait, Saskatchewan — Canada (sister to Olive — young girl of age 9)

Front Row L to R: Ralph Johnson, Ronald Johnson, Olive Finstad, Ruby Johnson, Doris Finstad. Seated Row: Aunt Esther Finstad, Annie Johnson, Floyd Johnson, mother Mary Larson. Back Row: Uncle Eli Johnson, Lloyd Larson, Olaf Larson, William Larson.October 1940 Johnson Family Picnic — Recreation Park in Williston, North Dakota

DIVIDE COUNTY FLYER MISSING IN THE PACIFIC

Lieutenant Wm. R. Larson Believed Lost Following Crash—Nearly Five Years Of Service

Mr. and Mrs. Olaf Larson, well known farmers of Sioux Trail township, are in receipt of one of those messages from the War Department that so many parents are in dread of—conveying the sad news that their son, William R. Larson, is missing in action. The message was received early last week and is as follows:

Washington, D. C., 1-3-44
Mr. and Mrs. Olaf M. Larson,
Hanks, N. Dak.

The Navy Department deeply regrets to inform you that your son, Lieut. William Rudolph Larson, USNR, is missing in the performance of his duty and in the service of his country, following plane crash. Conditions indicate that your son probably lost his life, but due to in evidences, he will be carried in the missing status until further word is received. You will be promptly advised of any change of status. Sincere sympathy is extended to you in your great anxiety.

Rear Admiral Randall Jacobs,
Chief of Navy Personnel

First Lieutenant Larson has been in the Naval Air Service about four and one-half years. He joined at Minneapolis, Minn., and took the greater part of his training at Pensacola, Fla. After receiving his wings, he saw plenty of active duty, serving at Bermuda and in Iceland, on the Atlantic patrol. Later he was transferred to the Pacific area and spent the spring and summer of 1942 in the Aleutian Islands.

He was subsequently sent to the far East, where it is believed the crash occurred.

Lieut. Larson was the oldest son of Mr. and Mrs. Olaf Larson and was born at Osakis, Minn., on December 1st, 1916. As an infant he came to Divide County and lived here until entering the service. His last visit home was in the month of October, 1942. Other members of the family are his parents and a brother, Lloyd, now in training at Great Lakes, Ill.

The Journal joins with the many friends of the Larson family in extending sympathy to them in their great anxiety and all join in offering their prayers that "Bill" will turn up safe and sound.

SIOUX TRAIL NEW

Mr. and Mrs. Olaf Larsen received a telegram on Tuesday from the Navy Department in Washington, D. C., that their son, Lt. William R. Larsen, a navy aviator, had crashed, and has probably lost his life. But due to insufficient evidence he will be reported missing. The writer hopes no other parents here may get such a message as it leaves an ache in the heart that does not leave day or night. But we hope he may yet be alive and return safely in time.

More About Lieut. Larson

Mr. and Mrs. Olaf Larson, well known farmers of Sioux Trail township in southern Divide county, are in receipt of a message from the war department stating that their son, William R. Larson, is missing in action. The message states that "Lieut. William Rudolph Larson, USNR, is missing in the performance of his duty and in the service of his country, following plane crash. Conditions indicate that your son probably lost his life, but due to insufficient evidence, he will be carried in the missing status until further word is received."

Lieut. Larson has been in the naval air service about 4½ years. He joined at Minneapolis, Minn., and took the greater part of his training at Pensacola, Fla. After receiving his wings, he saw plenty of active duty, serving at Bermuda and in Iceland, on the Atlantic patrol. Later he was transferred to the Pacific area and spent the spring and summer of 1942 in the Aleutian islands.

He was subsequently a navy pilot on a carrier in the Solomon islands territory, where it is believed the crash occurred.

Lt. Larson, oldest son of Mr. and Mrs. Larson, was born at Osakis, Minn., on Dec. 1, 1916. While an infant he came with his parents to make his home in Divide county. His last visit was in October, 1942. Other members of the family besides his parents, is a brother, Lloyd, now in training at Great Lakes, Ill.

(Previous page) January 14, 1944 news articles in Divide County Journal reporting Lucky missing in action. The news clipping titled, Sioux Trail News, was written by mother Mary Larson. She was a contributor to the Divide County Journal paper for over 40 years, writing about activities and events in Sioux Trail Township, North Dakota.

WILLIAM LEMKE
AT LARGE
NORTH DAKOTA

W. O. SKEELS
SECRETARY

COMMITTEES:
IRRIGATION AND RECLAMATION
REVISION OF THE LAWS
PUBLIC LANDS

HOME ADDRESS:
FARGO, N. DAK.

Congress of the United States
House of Representatives
Washington, D. C.

January 17, 1944

Mr. and Mrs. Olaf M. Larson
Hanks, North Dakota

Dear Mr. and Mrs. Larson:

Just received official notice from the Navy Department that your son, William, is missing.

I wish to extend to you my sympathy in your anxiety. Let us hope that he has not been injured and that, he has been rescued and will be reported found in the near future.

May I also suggest to you that the Red Cross and the representatives of neutral countries under arrangements with our Department of State will endeavor to get information as to the whereabouts and condition of your son.

Again hoping that your son is well and with my personal regards, I am

Very truly yours,

Wm Lemke

STATE OF NORTH DAKOTA
OFFICE OF THE GOVERNOR
BISMARCK

JOHN MOSES
GOVERNOR

January 18, 1944

My dear Mr. and Mrs. Larson:

It has just been brought to my attention that your son, Lieut. William Rudolph Larson, has been reported missing.

All of us who are parents, especially of men in the service, can in a measure appreciate the anxiety you are suffering, and can share with you the hope that later word may tell you of his safety.

The fate of this Nation, and of the ideals of liberty and justice we all hold so dear, depends upon the courage and the heroic devotion of young men like your son—upon the patriotic sacrifice of parents like yourselves.

May God grant that we at home may prove worthy of that sacrifice, and that your son may yet be found and return safe to you in the not too distant future.

Sincerely,

John Moses

Governor

Mr. and Mrs. Olaf Larson
Crosby, North Dakota

BUY "DAKOTA MAID" FLOUR

*"**Mr. & Mrs. Olaf Larson,** My Dear Friends, I have just received word that your son, my good friend William, has been reported missing in action. We hope and pray with you that his life has been spared and that someday he can be back with us again. If he is alive we know that God is with him and if not, he is with God. We all had a high regard for William when he was at Concordia. He was the industrious, able and conscientious, Christian young man whom every one loved and respected. I know that he took with him, where ever he walked his faith in Jesus as his Savior. … May the Master be especially close to you in these days. Yours in Christ, J.N. Brown."*

January 19 1944 J.N. Brown, President of Concordia College — Moorhead Minnesota

*"**My Dear Olaf and Mrs. Larson,** Believe me, my dear friends it was with the deepest regret and sense of bereavement, that I read the clipping from the Williston Herald that Stella sent to me. And I really don't know how to say anything that would make it any easier for you but I shall try my best.*

Last night when I was on the bus going ashore for my 36 hour liberty I chanced to have for a seat mate a Lt. in the regular Navy, stationed on the Navy Air at Quonset Point. In the course of our conversation I asked him if he had ever

heard of Lucky Larson. His answer was "Hell, yes everyone in the Naval flying branch has heard of him." *I then told him of the telegram you folks had received and he said that everyone in the Navy would hear of it with sorrow. So, my friends you may be sure, that Bill, if he is lost will not be forgotten very soon by his mates and associates. But as long as he is not actually known to be killed, we shall all hope and pray, that somehow or somewhere, he is on top and will come back to us some day. And if not we know that Bill went west in the way he would have liked to. Also that he had struck hard at our enemies, and done his bit and willingly. I shall always remember Bill as a swell kid as a boy, and as a man he was a splendid gentleman held in esteem by all who knew him. ...But I shall continue to think of Bill as being one of us mates, till I know different for sure I should be very happy to hear from you when you get time to write. My best regards from an old friend and from all my mates in this Navy. Warner Peterson."*

January 23 1944 –Chief Petty Officer Warner Peterson — Camp Thomas Rhode Island — William's High School teacher at Sioux Trail Consolidated

"**Dear Mary and Olaf:** *It is not so easy to write an answer to your letter except to thank you so kindly for remembering my birthday. That is always appreciated. There has been small articles in the Forum about William missing in action, presumably having crashed somewhere in the Far East. Such reports have come often and later found them prisoners of war. News about war prisoners are slow especially from the Japs. We should not anticipate the worst until we are sure. There is always hope until then. In the midst of war it is not so easy to get news from the immediate fronts. We are not helpless in circumstances, but seems we are helpless about the whole* *thing. War starts and we are in it whether we like it or not. So far, the world has been that way and will be now until this is finished. Nobody can quit. Neither the Germans, Japs, or the Allies will quit at this stage. It is going to take a knock out to stop it. There is pride, honor, and profit all involved. They are powerful forces and do not surrender willingly. . . . The feeling of losing a member of the family is something words can not explain. I went thru it once and, of course, one never really gets over it. We will live in hope until we are sure."*

January 24 1944 Letter from William's Uncle William (Willie) Johnson — Mary's Brother — Fargo North Dakota

C.E. Brunton, Comdr., U.S.N.,
Commander V.C. Squadron 38,
Fleet Post Office,
San Francisco, California,
January 5, 1944.

Mr. Olaf M. Larson,
Hanks, North Dakota.

Dear Mr. Larson:

It is my sad duty to have to inform you of the circumstances surrounding the death of your son William Rudolph Larson on 27 December 1943. I feel sure that for your own peace of mind you wish to know regardless of the hurt. In behalf of the entire squadron and myself I want to tell you that Bill's loss was a very sad occassion to us; there was no finer boy in the world; there were very few better pilots and naval officers. To myself, his commanding officer, Bill was a capable officer who gave me complete support and cooperation and never let me down. I know that had he lived he would have had his own squadron in a very short time. It would have been a fine squadron.

Our squadron had recently completed a tour of duty in an active combat zone. While there we participated in many bombing missions against Japanese held airfields and gun positions as well as missions against Japanese troops. Bill went on these missions and did his duty without fanfare. Having completed a tour, the pilots and plane crews were sent to Sidney, Australia for leave and recreation. While returning to duty from this leave the aircraft in which Bill was traveling as a passenger crashed in the water ten miles south of the Island of Uvea in the Loyalty Group. There were no survivors; none of the bodies were recovered. It is not definitely known what caused the aircraft to crash as radio contact was lost with the aircraft shortly after it departed from Tontouta, New Caledonia. The weather was not too good and from reports of native eyewitnesses the aircraft spun into the water out of control. There were no rescue facilities at hand at the remote scene of the crash. Any statement as to cause would be mere conjecture.

It is little solace to you or anyone else that every effort is made to prevent such accidents - the fact remains that they do occur and on a regular percentage basis. This percentage is low and going down steadily but there is an irreducible minimum.

In regard to Bill's personal effects, the clothing and similar equipment will be packed and shipped by Navy Freight. Valuables are forwarded by registered mail. It often takes a rather long period of time for these matters to be settled but you will eventually receive everything.

-1-

Letter Received by Family on March 15 1944

Source: Gregory Pons Collection

Commander Charles E. Brunton (4/29/1906 to 1/7/1993): Charles was the Commander of VC 38. He was awarded the Distinguished Flying Cross (D.F.C) for action at Rabaul Harbor. On 17 February 1944, while leading a combined Navy and Marine mast-head bombing attack against enemy shipping in Rabaul Harbor, New Britain, he picked for his target an un-engaged enemy destroyer. In his approach to the target through heavy and intense anti-aircraft fire he was seriously wounded. Disregarding his own pain and personal safety he pressed home his attack with courage and determination securing a direct hit on the destroyer. This destroyer was later photographed close ashore with its stern awash. With the same courage and determination shown above, he flew his plane to its home base returning the other members of his crew to safety

Charles also served in Korea and became a Rear Admiral. Richard Wagner, Lucky's radioman, immediately flew with Commander Brunton following William's death and accompanied Cdr. Brunton during the Rabaul Harbor dive attack on February 17, 1944.

THE DEPUTY CHIEF OF NAVAL OPERATIONS (AIR)
WASHINGTON

January 25, 1944

My dear Mr. Larson:

It was with deep regret I learned the sad news that your son, Lieutenant William Larson, has been reported missing as the result of an aviation accident at sea. I fully realize your anxiety and grief and want you to know that you have my sincere sympathy.

Words are of little help at such a time, but it is my fervent hope that the knowledge of your son's loyalty to our country and his patriotic participation in the essential work of the aviation branch of its defense forces will comfort you in your sorrow.

I wish to extend to you the deepest sympathy of the officers and men of naval aviation.

Sincerely yours,

J. S. McCAIN
Vice Admiral, U. S. Navy

Mr. Olaf M. Larson
Hanks, North Dakota

Vice Admiral, John Sidney McCain (1884 — 1945). Died 4 days after Japanese surrender — Grandfather of Senator John McCain of Arizona

*"**Dear Mr. Lemke:** Lieutenant Larson has been in the status of missing since 27 Dec. 1943. He was one of a party of officers and enlisted men of his squadron who had been given rehabilitation leave at Sydney, Australia. On Dec. 27, 1943 the party was returning to the combat area as passengers on a scheduled flight in one of the government transport planes, regularly operating in that area. About an hour and a half after the plane had taken off from one of the island stops, all radio contact with it was lost, and it was not hear from again. After the scheduled time for its arrival at the base had been passed, extensive searches were begun by Army, Navy, and Marine planes which continued throughout 28 December 1943. On the evening of that day, word was received that wreckage of a transport of the type that was lost had been found near the place where the last radio contact with the plane had been made, a few miles off one of the islands in the Loyalty Group, northwest of New Caledonia. The wreckage was identified as that of the missing plane by a flier's log book bearing the name of one of the enlisted men of the party who was a passenger in the plane and by other circumstances. At the time of this report no survivors have been found; extensive searches were continued for several days, but none of them brought forth any results.... If at the end of that time (one year) his fate has not been determined, the Secretary of Navy will give consideration to his status on the basis of the facts then available. ..."*

February 16 1944 letter from A.C. Jacobs, Cdr. USNR, Head of Casualties and Allotments Section, to Congressman William Lemke of North Dakota

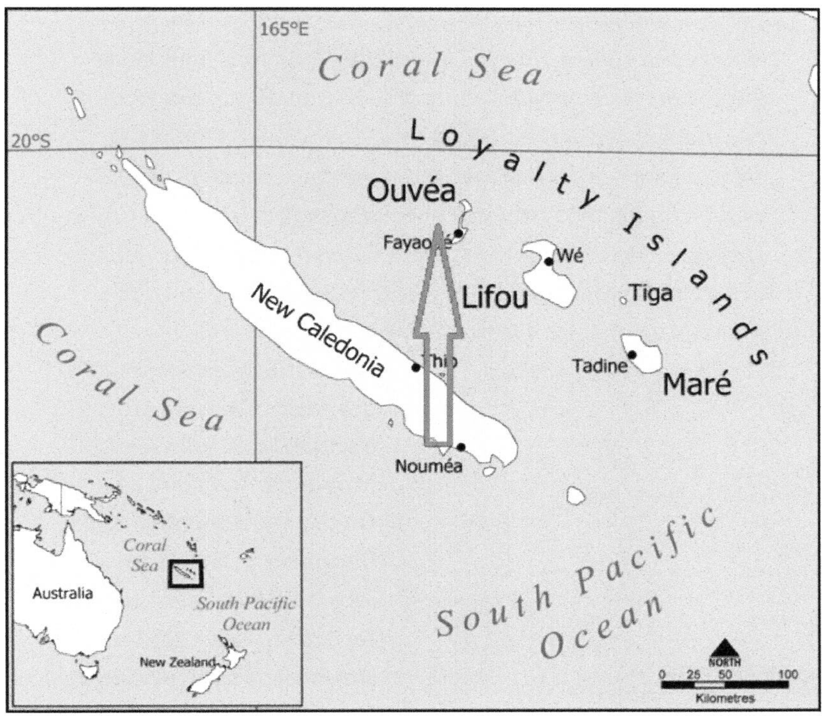

Flight Path of Lucky's Transport Plane December 27 1943

*"**Dear Mr. Larson,** Yesterday I received your letter and will answer your questions and tell you what I know of your son's loss. I'm sorry that you were not told more definitely before. Of course, anything I write is personal and unofficial. But I understand your anguish and feel it is best to dispel any false hopes. Your son has been reported "missing" because his body was never recovered. However, none of us holds any hope that he, nor any of the other passengers on the last plane, is alive. I have your letter in front of me now and I will answer your questions in the order that they are written in your letter. No, I don't think he is alive on any island. His plane was not shot down by Japs as it was not near any place where it could have been shot down. Yes, as far as I know the plane crashed and the*

cause had not been determined. Yes, there were several other officers and enlisted men on board the plane. No, I don't think there is the remotest possibility of sabotage. That plane had adequate life preserving equipment. They carry an individual preserver for each passenger and crewman and rafts large enough for all. Bill's personal belongings will be sent to you. They are inventoried in the squadron and forwarded according to regular Navy procedure. I am sure you will receive all his personal belongings eventually.

U.S. NAVY AIR CORPS

VC 38 Fleet P.O.
San Francisco
17 March, 1944

Dear Mr. Larson,
Yesterday I received your letter and will answer your questions and tell you what I know of your son's loss. I'm sorry that you were not told more definitely before. Of course, anything I write is personal and unofficial. But I understand your anguish and feel it best to dispel any false hopes. Your son has been reported 'missing' because his body never was recovered. However, none of us holds any hope that he, nor any of the other passengers on the lost plane, is alive. I have your letter in front of me now and I will answer your questions in the order that they are written in your letter. No, I don't think he is alive on any island. His plane was not shot down by Japs as it was not near any place where it could have been shot down. Yes, as far as I know the plane crashed and the cause had not been determined. Yes, there were several other officers and enlisted men on board

Here is the story of the crash. We were on our way back from leave in Sydney, Australia. On the morning of 27 December 1944, we took off on different planes from Tontouta, New Caledonia enroute to Espiritu Santo, New Hebrides. My plane left a few hours before that on which Bill was a passenger. We arrived safely at Espiritu Santo and soon heard that Bill's plane was over-due. He was the only member of our squadron on board that plane. The rest of the passengers belonged to another squadron. No one was ever recovered. This plane was seen to crash into the water near a small island north of New Caledonia. I heard, also unofficially, that part of the wreckage was sighted. Most likely all the bodies were pinned to the wreckage and went to the bottom as neither the plane nor any of the passengers

or crew were recovered, it is impossible to say what the cause of the crash was. We who fly understand the many possible causes of such a crash. *However, as I know no more details I wouldn't hazard a guess. But I am satisfied that no foul play was involved. As I said before, this information is not official. We got it from pilots who searched for the plane and by word of mouth from others who had knowledge of the crash.*

I hope this letter doesn't hurt you too much; but I would not want you holding to hopes which don't exist. I always tell the fellows that if I ever get killed that I don't want my folks to be told that I am just "missing" I want them to know what happened. I feel that you would like to be told in the same way. Thank you for the good wishes for our squadron. However, I'm sorry to say that we have lost two more of our flying mates and had three more seriously wounded. . . . Hoping that this letter gives you the information you desired, I am, Robert Giblin."

March 17 1944 — Lt. R.B. Giblin — VC 38

CDR. ROBERT B. GIBLIN
CO, VA-196

Lt. Robert B. Giblin: (11/13/1917 to 7/2/1984): Robert was a fellow aviator in VC 38 and born in St. Paul, Minnesota. He enrolled in the Navy in August 1940. Lt. Giblin took advanced operational training with Advanced Carrier Training Group, NAS Norfolk, Virginia. He then joined VGS-21 on the west coast. This squadron successively was designated VC-21 and then VC-38. With VC-38 he made a tour of duty in the Solomon Islands off land bases at Guadalcanal, Munda, and Empress Augusta Bay, Bougainville. He flew 25 attacks and was awarded the Distinguished Flying Cross (D.F.C.) after returning to the USA. –Declassified papers from VT-85. Robert also served in Korea and Vietnam.

*"**Dear Mrs. Larson,** I received your fine letter in January and would have answered it long ago if my duties had permitted, but things were moving so fast and so compellingly that there was no time for the kind of letter I wanted to write in reply to yours. And then, too, I was hoping against hope for some sort of miracle that would bring Mr. Bill (as I and the boys used to call him affectionately) back to us. But there is no room for hope now, and I hate to be the one to tell you this. Bill was lost in the accident that you were informed of; he was not over enemy territory at the time but over the ocean and the end must have come mercifully and quickly, and my conviction is that he nor anyone else knew what happened. The shock was one of the deepest I have ever received when I heard the terrible news. He was my best friend in the squadron and **the best friend I've ever had anywhere in my life**. From the very first when I joined the squadron, we were drawn to each other by mutual philosophies of life and mutual likes and outlooks; and the good times we had together, walking and talking in the evening, playing cribbage (he taught me how to play, and I had a hard time ever getting the best of him — he was sharp!), and discussing life both past, present, and future — those good times, I say, and the rare, fine comradeship we had will always stand out in my memory as superlatively tall, and fair, and shining. He*

reflected in his actions, and thoughts, and manners the kind of upbringing that must have been very similar to mine, and I felt as close to him as to one of my own brothers. He was a man in the very best sense of the word and noble through and through. In all of the time I knew him, I never heard him once speak ill of anyone. He was conscientiously devoted to his duty and as good a Christian as I ever hope to meet. We always attended church together whenever we had the opportunity. His loss to the squadron is one that can never be remedied — he was loved and respected by everyone, enlisted men and officers alike.

I hope someday that I shall have the opportunity to come by to see you in Hanks. I would like very much to meet personally the family of such a man and friend as Mr. Bill was. It is impossible for me to understand his having been taken, but my faith in the strength and tenderness of His Everlasting Arms is unshaken and I know that Mr. Bill is with Him, and I pray that He will give us the strength to continue in our duty and join Mr. Bill when our time comes. I am speaking for Mr. Bill now when I tell you to take good care of yourselves and be as happy as you can — that is what he would want you to do most of all, Mrs. Larson, and he wouldn't want you to worry and grieve yourselves until you impaired your health and life became a burden. That would make his sacrifice a little in vain if you should not continue to live and serve happy in your faith in the internal values. Please forgive me if I seem to be "preaching", I talked with Mr. Bill on this subject and I know how he felt and how he wanted you to feel and live now. And please know that I share your grief to an extent beyond the power of words to express.

With very good wishes for you and yours and hoping to see you one of these days, I am Sincerely your friend, J.N. Truesdale."

March 16 1944 — Lt. J.N. Truesdale — VC 38 — Pacific Area

Lt. James Nardin Truesdale: (10/8/1907 to 11/7/1987): Jim was a university professor of Greek studies at Duke University, Durham, North Carolina. He started a Methodist school. Jim was the Air Combat Intelligence Office (ACIO) of VC 38. He met Lucky during training at NAAS Otay Mesa, California, in March of 1943, while they were both in VGS-21 and were roommates at Otay Mesa. Jim had two children — Robert and Carolyn. His son, Robert Truesdale, currently lives in the house his father built on Pinecrest Road in Durham, North Carolina. (Photo source: Carolyn Truesdale)

*"**Dear Mrs. Larson,** After my last letters came back "Unclaimed" from Bill, I wrote to Concordia. Today I received word from the Registrar that he was reported "Missing in Action." Sympathy, though so inadequate and futile at a time like this, is what I felt I must send to you and your family. Probably Bill never mentioned me to you in his letters — but I am a Schoolmarm he met while stationed here in Alameda. We had such a good time before he was sent over. He always said that when the war was over he wanted to go back to the farm and raise wheat. I would greatly appreciate your letting me know if any other report is sent to you. Am going into Red Cross Clubmobile[25] work overseas next month but the letter would be forwarded if you sent it here. Most Sincerely, Ruth Cronkite."*

March 20 1944 — Ruth Cronkite — Alameda California

---

25 The American Red Cross Clubmobile Service was a mobile service club created during World War II to provide servicemen with food, entertainment and a connection home. The original Clubmobiles operated from late 1942 until 1946, traveling all throughout Great Britain and Europe.

Letter from Mary & Olaf Larson to Lt. J. Truesdale, Pacific Area

"Dear Friend. *We want to thank you very very much for your wonderful letter. It gave us much comfort. It is hard for us to realize William is gone, but it must have been his fate. We are so glad you talked together of eternal things. That is what has especially worried me. Wondering if William was prepared to go. We know, if we are only prepared, then it makes no difference when we leave this earth. But it is hard and a terrible blow for parents to lose a child. We try to bear up, and ask God to give us strength. We heard from Giblin [Lt. Robert B. Giblin] that William was the only passenger from squadron 38 on that plane. Strange he should be the only one. It must have been God's will he should go that way. Also want to thank you for the tribute given William. We know he deserves them. He was a model son, and we loved him so much. Mention was made of William's personal things. They will be sent home. Sure would hate getting back the things we sent him for Christmas. Won't you keep them? And that exercising gadget we sent him. We have no use for it here, and you and the boys there can make use of it. So please keep it. You also can make use of his stationary. We will be happy to hear from you again when you have time to write. William wrote once you were one friend he would never forget, and mentioned you so many times in his letters. We feel thankful to you for being his friend, and for all you did to make life there more pleasant and bearable. How we hope peace comes soon, so boys can come back to their native land. We hate seeing them sent away all over the world. Hope this letter gets there before William's things are sent, so you can keep what I mentioned. Hope you stay well, and never get hurt. And when you have the chance we will be happy to have you visit us. Will send you a picture of William we had taken last time he was home. May God protect you and bless you, is our prayer."*

March 30 1944 (source: Ms. Carolyn Truesdale — Medford Lakes New Jersey)

*"**Dear Mr. and Mrs. Larson:** Naturally, I was very shocked and distressed when I read your letter. When I wrote you asking for his address I was worried, because a letter I had written to him had just been returned to me. Also Mrs. Burkett (the wife of an aviator that was lost while serving with us on the Nashville) told me that a letter she had written was returned. I hadn't seen Lucky since he left the Nash, but my wife met him in San Francisco last spring. I left the Glamour Ship last May, and have been on other cruisers. My address after April 15th will be U.S.S. Detroit, care of Fleet P.O., San Francisco. I should like to hear from you again. I know you will write if you should hear anything new. Best Wishes, Barbara and Jimmy Holladay."*

April 2 1944 — Lt. J.M. Holladay — Seattle Washington

Lt. James M Holladay, Jr. (8/22/1918 to 12/15/1967): Jimmy (nicknamed Virginia Jim) was shipmate & roommate with Lucky on the USS Nashville and later a Commander. He was from Virginia and is buried at Maplewood Cemetery near Gordonsville, Virginia.

***Dear Mr. and Mrs. Larson**, My name is Dorothy Burkett. I knew your son, William, (altho we usually spoke of him as "Lucky or Bill") and I last heard from him in a letter dated December 1 1943. May I explain — my husband's name was Howard Ray Burkett[26] and he was a pilot with Lucky aboard the "Glamour Ship." I don't know if Bill ever mentioned him — he was missing from the ship on a patrol flight on May 5, 1942.*

---

26 On May 5, 1942, SOC pilot Ensign Burkett and radioman, Paul Phillip Ewell Jr., radioed USS Nashville that they were in a rain squall and heading to nearest land at Lisianski Island. At 2150 plane reported that he had landed safely on the water to await daylight. The plane was approximately 64 miles from the Nashville. On May 6, 3 planes and ship [Nashville] searched for the lost plane and in mid-afternoon, search was abandoned and the Nashville continued on for Midway Island. Both men were listed as M.I.A. (Source: USS Nashville War Diary, dated May 5 and 6, 1942)

He thought the world of Lucky and I can remember so well his chuckle when I asked why Bill's nickname was "Lucky." Howard said he guessed he was the best darn flier in the outfit and never missed a gun run. Then a few days ago I was reading Howard's diary and he mentioned having gone out to Bermuda (before the war, when my husband had just joined the Nashville) with Lucky and bicycling all over the island — how much he liked this "flier whose name is Larson and I guess is as quiet as I am." He mentions him several times and later in his diary and in letters.

Then last summer Lucky came to San Francisco as soon as he got my address from Jimmy Holladay and looked me up at the place I was working. He was the first flier I had seen since I heard of Howard's bad luck — in fact he was the first person from the ship and you have no idea what it meant to me — or how grateful I was to him. But it was just one of those things he did so easily and so well. I have had quite a few letters from Lucky since we kept tabs on everyone we knew that way. I remember particularly how proud he was of leading a flight of his lovely TBFs down to San Diego "and I didn't lose my way" — and believe me when he shows up <u>this</u> time I shall really tease him. . . . Jimmy Holladay sent on to me the letter you had written him. . . . I asked Lucky when I talked with him if Howard had a chance and he answered me by saying " Dorothy, I don't know — no one knows — but believe that if he <u>had</u> a chance, he <u>will</u> make it." And I feel in my heart, that, if there was a chance — Lucky will make it. . . . I want to quote you a part of my last letter from Lucky to date. ---- 'Am still kicking the TBF around and like it fine. This is quite a spot. Rain pours on the slightest provocation — salt never. The sun is unmercifully hot and because of its unusual position in the sky, most confusing. — Mud, dust, coral, innumerable strange insects, lizard-like fly catchers, a social game of cards, male companionship (a bit stale by now), airplanes, bunk *time, vitamin pills, coffee, two month old newspapers — all part of the environment in which we are so fortunate to find ourselves. A Very Merry Christmas!! And if you venture to join the Waves — best of luck! As ever, Bill L.' So you can see Lucky is quite a home down "round those parts" and he'll probably have quite a tale to tell. . . . Affectionately, Dorothy M Burkett."*

April 4 1944 Dorothy Burkett — San Francisco California

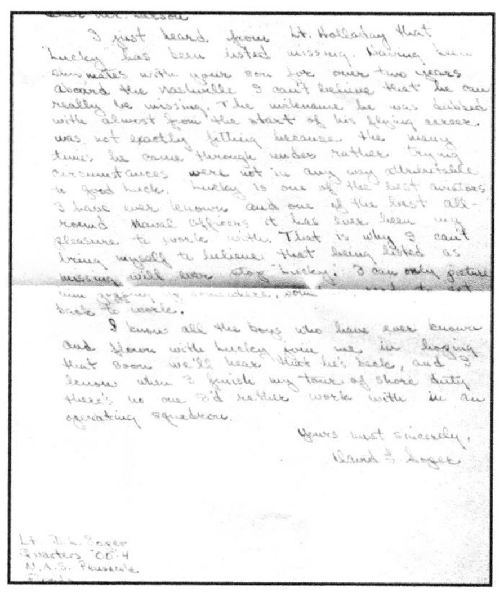

I just heard from Lt. Holladay that "Lucky" has been listed missing. Having been shipmates with your son for over two years aboard the Nashville I can't believe that he can really be missing. The nickname he was dubbed with almost from the start of his flying career was not exactly fitting because the many times he came through under rather trying circumstances were not in any way attributable to good luck. Lucky is one of the best aviators I have ever known and one of the best all-round Naval officers it has ever been my pleasure to work with. That is why I can't bring myself to believe that being listed as missing will ever stop "Lucky." I can only picture him popping up somewhere, som[illegible] to get back to work.

I know all the boys who have ever known and flown with Lucky join me in hoping that soon we'll hear that he's back, and I know when I finish my tour of shore duty there's no one I'd rather work with in an operating squadron.

Yours most sincerely,
David L. Soper

Lt. D. L. Soper
Quarters "CO"-4
N.A.S. Pensacola

*"**Dear Mr. Larson,** I just heard from Lt. Holladay that "Lucky" has been listed missing. Having been shipmates with your son for over two years aboard the Nashville I can't believe that he can really be missing. The nickname he was dubbed with almost from the start of his flying career was not exactly fitting because the many times he came through under rather trying circumstances were not in any way attributable to good luck. "Lucky" is one of the best aviators I have ever known and one of the best all-round naval officers it has ever been my pleasure to work with. That is why I can't bring myself to believe that being listed as missing will ever stop "Lucky." I can only picture him popping up somewhere, somehow, ready to get back to work. I know all the boys who have ever known and flown with Lucky join me in hoping that soon we'll hear that he's back, and I know when I finish my tour of shore duty no one I'd rather work with in an operating squadron. Yours most sincerely, David L Soper."*

April 15 1944 — Lt. D.L. Soper — Quarters — NAS Pensacola Florida

Lt. David L Soper: (8/21/1915 to 1/5/2014): David was shipmate with William on the USS Nashville and later Commander of the USS Wright, San Marino CA. He retired to San Diego and had four daughters — Pat, Carol, Linda, and Debbie. Upon contacting his daughter, Debbie, in August 2014, she asked if my uncle was, "named Lucky Larson?".

"***My dear Mrs. Larson,*** *Recently my son, Ben Wright, was at home on leave, and intended writing you a note, but in some way misplaced your address, which I have since found. So I am taking the liberty of writing for him. Ben was Lieut. Larson's turret gunner, and had great confidence in him both as a pilot and a man. He spoke of him as being "a swell guy" — this younger generation's greatest compliment. As ranking ordnance man in Squadron VC38, Ben had the privelage of choosing his pilot, and selected your son as the one he thought best of all. He said he had never had cause to regret his selection, because Lieut. Larson was surely "tops" as a pilot. It fact since then, Ben has had no desire to fly, and hopes that he will not have to so — at least not after the mil. of course if necessary. (by then, I mean your son's accident). Lieut. Larson's loss was a blow to VC38, both as a pilot and as to morale for he was loved and respected by all. Ben told me that their radio man was to go to see you while he was on leave, so I'm sure he told you about how good a record the squadron had made. We are so proud of it. Ben reported back to Seattle on May 8, being one of the 20 odd to form a nucleus for new VC38. This was his first leave in 20 months, so you can know how overjoyed his dad and I were to have him those two weeks. My older son is also in the Navy, on the aircraft carrier Lexington, now in the thick of the fight in the Pacific.... With the deepest symphathy from Ben and me, and with appreciation for all that Lieutenant Larson meant to Ben, who being younger, looked up to him and* *respected and admired him so, Very Sincerely Yours, Estelle Wright."*

May 8 1944 — Mrs. B. W. Wright — Jacksonville Florida

Benjamin Winn Wright: (2/10/1923 to 12/24/1978): Ben was Lucky's turret gunner on their TBF. He is buried in Jacksonville, Duval County, Florida.

*"**My Dear Mr. Larson,** For a year and a half I was captain of the Nashville, and so an associate of your boy William. Only recently, through Dorothy Burkett, whose husband also was an aviator attached to the Nashville and who lost his life while I was in command, I learned that William is missing. I felt that that I should write you, because I was very fond of him.*

I suppose you know of his nickname, Lucky. I don't know whether it was given to him on the ship or whether he brought it with him, but it seemed to be a good name for him. He survived some astonishing adventures. *Two of them were amazing: one was a 3500-foot descent through thick fog, to land safely after nightfall; the other comprised two dreadful nights alone in his plane, riding out an Alaskan storm in a bay of a strange island, while his radioman was marooned on the beach, unable to get back. I am going to ask Bernard **McQuaid of the Chicago Daily News**, who was with us on both occasions, to send you the stories he wrote about them.*

However, what I really had in mind, Mr. Larson, was that it

Navy Yard, Navy #128
Care FPO, San Francisco
15 May 1944

My dear Mr Larson,
For a year and a half I was captain of the Nashville, and so an associate of your boy William. Only recently, through Dorothy Burkett, whose husband also was an aviator attached to the Nashville and who lost his life while I was in command, I learned that William is missing. I felt that I should write you, because I was very fond of him.
I suppose you know of his nickname, Lucky. I don't know whether it was given him on the ship or

wan't luck but great skill, great courage and endurance and splendid judgement which brought your son through these experiences. He was a great aviator, a fine man and a shipmate whom none who served with him in the Nashville will forget. I loved him like a son, and I share your distress and grief at what has happened. You can at least be proud to have had such a son.

If William's mother is living, will you please extend to her my deep sympathy? Most sincerely yours, Francis S Craven."

May 15 1944 — Captain Francis S Craven — Navy Yard, Navy 128

Capt. Francis Sanderson Craven: (8/16/1890 to 2/18/1969): Captain Craven was from New York and served in the US Navy in World War I and II. He was the captain of The Glamour Ship (*Nashville*) May 1, 1941 to September 30, 1942.

In reply address not the signer of this letter, but Bureau of Naval Personnel, Navy Department, Washington, D. C.
Refer to No.
83169
Pers-5353a-OC

NAVY DEPARTMENT
BUREAU OF NAVAL PERSONNEL
WASHINGTON 25, D. C.

28 March 1944

Mr. Olaf M. Larson
Hanks, North Dakota

Dear Mr. Larson:

You have previously been informed of the details surrounding the disappearance of your son, Lieutenant William Rudolph Larson, United States Naval Reserve, who was reported missing on 27 December 1943 as the result of a plane crash in the South Pacific area.

It is with deep regret you are now informed that after a complete review of all available information surrounding the disappearance of your son, it has been officially determined that he lost his life on 27 December 1943.

All the agencies of the government having jurisdiction over the payment of death benefits and insurance are being informed of the death of your son. They will forward directly to you the necessary forms upon which to file claim for payment of any benefits to which you may be entitled.

The Bureau regrets that the hope which you have held during these intervening months for the safe return of your son must now be concluded. Sincerest sympathy is extended to you in your sorrow.

By direction of the Chief of Naval Personnel.

Sincerely yours,

A. C. Jacobs

A. C. JACOBS
Commander, U. S. N. R.
Head of the Casualties
and Allotments Section

In reply address not the signer of this letter, but Bureau of Naval Personnel, Navy Department, Washington, D. C.
Refer to No.

83169
Pers-5352a-hc

NAVY DEPARTMENT
BUREAU OF NAVAL PERSONNEL
WASHINGTON 25, D. C.

5 May 1944

LIEUTENANT WILLIAM RUDOLPH LARSON, A-V(N), U. S. NAVAL RESERVE
ACTIVE, DECEASED

Re: Service of

- -

1915	Dec	1	Born in Osakis, Minnesota.

ENLISTED SERVICE

1939	Jun	2	Enlisted in the U. S. Naval Reserve as S2c.
	Jun	15	Reported for active duty at the Naval Reserve Aviation Base, Minneapolis, Minnesota.
	Jul	14	Released this date from elimination flight training.
	Sep	20	Enlisted service terminated to accept appointment as Aviation Cadet.

OFFICER SERVICE

1939	Sep	21	Accepted appointment and executed oath of office as Aviation Cadet, U. S. Naval Reserve, to rank from 5 September 1939.
	Sep	25	Reported to the U. S. Naval Air Station, Pensacola, Florida for active duty undergoing training.
1940	Jul	1	Accepted appointment and executed oath of office as Ensign, A-V(N), U. S. Naval Reserve, to rank from 15 April 1940.
	Jul	1	Detached from Pensacola, Florida and transferred to the USS NASHVILLE for duty involving flying in Cruiser Scouting Squadron EIGHT. Rep 23 Jul.
1942	Jun	25	Accepted appointment and executed oath of office as Lieutenant (junior grade), A-V(N), U. S. Naval Reserve, to rank from 15 April 1942.
	Sep	25	Detached from the USS NASHVILLE and transferred to Escort Scouting Squadron TWENTY-ONE for active duty involving flying in that squadron. Rep 19 Oct.
	Oct	1	Appointed Lieutenant, A-V(N), U. S. Naval Reserve, for temporary service. Appointed by the President under Alnav 209 dated 1 October 1942.
1943	Jun	12	Ordered detached from Escort Scouting Squadron TWENTY-ONE and transferred to a composite squadron for active duty involving flying in that squadron.

Concordia College - B. A. Degree.

- 1 -

American Defense Service Medal - Bronze A.
Asiatic-Pacific Area Campaign Medal.

Died: 27 December 1943. (Previously reported missing 27 December 1943).

Place: Pacific area. (Enroute from Tontouta, New Caledonia to Espiritu Santo, New Hebrides.

Cause: Plane crash at sea. Not Enemy Action.

Next of kin: Mr. Olaf M. Larson, Father
Hanks, North Dakota.

Presented Air Metal - Dec. 13, 1945 - for action in the Solomon Islands in Sept, Oct., and Dec. 1943.

- 2 -

Awards & Citations

Air Medal

American Defense Service Medal

Asiatic Pacific Campaign Medal

World War II Victory Medal

THE SECRETARY OF THE NAVY
WASHINGTON

The President of the United States takes pride in presenting the AIR MEDAL posthumously to

LIEUTENANT WILLIAM RUDOLPH LARSON, UNITED STATES NAVAL RESERVE

for service as set forth in the following

CITATION:

"For meritorious achievement in aerial flight as Pilot of a Torpedo Bomber in Composite Squadron THIRTY-EIGHT during action against enemy Japanese forces in the Solomon Islands Area, from September 13 to 18, and from October 17 to December 16, 1943. Participating in numerous daring missions over enemy-controlled territory, Lieutenant Larson struck repeatedly at Japanese airfields, supply installations and troop concentrations despite intense anti-aircraft fire and heavy fighter opposition, inflicting severe and costly damage on the enemy. A brilliant and intrepid airman, Lieutenant Larson rendered invaluable assistance in the complete neutralization of the vital Vila, Kara, Kahili, Ballale, Buka and Bonis Airfields and, by his superb tactics and cool courage, contributed immeasurably to the outstanding success of his squadron throughout a critical period of war in the Pacific. His resolute determination and indomitable fighting spirit were in keeping with the highest traditions of the United States Naval Service."

For the President,

James Forrestal

Secretary of the Navy

William's Medals (R to L across: Air Medal, WW II Victory Medal, Asiatic-Pacific Campaign Medal, American Defense Service Medal), Wings, and Air Medal Engraving: "Lt. William Rudolph Larson, USNR, Sept. 13-18, and Oct. 17-Dec. 16, 1943" (below).

IN GRATEFUL MEMORY OF

William Rudolph Larson

WHO DIED IN THE SERVICE OF HIS COUNTRY AT

Sea, Pacific Area, Composite Squadron 38, 27 December 1943

HE STANDS IN THE UNBROKEN LINE OF PATRIOTS WHO HAVE DARED TO DIE

THAT FREEDOM MIGHT LIVE, AND GROW, AND INCREASE ITS BLESSINGS.

FREEDOM LIVES, AND THROUGH IT, HE LIVES–

IN A WAY THAT HUMBLES THE UNDERTAKINGS OF MOST MEN

Franklin D Roosevelt

PRESIDENT OF THE UNITED STATES OF AMERICA

In reply address not the signer of this letter, but Bureau of Naval Personnel, Navy Department, Washington 25, D.C.

Refer to No.

NAVY DEPARTMENT
BUREAU OF NAVAL PERSONNEL
WASHINGTON 25, D.C.

83169
Pers-5321-ieb

27 September 1946

Mr. Lloyd J. Larson
Hanks, North Dakota

Dear Mr. Larson:

Receipt is acknowledged of your recent letter requesting information concerning your brother, the late Lieutenant William R. Larson, United States Naval Reserve.

Immediately after the surrender of Japan, the Chief of Naval Operations directed the Commander-in-Chief of the Pacific Fleet to arrange a search of islands and atolls in the Pacific to locate any missing personnel who may have survived. On 22 April 1946 this Bureau received a report from the Commander-in-Chief of the Pacific Fleet stating that the Pacific Ocean area, which includes the Loyalty Islands, has been searched completely. The search as prosecuted was intensively conducted by ships, planes and landing parties. You may be assured that every clue to the possible whereabouts of surviving personnel in the Pacific Ocean area was thoroughly investigated by the Navy and that everything possible was done to locate any survivors who might have been marooned in the islands. It is regretted that these searches have failed to reveal any information regarding your brother.

The information received in this Bureau states that there were no survivors of the plane which crashed on 27 December 1943 in which your brother was a passenger. Complete casualty lists are not available for distribution by this Bureau. However, in response to your request, the names and addresses of four of the next of kin of men aboard the plane are as follows:

Lieutenant Commander John Risse LITTLE, USNR(Deceased)
Commanding Officer of Bombing Squadron NINETY EIGHT
Next of kin-wife Mrs. Voris M. Little
256 Linden Avenue, Southgate
Newport, Kentucky

Lieutenant Kenneth Robert SPEER, USNR(Deceased)
Next of kin- wife Mrs. Jean D. Speer
Apt. 224, Dracker Apartments
C/o Village Station
Los Angeles, California

-1-

83169
Pers-5321-ieb

27 September 1946

Lieutenant(junior grade) Norman William MACKIE,USNR(Deceased)
Next of kin-wife Mrs. Norma W. Mackie
4840 Lake Park Avenue
Chicago, Illinois

Lieutenant(junior grade) Donald Everett WINTERS,USNR(Deceased)
Next of kin-father Mr. Jacob E. Winters
2904 - 17th Street
Huntington Beach, California

The Navy Department again extends sincere sympathy to you in your great loss.

By direction of Chief of Naval Personnel.

Sincerely yours,

W. A. Semmes
W. A. SEMMES
Lieutenant Commander, USNR
Acting Officer in Charge
Casualty Section

-2-

NOTE: The full casualty report, including 14 additional personnel, is presented on page 190.

Route 1 Box 313
Bellevue, Wash.
6 May 1951

Dear Mr. + Mrs. Larson,

A few days ago, Captain and Mrs. Fradd spent a day with us, which led to my going into some envelopes of Nashville relics. This picture of William turned up and I thought you would like to have it.

Captain Fradd was chief engineer of the Nashville when I had her. He now commands a transport recently back from Korea.

I am now retired and in busi-

NOTE FROM CAPT. CRAVEN IN 1951 TO MARY AND OLAF

*"**Dear Mr. and Mrs. Larson,** A few days ago, Captain and Mrs. Fradd spent a day with us, which led to my going into some envelopes of Nashville relics. This **picture of William** turned up and I thought you would like to have it.*

Captain Fradd was chief engineer of the Nashville when I had her. He now commands a transport recently back from Korea.

I am now retired and in business in Seattle with a friend. It is strange occupation for one who spent forty years as a naval officer, but I find it interesting and the income is a necessary addition to my retirement pay.

You know, from the letter I wrote you in 1944 on learning that William was missing, that I I was deeply fond of your son. That has given me a special feeling of sympathy for you, his parents. I hope you will like the picture, in case you do not already have one. Sincerely, Francis S. Craven, Captain USN (retired)."

May 6 1951 Captain F.S. Craven — Bellevue Washington

Lucky and his fish — Aleutian Islands, Alaska

The declassified War Diary of Bombing Squadron 98 (discovered November 16, 2013), Finding of Facts document, and Secret Dispatch Report, dated January 11, 1944 (both obtained in March 2014 from the National Personnel Records Center), provide details of the full human loss of the plane crash of December 27, 1943, off the Island of Ouvea, Loyalty Group, in the Pacific Ocean:

WAR DIARY—1 DECEMBER 1943 TO 31 DECEMBER 1943 INCLUSIVE
BOMBING SQUADRON NINETY EIGHT
CONFIDENTIAL CONFIDENTIAL

27 December On this date, it was subsequently reported, the following six pilots and twelve gunners of Detachment A, stationed at Espiritu Santo, were reported "missing, facts warrant presumption of death," as a result of the loss of Scat[27] plane off Uvea Island [Ouvea], coming from Tontuta [Tontouta-New Caledonia] to Santo [Espiritu Santo], in the process of transporting squadron personnel back from Sydney, Australia:

Lt—Cdr. John Risse Little
Lieut. Kenneth Robert Speer
Lt (jg). August George Kafer
Lt (jg). Norman William Mackie
Lt (jg). Donald Everett Winters
Lt (jg). Glenn Guy Parker
Lieut. William Rudolf Larson

27 South Pacific Combat Air Transport Command. Plane #12432 was assigned to VMJ-253, a Marine Corps combat transport squadron.

William Harold Beltz, ARM2c
Lewis James Fenton, ARM2c
John Joseph D'Huyvetters, ARM2c
Eugene Franklin Sutton, ARM2c
John Frederick Werner, ARM2c
William LeRoy Daugherty, ARM2c
Dirk Berend Boonstra, ARM1c
Earl Brice Fuller, AMR1c
Francis John Storm, ARM1c
William Edward Luby, ARM2c
Mauritx Henry Nelson, ARM2c
Edwin Lawrence Spangler, ARM2c

R4D Skytrain Plane (Source: ww2db.com)

R4D Skytrain Plane (Source: ww2db.com)

Seventy years after my grandparents received the Western Union telegram notification of Lucky's plane crash and status of missing, my family finally discovered the details of the accident.

The R4D-5 airplane (Bureau #12432) flight of December 27, 1943, from Tontouta, New Caledonia to Espiritu Santo, New Hebrides (now Vanuatu), departed 1338 local time and last radio contact was at 1350. Finding of Facts opinion was "that airplane number 12432 crashed into the sea and sank at approximately latitude 20 degrees 30 minutes South and longitude 166 degrees 15 minutes East. Location established 1424 off south tip of Uvea Island, Loyalty Group. The wreckage was discovered about noon on December 28, 1943, in the vicinity of the last reported position of plane number 12432." The secret dispatch reported, "wreckage consisting of pilots log book signed by E.L. Spangler, thermos jug marked VMJ, red rubber aileron baton, burned wood, and wood painted silver with word "oxygen" painted in black letters. Natives say they heard engines about 1500, on going to beach they saw a plane in spin. They [natives] did not go to wreckage as they estimated the distance about 10 miles. No survivors." The Finding of

Facts opinion was "that a fire existed in the crew's compartment and the cargo-passenger space of the airplane some time during the last few minutes before it crashed." Appendix B includes the Finding of Facts and Secret Dispatch Report documents of the crash investigation.

Plane accidents were sadly not uncommon during WWII. According to the US Army Air Forces (AAF) Statistical Digest[28], in less than four years (December 1941-to-August 1945), the AAF lost 14,903 pilots, aircrew, and assorted personnel plus 13,873 airplanes—all inside the continental United States. These were the result of 52,651 aircraft accidents (6,039 involving fatalities). An eye-watering 43,581 aircraft were lost overseas, including 22,948 on combat missions and 20,633 attributed to non-combat causes overseas. Non-combat losses were over 47% of all accidents overseas. Lucky's plane crash was one of those 20,633 dire accidents during WWII.

The R4D transport plane crash of December 27, 1943, included the loss of Lucky and 18 other naval personnel from VB-98, along with the USMCR flight crew of 5 soldiers from VMJ-153. God bless them all and their peaceful slumber at sea.

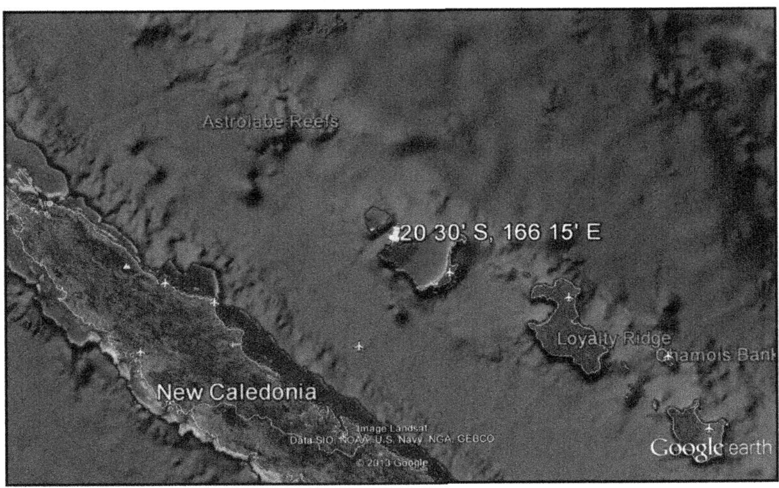

Approximate location of plane crash—west of Ouvea Island

28 www.wwiifoundation.org

List of USNR & USMCR Casualties
R4D-5 Airplane (Bureau #12432)
Flight of December 27 1943

First Name	Middle	Last	Rank	Service No.	Birth Date	Age	Squadron No.	Home State	Home City	Next of Kin	Additional Info
John	Risse	Little	Lt - Cdr.	77735	5/17/1915	28	VB 98*	Kentucky	Southgate	Son of Clarence and Mable Little, Husband of Mrs. Voris Margaret Little, 256 Linden Ave, Southgate, KY	VFW Post 3186 of Southgate, KY is named in his honor. Awarded Distinguished Flying Cross, posthumously
William	Rudolf	Larson	Lt.	83169	12/1/1915	28	VC 38	North Dakota	Hanks	Mr. and Mrs. Olaf M. Larson, Hanks ND	VFW Post 6139 of Zahl, ND is named in his honor. Awarded Air Medal, posthumously
Kenneth	Robert	Speer	Lt.	98716	1/2/1920	22	VB 98	California	Tulare County	Wife: Mrs. Jean Douthit Speer, 338 Laurel Drive, Corpus Christi, TX	Awarded Air Medal, posthumously
August	George	Kafer	Lt. (jg)	114600	12/25/1917	26	VB 98	West Virginia	Jane Lew	Mr. and Mrs. John Kafer, PO Box 399, Jane Lew, WV	 Awarded Air Medal, posthumously
Norman	William	Mackie	Lt. (jg)	125503	3/12/1920	23	VB 98	Illinois	Chicago	Wife: Mrs. Judith King Mackie, 4840 Lake Park Ave., Chicago, IL	
Donald	Everett	Winters	Lt. (jg)	130333	11/17/1918	25	VB 98	California	Huntington Beach	Stepmother: Sara Ann Winters, 2904 17th Street, Huntington Beach CA	Awarded Air Medal, posthumously
Glenn	Guy	Parker	Lt. (jg)	125393	5/4/1920	22	VB 98	District of Columbia		Mr. and Mrs. Glenn Lane Parker, 2706 N.W. 44th St., Washington D.C.	 Awarded Air Medal, posthumously
Dirk	Berend	Boonstra	ARM1c	2244120	1/2/1924	19	VB 98	New York	Montrose	Brother: Piet Boonstra, 151 Seward St, Buchanan, NY 10511	
Earl	Brice	Fuller	ARM1c	3000460	2/3/1918	24	VB 98	Wisconsin	Oshkosh	Mr. and Mrs. Earl E Fuller of Oshkosh, WI	Cook-Fuller Post of the American Legion named in his honor
Francis	John	Storm	ARM1c	6464246	4/3/1916	27	VB 98	New Jersey	Jersey City	Brother: Walter J. Storm, 280 Columbia Ave., Jersey City, NJ	
William	Edward	Luby	ARM2c	6420289	7/14/1918	25	VB 98	Connecticut	Wallingford	Father: Mr. William Barnard Luby, PO Box 387, Wallingford, CT Sister: Anna May Luby, 20 Christian St., Wallington, CT	
Mauritz	Henry	Nelson	ARM2c	6200889			VB 98	Iowa	Forest City	Mr. and Mrs. Henry H. Nelson, Rt4, Forest City, IA	
Edwin, Jr.	Lawrence	Spangler	ARM2c	6502443			VB 98	Pennsylvania	York	Mr. and Mrs. Edwin Lawrence Spangler, Sr., 35N Highland Ave, York, PA	
William	Harold	Beltz	ARM2c	6506436			VB 98	Pennsylvania	Philadelphia	Son: Frank Alexander	
Lewis	James	Fenton	ARM2c	6688048			VB 98	Missouri	Bonne Terre	Mr. and Mrs. John W. Fenton, 215 Hillstreet, Bonne Terre, MO	
John	Joseph	D'Huyvetters	ARM2c	6502691			VB 98	Pennsylvania	Easton	Mr. Julius D'Huyvetters, 148 Lincoln St., Easton, PA	
Eugene	Frankline	Sutton	ARM2c	3860564		17	VB 98	California	San Bernardino	Mother: Mrs. Mattie Lee Sutton, 1343 D Street, San Bernardino, CA Brother: Lt. S.L. Sutton - Navy torpedo instructor at Miami, FL Sister: Mrs. Juanita Stepp of San Bernardino, CA	
John	Frederick	Werner	ARM2c	6507082			VB 98	New Jersey	Penns Grove	Wife: Mrs. Christine Elizabeth Werner, 202 Avenue B, Carney's Point, Penns Grove	
William	Leroy	Daugherty	ARM2c	6529394		19	VB 98	Pennsylvania	Butler	Mother: Mrs. Olive Daugherty, Meridian PA	
Reynolds	Hill	Knotts	Captain USMCR	10611	4/24/1916	27	VMJ 153**	Delaware	Wilmington	Mother: Mrs. Mildred Pratt Knotts, 305 W 7th Street, Wilmington, Delaware	 Pilot - Awarded Air Medal, posthumously
Louis	White	McCay	MT SGT USMCR	259806	3/3/1918	25	VMJ 153	Florida	Miami	Mother: Mrs. Mable L McCay, 2249 SW 13th Street, Miami FL	 Co-Pilot
John	Thomas Jr.	Felts	2nd Lt USMCR	26187	10/22/1923	20	VMJ 153	Texas	Clarkville	Father: Mr. John T. Felts Sr., Box 625, Clarksville, TX	 Navigator
James	Guernsey	Duignan	SGT USMCR	450996	3/3/1922	21	VMJ 153	New York	Brewster	Father: Mr. Henry E Duignan, Old Turk Hill Rd, Brewster, NY	Radioman
Opal	C.	Hughes	MT SGT USMCR	364813	10/12/1921	22	VMJ 153	Mississippi	Magee	Mr. & Mrs. John W Hughes, Route #1, Magee, MS Sister: Johnye Hughes Johnson	Crew Chief - Mechanic

* Bombing Squadron 98 (VB 98) was part of VC 24. Unit consisted of 18 SBD-5 planes stationed at Munda Airfield in Dec 1943
The Joe Baugher list of US Navy planes lists a total of 24 missing personnel on BuNos 12432 (c/n 9529) plane crash.
ARM = Aviation Radioman, First or Second Class
** Flight crew of Marine Utility Squadron 153 (VMJ 153), Marine Air Group 25, First Marine Aircraft Wing

VETERANS OF FOREIGN WARS
POST 6138
William R. Larson
DECEMBER 1, 1915 - DECEMBER 27, 1943
NAVY AIR CORPS - 1939
AIR GROUP - PC 38
SERVED IN ALASKA AND SOUTH PACIFIC
MISSING IN ACTION - DECEMBER 27, 1943

Epilogue

My uncle Lucky was never found. After four-and-a-half years in the US Navy Reserve, including astonishing adventures and countless recoveries in the impenetrable fog of the Aleutian Islands and the Bering Sea, island hopping in the Solomon Islands off carrier decks and jungle airfields, and dive bombing Japanese troops, ships, and airfields on 22 TBF combat missions, Lucky's flight log record suddenly stopped. 1,860 total flights hours were recorded. A brilliant, courageous, and skillful aviator, beloved son and brother was gone. As his fellow squadron member, Lt. Graham "Ham" Tahler put it so eloquently, "the Navy, Squadron VC-38 in particular, lost one of its best members, and the world in general lost one of its favorite people." After reading William's letters home and gaining an understanding and true respect for the uncle I never met, I couldn't agree more with Ham. Lucky was just 28 years old and his amazing future was lost with him.

If Lucky had taken the early flight from Tontouta, New Caledonia, with his fellow VC-38 squadron pilots on December 27th, 1943, or if Lucky had been in the pilot seat of that DC-3 transport plane (R4D-5 airplane, Bureau #12432), instead of a passenger, the world would be a different place for sure. After researching the splendid record of VC-38 and discovering the full World War II record of Lucky's adventures, I can't help but believe that he would have been wingtip — to — wingtip with Commander Brunton and his fellow TBF Avenger pilots just 52 days later on VC-38's heroic "skip bombing" mission against Japanese enemy ships in Rabaul Harbor, New Britain, on February 17, 1944[29]. That day accounted for at least ten awards of the Distinguished Flying Cross to fellow members of the VC-38 TBF squadron. That is truly an amazing achievement and one that is not well known in the history of World War II.

As far as we know, his fiancée Bette Burton never traveled out to Hanks, North Dakota, to visit her new family. I sincerely hope she got over the loss of William, married, and lived a long, happy, and prosperous life after 1944. We will never know...but I can't help thinking she is still out there with hope in her heart and love for Lucky.

Based on several letter references, we have the same sentiment regarding William's radioman, Richard Wagner. We hope Richard visited Olaf and Mary in Sioux Trails Township on his leave to his home in nearby South Dakota — but we have no family memories or records of this event — those who would have known are gone now.

The family finally held a Memorial Service on May 30th, 1962, for William Rudolf Larson. The William R. Larson Post 6139 of Zahl, North Dakota (named in honor of Lucky), placed a wreath on the marker. The Commander was Dallas Smith. The memorial was held at Bethany Lutheran Church. The American Legion of Grenora, North Dakota, had their firing squad fire over the marker and played taps. The Zahl Post also presented my grandparents a large U.S. flag.

Olaf and Mary continued to live on the family farm until the early 1960s (50 years), when they rented a winter apartment in Williston, N.D. Olaf suffered a debilitating stroke in the early 1950s and passed away in 1964, just 2 years after Lucky's namesake and my oldest brother, William Lloyd Larson, was born.

---

29 A full account of that day is presented in Appendix F, along with VC 38's Scorecard of their South Pacific tour from August 1943 to April 1944.

In 1948 the house was enlarged and modernized with electricity and running water. Lucky's navy locker, with his letters home, was stored in the 2nd story bedroom on the left.

Mary continued to live in Williston after Olaf's passing, and began traveling the world over, including Africa, Egypt, Israel, Scandinavia, and Hawaii. During her trip with my middle brother David to Hawaii, she visited the National Memorial Cemetery of the Pacific in Honolulu and wept at the foot of the marble stone with the etched name of her eldest, beloved son — Lt. William Rudolf Larson, USNR, North Dakota. Mary lived to be 90 years old and was a strong, positive force in the lives of her three young grandsons.

Mother Mary Larson — 1978 (87 years old)

"Olaf Larson was born on a farm near Osakis, Minnesota July 20, 1885. His parents were Olena and Martin Larson who came from Trondheim, Norway. He was baptized and confirmed in Sauk Valley Lutheran Church there, and grew up there. In 1909 he homesteaded here in Sioux Trail Township, and lived here the rest of his life. He died May 24, 1964. He was a jolly fellow and always looking on the bright side of life. If he knew of something unfavorable about anybody,

he did not tell anyone, not even his wife. He was the first in the community to try new things. He had the first tractor, truck, combine, and sewer system. He and several others had big new barns built in 1918. In 1948 he remodeled his home and that year we also got dial telephones. We had the box on the wall type since 1919.

Olaf was a deep thinker. He could always solve knotty problems his boys brought home from school.

In 1914 on July 1, he married Miss Mary Johnson of Osakis, Minn. and she came out here then, and still lives here. They had two sons. William Rudolf who was killed in World War II on Dec. 27, 1943 and Lloyd Jerome who is a member of the Senior High School faculty in Williston, N.D. He is married and has 3 young sons. Olaf is buried at Bethany Lutheran Church where he was a member.

The first tractor was a Waterloo Boy. The first combine was a Nichols and Shepard. I believe he was also the first to have a side-discharge rake."

September 18 1970 — Mary Larson's Account

Feb 2 1949 — The day my Grandparents traded in William's Pontiac — after 42 days they bought it back.

Aerial View of Family Farm in Sioux Trail Township, Divide County. N.D. — 1958

Lucky's kid brother, Lloyd (my father), graduated from Concordia College, and finished US Naval Reserve Navy midshipmen's training (Ensign rank) at Notre Dame, Indiana, on May 31, 1944. He was ordered to Fort Pierce, Florida, and then stationed at a recruiting facility in Helena, Montana. Upon the request of Olaf and Mary, he was discharged on June 16, 1944, and returned to the family farm in Sioux Trail Township. He taught school at local towns, including Genora, Zahl, Epping, and Williston Junior High and Senior High. He married my mother, Mary Ann Valentine, in July 1961 and raised three fine boys; William Lloyd Larson, David Jeffrey Larson, and Donald James Larson. He was a successful business owner of the Kleen

Kar carwash in Williston, North Dakota, and taught history at the local high school and Williston State College. He continued to farm and ranch the family land until 1980. My father passed away in 1995, not knowing the full, detailed account of the World War II story of his older brother, William.

In 2011, my mother, Mary Ann V. Larson, gifted my two brothers and me with the letter history of William which she had painstakingly assembled during her time in an assisted living home in Williston, North Dakota, while recovering from a long hospital stay. Upon reading the treasured family letters that were safely kept for over 70 years in a naval trunk within the family–an idea and memorial was born. This is that Memorial to Lucky. Upon chance contact with Walt Wagner, the son of Lucky's radioman, Richard Wagner, and other VC 38 family members, the full history of Lucky's war experience was discovered. God bless all those who served in World War II and those who lost their loved ones. I obviously never met my uncle Lucky, but I sure wish I had. He'd have quite a tale to tell.

Donald James Larson
Author
December 27 2013
Portland, Oregon

William Rudolph Larson, son of Mr and Mrs Olaf Larson was born Dec I, I915 at Osakis, Minnesota. He was brot to his home here in the spring which was his home the rest of his life. He attended school at Sioux Trail and graduated from High School at Grenora recieving a scholarship.to Concordia College, Moorhead Minnesota. He was confirmed at Bethany Church by Rev M.O. Dybvik Nov I8, I928. He was a member of the first class to be confirmed in the new church. He attended Concordia College four years and graduated in I937. He then taught school for two years at Arnegard, N.Dak.

In the spring of I939 he enlisted in the Naval Reserve Air Force. He trained at Pensacola , Florida and was graduated there July I, I940.as an ensign. He was on the Cruiser Nashville for two years. Here he was catapulted in his plane from the ship on his missions. He had some narrow escapes while there such as the time he landed safely on the ocean thru thick fog after nightfall a decent of 3500 ft. This was in the Aleutians Islands. Another time he was nearly out of gas and sat for two nights alone in a strange bay during a storm , while his radio man was on the beach unable to get back. But they came thru safely and he was nick named Lucky. Also while there he flew one of the planes that accompanied Doolittle to Japan.

In I942 he asked to be transferred to a carrier and got his wish. While making the change he came home for two weeks. This was in October which was the last time he was home. He then went to San Diego where he trained for night flying and bombing and from there was sent to the South Pacific. There he flew Torpedo, Bomber and Fighter planes and saw much action. He was a liutenant in the 38 Squadron. His last letter home was written Dec I6, I943. He said they were getting I0 days of much needed rest and were going to Australia. It was on the way back to his base that the plane dissappeared . He was stationed in the New Hebrides Islands at the time. His flight log showed he had flown I860.2 hours. An Air Medal was given him for his action against the Japanese. Other medals were also sent after his death which was Dec 27, I943.

Lt. William R. Larson , son of Mr and Mrs Olaf Larson was born Dec I, I915 and gave his life for his country in the South Pacific area on Dec.27, I943 He graduated from college in I937, taught H.S. two years, then enlisted in the U.S.Navy Air Force in June I939. He took his training at Pensacola Florida,and graduated July I, I940. He spent two weeks leave at home then reported at San Pedro, Calif. He spent two years on the cruiser, Nashville then was transferred to carriers and flew TBF planes. He received the Air medal for his brace participation against the enemy, and several other medals were sent his parents after his death. In his transfer from cruiser to carrier he had his last leave and was home in October I942. He then had training in night flying at San Diego Calif a short time before leaving for the South Pacific where he lost his life.

written by Mary Larson

William Rudolf Larson, son of Mr. and Mrs. Olaf Larson was born December 1, 1915 at Osakis, Minnesota. He was brot to his home here in the spring which was his home the rest of his life. He attended school at Sioux Trail and graduated from High School at Grenora receiving a scholarship to Concordia College, Moorhead Minnesota. He was confirmed at Bethany Church by Rev M.O. Dybvick Nov 18, 1928. He was a member of the first class to be confirmed in the new church. He then taught school for two years at Arnegard, N.Dak.

In the spring of 1939 he enlisted in the Naval Reserve Air Force. He trained at Pensacola, Florida and was graduated there July 1, 1940 as an ensign. He was on the Cruiser Nashville for two years. Here he was catapulted in his plane from the ship on his missions. He had some narrow escapes while there such as the time he landed safely on the ocean thru thick fog after nightfall, a descent of 3500 ft. This was in the Aleutians Islands. Another time he was nearly out of gas and sat for two nights alone in a strange bay during a storm, while his radio man was on the beach unable to get back. But they came thru safely and he was nick named Lucky. Also while there he flew one of the planes that accompanied Doolittle to Japan.

In 1942 he asked to be transferred to a carrier and got his wish. While making the change he came home for two weeks.

This was in October which was the last time he was home. He then went to San Diego where he trained for night flying and bombing and from there was sent to the South Pacific. There he flew Torpedo Bomber and Fighter planes and saw much action. He was a lieutenant in the 38 Squadron. His last letter home was written Dec 16, 1943. He said they were getting 10 days of much needed rest and were going to Australia. It was on the way back to his base that the plane disappeared. He was stationed in the New Hebrides Islands at the time. His flight log showed he had flown 1860.2 hours. An Air Medal was given him for his action against the Japanese. Other medals were also sent after his death which was Dec 27, 1943.

Written by mother Mary Larson

Lt. William R. Larson, son of Mr. and Mrs. Olaf Larson was born Dec 1, 1915 and gave his life for his country in the South Pacific area on Dec. 27, 1943. He graduated from college in 1937, taught H.S. two years, then enlisted in the U.S. Navy Air Force in June 1939. He took his training at Pensacola Florida, and graduated July 1, 1940. He spent two weeks leave at home then reported at San Pedro, Calif. He spent two years on the cruiser Nashville then was transferred to carriers and flew TBF planes. He received the Air medal for his brave participation against the enemy, and several other medals were sent to his parents after his death. In his transfer from cruiser to carrier he had his last leave and was home in October 1942. He then had training in night flying at San Diego Calif a short time before leaving for the South Pacific where he lost his life.

Written by mother Mary Larson

William and Olaf- 1917

William's Initials Carved into Horse Stall within the Family Barn

Larson Family Barn — August 2010 (built 1918)

Some of the contents of Lucky's naval trunk: Aviator Flight Log, winter flight gloves, flight helmet, Mark II aviation goggles, Ray Ban shooting glasses, match books, leather toilet kit.

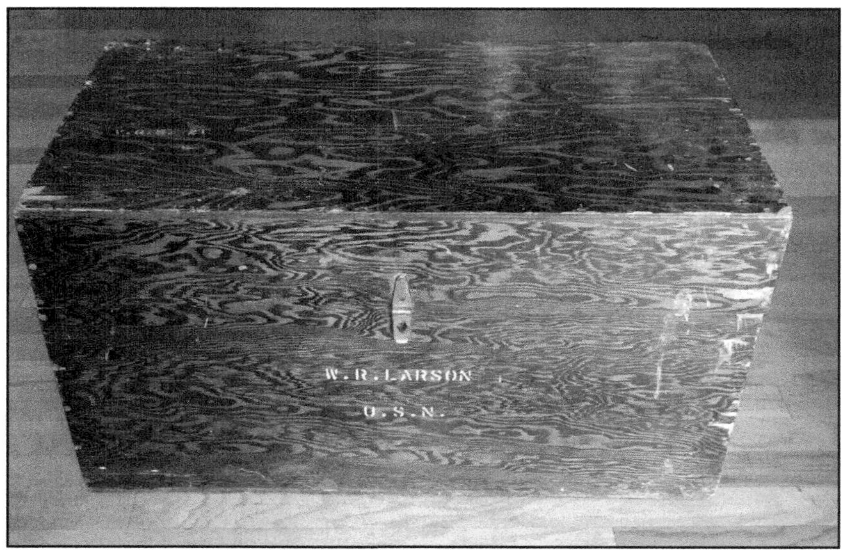

Lucky's pinewood naval trunk

Lt. William R. Larson — "Lucky" — December 1 1915 to December 27 1943

Contributors:

- Mary Ann V. Larson of Vancouver, Washington
- Walt Wagner of Carlsbad, California
- Leary Family Collection — John, Chris, and Daniel Leary of Hudson Falls, New York
- Rick Bryant of Portland, Oregon
- Lt. Col. Daniel Phillippi of Sacramento, California
- Gregory Pons of France — author of *USMC Aviators 1941 — 1945*
- Mark J Sheppard of Oxfordshire, England — WWII aircraft researcher
- Steven Bustin of San Francisco Bay area, California — author of *Humble Heroes — How the USS Nashville CL43 Fought WWII*
- Tamara Ashley of Atlanta, Georgia
- Carolyn Truesdale of Medford Lakes, New Jersey and Robert Truesdale of Durham, North Carolina
- Retired Judge Jack P. Scholfield of Mercer Island, Washington
- James Scholfield of Los Gatos, California
- Donna Mattson (Greslie) of Las Vegas, Nevada
- Raymond Barcala of Georgetown, California
- Pauline Winter (niece of Santiago Barcala) of Auburn, California
- Rick Bryant of Portland, Oregon
- Lonnie Schorer of Burke, Virginia
- Ray Blanchard of San Diego, California
- James Boyle of Pittsburgh, Pennsylvania

All photos and documents are from the Larson Family collection, except for when specific credits are cited.

Appendix A

Study Myself

STUDYING MYSELF

BY

WILLIAM RUDOLPH LARSON

To My
Loving Parents

CONTENTS

ILLUSTRATIONS

VII

PREFACE

I have written this, the story of my life, in order that I might become better acquainted with myself and my ancestors. In the light of my heritage, environment, and training, I can more readily understand my present traits. The story is divided into three main divisions: (1) my heredity; (2) my education; and (3) my present and future self. My family tree will be found in the rear of this book! With reference to the key, the family tree will be easily understood. The few pictures in the book will give the reader a better understanding of the author's physical development. A picture of my home and family is also contained in this book.

I wish to thank my parents, Mr. and Mrs. Olaf M. Larson, Hanks, North Dakota, for so kindly giving me the necessary information on my heritage.

November, 1934.

William Larson

STUDYING MYSELF

MY HERITAGE

Just a few months ago I stood within an old delapidated farm house near Osakis, Minnesota. I felt a sort of reverence and respect for that house, because it was here that I was born, on December 1, 1915. Shortly after my arrival, my mother took me out to the rugged prairies of northwestern North Dakota where my father had taken a homestead. I grew up on those prairies and learned to love them.

An efficient study of my life necessitates a somewhat summary study of my ancestors. I shall therefore attempt to portray their traits and environment to the reader in this chapter.

My great-grand parents on my father's side were all hardy, hard working Norsemen. They were carpenters and farmers. They had no diseases or abnormalties. They were pious people and lived to be very old. All of them were mentally alert. Family ties were strong. All of them died in Norway.

My grand-father on my father's side came to America and homesteaded near Osakis, Minnesota. He was a successful farmer and carpenter. He was

2

very healthy, and a hard worker throughout his life. He was very religious and read the Bible constantly. My grandfather, Martin Larson, died at the age of eighty-seven. He had one brother, Michael Larson, and one sister, Mrs. Anna Broughton. Michael Larson was also a carpenter and farmer and died in Norway. Mrs. Anna Broughton was a farmer's wife and died at an old age at Osakis, Minnesota.

Christian Holmlie, my great-grandfather on my father's mother's side, was also a farmer. He and his wife died at an old age in Norway. They had five children: (1) Martha Olson, their oldest child, became a farmer's wife and died in Canada; (2) Ellen, a farmer's wife. She died in Norway; (3) Olena Larson, my grandmother, who is now eighty-seven years old and lives at Osakis, Minnesota. Before her eyes became weak from old age, she read often, especially the Bible. She always had a keen, clear mind and has a wonderful memory. She had never been sickly; (4) Christina Hanson died at Osakis, Minnesota at an old age. Was a farmer's wife; (5) [illegible] Johnson lives in Norway and is the wife of a carpenter.

Jorgen Jorgenson, my great-grandfather on my mother's father's side, was a tailor and small farmer. He and his wife died at the age of eighty in

3

Denmark. His wife, Maren, wrote beautiful letters and poems. They were pious, joyful, and contented people. They had seven children: (1) Fred Johnson, as Jorgenson was changed to Johnson after coming to America, was the oldest child. He was a strong, healthy farmer. He died, a wealthy retired farmer, in Los Angeles at the age of eighty-two. (2) Peter Johnson was a tailor at Paris, Missouri. He had two children who are now instructors in high-school. He died at about eighty years of age. (3) Robert Johnson, my grandfather, was once a cook on a steamboat. He liked to eat and was fat ever since I can remember him. He took a homestead at La Moure, North Dakota and died a farmer. He did not believe in an education. If his children knew how to cook and work, he thought that was all that was necessary. He was in comfortable circumstances as long as he lived. He died at the age of seventy-two at Hirsch, Saskatchewan, Canada. (4) Nels Johnson died a prosperous farmer at the age of seventy at Osakis, Minnesota. (5) Christine Frederickson is a store keeper's wife in Copenhagen, Denmark. (6) Christian Johnson is a sergeant in the army at Copenhagen; (7) Mary Lowe is a retired farmer's wife and lives in comfortable circumstances at Oakes, North Dakota.

Maria Villads, my great-grandmother on my

4

mother's mother's side, was a poetess. She had dark eyes and black hair. After her husband died, she made her living by selling her books of poems. Some of her poems were written especially for the King of Denmark. She was very healthy, full of fun, and enjoyed living. When about sixty-five years old she came to America. She died at the age of seventy-five at La Moure, North Dakota. Her husband, Mr Villads, was a tailor and small farmer. They had four children: (1) Lars Villadson, a farmer, lives at Hardy, Saskatchewan, Canada. He also writes poems. (2) Hans Villadson is about sixty-eight years old and lives near La Moure, North Dakota. He too is a farmer. (3) Ellen Christine Johnson, my grandmother, is sixty-six years old and lives at Hirsch, Saskatchewan, Canada. She also writes poetry. She has firm moral convictions and is very pious. She enjoys reading very much. She believes in a good education and did her best to give her children an education. She has light hair and blue eyes. (4) Villads Villadson, a farmer, lives near La Moure, North Dakota. He is a happy-go-lucky sort of person and looks and acts like Andy Clyde of the movies. He is about fifty-eight years old.

My father was the fifth child of a

family of seven children. The children in order are: Carl Larson, Osakis, Minnesota; Mrs. Anna Johnson, Osakis, Minnesota; Mrs. Julia Johnson, Sherwood, North Dakota; Marius Larson, Hanks, North Dakota; Olaf M. Larson, Hanks, North Dakota; Mrs. Lena Brakken, Zahl, North Dakota; and Mrs. Mary Larson, deceased. My father has always been a healthy, strong man. He has black hair, brown eyes, high cheek bones, and is quite large. He likes to read papers and keeps well posted on the affairs of the day. He is a firm believer in a good education and I admire him for trying to give his children an education in spite of present difficulties. He has a keen, alert mind and is very good in mathematics. He does not smoke, drink, or chew, so has been a good example for his two sons, Lloyd, my younger brother, and myself. Although he does not attend church regularly, I am certain that he has firm religious convictions at heart. My father homesteaded in Northwestern North Dakota about 1914. He erected good buildings within a few years, secured good farm equipment, and has lived there ever since. He is now forty-eight years old.

My mother, Mary Larson, was the second child of a family of four. The children in order are: William Johnson, Fargo, North Dakota; Mrs. Mary

Larson, Hanks, North Dakota; Ole Johnson, Hirsch, Saskatchewan, Canada; and Mrs. Esther Kinstad, Hirsch, Saskatchewan, Canada. My mother is now forty-two years old, has brown hair and blue eyes, is quite stout, and is strong and healthy. As she taught school for five years before marrying my father, she has a good general education. She likes music, is a good singer, and can play the piano. She tries to attend church regularly and wants her children to do so too. It was my mother who had the greatest effect upon my religious life. When I was just old enough to understand the meaning of life somewhat, she taught me simple evening prayers and told me about God. As a direct result of this early instruction in prayer I have talked to my God in prayer each night throughout my life. My mother enjoys taking part in the social life of our community. She is an active and interested member of several clubs and associations in the community. She, too, believes in a good education and is making great sacrifices in order that her children might have the chance to obtain one.

Mostly all of my ancestors on my father's side were dark people. They were tall, thin, hardy, hard working, and long-lived. They were all religiously

8

inclined. All were mentally and physically sound. Many of my ancestors on my mothers side were light people. All were sound of body and of mind. Poetry seems to be a mental characteristic trait of the family. Most of my ancestors were farmers and carpenters. Several on my mothers side were teachers. All were pious people. None were sickly and there were no abnormalties.

Based on the foregoing discussion I should reasonably expect to be long lifed, hardy, strong of body, sound of mind, healthy and a Christian. The larger percentage of my ancestors have been successful farmers. I, therefore, could also expect to make a living by farming. Although I have an interest in farming I do not, at present, expect to enter this occupation.

10

MY EDUCATION

When I speak of my education, I refer to all my training and experiences mentally, morally, and physically, which have gone to mold my general character up to the present.

The aspects of my environment which influenced me the most were the kind and loving guidance of my parents, the school and the parochial school, and living in the country. My parents have always been lenient with me and have let me make decisions and think things out for myself. This gave me a self-reliant quality and a feeling of trustworthiness. It was from my parents that I first learned about God, the difference between right and wrong, and many important facts of life. Going to school taught me how to associate with others. Living in the country taught me to love animals and nature. The one negative effect on my development which may have been produced by living in the country is bashfulness. I have always been quite bashful and still am. However I am gradually overcoming this quality.

As a child, I enjoyed very much to

11

play with mechanical toys. As a youth I enjoyed working with tractors, trucks, cars, and machinery. I started working in the fields with machinery at a very early age. This was not because I had to, but because I wanted to, and felt as though I were grown up. I was only thirteen years old when I first hired out to run a Wallace tractor in the harvest fields. How grown up I felt as I was now actually running a tractor! And, incidentally, it was through this experience that I earned my first money, and learned the value of it. Because of this knowledge I have always used considerable judgment in spending money.

The entertainment I most enjoyed was playing games with the young people of my own age. In our immediate community, the young people never danced at their social gatherings, but played games instead. I also enjoyed seeing good movies and plays, and hearing talented speakers. The sports I have always enjoyed are skiing, sliding, roller-skating, ice-skating, boxing, baseball and basketball. I started boxing when I was in the fifth grade and am indebted to a neighbor boy, Boyd Brakken, for learning the manly art of self-

13

defense. He owned a set of boxing gloves and gave me a bloody nose so many times that I first had to learn to box in order to get even with him. I am extremely thankful for this early training in self defense, for it came in handy many times throughout grade school and will [illegible] in the future.

Having seen something of my general environment, I shall now discuss briefly my physical development. Until the age of sixteen, I developed a little slower than the average, physically. I have had no minor defects and no special illnesses. However, I have had several contagious diseases which every child usually contacts such as whooping cough, scarlet fever, measles, and common colds. In no case was any permanent damage done to my body. At the age of sixteen I began to develop very rapidly and began to be a man. My weight jumped from one hundred and ten pounds to one hundred and forty pounds in two years. My height increased by about nine inches in the same time. I was always strong, wiry muscled, and healthy. I became quite skillful in working with machinery and [illegible] at an early age. I had plenty of wholesome foods and fresh air.

14

I shall now turn to my mental development. I lived three miles from a consolidated country school, Sioux Trail Consolidated. I attended this same school from the time I was in the first grade until I was in the fourth year of high school. I graduated from the Grenora High School, Grenora, North Dakota and am now in my sophomore year at Concordia College, Moorhead, Minnesota. During the summers, I attended Norwegian, or parochial school. After a few summers' attendance at this school I was confirmed by Rev. Dydvik in 1928.

As compared with other children of my age I was a little above the average in mental ability. I had an average of ninety-three and a fraction in my four years of high school. I received a Concordia scholarship for maintaining this average. Last year I made seventy-five dollars by maintaining a B average during the first semester of college work. I have maintained good department and have been quite diligent in my studies. As my marks during the grades show, I could, however, have been more diligent in the grade school.

As the grade teachers provided no special play for the children during recess and noon, the children frequently rid themselves of surplus energy

16

by fighting. There was one boy whom I especially enjoyed fighting with — not because I could handle him but because he enjoyed fighting with me too. He was sort of a sneaky fellow always trying to get me on the sly. Later on, when grades were [illegible] among [illegible] and [illegible], we quit fighting, but we still are not so [illegible] of each other.

During my early years of school life I singled out two or three companions to chum with and they have been my friends ever since. Later on in my school life I chose a larger number of friends. I was not an outstanding scholar in school but hated to make a mistake while reciting.

In the grades, I didn't like civics or geography but liked spelling and reading. I also disliked grammar in the grades but learned to like it in high school. I had no special dislike for any subjects in high school. This is probably due to the way Mr. and Mrs. Warner Peterson, whom I consider as the best teachers I have ever had, taught them. Mr. and Mrs. Warner Peterson were my high school teachers up to the senior year. It was through them that I learned how to really study. It was they who organized the first basket-ball team at Sioux Trail, started a school paper, organized the S.Y.C., organized

17

the young citizens' league, put on plays), and woke Sioux Trail up generally.

Partly through the influence of my father and partly through the acquaintance of a dentist at Venora, North Dakota, I decided, while studying vocations in high school, that I would like to become a dentist. With this vocation in mind I entered Concordia College in the fall of 1933 as a pre-dental student. In my freshman year I studied religion, physics, mathematics, English, latin III, and graphics. This year I am studying chemistry, psychology, biology, church history, and german.

As I have stated before, my mother made the greatest impression on me in a religious way. However, the larger part of my knowledge of the Bible and the catechism was obtained by attending parochial school which was held each summer in our church six miles west of my home. I thought about God as being a divine, godly person who lived in that much-to-be-desired, far-removed, beautiful place called heaven. I thought of prayer as a necessary part of my daily life. I thought of sin as something which displeased God and was to be avoided. I remember that I used to swear quite a bit when I was small. I had learned it from various hired men. When I was just beginning to ice skate

I used to swear every time I fell down. My aunt, "Mrs. Anna Johnson," told me that God made me fall as a punishment for swearing. I immediately made every effort possible to prevent swearing or cussing. By the time I had learned to skate without falling I had also broken the habit of cussing. Ever since this experience I have sworn very little.

I believe I am an honest person. My first experience in honesty came about in the following way: When I was very young, I broke a steel tape-measure which my father had said I should not play with. As soon as I had broken it I became afraid, and hid it. Later, my father, knowing I had broken the tape-measure, asked me if I had broken it, I told him I hadn't. Then he told me it would be better for me to tell the truth than to tell a lie and try to escape punishment. By this time my conscience was bothering me very much. I burst into tears and told him the truth. He did not punish me but said it was always the best policy to tell the truth. This little lesson in honesty stuck with me ever since.

Physically I was a tough, hardy little fellow. I was also stubborn in some ways. I never wanted to put on new clothes, and my few old clothes,

19

even in the heart of winter. On a very cold day in the middle of a hard winter I walked out of the house without cap or coat, took my tobaggan, and struggled through deep snow on my way over to see a neighbor boy who lived one-half mile east of our place. When I finally arrived at his place, my ears were entirely frozen. A blister the size of a hen's egg soon appeared on each ear. If that neighbor boy's mother, Mrs. Holman, had not known just what to do for me I would have had some sorry looking ears today. Although I was in extreme pain, I made the most of it – I wanted to be tough! I have had to be tough, too, to go through some of my experiences such as having my lip and hand cut up by running into a barbed wire fence on a tobaggan, being run over by a drill, and falling eighty feet to the plank floor of a grain elevator.

When I was just old enough to walk, I used to sneak away from the house and walk way over to my cousin's place which was one mile west of my home. The only language that my cousin, Olaf Johnson, could talk and understand was Norwegian; the only language I could handle was English. In spite of this difficulty, we enjoyed our frequent play times together very much. It was through him that I became familiar with the Norwegian language. It was through her that he became familiar with the English language.

I have had no outstanding fears. However, I was afraid of the dark for several years during my childhood. This was due to a scare I received in the dark from one of our hired men. I believe I have had as much courage, though, as other children of my age.

As a child I was very sensitive; my feelings were easily hurt. If anybody said anything mean about me, or scolded me, I felt very much hurt. My parents never whipped me. A scolding served the purpose just as well, and, I believe, it was just as effective. Although I was sensitive I was not a nervous child.

Ever since I became old enough to go to school I have been rather quiet. Before I entered school I was a little selfish. Perhaps this was because I was the oldest child and was always given nearly anything I wanted. My brother came when I was five years old. In a short time I learned that I had to share things with him. Other traits I might mention are fairness, calmness, and cheerfulness.

My chief longing of my school years was to complete a successful school term. But still,

21

at the close of each vacation, I welcomed the approach of the beginning of another school year—with its new learning and many happy experiences.

MY PRESENT AND FUTURE SELF

Having learned something about my traits and experiences throughout my life, the reader might be interested in what I am like now, and what I would like to be in the future.

I am dark, and look like my father. My brother is light, and looks like my mother. I have black hair, brown eyes, am quite well built physically, weigh one hundred and forty pounds, and am sixty-nine inches tall. My heart, lungs, digestion, and voice are good. I try to sleep at least eight hours each night with my windows open. I eat almost every kind of food, but am especially fond of sweets. I do not use liquor or tobacco.

My favorite pastime is to play the guitar and sing. I also enjoy so-called "bull sessions" with student friends here in my room. I take great interest in reading newspapers and magazines, but not books. When I have plenty of time to spend I enjoy seeing good movies and plays, and listening to live speakers.

I am a home loving individual. There is no time that I am more happy than when I'm

24

going home! I am indeed thankful for a home, parents, and a brother. I never knew of an experience that was as hard to endure as staying away from home last year. Going to college was like being thrust into a new world. The environment was entirely different. I knew noone. I hated college; I wanted to go home. But still I had the determination to stick it out. By the end of the year I had adjusted myself to the environment, made new friends, and found that I liked college. This year I find that it is quite easy to remain away from home. Still, when Christmas vacation comes, I will be among the first of the students to dash for home!

As is shown by my present school work, I have the mental capacity to grasp nearly any subject. In a general free-for-all competition in special subjects I might expect to win in science and mathematics.

I cannot say that I am entirely agreeable to all people socially. This is probably because I am rather modest and quiet. Because I do not drink, I am not agreeable socially to those people who think that the only way they can have a really good time is to get drunk! I am most

26

satisfied with rather reserved, sensible young people of my own age.

Judging by my heritage, present traits, and education, I might reasonably expect to succeed in farming as a life work. If grain farming were a paying proposition, I believe I should enter this vocation. As it is today it is a losing proposition. I believe that I have the mental capacity and skill to enter into other lines of work. What this work will be I am not definitely certain of — I have been thinking of dentistry for some time. I have strong, keen eyes, steady, strong hands, am neat, patient, and accurate, and am overcoming my backwardness in meeting strange people. With these qualities I think that I could succeed in the profession of dentistry.

At the age of thirty I hope to be well established in a good, honest business. I hope to have a wife who is beautiful, loyal, intelligent, pious, neat, a good home-maker and a good cook. I hope to be blessed with two intelligent, healthy children, a boy and a girl. I hope to raise my children in a pleasant home with a Christian atmosphere.

At the age of sixty I hope to be able to retire with enough money to support my wife and

27

myself for the rest of our days. I would also like to have enough money to travel if I so desired. I hope to have given my children a good education by that time. Also that they are upright young citizens who are married, working, and happy.

28

APPENDIX

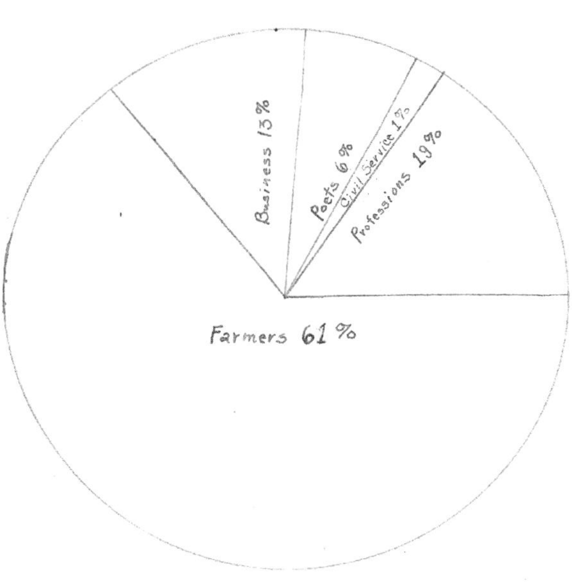

OCCUPATIONAL DISTRIBUTION OF ANCESTORS

Interesting Places, Things, Persons Seen And Heard

Places and Things	Persons
1. World's Fair, Chicago	1. Billy Sunday, evangelist
2. Charles Lindberg's birthplace, Minn.	2. Boyd Little, champion diver
3. Burning coal mines, N. Dak.	3. Bigelow Neal, author
4. John Dillinger's death spot	4. Barney Oldfield, auto daredevil
5. Oldest building in Chicago	5. The living duplicate of Abe Lincoln
6. World's largest stockyards, Chicago	6 Newman, hypnotist
7. The transparent man	7. Allen King, lion-tamer
8. Insane Asylum, Weyburn, Sask.	8 J. W. Zellnor, Impersonator
9. State Penitentiary, Bismarck, N. Dak.	9.
10. Monkey Island, Como park, Minneapolis	10.
11. Parliament building, Regina, Sask.	
12. Sand hills, Montana	
13. Qu Appelle Lakes, Canada	
14. Zephur the worlds fastest train	
15. The Talking Ford V-8	

31

The Family Tree

1934

THE FAMILY TREE

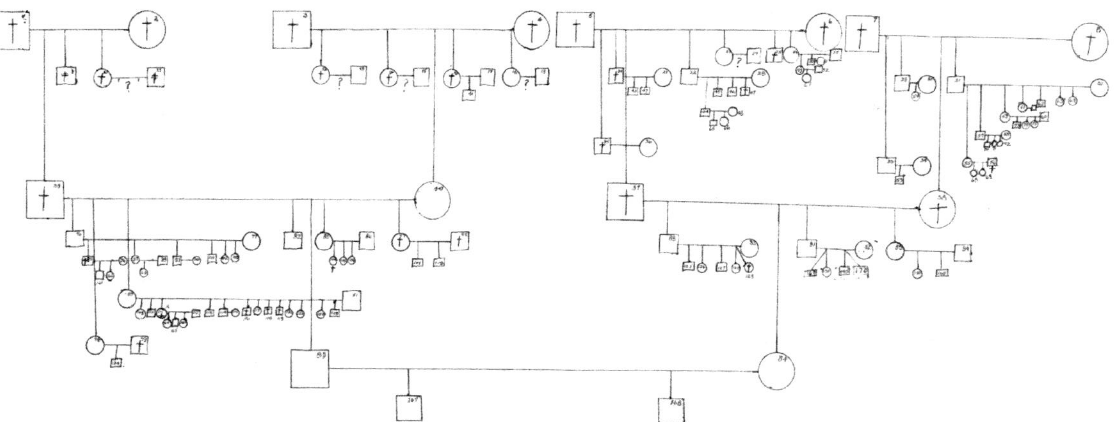

1. Great-Grandfather (Farmer)
2. Great-Grandmother Larson
3. Christian (Farmer) Holmlie
4. Name Unknown – Mrs Holmlie
5. Jorgen Jorgensen (Tailor and farmer)
6. Maren – (Poetess)
7. Willads (Tailor)
8. Marie Willads (Poetess)
9. Michael Larson (Carpenter)
10. Mrs Anna Broughton (Farmer's Wife)
11. Mr. Broughton (Farmer)
12. Mrs. Martha Olson
13. Mr. Olson (Farmer)
14. Ellen Holmlie
15. Ellen's husband (Farmer)
16. Mrs. Christiana Hanson
17. Mr. Hanson (Farmer)
18. Mrs Ingabrana Johnson
19. Mr. Johnson (Carpenter)
20. Peter Johnson (Tailor)
21. Mrs. P. Johnson
22. Nels Johnson (Farmer)
23. Mrs Christine Frederickson
24. Mr. Frederickson (Storekeeper)
25. Christian Johnson (Sergeant)
26. Mrs. Mary Lowe
27. Hans P. Lowe (Hotel, Storekeeper)
28. Mrs Nels Johnson
29. Hans Villadsen (Farmer)
30. Mrs. A. Villadsen
31. Villads Villadsen (Farmer)
32. Mrs. V. Villadsen
33. Lars Villadsen (Farmer, Poet)
34. Mrs. Lars "
35. Fred Johnson (Farmer)
36. Mrs. F. "
37. Robert Johnson (Cook, Farmer)
38. Mrs Ellen Johnson (Poetess)
39. Martin Larson (Carpenter, Farmer)
40. Mrs. Olena Larson
41. Carl Hanson (Hardware)
42. — Johnson (Teacher)
43. — Johnson (Teacher)
44. Alfred Johnson (Farmer)
45. Carl Johnson (Farmer)
46. Thorval Johnson (Farmer)
47. Joseph Johnson (Farmer)
48. Mrs Alfred Johnson
49. Clara Lowe
50. Fred Lowe (Business)
51. Mrs. Fred Lowe
52. Clara Lowe's husband (Barber)
53. Ludvig Villadsen (Farmer)
54.
55. Mary Malbaugh (Farmer's Wife)
56. Mr. Bob Malbaugh (Farmer)
57. Axel Villadsen (Farmer)
58. Mrs. Minnie Villadsen
59. Mrs Agnes Baker
60. Mr Baker (Farmer)
61. Mabel Villadsen (Farmer)
62. Alfred Villadsen (Farmer)
63. Larraine Villadsen
64. Jean Villadsen
65. — Johnson
66. — Johnson
67. Baby
68. Mary Ann Albaugh
69. Margaret Albaugh
70. Charles Villadsen
71. Anna "
72. Ruth "
73. Charles Baker (Farmer)
74. Alice
75. Kathleen
76. Carl Larson (Farmer)
77. Mrs. Carl Larson
78. Mrs Anna Johnson
79. Mr. J. T. Johnson (Farmer)
80. Mrs. Julia Johnson
81. Mr. Jens Johnson (Carpenter)
82. Marius Larson (Farmer)
83. Olaf M. Larson (Farmer)
84. Mrs. Mary Larson (Teacher)
85. Mrs. Lena Brakken
86. John Brakken (Farmer)
87. Mrs. Mary Aasboe
89. William Johnson (Teacher, Accountant)
90. Mrs. Fannie Johnson
91. Eli Johnson (Farmer)
92. Mrs. Annie Johnson
93. Mrs Esther Finstad (Teacher)
94. Knute Finstad (Farmer)
95. Melvin Larson (Farmer)
96. Mrs. Emma Larson
97. Mrs. Effie Witsoe
98. Glen Witsoe (Farmer)
99. Goffrey Larson (Farmer)
100. Mrs. Goffrey Larson
101. Lester Larson (Farmer)
102. Harriet Larson
103. Clara Larson
104. — Brakken
105. Hulda Brakken
106. Carla Brakken
107. Oswald Aasboe (Farmer)
108. Jerald Aasboe (Farmer, Camp)
109. Sophie Johnson – Cripple
110. Jeffrey Johnson (Electrician)
111. Mrs. Thorval Johnson
112. Thorval Johnson (Farmer)
113. Arthur Johnson (Butcher)
114. Wilbur Johnson (Clerk in store)
115. Mrs. W. Johnson
116. William Johnson
117. Ethel Johnson
118. Roy Johnson
119. William Johnson
120. Judith Johnson
121. Lily Johnson
122. Johnson
123. Lloyd Johnson
124. Olaf M. Johnson (Farmer)
125. Howard Johnson
126. Mildred Johnson
127. Robert Johnson
128. Louise Johnson
129. Elizabeth Johnson
130. Ruby Johnson
140. Ralph Johnson
150. Olive Rae Finstad
160. Doris Finstad
161. Oliver Larson
162. Larson
163. Witsoe
164. Johnson
165. Marvin Johnson
166. Evelyn Johnson
167. William Larson
168. Lloyd J. Larson
169. Ronald Johnson
170. Lloyd Johnson

Key to Chart

† — Dead
□ — Male
○ — Female
Λ — Twins
? — Children Unknown

STUDYING MYSELF

Author At Present

5

My First Picture (3 mo.)
(My Mother's mother, my mother, and myself)

The Author At Age of 2½ yrs.

12

My Family (1925)

15

Confirmation Picture
(13 yrs. Old)

My Home

25

The Author (Age16) And Brother

Appendix B

William Rudolf Larson Background Items

Daabs Attest.

William Rudolph
født den 1ste December 1915
af Forældrene Olaf M. Larson
og Hustru Mary Caroline Larson
blev den 27de Februar 1916
døbt i Sauk Valley n. luth. Mgh. Osakis, Minn.
I
FADERENS, SØNNENS OG DEN HELLIGAANDS NAVN.

Faddere Peter Edenlöf
Mrs. Lucy Edenlöf
Eli J. Johnson
Esther R. Johnson

Pastor.

Hvo der tror og bliver døbt, skal blive salig. Mark 16.16.

Lader de smaa Børn komme til mig og forhindrer dem ikke! Ev. Luk. 18.16.

No. 525

Certificate of Confirmation.

William Rudolph Larson

Born Dec. 1st 1915 and Bapt. Feb. 27th 1916.

Confirmed Sunday 18th of Nov. 1928 at

Bethany Luth. Church, Divide Co., N.D.

H. O. Dybvik

NEITHER is there salvation in any other: for there is none other name under heaven given among men, whereby we must be saved. Acts 4, 12.

Rock of ages, cleft for me,
Let me hide myself in thee!
Let the water and the blood,
From thy riven side which flowed,
Be of sin the perfect cure,
Save me, Lord, and make me pure!

Published and printed by LUTH. PUB. HOUSE, Decorah, Iowa.

15

North Dakota
Public Schools

SAKAKAWEA
OR "BIRD WOMAN"

This Certifies that

William Larson

has satisfactorily completed the Course of Study prescribed for the Public Schools of the State of North Dakota and therefore merits this

Diploma

which entitles the holder to admission to any High School in the State

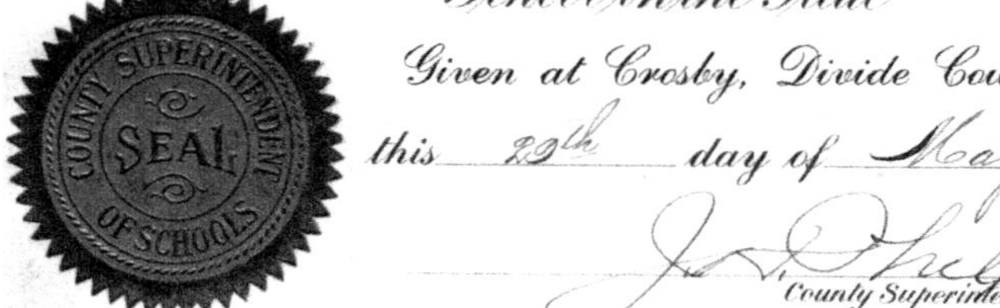

Given at Crosby, Divide County, N. D.

this 29th day of May 1922

J. L. Phelps
County Superintendent of Schools

Teacher

FORM S S 8½

Concordia College

Soli Deo Gloria

Know all men by these presents

that the Board of Directors on the nomination by the Faculty have conferred upon

William R. Larson

the degree of

Bachelor of Arts

and have declared him entitled to all the rights and privileges which pertain to that degree here or elsewhere. In Testimony Whereof and as evidence that he has fulfilled all requirements prescribed for that Degree this Diploma is granted.

Dated at the College in the City of Moorhead, State of Minnesota, this seventh day of June in the year of our Lord, nineteen hundred and thirty-seven

President of the Board of Directors

J. N. Brown
President of the College

Taken March 18, 1916.

Age 3 mo. 2 wk. 4 da.

William Rudolph Larson

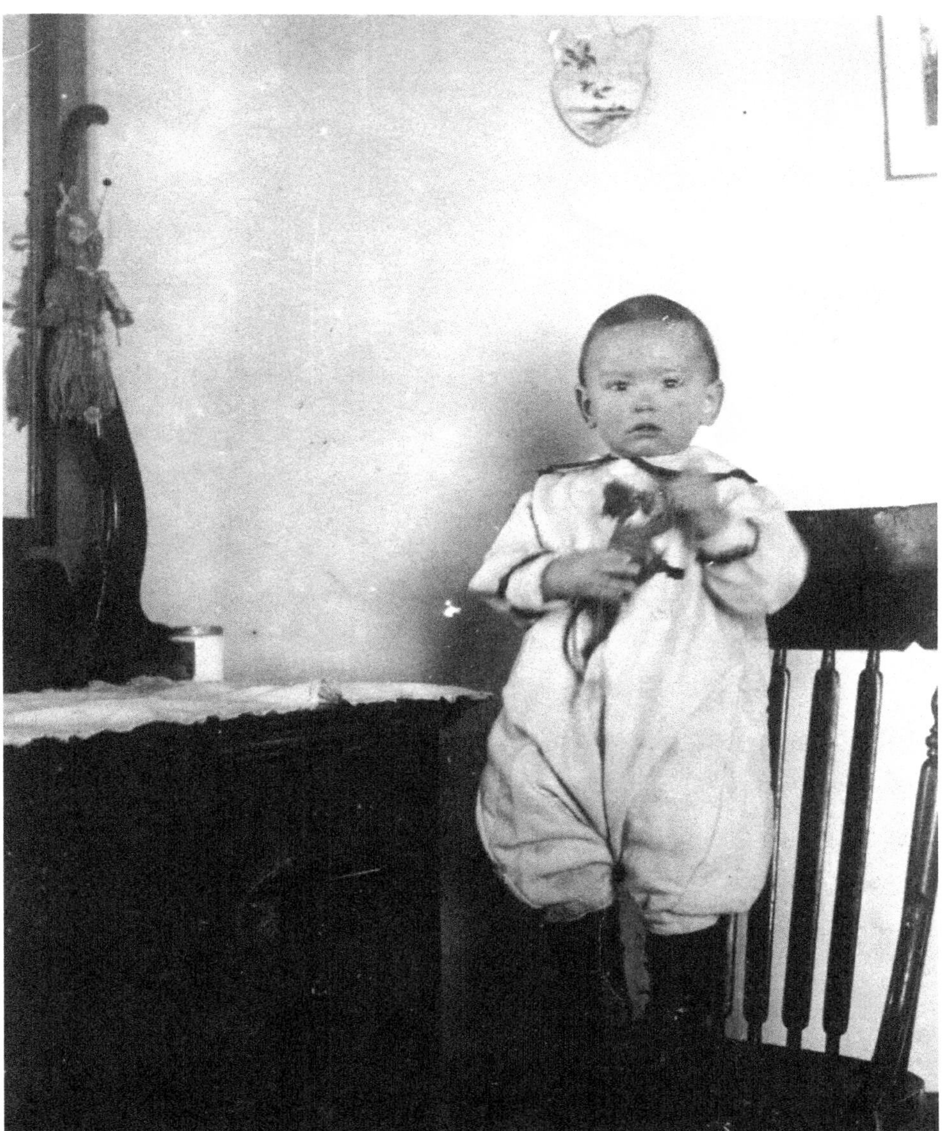

William at 2 ½ - June 1918

Olaf William Mary

1917 (2 yrs old)

Olaf, Lloyd, William, Mary – Larson Family - 1925

William and Lloyd playing in family farmyard

William and Lloyd, Hirsch, Saskatchewan, Canada

Bethany Church Confirmation Class November 1928: Front Row L to R, Sylvia Haug, Pastor Dybdvik, Hulda Brakken, Mildred Schenstad. Back Row L to R, Clarence Rodvold, William Larson, Arne Nelson, Melvin Schenstad, Thelma Witsoe, Ellis Berg, Erling Twete, Viola Witsoe, Leonard Twete

Sioux Trail Consolidated School Mates – Sophomore Class 1931 (Back left: Teacher Warner Peterson)

Grenora N.D. High School Graduation Picture – June 1, 1933 (17 years old)

Ed Nies and William – Concordia College

Concordia College – William 3rd from left

Concordia Graduation – 1937 (21 years old)

Lloyd & William with their band instruments

N. Nav. 378
Rev. Feb. 1938

8316

Enl 6-2-39

APPLICATION FOR AVIATION TRAINING IN THE U. S. NAVAL RESERVE

RECEIVED JAN NAV. RES. AVI. BASE MINNEAPOLIS, MINN.

410-5-5-36

Name William R. Larson   Permanent address Hanks, N. Dak.

Telephone No. ....   Temporary address Ambrose(?), N. Dak.

Date of birth Dec. 1, 1915   Place of birth Osakis, Minnesota

1. I hereby apply for flight training in the U. S. Naval Reserve.

2. I certify that no promises have been made me regarding assignment to or continuance on duty and I understand that my training will be undertaken, continued, and completed only if practicable under instructions to be issued by the Navy Department, from time to time.

3. I agree (with the consent of parent or guardian, if a minor) to serve for a continuous period of 4 years on active duty (including period of training duty at Pensacola), unless sooner released.

4. I am unmarried and agree to remain unmarried until the expiration of 2 years from the date of entering upon active duty undergoing training at Pensacola, unless sooner released from active duty by the Navy Department.

5. I agree to maintain my efficiency insofar as is practicable by associating myself with a naval reserve aviation organization after completion of active duty indicated above, and receiving commission in the Naval Reserve.

6. Attached hereto, I submit the following required documentary data (indicate by check mark (√) to left that (*a*) to (*h*) are attached and in acceptable form).

√ (*a*) Copy of birth certificate (or acceptable affidavit, giving date and place of birth).

___ (*b*) Evidence of citizenship (if not native born).

√ (*c*) Educational record (high school).

√ (*d*) Educational record (college).

√ (*e*) Three letters of recommendation and identification by persons of recognized standing in my home community.

___ (*f*) The consent of my parents or guardian to enlist for this training (required only in cases of minors).

√ (*g*) A résumé (at least 50 words) covering occupational and other experience, written in own handwriting on one side of 8 inch by 10½ inch sheet of paper. This must include statement of any military or naval training received, or statement that applicant has had no previous military or naval training.

√ (*h*) In the space provided is a 2½ inch by 2½ inch photographic print of myself.

7. I certify that I have not previously failed in flight training in the Army.

William Rudolph Larson
(Applicant sign full name here)

4—7377

FINISHED-LYNCH-FILE

File in Officer's Jacket

INSTRUCTIONS

Applications must be mailed to the commandant of the naval district in which applicant resides, or to Senior Member, Naval Reserve Flight Selection Board for the naval district. In no case will applications be considered by the Navy Department unless individuals have been nominated by the district Naval Reserve Flight Selection Board.

If an application is rejected the applicant will be so advised and the application retained in the files of the commandant.

If an application indicates probable qualification, the applicant will be advised to report, at his own expense, for interview and physical examination.

Applications of those found qualified after interview and physical examination will be forwarded to the Bureau of Navigation with the following form completed and signed by those officers responsible for the action taken on the application. Enlistments will be made only when specifically and individually authorized by the Bureau of Navigation.

Place N.R.A.B., Minneapolis, Minn., Date 8 April 1939

This applicant has been examined physically and psychologically and found qualified for flight training and for a commission in the Naval Reserve. Bureau of Medicine and Surgery Forms Y and N. M. S. Aviation No. 1 have been completed and forwarded to the Bureau of Medicine and Surgery.

L.M. Larson, Lieut. MC-O, USNR
(Medical officer sign here)

REPORT OF COMMANDANT'S BOARD

This applicant is recommended for flight training in the Naval Reserve.

In the opinion of the board he stands No. 6 among selections made by this board for Class No. 2 from the Ninth Naval District.

He is assigned a mark of 3.3 in potential ability as an officer and naval aviator.

The following is the board's estimate of this candidate:

(*a*) Officer material Good Officer material

(*b*) Personality and manner Pleasing personality, Frank and modest.

(*c*) Appearance and type of individual Good Appearance, stable.

(*d*) Qualifies under Art. H-10302, Paragraph (2)(c) Bu.Nav.Manual.

C.S. Smiley, Lieut. Comdr. U.S. Navy

K.B. Salisbury, Lieut. U.S.N.R.

L.M. Larson, Lieut. MC-O, U.S.N.R.

U. S. GOVERNMENT PRINTING OFFICE 4—7377

No. 40—Certified Copy of Birth Register, 1911 Laws. FREE PRESS, MANKATO, MINN.

State of Minnesota, County of Douglas — Osakis, Township (City, Village or Township)

No.	NAME OF CHILD	SEX	Single Twins Triplets	No. in Order of Birth	No. of Child of this Mother	Legitimate	TIME OF BIRTH Month	Day	Year	Hour
399	William Rudolph Larson	M	S	–	1	yes	Dec.	1,	1915	

FATHER

NAME	AGE	COLOR	BIRTHPLACE	OCCUPATION
Olof Larson	30	White	Minn.	Farmer

MOTHER

FULL MAIDEN NAME	AGE	COLOR	BIRTHPLACE	OCCUPATION
Mary Johnson	24	White	N. Dak.	H-wife

PHYSICIAN, MIDWIFE OR OTHER REPORTER NAME	ADDRESS	DATE OF REPORT	REGISTRAR NAME	ADDRESS	DATE OF FILING
~~W. H. Hengstler~~			- -		- -
W. H. Hengstler		------	A. A. Rooney,	Osakis,	1-14-16

State of Minnesota,
County of Douglas } ss.

IN DISTRICT COURT
Seventh Judicial District

I, Albert T. Olson *Clerk of the District Court in and for said County and State, do hereby certify that the foregoing is a full and complete transcript of the entries appearing of record in the Register of Births now remaining in my said office relating to the birth of said* William Rudolph Larson *and of the whole thereof.*

WITNESS my hand and the seal of said Court hereto affixed at Alexandria, *Minn., this* 1st *day*

AFFIDAVIT

County of McKenzie)
)
State of North Dakota)

Olaf M. Larson and Mary Caroline Larson, being duly sworn, depose and say that William Rudolph Larson is born on the first day of December, Nineteen Hundred Fifteen(1915) in the township of Osakis, county of Douglas, state of Minnesota. Post Office address Osakis, Minnesota.

Olaf M. Larson
Mary C Larson
Parents

Subscribed and sworn to before me a Notary Public this 11th. day of January 1939.

Ivar Dvoidal

Notary Public, North Dakota
My Commission Expires Dec. 4th, 19 40

Form 13

Transfer Certificate of High School Credits

This is to certify that William Larson (Give name in full)

of Grenora, North Dakota (Number and street) (City) (State)

who was born ______, 19___, at ______(City) ______(County) ______(State)

attended the Grenora High School of Grenora, N. Dak.

from Sept., 1932, to June, 1933 and was graduated June 1933

He/She was enrolled in this school 2 semesters. Below is a correct statement of his/her record in

Grenora High School. Signed by E. R. Hilde

Dated May 25 1938 Superintendent of Publis Schools Official Position.

SUBJECTS	Year Taken (1,2,3,4,)	No. of Weeks Pursued	No. of Periods per Week	Grade	Units of Credit
English—First Year	1	36	5	85-90	1
Second Year	2	36	5	88-90	1
Third Year	3	36	5	91-91	1
Fourth Year	4	36	5	96-96	1
Latin—First Year	1	36	5	95	1
Second Year	2	36	5	90	1
Third Year					
Fourth Year					
French—First Year					
Second Year					
Third Year					
Fourth Year					
German—First Year					
Second Year					
Third Year					
Fourth Year					
Spanish—First Year					
Second Year					
Third Year					
Fourth Year					
History—Ancient					
Medieval and Modern	3	36	5	92	1
English					
General					
United States	4	36	5	97	1
Civics	2	18	5	89	1/2
Economics					
Sociology					
Other Subjects					
Note: Credits for first three years were accepted from Souix Traill High School.					

SUBJECTS	Year Taken (1,2,3,4)	No. of Weeks Pursued	No. of Periods per Week	Grade	Units of Credit
Mathematics					
Elementary Algebra	1	36	5	94	1
Advanced Algebra					
Plane Geometry	3	36	5	95	1
Solid Geometry					
Science					
Physics					
Chemistry					
Botany					
Zoology					
Physiology					
Physical Geography					
General Science					
Agriculture—First Year	2	36	5	91	1
Second Year					
Third Year					
Bookkeeping—First Year	1	36	5	89	1
Second Year					
Shorthand—First Year					
Second Year					
Typewriting—First Year	4	36	5	95	1/2
Second Year					
Clothing					
Foods					
Drawing					
Manual Training					
Music Orchestra	4	36	2	96	1/4
Other Subjects					
Vocations	2	18	5	91	1/2
Pro. Democracy	3	36	5	93	1
Com. Law	4	18	5	97	1/2
Biology	4	36	5	97	1
Com. Geography	4	18	5	96	1/2
Phys. Ed.	1234	144	2	94	1
Total Credits Earned					

Passing grade in school 75 Number of units of credit required for graduation 16 Length of recitation period 40

Did this pupil ever fail in any subject? No If so, what subject? (Give name of subject, length of time pursued, and failing grade) ______

Explanation of grading system if figures are not used ______

School Service Co., 154 E. Erie St., Chicago, Ill.

CONCORDIA COLLEGE

Moorhead, Minnesota

OFFICE OF THE REGISTRAR

The following is a complete transcript of the record of Larson, William R.

in Concordia College, together with credits presented at entrance from Grenora, North Dakota High School

Date of entrance 9-11-33 Degree granted Will graduate -- 1937

PREPARATORY RECORD

Subject	Units	Subject	Units	Subject	Units	Subject	Units	Subject	Units	Subject	Units
English	4	Hist. Ancient	1	Algebra, Elem.	1	Physics		Man. Training		Stenography	
Sr. Grammar		Hist. Modern		Algebra, Higher		Chemistry		Dom. Science		Typewriting	1
Pub. Speak.		Hist. American	1	Geometry, Plane	1	Biology	1	Cooking		Shorthand	
Latin	2	Hist. General		Geometry, Solid		Gen. Science		Sewing		Religion	
French		History		Arithmetic		Botany		Com. Geography	1/3	Pen. and Spelling	
German		Social Problems	1/2	Psychology		Zoology		Com. Law	1/3	Music	
Norse		Civics	1/2			Physiology		Bookkeeping	1		
		Economics				Agriculture	1	Vocations	1/3	Drawing	
		Sociology						Physical Ed.	4 yrs.	TOTAL	17

COLLEGE RECORD

Department and Course Number	Descriptive Title of Course	No. of Weeks	Cr. Hrs. Per Wk.	Grade 1 Sem.	Grade 2 Sem.	Year
English 1-2	Composition	36	3	B	A-	33-4
Latin 3-4	Third Year Latin	36	3	C-	B	
Religion 1-2	Bible	36	2	B-	C	
Mathematics 3-4	Elementary Functions	36	3	A-	A	
Mathematics 5-6	Graphics	36	3	B	B	
Physics 1-2	General College	36	4	A-	B⊥	
Personal Hygiene		18		B		
Physical Education		36		C	A	
German 1-2	Elementary	36	3	B⊥	A	34-35
Economics 11	Principles	18	3		B	
Psychology 11-12	General; Educational	36	3	B⊥	A-	
Religion 11, 14	Church History; Church in Mod. World	36	2	B	C	
Biology 1-2	Animal	36	4	B⊥	A	
Chemistry 3-4	General Inorganic	36	4	B	B⊥	
Physical Education		36		Ex.	Ex.	
English 11-12	History of English Literature	36	3	B	B	35-36
German 3-4	Intermediate	36	3	B-	C⊥	
Education 33, 44	Principles and Prob. of Sec. Educ.; High School Administration	36	3	B	B	
Public Speaking 12	Principles and Practice	18	3		C	
Religion 21-22	Christian Doctrines	36	2	B-	B	
Chemistry 11	Qualitative Analysis	18	3	B-		
Chemistry 21-22	Organic	36	3	A	A	
Physical Education		18		C		
German 29	Scientific	18	3	B-		36-37
Education 47	General Methods	18	3	B		
Religion 25	Christian Apologetics	18	2	B		
Mathematics 17	Mathematics of Finance	18	3	B-		
Mathematics 23	Teachers Course	18	2	C⊥		
Chemistry 33	Theoretical	18	3	B		
Chemistry 41	Methods	18	2	B		
Physical Education		18		Ex.		
PRESENT SCHEDULE OF COURSES:	(Second Semester 1936-37.)					
Psychology 22	Applied	18	(3)			
Chemistry 34	Theoretical	18	(3)			
Philosophy 12	Logic	18	(3)			
German 30	Scientific	18	(3)			
Chemistry 16	Quantitative Analysis	18	(3)			
Biology 22	Comparative Anatomy	18	(3)			

Arnegard School Dist. No. 11

DIRECTORS:
Edwin S. Sanders
Harold Bolken
Geo. Leiseth

A Classified High School

ROLF D. BRANDT, SUPERINTENDENT

OFFICERS:
Edwin S. Sanders, President
Marie Boe, Treasurer
Ivar Drovdal, Clerk

Arnegard, North Dakota

January 11, 1939

The United States Naval Reserve
Aviation Base
Minneapolis, Minn.

Re: Identification and Recommendation of Mr. William R. Larson

Gentlemen:

Mr. William R. Larson has asked me to write you a letter of identification and recommendation. This I willingly do.

Mr. Larson, whose home is at Hanks, North Dakota, is a graduate of Concordia College, Moorhead, Minnesota, and has taught school in Arnegard under my supervision for one full school term, teaching his second term here at the present time.

He is intelligent, athletically inclined, healthy, and of impeccable honesty. He cooperates well, is willing to take and act upon suggestions and orders, and has a personality which wears well.

Mr. Larson is deeply interested in things aeronautical, and it is my belief that he will become a very efficient member of the naval forces of the United States.

Sincerely,

Rolf D. Brandt

Rolf D. Brandt.

RECEIVED
JAN 13 1939
NAV. RES. AVI. BASE
MINNEAPOLIS,

Arnegard, North Dakota
January 12, 1939

U. S. Naval Reserve Aviation Base
Minneapolis, Minnesota

Gentlemen:

Mr. William Larson, of Arnegard, North Dakota, has asked me to recommend him to you. Mr. Larson has taught under my supervision for the past two years. I have found him to be a very trustworthy person who carries his responsibility well.

Besides being of good personality, Mr. Larson is a neat dresser. His pupils like him, and that--I believe--is almost sufficient recommendation for anyone.

I am sure you will find Mr. Larson both mentally and physically fitted for the work he is planning to take up.

Yours very truly,

(Miss) Ruth A. Mittelstadt
Principal of High School

RM:RM

U.S.Naval Reserve Aviation Base,
Minneapolis, Minn.

To Whom It May Consern;-

The undersigned take pleasure in stating, that Mr. William Rudolph Larson has been in the employ of the Arnegard School District No.11 of Arnegard N.D. for the past 18 month as a teacher and athletic coach of our High School Department.

He has proven himself of being capable, energetic and faithfull , he ~~has~~ is a young man of very good habits, and a fine Christian character.

I highly recomend him to the service he is seeking with our Federal Government.

Yours Very Respectfully.

Ivar Drovdal

Ivar Drovdal, Clerk
Arnegard School District No.11.

1

April 22, 1939

Occupational Resumé

I was raised on a Western North Dakota farm so that my time outside of school has been spent, largely, driving horses and tractors and running all types of farm machinery. Two summers were spent running trucks for gravel road-surfacing contractors.

By clerking in the Red Owl Food Stores and doing other odd part-time jobs, I worked my way through Concordia College.

I have had no military training.

At present I am employed as science and mathematics teacher and coach in the Arnegard High School.

William R. Larson

Hand-sketched Map of Corry Field by William – NAS Pensacola Florida 1940

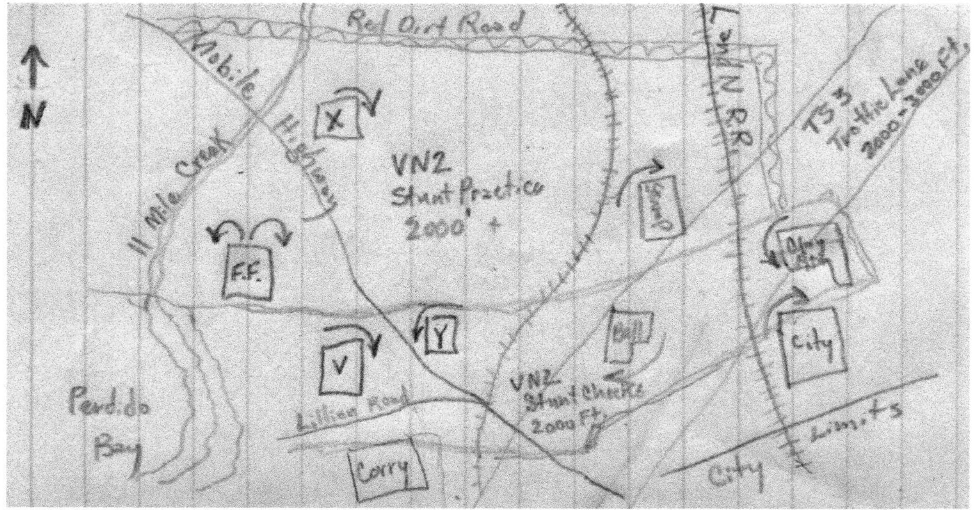

Soloed at Pensacola Mon. Nov. 6, 1939
Instructed by Capt. Grevemeyer.

ORDER FORM

THE HAAS TAILORING COMPANY - Paca + Redwood Sts.

BALTIMORE, MD.

Coat + Pants Green Elastique	48.00
Best Gold Emb. Wings	4.50
2 suits Best Cramerton Khaki	31.00
2 Button Sets for Khaki	2.00
1 Cravanette Raincoat	44.50
1 Sword + Scabbard 30"	24.50
1 Sword Belt	5.25
1 Sword Knot	3.00
1 Chamois Sword Case	2.50
1 pr. Ens. Sh. Mks.	3.00
1 Cap Complete - White 7 1/8	9.00
1 Cap Complete - Green	10.00
1 pr. Metal Wings	.75
1 pr. Ens. Collar Bars	.75
1 pr. High Grade Leather Gloves 8 1/2	3.75
1 pr. White Lisle Gloves 8 1/2	1.00
1 suit Blues Converted (Wings, lace, new stars)	8.75
	202.25

$10.00 Free Cleaning Credit with This order.

Both parties understand that this order is conditional only on the purchaser receiving wings upon completion of Aviation Training. In the event that training is not completed for any reason, the purchaser is under no obligation. Payment for the above is to be made in 6 equal monthly payments, the first due 30 days after delivery.

Monthly payment $ 33.71

W R Larson Purchaser

J B Miller

9-29-39-22000

N-16

U. S. NAVAL AIR STATION
PENSACOLA, FLORIDA

BUREAU OF NAVIGATION
NAVY DEPARTMENT
RECEIVED
83169-
1940 JUL 22 AM 10 36

FINAL REPORT OF AVIATION TRAINING
(Heavier-than-Air)

Name LARSON, William R. Rank or Rate Ensign, A-V(N)

Corps U.S.N.R. Class Number 130-C

Commenced Training 24 Sept. 1939 Completed Training 1 July 1940

Division			Relative Weight	Mark
GROUND SCHOOL			40	3.1440
FLIGHT SCHOOL				
	Relative Weight	Mark		
Primary Training	20	2.910		
Basic Training	10	3.047		
Advanced Training Specialized VO-VS	30	2.89		
Advanced Training Specialized Patrol				
Advanced Training Specialized Carrier Group				
Final Mark, Flight School			60	2.923
FINAL MARK, COURSE OF AVIATION TRAINING			100	3.011

REMARKS: Completed XXXXXXXX Specialized Course in VO-VS type airplanes.
Qualified catapult pilot.
Flight Time: Solo - 184.6
Dual - 71.4
Passenger - 28.0
Total - 284.0

FINISHED-LYNCH-FILE

W D Anderson
W. D. ANDERSON,
Lieut. Comdr., U. S. Navy,
Superintendent Aviation Training
Acting.

39-9

U.S.S. NASHVILLE 29-lec

CL43/P17-2/MV-1 ( ) May 8, 1942.

From: Ensign William R. Larson, A-V(N), USNR.
To : The Chief of Bureau of Navigation.
Via : Commanding Officer.

NAVY DEPARTMENT RECEIVED 1942 JUN 6 PM 12 00

Subject: Change of Duty - request for.

1. It is requested that I be transferred to Aircraft Carrier Training Group on either coast for further transfer to an Aircraft Carrier.

2. At present there are nine aviators on board this vessel. I have been in Cruiser Aviation aboard this vessel for twenty-two (22) months.

3. I believe that I would be of greater service to the aviation activity if granted this change of duty.

W. R. Larson
W. R. LARSON

- -

FIRST ENDORSEMENT
CL43/P17-2/MV-1/(188)

U.S.S. NASHVILLE
c/o Postmaster,
San Francisco, Calif.
MAY 1 1942

From: Commanding Officer.
To : The Chief of Bureau of Navigation.

1. Ensign Larson is an excellent pilot who would do well in any branch of Naval Aviation. However, he is one of the more experienced pilots in this ship's aviation detachment, and the Commanding Officer would not want to lose his services until the newer pilots had gained more experience.

F. Craven
F. S. Craven.

Finished File

MEDICAL CLEARANCE SLIP

UNITED STATES NAVAL AIR STATION, SEATTLE, WASHINGTON

10/20/ ,1942

MEMORANDUM FOR COMMANDING OFFICER, VGS 21

1. The below named Naval Aviator ~~Nxxxxxx.~~ (~~xxxx~~) has reported to the Dispensary this date and was found physically qualified for duty involving actual control of aircraft. LARSON, William Rudolph Lt.(jg) A-V(N) USNR

C. E. R. # 13

Vision: O.U. 20/20

R.W. Whitley (MC)USN
FLIGHT SURGEON

EXPENDITURE INVOICE October 23, 1942

From S. O. 257 NAS, Seattle, Washington (Yard or Vessel) To Flight Clothing Issued Aviators

Account from which expended 13 X 2 To title and account 11-V-53

Authority Art. 2750-4, Bu. S&A Manual Appropriation chargeable Aviation Navy

Item No.	Standard Stock Catalogue No. or Class No.	Description of Article	Quantity Delivered	Unit of Quantity	Unit Price	Extension
	Class 37					
1	B-	BAG, carry-all		No.		
2	B-	BAG, suit		No.		
3	B- M-	BOOTS, or MOCCASINS, furlined		Pr. Pr.		
4	F-	FRAMES, goggles, pilot type		Pr.		
5	G-	GLOVES, summer, size		Pr.		
6	G-	GLOVES, winter, size		Pr.		
7	H-	HELMET, summer, unlined		No.		
8	H-	HELMET, medium, lined		No.		
9	H-	HELMET, winter, lined		No.		
10	J-	JACKET, medium flight		No.		
11	J-	JACKET, summer flight		No.		
12	L-	LENSE, goggle, clear		Pr.		
13	L-	LENSE, goggle, colored		Pr.		
14	S5364	SUIT, flying, summer, Size 38 Med.	1	No.		
15	S-	SUIT, flying, winter, 1-piece, size or 3-piece as follows:		No.		
15a	J-	JACKET winter, heavy		No.		
15b	J-	JACKET, winter, light		No.		
15c	T-	TROUSERS, winter, heavy		Pr.		
16	P-	PHONE ASSEMBLY, radio helmet		No.		
					Total,	

To cover Survey No. 3-43

G.E. Moore II
LT. (SC) USN, U. S. Navy.
Stores Officer

Received October 23, 1942, the above-mentioned articles ~~accompanied by priced invoice~~ which are not in excess of

N. Nav. 296
(June 1928)

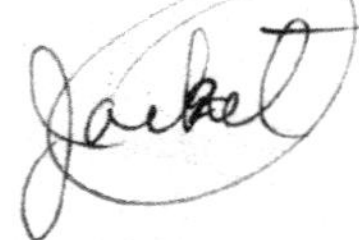

REPORT OF LEAVE OF ABSENCE

(SEE INSTRUCTIONS BELOW)

Escort Scouting Squadron - 21 (Ship or Station) November 14, 1942. (Date)

From: Commanding Officer. (Commanding Officer)

To: BUREAU OF NAVIGATION, NAVY DEPARTMENT.

Subject: { Report of leave of absence.
Report of authorized delay counting as leave of absence.

In conformity with requirements of U. S. Navy Regulations, I report the following leave of absence taken by:

LARSON, William R. (Name, surname first) Lt. A-V(N), USNR (Rank and corps) (Signal number)

under orders of CL43/P16-4/00, dated Sept. 25, 1942.

NOTE.—Use either (*a*) or (*b*). Do not use both for same leave.

(*a*) Leave: Total number of days, *including* any travel time

(*b*) Delay counting as leave or leave between stations: Total number of days, *excluding* preparation period of 4 days and *excluding* allowance for travel time from old to new station via shortest usually traveled route 14

Commencing with October 7 (See instructions), 1942

Expiring with October 22 (See instructions), 1942

Insert inclusive dates to agree with number of days leave.

L.K. GREENAMYER., Lieut.Comdr, USN (Signature of Commanding Officer)

INSTRUCTIONS

1. The day of departure from station or duty counts as a day of duty; the day of return as a day of leave. This refers to leave taken when not detached from ship or station (see Article 1727, Navy Regulations).
2. In cases of authorized delay counting as leave, this form should be submitted in *addition* to the B-slip form.
3. This report will be made at expiration of leave by the immediate superior of the officer to whom the leave is granted and forwarded immediately to the Navy Department (Bureau of Navigation). Care must be taken to insure that correct number of days of leave is reported and corresponds with the inclusive dates reported.

4—6271

FORM 1040
Treasury Department
Internal Revenue Service

UNITED STATES
INDIVIDUAL INCOME TAX RETURN

Page 1
1942

OPTIONAL FORM 1040A MAY BE FILED INSTEAD OF THIS FORM IF GROSS INCOME IS REPORTED ON THE CASH BASIS FOR THE CALENDAR YEAR, IS NOT MORE THAN $3,000, AND CONSISTS *WHOLLY* OF SALARY, WAGES, OTHER COMPENSATION FOR PERSONAL SERVICES, DIVIDENDS, INTEREST OR ANNUITIES.

FOR CALENDAR YEAR 1942

or fiscal year beginning 1 Jan., 1942, and ending Dec 31, 1943

PRINT NAME AND ADDRESS PLAINLY. (See Instruction C)

Larson, William R.
(Name) (Use given names of both husband and wife, if this is a joint return)

VC-21 c/o Postmaster
(Street and number, or rural route)

San Francisco, (Post office) (County) California. (State)

Naval Aviator, (Occupation) (Social Security number, if any)

U.S.N.R. (Name and address of employer)

(If more than one employer, attach statement showing name and address and amount received from each)

(Do not use these spaces)
File Code
Serial No.
District
(Cashier's Stamp)
Cash—Check—M. O.
First Payment
$

Item and Instruction No.	INCOME	Amount	Deductible Expenses (Attach itemized statement)		
1.	Salaries and other compensation for personal services,	$ 3142	$	$	
2.	Dividends				
3.	Interest on bank deposits, notes, etc.				
			Less amortizable bond premium		
4.	Interest on corporation bonds, etc.	$	$		
5.	Interest on Government obligations, etc.:				
	(a) From line (h), Schedule A	$	$		
	(b) From line (i), Schedule A	$	$		
6.	Rents and royalties. (From Schedule B)				
7.	Annuities				
	ITEMS 8, 9, AND 10, BELOW (AND PAGES 3 AND 4) NEED NOT BE CONSIDERED UNLESS YOU HAVE INCOME (OR LOSSES) IN ADDITION TO ITEMS ABOVE.				
8.	(a) Net gain (or loss) from sale or exchange of capital assets. (From Schedule F)				
	(b) Net gain (or loss) from sale or exchange of property other than capital assets. (From Schedule G)				
9.	Net profit (or loss) from business or profession. (From Schedule H) (State total receipts, from line 1, Schedule H, $)				
10.	Income (or loss) from partnerships; fiduciary income; and other income. (From Schedule I)				
11.	Total income in items 1 to 10				$ 3142
	DEDUCTIONS				
12.	Contributions paid. (Explain in Schedule C)			$	
13.	Interest. (Explain in Schedule C)			~~25~~ —	
14.	Taxes. (Explain in Schedule C)			18 —	
15.	Losses from fire, storm, shipwreck, or other casualty, or theft. (Explain in Schedule C)				
16.	Bad debts. (Explain in Schedule C)				
17.	Other deductions authorized by law. (Explain in Schedule C)				
18.	Total deductions in items 12 to 17				18
19.	Net income (item 11 minus item 18)				$ 3124

COMPUTATION OF TAX

20. Net income (item 19 above)		$ 3124	
21. Less: Personal exemption. (From Schedule D-1)	$ 500 —		
22. Credit for dependents. (From Schedule D-2)		500	
23. Balance (surtax net income)		$ 2624 —	
24. Less: Item 5 (a) above	$		
25. Earned income credit. (From Schedule E-1 or E-2)	312 40	312	40
26. Balance subject to normal tax		$ 2311	60

27. Normal tax (6% of item 26)	$ 138	70
28. Surtax on item 23. (See Instruction 28)	359	84
29. Total (item 27 plus item 28)	$ 498	54
30. Total tax (Item 29 or line 16, Schedule F)	$ 498	54
31. Less: Income tax paid at source	$	
32. Income tax paid to a foreign country or U.S. possession. (Attach Form 1116)		
33. Balance of tax (Item 30 minus items 31 and 32)	$ 498	54

I/we declare, under the penalties of perjury, that this return (including any accompanying schedules and statements) has been examined by me/us, and to the best of my/our knowledge and belief is a true, correct, and complete return, made in good faith, for the taxable year stated, pursuant to the Internal Revenue Code and the regulations issued under authority thereof.

(Signature of person (other than taxpayer or agent) preparing return) (Date)

William R Larson 2/21/43
(Signature of taxpayer) (Date)

(Name of firm or employer, if any)

(If this is a joint return (not made by agent), it must be signed by both husband and wife) A return made by an agent must be accompanied by power of attorney. (See Instruction F)

16—24246-1

124.64 quarterly

N. Nav. 296
(June 1928)

REPORT OF LEAVE OF ABSENCE
(SEE INSTRUCTIONS BELOW)

Composite Squadron Thirty Eight — July 28, 1943
(Ship or Station) (Date)

From: Commander, Composite Squadron Thirty Eight.
(Commanding Officer)

To: BUREAU OF NAVIGATION, NAVY DEPARTMENT.

Subject: { Report of leave of absence.
~~Report of authorized delay counting as leave of absence.~~

In conformity with requirements of U. S. Navy Regulations, I report the following leave of absence taken by:

LARSON, William R. — Lieut. AVN, USNR — 83169
(Name, surname first) (Rank and corps) (Signal number)

under orders of Commanding Officer, dated June 23, 1943

NOTE.—Use either (*a*) or (*b*). Do not use both for same leave.

(*a*) Leave: Total number of days, *including* any travel time (7)

(*b*) Delay counting as leave or leave between stations: Total number of days, *excluding* preparation period of 4 days and *excluding* allowance for travel time from old to new station via shortest usually traveled route ______

Commencing with June 25, 1943 (See instructions)
Expiring with July 1, 1943 (See instructions)
} Insert inclusive dates to agree with number of days leave.

C.E. BRUNTON, Comdr., USN.
(Signature of Commanding Officer)

INSTRUCTIONS

1. The day of departure from station or duty counts as a day of duty; the day of return as a day of leave. This refers to leave taken when not detached from ship or station (see Article 1727, Navy Regulations).
2. In cases of authorized delay counting as leave, this form should be submitted in *addition* to the B-slip form.
3. This report will be made at expiration of leave by the immediate superior of the officer to whom the leave is granted and forwarded immediately to the Navy Department (Bureau of Navigation). Care must be taken to insure that correct number of days of leave is reported and corresponds with the inclusive dates reported.

4—6271

VC38/P18/MM

COMPOSITE SQUADRON THIRTY EIGHT
FLEET POST OFFICE
SAN FRANCISCO, CALIFORNIA

CEB/jph

June 23, 1943

From: Commander, Composite Squadron Thirty Eight.
To : **Lieutenant W.R. LARSON, AVN, USNR.**

Subject: Leave.

1. You are hereby granted Seven days leave.

2. You have given as your leave address: **Leamington Hotel, Oakland, Calif.**

3. Any change in the above address shall be promptly reported to your commanding officer.

4. You have stated that you have sufficient funds to defray all expenses incurred while on this leave.

5. You are not entitled to incure any expense for medicine or medical treatment that may be made the basis of a claim against the navy department. Should you become ill while on leave you shall report the time, place and extent of such illiness to your commanding officer and necessary instructions will be issued you.

6. You are informed that a request for extension of leave must be addressed to your commanding officer and not to the navy department or any other activity. Such extension shall be requested only in an emergency.

7. You shall report the commencement and expiration of this leave to the officer-of-the-day, who will enter hereon in ink the hour and date of departure and the hour and date of return from leave.

8. You are instructed not to divulge the location of any U.S. Naval vessels or unit to any unauthorized persons.

C.E. BRUNTON.

Time departed ______ date ______ SIGNATURE ______
Time returned ______ DATE ______ SIGNATURE ______

NOTE: You are warned that transportation facilities are very uncertain and that failure to return on time due to transportation difficulties will not be accepted as an excuse.

L19 (PEDC)
SERIAL (1410)
hmp

NAVAL UNIT
Personal Effects Distribution Center
Clearfield, Utah

27 July 1944
(Date)

(Deceased)

Subj: LARSON, William R., Lieut., A-V(N), USNR.
Inventory of Personal Effects; Certified copy of.

1. An inventory of the subject's personal effects was held this date and consists of the following items as listed hereon. These effects have been turned over to the Supply Officer for shipment to next of kin,
Mr. Olaf M. Larson, (Father)
Hanks, North Dakota.

CLOTHING

1 Belt, webb
1 Belt, leather
1 Cap, officer, complete
1 Cap, overseas, green
1 Cap, aviators
1 Coveralls, green
28 Handkerchiefs
1 pr. Overshoes, rubber
1 Robe, bath
5 Shirts, khaki
1 pr. Shoes, brown, low
1 pr. Sneakers
20 pr. Socks, black
4 pr. Socks, brown
1 pr. Socks, green
1 Tie, black
6 Trousers, khaki
1 Trunks, swim
8 Undershirts
22 Undershorts

MISCELLANEOUS

1 Bag, containing: (fishing line & fishing equipment)
1 Band, wrist watch
3 Bars, soap
1 Belt, money
1 Board, cribbage
1 pkg. Blades, razor
1 Book, address
1 Book, prayer
1 Box, stationery
1 Bracelet, souvenir
2 Brushes, hair
1 Can, peanuts
1 Can, powder, antiseptic
2 Cans, powder, talc.
2 decks Cards, playing
1 bdl. Correspondence
2 Covers, pillow
1 bdl. Drawings
5 Envelopes, stamped airmail 6¢
2 Kits, leather, toilet
1 Knife, pocket
2 pr. Laces, shoe
1 Lighter, cigarette
1 Mat, floor, souvenir
1 Pad, knee
4 Pencils, lead
1 Photo
1 Pipe
1 Plate, leather, name
12 Postcards
5 Postcards, stamped 1¢

-1-

L19 (PEDC) NAVAL UNIT
SERIAL(1410) Personal Effects Distribution Center
hmp Clearfield, Utah

27 July 1944
(Date)

Subj: (Deceased)
LARSON, William R., Lieut., A-V(N), USNR.
Inventory of Personal Effects; Certified copy of.

CLOTHING

NOTE: Following items were unaccounted for as listed on inventory by Composite Squadron THIRTY-EIGHT (38) dated 3 January 1944

22 Shirts, white
1 Combination Rain & Topcoat
1 Khaki, cover, cap
1 Negative
1 Band, watch

MISCELLANEOUS

1 Purse, coin, containing: (1 token, 3 foreign coins, 1 marine emblem, 1 (Lt.) collar bar, 1 pr. small gold navy wings.)
1 Razor, safety & case
1 Sharpener, razor blade
1 Sheet, music
15 Snapshots
2 Springs, steel
3 Stamps 3¢
5 Stamps, airmail 6¢
1 pkg. Stationery
1 Thread, spool
1 Towel
3 Tubes, lypsyl
5 Tubes, shaving cream

A. V. Zaccor

A. V. ZACCOR,
Lieut. Comdr., USN(Ret.),
Officer in Charge.

cc: BuPers (Casualties & Allotments)
Mr. Olaf M. Larson
File

-2-

FINDING OF FACTS

1. R4D-5 airplane, Bu. #12432, operating under the control of South Pacific Combat Air Transport Command, took off from Tontouta, New Caledonia, at about 1338 local time, 27 December 1943, bound for Espiritu Santo, New Hebrides, on an authorized flight, and has been missing since about 1424 local time, 27 December 1943.

2. The engineering records show the airplane and engines were in satisfactory mechanical condition.

3. The airplane was properly serviced and equipped.

4. The entire flight crew was experienced in this type of aifcraft, and eachmember was qualified to perform the duties required of him.

5. Flying conditions along the route were average. A local thrunderstorm existed in the vicinity of Uvea Is. about 1400 local time, 27 December 1943.

6. The flight of this plane was properly guarded by radio and radar shore facilities.

7. The lost plane procedure and lost plane search were properly carried out.

8. According to the records of the South Pacific Combat Air Transport Command, the following Naval personnel were authorized by proper Naval authority to be, and were, on board the missing airplane when it departed from Tontouta;

SPEER, K.R. Lt. USNR VC-24
PARKER, G. G. Lt. USNR VC-24
BELTZ, W.H. ARM2c USNR VC-24
DAUGHERTY, WL.ARM2c USNR VC-24
D'HYNVETTERS, J.J. ARM2c USNR VC-24
LUBY, W.E. ARM2c USNR VC-24
NELSON, M.H. ARM2c USNR VC-24
SPANGLER, EL. ARM2c USNR VC-24
STORM, F.J. ARM1c USNR VC-24
SUTTON, F.J. ARM2c USNR VC-24
WERNER, J.E. ARM2c USNR VC-24
FULLER, E.B. ARM2c USNR VC-24
FENTON, L.H. ARM2c USNR VC-24
LITTLE, J.R. Lt. Comdr. USNR VC24
KAFER, A.C. Lt. USNR VC-24
MACKIE, N.W. Lt. USNR VC-24
WINTER, D.E. Lt. USNR VC-24
LARSON, W.R. Lt. USNR VC-24
BOOSTRA, O.B. ARM2c USNR VC-24

OPINION

1. That R4D airplane number 12432 crashed into the sea and sank at approximately latitude 20o 50' South and longitude 166o 15' East,on the afternoon of 27 December1943.

2. That every person in the aircraft was killed as a result of this crash, and that death occurred in line of duty and was not the result of his own misconduct.

3. That the wreckage discovered about noon on 28 Dec. 1943, in the vicinity of the last reported position of plane No. 12432 was part of this airplane.

4. That, from the board's examination of the wreckage, a fire existed in the crew's compartment and the cargo-passenger space of the airplane some time during the last few minutes before it crashed.

5. That the cause of the accident is not apparent from the facts available to the board, and, therefore responsibility for the loss of the airplane cannot be fixed.

"Finished File, Casualties
and Allotments Section"

Finding of Facts Document – Received from National Personnel Records Center March 2014

FROM: VC 38 PERS-53512-WRL (PACIFIC)

ACTION: SECNAV

INFO: CNO BUPERS BUAER COMSOPAC CINCPAC COMAIRPAC COMAIRSOPAC COMFAIRSOUTH COMSERVPAC

DATE: 11 JAN 1944 12-27-43

LARSON, William Rudolph, Lieut., AVN USNR 83169. MISSING UNDER CIRCUMSTANCES THAT WARRANT THE PRESUMPTION OF DEATH, WHILE RETURNING FROM LEAVE IN AUSTRALIA . WAS MANIFESTED PASSENGER IN SO PAC AAIR TRANSPORT PLANE ON REGULAR OPERATIONAL FLIGHT FROM TONTOUTA NEW CALEDONIA TO ESPIRITU SANTO NEW HERBEDIES. DEPARTED 1338 L DEC 27 1943. LAST RADIO CONTACT 1350 L. LOCATION ESTABLISHED 1424 OFF SOUTH TIP UVEA ISLAND LOYALTY GROUP. SECRET DISPATCH REPORTED WRECKAGE AT 20 DEG 30 MIN SO 166 DEG 15 MIN EAST CONSISTING OF PILOTS LOG BOOK SIGNED BY E L SPANGLER, THERMOS JUG MARKED VMJ, RED RUDDER AILERON BATON , BURNED WOOD, WOOD PAINTED SILVER WITH WORD OXYGEN PAINTED IN BLACK LETTERS. NATIVES SAY THEY HEARD ENGINES ABOUT 1500L.ON GOING TO BEACH THEY SAW PLANE IN A SPIN. THEY DID NOT GO OUT TO WRECKAGE AS THEY ESTIMATED THE DISTANCE ABOUT 10 MILES. NO SURVIVO TO THIS TIME. LINE OF DUTY NO MISCONDUCT.

NOK OLAF M LARSON HANKS NORTH DAKOTA. FATHER NOT NOTIFIED.

PAY 366.00 BENEF: UNKNOWN INSL 10,000.00 PREMIUMS PAID THRU DEC 1943.

LOG # 3355

NOK WERE NOTIFIED BY BUPERS ON 3 JAN 1944

Secret Dispatch Report of Wreckage – Received from National Personnel Records Center March 2014

List of USNR & USMCR Casualties
R4D-5 Airplane (Bureau #12432)
Flight of December 27 1943

First Name	Middle	Last	Rank	Service No.	Birth Date	Age	Squadron No.	Home State	Home City	Next of Kin	Additional Info
John	Risse	Little	Lt - Cdr.	77735	5/17/1915	28	VB 98*	Kentucky	Southgate	Son of Clarence and Mable Little, Husband of Mrs. Voris Margaret Little, 256 Linden Ave, Southgate, KY	VFW Post 3186 of Southgate, KY is named in his honor Awarded Distinguished Flying Cross, posthumously
William	Rudolf	Larson	Lt	83169	12/1/1915	28	VC 38	North Dakota	Hanks	Mr. and Mrs. Olaf M. Larson, Hanks ND	VFW Post 6139 of Zahl, ND is named in his honor. Awarded Air Medal, posthumously
Kenneth	Robert	Speer	Lt.	98716	1/2/1920	22	VB 98	California	Tulare County	Wife: Mrs. Jean Douthit Speer, 338 Laurel Drive, Corpus Christi, TX	Awarded Air Medal, posthumously
August	George	Kafer	Lt. (jg)	114600	12/25/1917	26	VB 98	West Virginia	Jane Lew	Mr. and Mrs. John Kafer, PO Box 399, Jane Lew, WV	Awarded Air Medal, posthumously
Norman	William	Mackie	Lt. (jg)	125503	3/12/1920	23	VB 98	Illinois	Chicago	Wife: Mrs. Judith King Mackie, 4840 Lake Park Ave., Chicago, IL	
Donald	Everett	Winters	Lt. (jg)	130333	11/17/1918	25	VB 98	California	Huntington Beach	Stepmother: Sara Ann Winters, 2904 - 17th Street, Huntington Beach CA	Awarded Air Medal, posthumously
Glenn	Guy	Parker	Lt. (jg)	125393	5/4/1920	22	VB 98	District of Columbia		Mr. and Mrs. Glenn Lane Parker, 2706 N.W. 44th St., Washington D.C.	Awarded Air Medal, posthumously
Dirk	Berend	Boonstra	ARM1c	2244120	1/2/1924	19	VB 98	New York	Montrose	Brother: Piet Boonstra, 151 Seward St, Buchanan, NY 10511	
Earl	Brice	Fuller	ARM1c	3000460	2/3/1918	24	VB 98	Wisconsin	Oshkosh	Mr. and Mrs. Earl E Fuller of Oshkosh, WI	Cook-Fuller Post of the American Legion named in his honor
Francis	John	Storm	ARM1c	6464246	4/3/1916	27	VB 98	New Jersey	Jersey City	Brother: Walter J. Storm, 280 Columbia Ave., Jersey City, NJ	
William	Edward	Luby	ARM2c	6420289	7/14/1918	25	VB 98	Connecticut	Wallingford	Father: Mr. William Barnard Luby, PO Box 387, Wallingford, CT Sister: Anna May Luby, 20 Christian St., Wallington, CT	
Mauritz	Henry	Nelson	ARM2c	6200889			VB 98	Iowa	Forest City	Mr. and Mrs. Henry H. Nelson, Rt4, Forest City, IA	
Edwin, Jr	Lawrence	Spangler	ARM2c	6502443			VB 98	Pennsylvania	York	Mr. and Mrs. Edwin Lawrence Spangler, Sr., 35N Highland Ave, York, PA	
William	Harold	Beltz	ARM2c	6506436			VB 98	Pennsylvania	Philadelphia	Son: Frank Alexander	
Lewis	James	Fenton	ARM2c	6688048			VB 98	Missouri	Bonne Terre	Mr. and Mrs. John W. Fenton, 215 Hillstreet, Bonne Terre, MO	
q	Joseph	D'Huyvetters	ARM2c	6502691			VB 98	Pennsylvania	Easton	Mr. Julius D'Huyvetters, 148 Lincoln St., Easton, PA	
Eugene	Frankline	Sutton	ARM2c	3860564		17	VB 98	California	San Bernardino	Mother: Mrs. Mattie Lee Sutton, 1343 D Street, San Bernardino, CA Brother: Lt. S.L. Sutton - Navy torpedo instructor at Miami, FL Sister: Mrs. Juanita Stepp of San Bernardino, CA	
John	Frederick	Werner	ARM2c	6507082			VB 98	New Jersey	Penns Grove	Wife: Mrs. Christine Elizabeth Werner, 202 Avenue B, Carney's Point, Penns Grove	
William	Leroy	Daugherty	ARM2c	6529394		19	VB 98	Pennsylvania	Butler	Mother: Mrs. Olive Daugherty, Meridian PA	
Reynolds	Hill	Knotts	Captain USMCR	10611	4/24/1916	27	VMJ 153**	Delaware	Wilmington	Mother: Mrs. Mildred Pratt Knotts, 305 W 7th Street, Wilmington, Delaware	Pilot - Awarded Air Medal, posthumously
Louis	White	McCay	MT SGT USMCR	259806	3/3/1918	25	VMJ 153	Florida	Miami	Mother: Mrs. Mable L McCay, 2249 SW 13th Street, Miami FL	Co-Pilot
John	Thomas Jr	Felts	2nd Lt USMCR	26187	10/22/1923	20	VMJ 153	Texas	Clarkville	Father: Mr. John T. Felts Sr., Box 625, Clarksville, TX	Navigator
James	Guernsey	Duignan	SGT USMCR	450996	3/3/1922	21	VMJ 153	New York	Brewster	Father: Mr. Henry E Duignan, Old Turk Hill Rd, Brewster, NY	Radioman
Opal	C.	Hughes	MT SGT USMCR	364813	10/12/1921	22	VMJ 153	Mississippi	Magee	Mr. & Mrs. John W Hughes, Route #1, Magee, MS Sister: Johnye Hughes Johnson	Crew Chief - Mechanic

* Bombing Squadron 98 (VB 98) was part of VC 24. Unit consisted of 18 SBD-5 planes stationed at Munda Airfield in Dec 1943

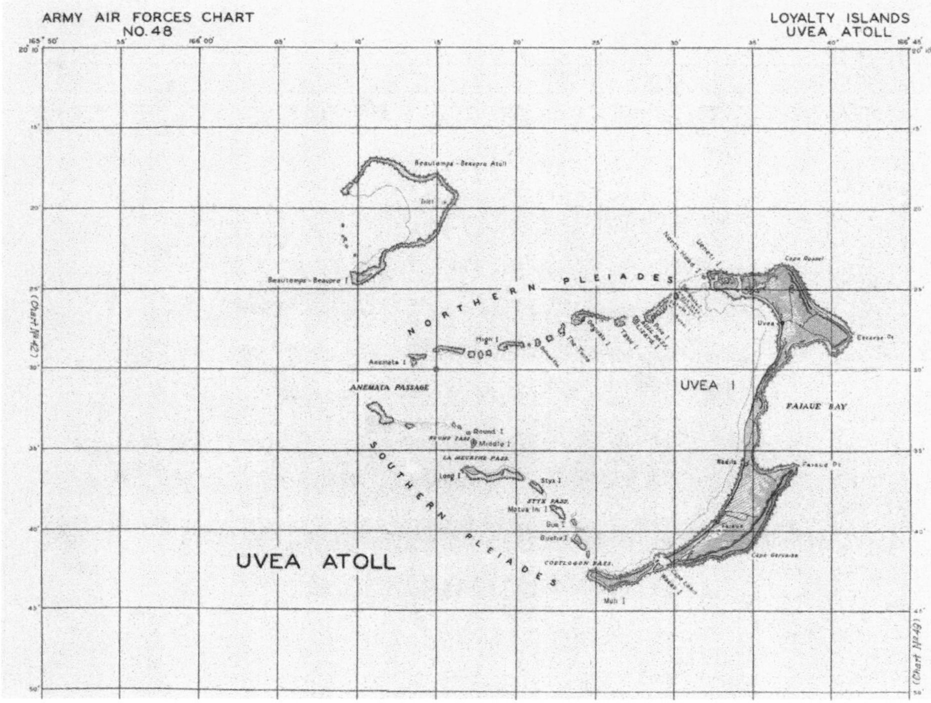

Approximate location of Plane Crash near Uvea Island [Ouvea] – Source: Jean-Paul Mugnier of Fortunes de Mer Caledoniennes

William and Lloyd on "Alley Oop" tractor

Olaf and Lloyd Combining 1941

YOU, TOO, CAN BECOME A SUCCESSFUL LETTER WRITER!

IN TWO EASY LESSONS

LESSON NO. 1:
IF YOU WRITE ABOUT THESE
Your letter will get "thumbs down:"

- The location, identity, movement, or prospective movement of any merchant ship, aircraft, naval vessel, or naval or military force. . . .
- The defensive or offensive forces, weapons, installations or plans of the United States or her allies. . . .
- The production, movement, or supply of munitions, or the location or progress of war industry. . . .
- The routing or employment of any naval or military unit of the United States or her allies.
- The effect of enemy operations, or casualties to personnel or material suffered by the United States or her allies, previous to official publication of such information.
- The criticism of equipment, appearance, physical condition, or morale of the . . . armed forces of the United States or her allies.
- Matter, the dissemination of which might benefit enemy military, economic, or financial interests, or which might interfere with the national effort of, or disparage the foreign relations of, the United States or her allies.

(From Section I, Article 14, Censorship Regulations, U. S. Navy, 1943)

LESSON NO. 2:
IF YOU WRITE ABOUT THESE
Your letter will get "thumbs up:"

- Love.
- Friends, shipmates and relatives, including your mother-in-law, if you have one.
- Entertainment, recreation, sports and the movies.
- Love.
- Education, religion, art, music, books and hobbies.
- Matters of business, personal finances, your plans after the war is won (unless these plans include revenge upon the censors).
- Your personal needs or wants for soap, fruit cake, razor blades or whatnot.
- The latest jokes — but keep them clean enough to stay on the right side of the postal laws.
- Love.

(Prepared by Fleet Chief Censor, U. S. Pacific Fleet)

WRITE HOME OFTEN... BUT WRITE IT RIGHT!

Memorial Marker - Bethany Lutheran Church, Divide County, North Dakota

Appendix C

USS Nashville War Diary April 18 1942 Doolittle Raid

Photo # NH 53289 USAAF B-25B bombers on board USS Hornet for the Doolittle Raid, April 1942

SECRET

WAR DIARY

U.S.S. NASHVILLE

SECRET

Date: Saturday April 18, 1942.

Task Force or Unit: Task Force 16

Enroute to/At // Western Pacific

Operder or Opplan in effect: CincPac Opplan 20-42.

Position	Lat.	Long.	Distance steamed since:	
:0800	35-55N	153-40E	:2000	258
:1200	36-13N	154-11E	:0800	90
:2000	36-08N	157-43E	:1200	158

Made good 1200 to 1200: Course 086 Speed 10.5

Logistics

Fuel expended 38,482 Received Transferred

ENCLOSURES:

NARRATIVE AND REMARKS:

At dawn the NASHVILLE was steaming in company with aircraft carriers ENTERPRISE and HORNET and cruisers NORTHAMPTON, SALT LAKE CITY, and VINCENNES enroute to a point at which the bombers on the HORNET were to be launched. At 0632 the course was 220 T. and speed was 23 knots. At 0741 an enemy ship was sighted bearing 350 relative at a distance of about 10,000 yards. The following is a chronological record of the engagement:

0744 General Quarters sounded.

0748 Enemy ship bore 201 T. at a range of 9,000 yards.

0752 Received order from Admiral Halsey to attack vessel and sink same.

0753 Opened fire with main battery, firing salvo fire at a range of 9,000 yards.

0754 Shifted to rapid fire.

No. 2 of 2 Copies

20

Saturday April 18, 1942.

0755 Checked fire. Target could not be seen.

0756 Resumed firing. Bombing planes made attack on enemy vessel. The returned the fire of the planes with machine guns and a light cannon.

0757 Enemy headed toward the NASHVILLE

0801 Bombing planes made another attack on enemy ship. This fire returned by the enemy.

0804 Opened fire. This fire was returned but enemy shells fell short.

0809 Bombing planes made another attack. Changed course to the left in order to close the enemy.

0814 Increased speed to 25 knots.

0819 Commenced firing salvo fire.

0821 Steadied on course 095 T. Enemy vessel on fire.

0823 Enemy ship sunk.

0827 Commenced maneuvering to pick up survivors. Attempts to rescue one man sighted proved unsuccessful.

0846 Went to 25 knots to rejoin formation.

0847 Set material condition Baker.

0857 Set the watch in condition of readiness II.

1102 Sighted Task Force bearing 235 T.

1153 Resumed station in formation.

During this engagement 938 rounds of 6" ammunition were expended due to the difficulty in hitting the small target with the heavy swells that were running and the long range at which fire was opened. This range was used in order to silence the enemy's radio as soon as possible. The ship sunk was a Japanese patrol boat and was

No. 2 of 2 copies.

Saturday April 18, 1942.

equipped with radio and anti-aircraft machine guns.

During the encounter with the craft the Army bombers carried on the HORNET were launched to make their attack on Tokyo. When the NASHVILLE rejoined the formation the ships had reversed course and were steaming on course 092T. at 25 knots.

During the afternoon the following action took place:

1409 Went to General Quarters, OTC having ordered this ship to sink two Japanese sampans reported by aircraft.

1411 Sighted ship bearing 350, range 10,700 yards.

1415 Dive bombers made attack on enemy.

1417 Planes made second attack on enemy; their fire was returned by the enemy.

1422 Opened fire with main battery firing salvo fire at range of 4,500 yards.

1424 Checked fire.

1425 Resumed fire.

1427 Checked fire.

1429 Opened fire with 5" battery.

1435 Checked fire.

1439 Opened fire with main battery.

1440 Ceased fire as vessel was sinking. Prepared to pick up survivors.

1446 Enemy vessel sank. Five survivors were seen. These men were all picked up by this ship. All but one were uninjured and suffered only from shock and immersion.

1500 Picked up last survivor and began maneuvering to rescue pilot and passenger of ENTERPRISE plane which crashed in water astern of ship.

No. 2 of 2 copies 22

Saturday April 18, 1942.

1517 Rescued two fliers.

1518 Commenced maneuvering to rejoin formation.

The second ship sunk was a patrol craft similar to the first. 65 rounds of 5" ammunition and 102 rounds of main battery ammunition were used in this engagement.

No. 2 of 2 copies.

W.A.B.
23

SECRET

U.S.S. NASHVILLE

CL43/A16-3/(0845)

~~CONFIDENTIAL~~

At sea,
April 21, 1942.

From: Commanding Officer.
To: Commander in Chief Pacific Fleet.
Via: Commander Task Force SIXTEEN.
Commander Task Group 16.2 (ComCruDiv FIVE).
Subject: Report of Sinking of Two Enemy Patrol Boats on 18 April, 1942.

References: (a) Article 712, U.S. Navy Regulations.
(b) Article 874(5), U.S. Navy Regulations.
(c) CTF-16 Cruising Instructions, Serial 0127 of 12 April, 1942.
(d) NASHVILLE 180300 of April to CTF-16.

Enclosure: (A) Report of Gunnery Officer.

1. On 18 April this vessel sank two enemy (Japanese) motor patrol vessels pursuant to orders received by signal from the Commander Task Force SIXTEEN. The circumstances were as follows:

2. The first vessel was sunk by 6-inch gunfire in latitude 35-50 N, longitude 153-40 E at 0823 (zone minus 10 time). It probably was a steel vessel of conventional fishing-sampan type, about 70 feet long, name unknown. It was equipped with radio, machine guns and a small cannon. It apparently had escaped the notice of our air patrol and was first sighted at about 0741 from this vessel, on a bearing about 350 degrees, relative to the base course (220, true), distance about 16,000 yards from the disposition guide (HORNET). It was reported by flag hoist at about 0745; permission to open fire was requested by flag hoist at 0750; orders to sink it were received by TBS and flags at 0752; fire was opened at 0753. Two survivors were reported in the water but neither could be recovered. The Commanding Officer personally saw only one who apparently was wounded and sank before he could be reached.

3. The second vessel was sunk by 6-inch and 5-inch gunfire in latitude 36-21 N, longitude 155-14 E, at 1446. It was a wooden vessel (name unknown) about 90 feet long with a clipper bow, painted generally black but with a white deck house which when first seen was mistaken for a white flag. The vessel was first sighted and reported by planes, and at 1409 we were directed by TBS to sink it and also another one located about 15,000 yards on our port beam. We left the formation at 1409 and at 1411 sighted the vessel, bearing 020 true, distant 9,000 yards. Fire was withheld to close the range, for reasons discussed in par. 9. Meanwhile, the supposed white flag had been reported by TBS; and soon after we were told by TBS to take prisoners and then sink the vessel if practicable, otherwise to sink it without delay; and to remain in sight contact of the Task Force. The latter was then distant about 18,000 yards, and although then on an approaching course recovering planes, was expected soon to take up a retiring course at 25 knots. Also the enemy vessel was firing at planes attacking it. The decision therefore was made to sink first and recover survivors if time permitted. At 1424 fire was opened, and at 1434 the vessel was seen to be sinking. At about 1446, just as she sank, we recovered 5 survivors and proceeded to rejoin. From the

- 1 -

24

C-O-N-F-I-D-E-N-T-I -L U.S.S. NASHVILLE

CL43/A16-3/(045) April 21, 1942.

Subject: Report of Sinking of Two Enemy Patrol Boats on 18 April, 1942. (Continued).

- -

survivors it was ascertained by the sign language that the original crew had totalled eleven. Presumably the names of the prisoners and also of those lost can be obtained from the survivors by a Japanese interpreter. The other enemy patrol vessel was not seen, but the ENTERPRISE pilot, whom we rescued soon afterward, said he had set it on fire and believed he had sunk it. Search for it therefore was abandoned.

4. The circumstances outlined above are in themselves trivial, but they served as the bases of several observations and conclusions which are believed of practical value. These are outlined in following paragraphs.

5. The proper procedure of a screening vessel, in a situation such as our contact with the first patrol vessel, could be included with advantage in reference (c) or in special instructions for an operation. The Commanding Officer now feels that he would have been justified in closing and firing on the vessel at once without awaiting permission, in order to destroy its radio; but it would have been helpful if such a directive had existed.

6. Ammunition expenditure. To sink the first vessel required 928 rounds of 6-inch ammunition, of which 13 rounds had to be expended in clearing loaded guns after the action. Expenditure of 915 rounds to sink a sampan appears ridiculous, and obviously was excessive; but in this instance was not wholly inexcusable, for the following reasons:

(a) In the circumstances, immediate destruction of the vessel's radio was of vital interest. This appeared to justify immediate opening of fire, as the sighting range was only about 15,000 yards.

(b) The vessel received effective protection from heavy swells then running, and apparently escaped serious injury for a long time. The radio room reports hearing transmissions on 393 kcs, believed to have been from the enemy vessel, which did not stop until 27 minutes after we first opened fire.

(c) There was no external evidence of damage to the ship until 29 minutes after we opened fire, and fire was ceased one minute later when it was apparent that she was sinking rapidly.

7. The Commanding Officer, who has been closely associated with small-calibre gunnery over many years, does not attribute our failure to hit to poor spotting, poor pointing or poor control. These all looked reasonably good from the ship, although the comments of the pilots of planes who were diving on the ship, requested in reference (d), should throw light on the subject. Delay in hitting probably was a consequence of protection given by the swells, which had a height from crest to trough of about 20 feet; rapid and appreciable vertical movement of the target imparted by the swells; and luck. The Commanding Officer finally realized he would have to close, and also to bring the target to bear along the direction of the troughs instead of nearly at right angles to them, in order to hit.

25

C-O-N-F-I-D-E-N-T-I-A-L U.S.S. NASHVILLE

CL43/A16-3/(045) April 21, 1942.

Subject: Report of Sinking of Two Enemy Patrol Boats on 18 April, 1942. (Continued).

---

8. The heavy ammunition expenditure can be attributed to the above-described difficulty in hitting, plus inexperience in gunnery under the existing sea conditions, which never are even approached in peace-time gunnery. By difficulty in hitting is not meant difficulty or inaccuracy in gun laying and turret training, since our automatic control system took care of these well, in spite of considerable motion of this ship; but rather to our initial failure to realize the wastefulness of continuous fire under such sea conditions. With a rate of fire approaching 150 shots per minute, many were wasted during long intervals while the target was shielded by swells. After we realized this and used salvo fire, there was less wastage. Another point is the difficulty of realizing the enormous volume of fire which these ships deliver with "continuous fire". Six minutes of continuous fire would account for our total expenditure. We actually fired in bursts, over a total period of about 30 minutes; and in retrospect this also is difficult to realize. It is evident that the Commanding Officer of a ship of this type must keep ammunition expenditure constantly in mind.

9. In sinking the second ship only 102 rounds of 6-inch and 65 rounds of 5-inch were expended. Applying lessons from the first experience, we closed to a hitting range before commencing fire (by that time it was known that the first ship had gotten off radio report) and took a position along the troughs. The 5-inch were used to conserve 6-inch ammunition and to give experience to the 5-inch battery, but only the second of these objects was attained, as the 5-inch muzzle velocity was too low for a target moving 20 feet vertically with the swells. Only one or two 5-inch hits were made.

10. Wind shields came off many 6-inch projectiles, close to the ship. The Gunnery Officer estimates these at 5 percent.

11. The Gunnery Officer's report is enclosed. It should be of value to the Bureau of Ordnance and to other ships of this type, and the question of its promulgation to them is raised.

12. Diving by planes against a target under gun fire. ENTERPRISE planes were attacking the first vessel, and planes from one of the carriers were attacking the second vessel, during the time we were firing. This was rendered hazardous by the erratic performance of projectiles which lost their wind shields, and by very low dives of the planes. Pulling out at a greater height is recommended. Many dives were to within 100 feet of the water or less.

13. Recovery of survivors. The five prisoners taken from the second ship were brought aboard over the forecastle, and this same method was soon afterward used effectively and expeditiously (13 minutes from crash to rescue) in getting aboard two aviators from a crashed plane. For these reasons, and in view of the sea conditions, the following description is considered of probable interest.

- 3 - 26

C-O-N-F-I-D-E-N-T-I-A-L U.S.S. NASHVILLE

CL43/A16-3/(045) April 21, 1942.

Subject: Report of Sinking of Two Enemy Patrol Boats on 18 April, 1942. (Continued).

- -

14. In rescuing the survivors of the patrol vessel, approach was made from up wind. The men were well clustered, and on reaching them the heading was changed slightly to the left, to bring them under the starboard bow which became the lee bow. They were thrown lines, and were brought aboard with these lines and also over a sea ladder comprised of a cargo net one of which is permanently stopped to our life lines on each side of the forecastle. The ship drifted down wind faster than the men, and so brought them all gradually within reach. One was wounded and another virtually exhausted, yet all were recovered without great difficulty although the ship was rolling heavily. She soon fell off into the trough of the sea, and the actual rescues were effected while lying in the trough.

15. Realizing from this that she usually would fall off into the trough, we did not wait to approach the aviators from up wind but simply brought them under the lee bow while heading along the troughs. Both aviators came aboard over the cargo net.

16. There was some confusion on the forecastle, together with difficulty in locating quickly the proper gear for effecting rescue. While the confusion resulted partly from curiosity to see the survivors, it was a consequence also of the ship's being still at general quarters, so that normal administrative arrangements on the forecastle were lacking, as were good communications. For these reasons, and since future war-time rescues over the forecastle appear not improbable, a special Rescue Bill is being developed to meet such occurrences. This will be a General Quarters bill, with the Gunnery Officer detailing personnel from forward turrets or a 5-inch battery and providing battle-telephone communications from a turret. Necessary gear will be made up and stowed in convenient locations on the main deck in the vicinity of the 5-inch guns.

F. S. Craven

Copies (extra), herewith: 12.

27

U.S.S. NASHVILLE

CONFIDENTIA .

April 19, 1942.

REPORT BY GUNNERY OFFICER ON FIRING AT JAPANESE PATROL BOATS ON 18 April, 1942.

- -

GENERAL AND FIRE CONTROL, FIRST ACTION.

At 0720, 18 April, sighted small Fishing or Observation vessel of about 60 - 100 tons on the port bow. The Task Force was at this time approximately 600 miles off the Japanese coast. The sea was rough with a heavy swell from Northwest. The ship was in Condition of Readiness II. General Quarters was sounded and commence firing ordered at 0750, opening range 9000. The target was quickly crossed and continuous fire was ordered; course converging; range about 8000. Fire was soon checked as the target was totally obscured by splashes. The target reappeared and continuous fire was resumed. This procedure was repeated several times and each time the enemy emerged from the splashes apparently undamaged. It is inconceivable that he was not hit. Meanwhile the range was closing and the heavy swells at times obscured the entire target, except the mast tops. At this point it became painfully apparent that by reason of the flat trajectory and the screening effect of the swells many projectiles were hitting wave tops short of the target. Fire was checked and the ship swung to port to bring the turrets to bear to starboard. The Gunnery Officer and Spot I agreed that deliberate salvos would produce more effective results. Fire was reopened with gun range of about 4500 yards. This fire was effective and the vessel sank after the third salvo.

There was much motion on the ship during the action. This produced extreme values of level and cross-level in continuous fire which tended to increase the pattern in range and deflection. With the guns in automatic, the heavy roll at times brought them up full against their depression stops which greatly increased the pattern size in continuous fire. In many cases the turrets were shifted to local in elevation and firing circuits opened under the above conditions but in others the fire continued. Firing at maximum depression places the deck lugs under severe stress and should not be resorted to under conditions such as obtained in these actions. Conditions above together with the interference of projectile flight by wave crests, tended to give an exaggerated idea of the pattern size, not confirmed in salvo fire. In the latter case the patterns were normal and tight.

MATERIAL AND PERSONNEL.

Personnel behaved in the accepted tradition demonstrating coolness and ability. Material performed perfectly with minor exceptions. The many drills held in Ammunition Supply bore noble fruit. In no case was there any delay in supplying shells or powder to the guns. In this connection there were 4000 rounds of 6-inch powder and shell aboard at the start of the action. 75% of this was immediately available. No shellman or powderman in any station showed evidence of hindering fatigue when the action was closed. Magazine personnel requested fresh air in the after magazines after approximately 30 minutes of supplying powder.

C-O-N-F-I-D-E-N-T-I-A-L U.S.S. NASHVILLE

April 19, 1942.

REPORT BY GUNNERY OFFICER ON FIRING AT JAPANESE PATROL BOATS ON 18 April, 1942 (Continued).

- -

AMMUNITION

928 rounds were expended. It is well realized that this is an excessive expenditure of ammunition considering the target and the importance of conserving the supply during protracted cruises in war-time. In this instance however valuable lessons were learned which are considered to justify this seemingly extravagant use of so large a percentage of the available supply. First and most important continuous fire was ordered in attempt to hit him quickly and hard, so as to disable his radio. By so doing, information of our primary mission would have been denied the enemy at home. Unfortunately he was able to use his radio and thus gave warning of the presence of the Task Force. Second, although frequent check fires were ordered, there was no lull as such. Shellmen and powdermen who had handled 75-80 rounds showed no evidence of fatigue. Finally it has been demonstrated that the method of ammunition supply for this type ship is satisfactory and adequate. There were few misfires, even in the drill service.

PROJECTILES

It is believed at least 5% of projectiles fired threw windshields in flight. Probably seven others came off while loading, of which some were fired. These "shorts" (unshielded projectiles) appeared erratic in flight and undoubtedly increased the pattern size out of proportion to that expected. NASHVILLE has no dye in 6" projectiles but those vessels so equipped are faced with a definite impediment in the gun room from loose dye. I do not consider the proper solution to be in more careful loading or gentler handling of projectiles, but feel that the windshields should be fixed more firmly to the bourrelet, either by spot welding or screw threads. Some corrective action is necessary.

SECOND ACTION

At about 1430 the same day another small vessel was sighted. Range was closed to 6000 and fire commenced. The second and subsequent salvos hit, and she was sinking after the fifth. The 5" battery (port) fired 63 rounds but hits were few due to wave crests. 102 6-inch rounds were expended in the second action. 5 survivors were recovered.

TARGETS, BOTH ACTIONS

The first target was of metal construction, the second of wood. In each case it is believed that many hits were made which completely pierced the vessels but did not explode. This would account for their phenominal ability to stay afloat even if holed several times at the water line. In the case of the second target, her whole starboard side was riddled before she finally sank. It may be that the 6"/47 projectile is not designed to explode on contact with such light weight construction. (Bureau comment is requested).

C-O-N-F-I-D-E-N-T-I-A-L U.S.S. NASHVILLE

April 19, 1942.

REPORT BY GUNNERY OFFICER ON FIRING AT JAPANESE PATROL BOATS ON 18 April, 1942 (Continued).

CONCLUSIONS AND RECOMMENDATIONS

CONCLUSIONS

1. In heavy weather avoid using continuous fire unless the target is large and presents a good background. Selected level, or selected director fire on the down roll, is recommended.

2. Radar ranging is not satisfactory against small targets when frequently obscured by swells.

3. Ammunition can be supplied to all turrets as fast as required until it becomes necessary to clear empties.

4. Case ejection from turret three is definitely unsatisfactory at medium ranges. It was frequently necessary to check fire and elevate the guns to clear the cartridges. Two men outisde are not sufficient; at least three are required.

5. Deflection spreads are feasible and useful in opening salvos. They were used in both actions. They were produced by setting convergence-range a predetermined amount.

6. Director in automatic in heavy weather causes increased dispersion in deflection.

RECOMMENDATIONS

1. Provide better method of securing windshields to bourrelets of 6-inch projectiles. I consider 5% windshield failures as too high. (Bureau comment requested).

2. Improve case ejection to turret three. It should be positive at all angles of elevation. (PHILADELPHIA arrangement may be satisfactory. PHILADELPHIA and Bureau comment requested).

3. Increase 6-inch ammunition to 4000 rounds for ships of the type. It can be stowed (BROOKLYN Class) so that 75% is immediately available. We stowed it, without difficulty.

4. Avoid leaving cartridges in extremely hot guns. It was discovered after the morning action (all guns loaded) that in most cases when the cartridge was removed the cork adhered to the base of the projectile. This of course definitely puts the gun out of action until the cork is cut away or the projectile backed out. After the action is concluded it is recommended that loaded guns always be cleared immediately through the muzzles.

5. Provide gun counters for all quick firing guns. NASHVILLE has installed counters purchased from 10 cent store. With two exceptions they worked perfectly, thus providing quick count of ammunition expended.

- 3 -

ENCLOSURE (A) OF NASHVILLE SERIAL CL43/A16-3/(045) of April 21, 1942. 30

C-O-N-F-I-D-E-N-T-I-A-L U.S.S. NASHVILLE

April 19, 1942.

REPORT BY GUNNERY OFFICER ON FIRING AT JAPANESE PATROL BOATS ON 18 April, 1942 (Continued).

GENERAL

As an item of interest to the forces afloat and ships of this type, a brief summary sheet of each turret and important control station is included herewith.

W. KIRTEN, jr.

ENCLOSURE (A) OF NASHVILLE SERIAL CL43/A16-3/(045) of April 21, 1942.

31

SECRET WAR DIARY SECRET

U.S.S. NASHVILLE

Date: Sunday April 19, 1942.

Task Force or Unit: Task Force 16 Enroute to/At // Pearl Harbor, T.H.

Oporder or Opplan in effect: CincPac Opplan 20-42

Position :0800 Lat. Long.
:1200 Lat. Long.
:2000 Lat. Long.

Distance steamed since :0800 :2000 313
:0800 :1200 62
:1200 144

Made good 1200 to 1200: Course 086 Speed 22.2 kts.

Logistics
Fuel expended 76,478 Received Transferred

ENCLOSURES:

NARRATIVE AND REMARKS: Sighted destroyers of own force bearing 040 T. distance about 10 miles. Completed rendezvous with destroyers BALCH, FANNING, BENHAM, GWIN, GRAYSON, and MEREDITH and formed formation 7-V. NASHVILLE took station 2300. Proceeded on course 090 T. at 20 knots ENTERPRISE aircraft maintained scouting and inner air patrols.

B.H.

No. 2 of 2 Copies 45

Photo # NH 53293 B-25Bs parked on board USS Hornet during the Doolittle Raid. April 1942

Aft flight deck of USS Hornet while en route to the launching point of the Doolittle Raid – USS Gwin & USS Nashville nearby.

Nito Maru on Fire and Sinking (Source: S Bustin)

USS Nashville Firing at Japanese Picket Ships November 18, 1944 (Source: S Bustin)

Japanese Prisoner from sunk picket ship on Doolittle Raid – the 2nd Japanese POW of WW II
(Source: Steven Bustin, Author of Humble Heroes, How the USS Nashville CL43 Fought WW II)

SOC Planes on Catapults

USS Nashville during the Doolittle Raid (Source: National Archives phono no. 19-LCM-271-28412)

APPENDIX D

Lucky's Flight to Tanaga

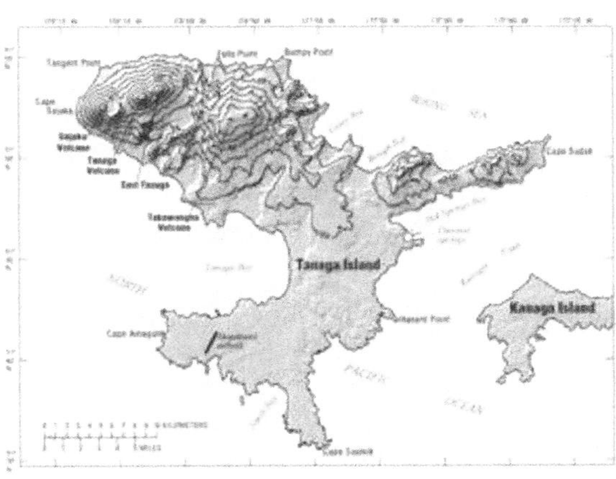

We were catapulted for Kuluk Bay at 1630 on August 31, 1942. Bearing and distance Kuluk Bay was given as 196 and 122 miles, wind was 18 kts from 135°T.

The wind was picking up rapidly and the weather was closing in more and more the closer we got to the islands. At about 1800 we spotted a small island to our right. Visibility had decreased to approximately ¾ of a mile. I believed this island to be Great Sitkin (later identified as Bobrof Is.), so swung southwestward. In about seven minutes we sighted land again – we followed the coastline of this island and went completely around it in about one hour. Meanwhile we landed once or twice in an attempt to get our position. Flying conditions were exceedingly poor – we bounced around like a rubber ball in a washing machine, and we passed through rain squalls every few minutes.

As my gas was getting low and it was getting dark I decided to sit down in the first bay I could find. We landed about 2015 with 30 gallons gasoline remaining. The beach was covered with huge rocks which formed a white wall of breakers as the swells came in.

We anchored some distance from shore. As the anchor dragged, I had to start the motor several times to keep the plane from being dashed to pieces on the rocks. We had spotted a small cabin on the beach, so I sent my radio-man Schledwitz ashore to investigate on the morning of the 1st. He inflated the life raft by hand pump and got ashore without much trouble.

Schledwitz reported finding two names written on the wall of this cabin – "North End Bay" and "Hot Springs Bay." In the meantime I had studied the charts carefully and checked my navigation. I concluded that this must be Hot Springs Bay on the Island of Tanaga.

I told Schledwitz to return to the plane. He was quite a way down-wind from the plane. Schledwitz got out in the raft and rowed for at least 30 minutes without gaining a foot in the direction of the plane. I motioned him back on the beach and told him to relaunch upwind. Schledwitz threw the life-raft on his back and proceeded to stumble his way over the rocks to gain a more favorable launching position.

After several minutes, I heard a terrific explosion and saw the yellow lift raft disappear. The CO2 bottle on the raft was accidently tripped. The raft, as a result, was blown to bits. Schledwitz threw his arms into the air and shouted "What do I do now?" I suggested building a wooden raft out of the driftwood scattered around the shore-line.

The weather was miserable all day the 1st. Schledwitz spent a good part of the day building a raft. I told him to take his time as I did not intend to take off until the weather cleared. In the evening he launched his raft – which promptly sank to the bottom. He again threw up his arms. I told him to return to the trapper's cabin, build a fire, and stay there all night.

As I did not have enough gasoline to keep starting the plane every so often, and the plane insisted on drifting into precarious positions, I decided on the afternoon of the 1st, to use the free gun as an additional anchor. This worked out very well.

From 2100 on the evening of the 1st to 0300 on the morning of the 2nd, the altimeter dropped 800 feet, indicating a return of normal atmospheric pressure. I was thankful to the Lord for being able, at 0300, to see the moon & stars as the overhead began to break. By 0700 on the morning of the second the sun was shining brightly. Schledwitz fell asleep and did not come out to the beach until about 0800.

We were again faced with the problem of getting Schledwitz to the plane. He offered to attempt swimming. I knew it was exceedingly risky, but it seemed the only way out. I told him to inflate his life jacket and give it a trial. He started out very well, got about half way out to the plane and stopped – completely exhausted. He shouted "Start the plane." I started immediately, dragged anchor, and stopped alongside Schledwitz. I helped him out of the water, and in a few minutes he gained strength enough to get into the rear cockpit. He stripped immediately, rubbed down with a dry towel, and put on some dry clothes which we fortunately had carried along. After smoking a cigarette he began to feel comparatively comfortable again.

I figured that we had gasoline enough to carry us 80-100 miles. If we were right in the assumption that this bay was Hot Springs we had only 44 miles on course 085° to go. I started the plane and attempted to pull anchor as fast as possible. However, I found that I was exceedingly short on patience and strength so decided to cut the line.

We took off at 0905 and landed at Kuluk Bay with 10 gallons gasoline at 0935 – both uttering a prayer of thanks. Schledwitz[1] suffered many discomforts during the experience but other than a head cold, apparently sustained no seriously ill effects.

[1] Raymond John Schledwitz was born August 14, 1921 in Colorado, and died July 3, 1970. He served in both WWII and Korea. He is buried at the Memphis National Cemetery.

USS Nashville War Diary for September 4, 1944 reporting recovery of Lucky's plane at 1207.

SECRET WAR DIARY SECRET

U.S.S. NASHVILLE

Zone Description: Plus 10 Date: September 4, 1942.

Task Force or Unit: ComTaskGroup 8.~~[struck out]~~ Off Adak Island

Oporder or Opplan in effect: ComTaskFor 8 Opplan 10-42.

	:0800 Lat. 53-21.4 N	Long. 174-02.5 W	Distance Steamed since :2000	180.9
Position	:1200 Lat. 53-55.6 N	Long. 175-42 W	:0800	61.0
	:2000 Lat. 53-05 N	Long. 173-29 W	:1200	124.2

Made good 1200 to 1200: Course 175.5 Speed 2.3

LOGISTICS

Fuel expended 26,281 Received -none- Transferred -none-

ENCLOSURES: -none-

NARRATIVE AND REMARKS: Operating in the Bering Sea north of Adak Island in company with the INDIANAPOLIS (SOPA), McCALL, BROOKS and GRIDLEY (TaskGroup 8.6). During the morning friendly aircraft were sighted (PBY, B-24). At 1134 three ships were sighted on the other side of the horizon bearing 152 T. (CUYAMA, WASMUTH, and a destroyer). At 1333 two transports (BELL and ST. MIHIEL) and one destroyer were sighted bearing 070 T., 5½ miles.

At 1207 we recovered our plane sent to Adak two days ago. (Reference to picking up Lucky and crew)

At 1811 a formation of ships was sighted (140 T., 22,000 yards). We left formation at 1910 on orders of ComTaskGroup 8.6 and joined the following ships at 2000; two cruisers, ST. LOUIS, HONOLULU; six destroyers; WATERS, SANDS, DENT, HUMPHREYS, KANE and KING; three cargo ships; STANLEY GRIFFITHS, THOMAS JEFFERSON and NORTH COAST. At the same time the HONOLULU was directed to rejoin Task Group 8.6. The NASHVILLE took charge of the convoy as O.T.C.

Wind was from the SE at 12 knots increasing to 25 knots late in the afternoon. Clouds overhead but good visibility.

No.____of____copies. 6

CL43/P20-1/(088) September 5, 1942

CONFIDENTIAL

From: Commanding Officer.
To: Commander in Chief Pacific Fleet.
Via: Commander Task Force EIGHT.

Subject: Report of excellent judgment and performance of duty by Lieut.(jg) W. R. Larson, A-V(N), USNR, during recent flights.

Reference: (a) NASHVILLE letter CL43/A6-2 of 13 July 1942, on Procedure for recovery of a lost plane in a fog.

Enclosures: (A) Copy of report of Lieut. Larson dated 4 Sept. 1942.
(B) Copy of statement by R. J. Schledwitz, ARM2c.
(C) Copy of reference (a).

1. In the reference the Commanding Officer had occasion to report the recovery of a plane under difficult conditions. An important element in the recovery of the plane was the expert airmanship and good judgement displayed by the pilot, Lieutenant (jg) W. R. Larson, A-V(N), USNR.

2. Now, once again, Lieutenant Larson, through excellent judgment, calmness, resourcefulness and endurance, has saved his plane and perhaps the lives of himself and his radioman. The circumstances are best understood from Enclosures (A) and (B).

3. The anchor which Lieutenant Larson used, to keep his plane off a lee shore during two nights and a day of bad weather, was his free machine gun, the plane's regular anchor having proved ineffective. By sacrificing the gun he saved the plane. He evidently made this decision quickly, since there obviously was little time for delay. It obviously was a difficult decision to anyone familiar with the money value of a machine gun and the Navy's peace-time emphasis upon responsibility for material. That it was a correct decision, reflecting excellent judgment under critical conditions, seems unquestionable.

4. The Commanding Officer believes that these two performances of Lieutenant Larson are worthy of a letter of commendation from the Commander in Chief, since they were largely instrumental in saving valuable aircraft and probably also valuable lives. Such a letter would be of great value to Lieutenant Larson in the event that he requests transfer to the regular Navy, as the Commanding Officer has suggested that he do.

F. S. Craven

U.S.S. NASHVILLE

4 September, 1942

CONFIDENTIAL

From: Lieutenant (jg) W. R. LARSON, A-V(N), USNR.
Commanding Officer.

Subject: Report of difficulties attending flight to ADAK on
31 August 1942.

Schledwitz and I were catapulted at 1630 on August 31 for ADAK. Weather was closing in the closer to land we got. We sighted land at 1200 which I thought to be GREAT SITKIN. Turned west and flew for ten minutes, sighted land again, found nothing familiar. Flew around island; was getting low on gasoline. It also was getting dark, and I landed in first bay I could find, with 30 gallons of gasoline. Dropped anchor 100 yards off shore which was composed of boulders, and breakers were coming in on the beach. Sat in plane all night, getting wet every fifteen minutes. In the morning Schledwitz took the life raft and went ashore and investigated trapper's cabin. He found two names written on wall -- NORTH END BAY and HOT SPRINGS. I checked all navigation, studied the charts, and concluded that this must be TANAGA ISLAND and that this was HOT SPRINGS BAY. Schledwitz's life raft exploded and he was stranded on the beach. He spent all day building a wooden raft out of drift wood. He launched it that evening, and it sank to the bottom, Weather was closed in all day, raining frequently, Schledwitz went back to the cabin, built a fire and stayed all night. During the night the weather cleared. Schledwitz came out early in the morning, inflated his life belt, and started to swim to the plane. He was exhausted half way out. I started plane and picked him up. He put on dry clothes immediately. I could not pull up anchor (free machine-gun), so cut line. Took off immediately on course 085. Landed ADAK with 10 gallons of gasoline.

William R. Larson

ENCLOSURE (A) TO NASHVILLE SERIAL CL43/P20-1/(0SS) of 5 September, 1942.

U.S.S. NASHVILLE

CONFIDENTIAL

4 September, 1942

August 31 - 1630: Catapulted from ship. Enroute to ADAK ISLAND we encountered very heavy fog. First land sighted wasn't ADAK, Mr. Larson figuring the wind drift caused us to miss our destination. We navigated slightly to the west. Shortly thereafter we sighted a large island which we explored thoroughly by flying around it, investigating each cove and harbor. After completing our search around the island we know it was not ADAK so we flew back to a large harbor previously sighted, landed, and immediately anchored the plane. By this time it was quite dark. Both Mr. Larson and I spent first night in plane, Had a lot of trouble with anchor due to rough water and strong winds. At sunrise I inflated life raft and rowed ashore, securing raft far upon the beach and proceeded to a small trappers cabin to investigate for possible clues as to our whereabouts. Found some writing in cabin, much being in Russian. I could make out two names of bays - OLD NORTH BAY and HOT SPRINGS BAY. Relayed this information to Mr. Larson who is still in the plane. Attemtping to return to plane in rubber life raft, it exploded leaving no transportation to plane. I immediately started building a raft and by time I finished, it was dark. I attempted once to launch it but undertow of surf made it impossible. Telling Mr. Larson my predicament he suggested I return to cabin and start a fire to dry my clothing. Also to spend night in cabin and return to beach in morning and make another attempt to launch raft. Next morning I tore one bunk from cabin to enlarge raft and after doing so triedto launch once again and encountered same trouble. The wind still strong and surf was very heavy. Telling Mr. Larson my trouble I asked his permission to swim back to plane as weather was clearing and Mr. Larson wanted to take off as soon as possible. After receiving his consent I took off my heavy clothing and started to swim towards plane which was still anchored. About half way to plane I started getting cramps and hollered to Mr. Larson to turn up plane and come to my assistance. He done so with remarkable speed. As the plane neared he cut the engine, climbed out of cockpit and pulled me aboard the wing. I took off my wet clothing and put on some of Mr. Larson's dry clothes. Mr. Larson attempted to raise anchor but was too weak so he cut the line. Shortly thereafter we took off and followed a hunch of Mr. Larson's. We flew approximately 40 miles and then sighted ADAK ISLAND. We shook hands and then landed by the U.S.S. TEAL. After securing plane we went aboard ship where we were given food, a shower and a bed. "Thank God"

Respectfully,

R. J. Schledwitz, ARM2c

ENCLOSURE (B) TO NASHVILLE SERIAL CL43/P20-1/(OSS) of 5 September, 1942.

OAKLAND TRIBUNE, FRIDAY, NOVEMBER 6, 1942

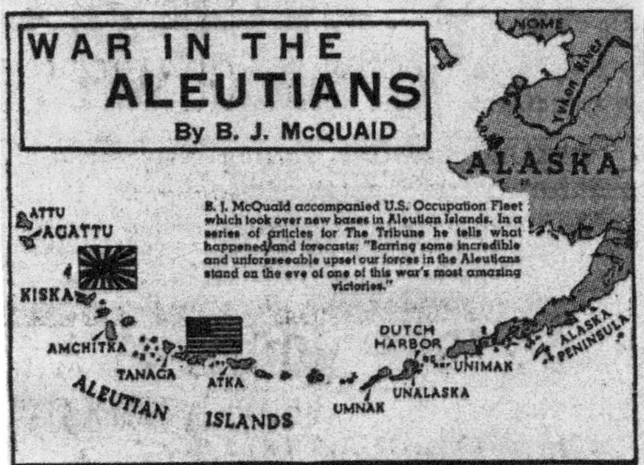

No. 8: Japs Unlucky if 'Lucky' Lands on Kiska

Special to The Tribune and the Chicago Daily News, Inc.

ABOARD A U.S. WARSHIP IN THE BERING SEA, Sept. 30.—"Now, once again, Lieut. L——, through excellent judgment, calmness, resourcefulness and endurance, has saved his plane and perhaps the lives of himself and his radioman. The commanding officer believes that these two performances of Lieut. L—— are worthy of a letter of commendation from the commander in chief."—From a memorandum to the "Cincpac" by the skipper of this cruiser.

Lieut. L—— is "Lucky," the young North Dakotan previously celebrated in your correspondent's dispatches for his almost unbelievable feat of getting his plane back to the ship after he had become lost, at night, in impenetrable fog.

This story starts out the same way: Lucky got lost. He had been catapulted from the cruiser on a communications mission to the place where U.S. troops, under the protection of this naval task force, are establishing an advanced base to carry the Aleutian war to the Japs.

Weather out here where the ships are operating was excellent at the time of his takeoff. At the other end of the mission—only a few miles away — everything was shut in tightly by fog. However, there was no way of checking the weather at the other end, because these ships are under the obligation of maintaining a strict radio silence.

LOW ON GAS

Shortly after launching, Lucky's plane encountered strong beam winds, whose strength he underestimated. These carried him considerably west of his destination. When, finally, he sighted a few land elevations muzzling up through the fog, he could recognize none of the contours.

"Flew around island," says Lucky's written report. "Was getting low on gasoline. It was also getting dark, and I landed in first bay I could find, with 30 gallons of gasoline." (Enough for about an hour of flight.) "Dropped anchor 100 yards off shore, which was composed of boulders, and breakers were coming in on the beach.

"Sat in plane all night, getting wet every 15 minutes. In the morning, S. (the radioman) took the liferaft and went ashore and investigated trapper's cabin. We found two names written on wall: North End Bay and Hot Springs. I checked all navigation, studied the charts and concluded that this must be Tanaga Island . . . S.'s liferaft exploded and he was stranded on the beach. He spent all day building a wooden raft out of driftwood. He launched it that evening, and it sank to the bottom.

BACK TO BASE

"Weather was closed in all day, raining frequently. S. went back to the cabin, built a fire and stayed all night. During the night the weather cleared. He came out early in the morning, inflated his lifebelt and started to swim to the plane. He was exhausted halfway out. I started plane and picked him up. We put on dry clothes immediately. I could not pull up anchor (machine gun), so cut line. Took off immediately on course. Landed at base with 10 gallons of gasoline."

This is in Lucky's best laconic style, but manages to convey one or two hints of the hazards and hardships faced by the stranded plane crew. Note that Lucky's anchor was his "free machine gun." Cruiser planes are, of course, equipped with anchors, and Lucky put down his when he first landed, but it proved inadequate to the job of holding the plane against the heavy swell. His unhesitating use of the machine gun may be a commentary on the Navy's changing sense of economic values. In former days, Navy emphasis on money values and individual responsibility for material would have caused a pilot to think twice in this situation.

MODESTY

The best bit of understatement is Lucky's description of his rescue of the radioman.

"He was exhausted . . . I started plane and picked him up."

Maybe you think that's a simple matter, in a small biplane tossed about by raging surf and requiring all an ordinary man's efforts just to keep it afloat and in one piece. Lucky, by this time, had sat out in an open cockpit, drenched by rain and spray from the cold Bering sea, for two nights and a day.

(More Tomorrow)

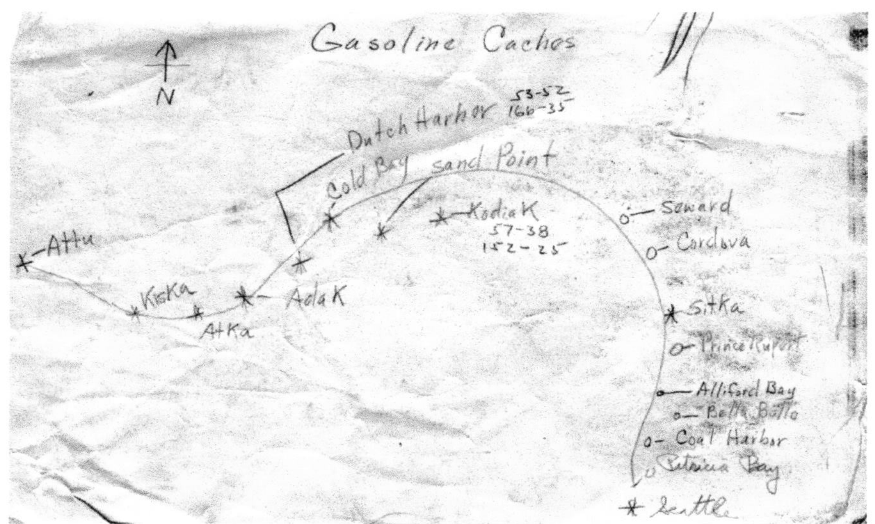

Lucky's handwritten map of gasoline caches for his flight from Kodiak, Alaska to Seattle, Washington to report to the Thirteen Naval District, September 1942.

Appendix E

Intelligence Reports & War Diaries

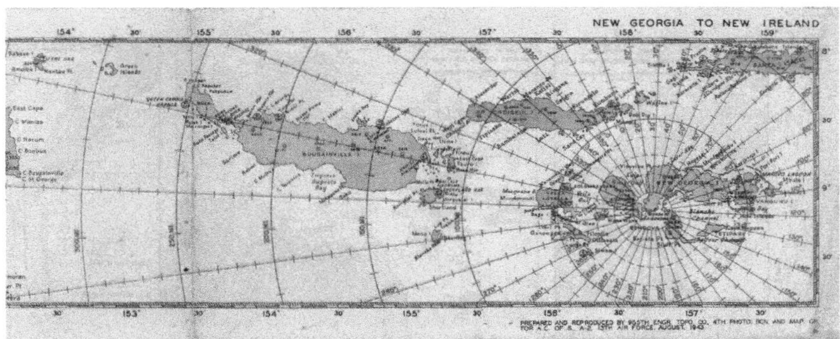

VC 38 Lt. John Leary's Pilot Reference Strip of Munda (New Georgia) to New Ireland (Source: Leary Family Collection)

Contents:

1.	9/14/1943	Ballale Island Airfield Mission
2.	9/15/1943	Ballale Island Airfield Mission
3.	9/16/1943	Ballale Island Airfield Mission
4.	10/23/1943	Kara Airfield Mission
5.	10/24/1943	Kahili Airfield Mission
6.	10/26/1943	Kahili Airfield Mission
7.	10/26/1943	Bomb Kara Airfield (Strike No. 2)
8.	10/28/1943	Kara Airfield Mission
9.	10/30/1943	Bombing of Kara Airstrip
10.	10/31/1943	Kara Airfield Mission
11.	11/2/1943	Search for Enemy Shipping –Bougainville Island
12.	11/2/1943	Bombing of Kara Airfield
13.	11/7/1943	Bomb Jaba Village Area
14.	11/10/1943	Buka and Bonis Airfield Mission
15.	11/12/1943	Buka Passage Mining Operation
16.	11/14/1943	Support Ground Troops – Empress Augusta Bay
17.	11/16/1943	Mine Laying – Buka Area
	a.	Statement from Lt. McLaughlin of VMTB-143
18.	11/20/1943	Mosigetta Village Mission
19.	11/22/1943	Kahili Airfield and AA Positions Mission
20.	11/24/1943	Chabai Airfield Mission
21.	11/26/1943	Kangu Hill Anti-Aircraft Guns
22.	11/30/1943	Mosigetta
23.	12/1/1943	Kara and Ballale Island Airfields
24.	12/4/1943	Mosigetta – Bivouac and Supply Area
25.	12/11/1943	Jokohina Supply & Kangu Hill Gun Positions
26.	12/12/1943	Ratsoa and Soraken Missions
27.	12/12/1943	Kieta Village- Toborei Bay
28.	12/13/1943	Porton Plantation
29.	1/27/1944	Jap Bivouac between Ibu and Sisivie
30.	1/28/1944	Tobera Airfield Mission
31.	1/31/1944	Tobera Airfield Mission
32.	2/5/1944	Lakunai Airfield Mission
33.	2/10/1944	Lakunai: Rapopo and Tobera Airfields
34.	2/11/1944	Vunapope Mission
35.	2/12/1944	Mining Oper. Memo in Simpson Harbor, Rabaul Area

36.	2/14/1944	Mining Operation in Simpson Harbor (VMTB 233)
37.	2/14/1944	Tobera, South Revetment Area
38.	2/17/1944	Keravia Bay Mission
39.	2/20/1944	Monoitu Mission Area near Hongorai River
40.	2/24/1944	Kuraio Mission
41.	2/26/1944	Vunapope Mission
42.	2/29/1944	Mawaraka and Jaba River Missions
43.	3/3/1944	Lakuai Gun Positions

S E C R E T

TBF OPERATIONS
GUADALCANAL

INTELLIGENCE REPORT

Date: September 14, 1943

Mission: Strike Ballale

Planes: 24 TBF's (6--VC-38; 6--VC-40; 12--VMTB-233)
30 SBD's
42 VF

Loadings: 12 TBF's with 2000 lb. inst.
12 TBF's with 2000 lb. 1/10 sec. delay.

Times: Take off--1039
Rend.--1220
Over target--1315
Landing--1648

AA: Moderate--heavy and light from Ballale and surrounding Islands.

Weather: Good.

SUMMARY

The TBF's were off at 1049, rendezvoused with the SBD's and fighters over Munda at 1220, and continued up over Vella Gulf to Fauro Island and were over Ballale at 1315.

After the planes had passed over the southern tip of Fauro they pushed over into a high speed approach from north to south, making the final pushover from about 8000 feet, releasing at 2000 feet and pulling out at 1500 feet generally.

The twenty-four planes dropped 24 x 2000 lb. bombs on Ballale. Twelve of the bombs had instantaneous fuses, and twelve had 1/10 second delay fuses. Of the bombs released, 10 hit the runway, 2 were on AA position on the north tip of the island, one on a fuel or ammunition dump in the SW revetment area, 3 on AA positions on SE shore and the others were unobserved. Both the pilots and gunners strafed during the diving run, and several fires and explosions were seen. Two bombs failed to release; one jetusived, one brought back to Henderson.
One Tony and several Zekes were seen by the TBF's. Two zeros made half-hearted passes at the TBF's, making sure that they kept out of range of the turret gunners.

AA was observed from Ballale, Poporang, Faisi, and Shortlands with a few bursts from Fauro. All of it was moderate in intensity, and inaccurate.

With the exception of possible 40 mm on NE end of the strip and some heavy AA at SE end, no change in positions were observed.

7-10 VF were seen on the field and one MF was sighted on the north end of the strip, with its back broken. Another MB was seen in the NE revetment area and was strafed.
Four TBF's landed at Munda on the return trip and two landed at the Russells due to engine trouble. However, all planes had returned safely to Henderson Field by 1648.

W. M. BURNS
1st Lt. USMCR
Intelligence Officer
VMTB-233

101

VMTB - 233

PLANE BU NO.	PILOT	RADIOMAN	TURRET	TAKE OFF	LAND
23873	Coln	Green	Snyder	1034	1523
06406	Kirincich	Anderson	Gunning	1034	1523
47504	Gennerman	Fenton	DeMoss	1034	1524
06420	Little	Ivers	Miller, H.A.	1035	1524
064299	Johnson	Fleming	Herndon	1035	1524
06190	Landae	Guinea	Daniels	1035	1525
06432	Haxton	Bullock	Doss	1035	1646
06411	Keiter	Brunnhoeffer	Larson	1036	1648
06311	Milling	Hall, B.C.	Benson	1037	1603
47501	Voyles	Provenzano	Gilbert	1037	1605
06118	Jaque	Cannon	Cox	1039	1605
06115	Boydon	Conyers	Keer	1038	1648

VC - 38

PLANE BU NO.	PILOT	RADIOMAN	TURRET	TAKE OFF	LAND
24244	Brunton	Sunday	Paul	1046	1526
47502	Scholfield	Ulrich	Dills	1041	1528
23959	Giblin	Lee	Perkins	1041	1526
47553	Phillippi	Bond	Tylor	1043	1527
24182	Leake	Greslie	Dale	1043	1527
06145	Tahler	Brewer	Jeffrey	1044	1526

VC - 40

PLANE BU NO.	PILOT	RADIOMAN	TURRET	TAKE OFF	LAND
24283	Jackson	Adams	Powell	1045	1527
47995	Hahn	Dunn	Ellis	1045	1523
23970	Locklider	De Mott	Zollinhofer	1047	1529
06454	Truly	Joacloim	Temple	1047	1529
23910	Behl	Draudon	Dunning	1048	1529
23909	LaPierre	De Vou	Faust	1048	1529

102

WAR DIARY
VMTB- 233

14 September 1943

1. Orders Received.

Starting on this day Strike Command plans a three day assault on enemy held positions on Ballale Airfield. VMTB-233 is operating TBF's with two Navy Groups, VC-38 and VC-40 in this all-out attack by Torpedo Bombers and Dive Bombers.

2. Operations.

Twelve planes of this squadron and six planes from VC-38 and six planes from VC-40 struck Ballale Airfield. The pilots covered the target areas well despite intense anti-aircraft fire and determined enemy fighter opposition. All planes returned safely to Henderson Field.

3. Special Action Reports.

See Special Action report for September 14, 1943, attached to back of War Diary.

4. Changes in Personnel.

None.

5. Relationship of Subordinate Units.

No change.

- 15 -

62

S E C R E T

TBF OPERATIONS
GUADALCANAL

INTELLIGENCE REPORT

Date: September 15, 1943

Mission: Strike Ballale.

Planes: 24 TBF's (6--VC-38; 6--VC-40; 12--VMTB-233)
30 SBD's
72 VF

Loadings: 12 TBF's with 2000 lb. inst. fuse.
12 TBF's with 2000 lb. 1/10 delay fuse.

Times: Take off--0912
Rendezvous--1030
Over target--1115
Landing--1320

Weather over target: GOOD. Scattered Cumulus from 3-5000 feet.

AA: Medium and heavy-- moderate to slight.

SUMMARY

The 24 TBF's had joined the 30 SBD's at the Russells after taking off from Henderson Field at 0912. At 1030 they made the rendezvous with the 72 fighters over Munda, and proceeded to the target over Vella Gulf, to southwest tip of Fauro before making the high-speed NS approach over Ballale, pushing over at 10,000 releasing at 2000 and pulling out at 1500 feet.

Of the 24 TBF's dropped 24 x 2000 lb. bombs on various targets on Ballale. Nine of the one-tenth second delay bombs were strung down the runway. One two thousand pounder hit squarely in a revetment area SE of the runway, and one 2000 lb. bomb was dropped in a group of trucks at the SW end of the runway. The other bombs were dropped in the target areas which consisted of gun positions and supply dumps. A large fire was started at the SW end of the runway, and a fire was seen on the E side of the island.

The TBF's reported that the fighter cover was excellent. Although several fighters jumped them, none of them made passes. A fire was seen on the N end of the runway at Kahili, and an AK about 200 feet long was seen in Tonolei Harbor. Three planes were seen to go into the water. It is certain that two of them were Zekes.

Twenty-two TBF's landed at 1320 at Henderson Field. Two landed at Munda because one plane had a leak in his oil line. These two finally pancaked on Henderson at 1720.

W. M. BURNS
1st Lt. USMCR
Intelligence Officer
VMTB-233

103

VMTB - 233

PLANE BU. NO.	PILOT	RADIOMAN	TURRET	TAKE OFF	LAND
06474	Bright	Dearing	Horne	0858	1316
23873	Dowd	Brownfield	Rosenthal	0859	1317
06432	Cornelius	McCarthy	Slipkas	0859	1318
23871	Croker	Schroeder	Casper	0859	1317
06406	DeLancey	Kozakewich	Butchorn	0900	1317
47510	Phillips	Susedik	[illegible], H.C.	0900	1318
06429	Fuller	Roselli	Embry	0900	1319
06329	Morris	McGee	Hundricks	0901	1320
06115	Takacs	Hall, E.J.	Ison.Rourke	0901	1725
06420	Harris	Henderick	McElhoes	0901	1728
06472	Bartholf	Bendschneider	Shoul[illegible]	0902	1320
47501	Bauder	Fyock	DeRouen	0902	1320

VC - 38

PLANE BU. NO.	PILOT	RADIOMAN	TURRET	TAKE OFF	LAND
24244	Larson	Wagner	Wright	0906	1329
47502	Regan	Misner	Bradt	0906	1325
23959	Leary	Groslie	Dale	0907	1322
47553	Wilson	Heller	Wilson	0907	1323
24182	Bishop	Schramm	Barnes	0908	1323
47504	Bohn	Dill	Buis	0909	1324

VC - 40

PLANE BU. NO.	PILOT	RADIOMAN	TURRET	TAKE OFF	LAND
24283	Jackson	Adams	Powell	0903	1324
23970	Collura	Ruiard	Pittman	0903	1327
47599	DeVeer	Schneider	Mogl[illegible]	0904	1327
06145	Fre[illegible]s	Tufenkjian	Wrebbens	0904	1326
23910	Bennett	Whitworth	Brantingham	0905	1325
23987	Tracey	Joscelein	Temple	0905	1326

104

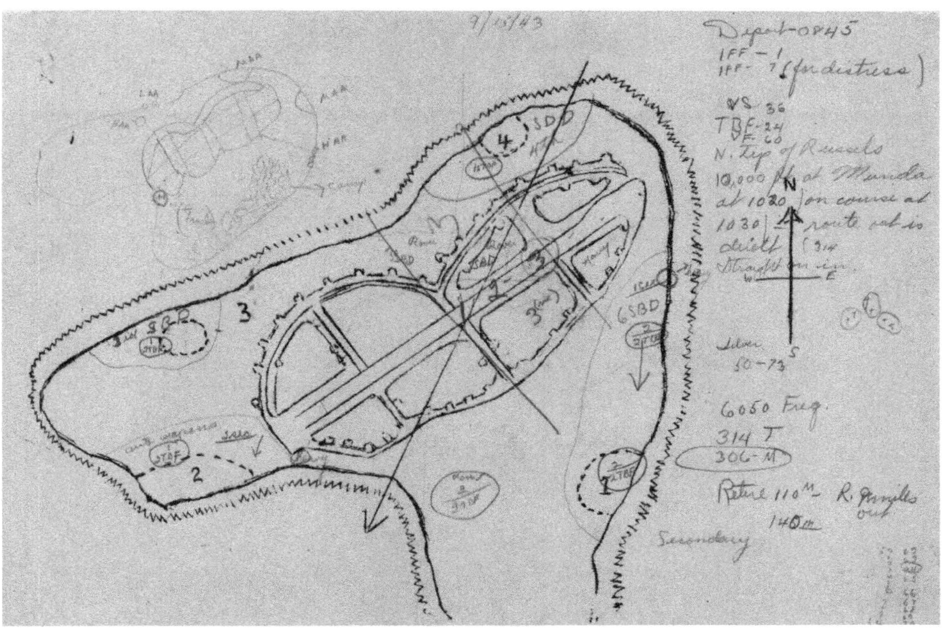

VC 38 Lt. John Leary's Map of Ballale (Source: Leary Family Collection)

WAR DIARY
VMTB - 233

15 September 1943

1. Orders Received.

Twelve planes of this squadron and six planes from each of the Navy Groups (VC-38 and VC-40) are to strike Ballale Airfield.

2. Operations.

Twelve planes of this squadron with six planes of VC-38 and six planes of VC-40 struck Ballale Airfield. All planes were loaded with 2000# bombs. The TBF's reported that the fighter cover was excellent. Several enemy fighters were seen, but none of them made passes. The bombs were well dispersed over the target areas. All planes returned safely to Henderson Field.

3. Special Action Reports.

See special action report for September 15, 1943, attached to back of War Diary.

4. Changes in Personnel.

None.

5. Relationship of Subordinate Units.

No change.

- 16 -

63

S E C R E T

TBF OPERATIONS
GUADALCANAL

INTELLIGENCE REPORT

Date: September 16, 1943

Mission: Strike Ballale

Planes: 24 TBF's (6--VC-38; 6--VC-40; 12--VMTB-233)
30 SBD's
72 VF

Loadings: 11 TBF's with 4x500 lb. inst.
13 TBF's with 2000 lb. inst.

TIMes: Take off--1233
Rendezvous--1350
Over target--1450
Landing--1737

AA: Moderate, heavy and light---accurate.

Weather: Good

SUMMARY

The twenty-four TBF's were off at 1233 to strike Ballale for the third consecutive day. They rendezvoused with the SBD's and 72 fighters over Munda at 12,000 feet at 1350 and were on course at 1400 on a bearing of 305° magnetic, proceeding up over Vella Gulf, midway between Fauro and Shortland Islands, circling Ballale to the south and west to make a general northwest-southeast approach. The pushover was made, after a high speed approach, from 8,000 feet; the release was made from 1800-1000 feet with a pull out from 1200-500 feet.

Of the 44 x 500 lb. bombs, 33 were dropped in the target areas, 5 fell into the water, 4 failed to release and two were unaccounted for (these are from one of the lost TBF's). Twenty-four of the 500's were put in the revetments and in the runway area with 7 others landing in the gun positions and supply areas south and west of the strip's southern end. Two others were in the jungle area on the southeastern end of the island.

One 2000 pounder landed squarely on the runway. Five of them were in a semi-circle off the southwest end of the strip, and 6 were in the supply, personnel areas and gun postions in the southern bulge of the island. One 2000 pound bomb was unaccounted for.

One TBF was flying at a low altitude across the island when an explosion, apparently from two bombs which it had just dropped, blew off its right wing, flipped it over on its back and sent it crashing into the water at which time it burst into flames. The pilot was Lt. (jg) Rowland D. Hahn, AV(N), USNR. The crew consisted of W. M. Ellis, AMM2/c, turret gunner, R.T. Dunn, ARM2/c, radioman and C.E. Wells, AMM1/c who was riding as a passenger. This plane, pilot, and crew were attached to VC-40. Another TBF, piloted by Lt. E.A. Croker of VMTB-233, is unaccounted for. No one saw this plane after the dive, and its fate is undetermined.

The TBF's pilots expressed their appreciation for excellent fighter cover during and after the dive. Four fires were seen burning on the island, onein target area #4, one in the area to the southwest of the runway, and two in the area to the south of the runway. An explostion was seen on the southwestern end of the island.

105

A burning object, which appeared to be a ship, was seen near the shipping ramps south of the field. Several planes (probably all enemy), were seen to crash into the water as the TBF's were making their runs.

The TBF's received several accurate bursts of AA fire from Poporang and Shortland Islands as they made their approach to the target. The AA from Ballale was reported as moderate in intensity, both heavy and light, but more accurate than on the previous strike.

One TBF had a piece about four inches in diameter shot out of the leading edge of its wing. Another TBF received a burst of fire from a zero that entered the fuselage just behind the bomb bay and smashed the radio. An explosive shell hit the stabilizer of yet another TBF, jamming the elevator so that the pilot had difficulty in pulling it out of the dive. He landed at the Russells along with three other planes and all returned to Henderson Field at 1730.

W. N. BURNS
1st Lt. USMCR
Intelligence Officer
VMTB-233

106

VMTB - 233

PLANE BU NO.	PILOT	RADIOMAN	TURRET	TAKE OFF	LAND
23871	Cunningham	Wikora	Schillinger	1233	1654
06118	Jaqua	Cannon	Cox	1234	1736
23873	Ward	Marshall	Rice	1234	1654
06472	Hollis	Howard	Cunningham	1235	1655
06190	Molby	Conner	Keer	1235	1737
47592	Boyden	Conyers	Pardon	1236	1657
24283	Bright	Dearing	Horne	1237	1656
06416	Pennestri	Beiderman	Boardman	1237	1718
47504	Cornelius	McCarthy	Slipkas	1238	1655
06429	Croker	Schroeder	Casper	1238	----
06438	DeLancey	Kozakewich	Dutchorn	1238	1657
47501	Lamade	Guinea	Daniels	1239	1718

VC - 30

PLANE BU NO.	PILOT	RADIOMAN	TURRET	TAKE OFF	LAND
24244	Brunton	Sunday	Paul	1228	1648
23959	Scholfield	Ulrich	Dills	1229	1650
47553	Marshall	Lane	Tye	1229	1649
24182	Phillippi	Bond	Tyler	1230	1651
23975	Leake	O'Daniel	Boyle	1231	1649
47458	Goblin	Lee	Perkins	1230	1651

VC - 40

PLANE BU NO.	PILOT	RADIOMAN	TURRET	TAKE OFF	LAND
23987	Leckleder	De Mott	Zollinhofer	1231	1652
06145	Willeman	Garwood	Irwin	1233	1652
23910	Behl	Drauden	Dunning	1231	1652
06454	Truly	Joachin	Temple	1232	1653
23909	Hahn	Dunn	Ellis	1232	----
47599	La Pierre	De Vore	Faust	1240	1530

107

WAR DIARY
VMTB - 233

16 September 1943

1. Orders Received.

Twelve planes of VMTB-233 to strike Ballale for the third consecutive day, accompanied by six planes from VC-38 and six planes from VC-40.

2. Operations.

Twelve planes of this squadron with six planes from VC-38 and six planes from VC-40 struck Ballale Airfield, Ballale Island, for the third day in succession in the all-out attack against the enemy held positions in the Shortland Island, South Bougainville areas. Twelve planes were loaded with 4x500# bombs, and twelve were loaded with 2000# bombs. Due to excellent fighter cover, enemy fighters were again unable to come within range of the TBF's.

On this strike Lt. E.A. Croker of VMTB-233 did not return. His plane was not seen after the dive bombing run was begun. Lt. Hahn of VC-40 also failed to return. His plane was seen to crash off the southeastern end of Ballale with a wing blown off, probably from the explosion of his own bombs. The other planes returned to Henderson Field, Guadalcanal. This concluded the three-day attack on Ballale.

3. Special Action Reports.

See special action report for September 16, 1943, attached to back of War Diary.

4. Changes in Personnel.

None.

5. Relationship of Subordinate Units.

No change.

- 17 -

64

AIR DEPARTMENT PLAN OF THE DAY

Tuesday, 28 Sept. 1943

0615 Flight Quarters. Turn on YE.

0700 Launch Attack group (6 VF, 6Vt)

T 1 BRUNTON T 6 LEAKE
T 3 SCHOLFIELD T 7 GIBLIN
T 5 MARSHALL T 8 BEHN
Call V151,335,6 etc.

F 1 ANDERSON F 3 MOORE F 5 CORNELL
F 2 SPAULDING F 4 BEAUMONT F 6 HAGANS
Call Green 1,2,3,4, etc.

0745 Combat Air Patrol

F 7 CHENOWETH F 9 MCNEIL F 11 ENGLADE
F 8 KELLEY F 10 KASTRZEWSKY F 12 MCMAHON
Plane Call Green 7, 8, 9, etc.
Group proceed at least 100 miles to eastward; then return and make coordinated simulated air attack on Disposition.

About 1000 At completion of attack, recover group (landing order VF, VT), strike below 12 VF; respot as directed.

—— Launch Group 7 VT, 12 VF, return to shore base.

T 1 BRUNTON T 5 LEAKE T 8 LARSON
T 2 SCHOLFIELD T 6 GIBLIN
T 3 MARSHALL T 7 BEHN

F 1 ANDERSON F 5 CHENOWETH F 9 SENFT
F 2 SPAULDING F 6 KELLEY F 10 CONDO
F 3 MOORE F 7 MCNEIL F 11 THOMPSON
F 4 BEAUMONT F 8 KOSTRZEWSKY F 12 McMAHON

—— Secure from Flight Quarters.

E. B. NOBLE, Lt. Cdr. USN
Air Officer

September 28, 1943 VC 38 Orders of the Day - To Espiritu Santo Island (Buttons) from USS Brenton (Source: Leary Family Collection)

S-E-C-R-E-T COMMANDER AIRCRAFT SOLOMONS S-E-C-R-E-T
STRIKE COMMAND
INTELLIGENCE SECTION

Date: 23 October 1943

Squadrons: VC - 38
VC - 40
VMTB - 143

Type of Mission: Bombing and strafing Kara Airfield and AA gun positions and area.

Planes & Loadings: 18 TBF'S - 1x2000 lb. 1/10

Times: Take Off - 1353-1359, Over Target - 1600, Landed - 1650 (6 planes here),
1800 (12 planes at Cactus).

Anti-Aircraft: Heavy and light AA of medium intensity. 20 to 30 black puffs between 1000-15000 ft. Heavy AA noted on pull outs. AA fire came from: near ammunition dump at Northwest corner of strip - about five 40MM guns near lake about 7 miles Northeast of strip - at head of Tonolei Harbor - at known positions South of strip - automatic AA at Northeast corner of strip and West of center of strip - 1 tracer observed coming from Northeast corner of runway - 30 and 50 caliber AA noted on both ends of runway.

Interception: None

M/G Ammo expended: Not available

Damage to Planes: One TBF at escape hatch. One SBD caught fire and crashed about one mile West of South end of Kara Airstrip.

Weather: Cloudy North of Bougainville. Clear over target. Overcast 14000 ft. over Kara strip.

Target Areas: Kara Airstrip assigned to TBF'S.

Attack: Rendezvous at Ringana Island off Choiseul. Flight proceeded to target East of Choiseul, and approach made from Northeast of Bougainville and North of Tonolei. Dove North to South and turned West across target. Push overs from 6000-4500 ft.; releases from 1500-2500ft.; pull outs from 1000-1500 ft. Bomb hits were as follows:
Ten on center of strip.
Two on North 1/3 of strip.
Two on South 1/3 of strip.
Three near edge of strip.
One off strip.
Area West of strip and 6 huts about 2 miles Southwest of Uquimo River were strafed.

Observations:
1. 4 or 5 small AK in Tonolei Harbor.
2. AA - Known positions Southwest of strip hit by SBD'S.
3. South half of runway hit better.

Route Back: Via Moila Point then South Route.

Myron Sulzberger
Intelligence Duty Officer
VMTB 143

8

VC - 38

Plane Bu.No.	Pilot	Radioman	Turret man	Take Off	Land
24244	BRUNTON	Sunday	Kempers	1353	1800
23981	SCHOLFIELD	Ulrich	Dills,J.F.	1353	1800
23981	DAUGHTON	Deal	Paul	1353	1800
24242	GIBBILON	Lee	Perkins	1354	1800
24182	BEHN	Buis	Dills,C.F.	1354	1800
23975	MARSHALL	Lane	Tye	1354	1800
24194	BISHOP	Schramm	Barnes	1358	1651
24208	TAHLER	Jeffrey	Brewer	1358	1651
24265	McDONALD	Blank	Young	1358	1651

VC - 40

Plane Bu.No.	Pilot	Radioman	Turret man	Take Off	Land
24334	JACKSON	Powell	Adams	1355	1800
23907	BENNETT	Brautingham	Whitworth	1355	1800
47595	KNOCHE	Crabtree	Camp	1356	1800
24403	BEHL	Dinning	Drauden	1356	1800
23970	LaPIERRE	Faust	DeVore	1356	1800
24356	LECKLEIDER	Zollwhefer	DeMott	1357	1650
24195	TRULY	Temple-Menzies-	Joachen	1357	1650
24212	FALLS	Wubbrus	Tufenkjian	1357	1651

VMTB - 143

Plane Bu.No.	Pilot	Radioman	Turret man	Take Off	Land
	MORRIS			1355	1800

9

S-E-C-R-E-T COMMANDER AIRCRAFT SOLOMONS S-E-C-R-E-T
STRIKE COMMAND
INTELLIGENCE SECTION

Date: 24 October 1943

Squadron: VMTB 232, 18 Planes - VC 38, 3 Planes - VC 40, 3 Planes.

Type of Mission: Bombing and strafing of Kahili Airstrip, Bougainville Island.

Planes: 24 TBF'S - 47 SBD'S

Loadings: 24 TBF'S with 1x2000LB 1/10.
47 SBD'S with 1x1000LB Inst.

Times: Take Off - 0922-0938, Over target - 1105, Landed - 1205-1211.

Anti-Aircraft fire: Heavy and light of medium intensity. (See observations)

Interception: None.

Damage to Planes: Plane piloted by Lt. Al Moret was hit by a 40 millimeter shell which entered the left side of bomb bay and penetrated cockpit and tunnel.

Injury to personnel: First Lieutenant Alfred Moret,Jr. and the turret gunner George T. France received flash burns from exploding shell.

Weather: 2/10 scattered over target 4000 feet to 6000 feet.

M/G Ammo expended: 5000 rds. 30 calibre.
2600 rds. 50 calibre.

Target area: Airstrip at Kahili.

Attack: After rendezvousing with fighters over Baga Island on West coast of Vella LaVella, flight proceeded around southwest corner of Shortlands and to a point North of target area. From this position push overs from North to South were made at altitudes varying from 8000 feet to 10,000 feet; releases at 1500 feet to 2500 feet; and pullouts from 1000 feet to 2000 feet. Bomb hits were as follows:

Nineteen hits on runway with about equal distribution on North and South halves of strip.

Three hits on taxiway West of strip. (Two in the North end and one in South end.

Two bombs hung up and were jettisoned enroute to base.

Observations: Light AA gun emplacements at Southeast edge of strip; twelve flashes from heavy AA Southeast edge of top of Kangu Hill; Light AA from beach Southwest of strip; Heavy AA positions in Eberly's Lease; AA positions about one and one half miles East of South end of runway; Some heavy AA bursts from North end of strip; Heavy AA from West of strip and from square clearing one quarter mile West of middle of Kara strip; 40 millimeter firing from West side of Kahili strip near North end; AA positions Northwest of Malibita Hill in clearing towards Kara; Some heavy AA seen coming from Evventa.

Miscellaneous: On North end of small island West of Shortlands,,Lt. Everson's Radio gunner, Herman S. Pell, saw flashes from a mirror. After observing it he flashed an answer of OK with the Aldis Lamp.

13

A Yellow raft having two men in it was seen by turret gunner Temple about half way between Moila Point and Komaleai Point(North tip of Shortlands).

A fire was observed South of end of Kahili strip. The tower at the Northwest corner of the strip was seen to explode. Four or five Betty's were seen on the South end of the runway.

Route Out: Rendezvous over Baga Island-around Southwest tip of Shortland Island and North to target area.

Route Back: Rally over Moila Point direct to base.

****

SPECIAL REPORT RE-INJURIES OF LT. ALFRET T. MORET,JR. AND TURRET GUNNER GEORGE T. FRANCE

Their injuries were caused by an exploding 40 millimeter shell within the plane resulting in flash burns on neck, left and right arm of first and second degree, for Lt. Moret and leg burns for Gunner France.

Lt. Moret strongly recommends that all flying personnel be fully clothed with sleeves rolled down and goggles in use.

Lt. Moret had his flight suit sleeves rolled down but even so he suffered burns.

Kenneth R. Johnson
A.C.I.O.
VMTB 232

14

VMTB 232

Plane Bu.No.	Pilot	Radioman	Turret Man	Out	In
24406	SMITH	Waldvogel	Stanner	0922	1205
06425	STAMETS	Severson	Brodeski	0922	1206
06411	EVERETT	Ward	Norby	0922	1206
06190	DAUGHERTY	Railey	Donovan	0922	1207
06311	HUMPHREY	Martin	Adams	0938	1213
064714	LAUGHLIN	Akroyd	Spychalla	0923	1207
24358	RUBINCAM	Barker	Nichols	0924	1256
06353	OLSON	Hoke	Mitchell	0924	1211
47504	METZELAARS	Pollow	Eldridge	0925	1208
06406	SCHRADER	Seamonds	Jenkins	0925	1213
06472	GOODMAN	Wood	Cardno	0925	1211
24264	FIELD	Miller	Dzama	0925	1208
06432	EVERSON	Poll	Marker	0928	1213
06489	DEXHEIMER	Jackson	Nilson	0928	1213
24268	SPARKS	Rader	Sauter	0929	1213
06341	THOMAS	Schlueter	Akey	0929	1211
06438	MORET	Shelton	France	0929	1208
47510	GARILLI	Schafer	Hall	0929	1151

VC-40

Plane Bu.No.	Pilot	Radioman	Turret Man	Out	In
24358	LECKLEIDER	Zollinhofer	DeMott	0932	1214
24195	TRULY	Temple	Joachim	0932	1206
24212	FREES	Wubbens	Tufenkjian	0932	1214

VC-38

Plane Bu.No.	Pilot	Radioman	Turret Man	Out	In
24194	BISHOP	Schramm	Barnes	0932	1215
24208	TAHLER	Jeffrey	Brewer	0936	1214
24265	MC DONALD	Blank	Young	0933	1215

15

S-E-C-R-E-T COMMANDER AIRCRAFT SOLOMONS S-E-C-R-E-T
STRIKE COMMAND
INTELLIGENCE SECTION

Date: 26 October 1943

Squadron: VMTB-232 (20 planes), VC-38 (7 planes), VC-40 (9 planes).

Type of Mission: Bomb Kahili Airfield.

Planes: 36 TBF'S

Loadings: 36 TBF'S with 1x2000 lb. 1/10

Times: Take Off - 0716-0724, Rendezvous - 0820 (Baga, 10,000 ft.), On Course - 0825, Over Target - 0905, Return - 0955-1006.

Anti-Aircraft: Intense heavy, moderate light.

Interception: None; 2 damaged twin engined bombers were observed at South end of runway.

M/G Ammo expended: 2700 rds. 50 cal. - 9800 rds. 30 cal.

Damage to Planes: Empennage of one plane damaged by AA; tail of another plane severely damaged by heavy AA; one plane shot down.

Weather: Excellent; light scattered clouds at 3000 ft.

Target areas: Kahili runway and taxiway to West.

Attack: Approach course 300 degrees M to Southwest tip of Shortland Is.; thence 000 degrees M East of Kara Airfield, making "S" turn to gain distance and avoid AA; final approach from 11,500 ft. courses of 135, 180, 225 degrees. Push overs from 7000-8000 ft.; releases from 1100-2500 ft.; pull outs from 800-2000 ft. Route back - direct to Base. Strafed strip, West taxiway and area, targets #2 and #4 and all along beach; also beached ship firing AA. Also strafed road between Targets #4 and #6, barges and gun positions 1/2 way to Moila Pt. Bomb hits were as follows:

26 on strip, well spaced except for South end.
1 on Northwest edge of strip.
1 near miss on beached ship.
1 jettisoned North of Kangu Hill on approach.
1 brought back.
1 unaccounted for (this of plane shot down).

Observations: AA guns: 4 heavy guns on Kangu Hill and 4 automatics on East side thereof. 4 heavy guns at Southerly edge of Eberly's base; one heavy gun at North side thereof. 2 heavy guns in Target #3; 2 guns to East thereof. Light guns in Targets #2 and #4 and along both sides of strip. Light guns on beached ship between Targets #2 and #4. Twin light guns on beach, one halfway between Kahili and Moila Pt.; light guns on barges immediately off shore therefrom (apparently beached). 2 heavy guns in clearings South west of Malabita Hill. Heavy guns at North end of strip.

20

Ten barges along beach half way between Kahili and Moila Pt. Four ships off beach at Target #6. Two ships in Tonolei Harbor. Bomb hits observed: Accurate hits by SBD'S bombs on the AA guns on either side of the neck of the strip, designated Target #8 were observed.
Prior damage to runway: The pilot of the first TBF observed 6 large craters in the runway, the result of previous strikes, indicating that the strip is not being repaired promptly.

Lost Plane: First Lieutenant Philip Field, N.A., U.S.M.C., VMTB 232, pilot, Sergeant Edward R. Dzama, U.S.M.C., turret gunner, and Private Joseph D. Miller, U.S.M.C., radio gunner, flying in Plane Bu.No. 06416 were observed to pull out of glide at 1000 ft. The engine was on fire, and, after making a turn to the left, the plane dove into the water at a 20 degrees angle about half way between the beach and Erventa Island. Two men were seen to jump; one chute opened; the other did not and the man was seen to go into the water. No other information was obtainable.

Frederick Frelinghuyson
Lt. USNR, VC-40
Intelligence Duty Officer.

VMTB-232

Plane Bu.No.	Pilot	Radioman	Turret Man	Out	In
06406	Schrader	Seamonds	Jenkins	0729	1002
06499	Goodman	Wood	Cardno	0729	1002
24264	SMITH, Maj.	Waldvogel	Stanner	0721	0955
47504	METZELAARS	Pollow	Eldridge	0721	0955
06411	EVERETT	Ward	Norby	0723	0956
06190	DAUGHERTY	Railey	Donovan	0724	0956
06475	STAMETS	Severson	Brodeski	0722	0959
24268	HUMPHREY	Martin	Adams	0722	0956
47501	WHITE	Crumpton	Moon	0727	0957
06118	McCOLE	Sears	Blackerby	0727	0958
06341	BURRIS	Lossie	Wagner	0727	0958
064714	LAUGHLIN	Akroyd	Spychalla	0728	0958
06420	CAREY	Downey	Copeland	0728	0957
06416	FIELD	Miller	Dzama	0728	----
06432	EVERSON	Pell	Marker	0728	1001
06359	DEXHEIMER	Jackson	Nilson	0729	0959
06125	SPARKS	Rader	Sauter	0729	1001
06489	THOMAS	Schlecter	Akey	0729	1001
24358	OLSON	Hoke	Mitchell	0729	1001
47510	GARILLI	Schafer	Hall	0729	0959
VC-38					
24244	LARSON	Wagner	Wright	0717	1005
23981	GANIMAGE	Morrissey		0717	1005
47494	LEARY	Groslie	Dale	0717	1006
24242	WILSON	Haller	Wilson	0717	1000
24182	REGAN	Misner	Brant	0717	1006
23975	LEAKE	Boyle	[illegible]	0718	1006
~~24265~~	~~PHILLIPI~~	~~Bond~~ Did not attack	Tyler	0718	0839
24194	DRAUGHON	Deal	Paul	0720	1002
VC-40					
24334	JACKSON	Powell	Adams	0716	1008
06034	COLLURA	Pittman	Accardi	0716	1008
23987	BENNETT	Brantingham	Whitworth	0716	1008
47595	KNOCHE	Crabtree	Camp	0716	1005
24403	BEHL	Dunning	Draudon	0716	1008
23870	LaPIERRE	Faust	DeVore	0716	1008
24358	DEVEER	Moglomre	Schneider	0718	1004
24195	TRACY	Boyer-	Rhodes	0718	1004
06311	WILLIMAN	Irwin	Garwood	0718	1014

21

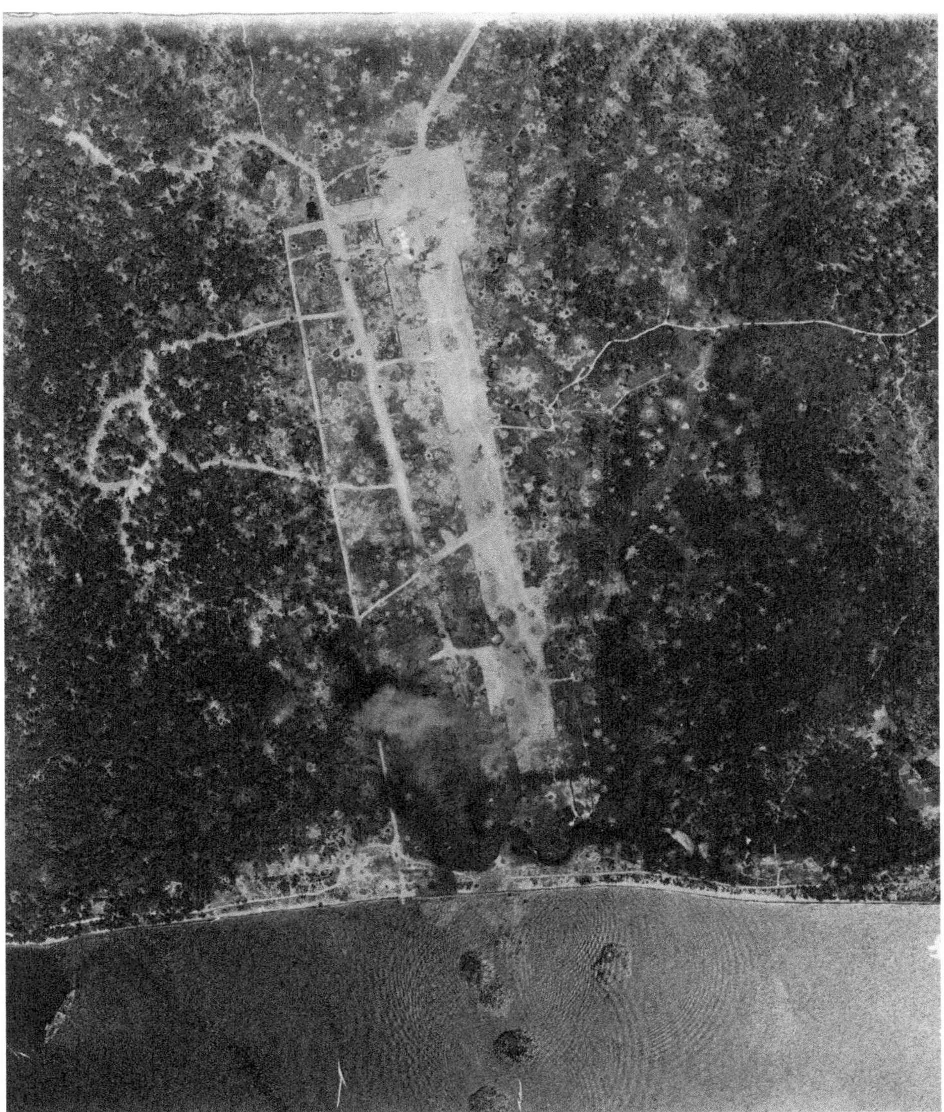

Kahili Airfield Bombing (Source: Lt. John Leary's photograph provided by the Leary Family Collection)

S-E-C-R-E-T COMMANDER AIRCRAFT SOLOMONS S-E-C-R-E-T
STRIKE COMMAND
INTELLIGENCE SECTION

Date:	26 October 1943 (Strike No. 2)
Squadrons:	VMTB - 232 (6 planes); VC-38 (6 planes) VC-40 (6 planes)
Type of Mission:	Bomb Kara Airfield.
Planes & Loadings:	18 TBF's - 1x2000 lbs. 1/10
Times:	Take Off - 1410-1416, rendezvous - 1455 (Baga Island, 12,000); On course - 1510; over target - 1555; return 1655-1700.
Anti-Aircraft:	Moderate heavy: Intense light.
Interception:	None
M/G Ammo expended:	8250 rds. 30 calibre - 4260 rds. 50 calibre.
Damage to Planes:	
Weather:	Thunderstorm on course out; over target good.
Target Areas:	Kara runway.
Attack:	Approach - direct from Baga, south around thunderstorm on route; swing to right 5 miles West Moila Point to attack down runway. Push-overs: 5000 - 9000'; Releases: 1100 - 2500'; Pull outs: 1000 - 2000'; Route back: Direct to Base.
Bomb Hits:	Runway - 16 (with the majority on South half of strip) South AA position West side strip - 1 Buildings West North end of strip - 1
Observations:	1: AA guns: 1 heavy Northwest corner of strip; 1 heavy and automatics in known position West of center of strip; Automatics at North and South ends of strip. 2: Shipping: Possible ship on South side Treasury Island. It was reported that the shipping observed off Kahila and in Tonolei Harbor earlier in the day had disappeared.

Frederick Frelinghuysen,
Lieut., USNR., VC-40
Intelligence Duty Officer.

34

VMTB- 232

Plane Bu.No.	Pilot	Passengers	Out	In
23873	SMITH	Waldvogel-Stanner	1414	1659
06489	DALBY	Broome-Knight	1415	1700
06411	EVERETT	Ward-Norby	1415	1659
06190	DAUGHERTY	Railey-Donovan	1415	1700
24268	HUMPHREY	Martin-Adams	1415	1700
06475	STAMETS	Severson-Brodeski	1414	1700

VC-38

Plane Bu.No.	Pilot	Passengers	Out	In
24244	BRUNTON	Sunday-Kemper	1410	1655
23981	SCHOFIELD	Ulrich-Dills	1410	1655
24182	GIBLIN	Lee-Perkins	1411	1657
23975	BEHN	Buis-Dills	1411	1657
06125	MARSHALL	Lane-Brewer	1412	1656
06472	MCDONALD	Blank-Young	1412	1656

VC-40

Plane Bu.No.	Pilot	Passengers	Out	In
23970	JACKSON	Powell-Adams	1412	1658
47506	COLLURA	Pittman-Accardi	1412	1658
24358	FREES	Wubbens-Tufenkjian	1422	1659
23987	MORRISON	Loughridge-Joyce	1416	1659
24403	DEVEER	Meglemre-Schneider	1413	1659
06359	COLLINS	Mocker-Rivard	1414	1659

35

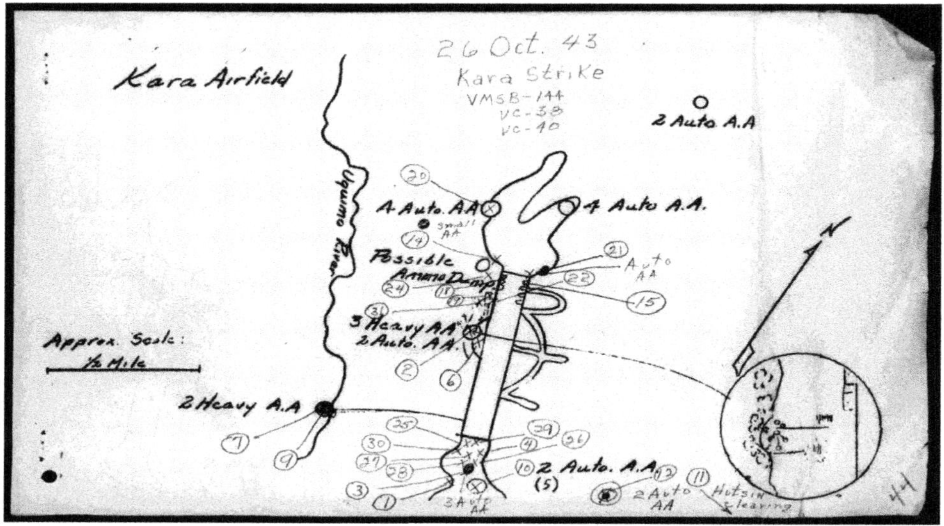
Kara Airfield
26 Oct. 43
Kara Strike
VMSB-144
VC-38
VC-40
2 Auto A.A
Uquimo River
4 Auto. AA
4 Auto A.A.
small AA
Possible Ammo Dump
Auto AA
3 Heavy AA
2 Auto. AA.
Approx. Scale:
½ Mile
2 Heavy A.A
2 Auto. A.A.
(5)
2 Auto AA
3 Auto AA
Hutsin clearing
N

S-E-C-R-E-T COMMANDER AIRCRAFT SOLOMONS S-E-C-R-E-T
STRIKE COMMAND
INTELLIGENCE SECTION

Date: 28 October 1943

Squadrons: VMTB-143 (1 pilot), VC-38 (9 pilots), VC-40 (9 pilots).

Type of Mission: Bombing and strafing of Kara Airfield and anti-aircraft positions.

Planes: 19 TBF'S

Loadings: 13 planes with 1x2000LB. Inst. &1/10.
2 planes with 4x500LB. Inst.
4 planes with 4x500LB. Delayed fuzes -
2 with 6 hrs. delay
2 with 12 hrs. delay.

Times: Take Off - 0559-0620 (1 planes took off at 0641 and returned without going on strike.), Over target - 0740, Landed - 0847-0850.

Anti-Aircraft:
1. Light automatic AA intense.
2. Automatic AA from known positions. NW of strip, SW of center of strip, SE of strip (possibly 50 caliber and 20 MM).
3. New positions: NE and NW corners of strip, SE end of strip.

Interception: None except: (a) two unidentified planes observed going West about 2000 ft. before TBF'S attacked and while SBD'S were diving (1 pilot's observation); (b) after passed Shortland-Faisi area saw 8 planes going SE toward TBF'S. These planes, at 10,000 ft. just over the clouds, could not be indentified and when about 5 miles away these planes turned back (1 pilot's observation).

M/G Ammo expended: 4200 rds. - 30 cal.
1500 rds. - 50 cal.

Damage to Planes: 4 planes were hit by AA. 1 plane made a forced water landing and 3 are out of commission for an indefinite length of time, specifically -
#121 - 20 MM shell exploded in rear compartment (radio man and gunner injured).
#103 - Faring on wing pulled back during dive.
#109 - Shot up badly, in tail, hydraulic system, flaps - hit by 20 MM at 2500 ft. over strip at moment of release.
#120 - Shot in right wing and engine. Made water landing off Volla LaVella. Pilot and crew rescued.

Weather: 4/10 high 13,500 ft. Broken clouds 1500 to 11,000 ft. enroute in a right hand approach.

Target areas: Airstrip and AA gun positions.

Attack: High speed approach, dove North to South, push overs from 7000to 10,000 ft., releases at 1800 to 2500 ft., and pull outs from 1000 to 1200 ft. Bomb hits were as follows:
14x2000 lb. hit and covered strip.
4x500 lb. inst. on buildings and gun positions west of north 1/3 or strip.

27

Bomb hits (continued)
8x500 lb. delay on north 1/3 of strip.
4x500 lb. delay on north center of strip (probable).
4x500 lb. inst. on south half of stip.
Areas strafed were: strip; huts on river and beach; gun emplacements; Moila Pt. area; huts Southwest of strip; bivouac area.

Observations: 1 Corvette at Tonolei. One 10,000 ton ship 600 yards off Kahili (1 pilot's observation).

Route Out: Southern.

Route Back: Southern.

Note: 1. Plane #118 crashed on take off at 0619 and was damaged beyond repair. Its pilot, Lt. (J.G.) Harry W. Wilson was killed. Minor injuries were sustained by W. M. Haller, ARM2/c and L. E. Wilson, AOM3/c. This crew was attached to VC-38. The Bureau Number of the afore-mentioned plane is 06118.

2. Plane #120, Bureau Number 06475 - Lt. (J.G.) Douglas B. LaPierre A-V(N), pilot, turret gunner R. E. Faust, AMM2/c, J. E. DeVore, ARM2/c - was hit by 40 MM anti-aircraft fire froma a gun at the NE or NW corner of the strip immediately after the push over at an altitude of 5000-6000 feet. A piece, 2 feet square, was blown out of the leading edge of the starboard wing outward of the fold, and the engine was damaged. The pilot continued in his glide and is believed to have dropped his bombs on the strip. The plane continued on the route home but the engine and tail vibrated increasingly badly. Crash-boat USS C-9495 was observed in Wilson Strait, directly south of Baga Island. The pilot made a water landing; but, due to the hole in the wing the plane stalled and cartwheeled 180 degrees. The radioman's left leg was broken by gear which broke loose in the cartwheel. The plane floated for two minutes, permitting the pilot and gunner to remove the life raft and radioman. The crew was picked up by the crash-boat a few minutes later. The pilot and gunner were uninjured.

Myron Sulzberger
Captain U.S.M.C.R., VMTB-143
Intelligence Duty Officer.

VMTB-143

Plane Bu.No.	Pilot	Radioman	Turret Man	Out	In
06341	MC QUADE	Clark	Heager	0607	0853
		VC-38			
24244	BRUNTON	Sundey	Kemper	0618	0847
23981	SCHOLFIELD	Ulrich	Dills	0618	0847
23959	GIBLIN	Lee	Perkins	0622	0848
24265	MARSHALL	Lane	Tye	0618	0848
24194	DRAUGHAN	Deal	Paul	0618	0851
06472	LARSEN	Wagner	Wright	0601	0851
06406	PHILLIPPI	Bond	Tyler	0601	0852
24358	BISHOP	Schramm	Barnes	0605	0853
06489	TAHLER	Jeffrey	Brewer	0620	0844
		VC-40			
23987	BENNETT	Brantingham	Whitworth	0559	0850
24334	JACKSON	Powell	Maloney	0559	0852
24358	COLLINS	Mocker	Rivard	0559	0852
24195	COLLURA	Pittman	Accardi	0559	0850
24390	MORRISON	Loughridge	Joyce	0626	0845
24403	BEHL	Dunning	Drauden	0600	0853
24264	DeVEER	Meglemre	Schneider	0605	0850
06432	FREES	Wubbens	Tufenkjian	0600	0850
06475	LaPIERRE	Faust	DeVore	0619	****

28

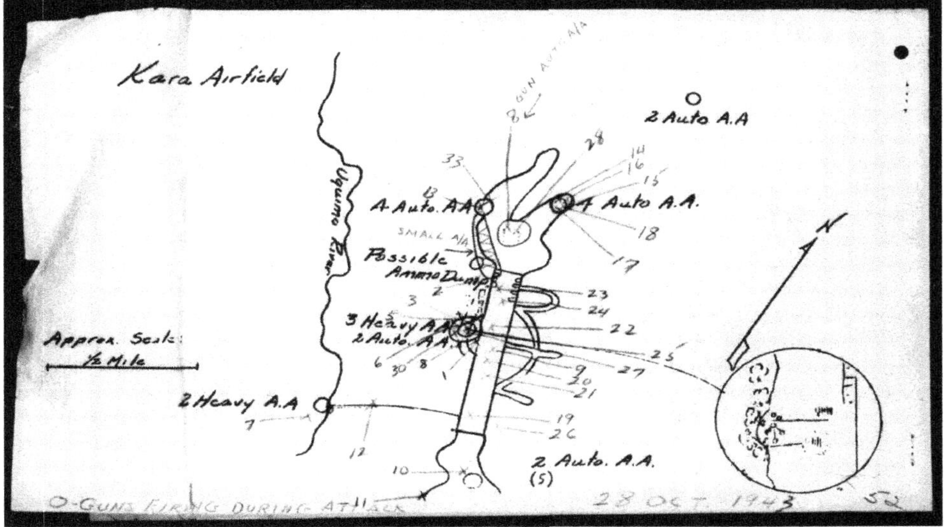
Kara Airfield
Uquimo River
2 Auto A.A
4 Auto. AA
4 Auto A.A.
SMALL A/A
Possible Ammo Dump
3 Heavy A.A
2 Auto. A.A
Approx. Scale:
½ Mile
2 Heavy A.A
2 Auto. A.A.
(5)
N
O-GUNS FIRING DURING ATTACK
28 OCT. 1943
52

Exhibit No. 8

S-E-C-R-E-T COMMANDER AIRCRAFT SOLOMONS S-E-C-R-E-T
STRIKE COMMAND
INTELLIGENCE SECTION

Date: 30 October 1943.

Squadron: VC-38, 9 planes; VC-40, 9 planes; VMTB 143, 9 planes.

Type of Mission: Bombing and strafing of Kara Airstrip and vicinity, Bougainville Island.

Planes: 27 TBF'S.

Loadings: 15 TBF'S with 1x2000LB. 1/10.
6 TBF'S with 4x500LB. Inst.
6 TBF'S with 4x500LB. delayed fuses as follows:
Each plane with 2-2 hour delay, 1-6 hour delay, 1-12 hour delay.

Times: Take Off - 0755-0803, Over target - 0945, Landed - 1055-1102.

Anti-Aircraft fire: Light heavy AA; Moderate light AA; some machine gun fire.

Interception: None.

M/G Ammo expended: 13,500 rds. 30 calibre.
6,975 rds. 50 calibre.

Damage to planes: Two planes received small holes from own shrapnel and machine gun fire.

Weather: 6/10 scattered cumulus clouds over target; base 2000 feet and top 4000 feet. North end of target obscured by clouds.

Target area: Kara runway and gun positions immediately adjacent to strip.

Attack: A high speed approach was made to a point directly North of the target. Push overs at altitude ranging from 7000 feet to 10,000 feet were made from North to South down the runway; releases on 2000LB. bombs and Inst. bombs at altitudes from 1500 feet to 2500 feet; releases on delayed fuse bombs, 900 feet to 1500 feet; pull outs on 2000LB. 1/10 and 4x500LB. Inst. were from 1200 feet to 1800 feet; pull outs on delayed fuse bombs were from 800 feet to 1200 feet.
Bomb hits were as follows:

12 2000Lb. bomb hits were well dispersed along entire runway. (1/10)
22 500LB. delayed bombs on the South three quarters of the field.
1 500 LB. delayed bomb on North quarter of strip.
12 500LB. Inst. bombs on gun positions and buildings adjacent to the North half of strip.
7 500LB. Inst. in vicinity of gun positions South Southeast of South end of strip.
4 500LB. Inst. bombs in the taxiway approaching center of Airfield from the East.
1 2000LB. was dropped in East end of revetment directly East of South one-third of Strip.
1 500LB. delayed and 1 500LB. Inst. hung up and were jettisoned enroute to base.

EXHIBIT NO. 8 26

Observations: Some light AA West of center of strip; heavy AA and small amount of automatic AA was observed coming from Northeast corner of strip. One pilot believes that an AA position directly West of center of strip was hit. He also noticed automatic 40 millimeter firing from same area. One pilot stated that he observed what appeared to be a 40 millimeter gun directly West of North one-quarter of strip on bank of Uguimo River firing from wooded area. A possible hit in an ammunition dump Northwest of strip followed by black smoke was reported by a pilot. A large fishing boat adjacent to a small island reef on the West coast of Shortland Island was seen. One gunner reported possible transport on Northeast coast of Bougainville Island at Rorawana Bay. A single engine plane well camouflaged was spotted in the revetment directly East of center of strip. Three barges and two AK in cove West of Tonelei was reported. Many bomb craters were observed on the runway. All pilots strafed gun positions and bivouac areas.

Route Out: To Baga; Northwest to a point West of Shortland Island and North to target area.

Route Back: Direct to base.

Kenneth R. Johnson
A.C.I.O.
VMTB 232

VC-38

Plane Bu.No.	Pilot	Radioman	Turret man	Out	In
24406	BRUNTON	Sunday	Kemper	0755	1102
06190	SCHOLFIELD	Ulrich	Dills	0755	1057
24358	GIBLIN	Lee	Perkins	0755	1102
24265	BEHN	Buis	Dill	0755	1057
24194	BISHOP	Schramm	Barnes	0756	1056
06420	TAHLER	Jeffrey	Brewer	0756	1056
24242	MARSHALL	Lane	Tye	0759	1059
06359	PHILLIPPI	Bond	Tyler	0759	1059
24282	LEARY	Groslie	Dale	0759	1059

VC-40

Plane Bu.No.	Pilot	Radioman	Turret man	Out	In
24334	JACKSON	Powell	Adams	0756	1058
24403	TRACY	Boyer	Rhodes	0756	1058
24264	BENNETT	Brantingham	Whitworth	0757	1101
23987	KNOCHE	Crabtree	Camp	0757	1101
24358	COLLURA	Pittman	Accardi	0757	1058
24268	MORRISSON	Loughridge	Joyce	0757	1058
06024	BELL	Dunning	Drauden	0758	1059
47595	COLLINS	Mocker	Rivard	0758	1059
23970	DE VEER	Meglemre	Schneider	0758	1058

VMTB 143

Plane Bu.No.	Pilot	Radioman	Turret man	Out	In
06270	SMITH	Gates	Thomas	0800	1100
06473	DAVIS	Fisher, L.G.	West	0800	1100
06341	LEIDECKER	Danielson	Hensen	0800	1055
06455	WEBB	Visvardio	Miller	0801	1053
06093	STEINAKER	Howe	Spickard	0801	1102
47506	GLENN	Sticksel	Whiteanack	0802	1100
47551	MORRIS	Duchesneau	Whitacre	0803	1050
06125	MC LAUGHLIN	Suchy	Smith	0803	1055
064714	YEAST	White	Oertle	0803	1101

27

S-E-C-R-E-T COMMANDER AIRCRAFT SOLOMONS S-E-C-R-E-T
STRIKE COMMAND
INTELLIGENCE SECTION

Date 31 October 1943.

Squadrons: VMTB-143 (0 pilots); VC-38 (9 pilots); VC-40 (8 pilots).

Type of Mission: Bombing of Kara Airstrip and AA, and strafing of area.

Planes: 24 TBF'S

Loadings: 12 planes with 1x2000 lb. 1/10.
6 planes with 4x500 lb. Delay (1,2,6,12 hrs).

Times: Take Off - 0715, Over target - 0900, Landed - 1024.

Anti-Aircraft fire:

1. Heavy and light at point 1/4 distance North of South end of strip and 1/2 way between Uquimo River and at a point a short distance NE of this.
2. 1 automatic AA at a point South of the road West of the South end of the strip 1/2 distance between Uquimo River and strip.
3. 1 light machine gun 1 mile South of strip
4. Light AA South of strip.
5. 2 or 3 machine guns West of Moila Pt.
6. Heavy AA at leavies from Tonolei and Eberle's Lease.
7. AA puff noticed between 4000/5000 ft.
8. Light AA tracers seen 1/2 way between South end of strip and Moila.
9. 10/15 puffs seen at 13000 ft.
10. AA of light intensity.

Interception: None.

M/G Ammo expended: 6900 rds. of 30 cal.
3070 rds. of 50 cal.

Damage to Planes: 2 planes sustained minor damage by AA - one had starboard flipper shot away, and one hit in green house to rear of pilots' head.

Weather: Over target good; over route scattered clouds 3000-15000 ft. solid overcast 30000ft.

Target area: Kara strip and AA guns.

Attack: Rendezvous at 0814 at Baga at 12000 ft., on course 0820; high speed approach. Came from SW of Moila Pt. Attacked from N of strip, runs South and Southwest. Push overs 6000-9000 ft.; releases 1500-2500 ft. Pull outs 200-2000 ft. Made right turn going out. Bomb hits were as follows:

1x2000 lb. 1/10 on N 1/3 of strip.
4x2000 lb. 1/10 on center of strip.
2x2000 lb. 1/10 on S 1/3 of strip.
1x2000 lb. 1/10 on West of N end of strip.
1x2000 lb. 1/10 on heavy AA west of center of strip.
1x2000 lb. 1/10 on East of S end of strip.
2x2000 lb. 1/10 hung up and returned.
14x500 lb. delayN 1/2 strip.

33

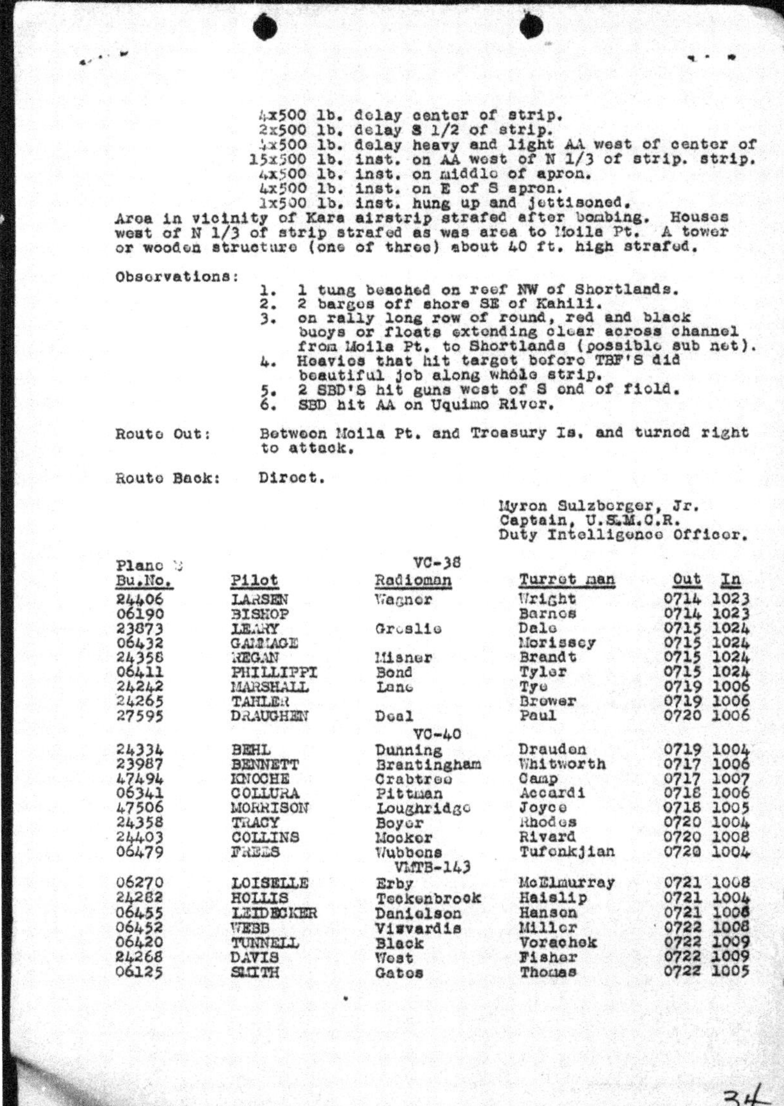

4x500 lb. delay center of strip.
2x500 lb. delay S 1/2 of strip.
4x500 lb. delay heavy and light AA west of center of
15x500 lb. inst. on AA west of N 1/3 of strip. strip.
4x500 lb. inst. on middle of apron.
4x500 lb. inst. on E of S apron.
1x500 lb. inst. hung up and jettisoned.

Area in vicinity of Kara airstrip strafed after bombing. Houses west of N 1/3 of strip strafed as was area to Moila Pt. A tower or wooden structure (one of three) about 40 ft. high strafed.

Observations:

1. 1 tung beached on reef NW of Shortlands.
2. 2 barges off shore SE of Kahili.
3. on rally long row of round, red and black buoys or floats extending clear across channel from Moila Pt. to Shortlands (possible sub net).
4. Heavies that hit target before TBF'S did beautiful job along whole strip.
5. 2 SBD'S hit guns west of S end of field.
6. SBD hit AA on Uquimo River.

Route Out: Between Moila Pt. and Treasury Is. and turned right to attack.

Route Back: Direct.

Myron Sulzberger, Jr.
Captain, U.S.M.C.R.
Duty Intelligence Officer.

Plane Bu.No.	Pilot	Radioman	Turret man	Out	In
		VC-38			
24406	LARSEN	Wagner	Wright	0714	1023
06190	BISHOP		Barnes	0714	1023
23873	LEARY	Greslie	Dale	0715	1024
06432	GAMMAGE		Morissey	0715	1024
24358	REGAN	Misner	Brandt	0715	1024
06411	PHILLIPPI	Bond	Tyler	0715	1024
24242	MARSHALL	Lane	Tye	0719	1006
24265	TAHLER		Brewer	0719	1006
27595	DRAUGHEN	Deal	Paul	0720	1006
		VC-40			
24334	BEHL	Dunning	Drauden	0719	1004
23987	BENNETT	Brantingham	Whitworth	0717	1006
47494	KNOCHE	Crabtree	Camp	0717	1007
06341	COLLURA	Pittman	Accardi	0718	1006
47506	MORRISON	Loughridge	Joyce	0718	1005
24358	TRACY	Boyer	Rhodes	0720	1004
24403	COLLINS	Mecker	Rivard	0720	1008
06479	FREES	Wubbens	Tufenkjian	0720	1004
		VMTB-143			
06270	LOISELLE	Erby	McElmurray	0721	1008
24282	HOLLIS	Teckenbrock	Haislip	0721	1004
06455	LEIDECKER	Danielson	Hanson	0721	1008
06452	WEBB	Viavardis	Miller	0722	1008
06420	TUNNELL	Black	Vorachek	0722	1009
24268	DAVIS	West	Fisher	0722	1009
06125	SMITH	Gates	Thomas	0722	1005

34

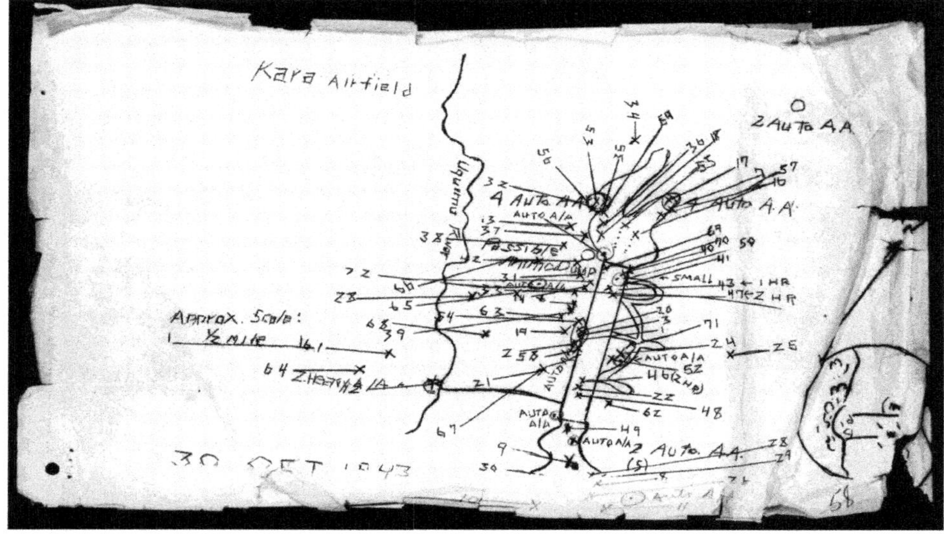
Kara Airfield
2 Auto A.A
4 Auto A.A
Auto A.A.
Possible
SMALL
Approx. Scale:
1/2 mile
2 Auto. A.A.
30 OCT 1943

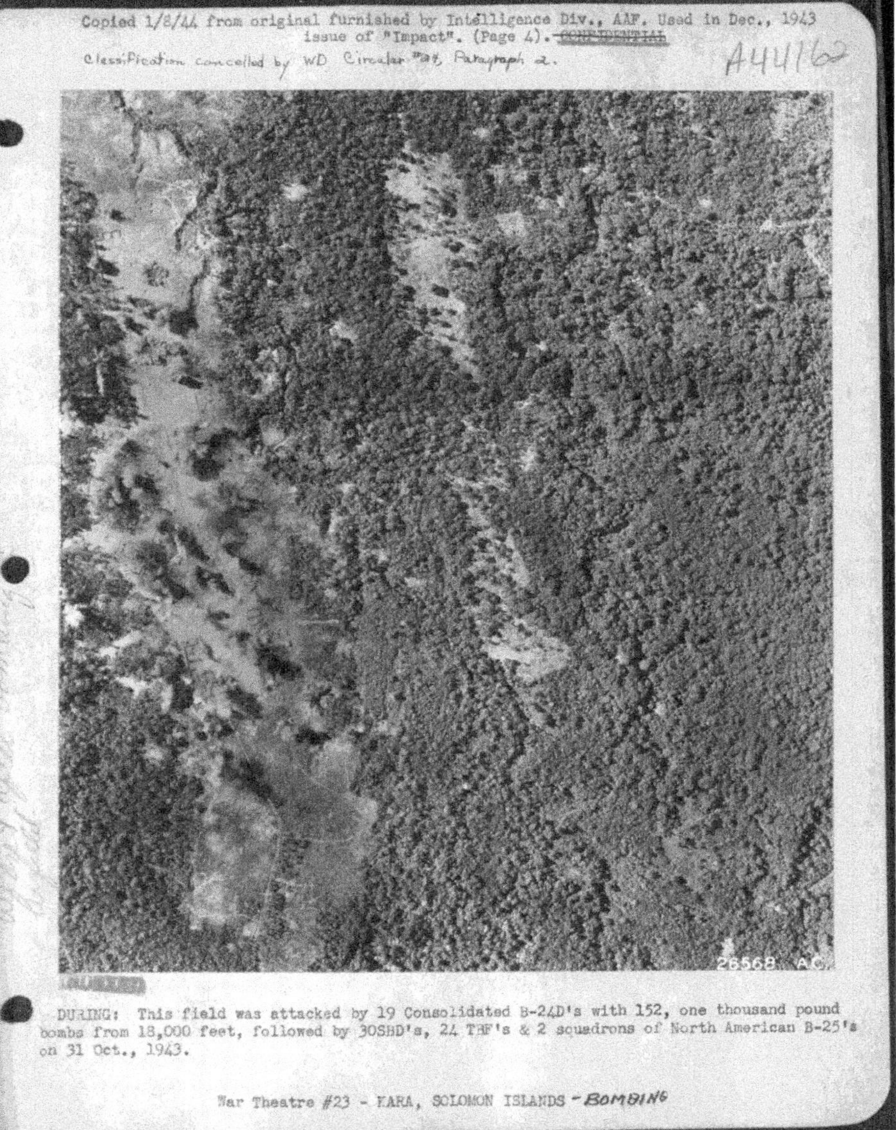
Copied 1/8/44 from original furnished by Intelligence Div., AAF. Used in Dec., 1943 issue of "Impact". (Page 4). ~~CONFIDENTIAL~~

Classification cancelled by WD Circular #?, Paragraph 2.   A44162

26568 A.C.

DURING: This field was attacked by 19 Consolidated B-24D's with 152, one thousand pound bombs from 18,000 feet, followed by 30SBD's, 24 TBF's & 2 squadrons of North American B-25's on 31 Oct., 1943.

War Theatre #23 - KARA, SOLOMON ISLANDS - BOMBING

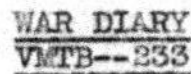

WAR DIARY
VMTB--233

2 November 1943

1. Orders Received.

Twelve planes of this squadron and six planes of VC-38 were ordered to a point northwest of the northern point of Bougainville Island in search of enemy shipping.

2. Operations.

Twelve planes of VMTB-233 with six planes from VC-38 went on a 4.5 hour search for enemy shipping. None was encountered.

3. Special Action Reports.

None.

4. Changes in Personnel.

None.

5. Relationship of Subordinate Units.

No change.

- 2 -

4

S-E-C-R-E-T

COMMANDER AIRCRAFT SOLOMONS
STRIKE COMMAND
INTELLIGENCE SECTION

S-E-C-R-E-T

EXHIBIT NO 11

Date: November 2, 1943.

Squadron: VMTB-143, 14 planes; VC-38, 2 planes, VC-40, 4 planes.

Type of Mission: Bombing of Kara Airfield and gun positions and strafing of area.

Planes: 20 TBF's.

Loadings: Sixteen TBF's with 1 X 2000 lb. 1/10. Four TBF's with 4 X 500 lb. Delay (2-6-12 hrs. delay).

Times: Take Off - 0815-0845. Rendezvous0904. On Course 0910. Over target. 1000. Landed 1118.

Anit-Aircraft Fire:

1. 1500' burst from known position west of strip.
2. Machine gun fire from; woods one mile west of south half of strip.
3. AA puffs noted; at 1000' ½ mile from South apron - over north apron - 1500' & 3000' over strip - 10/15 over Tonolei Harbor - couple of hundred (heavy intense barrage) over Kahili.
4. Tracer fire on pull out over strip.
5. Kara AA of light intensity.

Interception: None except 18 unidentified planes seen flying North 18 miles east of strip just inside the coast.

M/G AMMO. Expended: .50 Cal. 4240 rounds. . 30 Cal. 4650 rounds.

Damage to planes: None.

Weather: Bad weather all way. Rain squals over target. 7/10 cummulus with base at 3000' and top at 12000'.

Target area: Airfield and gun positions.

Attack: Circled area due to weather. High speed approach from 12000 ft. Direction of attack, South, pull out with right turn. Dove at target through holes in clouds. Push overs 4000' - 12000'. Release for 500 pounders 900' - 1100', for 2000 pounders 1000' - 3000'.

Bomb hits:

5 X 2000 lb. South 1/3 of strip.
2 X 2000 lb. Center 1/3 of strip.
7 X 2000 lb. North 1/3 of strip.
1 X 2000 lb. Northeast North end of strip on apron.
1 X 2000 lb. Southeast taxiway.
8 X 500 lb. North 1/2 of strip.
2 X 500 lb. South 1/3 of strip.
4 X 500 lb. Gun west of center of strip.
2 X 500 lb. Hung up and jettisoned.

General Kara area including huts and bivouac area strafed.

EXHIBIT NO. 11

32

Observations:

1. A good barrage of intense AA over Kahili.
2. Kara in good condition and operational before attack. West half of strip (half running from North to South) surfaced. East half not surfaced.
3. One plane's gunner observed four ships (cruisers or destroyers) zig zagging west of Shortlands.

Route out: Southern.

Route back: West of Treasury then direct.

Myron Sulzberger, Jr.,
Captain, U.S.M.C.R.,
Duty Intelligence Officer.

VMTB - 143

Plane Bu.No.	Pilot	Radioman	Turret Man	Out	In
06411	GLENN	Sticksel	Whiteanack	0815	1110
06479	PAINTER	Day	Brewer	0815	1110
24194	WEBB	Visvardis	Miller	0815	1110
064714	YEAST	White	Oertle	0816	1118
06369	STALNAKER	Howe	Spickard	0816	1116
24282	HOLLIS	Teckenbrock	Haislip	0819	1110
24358	SMITH	Gates	Thomas	0830	1112
24482	DAVIS	Fisher	West	0838	1112
47501	NAGODA	Hoolzel	Donaldson	0817	1111
06311	LEIDECKER	Danielson	Hansen	0817	0930
06452	MORRIS	Duchesneau	Whitacre	0819	1111
24244	TURNER	Lockridge	Parris	0820	1111
24195	ALTIZER	Thokar	Armacost	0820	1117
23987	TUNNELL	Black	Vorachek	0820	1118
24334	HORGAN	Moffitt	Bosco	0838	1113

VC - 38

Plane Bu.No.	Pilot	Radioman	Turret Man	Out	In
24212	BISHOP	Haller	Barnes	0830	1113
24403	BAHN	Buis	Dill	0818	1113

VC - 40

Plane Bu.No.	Pilot	Radioman	Turret Man	Out	In
24406	BEHL	Dunning	Drauden	0830	1113
24486	LAPIERRE	Faust	Devore	0843	1114
23873	TRULY	Temple	Joachim	0846	1110
47494	WILLIMAN	Irwin	Garwood	0846	1111

33

S-E-C-R-E-T

TBF OPERATIONS
MUNDA AIRFIELD

INTELLIGENCE REPORT

Dated	7 November 1943
Squadron:	VC-38 (4) VC-40 (7) VMTB-233(7)
Type of Mission:	Bombing and strafing of Gun Positions.
Planes:	14 TBF's.
Loading:	14 x 2000# Instan. fuse.
Times:	T O -- 1151 On course -- 1220 O T -- 1330
Anti Aircraft:	None.
Interception:	None except inconfirmed report of gunner that 2 Ø attacked an SBD.
MG Ammo. Expanded:	30 cal. --- 950 rounds. 50 cal. ---1170 rounds.
Damage to planes:	None.
Weather:	Rain squals up and back. O.T.-- Cumulus clouds 5/10,000, 5/10.
Target areas:	2 guns in Jaba Village area.
Attack:	High speed approach from 10,500. Push over from 4000 - 10,000. Release from 1000-2500. Dove E to W. Target area evident. SBD's hit village area strafed.
Bomb Hits:	7 x 2000# in N gun target area (no gun observed there). 3x2000# in S gun target area (only 1 pilot observed gun here - he observed 1 large gun. It was not firing.) 1 x 2000# Near miss in S gun target area. 2 x 2000# in area between most southernly part of trail and the most westernly part of the river east of the S end of the trail.
Observations:	1. 2 small boats 15 miles of river on course 270°. 2. 2 small boats 2/3 mile W of Jaba Village going fast and putting up smoke screen. 3. 2 DD and transports on course 120° from Treasury Island. 4. 4 badly camouflaged barges on the river 1 mile S of Jaba river. 5. Yellow something seen at 8000', 15 miles S & W of Jaba River. Possibily B24 raft. 6. Explosion and smoke in S gun target area. 7. No activity in area. 8. Small dock on river in S gun target area.

MYRON SULZBERGER
CAPT. USMCR Intelligence O.

8

TBF OPERATIONS

SQD NO.	PLANE BU.NO.	PILOT	PASSENGERS	OUT	IN	MISSIO
101	06190	McDonald	Blank-Woung	1147	1456	Bomb
126	06359	Scholfield	Ulrich-Dills	1147	1456	Juba
128	06411	Draughon	Deal-Paul	1147	1456	Vill-
129	47510	Giblin	Lee-Perking	1147	1456	age.
18	23987	Milling	Hall-Benson	1148	1456	
22	24490	Pennestri	Beiderman-Bordman	1148	1456	
110	064714	Cornelius	McCarthy-Slipkas	1148	1456	
17	24403	Watson	Crawford- Lavino	1149	1456	
118	24486	LaMade	Guinea-Daniels	1149	1456	
115	47501	Lecklider	Zollinhoffer-DeMott	1148	1456	
119	24358	Truly	Temple-Joachim	1150	1456	
113	24268	Tracy	Boyer-Rhodes	1150	1456	
130	06341	Knoche	Crabtree-Camp	1150	1456	
116	06311	Willamn	Irwin-Garwood	1151	1456	

9

S-E-C-R-E-T   TBF OPERATIONS
MUNDA AIRFIELD   S-E-C-R-E-T

INTELLIGENCE REPORT

Date: 10 November 1943

Squadrons: VMTB-233 (5) VC-38 (11) VC-40 (9) VMTB-143 (8)

Mission: Bomb and strafe Buka and Bonis Airfields, Buka Passage area.

Planes: 33 TBF's (18 on Buka) (15 on Bonis)
60 SBD's

Loadings: 33 TBF's with 1x2000# 1/10
60 SBD's with 1x1000# Inst.

Times:
Ren
Take Off--- 0615
Rendezvous --- 0720
Over Target --- 0808
Landed--- 0950

AA Fire: Heavy of medium intensity from 5-6 guns on north tip of Sohana Island. Heavy of light intensity from known positions E and N of Bonis Strip. Automatic of light intensity from known positions about both strips.

Interception: None.

Weather: To target, overcast at 12000'; showers; 6/10 low cu. 3000' - 6000'. Over target: 8/10 stratus at 17000'; 2/10 low scattered Cumulus. Visibility to target clear.
From target; Treasury Island south 5/10 - 7/10 low broken cu. 2000-3500.

Bomb Hits: Buka Airfield.

7--Confirmed hits on strip, concentrated on west and center 1/3.
6--Unconfirmed probable hits thru the length of Airstrip.
5--Unobserved.

Bonis Airstrip.

4--Confirmed hits, center and west 1/3 of strip.
4--Unconfirmed probable hits center and E 1/3 of strip.
2--Hits close to north edge strip, center.
2--Hits revetment area south of strip.
1--Miss in hut cluster, 2000 feet N/W of strip. 13
2--Bombs carried arming wires with them,

Observations: Heavy AA inaccurate fire noted from known positions on N tip of Sohana Island on approach. Accurate bombing by SBD silenced these. Other SBD hits seen on assigned targets E and W of Bonis strip and along N and S beaches of Buka Passage.
Two misses noted in water at E mouth of Passage. A large explosion and fire at W and of Buka Strip, by SBD hit on probable gas or ammo dump. Other SBD hits on Chinatown Village near piers, north beach of Buka Passage; a probable corvette seen anchored off beach of Matchin Bay, 5-6 miles south of Buka Passage.
3-4 medium bombers parked near south edge of Buka strip were well strafed by turret gunners. Bonis Airstrip probably serviceable, after attack.

Route Out: Course direct to rendezvous at West Cape (N tip of Choiseul) and up north coast of Bougainville. No shipping noted in Kihili- Tonolei area.

Attack: From 13000', left turn from N/E to S/W. Bonis Attack made from close over strip, necessetating dives too steep and fast for accuracy.

Route Back: Rally 3 miles S/W of Madchas Island thence down Southern coast of Bougainville and direct to base.

D.J. ROURKE
LT. USNR.
INTELLIGENCE O.

14

SQD. NO.	PLANE BU.NO.	PILOT	PASSENGERS	OUT	IN
116	06311	Gammage	Morissel	0612	0950
4	24242	Marshall	Lane, Tye	0612	0936
5	24182	Giblin	Lee, Perkins	0612	0950
6	23975	Tahlor	Jeffery, Brewer	0612	0939
7	24265	Larson	Wagner, Wright	0612	0950
22	24490	Bishop	Schramm, Barnes	0622	0950
8	24198	Leary	Greslie, Dale	0613	0940
125	06353	Rogan	Misher, Brandt	0613	0944
130	06341	Phillippi	Bond, Tyler	0613	0945
111	24480	Milling	Hall, B.C., Benson	0614	0941
102	23873	Watson	Crawford, Levine	0614	0947
103	06432	Lanace	Guinea, Daniels	0614	0947
104	47504	Harris	Henderick, Whiteis	0614	0951
106	06420	Cornelius	McCarthy, Slipkas	0615	0951
101	06190	Leidecker	Danielson, Karson	0615	0953
11	24332	Jackson	Powell, Adams	0616	0953
13	27595	Knoche	Crabtree, Camp	0616	0953
17	24403	Collura	Pittman, Accardi	0617	0951
12	06024	Morrison	Loughridge, Joyce	0617	0950
131	47506	Leake	Boyle, O'Daniel	0618	0945
14	24358	Leelider	Zollinhofer, DeMott	0618	0943
16	24212	Frees	Wobbins, Tufenjian	0619	0943
15	24495	Truley	Temple, Joachim	0619	0953
18	23987	Willaman	Irwin, Garwood	0620	0943
112	24482	DeVeer	Meglenre, Schneider	0620	0943
113	24268	Draughon	Deal, Paul	0620	0951
204	24489	Horgan	Moffitt, Bosco	0620	0951
206	06404	Yeast	White, Oertle	0620	0943
207	06455	Ranson	Fisher, J.J., Weeks	0620	0951
208	06452	McLauhlin	Suchy, Smith	0621	0952
202	06270	Smith	Gates, Thomas	0622	1003
107	24264	Stalnaker	Howe, Spickard	0622	1000
108	06472	Webb	Visvarois, Miller	0622	0951

15

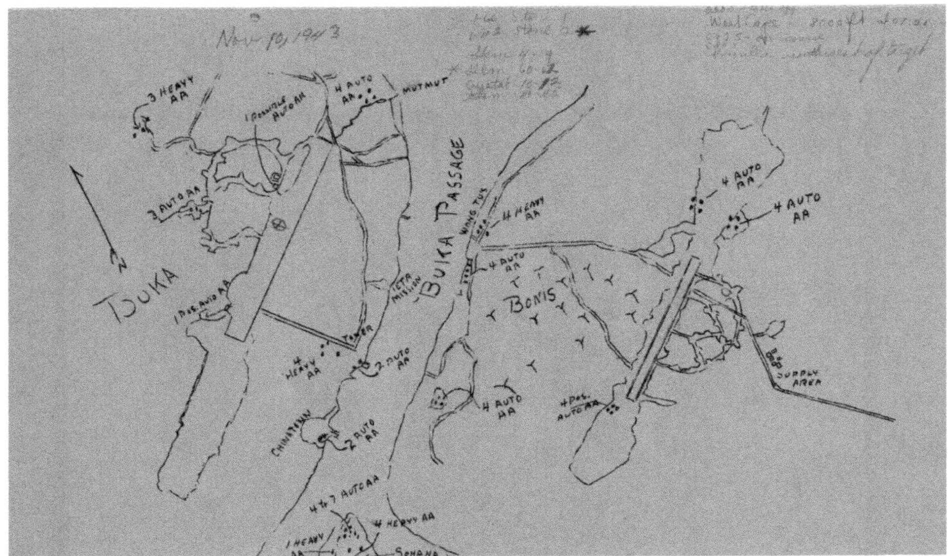

VC 38 Lt. John Leary's Map of Buka and Bonis Airfields Buka Passage Area, November 10, 1943
(Source: Leary Family Collection)

WAR DIARY
VMTB--233

10 November 1943

1. Orders Received.

Two strikes were ordered by strike command for this day, one on enemy forces on Empress Augusta Bay in support of our ground forces, and a strike on Buka and Bonis Airfields.

2. Operations.

Six planes of this squadron with six planes of VMTB-143 participated in a strike on Empress Augusta Bay in support of our ground forces. The pilots released their bombs at the assigned positions, strafed the area, and returned with no damage done to our planes.

Five planes of VMTB-233 with eleven planes from VC-38, nine planes from VC-40, and eight planes from VMTB-143 struck Buka and Bonis Airfields, releasing 18 tons of bombs on Buka Airfield and 15 tons of bombs on Bonis Airfield, and strafing the area. All our planes returned safely.

3. Special Action Reports.

See Speci l Action Reports for 10 November 1943 attached to back of War Diary.

4. Changes in Personnel.

None.

5. Relationship of Subordinate Units.

No Change.

STRIKE COMMAND,
COMMANDER AIRCRAFT SOLOMONS.

SECRET

12 November 1943.

OPERATIONS MEMORANDUM

Subject: Mining Operations in Buka Area.

Enclosures: (A) Mining Plan for Buka Passage
(B) Mining Plan for Channel Northwest of Madehas Island.
(C) Mining Plan for Channel East of Madehas Island.
(D) Time Schedule for Tactical Units.
(E) Routes to and from Target.

1. As ordered by ComAirSoPac (Secret despatch 081223) mining operations will be conducted in the eastern entrance to Buka Passage (Enclosure (A)), the cahnnel northwest of Madehos Island (Enclosure (B)), and the channel east of Madehas Island (Enclosure (C)). Defense and division support will be provided by B-25 and VB(H) aircraft.

2. This mining operation will take place during the night of 13-14 November 1943. Deferment due to weather may be necessary.

3. The tactical units employed will be:

9 PV-1, VB-140
9 PV-1, RNZAF Squadron No. 1
39 TBF-1, VMTB-233 & 143, VC-38 & 40
20 B-25, 42nd Bombardment Group
4 VB(H), 13th Bomber Command.

4. Takeoffs, rendezvous, attack, and tactical unit organization will be as indicated in Enclosure (D). Routes to and from the target will be flown as indicated in Enclosure (E). Details of attacks will be given in verbal briefing at 1400, 13 November, 1943.

5. Takeoffs will be made using the 3 ball course, landings as directed by tower or voice radio.

6. Group "D", diversion VB(H) will make simulated bombing runs from the northeast and southwest, 3 aircraft each on Buka airfield and Bonis airfield at 2335, 2350, 0005, and 0020. Bombs may be dropped on these fields after 0030. Bombs dropped prior to 0030 will strike only in areas 1 miles north-west of Buka airfield or 1 mile southeast of Bonis airfield.

7. Flight and division leaders will report to Strike Command at 2000, 13 November 1943 for final instructions, final weather information, and a time check.

8. Mines must be dropped, consistent with limitations stated below. In the event tactical units are prevented from attacking due to inclement weather or low visibility, time variations in time of attack up to 5 minutes are permitted. In the event the attacks cannot be made within these time limits tactical units will return to base. Do not jettison mines unless forced to do so to conserve fuel in order to assure safe return.

- 1 -

Source: VC 38 Lt. John Leary's Operations Memorandum (Source: Leary Family Collection)

SECRET

OPERATIONS MEMORANDUM

Subject: Mining Operations in Buka Area.

- -

9. Rendezvous after takeoff will be effected with lights on; turn off lights after 10 minutes on course. Keep all lights extinguished until within 20 miles from JACODET on return when running lights will be turned on.

10. All aircraft use 3415 Kcs.

CALLS

GROUP A	PV B-25	1 to 9 Stone 1 10 to 17 Stone 1
GROUP B	PV B-25	1 to 9 Stone 2 10 to 17 Stone 2
GROUP C	TBF	1 to 24 Stone 3
GROUP D	TBF B-25	1 to 15 Stone 4 16 to 19 Stone 4
GROUP E	2 B-24 2 B-24	Buka 1-2V26 Bonis 1-2V27

11. Observe normal Condition Red flight procedure if necessary when in vicinity of JACODET. Utilize all navigational radio aids to best advantage.

By direction Commanding Officer:

H H Larsen

H.H. LARSEN,
Lt-Comdr., USN.
G-3, Strike.

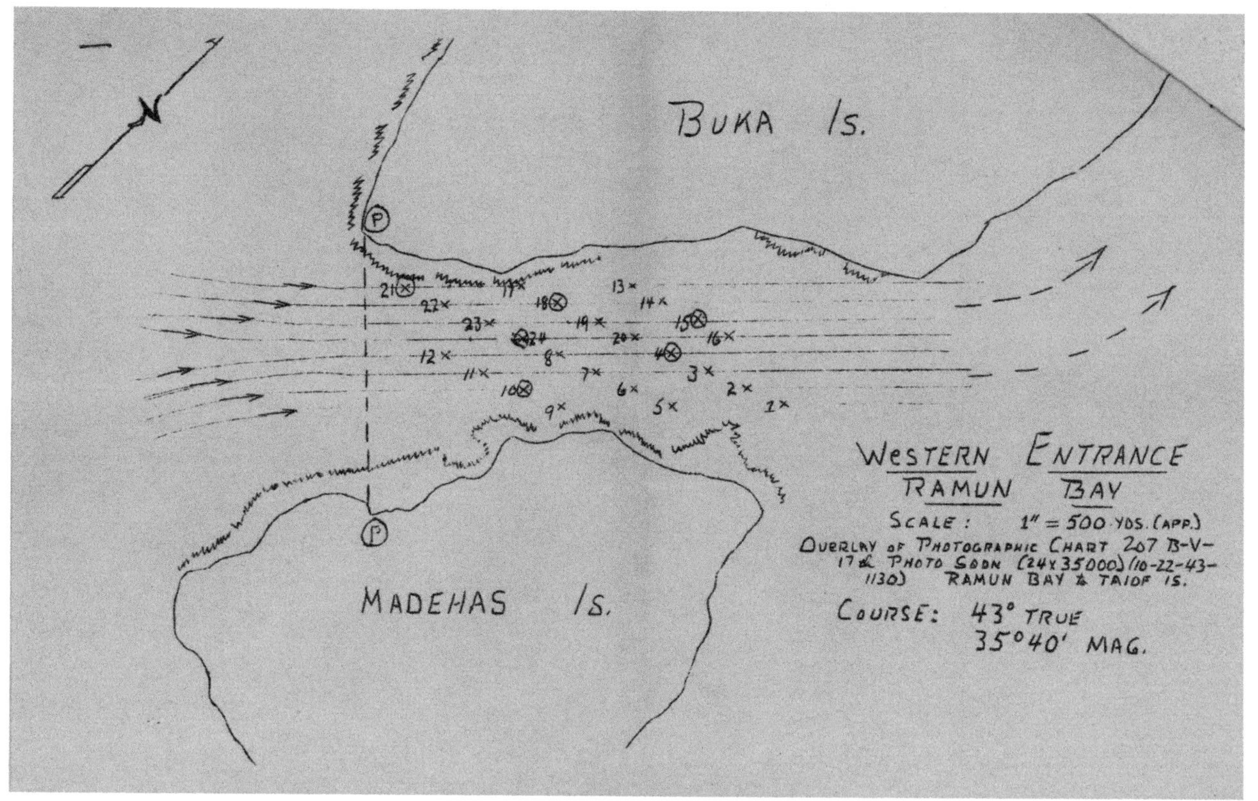
BUKA IS.
MADEHAS IS.
WESTERN ENTRANCE
RAMUN BAY
SCALE: 1" = 500 YDS. (APP.)
OVERLAY OF PHOTOGRAPHIC CHART 207 B-V-17 & PHOTO SQDN (24X35000)(10-22-43-1130) RAMUN BAY & TAIOF IS.
COURSE: 43° TRUE
35°40' MAG.

ENCLOSURE D.

SECRET

Time Schedule for Tactical Mining Units.

Group A: 9 PV-1, Load one Mk 12-1 mine – VB-140.
8 B-25 – Strafers, loaded with para frag bombs.

Group B. 9 PV-1, load one Mk 12-1 mine, RNZAF, No. 2.
8 B-25 – Strafers, loaded with para frag bombs.

Group C. 24 TBF, load Mk 12-1 mine.

Group D. 15 TBF, load one Mk 12-1 mine.
4 B-25 Strafers, loaded with para frag bombs.

Group E. 4 VB(H) loaded with 500 Lb. Inst. Fuze bombs.
Target Buka and Bonis Air Fields. Take Off prior 2100.
Land at Bevy

	A	B	C	D
TAKE-OFF	2130-45	2200-2215	2145-2200	2215-2230
Rendezvous Lights On.	2150 3000 Ft. Over Fld	2220 3000 Ft. Over Fld. Go out 5 Mi then turn.	2205 1000 Ft. over Fld.	2235 1000 Ft. over Fld.
On Course Lights Off +10	2155	2225	2210	2240
Route Up	N Coast B 1-40 ET	N Coast B 1-40 ET	S Coast B 1-40 ET	S Coast B 1-40 ET
Time Attack	2335	0005	2350	0020
Target	Buka Pass Encl. A	Buka Pass. Encl. A	Channel NW of Madehas Isle.	Channel E of Madehas Isle. Encl. C.
Route Back	1-45 ET S Coast B	1-45 ET S Coast B.	1-45 ET S Coast B.	1-45 ET S Coast B.
Land	0120	01-50	0135	0205
Pre-Landing Inst.	Land 1 Circle at 1000 Ft Over Fld.	Land 3 Circle at 1000 Ft. 5 miles SW of field until directed by tower to enter 1000' landing Cir over field then land.	Land 2 Circle at 2000' over field-enter 1000' circle then directed by tower then land.	Land 4 Circle at 1000' 5 miles west of field until directed by tower to enter 1000' circle over field then land

- -

L

SECRET ENCLOSURE (E)

ROUTES TO AND FROM THE TARGET

1. The point of departure for all missions will be JACODET airfield.

(a) Groups "A" and "B" will initially proceed north through Kula Gulf to the center of the main channel, thence to a point 8 miles west of West Cape thence to parallel the east coast of Bougainville 15 miles off the coast to a point 8 miles northeast of Buka Passage thence to the target. Do not exceed 1500 feet altitude. Retirement will be in accordance with the diagram furnished. From Mikmik Island to JACODET proceed direct - B-25's at 800 feet, PV's at 1200 feet 7 miles off of the general west coast of Bougainville.

(b) Groups "C" and "D" will initially proceed through Wilson Strait direct to a point 5 miles west of Mikmik Island. Keep 6 miles off of the general west coast of Bougainville. Thence proceed, attack and retire in accordance with the diagram furnished. From MikMik Island to JACODET Group "C" TBF's proceed at 1500 feet, Group "D" TBF's proceed at 1400 feet, and Group "D" B-25's proceed at 800 feet, keeping miles off of the general west coast of Bougainville.

(c) Group "E" will proceed independently to and from the target area remaining above 3000 feet.

2. Note small islands to be used as navigational check points.

3. Planes will proceed to the target as entire tactical units. Planes will return to JACODET in groups as convenient. Single aircraft unable to effect rendezvous within 50 miles of targets will return to base.

4. Keep IFF on at all times. Check Frequently.

5. Night Fighters will be cleared from the Cherryblossom-Jacodet route and areas from 2200 to 0200.

6. Verbal instructions will be given at the 2000/13 conference relative to the position of TF39 in the Cherryblossom Area in order that aircraft tracks in this area will clear this task force by 20 miles.

7. See Diagram attached to Enclosure E for retirement courses tracks and altitudes while in the Buka Area.

WESTERN ENTRANCE - RAMUN BAY

Section 1	Time of Runout*	Mine Number
Plane 1	22 sec.	1
2	20 "	2
3	18 "	3
4	16 "	4
Section 11		
Plane 1	16 sec.	5
2	14 "	6
3	12 "	7
4	10 "	8
Section 111		
Plane 1	10 sec.	9
2	8 "	10
3	6 "	11
4	4 "	12

Section 1V	Time of Runout	Mine Number
Plane 1	14 sec.	13
2	16 "	14
3	18 "	15
4	20 "	16
Section V		
Plane 1	8 sec.	17
2	10 "	18
3	12 "	19
4	14 "	20
Section VI		
Plane 1	2 sec.	21
2	4 "	22
3	6 "	23
4	8 "	24

* From pinpoint P-P

S-E-C-R-E-T — TBF OPERATIONS — S-E-C-R-E-T
MUNDA AIRFIELD

INTELLIGENCE REPORT

Date: 14 November 1943

Squadrons: VC-38 (12) VC-40 (8).

Type of Mission: Bombing in support of ground troops.

Planes: 20 TBF's.

Loadings:
2 TBF 10x100# fuse; nose 1/10 -- tail .025
2 TBF 11x100# fuse; nose 1/10 -- tail .025
16 TBF 12x100# fuse; nose 1/10 -- tail .025

Times:
Take off ------ 0601-0609.
On station----- 0730
Attack--------- 0902-0920
Land----------- 1033-1038

Anti-Aircraft fire: None. Tracer bullets reported are believed to have been ricochets from strafing. One gunner reported a field piece flashing on a bluff at 135.5 - 219.1 on map hereinafter referred to.

Interception: None.

Damage to Planes: Two planes received shrapnel and bullet holes in their tails, believed to have resulted from our own bombs and strafing ricochetes.

M/G Ammo Expended:
30 cal.-- 4070
50 cal.-- 2050

Weather: On way up: ceiling 800'; rain over Treasury Island. Over target: clear to 15000'. Return; 3/10 cumulus, ceiling 1000' - 1500'.

Target Area: Area shown on FMAC Hasty Terrain Map 141, Puruata within coordinates 135.2 - 217.9; 135.7 217.9; 135.4- 218.4.

Attack: Course up direct. Upon arrival, contacted Bomb Base and Aircraft Liaison Party # 21. Instructed by radio to orbit until 0830 over Cape Torokina; given coordinates of target area and instructed to bomb triangular area (approximately 500 yards to E side) north of base line upon smoke signals being given. Planes orbitted at 3500' - 4000' until 0900 when three smoke signals were given, those at base on coordinates, that at ajex short of coordinate. Planes decended to make level run over target area from E to W, parallel with base line, in sight of echelon.

16

Released bombs at 600-1100 feet. After bombing run, planes circled and made strafing run over target area. All but one gunner strafed to north (away from base line); it is belcived that all of that gunners shots landed within the target area.

Bomb Hits: 210 bombs in target area.
22 bombs hung up and wire jettisoned.
2 bombs hung up and were brought back (one to Munda; one to Barakoma.

Note: 13 arming wires of bombs dropped in the target area were not brought back; it is not known whether these bombs exploded.

Observations: 17 planes returned directly to base. 3 planes landed at Barakoma: one for engine trouble, another to accompany him. The third for fuel shortage. All planes later returned to base.

Shipping: Friendly PCs and small craft observed in vicinity of Cape Torokina.

FREDERICK FRELINGHUYSEN
Lt. USNR. VC-40
Intelligence Duty O.

17

SQD. NO.	PLANE BU.NO.	PILOT	PASSENGERS	OUT	IN
1	24244	Brunton	Sunday, Kemper	0610	1033
2	23981	Scholfield	Ulrich, Dills	0601	1033
3	23959	Giblin	Lee, Perkins	0601	1033
4	24242	Tahlor	Jeffery, Brewer	0601	1033
5	24182	Draughon	Deal, Paul	0609	1034
6	23975	Bishop	Schramm, Barnes	0603	1034
7	24265	Larson	Wagner, Wright	0608	1034
8	24194	Phillippi	Bond, Tyler	0608	[illegible]
9	24208	Leake	Boyle, O'Daniel	0603	1035
21	24515	Leary	Greslie, Dale	0603	1325
22	24490	Regan	Misner, Brandt	0609	1035
19	23970	Marshall	Lane, Tye	0605	1507
14	24358	Locklider	Zollinghofer, DeMott	0605	1036
12	06024	Morrison	Loughridge, Joyce	0605	1037
17	24403	Bohl	Dunning, Drauden	0606	1325
15	24195	Tracy	Boyer, Rhodes	0606	1036
18	23987	Bennett	Brantingham, Whitworth	0607	1037
11	24334	Knoche	Crabtree, Camp	0607	1038
207	06455	Collura	Pittman, Accardi	0607	1035
210	06223	Willmann	Irwin, Garwood	0607	1035

18

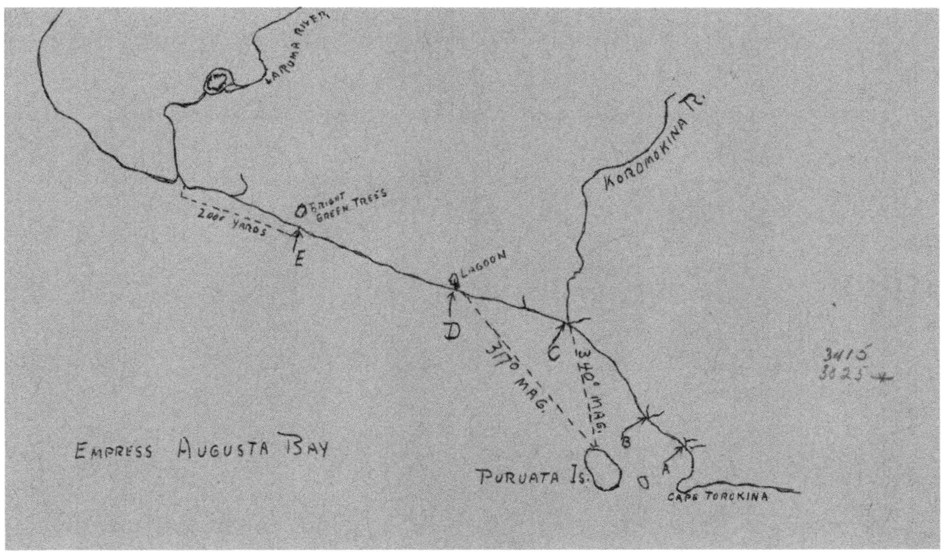

VC 38 Lt. John Leary's Map of Empress Augusta Bay (Source: Leary Family Collection)

EXHIBIT 16

CONFIDENTIAL — TBF OPERATIONS, MUNDA AIRFIELD — CONFIDENTIAL

INTELLIGENCE REPORT

Date: 16 November 1943

Squadrons: VMTB-143 (11) ; VMTB-233 (17); VC-40 (11).

Type of Mission: Mine laying.

Planes: 39 TBF's

Loadings: 39 x MK 12-1 mines.

Times: (1) West channel flight.

T.O.------0138 - 0152
O.T.------0350 - 0355
Land------0531 - 0705

(2) East channel flight.

T.O.----- 0213 - 0227
O.T.----- 0345 - 0355
Land----- 0557 - 0606

Anti-Aircraft Fire:
1. All AA and MG fire of slight intensity.
2. Light AA or MG fire at Cape Moltke and light AA from Sohana, Empress Augusta Bay, (also heavy) west shore of Ramon Bay, (also MG fire), Bonis and Buka Strip area, shores of Buka Passage, Kahili, and Ballale.
3. MG fire from both shores of west channel, SE coast of Ramon Bay and from hill in SW tip of Buka.
4. Tracers observed coming from Treasury.
5. Slight heavy observed over Buka at 4000'.

Interception: Indeterminate number of enemy planes. An enemy plane made passes and shot tracers at TBF's around Cape Moltke. An enemy plane made 2 passes on TBF of same flight and fired on second pass as TBF was making right turn to hit target. One plane fired tracers at TBF about 5 miles from target--round wing tips and single engine. One plane encountered a plane with lights flickering on and off, it followed the TBF one half way dwon Bougainville One plane encountered plane with all recognition lights go in at Taraokh,.A TBF kept with this plane at short distance down Bougainville when it went inland.

Damage and Casualties:
1. Plane # 223 (pilot 1st. Lt. Earle R. McLaughlin, USMCR ; Russel J. Suchy, Pvt. (461596) USMCR radioman ; George R. Smith Jr Sgt. (371678) USMC , all of VMTB-143) did not return. The plane it is believed was last seen NW of the Buka area.

EXHIBIT NO. 16 45

2. Plane # 101 (Pilot was 1st. Lt. DeLancey and his gunner and radioman, all of VMTB-23 did not return on schedule. A water landin was made about thirty miles northeast of Treasury. At 0830 they all were picked up by Dumbo uninjured.
Plane # 101's engine vibrated slightly after take off. This was followed by a pop from the exhaust manifold, however thereafter the motor ran well. All instruments checked. The motor quit at 0615 about 14 miles NE of Treasury while flyi at 1200'-1300'. Five minutes before the pilot had switched the main center fuel tank. There were no instrument indicati before the engine quit. The pilot immediately swiched back to all other tanks and back to center main. There was no reacti The pilot glided down and made a good water landing. The water landing was made with flaps down. The life raft was quickly removed from the plane however difficulty was encountered in removing it from the case. The plane floated for over a minute. There was sufficent time to remove from the plane; plotting board, parachutes, very pistol, and flares.

Weather: Clear, tho slightly hazy over channel.

Target areas: Channel between Buka and Madehas Islands and Channel east of Madehas Island.

1. West channel flight: Thru Wilson Strait direct about 6/8 miles off SW Bougainville to point west of Madehas Island. Glide down from 1600' to 600'. Release from 450' to 700' at speeds ranging from 165 to 185 knots. Retired with left turn over Buka at 1600'.
Mines were dropped as follows:

16 x channel.
4 x Between Madehas and Toiokh Islands.
1 x North of Madehas Island.
Overlay with more exact positions attached to original.

2. East channel flight: Thru Wilson Strait direct along west coast Bougainville about 6 miles out to point 3 miles W of Miknik, then N to [illegible] Then turned right over Buka, glided to 600' and went thru channel east of [illegible] ias where mine drop made and then made exit. Drops made between 170 - 180 knots, from 500'-800'.
Mines dropped as follows:

16 x channel
1 x hung up and jettisoned.
Overlay with more exact positions attached to original.

46

Observations:

1. Search light observed at: One at Cape Maltko, two at Empress Agusta Bay and one at Buka and one at Bonis.
2. Some difficulty experienced by east channel flight in finding the easterly landmark.
3. Area at which Mines No. 14, 15 and 17, (Eastern Channel) dropped seemed like a shallow spot.
4. B25's proceeding to fast for group "D".
5. Rendezvous for West Channel group poor.
6. Red alirt at Cherry Blossom up and back.
7. MG fired at B25's.
8. The west channel pilots went in Singly and in different sections.

Note: Overlay with mine positions plotted is attached to original.

MYRON SULZBERGER, JR.
Captain, USMCR.
Intelligence O. VMTB-143

47

SQD. NO.	PLANE BU. NO.	PILOT	PASSENGERS	OUT	IN
1	24244	Brunton	Sunday, Kemper	0138	0531
[illegible]	23961	Phillippi	Bond, Tylor	0139	0532
3	23959	Giblin	Leo, Perkins	0143	0550
4	24242	Scholfield	Ulric, Dills	0141	0533
5	24182	Marshall	Lane, Tye	0142	0533
6	23975	Bishop	Schram, Barnes	0143	0543
7	24265	Leary	Froslie, Dale	0144	0534
[illegible]	24194	Leake	Boyle, O'Daniel	0145	0535
[illegible]	24490	Rogan	Fisher, Brandt	0146	0535
[illegible]	06455	Draughon	Deal, Paul	0147	0535
[illegible]	06233	Tanler	Joffrey, Brower	0148	0535
[illegible]	06479	Hagoda	Hoelzel, Donaldson	0149	0620
[illegible]	24403	Smith	~~Gates~~ Shuey, Thomas	0150	0536
[illegible]	23970	Hanson	Fisher, J.J., Locks	0150	0705
[illegible]	24390	Painter did not	Joey, Brewer	0150	0237
[illegible]	06024	Webb	Visvardis, Miller	0150	0540
[illegible]	24358	Morgan	Moffitt, Bosco	0151	0536
[illegible]	24208	Stalnaker	Howe, Spickard	0151	0617
15	24195	Morris, T.	Duchesneau, Whitacre	0151	0230
[illegible]	24515	Hollis	Tuckenbrock, Hainlip	0151	0611
208	06452	Altizer	Thokar, Almacost	0152	0536
202	06270	Yeast	White, Oertle	0152	0542
[illegible]23	47551	McJanhlin	Sucky, Smith	0152	Did not return
212	06093	Turner	Lockridge, Farris	0152	0556
113	24268	Cole	Green, Morac	0213	0603
102	23873	Sloan	Bruce, Myers	0214	0604
107	47504	Pylant	Blum, Meyer	0215	0550
11[illegible]	24482	Takacs	Hall, J.J., Is.	0216	0555
117	47494	Colby	Connor, Kerr	0217	0605
10[illegible]	06472	LaSalle	Marshall, Schillinger	0218	0604
110	06471	Jaqua	Cannon, C[illegible]	0219	0603
115	47501	Johnson	Fleming, Herndon	0220	0601
116	06311	Strieby	Rickard, Rice	0221	0600
101	06190	Delancey	Kozakwich, Hutchorn	022[illegible]	not retur
128	06411	Hathaway	Thompson, Edwards	0223	0606
129	47510	Saxton	Bullock, Doss	0224	0601
130	06341	Lauder	Fyock, DeRouch	0225	0602
125	06353	Billing	Hall, E.C., Benson	0226	0602
100	24406	Hollis	Howard, Cunningham	0227	0603
105	06125	Gonterman	Sanjavic, Kasprzak	0227	0557
106	06420	Cornelius	McCarthy, Slipkas	0227	0600

48.

STATEMENT OF EARL R. MC LAUGHLIN

EXHIBIT NO 21

NOV. 16TH AT 0535, MINES WERE TO BE LAID IN THE BUKA PASSAGE AREA BY THE FLIGHT TO WHICH I WAS ATTACHED. THE EIGHT PLANE FLIGHT IN WHICH I WAS THEN FLYING REACHED A POINT ABOUT FIVE MILES S.W. OF MADEHAS ISLAND ABOUT TEN MINUTES AHEAD OF TIME. I WAS IN THE LAST SECTION AND TRAVELLING AT ABOUT 165 KNOTS INDICATED. I WENT DOWN TO 500 FEET, THE ALTITUDE AT WHICH THE MINES WERE TO BE LAID. I NOTICED A WHITE LIGHT TO THE EAST. I TROUGHT IT WAS A STAR. I MADE AN EASY CIRCLE. I SAW SEVERAL PLANES DOING THE SAME THING; I ASSUMED THAT THEY WERE OURS. IT WAS VERY DARK. WHEN HALF WAY THROUGH THE FIRST CIRCLE, I REALIZED THAT THE WHITE LIGHT WAS A PLANE AND NOT A STAR. IT WAS THEN AT 1000 FEET. I STILL BELIEVED THAT IT WAS ONE OF OUR PLANES. IT CONTINUED TO CIRCLE AS I DID. ON THE SECOND CIRCLE IT GOT INSIDE ME AND ON MY TAIL. I IMMEDIATELY MADE FOR A CLOUD. IT WAS THEN FLYING AT 800 FEET. THE PLANE HAD A SEARCHLIGHT WHICH LOOKED LIKE A LANDING LIGHT. THO I WAS THEN DOING OVER 200 KNOTS THE PLANE STILL STUCK WITH ME AND THE SEARCHLIGHT WE AIMED ON ALL THE WHILE. I TRIED EVERYTHING I KNEW TO AVOID THE PURSUER. I TRIED TO STAY IN THE SAME CLOUD, BUT IT WAS TOO SMALL; I MADE SHARP CLIMBING TURNS, REVERSE TURNS, AND DIVING TURNS.; AND CONTINUED EVASIVE TACTICS FOR FULLY 45 MINUTES. DURING THESE MANUEVERS I GOT UP AS HIGH AS 2500 FEET. NOT ONLY WAS I UNABLE TO SHAKE THIS PLANE, BUT I PICKED UP OTHERS. AT ONE TIME TWO PLANES WITH SEARCHLIGHTS WERE AFTER ME; ONE SEARCHLIGHT AT MY SIDE, AND ONE FLOODING ME FROM OVERHEAD. THE SEARCHLIGHT PLANES ALWAYS REMAINED OUT OF MY GUNNERS RANGE, THO ON ONE OCCASION ONE OF THE PLANES DID FIRE A BURST AT ME. A NIGHT FIGHTER WITH-OUT A SEARCHLIGHT MADE AT LEAST THREE RUNS ON ME FROM BELOW. THESE SEARCHLIGHT PLANES MUST HAVE WONDERFUL RADAR TO STICK WITH ME THE WAY THEY DID. NOT WITHSTANDING EVERYTHING I DID A SEARCH-LIGHT PLANE WASALWAYS WITH ME AT 7 O'CLOCK. VISIBILITY AT ALL TIMES WAS NOT IN EXCESS OF 500 FEET. I HAD TURNED OFF ALL MY LIGHTS.

I DID NOT DROP MY MINE BECAUSE I FELT THAT I COULD EVADE THESE ENEMY PLANES AND DROP THE MINE AT THE ASSIGNED LOCATION.

FINALLY I DECIDED TO COME HOME; I WAS THEN LOW ON GAS HAVING ONLY AN HOUR AND A HALF'S SUPPLY LEFT. I DETERMINED TO FLY HOME AT 100 FEET. WHEN THE ALTIMETER READ 100 FEET I STARTED TO LEVEL OFF. AT THAT INSTANT MY PLANE HIT THE WATER AND BOUNCED IN THE AIR. I GAVE IT THE GUN IMMEDIATELY. MY PLANE WAS MUSHING AS IT HIT THE WATER AND WAS THEN MAKING 165 KNOTS. AFTER HITTING THE WATER THE PROP HAD NO POWER. I JUST

EXHIBIT NO. 21 62

-2-

HEAD A [illegible]. THEN I MADE A FAIRLY SMOOTH WATER LANDING. WHEN THE PLANE FIRST HIT THE WATER I WAS THROWN FORWARD AND BANGED MY EYE ON THE INSTRUMENT PANEL. WHEN I FINALLY LANDED I KNOCKED MY HEAD ON THE PANEL. I TRIED TO PUT DOWN MY FLAPS BEFORE LANDING. I HAD [illegible] MY [illegible] OFF TEN MINUTES BEFORE LANDING.

I JUMPED OUT OF THE PLANE QUICKLY (WITH MY PARACHUTE AND [illegible]) AND STARTED TO PULL OUT THE LIFE RAFT. IT JUST TOOK ABOUT FIVE SECONDS TO REMOVE IT. MY TURRET GUNNER, SMITH, WAS CLIMBING OUT OF THE TURRET ESCAPE HATCH BY THE TIME I HAD GOTTEN THE RAFT OUT. THE REAR OF THE FUSELAGE WAS THEN HALF UNDER WATER. SMITH TOLD ME THAT [illegible], THE RADIOMAN, HAD [illegible] [illegible] [illegible] [illegible] A FEW MINUTES BEFORE THE CRASH. [illegible] MAY HAVE BEEN HIT BY ONE OF THE [illegible] THE NIGHT FIGHTER. I DO NOT KNOW IF MY PLANE WAS [illegible] HIT. I TRIED TO DIVE DOWN AND OPEN THE DOOR TO [illegible] INTO THE FUSELAGE. MY PARACHUTE KEPT ME AFLOAT AND I COULD NOT GET FAR ENOUGH UNDER WATER. SMITH DOVE FOR THE DOOR TOO, BUT HE COULDN'T FIND THE DOOR OR ITS LATCH. [illegible] THE PLANE [illegible] OVER AND SANK. THE TAIL HIT ME IN THE [illegible] AND DRAGGED ME [illegible], BUT I [illegible] TO GET AWAY.

[illegible] ABOUT [illegible] AFTER THE CRASH.

[illegible] HAD A LITTLE DIFFICULTY IN GETTING THE COVER OFF OF THE LIFE RAFT. AFTER GETTING IT OFF WE HAD DIFFICULTY IN INFLATING IT. THE VALVE WAS [illegible] AND THE RAFT WAS ONLY HALF INFLATED. WE [illegible] OVER THE VALVE AND AFTER ABOUT HALF AN HOUR OF THIS WE [illegible] TO FULLY INFLATE IT. THE RAFT COVER AND MY CARTRIDGE [illegible] LOST IN THE PROCESS. WE LATER FOUND THAT ALL THE RATIONS [illegible] ATTACHED TO THE COVER.

WHILE TRYING TO INFLATE THE RAFT I [illegible] THE "[illegible]" [illegible] IS [illegible] MY FINGER [illegible] THE GLASS TUBE. THESE GLASS TUBES ALWAYS GIVE A FELLOW TROUBLE.

WHEN WE FINALLY GOT INTO THE BOAT IT WAS 0[illegible]. WE [illegible] THE [illegible] OF [illegible], ABOUT FIFTY MILES OFF SHORE-- [illegible].

THE BOAT WAS THEN HALF FULL OF WATER. [illegible] IT OUT AND THEN NOTICED THAT WE BOTH FELT SICK AND BOTH OF US VOMITTED. WE JUST LAID [illegible] RESTED FOR A COUPLE OF HOURS.

BETWEEN 0[illegible] AND 0900 WE SAW A PV HEADED TOWARD RABAUL. IT WAS FLYING AT [illegible] FEET ABOUT 2[illegible]0 FEET TO OUR STARBOARD. I FIRED TRACERS AT THE PLANE WHICH WENT RIGHT PAST ITS NOSE, BUT THE PLANE NEVER STOPPED.

63

-5-

EVERYBODY IN THE PLANE INCLUDING THE PILOT MUST HAVE BEEN ASLEEP.

WE THEN CONCLUDED THAT IF WE WERE TO BE SAVED WE WOULD HAVE TO SAVE OURSELVES. WE COMMENCED ROWING-- WE ALTERNATED HOURLY-- AND CONTINUED THIS UNTIL 1100. THEN IT GOT TOO HOT. THERE WAS A ONE OR TWO KNOT WIND FROM THE SOUTH. THE CURRENT FLOWED SSE.

FORTUNATELY WE WERE NOT HUNGRY THAT MORNING. OUR TOTAL FOOD SUPPLY CONSISTED OF ONE CHOCOLATE RATION. WE ALSO HAD ONE CANTEEN FILLED WITH WATER. WE PUT UP THE PARACHUTE AS A CANOPY AND DRIFTED. DURING THE MORNING WE FOUND EIGHT COCONUTS DRIFTING IN THE WATER. WE DRANK THE WATER FROM ONE OF THEM. ALL THE OTHERS WERE RANCID. THE MEAT WASN'T ANY GOOD IN ANY OFTHEM.

A FIVE FOOT SHARK PERSISTED IN SWIMMING WITHIN A FOOT OF OUR BOAT FOR QUITE SOME TIME. WE FOUND THIS MOST UNPLEASANT. SMITH FINALLY SHOT HIM AND HE ROLLED OVER AND DIED.

ABOUT 1830 WE COMMENCED ROWING AGAIN. WE CONTINUED TO DO THIS UNTIL THE NEXT MORNING. DURING THE NIGHT EACH OF US TRIED TO SLEEP WHILE WE WEREN'T ROWING. EACH OF US MANAGED TO SLEEP FOR ABOUT 30 MINUTES.

WE DETERMINED TO RATION OUR FOOD AND WATER IN THIS WAY: 1/2 SQUARE OF CHOCOLATE FOR EACH OF US PER DAY, AND A SIP OF WATER IN THE MORNING AND A SMALL DRINK AT NIGHT. WE STUCK TO THIS. WE WERE BOTHERED MORE BY THIRST THAN HUNGER.

NOV. 17TH ABOUT 0100 AN EASTERLY BREEZE DEVELOPED AND WE USED THE PARACHUTE AS A SAIL. IT BLEW US ALONG UNTIL 0600. MY COMPASS, WHICH WORKED THOUGH IT GOT VERY WET, PROVED INVALUABLE. WE FOUND THAT BY THROWING THE NET OVER THE SIDE-- WITH THE FAVORABLE SSE CURRENT-- THAT WE MADE BETTER SPEED THAN WITH OUT IT. ABOUT 0230 WE HEARD PLANES. AT FIRST WE THOUGHT THAT THEY WERE OURS AND FIRED TRACERS AT THEM. AFTER THEY GOT CLOSER WE SAW THAT THEY WERE TWO "BETTYS" AND AN ENEMY FLOAT PLANE. THEY WERE FLYING AT 200 FEET ABOUT 1000 FEET AWAY AND HEADING EAST. LUCKILY THEY DID NOT SEE US. LATER WE COULD SEE TRACERS FIRED OVER THE HORIZON.

WE CONTINUED THE SAME ROUTINE. SMITH SHOT A BIRD. IT WAS PRETTY GAMEY. WE SAVED THE ENTRAILS; THOUGHT THAT WE COULD USE THEM FOR FISHING. WE CAUGHT A FEW SMALL FISH WITH OUR NET. THESE WE ATE PRINCIPALLY FOR THEIR JUICE VALUE.

64

-4-

THREE SHARKS STARTED TO FOLLOW US DURING THE DAY. WE FIGURED THAT THEY SMELLED THE BLOODY BIRDS ENTRAILS. THEY WERE ABOUT SIX FEET LONG AND SWAM ABOUT EIGHT FEET BEHIND OUR BOAT. WE THREW THEM THE BIRD'S ENTRAILS AND THEY DISAPPEARED.

NOV. 18TH TODAY THROUGH THE CLOUDS WE WERE ABLE TO SEE WHAT WE BELIEVED WERE MOUNTAINS IN THE DISTANCE. WE CONTINUED TO EAT RAW FISH AND FOLLOWED THE SECOND DAY'S ROUTINE. WE BELIEVED THAT WE WERE AVERAGING ABOUT 20 MILES A DAY. THE BREEZE PROBABLY INCREASED THE SECOND DAY'S MILEAGE TO 30 MILES.

IN THE EVENING WE SAW THE COAST. IT WAS 15 OR 20 MILES AWAY. WE THEN PROCEEDED TO PADDLE ALONG THE COAST.

NOV. 19TH AFTER THE MOON CAME UP WE SAW AA FIRE COMING FROM THE SHORE AND SEARCHLIGHTS SWEEPING THE SKY, AND PLANES HIGH OVER HEAD. SHRAPNEL WAS FALLING ALL ABOUT US. I COVERED MY HEAD WITH THE RUBBER SEAT OF MY PARACHUTE AND SMITH USED A BACK PACK. THIS NIGHT'S ACTIVITY CONTINUED UNTIL DAYLIGHT.

AFTER DAYLIGHT WE ROWED TO WHERE WE THOUGHT THAT THE SEARCHLIGHTS WERE LOCATED. A DESTROYER (THE TERRY) PICKED US UP AT 0630 ABOUT FOUR MILES FROM SHORE. THEY GAVE US A PLEASANT BIT OF NEWS-- THAT WE WERE HEADED DIRECTLY FOR A JAP POSITION. WE WERE GIVEN BRANDY AND GENERALLY TREATED IN FINE STYLE ABOARD SHIP.

NOV. 20TH WE DISEMBARKED AT CACTUS.

NOV. 21ST WE WERE RETURNED TO MUNDA VIA BOAT. WHEN I REACHED MY QUARTERS I FOUND THAT MY FELLOW PILOTS HAD DIVIDED UP MY LIQUOR, BEER, RAZOR BLADES, AND SIMILAR USEFUL PROPERTY. THEY TOLD ME THAT THEY WERE KEEPING THE THINGS SAFE FOR ME. I TOLD THEM THAT I THOUGHT THEY "OUGHT TO LET THE BODY GET COLD FIRST."

COMMENTS:

1. THE RATIONS SHOULD BE TIED TO THE RAFT AND NOT TO THE COVER; OR IF THEY ARE TIED TO THE COVER, THE COVER SHOULD BE SECURELY TIED TO THE RAFT.

2. THE CHERRY BLOSSOM FIGHTERS SHOULD MAKE A SEARCH AFTER EACH PATROL FARTHER OUT TO SEA BEFORE PANCAKING. THIS SHOULD BE FOLLOWED BY EACH PATROL WHEREVER BASED, ESPECIALLY WHEN A PILOT IS REPORTED AS MISSING.

65

WAR DIARY
STRIKE COMMAND
AIRCRAFT, SOLOMONS

20 November 1943 - 13 March 1944

On 20 November 1943, Strike Command was based at Munda, New Georgia, under command of Colonel D.F. O'Neill, who assumed command on 26 July 1943 at Guadalcanal. On 25 January 1944, headquarters of Strike Command was moved to Piva, Bougainville. This command for varying periods of time directed operations of and exercised tactical control of the following squadrons:

1. Attack Bomber Squadrons:

(A) SBD's
(B) TBF's

(A) SBD'S; VC-38--Lieut. A.R. Barber, USN and Lieut. Ben Tappan, USNR; VC-40--Lt.Comdr. John H. Pennoyer, USN; VB-98A-Lieut. Comdr. J. R. Little, USNR, Lieut(jg) W.G. Maerki, USNR, and Lieut. R.T. Lord, USNR: VB98B-Lieut.Comdr. J.R. Little, USNR, and Lieut. E.T. LaRoe, USNR: VMSB-144--Major F.E. Hollar, USMCR; VMSB-234--Major H.B.Penne, USMCR; VMSB-235--Major E.E. Munn, USMCR; VMSB-236A--Major E.P. Paris, Jr., USMC; VMSB-236B--Major W.A. Cloman, Jr.,USMC; VMSB-241--Major James A. Feeley, Jr., USMC; VMSB-243--Major Thomas J. Ahern, USMC; VMSB-244--Major R.J. Johnson, USMC, and Major Harry W. Reed, USMCR: VMSB-341--Major George J. Waldie, USMCR, and Major James T. McDaniel, USMC.

(B) TBF'S: VMTB-143--Capt. G.U. Smith, USMCR and Capt. H.W. Hise, USMCR: VMTB-232--Major R.W. Smith, USMCR: VC-40 --Lt.H.S. Jackson, USN: VC-38--Comdr. C.E. Brunton, USN, who also was Group Commander; VMTB-233--Major R.W. Coln, USMC; VMTB-134--Major A.C. Robertson, USMC.

2. Search and Reconnaissance:

RNZAF #1 (PV-1)--Squadron Leader H.C. Walker.
RNZAF #2 (PV-1)--Squadron Leader Greenway.
VS-64 (SBD) --Lt.Comdr. Alfred D. Morgan, USNR.
VB-138 (PV-1) --Lt.Comdr.Hanson, USN.
VB-140 (PV-1) --Lt.Comdr.V. Williams.

Missions carried out included bombing and strafing attacks against enemy installations, positions, airfields and shipping, support for our ground forces in the Bougainville campaign, reconnaissance, area searches, patrols, artillery spotting, liaison with ground forces and direction of rescues.

The following are brief accounts of the specific missions carried out during the period:

SECRET

3

EXHIBIT NO 17

CONFIDENTIAL — TBF OPERATIONS MUNDA AIRFIELD — CONFIDENTIAL

INTELLIGENCE REPORT

Date: 20 November 1943

Squadrons: VMTB-143 (15) VMTB-233 (8) VC-38 (13)

Type of Mission: Bombing and Strafing.

Planes: 36 TBF's.

Loadings: 12x2000# Inst.
12x4-500# Inst.
12x12-100 Inst.

Times: T.O. ----- 1548 - 1419
O.T. ----- 1555
Land ----- 1652 - 1713

Anti-Aircraft Fire: 2 MG located 3 miles E of Motupena Point.
1 MG located in Mosigetta Village.

Interception: None.

MG/Ammo. Expended: .30 cal --- 2600
.50 cal --- 2475

Casualties and Planes Damage: Shrapnel holes in wing of one plane.

Weather: There was a 9/10 cloud cover over the target from 2500 feet.

Target area: Mosigetta Village.

Attack: Approach made from the sea. The village area was circled. Ammunition or gasoline dump may have been hit. Releases from 2000' - 1300'. A number of fires was started.

Bomb Hits: 12x2000# --- Mosigetta Village area.
4x12-100 -- Mosigetta Village area.
10x4-500# -- Mosigetta Village area.
3x12-100# - Maigi mission area.
1x4-500# -- Maigi mission area.
1x4-500# -- 8 huts inclearing 10 miles E of Motupena Point.
1x12-100# - 8 huts inclearing 10 miles E of Motupena Point.
4x12-100# - Hung up.

Observations:
1. Mosigetta Village containedover 100 buildings and occupied an area of about 2 square miles.
2. About 30 piepls were seen diving into the water during the bombing run.

EXHIBIT NO. 17 49

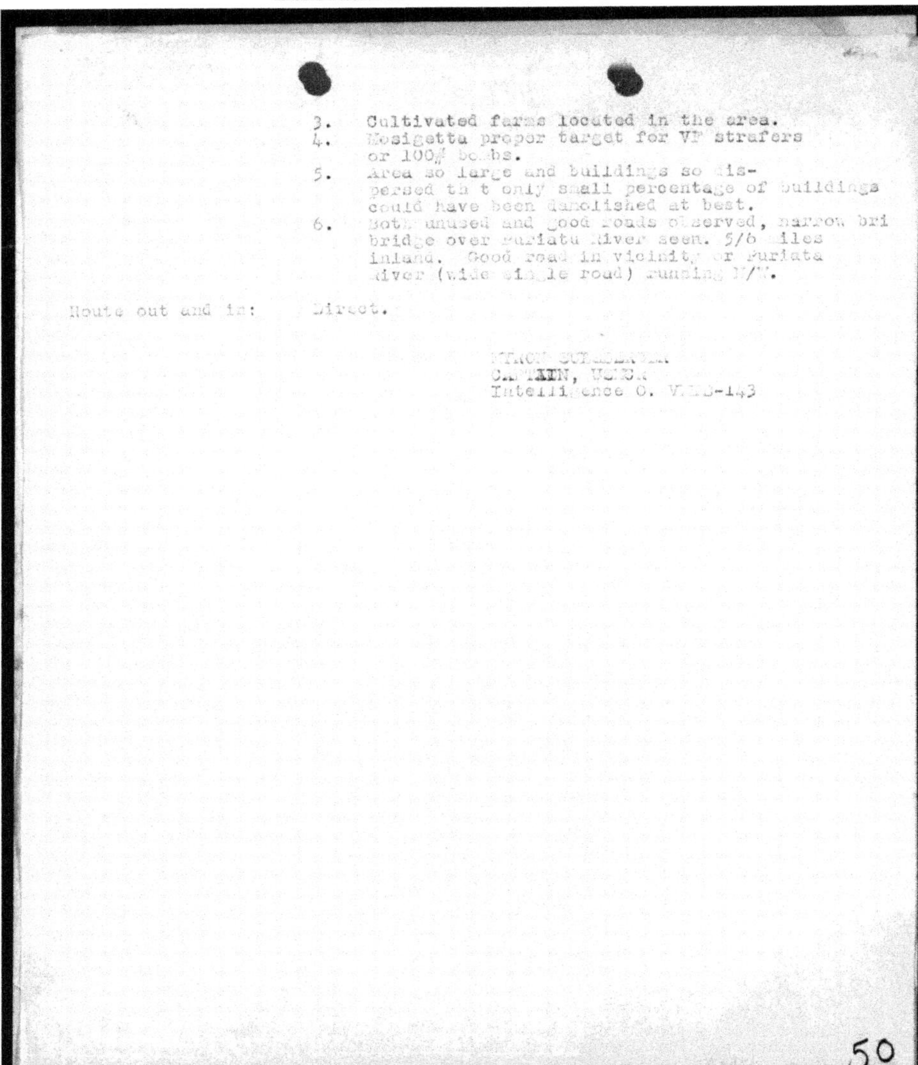

3. Cultivated farms located in the area.
4. Mosigetta proper target for VF strafers or 100# bombs.
5. Area so large and buildings so dispersed that only small percentage of buildings could have been demolished at best.
6. Both unused and good roads observed, narrow bri bridge over Puriata River seen. 5/6 miles inland. Good road in vicinity of Puriata River (wide single road) running N/W.

Route out and in: Direct.

[illegible]
CAPTAIN, USMCR
Intelligence O. VMTB-143

50

SQD. NO.	PLANE BU.NO.	PILOT	PASSENGERS	OUT	IN
111	[illegible]	[illegible]	[illegible]	1348	1651
115	24496	Giblin	[illegible]	1419	1700
10[illegible]	23873	Bishop	[illegible], Barnes	134[illegible]	1701
107	24464	[illegible]	[illegible]	1348	170[illegible]
109	06471	Marshall	[illegible]	1348	1700
117	24492	[illegible]	[illegible]	1425	1702
205	24471	[illegible]	[illegible]	1349	1700
123	06411	[illegible]	[illegible]	1349	1700
201	244[illegible]7	Dasher	Sutton, Clary	1349	1700
202	06270	Morgan	Moffitt, Bosco	1350	1701
203	06473	Turner	Lockridge, Ferris	1350	1701
20[illegible]	06452	[illegible], 143	[illegible]	1350	1649
112	[illegible]	Smith	~~[illegible]~~ SHURI, Thomas	1350	1650
106	064[illegible]0	Stainaker	Howe, [illegible]	1352	1704
108	06472	Webb	[illegible]	1352	1702
115	47501	Glenn	Sticksel, [illegible]	1352	1704
118	24486	[illegible]	White, [illegible]	1352	1705
119	[illegible]	Painter	[illegible]	1353	1713
113	24268	Altizer	[illegible]	1353	1705
1	24244	[illegible]	[illegible]	1353	1709
7	24265	Davis	Fisher, L.[illegible]., [illegible]	1354	1710
9	24260	Morris, T.	[illegible]	1354	1709
21	24515	McQuade	Clark, [illegible]	1354	1710
8	24294	Leidecker	[illegible]	1354	1710
2	23981	Larson	Wagner, Wright	1354	1708
3	23959	[illegible]	Bond, Tyler	1354	1709
20	24390	Leary	[illegible], Dale	1356	1709
220	06479	[illegible]	Jeffrey, Brewer	1365	1710
104	06024	Leake	Boyle, O'Daniel	1357	1710
206	24403	Draughon	Deal, Paul	1357	1710
4	24242	Voyles	Provenzano, Gilbert	1357	1640
222	06456	Radcliffe	Page, Mack	1357	1649
6	23975	Dowd	Brownfield, Rosenthal	1359	1648
130	06341	[illegible]	Fisher, J.J., Weeks	1359	1649
22	24490	Melby	Connor, Keer	1359	1649
5	24182	Boyden	Patrickus, Pardun	1359	1650

51

EXHIBIT 18

CONFIDENTIAL TBF OPERATIONS MUNDA AIRFIELD CONFIDENTIAL

INTELLIGENCE REPORT

Date: 22 November 1943

Squadrons: VMTB-143 (14) VC-38 (10)

Type of Mission: Bombing and strafing.

Planes: 24 TBF's.

Loadings: 19x2000# 1/10 nose ; .025 tail.
5x4-500# 1/10 nose ; .025 tail.

Times: T.O. ----- 1239 - 1250
O.T. ----- 1445
Land ----- 1530 - 1554

Anti-Aircraft Fire: Light AA from targets No. 4 and 6. Light and heavy AA, 3500' N/W of N end of strip. Two MG at west end of target No. 6 (75 yards from beach). Light and heavy AA at center of target No. 5. Two heavy AA at the top of Kangu Hill. 4 - 5 light AA E of Kangu Hill. Automatic AA from bomb crater in N apron. One auto just S of strip. AA, N/E side of Kangu Hill. Light and heavy from N/E/ of the N end of the strip at target No. 8 . Light AA from S end of target No. 7. There was moderate heavy and light AA except that the light AA (20/40 MM) from target No. 4 was intense as a plane passed over it.

Interception: None.

MG/Ammo. Expended: .30 cal ------ 3750
.50 cal ----- 5605

Casualties and Damage to Planes:

1. Tylor AOM 3/c (VC-38) sustaned shrapnel wound on hand. He was in plane # 19.
2. Plane # 19 damaged by shrapnel in left side top gun turret.
3. Plane # 118 hit in engine cowling from 20 MM or 40MM shell at 900 feet.
4. Plane # 113 MG shot off rudder cable .

Weather: Over target; 6/10 clouds from 3000'-9000' N of target and over N part of strip.

Target area: Kahili Airfield and gun positions.

Attack: Approached at 11000' from NE of Tonolei, made series of left turns and then made run down strip. Pushovers 9000'-5000'. Release 2500' -1200'. Pullouts. EXHIBIT NO. 18

52

Bomb Hits:

7x2000# North third of strip.
5x2000# South third of strip.
5x2000# center third of strip.
1x2000# west edge of south third of strip.
4x500 # at AA at NE end of target No. 7.
8x500 # South third of strip.
4x500 # Between S end of strip and beach.
4x500 # Just west of N part of west taxiway at gun positions in target No. 5.
Area generally strafed.

Observations:

1. Ammunition dump hit at center of the road located W of the strip.
2. Empty gun pits located NE of the N end of the strip 2/3 the way from the strip to Muliko River.
3. Shell splashes in sea off Morla Point (200 yards off) and 3/4 mile from Shortlands on line with Moila Point. Some firing definitely from Shortlands.
4. Three planes (2 Betties in good condition) on S apron. Probably hit by bomb.
5. Smoke from Erventa Island.
6. R/W unserviceable before attack at least 12 craters filled with water.
7. Submarine seen 20 miles W of N end of Ganngga Island.

Myron Sulzberger
Captain, USMCR.
IntelligenceO. VMTB-143

53

SQD. NO.	PLANE BU.NO.	PILOT	PASSENGERS	OUT	IN
8	24194	Scholfield	Ulrich, Dills	1239	1535
9	24208	Giblin	Lee, Perkins	1239	1536
20	24390	Tahler	Jeffrey; Brewer	1240	1538
22	24490	Bishop	Schra..., Barnes	1240	1538
19	23987	Phillippi	Bond, Tylor	1240	1439
101	24334	Larson	Wagner, Wright	1241	1530
103	06432	Leake	Boyle, O'Daniel	1241	1531
107	24264	Ga...age	Mriseey	1242	1532
108	06472	Regan	Misner, Brandt	1242	1533
109	24358	Draughon	Deal, Paul	1242	1534
112	24482	Altizer	Thekar, Ai..ocast	1243	1540
3	23959	Nagoda	Hoelzerl, Donaldson	1243	1541
4	24242	Davis	Fisher, L.O., West	1243	1542
5	24182	Morris, T.	Duchesneu, Whitacre	1244	1543
2	23981	Hollis-143	Teckjnbrock, Haialipl	1243	1544
113	24268	Glenn	Sticksel, Whiticanck	1245	1545
110	06471	Horgan	Moffitt, Bosco	1245	1546
115	47501	Yoast	White, Oertle	1246	1548
117	24492	McQuade	Bl..rk, Hedger	1246	1549
118	24486	Painter	Dey, Brewer	1247	1549
119	24358	Stalnaker	Howe, Spickard	1247	1550
128	06411	Smith	~~Gates~~ SHURI, Thomas	1248	1551
202	06270	Turner	Lockridge, Farris	1248	1553
206	24403	Webb	Visvardis, Miller	1249	1554

54

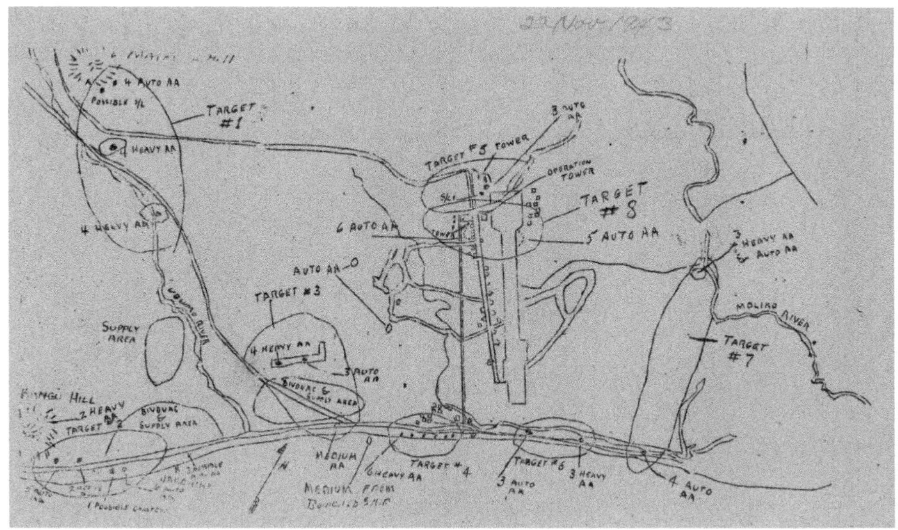

VC 38 Lt. John Leary's Map of Kahili Airfield, November 22, 1943 (Source: Leary Family Collection)

CONFIDENTIAL TBF OPERATIONS MUNDA AIRFIELD EXHIBIT NO 19 CONFIDENTIAL

INTELLIGENCE REPORT

Date: 24 November 1943

Squadrons: VMTB-143 (15) VMTB-233 (8) VC-38 (14)

Type of Mission: Bombing and strafing

Planes: 37 TBF's

Loadings: 14x2000# Inst.
12x4-500# Inst.
11x11-100# Inst. and one incendiary with each load or 11x100#

Times: T.O. ----- 0759 - 0813
O.T. ----- 1005
Land ----- 1140 - 1205

Anti-Aircraft Fire: One Heavy AA known position at Porton Plantation (still firing). One heavy AA at known position at Chabai 300 yards inland. One heavy AA at known Position 400 yards SE of center of strip. Four heavy AA and three light AA at Sohanna Island (25 heavy burst), five auto guns (5 tracer streams) S end Chabai strip. Possible heavy AA at Gomai (one gun flash). AA from islands off Chabai (MG). Moderate inaccurate heavy AA over Bonis. Heavy AA over targets slight and at 12000' and 2500'.

Interception: None.

MG/Ammo. Expended: .30 cal ----- 5200
.50 cal ----- 3700

Casualties and Plane Damage: Minor damage to two planes. One plane had MG holes at right wing and one had shrapnel holes in tail.

Weather: Clear over target area. 6/10 cloud cover 3000' - 7000' NE of target.

Target area: Supply and personnel area, storehouses and gun positions at Tarlena and Tsirogei.

Attack: High speed S/W approach at 11000' from east of Buka Passage then west over the target. Push overs from 8000' - 2000'. Releases from 2500' - 300'. Area strafed included target areas, buildings, at N end of Katitu Island (included this near Taiof Island), Sorokon Plantation and islands off Sorokan.

EXHIBIT NO. 19

55

Bomb Hits:

I Chabai

	Bombs	Target / Results
(a)	16x500# 33x100# 3 Inc'd	Storehouses and small buildings in area just east of Main road running NE, 700 yards inland. Many buildings destroyed, and blown up.
(b)	5x2000# 4x500# 42x100# 3 Inc'd	Supply area just west of the main road running NE, 500 yards inland. Buildings were destroyed.
(c)	4x500#	Just NE of the supply area just west of the main road running NE.
(d)	1x2000#	Just SW of the supply area just west of the main road running NE.
(e)	1x2000#	Gun position 200 yards N of the village.
(f)	1x2000#	Buildings E of main road, 150 yards inland. Some destroyed.
(g)	3x500#	Near known gun positions at Porton Plantation. Gun still firing.

II Tarlena

	Bombs	Target / Results
(a)	2x2000# 11x100 1 Inc'd	Supply and personnel area 750 yards NE of village. Many buildings destroyed.
(b)	4x500#	A 500' string running south beginning at the southerly end of the supply area 750 yards NE of village one or more buildings destroyed.
(c)	1x2000# 11X100# 1 Inc'd	Buildings in the village just off the pier.
(d)	11x100# 1 Inc'd	Supply area 400 yards N of village. Some buildings were destroyed.
(e)	3x500#	Buildings in the village

III Tsirogei

	Bombs	Target / Results
(a)	2x2000#	Supply and personnel area 1000 yards NE of the village. Buildings were destroyed.
(b)	3x500#	On the road intersection 500 yards NE of the village.
(c)	4x500# 11x100# 1 Inc'd	Supply area 1800 yards N of village. Buildings were destroyed.

IV Miscellaneous

	Bombs	Target / Results
(a)	1x2000# 2x100# 1 Inc'd 3x500#	Hung up ; 1x500# jettisoned.
(b)	4x500#	Row of houses in the beach at Tortai village on NE coast of Bougainville.

Bomb Summary:
14x2000# Inst.
48x500# Inst.
121x100# Inst.
11 Inc'd.

Observations:
1. Fire near pier at Tarlena.
2. Fire near Porton AA position.
3. Smoke and two fires from Chabai supply area.
4. 2 DD and 50 small craft in, harbor at Cape Torakina.
5. Fire and 1500' black smoke column 1500 yards east of Motupena Point on beach at Gazelle H[illegible]
6. Fires (possibly oil) at Tarlena and Tsiregei.
7. Bonis field not serviceable.
8. 3x50' barges east of Chabai pier.
9. 3 barges 750 yards east of pier at Chabai.
10. 1 DD, 2 LST and 2 small craft on 120° course 4 miles west of S tip of Vella LaVella.
11. Huts on islands of Tsiregei.

Route out: Northerly.

Route In: Southerly.

NOTE:

1st. Lt. Pennestri, plane # 7 with 11x100# and one incendiary, turned back at Kieta becasue of a rough engine and abnormally high fuel consumption. He proceded from Kieta in a SW direction toward Kara at which he arrived at 0930. A high speed approach was made at 11000', a shallow dive was commenced at this altitude. He passed east of the two known auto AA positions N of the strip dropped 7x100# in a possible ammunition dump NE of the strip at 3000'. He made a sharp right turn and headed west. No fire was started. The only AA encountered were tracers past the left wing as he flew over the N apron. No gun flashes seen at Kara. The strip was definetely inoperative. The place was deserted. There were 18 or 20 holes in the strip. Four 100# and one incendiary were dropped 500 yards west of the Porro River at a point between Porro River and Aku. This was a clearing 500 yards square. There were about 15 new canvas topped huts-- not camouflaged-on the clearing. This clearing about 7 miles SW of Kara. One MG fired from the NW corner of the clearing. There were trucks and roads there. There are six clearings of the same size within a one square mile area. Huts are located in all these clearings.

MYRON SULZBERGER JR.
Captain, USMCR.
Intelligence O. VMTB-143

57

SQD NO.	PLANE BU.NO.	PILOT	PASSENGERS	OUT	IN
204	24489	Brunton	Sunday, Kemper	0759	1140
208	06452	Phillippe	Bond, Tyler	0759	1140
201	24487	Giblin	Lee, Perkins	0759	1140
107	24264	Tahler	Jeffrey, Brewer	0800	1142
2	23981	Bishop	Schrader, Barnes	0800	1142
3	23959	Schelfield	Ulrich, Dills	0800	1142
207	06455	Larson	Wagner, Wright	0801	1140
203	06473	Leake	Boyle, O'Daniel	0801	1142
220	06479	Leary	Greslie, Dale	0802	1340
128	06411	Gammage	Morissey	0802	1143
4	24242	Rogan	Misner, Brandt	0802	1144
5	24182	Draughon	Deal, Paul	0802	1145
102	23873	Marshall	Lane, Tye	0803	1143
130	06341	McDonald	Blank, Young	0803	1144
108	06472	Damiani	Pudil, White	0803	1144
109	24358	Dasher	Sutton, Clary	0804	1144
6	23975	Bartholf	Bendschneider, Shouley	0804	1144
7	24265	Pennestri	Beiderman, Boardman	0804	1021
112	24482	Smith	~~Gates~~ SHURI, Thomas	0805	1205
119	24359	Stalnaker	Howe, Spickard	0805	1148
104	06024	Webb	Vissvardis, Miller	0805	1147
8	24194	Turner	Lockridge, Farris	0806	1147
20	24390	Painter	Dey, Brewer	0806	1146
205	24471	Altizer	Thokar, Almquist	0807	1150
117	24492	Nagode	Hoelzel, Donaldson	0807	1148
202	06270	McQuade	Clark, Hedger	0807	1146
110	06474	Morris, T.	Duchesneau, Whitmore	0808	1146
21	24515	Hollis-143	Teckenbrock, Haislip	0808	1150
22	24490	Leidecker	Danielson, Hanson	0808	1147
206	06404	Horgan	Moffitt, Bosco	0809	1150
118	24486	Ranson	Fisher, J.J., Weeks	0809	1146
209		Davis	Fisher, L.G., West	0809	1145
222	06456	Yeast	White, Oertle	0810	1149
101	24334	Milling	Hall, B.C., Benson	0811	1145
103	23871	Cornelius	McCarthy, Slipkas	0811	1145
111	24480	Morris	McGee, Hendricks	0812	1144
113	24268	Melby	Conner, Keer	0812	1144
116	24495	Watson	Crawford, Levine	0813	1241

58

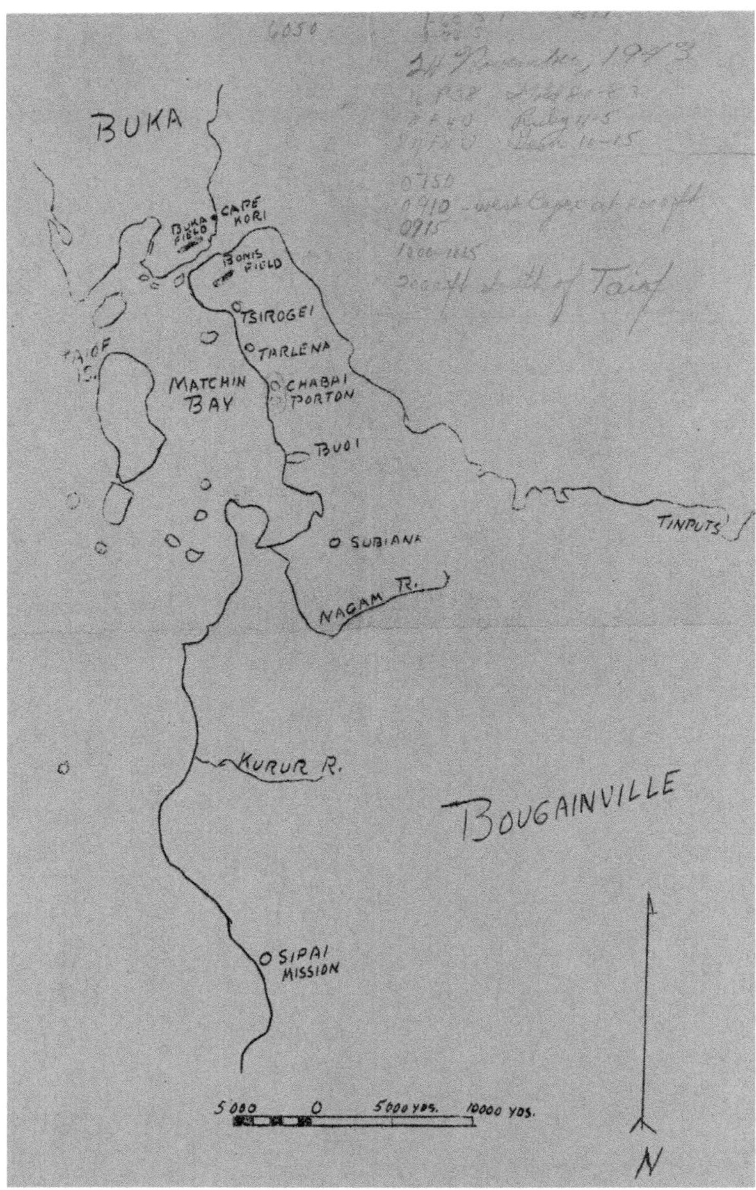

VC 38 Lt. John Leary's Map of Tarlena, November 24, 1943 (Source: Leary Family Collection)

CONFIDENTIAL

TBF OPERATIONS
MUNDA AIRFIELD

EXHIBIT No 20
CONFIDENTIAL

INTELLIGENCE REPORT

Date: 26 November 1943

Squadrons: VMTB-143 (13) VC-38 (6) VMTB-134 (18)

Target: Kara Airfield and gun positions.

Type of Mission: Kangu Hill anti-aircraft guns; Bombing and strafing.

Planes: 37 TBF's.

Loadings: 37x2000# 1/10 nose; .025 tail.

Times: T.O. ----- 1319 - 1330
O.T. ----- 1504
Land ----- 1612 - 1625

Anti-Aircraft Fire: 1. KARA.

(a) Meager inaccurate from one heavy known NW gun position.
(b) Meager inaccurate from one medium known NW 4 gun automatic position.
(c) Meager inaccurate from 3 light in known 4 gun automatic position S of the strip.
(d) Meager inaccurate light from 4 gun positions NE of the strip.
(e) Meager inaccurate from new MGs 1/2 mile east of center of strip.
(f) Meager inaccurate known medium from near NE auto gun position.
(g) 5 auto guns along the coast between Kangu and Uguma River.

2. KANGU HILL

(a) Intense inaccurate heavy (4 guns) from known positions ontop of hill. The number of guns firing from this position was demolished. There was one gun firing at the last TBF and none thereafter.
(b) Meager inaccurate from one heavy at Known heavy position NE of hill on the shore.
(c) Meager inaccurate light from one gun at knwon 5 gun automatic position NE of Kangu Hill.

Interception: None.

Damage and Casualties: None.

Weather: Clear up and back clear over target 8/10. Clouds 10000' - 12000' north of target.

Attack: 1. Kara-- A high speed approach made at 14,500'. Direction of attack was SW Direction out west. Push over 10000' - 6000'. Released 3600' - 1300'. Pull outs 300' - 2000'.

EXHIBIT No. 20 59

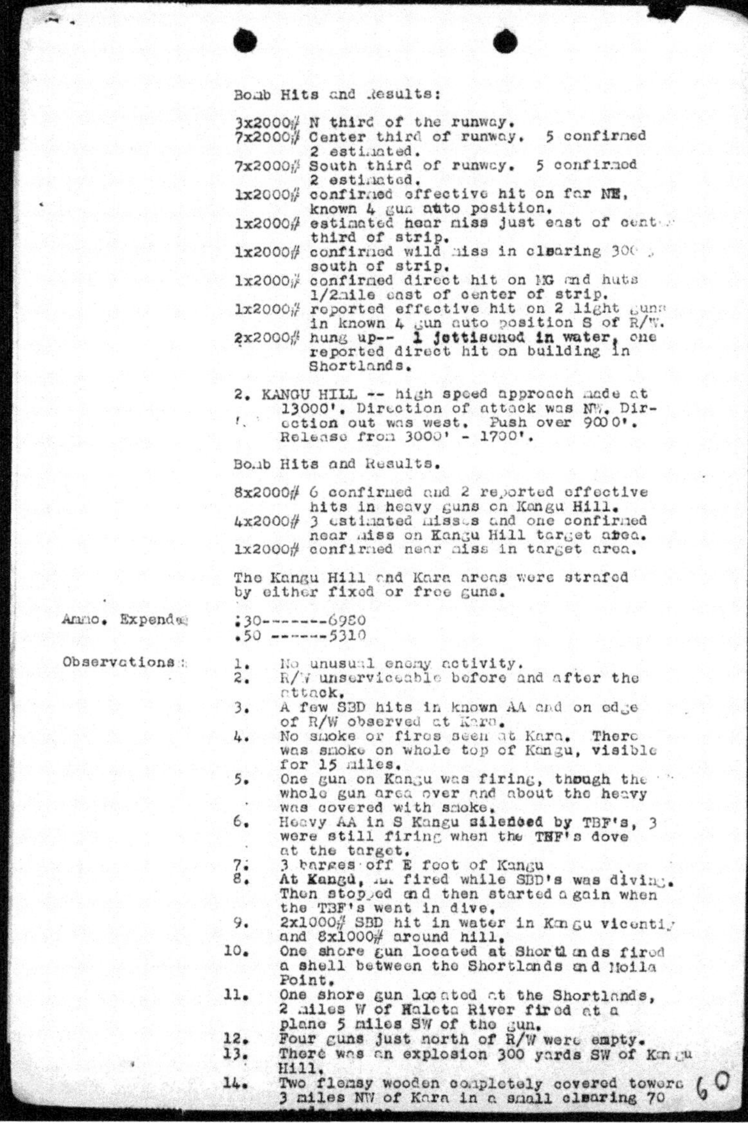

Bomb Hits and Results:

3x2000# N third of the runway.
7x2000# Center third of runway. 5 confirmed 2 estimated.
7x2000# South third of runway. 5 confirmed 2 estimated.
1x2000# confirmed effective hit on far NE, known 4 gun auto position.
1x2000# estimated near miss just east of cent[illegible] third of strip.
1x2000# confirmed wild miss in clearing 300 [illegible] south of strip.
1x2000# confirmed direct hit on MG and huts 1/2mile east of center of strip.
1x2000# reported effective hit on 2 light guns in known 4 gun auto position S of R/W.
2x2000# hung up-- 1 jettisoned in water, one reported direct hit on building in Shortlands.

2. KANGU HILL -- high speed approach made at 13000'. Direction of attack was NW. Direction out was west. Push over 9000'. Release from 3000' - 1700'.

Bomb Hits and Results.

8x2000# 6 confirmed and 2 reported effective hits in heavy guns on Kangu Hill.
4x2000# 3 estimated misses and one confirmed near miss on Kangu Hill target area.
1x2000# confirmed near miss in target area.

The Kangu Hill and Kara areas were strafed by either fixed or free guns.

Ammo. Expended: .30-------6980
.50 ------5310

Observations:

1. No unusual enemy activity.
2. R/W unserviceable before and after the attack.
3. A few SBD hits in known AA and on edge of R/W observed at Kara.
4. No smoke or fires seen at Kara. There was smoke on whole top of Kangu, visible for 15 miles.
5. One gun on Kangu was firing, though the whole gun area over and about the heavy was covered with smoke.
6. Heavy AA in S Kangu silenced by TBF's, 3 were still firing when the TBF's dove at the target.
7. 3 barges off E foot of Kangu
8. At Kangu, AA fired while SBD's was diving. Then stopped and then started again when the TBF's went in dive.
9. 2x1000# SBD hit in water in Kangu vicenti[illegible] and 8x1000# around hill.
10. One shore gun located at Shortlands fired a shell between the Shortlands and Moila Point.
11. One shore gun located at the Shortlands, 2 miles W of Haleta River fired at a plane 5 miles SW of the gun.
12. Four guns just north of R/W were empty.
13. There was an explosion 300 yards SW of Kangu Hill.
14. Two flemsy wooden completely covered towers 3 miles NW of Kara in a small clearing 70 [illegible]

60

SQD. NO.	PLANE BU.NO.	PILOT	PASSENGERS	OUT	IN
5	24182	Brunton	Sunday, Kemper	1319	1612
2	23981	Scholfield	Ulrich, Dills	1319	1617
3	23959	Giblin	Lee, Perkins	1320	1617
6	23975	Bishop	Schramm, Barnes	1320	1617
8	24194	Tahler	Jeffrey, Brewer	1320	1620
9	24208	Phillippi	Bond, Tyler	1320	1617
7	24265	Robertson	Dunelle, Ballard	1321	[illegible]
20	24390	Anderson, P.E.	Benjeck, Dunlop	1321	[illegible]
21	24515	May	Hull, McKenna	1321	[illegible]
22	24490	Shirley	Lords, Warren, Seule	1321	[illegible]
18	23987	Elliet	Gerbert, Stamm	1322	[illegible]
4	24242	Ball	Berryman, Kane	1322	161[illegible]
201	24487	Smith	~~Gates~~ SHURI, Thomas	1322	1612
207	06455	Stalnaker	Howe, Spickard	1322	1614
220	06479	Davis	Fisher, L.G., West	1323	1615
222	06456	Webb	Visvardis, Miller	1323	1612
118	24486	Hollis--143	Teckenbrock, Haislip	1324	1621
206	24403	Painter	Dey, Brewer	1324	1613
205	24471	Palmer	Drew, Covert	1325	1619
209	06189	McGann	Smith, Knott	1325	1619
102	23873	Bealfeld	Derursher, Best	1325	1619
103	23871	Glidden	Dunn, Murphy	1325	1619
106	06420	McLeish	Bernarcheck, Seregi	1325	1619
108	06472	Calfee	Caron, Brederson	1326	1620
204	24489	Altizer	Thoker, Aimacost	1327	1615
110	06471	Yeast	White, Oertle	1327	1615
130	06841	Turner	Lockridge, Farris	1327	1614
202	06270	Leidecker	Danielson, Hansen	1328	1614
115	47501	Mc Quade	Clark, Hedger	1328	1615
101	24334	Cole	Holmes, Mullen	1329	1615
100	06016	Kilgore	Dautel, Bartaukas	1329	1616
107	24264	Beasley	Durfee, Woodburn	1329	1616
109	24258	Patterson	Schmidt, Michales	1329	1616
203	06473	Garvey	Jargis, Wilson P.	1330	1616
113	24268	Cromwell	Ball, Wood	1330	1616
111	24480	Horgon	Moffitt, Bosco	1331	1619
119	24358	McLaughlin	Smith, VORACHEK	1332	1614

MYRON SULZBERGER JR.
Captain, USMCR
Intelligence O. VMTB-143

61

WAR DIARY
VMTB--233

15 November 1943.

1. Orders Received.

Twenty six planes of this squadron are ordered to strike Kara Airfield.

Seventeen planes in conjunction with twelve planes of VC-38 and twelve planes of VMTB-143 are to lay mines in the East Channel of Buka Passage. The plan is that they shall take off about 0130 and return for a daylight landing.

2. Operations.

Twenty six planes of VMTB-233 on a bombing mission over Kara Airfield released twenty six tons of bombs on the strip and the area around it leaving the strip unserviceable. All planes returned safely.

3. Special Action Reports.

See Special Action Report for 15 November 1943 attached to back of War Diary.

4. Changes in Personnel.

None.

5. Relationship of Subordinate Units.

No Change.

- 15 -

17

WAR DIARY
VMTB--233

16 November 1943.

1. Orders Received.

None.

2. Operations.

Seventeen planes of this squadron participated in a mine laying mission in Buka Passage. This mission was in operation from 0130 to 0700 this morning. First Lieutenant John B. DeLancey was forced to make a water landing on the return from the mine laying mission. He and his crew were picked up within two hours after the water landing and returned safely to Munda Airfield.

3. Special Action Reports.

See Special Action Report for 16 November 1943 attached to back of War Diary.

4. Changes in Personnel.

None.

5. Relationship of Subordinate Units.

No change.

18

November 20 - THIRTY-FIVE TBFs and 61 SBDs, escorted by 8 F4Us and 7 P39s, bombed and strafed Jap concentrations, supplies and transportation lines between the Mibo River and Mawaraka at 1550L/20th. Numerous small fires were started and many Japs were caught crawling into their foxholes. Heavy jungle growth made it difficult to assess definite damage done, but the area was well covered.

Bombs load for the SBDs was 1x1000 and 2x100 lb. instantaneous; and for the TBFs, 12x2000, 11x4x500, and 12x12x100 lb. instantaneous. Four of the TBFs carrying 12x100 lb. did not drop because the target was obscured by rain, and 4x1000 and 8x100 carried by the SBDs hung up and were jettisoned.

A few bursts of machine gun fire was the only AA encountered and no enemy planes intercepted. All planes returned to base.

Both the bombers and fighters report that this area is honeycombed with buildings of a permanent nature, concentrations of supplies and graded roads and tracks indicative of constant use.

Two of the Corsair escort returned via Kara and strafed the area from tree top level. A Betty, near the strip was hit and set afire.

November 21 - FIFTY-EIGHT SBDs and 35 TBFs escorted by 16 Corsairs dropped 59½ tons of bombs on Kara, and gun positions and installations at Kangu and Malabita Hills at 1400L/21st. Fifteen one-tonners and 2 half-tonners hit the runway, 4 fires were started in the bivouac area at Jakohina, 2 on the east side of Kangu Hill, and an oil fire between the Porarei River and Kangu Hill. Gun positions and buildings on top of Kangu Hill were demolished.

The SBDs were loaded with 1000 lb. 1/10 delay and the TBFs with 2000 lb. 1/10 delay bombs. Weather over the targets was overcast from 3000 to 10,000 feet so that the bombs were released in glides from 1500 to 2000 feet.

No AA was encountered at Kara, but moderate intensity medium and heavy came from known gun positions at Malabita and Kangu Hills. No enemy planes intercepted and all blue planes returned.

TWO SBD artillery spotter and ground liaison planes were over Cherry Blossom from 0703 to 1600L/21st, at which time the weather closed in. Trails, trenches and foxholes were seen 3000 yds. north of Old Piva Village and 4-50 ft. barges were seen concealed beneath trees in the lower Gazelle Harbor. Several trucks were seen and strafed with unobserved results just west of the bridge across the Mibo River. Huts in the Mawaraka area were also strafed with unknown results.

November 22 - FIFTY-TWO SBDs and 24 TBFs escorted by 16 F4Us dropped 52 tons of bombs on gun positions, installations and the runway at Kahili at 1445L/22nd. Twenty-six bombs hit on or near the runway, 18x2000 and 8x500 pounders, 2 fires were started near an ammo dump west of the south end of the strip, many hits were in the taxiways, and 1 direct hit was made on a gun position between the south end of the strip and Moisuru.

The SBDs carried 1x1000 1/10 delay and 2x100 lb. instantaneous and the TBFs, 19x2000 1/10 delay, 5x4x500 1/10 delay bombs. Weather over the target was clear and good dives were made.

Automatic and heavy AA was moderate from known gun positions with those at Kangu Hill especially active. A new position firing automatic was reported 50 yards east of the south tip of the runway. A few bursts of automatic was encountered at Moila Point and only automatic came from the mouth of Moliko River. Six SBDs and 3 TBFs were damaged by AA. No enemy planes intercepted and all blue planes returned. Photos taken after the strike indicate 9 new craters on the runway and many in taxiways. A direct hit was shown on a gun position. The runway is definitely unserviceable.

An enemy submarine was sighted at 1425 20 miles west of the north tip of Ganongga by the gunner in one of the returning TBFs. The sub was surfaced at the time of the sighting but had crash dived and disappeared by the time the plane circled for another look. The sub was painted black.

TWO SBD artillery spotters and 2 SBD ground liaison planes were over Cherry Blossom most of the day. AA was encountered from an automatic gun position 4000 yds. northeast by east of Old Piva Village This is the first AA from Jap positions at Cherry Blossom encountered by any of our planes. Seven barges were seen in the area: 4 beached

SECRET

4

at the mouth of the Laruma River, 2 beached at the lagoon south of Atsinima, and 1 beached near Kuraio Mission.

November 23 - TWO SBD ARTILLERY spotter were on station over Cherry Blossom from 0700 to 1700L/23rd, and 2 as ground liaison from 0650 to 1530L/23rd. Enemy shell fire was seen coming from a position 8000 yards north of the mouth of the Torokina River, and another position, either artillery or mortar was located 6000 yards NE of Old Piva village. Other activity was routine. One SBD developed motor trouble and made a crash landing off the north tip of Treasury. The pilot and gunner were rescued.

TWO SBDs, LOADED with 1000 pounders, were over Cherry Blossom in 2 hour patrols from 0645 to 1745L/23rd, except the last group which consisted of 4 SBDs. A total of 14x1000 pounders were dropped during the day on targets designated by the ground command. Several houses were destroyed in a clearing 4000 yards up the Suava River. Other results were unobserved.

November 24 - FIFTY-SEVEN SBDs and 37 TBFs, escorted by 48 fighters, bombed and strafed the Chabai area at 1000L/24th. The SBDs carried 1x1000 instantaneous plus 2x100 instantaneous; the TBFs, 14x2000 instantaneous, 12x4x500 instantaneous; and 11x11x100 instantaneous plus 1 incendiary cluster. Weather over the target was clear and good diving and strafing runs were made.

Numerous fires were started at Porton, Chabai, Tarlina and Tsirogei. A row of houses and a large warehouse were destroyed, and a large explosion in a supply dump caused at Chabai. Many buildings, believed to be supply storages, were destroyed at Tarlina, and several buildings and a fuel dump were set afire at Tsirogei. The entire area was well strafed causing considerable damage to installations at Soraken and Pau Plantations, Katitu Island, and Kateoa village. A row of buildings were destroyed at Tortai village (northeast coast of Bougainville) by 4x500 lb. bombs dropped there. AA was practically stopped during the attack by many direct or near misses on gun posits.

Intense light and medium AA, and slight heavy was encountered. AA was accurate as to altitude but leading. No enemy planes intercepted. One SBD was damaged by AA and made a successful emergency landing at Cherry Blossom. All other planes returned.

One TBF from the Chabai group, turned back from the primary target, dropped 11x100 lb. bombs and one indendiary cluster on Kara at 1000L/24th, starting a fire among a group of huts in a clearing. The only AA was machine gun fire. The plane returned safely to base.

TWO SBDs ARTILLERY spotters and 2 as ground liaison planes were over Cherry Blossom the 24th. No unusual sightings were made.

November 25 - The Mission for the SBDs and TBFs the 25th were cancelled on account of weather, and the B25s and Liberators were turned back from their target for the same reason.

November 26 - THIRTY-SEVEN AVENGERS and 57 Dauntless escorted by 8 fighters bombed and strafed Kara, Kangu and Malabita Hills at 1510L/26. Bomb load for the Avengers was 1x2000 lb. 1/10 delay and for the SBDs, 1x1000 lb. 1/10th and 2x100 lb. bombs. A total of 23 hits were made on the strip and gun positions at Kangu and Malabita Hills were well covered. Heavy smoke was seen coming from Kangu from 15 miles away. Photos show the strip to be definitely unserviceable. A group of huts 1/2 mile east of the strip were destroyed by one bomb hit.

AA from the vicinity of the Kara strip itself was light but appreciably more than has been encountered there in recent strikes. Known positions at Kangu and Malabita were firing with moderate to heavy intensity automatic and heavy caliber. Numerous hits were made on or near gun positions and the volume of fire decreased with at least 6 positions ceasing to fire altogether as the planes completed their attack. No enemy planes intercepted and all planes returned.

SBDs ON STATION over Torokina expended 700x50 caliber and 1000 x 30 caliber in strafing a fresh clearing near the inland defense line in the northeast sector (4000 yards, 60° from Old Piva Village). Another new clearing was reported just east of the Torokina River mouth.

Searches inland from the coast were generally negative.

WAR DIARY
VMTB--233

24 November 1943.

1. Orders Received.

None.

2. Operations.

Nine pilots, flying with VC-38 and VMTB-143, struck enemy ground positions and supply areas at Chabai Airfield.

Two planes went on a mine strafing mission off Shortland Island.

Six planes dropped bombs on Vila Airfield in an ordnance experiment.

3. Special Action Reports.

See Special Action Report for 24 November 1943 in back of the War Diary.

4. Changes in Personnel.

None.

5. Relationship of Subordinate Units.

No Change.

WAR DIARY
VMTB--233

27 November 1943.

1. Orders Received.

Thirty seven planes from TBF Operations were ordered on a strike on enemy supply and bivouac areas at Mosigetta Village, Bougainville Island. Eighteen of these thirty seven planes are from VMTB-233.

2. Operations.

Eighteen planes of this squadron participated in a raid on Mosigetta Village on the west coast of Bouganville Island. They were accompanied by nineteen other planes from VC-38 and VMTB-143. All planes returned safely.

3. Special Action Reports.

See Special Action report for 27 November 1943 in back of the War Diary.

4. Changes in Personnel.

None.

5. Relationship of Subordinate Units.

No Change.

COMAIRSOLS
STRIKE COMMAND
TBF INTELLIGENCE

Target: Mosigetta, Struck at 1545(LCT) 30 Nov 43
Mission: Bombing and strafing bivouac and supply area.
Flight Leader: Commander C.E. Brunton.
Squadrons: VC-38, VMTB-134.

Planes and bomb loadings: 12 TBF's with 4x500# instantaneous fuse.
Times: T.O.--1404; Over target--1545; Landing 1700.
Other aircraft coordinating: 10 SBD's.
Enemy Aircraft encountered: None.

Loss or damage (combat or operational) of own A/C: None.

Loss of or injury to own personnel: None.

Fuel and ammunition data: 1500 rounds .30 cal. 1950 rounds .50 cal. Miles out 150 over target 15 min. Miles in 150. Average fuel consumption 155 gal.

Brief narrative of attack tactics: Approach was from south to north passing target, making a 180° turn and breaking off. Each pilot made one individual run. Pushovers at 4000'. Releases at 1500'.

Summary of results: It is estimated that one warehouse, one large house and 8 small houses were demolished. One of the buildings destroyed is believed to be a radio station or lookout post.

Weather: 5/10 overcast at 6000' entire trip with intermittent rain enroute and return.
Observations: 1. Two cars were seen moving along road from Motupena Point to Mosigetta.
2. Smoke was observed on Motupena Point. Smoke and fire was seen on beach 5 miles south of Motupena.
Material Data: No malfunctioning of material reported.

CHARLES L. JONES
1st. Lt. USMCR
Intelligence O. VMTB-134

15

PLANE NO.	PILOT	PASSENGERS
101	Brunton	Kemper, Sunday
100	Scholfield	Dillis, Ulrich
116	Bishop	Barnes, Schramm
202	Tahler	Brewer, Jeffrey
7	Giblin	Perkins, Lee
102	McDonald	Young, Blank
107	Barker	Elder, Curran
2	Hollenbeck	Grell, Cleary
209	Phillips	Anderson, Webster
210	Hartzell	Wright, W., Colgan
22	Smith	Chiare, Camp
206	Hunt	Burrow, Conners

16

HBG/jn

COMAIRSOLS
STRIKE COMMAND
SBD INTELLIGENCE

C O N F I D E N T I A L C O N F I D E N T I A L

TARGET: Kara and Ballale Struck 1 December 1943.
(Chabai designated as primary target, but closed because of weather; Kara designated as secondary target).
MISSION: Bombing and strafing of enemy installations.
FLIGHT LEADER: Major E. P. Paris, Jr.
SQUADRONS: VMSB-236, VMSB-235, VMSB-243, VC-24, VC-38.
PLANES & LOADINGS: Ordered for mission: 48 SBD's plus 4 spares
1000# instant; 2 x 100# i.
Actually dropped bombs: 46 (32 on Kara, 14 on Ballale.
TIMES: Take-off: 1020. Attack: 1315, 1330. Return: 1420.
OTHER A/C UNITS COORDINATING: 26 TBF, 16 F4U's, 16 P-39's.
DATA ON ENEMY A/C ENCOUNTERED: None.
DAMAGE TO PLANES: 2 planes lost; 2 planes moderately damaged; 4 planes slight. damaged.
PERSONNEL CASUALTIES: Following pilots and gunners missing: Major Earl P. Paris, Jr., U.S.M.C.R; 1st. Lt. Earl R. Whiteley, U.S.M.C.R; Tech. Sgt. Alden Christiansen, (357425), U.S.M.C.R; Tech. Sgt. Charles A. Gotchling, Jr., (367401), U.S.M.C. Three persons were observed in the water three miles southwest of Ballale; a fourth was seen to land by parachute on Ballale.
RANGE: 475 nautical miles. FUEL: 210 gals average: AMMUNTION EXPENDED: .50 cal. 5,926, .30 cal. 13,803.
BRIEF NARRATIVE OF ATTACK TACTICS: Primary target of Chabai being closed in, one attack was made on secondary target, Kara, by Divisions 4-8, and by four planes in Division 3, all led by Lt. Cdr. J. R. Little; high speed approach from 9000'; executing a shallow dive with release at 1500', and pullout at 1000'. The remaing planes, led by Major E. P. Paris, attacked Ballale, with slow approach and planes in loose formation.
SUMMARY OF RESULTS:
1) Kara - clearings and settlement areas north and west of runway were well covered, with effective hits observed; some hits south of runway, and three on runway itself.
2) Ballale - known gun positions (particularly at western end of island) were bombed, with unobserved results; four hits in taxiway areas at southwestern end of runway; two fires observed, one due east of runway and the other off the southwestern end of runway.
WEATHER:
1) Enroute to target - thick thunderstorm formations over West Cape, Choiseul; solid and heavy cloud layer, 2000' to 8000'; over land all along north Coast of Bougainville; low thunderclouds over Chabai.
2) Over Kara - scattered clouds, 3/10 cover, ceiling 4000 to 5000'. Over Ballale - fair visibility; scattered clouds.
3) From target to base - slight squalls and gusts; steady rain from Barakoma to Munda.
OBSERVATIONS: 1. Runway at Kara seemed definitely unserviceable before attack; numerous holes on Ballale runway.
2. Attack execution seemed sound as to Kara, but confused and disorganized as to Ballale.
3. Possible automatic fire from east and southwest of Kara runway, but generally slight and intermittent.
4. Accurate and intense fire of all types from Ballale; heavy

15

MISSION REPORT: Cont'd BALLALE AND KARA STRIKE 1 December 1943.
Page No. 2.

fire, from known position at east and west and southwest of island, formed barrage pattern at 4000', 6000', 8000', and 10,000'; medium fire covered whole target area effectively.

5. Possible radio station observed off southeastern end of Kara runway.

MATERIAL DATA:

a. Guns - 7 planes had difficulty.
b. Bomb racks - 9 planes had difficulty.
c. Radio - 2 planes had difficulty.
d. Engine- 8 planes had difficulty.
e. Flaps - 2 planes had difficulty.
f. Instrument - 4 planes had difficulty.

LIST A/C INVOLVED IN MISSION:

Plane No.	Pilot	Squadron	Remarks
[illegible]31	Paris	VMSB-236	Missing (bailed out).
178	Lacey	"	Ballale taxiway (SE).
177	Quinlan	"	" AA (E).
A-11	Whiteley	"	Missing (bailed out).
A-31	Culler	"	Ballale AA (W).
A-21	Douglas	"	Ballale.
A-24	Belnap	"	Returned to base; engine trouble.
A-16	Bridges	"	Ballale
A-17	Jensen	"	Ballale AA (SW).
A-13	Meyers	"	Ballale (N).
A-15	Larkin	"	Ballale (SW).
176	Oughton	"	Ballale taxiway (SE).
A-23	Zouck	"	Kara bivouac area.
A-38	Shaw	"	"
A-26	Yeagley	"	"
169	Olson	"	Ballale AA (W).
167	Drostek	"	Ballale taxiway.
A-6	Todd	VMSB-235	Kara bivouac area S. of runway.
10	Cropley	"	"
12	Batoroff	"	"
164	Munn	"	"
23	Dalglish	"	"
A-22	McIntyre	"	"
20	Little	VC-24	Kara R/W (N).
13	Tobey	"	" - off R/W (N).
17	Durchfiel	"	" huts NW of R/W.
158	Shearer	"	"
159	Hansman	"	"
154	McLinden	"	Bombs hung.
15	Speer	"	Bombs failed to arm.
16	Parker	"	Kara clearing SW of R/W.
18	Maloney	"	"
152	Williams	"	"
151	Bates	"	"
150	Sherman	VMSB-236	"
19	Kafer	VC-24	Kara huts N and W of R/W.
21	Lloy d	"	"
22	Dunlap	"	"
24	Savage	"	Kara houses along road N. of R/W.
120	Banks	"	"
121	Persons	VMSB-243	"

16

LIST A/C INVOLVE[illegible]N MISSION: Cont'd. 1 [illegible]ember 1943.
DALLALE AND KARA STRIKE Page No. 3.

Plane No.	Pilot	Squadron	Remarks
130	Maerki	VC-24	Kara - house in clearing NW of R/W.
127	Knowles	VC-38	" buildings west of R/W.
105	Hedden	VC-24	" - west of R/W.
125	Sullivan	"	" "
10[illegible]	Young	"	" - SE of R/W.
12[illegible]	Ashman	VMSB-236	" "
1[illegible]	Olney	VC-38	Jettisoned.
112	Casey	VMSB-243	Ballale AA (W).
108	Ramsey	VMSB-235	Returned to base.

OTHER SQUADRON ACIO'S REPRESENTED:

JOSEPH R. McCARTHY,
Capt., U.S.M.C.R.,
A.C.I.O., VMSB-235.

LEON H. WEAVER,
1st. Lt., U.S.M.C.R.,
A.C.I.O., VMSB-243.

JAMES N. TRUESDALE,
Lieut., U.S.N.R.,
A.C.I.O., VC-38.

Report prepared by:
HAROLD B. GROSS,
Lieut., U.S.N.R.,
A.C.I.O., VC-24.

Assisted by:
FRANCIS T. KING,
Lieut., U.S.N.R.,
Strike Command Liason Intelligence
Officer.

17

WAR DIARY
VMTB - 233

1 December 1943

1. Orders Received.

Twenty-seven planes from TBF operations at Munda Airfield were ordered on a mission to bomb and strafe Chabai Airfield gun positions and supply areas.

2. Operations.

Twenty-two planes of this squadron and five planes of VC-38 participated in a bombing and strafing mission over Chabai Airfield, concentrating on supply areas in which fires were started.

Three planes of VMTB-233 bombed an enemy gun position on the Jaba River on the western coast of Bougainville Island.

All planes from both these missions returned safely.

3. Special Action Reports.

See Special Action Reports for 1 December 1943 attached to back of War Diary.

4. Changes in Personnel.

None.

5. Relationship of Subordinate Units.

No change.

Three SBDs were hit by AA fire and 2 of them had to make emergency landings at Barakoma, one of which was a belly landing. None of the pilots or crew was injured.

No enemy planes intercepted and all our team returned.

After the attack, the P39s in groups of 8, 7, and 8 strafed the northwest coast of Choiseul where reports indicate a large concentration of Japs. The western bank of the Warwior River and Redman and Taro Islands were strafed by 1 group. The west coast of Cape Alexander and huts in the Naleevoli and Malavogue Villages were also covered. Seven P39s strafed a plantation north of the Mulamabuli River and Torama Island and 2 fighters of 4 each made runs across islands in Choiseul Bay. Heavy foliage prevented observation of damage.

Three PVs, carrying 6 x 500 4-5 sec. delay bombs attacked Jap positions and stores in the Mawaraka area at 1525/L/30th from the tree top level. Three bombs were dropped on Tavera, 3 on Mawaraka, 6 in a bunch on Mamaregu, and 6 individually in clearing with huts in the general area. One large fire was started which was visible for many miles. Two planes were damaged by a 20 mm gun firing at Tavera. All returned.

December 1 - Chabai, the primary target, was closed to 51 SBDs and 26 TBFs which hit Kara and Ballale at 1310/L/1st. Thirty two fighters escorted the bombers. Two quarter tonners and 3 half tonners hit the Kara strip, and 4 half tonners hit the Ballale strip. One building was destroyed south of the Kara strip, and a group damaged or destroyed 1 1/2 miles northwest of the strip. An oil fire was started west of the Kara strip, and an explosion noted northwest of it. Several hits were made in taxiways at Ballale.

The SBDs carried 1 x1000 and 2 x 100 lb. bombs, instantaneously fuzed; the TBFs, 4 x 500 lb. bombs instantaneous.

All fire from Kara was inaccurate and slight. Automatic and light came from known AA positions, northeast of the strip. Automatic medium and heavy AA was reported from unobserved positions and machine gun fire from 200 yards in woods off southwest corner of strip A ccurate and intense AA came from known light and medium automatic and heavy positions on Ballale. Excellent barrages were noted at 6, 8, 10 and 12000 ft. levels.

Four SBDs were damaged by AA, one SBD crashed in the water and the crew were seen to bail out, landing in the water 3 miles west of Ballale. Another SBD is missing. All others returned.

Ten SBDs and 3 TBFs, escorted by 8 P39s, dropped 9 tons of bombs on a reported Jap gun position in the Jaba River area at 1545/L/1st. All bombs hit in the assigned area. Results were not visible.

The SBDs carried 1 x 1000 plus 2 x 100 instantaneous fuzed bombs and the TBFs 4 x 500 lb. instantaneous.

No AA or enemy planes were encountered and all blue planes returned.

Most of the time for these planes was spent in searching the area for possible targets but no enemy was reported.

New huts were seen 8000 and 10,000 yards inland from the Saua River mouth and 1500 yards northeast of Mopara 5 or 6 structures similar to Quonset huts, were reported. The buildings were identified as possible supply warehouses.

The mouth of the Atsinima River and the lagoon to the south were searched early in the morning. Two beached barges were on the coast west of the lagoon

One plane reported a probable 20mm between Maririci River and Mawaraka.

December 2 - No strikes this date.

December 3 - Japs at Monoitu Mission, Mosigetta, Porro River area, and in the Shishigatero Mibo Bridge area spent the day ducking bombs and bullets when 36 TBFs and 58 SBDs in groups of 6, 3, and 7 planes raided those areas at approximate 45 minute intervals from 0800 to 1600/L/3rd. Dives and strafing runs were deliberate with targets well spotted before. Thirty to 40 buildings were destroyed and numerous fires started in the area, which seemed alive with Jap activity, although no personnel were seen. The 250 ft. bridge over the Porro River near Aku was destroyed and [illegible] damaged.

Avengers carried 4 x 500 lb. inst. and the SBDs, 1 x1000 plus 2 x 100 lb. inst. bombs.

SECRET

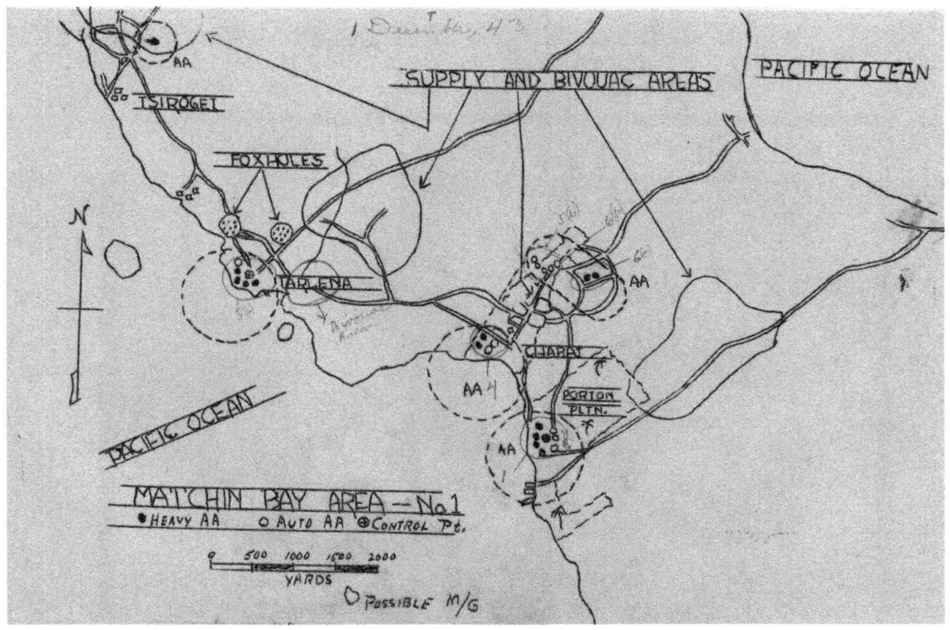

VC 38 Lt. John Leary's Map of Chabai Airfield (Source: Leary Family Collection)

CONFIDENTIAL COMAIRSOLS STRIKE COMMAND TBF INTELLIGENCE CONFIDENTIAL

Target: Mosigetta. Struck 4 December 1943
Mission: Bomb and strafe bivouac and supply area.
Destroy bridge over Porro River.
Flight Leader: Commander Brunton.
Squadrons: VC-38, VMTB-134
Planes and loading: 36 TBF's.
6-100# Inst. (Flight 2 1/10 sec)
6-250# Inst.
Ordered for Mission: 36 TBF's.
Actually dropped bombs: 36 TBF's.

Times:					
	First division	Take Off	0651	O.T.-- 0800	Land--0919
	Second "	" "	0753	" 0905	" 1020
	Third "	" "	0921	" 1035	" 1226
	Fourth "	" "	1042	" 1150	" 1356
	Fifth "	" "	1136	" 1245	" 1401
	Sixth "	" "	1250	" 1400	" 1538

Other A/C Units coordinating: 60 SBD's.
Data on enemy A/C encountered: None.
Loss or damage of own A/C actually attacking: None.
Personnel casualties: None.
Range, fuel, and ammo. data: Distance out 160 miles. Distance return 160 miles. Average hours in air 2.7 .
Ammonition expended .50 cal.--11,950
.30 cal.--15,980

Brief Narrative of attack tactics:
The strike was divided into six sections taking off and attacking as shown above. SBD's sections took off between TBF's sections. The second section was to destroy bridge over Porro River. All sections approached from SE to NW. Pushovers 8000'. Release 1500'-2000'.

Summary of Results: About thirty buildings were destroyed and many more damaged. The bridge on the east fork of the Porro River was not destroyed but the bridge on the west fork suffered a direct hit. (This bridge had already been claimed). Each section had sufficient time to strafe and the entire area was covered. Four or five fires were observed. One of these fires was caused by strafing.
Weather: Scattered cumulus at 6000' enroute and return. There was a light haze over the target at the time the first flight struck, but then cleared up for later flights.
Observations:
1. Enemy shipping activity noted: None.
2. Enemy ground activity noted: None
3. Condition of target befor and after attack: The area had been hit repeatedly in previous raids, however there were still a countless number of buildings, standing. This strike destroyed many of these buildings.
4. Brief comment on results obtained by coordinated attack of other A/C; also comment on efficiency of attack execution: The attack was executed in an effective manner. Each pilot had more time in which to spot his target and make the proper approach than is the case when a larger number of planes are over target at same time. They were able to do more efficient strafing for the same reason.
5. Unusual circumstances; enemy AA fire: None.
6. No enemy AA was encountered. Machine gun or rifle fire was observed but it was meagre and inaccurate.

Material Data: No malfunctioning of material reported.

Charles L. Jones

CHARLES L. JONES
1st. Lt. USMCR
Intelligence O. VMTB-134

14

PLANE NO.	PILOT	PASSENGERS
1	Brunton	Sunday, Kemper
5	Scholfield	Ulrich, Dills
7	Bishop	Schramm, Barnes
	Tahler	Jeffrey, Brower
119	Giblin	Lee, Perkins
	McDonald	Blank, Young
100	Palmer	Covert, Drew
200	McGann	Knott, Smith
111	Bealnfeld	Best, Derurscher
112	Glidder	Murphy, Dunn
128	Rockwell	Everard, Wagner
118	Gerard	Humphries, Canales
21	Zuber	Bland, Lindholm
22	Anderson	Sanches, Prothoe
201	Ayers	Shomatz, Greiner
207	Herndon	Roessler, Husteod
103	McAllister	Zavetz, Lucas
6	Patton	Sloan, Brooks
117	Robertson	Ballard, Dumolle
210	Anderson, P.	Dunlop, Benjeck
27-4	May	McKenna, Hull
8	Elliott	Stamm, Gebert
2	Lemmons	Beecher, Sutton
3	Boll	DeGeorge, Brouskiecky
109	Barker	Elder, Curran
4	Ballard	Justice, Schmitt, E.E.
208	Phillips	Anderson, Webster
116	Hollenbeck	Creel, Cleary
118	Hunt	Burrow, Conners
130	Hartzell	Wright, Colgan
119	Cole	Mullen, Holmes
102	Kilgore	Bartzckas, Deutel
111	Beasley	Woodburn, Duffee
112	Garvey	Wilson, Dargis
200	Patterson	Michonilles, Schmitt
7	Warner	Dunlap, Bernnek

15

CONFIDENTIAL COMAIRSOLS STRIKE COMMAND TBF INTELLIGENCE CONFIDENTIAL

Struck 11 December 1943

Target: Jakohina supply and bivouac areas; Kangu Hill gun positions.
Mission: Bombing and strafing gun positions, buildings, dumps, bridges, piers and ware houses.
Flight Leader: Major Rolland F. Smith.
Squadrons: VMTB-232 (22 planes) ; VC-38 (6).
Planes and loadings: 28 TBF's.
Major Smith division: 4x500# RDX - 2 inst.; 2 1/10 nose all four with 1/100 tail fu
Captain Cunningham division: 1x2000# 1/10 nose -1/100 tail.
Lt. Dougherty division: 1x2000# 1/10 nose - 1/100 tail.
Lt. Larsen (VC-38) division: 1x2000# 1/10 nose -1/100 tail.
Lt. Everson division: 2 planes 4x500# RDX : 2 planes 4x500 (2 bombs inst. nose and 2 1/10 All with 1/100 tail fuse).

Ordered for mission: 28 TBF's
Actually dropped bombs: 28 TBF's
Times: T.O.-- 1201-1210 ; O.T.-- 1330 ; Return-- 1435 - 1500.
Other A/C units coordinating: 55 SBD's.
Data on enemy A/C encountered: None.
Loss or damage own A/C: One TBF with hole in tail (probably 20mm); one TBF sustained damaged wing in runway collision on takeoff; one TBF sustained damaged tail in runway collision in landing; one TBF had portside of front and middle cockpit's shattered-cause unknown; two TBF each had both wing fairings damaged in dives. One TBF made a successful belly landing - propeller damaged. Left wheel would not lock. Roller ineffective, and emergency release failed to operate. See Material Data.
Personnel casualties: None.
Range, fuel and ammo. data: Enroute - 150 miles ; Return 150 miles; average hours airborne - 2.6 hours.
Ammo. expended: .30 cal -- 1500 rounds. .50 cal -- 1600 rounds.
Brief narrative of attack tactics: The four divisions plus four spares planes rendezvoused over Baga Island - proceeded NW around to the west of the Shortland Islands coming in from the south over Moila Point on Bougainville Island at an altitude of 13,600'. From this altitude a high speed approach was made to a point west of the target area. Push overs to the south east over target were made at 9000' to 10000'; Releases at 2000' to 2500'.
Summary of Results:

Kangu Hill

Three planes each carrying 4x500# RDX bombs scored eleven estimated effective hits on the crest in gun positions. 1x500# bomb was a wild miss and fell in water of coast. One plane with same load reported near miss on northeast side of top. One plane - same load failed to observe hits. One plane - same bomb load returned with 2x500# bombs and jettisoned 2x500# in the water enroute to base.

SE Sector of Jakohina Mission Area

Two planes each with 2000# bombs had confirmed hits on buildings in area. One plane (2000# bomb load) estimated effective hit on pier. One plane (2000# bomb load) reported effective hit on building. Two planes, one loaded with 4x500#, the other with a 2000# bomb reported unobserved results. Two planes each had loads of 1x2000# bombs which hung up. They were jettisoned in water enroute to base.

Circular clearing, NE corner

Three planes each with 2000# bombs load dropped in this area with unobserved results.

SW Secton of Jakohina Mission area

One plane - 2000# bomb load reported near miss on buildings. Four planes each with 2000# bomb load dropped in this area, - unobserved results. Two planes load (4x500# each) dropped in this area with unobserved results. One plane, (load of 4x500# RDX bombs) had a confirmed direct hit on building. Three of the bombs were unobserved.

19

Pororei River Area and Bridge
One plane with 4x500# bombs reported unobserved results with respect to two bombs and wild misses with respect to two bombs.

NE Sector of Jakahina Mission Area
One plane (2000# bomb load) reported unobserved results. One plane (4x500# bomb load) reported unobserved results.

For detail and location of hits see overlay attached.

Weather: Good visibility and clear enroute to target and return from target. 2/10 cumulus clouds at 2000' to 5000'.

Observations:
1. Enemy shipping activity noted: None.
2. Enemy ground activity noted: None.
3. Condition of target before and after attack: On approach Kangu Hill gun positions were seen to fire. One pilot reported explosion on top in middle of gun position which appeared to be caused by an SBD bomb. Gun positions fired sporadically during attack.
4. Comment on result of coordinating A/C: None.
5. Unusual circumstances: None.
6. Location of AA: All pilots reporting AA stated that it came from known heavy positions on Kangu Hill; was of merogre intensity and inaccurate; bursts were between 6000' and 9000'.

Material Data: Plane number 214 (pilot by Lt. Wesley McQueen, USMCR) was forced to make a belly landing at Munda Airfield because landing gear actuating cylinder was found to be warped and would not lock.

Kenneth R. Johnson
KENNETH R. JOHNSON
Captain, USMCR.
Intelligence, O. VMTB-232

PLANE NO.	PILOT	PASSENGERS
117	Smith	Waldvogel, Stanner
21	Burris	Lossie, Wagner
9	Humphrey	Matrin, Adams
2	Everett	Ward, Norby
6**⁂	Misamore	Boardman, Dirawor
204	Moret	Shelton, France
212	Cunningham	Cowling, Ryder
214	McQueen	Mitchell, W.K., Pero
200	Atkinson	Patterson, Zolla
202⁑	Goodman	Wood, Cardne
5⁑	Ryan	Hammond, Meek
205	Austin	Shea, Garrett
18	Dougherty	Railey, Donavan, G.J.
113	Carey	Downey, Copeland
116	Metzelaars	Pallo, Eldridge,
109	Stammetts	Severson, Brodeski
102	Fullop	Reed, Merola
103	Phillippi	Jackson, Nilsen
4	Larson	Wagner, Wright
3	Leake	Boyle, O'Daniel
112	Leary	Grealie, Dale
128	Gammage	Morissey,
100	Rogan	Misner, Brandt
110	Draughon	Deal, Paul
130	Everson	Bell, Marker
8	Gentry	Westoven, Galway
118	Jackson	Wolfe, Healy
115	Preister	Rotzl ff, McCowley

⁑ 1x2000# hung up and jettisoned.
* 1x500# hung up and jettisoned.
⁂ 1x500# hung up and brought back to base.

21

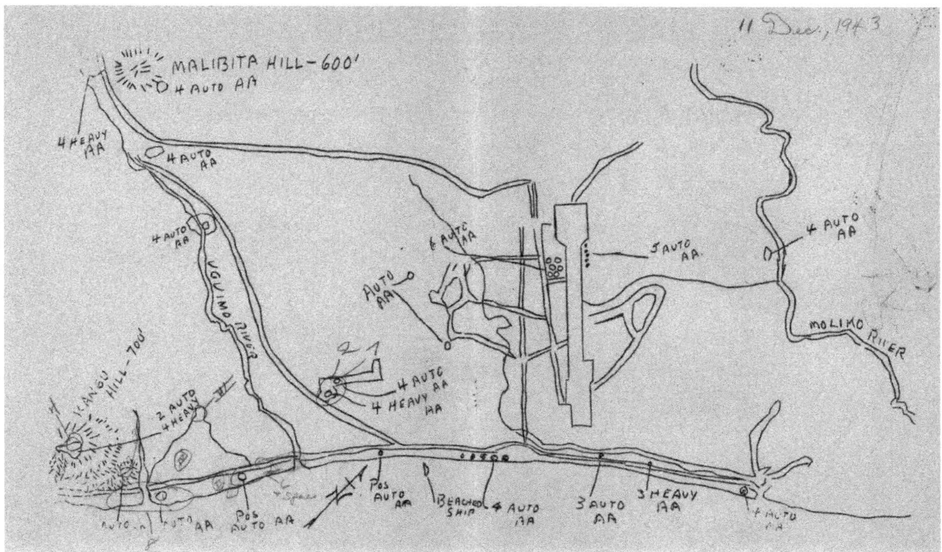

VC 38 Lt. John Leary's Map of Kangu Hill Gun Positions, December 11, 1943 (Source: Leary Family Collection)

COMAIRSOLS
STRIKE COMMAND
TBF INTELLIGENCE

CONFIDENTIAL CONFIDENTIAL

Target: Ratsoa, Soraken Plantation. Struck 12 December 1943
Mission: Bomb AA position at Ratsoa; Bomb and strafe bivouac and supply areas at Soraken.
Flight Leader: Commander Brunton.
Squadrons: VMTB-134 ; VC-38.
Planes and loadings: 28 TBF's. Ordered for Mission: 28 TBF's.
Actually dropped bombs, 26 TBF's.
Loaded: 16TBF's with 4x500#, 11 TBF's 1x2000#
Times: T.O.-- 0836; O.T.--1053; Land--1215.
Other A/C units coordinating: None.
Data on enemy A/C encountered: None.
Loss or damage own A/C: None.
Personnel casualties: None.
Range, fuel, and ammo. data: Out-220 mi.; Return-220 mi.; over target 15 min. Average hours airborn: 3.7; Ammo. expended: 30 cal-10710, .50 cal-7445.
Brief narrative of combat tactics: Approach was at 10,000' up the East of Bougainville. The flight made a complete circle and came out so that they were headed SW in which direction they made their run. Pushovers were made at 6,000' and bombs were released at 2500'.
Summary of results: The top of the hill, on which enemy AA positions were supposed to have been located, was hit by 40-500# bombs and 9-2000# bombs. However, no guns were seen at this position. A direct hit was scored on the pier at Soraken.
Weather: 3/10 cumulus enroute and return. There was a light haze at 10,000' over the target, but this did not interfere with the strike.
Observations:
1. Enemy shipping activity noted: None.
2. Enemy ground activity noted: None.
3. Conditionof target before attack not determined: After attack a large fire was seen on the top of the hill. The pier at Soraken was badly damaged.
4. Many SBD hits in the target area were seen, however, the TBF's were held up for about 10 minutes by the SBD's.
5. Unusual circumstances enemy AA: None.
6. Meagre and inaccurate fire from known positions in the Tarlina-Chabai area was observed with bursts at 4-7000'. Meagre and inaccurate automatic fire was seen on the south side of Ratsoa Hill. This automatic fire was not seen by later sections.

Material data: Garvey(9) was unable to drop or jettison his 2000# bomb and was forced to bring it back.
Commander Brunton(109) made belly landing because of failure of the hydraulic system.
Bell (100) was forced to return immediatly after [illegible] take off because of a leak in the cockpit.

Charles [illegible]. Jones
CHARLES L. JONES
1st. Lt. USMCR
Intelligence O. VMTB-134

19

PLANE NO.	PILOT	PASSENGERS
109	Brunton	Sunday, Kemper
108	Scholfield	Ulrich, Dills
[illegible]	Bishop	Schramm, Barnes
[illegible]	Tahler	Jeffrey, Brewer
[illegible]	Giblin	Lee, Perkins
[illegible]	McDonald	Blank, Young
[illegible]	Marshall	Lanê, Tye
[illegible]	Shirley	Warren, Lord
[illegible]	Robertson	Ballard, Duzelle
[illegible]	Patterson	Michaels, Schmitt
[illegible]	Cromwell	Wood, Batt
[illegible]	Warner	Dunlap, Beraneck
[illegible]	Cole	Mullen, Holmes
[illegible]	Kilgore	Bartzokas, Dautel
103	Beasley	Woodburn, Duffee
9*	Garvey	Wilson, P., Dargis
18	Palmer	Covert, Drew
[illegible]	Ayers	Shomatz, Greiner
[illegible]	Bealafield	Best, Derurscher
220	Gerand	Humphries, Canales
22	Glidden	Murphy, Dunn
3	Rockwell	Everard, Wagner
209	Calfee	Broderson, Caron
112	McLeish	Sergi, Barnarchek
101	Smith	Chisro, Camp
[illegible]	Bell	Degeorge, Brzuskiecky
[illegible]	Ballard	Kuzma, Schmitt
8	May	McKenna, Hull

* 1x2000# hung up and brought back to base.

20

CONFIDENTIAL — COMAIRSOLS STRIKE COMMAND TBF INTELLIGENCE — CONFIDENTIAL

Struck 12 December 1943

Target: Buildings and personnel areas Toborei Bay
Mission: Attack barges and AK reported in vicinity of Motong Pt. (No shipping located so attack was made on secondary target shown above)
Flight Leader: Major Smith
Squadrons: VMTB-232, VC-38.
Planes and loadings: 8 TBF'S with 2000# 1/10 nose, 1/100tail
8 TBF's with 4x500# 1/10 nose, 1/100 tail
Ordered for mission 16
Actually dropped bombs: 16
Times: T.O. 1551, O.T. 1805, Land 1900; Average hrs. 3.2
Other A/C units coordinating: 49 SBD's
Data on enemy A/C encountered: None encountered.
Loss or damage own A/C: None
Personnel casualties: None
Range, fuel, and Ammo Data: Distance out-200 Mi.;Return 160 Mi.
Brief narrative of attack tactics: The flights searched the area in which the enemy shipping had been reported, but the search was negative. The secondary target was then attacked. The approach was from the north through Kieta Harbor with runs made along shore.
Summary of results: One confirmed and one reported direct hits as well as three unobserved hits were scored on the cove south of Toromaro Point. Chinatown area suffered three direct hits and three unobserved. The Rigu Mission Area was blasted by three confirmed and four reported direct hits.. Eleven unobserved bombs fell on this area. AA positions and bldgs at Puanapa Head received one confirmed, two reported and one estimated direct hits. One effective confirmed, an effective miss and four unobserved hits were also scored on this area. Houses about 500 yds south of Puanapa Head were hit by 1 direct confirmed and three unobserved bombs.
Weather: Scattered cumulus at 8000'-10,000' were encountered enroute and return. A high overcast and haze was present at the targt the target.
Observations: 1. Enemy shipping activity noted PFC. Hammond reported sighting a small AK dead in water 500 yds north of Pui Pui Pt. This was not confirmed.
2. Enemy ground activity noted: None
3. Condition of target before and after attack: This area had been hit by previous strikes, however, a fire was observed at Rigu Mission which burned for 15 minutes. Fire and smoke was observed among huts behind pier east of Rigu Mission.
4.
5. Moderate, inaccurate fire was encountered from the known automatic position on the ridge at Puanapa Head. Meagre inaccurate fire was observed from a new position midway along shore of Toborei Bay. Meagre, inaccurate fire was noted form an MG at Rigu Mission.
Material Data: No malfunctioning of material reported.

CHARLES L. JONES
1st Lt. USMCR.
A.C.I.O. VMTB 134

Plane No.	Pilot	Passengers
113	Smith	Waldvogel, Stanner
212	Stulman	Washburn, Towe
213	Humphrey	Martin, Adams
3	Everett	Ward, Norby
4	Misamore	Boardman, Birawer
5	Moret	Shelton, France
7	Cunningham	Cowling, Ryder
103	Mc Queen	Mitchell, Pero
108	Atkinson	Patterson, Zolla
112	Goodman	Wood, Cardno
116	Ryan	Hammond, Mook
130	Austin	Shea, Garritt
200	Larson	Wagner, Wright
204	Dalby	Broome, Boland
205	Swenson	Betz, Brooks
117	Kizer	Donavon, Knight

COMAIRSOLS

CONFIDENTIAL STRIKE COMMAND IDENTIAL
TBF INTELLIGENCE

Target: Porton Plantation. Struck 13 Dember 1943
Mission: Bomb and strafe gun positions, supply bivouac areas.
Flight leader: Major Rolland F. Smith
Squadrons: VMTB-232 (20) ; VC-38 (8).
Planes and loadings: 28 TBF's.
11 planes loaded with 2000# ch, with inst. nose fuse and .01 tail fu.
13 planes loaded with 4x500# bombs, each with 2x4x5 second - inst. and 4x5 second - 1/1 nose fuse and all with . tail fuse.
Ordered for Mission: 28 TBF's.
Actually dropped bombs: 24 TBF's.
Times: T.O.--0954-1002 ; O.T.--1200 ; Return-- 5-1348.
Other A/C units coordinating: 46 SBD's.
Data on enemy A/C: None.
Loss or damage to own A/C: None.
Personnel casualties: None.
Range, fuel, and ammo. data: Enroute - 250 miles Return-- 225 miles.
Average hours airbo - 3.7 hours.
Ammo. expended: .3 - cal -- 5880 rds.
.5 - cal -- 5660 rds.

Brief narrative of attack tactics: Twenty-seven anes rendezvoused off Cape West, Choiseul Island; proceeded northw along Bougainville Island east coast ; the approach to the target o W coast of Bougainville was from the NE. Pushovers from 80 to 9000'. Releases at 1500' to 2000'.

Summary of Results:

A. One plane carrying a 2000# bomb scored a nfirmed direct hit on the HAA gun position near the beach.

B. There was one estimated effective hit wi 1x2000# bomb and four estimated effective hits with 4x500# bomb o he same gun position.

C. One 2000# bomb was reported as on effect hit on the pier south of the gun positions in Porton Plantation.

D. There were two confirmed effective hits 2000# bombs on the gun positions mentioned in (A).

E. Two planes each carrying 4x500# bombs (0# bombs) reported effective misses on gun positions. One own heavy AA and the other a new position about 100 yards nor of the beach positions.

F. 4x2000# bombs and 1x500# bomb were wild ses.

G. 34x500# bombs and 1x2000# bomb were dro with unobserved results.

H. 1x500# bomb hung up and was jettisoned.

I. 4x500# bombs were dropped on buildings he Chabai area with unobserved results.

SPECIAL NOTE:

One plane carrying a 2000# bomb dropped a .50 cal. position on the top of the highest point on Tautsin sland enroute to base.

Weather: Clear over target; over cast at 9000' 11000' over most of Bougainville; broken scattered clouds at 00' enroute to and return from target. Visibility approxim y 40 miles.

Observations:

1. Enemy shipping activity noted: None.

2. Enemy ground activity noted: Fifteen o ixteen buildings resembling quanset huts were observed between T and Tapsabawat, on east coast of Bougainville.

3. Condition of target before and after at k: On approach to target known gun positions in Porton target seen to fire; known gun positions in Chabai target were seen fire. On retirement by fourth division they stated that no AA was seen coming from target area in Porton.

4. Comment on result of coordinating A/C: e pilot reported a direct hit by SBD pilot on heavy AA gun posit near beach in Chabai area. One pilot stated that there were BD's bombs which hit in heavy AA positions on the beach-- Porton ea.

5. Unusual circumstances: None.

6. Location of AA: Heavy AA positions (kn) were observed in the Porton area along the beach. Fire was mode e and inaccurate Unknown position was observed about 100 yards n h of the known position between the two roads in Porton area. o pilot observed a 20mm position in edge of woods near NW corner Porton Plantation.

In the Chabai area known heavy AA positions were seen firing from position near coast; likewise from known position in area to north east in taxiway circle. Unknown automatic AA position observed, west of the 5 gun position in Chabai was observed. This position was hit by an SBD bomb.
Material data: No malfunction.

KENNETH R. JOHNSON
Captain, USMCR
Intelligence O. VMTB-232

PLANE NO.	PILOT	PASSENGERS
212	Smith	Waldvogel, Stanner
102	Stuhlman	Washburn, Towe
116	Humphrey	Martin, Adams
105	Everett	Ward, Norby
213	Misamore	Boardman, Birawer
112	Moret	Shelton, France
215	White	Crunton, Moon
203	Laughlin	Akroyd, Spyghala
216	Burris	Lossie, Wagner
1	McCole	Sears, Blackerby
4	Carter	McEnneny, Gruber
5*	Lynch	Brown, Gerber
103-	Ray	Young, Benedetti
100-	Olson	Hoke, Mitchell, J.A.
101	Schrader	Seamonda, Jenkins
201	Dalby	Broome, Boland
129	Swenson	Betz, Brooks
210	Kizer	Donavon, W.G., Knight
204	Larson	Wagner, Wright
128	Leake	Boyle, O'Daniel
205‡	Leary	Greslie, Dale
130-	Gammage	Morissey
200	Regan	Misner, Brandt
20	Phillippi	Jackson, Wilson
21	Thomas	Scheleter, Akey
7	Stone	Sarf, Henning
9	Draughon	Deal, Paul
22	Doxheimer	Jackson, Nelsen

* bombs hung up and jettisoned. 1x500#
‡ Dropped 2000# on a .50 cal. gun position on the top of Tautsina Island.
\- Returned to base because of overcast.

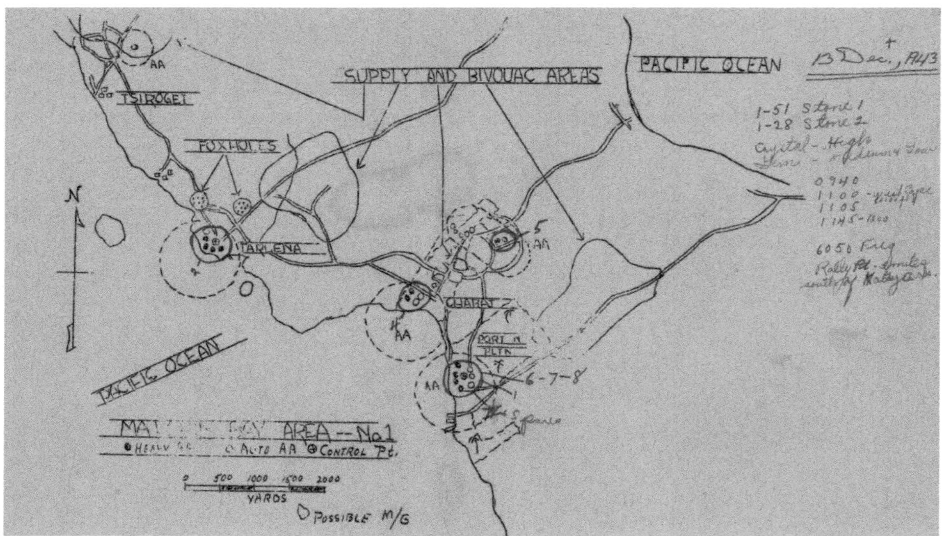

VC 38 Lt. John Leary's Map of Porton Plantation, December 13, 1943 (Source: Leary Family Collection)

VC-38
COMAIRSOLS
STRIKE COMMAND
TBF INTELLIGENCE

CONFIDENTIAL

Struck 27 January 1944

Target: Jap bivouac area between Ibu and Sisivie.
Mission: Bombing and strafing area.
Flight Leader: Lt. (jg) R. A. Marshall
Squadron: VC-38
Planes and Loading: Ordered for mission - 6 TBF's.
Actually dropped bombs - 6 TBF's.
Loadings - 12x100# inst.
Times: T.O. 0900 Attack: 0935 Return 1025.
Other A/C Coordinating: 6 SBD's
Enemy A/C: None
Damage to own A/C: None
Personnel Casualties: None
Ammo Expended: .50 cal. - 680 rds.
.30 cal. - 900 rds.
Attack Tactics: The target area was approached from the N.W., altitude 7000', speed 200K., bombs released around 3000', pull out towards the S.E.
Summary of Results: 67 out of 72x100# inst. fused bombs were dropped on the assigned target, an area 300 x 400 yds. The area was also strafed by both fixed and free guns The nature of the terrain and the thick jungle prevented observation of the results.
Weather: Route up: Good
Over target: Good
Return: Good
Observations: The coordination and the execution of the attack were efficient. No enemy ground activity was observed, and no A-A fire was encountered. A clearing with three or four native huts and a trail were observed 1 mile E. of the target area.

JAMES N. TRUESDALE, Lt. USNR.
A.C.I.O., VC-38
Intelligence Duty Officer

- -

Plane No.	Pilot	Passenger
103	Marshall	Lane-Tye
105	Phillippi	Bond-Rice
107	Bishop	Rourke-Schramm-Barnes
108	Thaler	Buis-Brewer
109	Leary	Greslie-Dale
113	Gammage	Durham-Morrissey

CONFIDENTIAL COMAIRSOLS STRIKE COMMAND TBF INTELLIGENCE CONFIDENTIAL

Struck 28, January 1944

Target: Aircraft in revetments Tobera Airfield.
Mission: Bomb and strafe.
Flight leader: Commander C. E. Brunton, USN
Squadrons: VMTB - 143 (12planes), VC - 38 (6 planes).
Planes: Ordered for mission: 18 TBF's
Actually dropped bombs: 17 TBF's
Loadings: 12x100 # inst.
Times: Take off: 0720
Over target 0907
Return: 1025
Other A/C coordinating: 48 SBD's.
Enemy A/C: Over the target, the fighter cover apparently functioned well in keeping off enemy A/C; however, on the way to the rally point, five or six zeros were reported to have made runs on the TBF's, particularly the last division. Some flashy overhead passes were made, but none resulted in any damage to our planes. Approximately 4 enemy A/ C were observed in the near vicinity during the high speed approach and about 12 on the way to the rally point. The following incident is a good example of cooperation between coordinating units. On the route to the rally point an F4U with a Zero on his tail led the enemy A/C close enough to a formation of 4 or 5 TBF's for the gunners to fire on the Zero; this they did which caused the Zero to turn away, and this enabled the F4U to get on the Zero's tail and shoot it down. One Zero was seen to go down in flames at the rally point, and a smoker was observed on the pull-out. Two F4U's blew up a Zero NE of the rally point. Anumber of dog-fights could be seen ataa distance. T

Ten enemy A/C were observed spotted on each side of the apron at the SW end of the strip, and a wrecked plane was seen at the NE end of the runway. Approximately 15 A/C were seen parked in tte revetment areas.

Pfc. Joe D. Williams, USMC , turret gunner in plane # 21, shot down a zero during the retirement form the target. It was seen to go in the water about 5 miles from shore.

Corporal Kenneth L. Johnson, USMCR, turret gunner in plane # 125 was credited with a smoker on way to rally.

Sgt. E. D. Spickard, USMCR , turret gunner in plane # 122, shot down a Zero at the rally point. The Jap plane was making an overhead run at 1000' when hit and was seen to explode and crash into the water.

Lt. Turner claimed a Zero which made a head on run on his plane when at an altitude of 500'. He opened up with his wing guns after which the Zero smoked havily, passed beneath his plane, and was last seen at 100' headed for the water indicating total loss of control. Lt. James R. Turner, USMCR.

Damage to own A/C: Plane # 1 was struck by AA (probably 40 MM.) on starboard side by turret gun, the burst making a hole about 2 feet in diameter.

Plane # 115 received 5 shrapnel holes in wings.
Plane # 105, 1 hole in right wing from AA at th NE end of runway.
Plane # 125, large hole in fromt of turret, 5 or 6 small holes in wings.
Plane # 122 returned with the radioantennae gone, reason unknown.
Plane # 4 had the bomb bay window and hydraulic system knocked out; but there was no evidence of bullets or shrapnel having struck plane.

Personnel Caualties: R. C. Wagner, ARM 2/c, USNR, radio gunner in plane # 1 was hit by shrapnel and received multiple wounds in head, hands, and leg, none of which proved to be serious.

Ammunition Expended: 2450 rounds - 30 calibre.
2915 rounds - 30 calibre.

Attack Tactics: Rendeznous Taioff Island, thence direct to target. High speed approach at 12,500', push over at 10,000', a second high speed approach, push over at 4,000' on to target at 300-315 K. from SW to NE, release 1500', retirement straight from airfield to rally point 5 miles east of Kabanga Point. Route back direct to Piva.

Results: In the area North of the strip, 3 confirmed direct hits, 2 estmated direct hits, and 1 reported effective hit were registered. In the revetment areas south of the strip, 2 confirmed direct, 3 estmated direct, and 6 reported effective hits were made. One plane did not drop and returned with bombs to base. 4 bombs hung and were jettisoned. Two fires were started inthe revetment area south of the runway,one of them an oil fire and 1 in the area north. Several small fires were reported. Three parked planes were seen to explode and several others were hit by the strings of bombs. The target area was strafed by both fixed and free guns, and the tower was left smoking as a result.

Weather: Route up: Generally good with a few scattered clouds.
Over target: Clear.
Return: 3/10 low scattered clouds 1000'-1500' encountered one-half

(Contd.)
way back.

Observations: 1. Enemy shipping: One pilot reported 1 large ship in center of Simpson Harbor; he could not identify it due to the distance. 3 unidentified ships were reported in Keravia Bay.

2. Enemy ground activity: None other than AA.

3. Condition of target before and after attack: runway serviceable.

4. Results of coordinated attack: The coordinated attack was executed efficiently. SBD hits were observed on buildings near control tower, and on AA positions at coffee plantation and NE end of strip.

5. Unusual circumstances: A white parachute was seen near rally point at 6,000'. A Jap was seen to bail out North of Cape Gazulle. A P-38 pilot was seen bailing out near rally point.

Over the target 2 phosporous bombs were reported dropped in the path of the SBD's too far away to do any damage, and another was seen NE of the NE end of the strip. 2 more burst at 3000' (approximately) near the rally point.

6. AA positions: In general the AA encountered over the target was both medium and heavy calibre of meagre to moderate intensity, from the following positions:

A. Moderate heavy AA from known position north of the garden plot, inaccurate, short in range bursting 2-4000' below SBD formation when it was making high speed approach. 3 or possibly 4 guns firing.
B. Known light auto position at control tower of meagre intensity, accuracy doubtful.
C. Known auto position NE end of runway of meagre to moderate intensity, accurate.
D. Know heavy and auto position Coffee Plantation, meagre intensity, inaccurate.
E. Known heavy position at NE end of runway, meagre, inaccurate.
F. New heavy position east of NE end of runway in known auto position, meagre, inaccurate.
G. New heavy (1gun) approximately 1200 yards east of N E tip of runway, meagre, inaccurate.

7. Miscellaneous: Over Kabanga Bay an unidentified plane was reported at 6,000' spinning down in flames; the pilot reporting stated that the plane had dark wings and appeared to have white star marking.

A great splash was reported in the water 1½ miles east of rally point, apparently from a plane that had been shot down or had spun in.

An F4U with right wing noticeably shot up joined up on a TBF at the rally point then pulled off after 2 or 3 minutes.

Dust was observed rising from Rapopo Airfield indicating a scramble there.

J. N. Truesdale
James N. Truesdale, Lt. USNR.
A.C.I.O. VC - 38
Intelligence Duty Officer

Plane No.	Pilot	Passenger
1	Brunton	Kemper-Wagner
4	Scholfield	Ulrich-Dills
12	Phillippi	Bond-Rice
3	Tahler	Buis-Brewer
2	Leaki	Boyle-O'Danials
115	Smith	Morey-Thomas
122	Stalnaker	Spickard-Howe
105	Bell	Drake-Burris
13	Webb	Miller-Visvardis
125	Ferguson	Johnson-Ayersman
118	Gundlack	Dunham-Duttie
120	Glenn	Whiteanank-Sticksel
126	Ransom	Mcadam-Fisher
21	Philbin	Williams-Blazi
113	Turner	Farris-Lockridge.
119	Richardson	Lane-Wilson
112	Teal	Otis-Russ

CONFIDENTIAL

COMAIRSOLS
STRIKE COMMAND
TBF INTELLIGENCE

CONFIDENTIAL

Struck 31 January, 1944

Exhibit I

Target: Tobera Airfield.
Mission: Bomb and strafe
Flight Leader: Commander Brunton
Squadrons: VC - 38 (6); VMTB - 143 (6); VMTB - 233 (6).
Planes: Ordered for mission - 18 TBF's
Released bombs - 18 TBF's
Loadings - 18x1x2000 # (4-5 second delayed fuze).
Times: T.O. - 0825
O.T. - 1030
Landed - 1155
Aircraft Coordinating: 24 SBD's and 72 VF.
Enemy Aircraft: 20 to 30 were sighted at the approach to Tobera Field. Only 6-10 enemy A/C pressed home the attack. One Zero got on the tail of Lt. S. W. Painter, the turret gunner opened fire and the Zero was seen diving toward the water. Lt. H. H. Keiter made his attack in the southern revetment area. His bomb exploded in a revetment containing one enemy plane. Lt. R. W. Sherman released his bomb on a plane taxing out into runway on south side of Tobera strip. His bomb made a direct hit on the U/I enemy plane. Lt. Stark possibly damaged or destroyed 10-12 enemy A/C on the ground by a estimated effective hit in a revetted area containing that number of planes. Lt. Painter made effective hit on a Betty in southern reveted area destroying it. His bomb also damaged an U/I enemy plane. T. G. Brewer, Lt. Painters gunner hit a Zero on his tail and it was last seen diving toward the water.
Damage to own A/C:

TBF Plane Number	Damage
1. 208	Hole from AA through right aileron
2. 204	Hole in right aileron

3. Four planes very slightly damaged from an enemy A/C.

Personnel Damage:
1. Captain E. Morgan, VMTB 143 received a minor injury in fleshy part of left arm near shoulder. He thinks it was from a 20 MM shell.
2. C. E. Brandt, AOM/2c, turret gunner in plane # 108 piloted by Lt. Regan of VC - 38 received lascerations in forehead from glass or 20 MM shell fragments.

Ammunition Expended: 30 calibre - 1275
50 calibre - 860
Attack Tactics: TBF's approached target from west 13,000' high speed approach. Push over at 8,000 feet, released at indicated 2500', pulled out 2000' indicated towards the east. Rally was made 10 miles east of Kabanga Bay.
Results: On the runway there were 5 estimated direct hits and 4 confirmed direct hits. In the revetment area to south of runway there were 4 estimated direct and 5 estimated effective hits. The target was strafed by 11 of 18 planes. No effects were observed.
Weather: 1. Route up: 3/10 to 5/10, low 1500' to 5000' - Over New Ireland west and over Rabaul Harbor a frontal condition. Harbor visible below overcast from west direction.
2. Over target: Clear.
3. Return: Same as route up.

Observations: 1. Enemy shipping.
A. 6-7 AK's and AO's in Keravia Bay 250-450 feet.
B. 4-5 U.I. ships in Simpson Harbor.
C. 1 large ship U. I. in Talili Bay.
2. Enemy ground activity:
A. Moderate to intense AA. Shipping in Simpson Harbor, Keravia Bay and Talili Bay.
3. Conditions of target.
A. Serviceable before strike but not serviceable afterwards.
B. Explosion and fire in south revetted area.
4. Results of coordinated attack: Not observed.
5. Unusual circumstances:
A. On approach intense AA apparently directed at B-24 strike on same target.
B. 20 to 30 enemy A/C sighted and attacked but only 6-10 pressed home.
C. Some phosphorous bombs dropped.
D. Weather conditions over Rabaul would permit a TBF shipping attack but too low for SBD attack.
E. Light A.A. generally accurate.

27

6. Anti-Aircraft.
A. Known auto NE end of strip, moderate and inaccurate.
B. New light in southernly revetted area east of strip-
C. Know light along N side of strip-Intense and inaccurate.
D. Known 4 heavies (descrobed as auto) northernly side of garden spot, moderate and accurate.
E. Known auto SW end of strip-moderate and accurate.

Lewis P. Kilbourne, Lt. USMCR.
A. C. I. O. VMTB - 233
Intelligence Duty Officer.

Plane No.	Pilot	Passengers
110	Brunton	Thatcher-Kemper
1[illegible]1	Scholfield	Ulrich-Dills
105	Giblin	Leo-Perkins
106	Draughon	Doal-Paul
108	Regan	Misner-Brant
2	Leake	Boyle, O'Danial
202	Haxton	Bullock-Doss
200[illegible]	Kieter	Boyd-Larsen
207	Bartholf	Lagro-Sullivan
208	Sherman	Cashman-Greene
209	Ward	Marshal-Rice
204	Roberts	Koloderf-Melvin
214	Morgan	Moffitt-Bosoo
215	Stark	Winn-Johnson
216	Davis	~~Bieher~~ Schaul-West
217	Painter	Doy-Brewer
218	Waddington	Arnold-Brogan
219	Belcher	McDonough-Cohoon

28

CONFIDENTIAL — COMAIRSOLS STRIKE COMMAND TBF INTELLIGENCE — CONFIDENTIAL

Struck 5 February, 1944

EXHIBIT K.

Target: Lakunai Airfield
Mission: Bomb and strafe.
Flight Leader: Commander C. E. Brunton, USN
Squadrons: VC-38 (14), VMTB-233 (7), VMTB-143 (3).
Planes: Ordered for mission: 24 TBF's
Actually dropped bombs: 23 TBF's
Loadings: 18x2000 # 1/10 second delay, and
6x2000 # 4-5 second delay.
Times: Take off - 0900
Over target- 1050
Return - 1215
Other A/C coordinating: 48 SBD's, 72 VF.
Enemy A/C: From 6 to 10 Zeros were seen at some distance off, two of which feinted but did not press home an attack on the TBF's.
Damage to Own A/C: Plane # 204 piloted by 1st Lt. Painter, USMCR. did not return from mission. Fighter Intelligence reported that a TBF was seen to make a successful water landing between Credner Island and Lesson Point.
Three planes received minor damage from light AA and shrapnel as follows:
Plane # 215 - 20MM hole through starboard wing.
Plane # 14 - small dents and scars on starboard wing and side of fuselage from shrapnel.
Plane # 126 - shrapnel or 20 MM hole through port stabilizer.
Personnel Casualties: 1st Lt. Stephen W. Painter, pilot, PFC. Harold A. Dey, USMC. (384581), turret gunner, and PFC. Charles S. Brewer, USMCR. (501697), radio gunner, are missing in plane # 204 (see supra) which was probably the TBF reported by Fighter Intelligence to have made a water landing between Credner Island and Lesson Point. No further information could be obtained.
Ammunition expended: 50 calibre - 1550 rounds
30 calibre - 1150 rounds
Attack Tactics: Rendezvous was made over Puruata Island and thence on course to SE New Ireland and St. George's Channel. The flight passed over the Duke of York Group and when N of the target turned left to make an approach from the NW. A high speed approach was made from 13,500' down to the pushover at 8,000'; a speed of 350 knots was attained in final dive, release at 2500', and pull out around 1200' towards the SE. Retirement to rally point 5 miles E of Cape Gazelle. Route back direct to Piva.
Results: On the concrete strip 4 estimated, 1 reported, and 4 confirmed direct hits were registered, and 5 hits were unobserved. 6 hits were well distributed on other parts of the runway. There was 1 wild miss, 1 dropped safe, and 1 hung and jettisoned on the route back. The target area was strafed by both fixed and free guns.
Weather: Route up - clear
Over target - clear with alto-stratus 18-20,000'
Route back - clear to within 50 miles of base, where a cumulus build up 1-2000' with an occasional thunderhead encountered.
Observations: 1. Enemy shipping.
A. 1 large AK SW Simpson Harbor.
B. 2 unidentified ships N part Simpson Harbor and a great many unidentified small ships.
C. 3 large (possibly damaged) AK or AO in N Keravia Bay.
D. 1 large AK (approximately 350') SE Keravia Bay.
E. 1 DD E of Praed Point.
2. Enemy ground activity: Moderate to intense AA; shipping as noted above.
3. Condition of target before and after attack:
Runway serviceable before attack and unserviceable afterwards. Two fires, one probably a large oil fire, observed in revetment area E of SE portion of runway, and another in SW revetment area.
4. Results of coordinated attack: The coordinated attack was executed efficiently. AA fire diminished appreciably after SBD attack. The Hirstein hulk was reported to have been hit heavily and left smoking. VF cover funtioned excellently.
5. Unusual circumstances: 2 VF were observed to strafe the tip of Cape St. George and an explosion of some sort resulted. 1 P-40 and 1 F4U were reported to have crashed in the water in St. George's channel; the F4U was burning.
6. Anti-Aircraft: On the approach to the target a heavy barrage was observed at 10-12,000' intense and accurate as to altitude AA fire was reported from the following positions:

(continued on next page)

10

(continued from preceding page)

6. A. South of Sulphur Creek, known heavy (2-4.7 dual Navy) position, of moder te intensity.
   B. West of Rabatana Crater an 1/3 of distance to strip, new heavy (2 guns) position, of moderate intensity.
   C. E of S end of runway, known heavy and auto, intense.
   D. S Matupi Island, known heavy and auto, intense.
   E. Praed Point and Ralu na Point, known heavy, of moderate intensity.
   F. E shore of St. George Channel (position mot pin-pointed) on New Ireland, new heavy of moderate intensity.

James N. Truesdale, Lt. USNR.
A. C. I. O. VC-38
INTELLIGENCE DUTY OFFICER

Plane No.	Pilot	Passenger
217	Brunton	Wagner, Kemper
105	Scholfield	Ulrich, Dills
107	Giblin	Lee, Perkins
109	Draughan	Deal, Paul
110	Regan	Misner, Brandt
111	Leake	Boyle, O'Daniel
202	Marshall	Lane, Tye
219	Mc Donald	Blank, Young
205	Phillippi	Bond, Rice
215	Tahler	Buis, Brewer
213	Leary	Greslie, Dale
216	Gammage	Durham, Morrissey
115	Bishop	Schramm, Barnes
119	Hollis	Howard, Dunningham
14	Bell	Burris, Drake
122	Teel	Russ, Otia
126	Behn	, Dill
8	Haxton	Bullock, Doss
3	Melby	Connor, Kerr
18	Bartholf	Lagro, Sullivan
12	Sherman	Cashman, Greene
13	Lamade	Mc Elhoes, Bellows
21	Strieby	Richard, Gooding

11

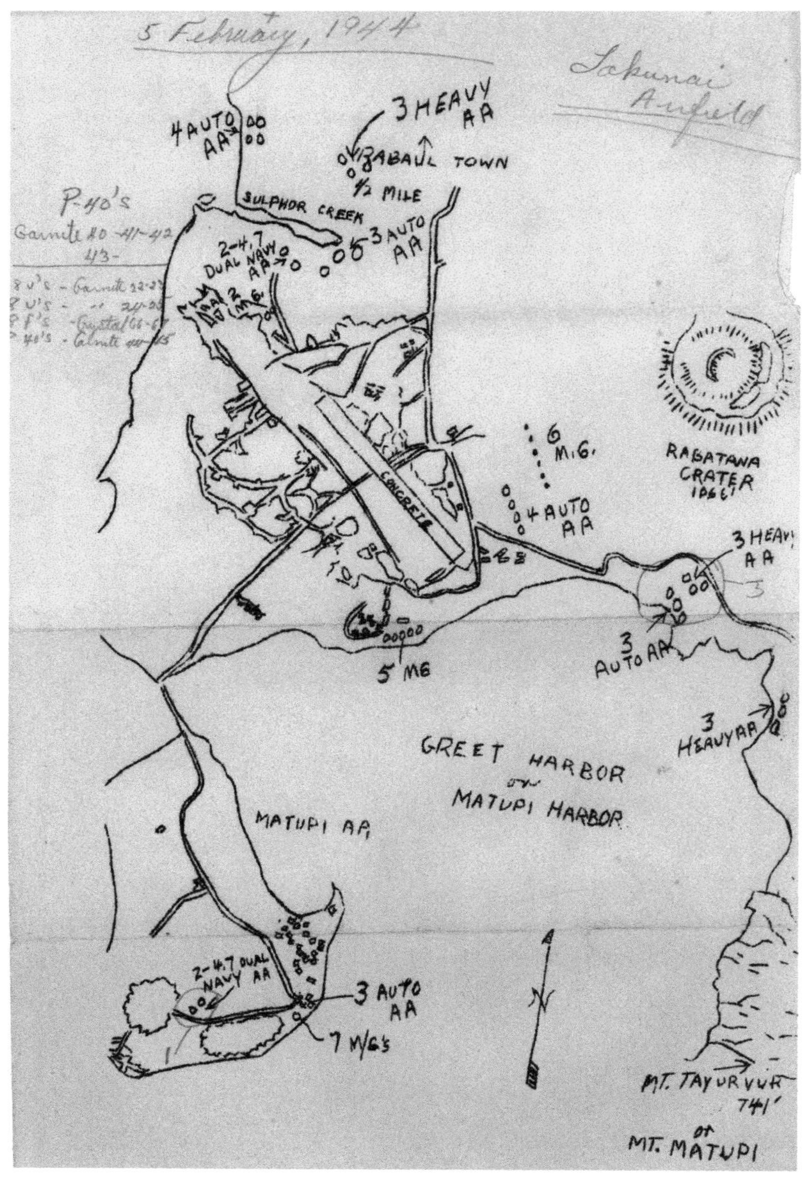

VC 38 Lt. John Leary's Map of Lakunai Airfield, February 5, 1943 (Source: Leary Family Collection)

TBF INTELLIGENCE

10 Febuary 1944

R/S 11/88

Target: Revetments at Lakunai; Ropopo and Tobera Airfields.
Mission: Bombing.
Flight Leader: Commander Brunton.
Squadron: VC 38
Planes and Loadings: Ordered for Mission - 6 TBF's.
Actually dropped Bombs - 6 TBF's.
Loadings each plane - 12 x 1000# 8-11 second delay.
Times: T.O. 0420
O.T. 0550
Arrived 0700
Other A/C Coordinating: None.
Enemy A/C: None.
Damage to own A/C: None.
Personnel Casualties: None.
Ammunition Expended: No Strafing.
Attack Tactics: Lakunai - Up Blanche Channel, at 6500' - 7000'. High speed approach from 7000' over Rabaul town from N. to S. Final pushover at 3000' Release at 1500'. Bombs hit in S.E. revetment area. S/L picked up planes immediately. They maneuvered out of spot light, S/L picked them up again. Route out, N. of Mt. Matupi and then direct.

Ropopo - High speed approach at 3000'. Released from 200' - 300' at 220 knots. Run made from S. to N.

Tobera - Following high speed approach, bombs released at 1000' above target.

Summary of Results: Assigned targets well covered with confirmed hits. Results unobserved.
Weather: Route up - Excellent.
O.T. - Clear. No clouds.
Route in - Light cumulus build up 1000' - 6000', 40 miles east of New Ireland. Thunderheads 50 miles south of New Ireland.
Observations:

1. Enemy Shipping: None.
2. Enemy Ground Activity: None except A-A and S/L. 15 S/L at Lakunai and 2 S/L at Tobera. Lakunai S/L picked up planes immediately and held planes thru out, blinding pilots. Lakunai alerted, lights out. At Tobera, lights still on in revetment area, mission a surprise, 2 S/L went on after planes passed R/W. Rapopo surprised.
3. Condition of Target before and after Attack: Unobserved.
4. Results of Coordinated Attack: None.
5. Unusual Circumstances: None.
6. Anti-Aircraft: Lakunai - Medium A-A moderate and inaccurate. Light A-A and MG fire moderate to intense, inaccurate over R/W and revetment areas.
Ropopo - None
Tobera - Light A-A, meager and inaccurate on retirement

Myron Sulzberger [signature]
Captain Myron Sulzberger, Jr.
USMCR., Intelligence Duty Officer
VMTB-143

- -

Plane	Pilot	Passengers
2	Brunton	Wagner, Kemper
18	Scholfield	Ulrich, Dills
117	Giblin	Lee, Perkins
101	Draughon	Deal, Paul
110	Regan	Misner, Brandt
14	Leake	Boyle, O'Daniel

CONFIDENTIAL   COMAIRSOLS
STRIKE COMMAND
TBF INTELLIGENCE   CONFIDENTIAL

Struck 11 February, 1944

EXHIBIT O

Target: Vunapope
Mission: Bomb and strafe.
Flight Leader: 1st Lt. F. C. Haxton.
Squadron: VMTB 233 (9), VC-38 (9), VMTB 143 (6).
Planes and Loadings: Ordered for Mission - 24 TBF's.
Actually dropped bombs - 24 TBF's.
Loadings: 1x2000 # 1/10 second delay.
Times: T.O. - 0915
T.O.T. - 1100
Return - 1225
Other A/C Coordinating: 36 SBD's, 64 VF.
Enemy A/C: Approximately 10 Zeros made passes at TBF's and several phosphorous bombs were dropped, three of which came close to TBF's but did no damage. One probable was scored by Sgt. Bryan L. Donaldson, turret gunner in plane # 123; 130 rounds were fired at Zero making a pass from the rear and the Zero was observed to smoke afterwards.
Damage to Own A/C: Plane # 9 sustained minor damage in aileron from shrapnel.
Personnel Casualties: None.
Ammunition expended: 30 calibre - 1750
50 calibre - 650
Attack Tactics: Rendezvous off Taioff Island at 6000', thence towards target passing over SE tip of New Ireland. The primary target Tobera was completely closed in by low cumulus clouds; hence Vunapope, the secondary target was attacked. High speed approach from SW at 13,000' to 11,000', final push over at 8,000; release at 1800-2000', pullout towards the NE. Rally 5 miles E of Cape Gazelle, route back direct to Piva.
Summary of Results: 19 hits were scored on Vunapope, 3 on supply area to west, 1 on Takubar, and 1 on alleged fuel dump (direct hit but no fire resulted). All hits were well within the target area, and many buildings were blown up and many fires started. The general area was strafed by both fixed and free guns.
Weather: Enroute: 2/10 low cumulus at 3500' with 5/10 cumulus haze at 7000'.
Over target: Clear except for cloud over Tobera from 1500' to 10,000'.
Return: Line of low cumulus SE of New Ireland, 3/10 scattered clouds from 1000'-3500' with a few rain squalls.
Observations: 1. Enemy shipping: Known hulks and 15-20 barges in vicinity of Vunapope.
2. Enemy ground activity: None, other than AA.
3. Condition of taret before and after attack: See summary of results supra.
4. Results of coordinated attack: Several SBD hits observed in target area with 1-2 in water. VF cover functioned excellently.
5. Unusual Circumstances: The direct hit registered on the alleged fuel dump did not result in a fire. A P-40 dropped a belly tank through the TBF formation.
6. Anti-Aircraft:
A. Over Tobera, meagre heavy and auto AA.
B. Rapopo, moderate auto over field at 1500'.
C. From shore E of Vunapope, meagre light auto.
D. Vunapope, light AA or M/G from town, meagre.
E. 225' beached hulk, small AA, intense and inaccurate.
7. Miscellaneous:
A. A splash was noted 5 miles E of Cape Gazelle, apparently caused by an U/I plane going in.
B. Prior to attack a Zero was observed going straight down out of control.
C. Large columns of smoke were visible over Vunapope from 20 miles out on retirement.

James N. Truesdale
James N. Truesdale, Lt. USNR.
A. C. I. O. VC-38
Intelligence Duty Officer.

17

Plane Number	Pilot	Passengers	
109	Haxton	Bullock, Doss	
104	Kieter	Boyd, Larsen	
105	Barthold	Lagro, Sullivan	
102	Roberts	Kolodey, Melvin	
107	Dowd	Brownfield, Butehorn	
111	Little	Ivers, Miller	
207	Marshall	Lane, Tye	
206	McDonald	Blank, Young	
215	Phillippi	Bond, Rice	
216	Tahler	Buis, Brewer	
218	Leary	Groelie, Morrison	
219	Giblin	Lee, Perkins	
115	Bishop	Lt. Rourke, Barnes	
113	Scholfield	Ulrich, Dills	
118	Hollis, A. E.	Howard, Cunningham	
120	Vollbrecht	McCarthy, Olevich	
2	Phillips	Drolsbaugh, Hobbs	(did not attack)
126	Hammer	Stanton, Surevy	
108	Altizer	Thokar, Armacost	
123	Nagoda	Hoelsel, Donaldson	
19	Kingery	Meade, Rogousky	
112	Loiselle	Erbe, McElmurray	
12	Harris	Altfillich, McDonald	
13	Loyd	Selvey, Delcamp	(did not attack)
8	Brunton	Wagner, Kemper	(did not attack)
4	Draughon	Deal, Paul	(did not attack)
5	Regan	Misner, Brand	(did not attack)
6	Leake	Boyle, O'Daniel	
7	Ranson	Fisher, McAdams	(did not attack)
9	Philbin	Blazi, Williamson	

18

STRIKE COMMAND.
COMMANDER AIRCRAFT SOLOMONS.

SECRET 12 February 1944.

OPERATIONS MEMORANDUM :

Subject: Mining Operations in Simpson Harbor, Rabaul Area.

Enclosures: (A) Mining Plan for Simpson Harbor.
(B) Time Schedule for Tactical Units.
(C) Routes to and from Target.

1. As ordered by ComAirSoPac (secret despatch 112252) mining operations will be conducted in the north half of Simpson Harbor (Enclosure A). Diversion support will be provided by PV-1 aircraft.

2. This mining operation will take place during the night of 13-14 February 1944.

3. The tactical units to be employed will be:

26 TBF-1 VMTB 134 - 233 and VC-38.
PV-1 as ordered.
VB(H)

4. Takeoffs, rendezvous, attack and tactical unit organization will be as indicated in Enclosure (B). Routes to and from the target will be flown as indicated in Enclosure (C). Details of attack will be given in verbal briefing at 1400 13 February 1944.

5. Takeoffs will be made using East to West Course; landings as directed by tower or voice radio.

6. Simulated bombing runs on Vunakanau will be made by diversion aircraft.

7. Flight and section leaders will report to Strike Operations one hour prior to take-off for final instructions, final weather information and time check.

8. Mines must be dropped consistent with limitations stated below. In the event tactical units are prevented from attacking due to inclement weather or low visibility, time variations in time of attack up to 20 minutes are permitted. In the event the attacks cannot be made within these time limits tactical units will return to base. Mines will not be jettisoned unless forced to do so to conserve fuel in order to assure safe return of aircraft.

9. Rendezvous after take-off will be effected with lights on; turn off lights after 10 minutes on course. Keep all lights extinguished until within 20 miles of Torokina on return, when running lights will be turned on.

10. All aircraft use 3415 KCS.

Calls:

Group "A" 1 to 9 Stone 1

Group "B" 1 to 8 Stone 2

Group "C" 1 to 9 Stone 3

11. Observe normal Condition Red flight procedure if necessary when in vicinity Torokina. Utilize all navigational radio aids to best advantage.

By direction of the Commanding Officer:

(10) Enc (C)

J. E. Butler

J. E. BUTLER,
G-3, Strike Command.

6

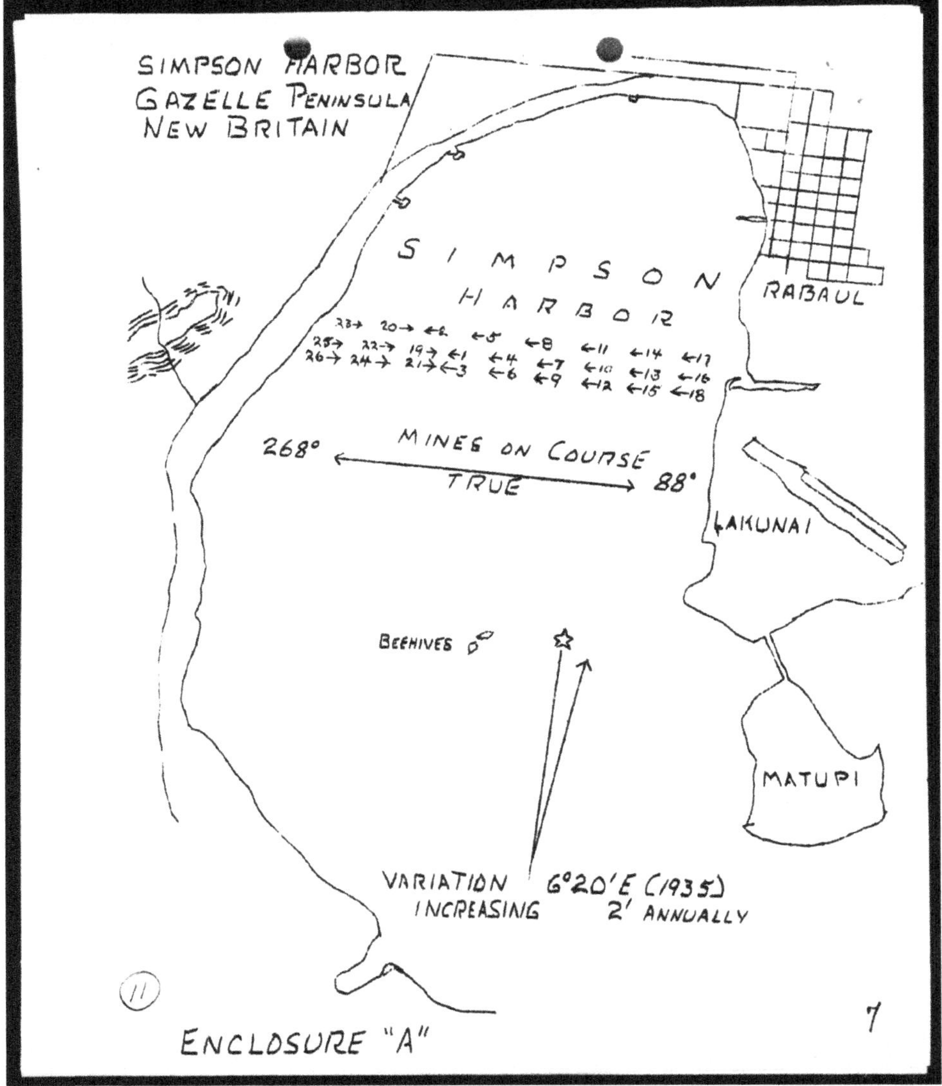
SIMPSON HARBOR
GAZELLE PENINSULA
NEW BRITAIN
SIMPSON
HARBOR
RABAUL
MINES ON COURSE
268°
TRUE
88°
LAKUNAI
BEEHIVES
MATUPI
VARIATION 6°20'E (1935)
INCREASING 2' ANNUALLY
11
ENCLOSURE "A"
7

ENCLOSURE (B)

TIME SCHEDULE FOR TACTICAL MINING UNITS:

Group A : 9 TBF's, loaded with one MK 12-1 mine.

Group B : 8 TBF's, loaded with one MK 12-1 mine.

Group C : 9 TBF's, loaded with one MK-12-1 mine.

Group D : VB(M) as ordered.

	A	B	C	D
Take Off	1230	0130	0230	As Ordered
Rendezvous, Lights on, Altitude	1240 1000 ft. over field	0140 1000 ft. over field	0240 1000 ft. over field.	
On Course	1245	0145	0245	
Lights Off	1255	0155	0255	
Route Up	Direct	Direct	Direct	
Time of Attack	0200 plus or minus 20 minutes	0300 plus or minus 20 minutes	0400 plus or minus 20 minutes	Over Target 0150 - 0210 0250 - 0310 0350 - 0410
Target	Center Area Simpson Harbor.	West Shore Simpson Harbor.	East Shore Simpson Harbor.	Simulated bombing runs Vunakanau
Route Back	Retire over Talili Bay around Tawui Pt.	Retire down Blanch Channel and St. George.	Retire over Talili Bay around Tawui Pt.	
Land	On arrival directions from tower.	On arrival directions from tower.	On arrival directions from tower.	

RUNOUT TIME FOR DROPPING MINES

Group "A"

Section I	Time of Runout*	Mine Number
Plane 1	14.0 Sec	1
2	15.4 Sec	2
3	15.4 Sec	3
Section II		
Plane 1	11.2 Sec	4
2	12.6 Sec	5
3	12.6 Sec	6
Section III		
Plane 1	8.4 Sec	7
2	9.8 Sec	8
3	[illegible]	9

Group "B"

Section I	Time of Runout*	Mine Number
Plane 1	7.2 Sec	19
2	5.4 Sec	20
3	6.2 Sec	21
Section II		
Plane 1	4.4 Sec	22
2	2.6 Sec	23
3	3.4 Sec	24
Section III		
Plane 1	1.6 Sec	25
2	.6 Sec	26

Group "C"

Section I	Time of Runout*	Mine No	Section II	Time of Runout*	Mine No	Section III		Mine No
Plane 1	5.6	10	Plane 1	2.8	13	Plane 1	0	16
2	7.0	11	2	4.2	14	2	1.4	17
3	7.0	12	3	4.2	15	3	1.4	18

(12)

*Time in seconds measured from waters edge.
Speed to be 190 knots.
Altitude of dropping - not under 500 feet.
Spacing between adjoining planes - not less than 200 feet.

ENCLOSURE (B)

8

(ENCLOSURE "D")

COL V STR CAS NR 37 FIT NR 33 OP SECRET

FROM: STRIKE COMMAND 132044

TO : COMAIRSOLS INTELLIGENCE

INFO: FIGHTER COMMAND, BOMBER COMMAND.

DATE: EARLY MORNING OF FEB. 14, 1944.

MISSION: MINING SIMPSON HBR., BETWEEN WESLEYAN MISSION AND SULPHUR CREEK COURSE 268 DEG - 88 DEG TRUE

PLANES: 25 TBF'S - THREE GROUPS 9, 7, 9 EACH EACH LOADED 1x MK 12-1 MINE. - VMTB 233

TO: 1230
Ø13Ø
Ø23Ø

ON STATION: Ø2ØØ
Ø3ØØ
Ø4ØØ

TA: Ø32Ø
Ø415
Ø545

ALL MINES DROPPED EXCEPT FOR ONE HUNG UP AND TWO BROUGHT BACK. DROPS, MOSTLY ON COURSE, MADE BY DUCKING DOWN IN COCKPIT TO ESCAPE SEARCHLIGHT GLARE AND COUNTING SECONDS.

SEARCH LIGHTS PICKED UP PLANES COMING OVER EAST RIDGE OF PENINSULA. SEARCH LIGHTS AND INTENSE ACCURATE AA WERE WELL COORDINATED.

SIX PLANES AND CREWS ARE MISSING, OF THESE, 4 PROBABLY SHOT DOWN, TWO IN HARBOR TWO ON LAND SIDE, THREE DEFINITELY FLAMERS.

PILOTS MISSING: LT. BARTHOFF
LT. CORNELIUS
LT. HATHWAY
LT. FOWLER
LT. BONDEN
LT. SHERMAN

TOD: NR 37 NR 32 21ØØ/13 DTG 132044
VCG AR

FITRR NR 32 13/21ØØ GMK K
CAS4 NR 37 13/21ØØ BLACKIE AR

(ENCLOSURE "D")

(14) 10

SECRET OPERATIONAL PRIORITY

FROM: COMAIRSOLS

TO : COMAIRSOPAC

140557

FIELD OF 16 MINES LAID SIMPSON HARBOR FROM WESLEYAN MISSION EAST TO SULPHUR CREEK X REF COMSOPAC 120625 X MARK 12 MOD ONE MINES

UWED WITH MARK 3 MOD ONE MECHANISMS SET AT SENSITIVITY OF 10 MILLIGAUSS X SHIP COUNTS AND DELAY SOLUBLE WASHERS EMPLOYED IN

SOME MINES X MINES FURNISHED BY MINE DETAIL 15 X MINES LAID BY FLIGHT OF 25 TBF BETWEEN 0400 AND 0500 LOVE NIGHT THIRTEEN DASH

FOURTEEN IN THE FACE OF INTENSE ACCURATE ACK ACK FIRE 6 PLANES LOST X 3 PLANES DID NOT RELEASE

ENCLOSURE (E)

(15)

11

Lt. Kilbourne
15 Copies

CONFIDENTIAL

COMAIRSOLS
STRIKE COMMAND
TBF INTELLIGENCE

CONFIDENTIAL

Struck 14, February, 1944

Target: Simpson Harbor.
Mission: Mining.
Flight Leaders: Major Coln, Capt. Milling, Capt. Voyles.
Squadron: VMTB - 233
Planes and loadings: Ordered for mission: 26 TBF's.
Actually dropped mines: 16 TBF's. (25 planes took off, 2 returned to base, 1 mine hung, and 6 planes did not return from mission).
Loadings: 1xMK12-1 mine per plane.

Times:	Group A	Group B	Group C
T.O.	1230	0130	0230
T.O.T.	0200	0310	0415
A.T.A.	0335	0435	0600

Enemy A/C: One night fighter at distance.
Damage to Own A/C: Plane # 211, Bullet hole in cowling.
Plane # 11, Bullet shattered windshield.
Planes # 14, #10, # 111, # 115, # 107, and # 102 did not return.
Four probable plane crashes, resulting from AA fire were reported in the following locations: N. shore Simpson Harbor, Center of Simpson Harbor opposite Bradgo Point, N of NW end of Lakunai Airfield, and Center of Blanche Bay E of Vulcan Crater.
Personnel Casualties: The following pilots and crews are missing:

Plane No.	Pilots and crews.
P10	*1stLt. Hugh L. Cornelius, Pilot, USMCR.; PFC. Edwin D. St. Germain, Radio Man, USMCR.; S/Sgt. Edward M. Slipkas, Turret Gunner, USMC.
14	*1stLt. John F. Bartholf, Jr., USMCR., Pilot; PFC. Raymond P. Lagro, Radio Man, USMCR.; S/Sgt. Joseph A. Sullivan, Turret Gunner, USMC.
102	1stLt. James W. Boyden, Pilot, USMCR.; PFC. Arthur J. Patrickus, Radio man, USMCR.; PFC. Bernard C. Pardun, Turret Gunner, USMCR.
107	1stLt. Robert W. Sherman, Pilot, USMCR.; PFC. William B. Cashman, Radio Man, USMCR.; Sgt. James W. Greene Jr., Turret Gunner, USMCR.
115	1stLt. James L. Fowler, Pilot, USMCR; Pvt. John J. Pudil, Radio man, USMCR.; Pvt. Cecil M. White, Turret Gunner, USMCR.
111	1stLt. Alonzo N. Hathway, Pilot, USMCR.; PFC. Willie C. Thompson, Radio Man, USMCR.; Cpl. John J. Edwards, Turret Gunner, USMCR.

Note: * Cornelius - shot down in flames, Center of Blanche Bay, E of Vulcan Crater.
* Bartholf - shot down in flames N of NW end of Lakunai Airfield.
Ammunition Expended: Did not Strafe.
Attack Tactics: Group A: Approach to harbor for run from E to W crossing Crater Peninsula N. of the Mother at 6-700' to mouth of Sulphur Creek. Mines were dropped in Center Area Simpson Harbor as follows:

Mine No.	Time of runout	Course			Speed	Atltitude
1	14 seconds	250 degrees	Magnetic		190 k	600'
2 (probably dud)	15.4 "	262	"	"	185 k	750'
3	15.4 "	255	"	"	192 k	600'
4	11.2 "	255	"	"	190 k	700'
6	12.6 "	260	"	"	180 k	650'
7	10 "	265	"	"	190 k	700'
8	10 "	260	"	"	185 k	700'

Group C: Approach similiar to that of Group A. Mines were dropped off E. shore Simpson Harbor as follows:

Mine No.	Time of runout	Course			Speed	Altitude
11	7 seconds	261 degrees M.			170 k	600'
13	2.8 "	260	"	"	180 k	550'
15	5 "	270	"	"	182 k	600'
16	0 "	260	"	"	180 k	700'

Groups A and C retired across Simpson Harbor and Maliguna Mission, Talili Bay, around Tawui Point and down St. Georges Channel, going up to 1000' at Cape St. George.
Group B attacked from W to E around Tawni Point , accross Talili Bay and the neck of Crater Peninsula. Mines were dropped off W shore Simpson Harbor as follows:

Mine No.	Time of runout	Course			Speed	Altitude
19	7 seconds	80 degrees M.			180 k	500'
20	5.4 "	85	"	"	175 k	700'
21	6.3 "	82	"	"	185 k	600'
23	2.6 "	85	"	"	180 k	600'
25	1.6 "	82	"	"	178 k	480'

Retirement was made down Blanche Channel and St. Georges Channel. Planes went to 1000' at Cape St. George.

80

11

Summary of results: 16 mines were dropped in Simpson Harbor as specified supra, 1 mine (No. 9), hung and was returned to base. Two planes did not reach target and returned to base with mines No. 10 and No. 18. Six planes did not return from mission; they were loaded with mines No. 5, 12, 14, 17, 22, and 24. Some of these may have been dropped in harbor.

Weather: Enroute: Good
Over target: Clear
Route back: Same as route up. One small front encountered off Buka extending E and W.

Observations: 1. Enemy shipping.
A. 1x350' AK NW coast Simpson Harbor.
B. 1x300' AK Center Simpson Harbor, S of mine lane.
2. Enemy ground activity: AA and S/L's. Approximately 30 S/L's were reported in the area, many of which were very accurate in picking up the planes and keeping them in the light. The following locations were pinpointed:
A. East Coast of Crater Peninsula: 7 S/L's, one of which was very accurate in picking up planes on approach.
B. N of Rabaul on edge of town, 4 S/L's.
C. NE of Rabaul between town and coast, 8 S/L's.
D. Cape Tawui; 1 S/L, and 2 SE of Cape on Coast.
E. Neck of Peninsula, 6 S/L in double row from Talili Bay to Simpson Harbor.
F. W coast Simpson Harbor N of Vulcan Crater, 3 S/L's.
G. Vicinity of the Mother, 2 S/L's.
H. Raluana Point, 1 S/L.
I. Lesson Point, 1 S/L.
J. Mouth of Sulphur Creek, 1 S/L.
K. Praed Point 1 S/L, Suphur Point, 1 S/L.
3. Condition of target before and after attack: Not observed.
4. Results of coordinated attack: None.
5. Unusual Circumstances:
A. Plane crashing on W shore Simpson Harbor was reported to have exploded and destroyed wharf.
B. Flares were seen in water SE of Matupi Island.
C. A fire was observed at N of SimpsoneHarbor in town. This may have been caused by a plane crashing.
D. Burning plane (probably piloted by Lt. Bartholf) went down N of NW end of Lakunai Airfield.
E. Lt. Cornelius' plane was observed to smoke and strike water in Center of Blanche Bay E of Vulcan Crater and then bounde. Later flames were observed at this spot.
F. A large splash was reported near E coast of Simpson Harbor, cause undetermined.
6. Anti-Aircraft:
A. N of Mother and N side of Mother, Known, meduim and light, very intense, accurate.
B. Neck of Crater Peninsula from Simpson Harbor to Talili Bay, known medium and light, intense, accurate.
C. Sulphur Creek, known 2x4.7 Naval guns firing.
D. E and N Simpson Harbor, known light and medium, intense, accurate.
E. Beehives or ship close by, light and medium, intense, accurate.

Note: An intense and accurate crossfire was encountered N of the Mother, over Simpson Harbor, and across the neck of the peninsula between Talili Bay and Simpson Harbor.

James N. Truesdale

James N. Truesdale, Lt. USNR.
A. C. I. O. VC - 38
INTELLIGENCE DUTY OFFICER.

81

Plane No.	Pilot	Passengers	
Group A			
202	Coln	Hanks, Greathouse	
216	Sloan	Bruce, Myers	
108	Kirincich	Belling, Gunning	
211	Little	Ivers, Miller	
210	Aaronson	Sombati, Webb	(did not get off)
206	Renton	Trahan, Yelton	
207	Johnson	Fleming, Herndon	
121	Kirsch	Sutton, Cleary	
13	Melby	Conner, Keer	
14 (spare)	Bartholf	Lagro, Sullivan	(did not return)
Group B			
113	Milling	Smith, Benson	
110	Hammer	Stanton, Surevy	
209	Dowd	Brownfield, Butehorn	(did not get off)
10	Cornelius	St. Germain, Slipkas	(did not return)
112	Volbrecht	McCarty, Olevitch	
111	Hathway	Thompson, Edward	(did not return)
11 (spare)	Keiter	Boyd, Larsen	(replaced Strieby)
219	Lamade	McElhoes, Bellow	
209	Strieby	Hickard, Gooding	(did not attack)
Group C.			
120	Voyles	Fitzgerald, Gilbert	(did not release mine)
117	Radcliffe	Page, Mack	
115	Fowler	Pudil, White	(did not return)
215	Gonnerman	Kazprazak, Benjavcic	
102	Boyden	Patrickus, Pardun	(did not return)
103	Savino	Matlock, Gumm	
101	Maxton	Bullock, Doss	
126	Ward	Marshall, Rice	(did not get off)
125	Hollis	Howard, Dunningham	(did not release mine)
107	Sherman	Cashman, Greene	(did not return)
104	Jaqua	Canhan, Cox	(returned to base)

82

COMSOPAC FILE

SOUTH PACIFIC FORCE
OF THE UNITED STATES PACIFIC FLEET
HEADQUARTERS OF THE COMMANDER

S81/(91)
Serial 39

33180

S-E-C-R-E-T

THIRD ENDORSEMENT on Strike Command, Com AirSols, Secret ltr. dated 18 February, 1944.

From: The Commander South Pacific.
To : The Chief of Naval Operations.
Via : (1) The Commander in Chief, U. S. Pacific Fleet.
(2) The Commander in Chief, United States Fleet.

Subject: Offensive Aerial Mining Operations Against Simpson Harbor, Rabaul, New Britain.

1. Forwarded.

2. The Commander South Pacific concurs in the conclusions stated in paragraph ten of the basic letter. He is of the opinion, however, that it should have been self-evident that no effective diversionary bombing could be obtained over such a heavily defended area by the employment of a single plane in such a mission. On the contrary, the result more probably would be the alerting of the anti-aircraft defenses of the harbor, with the minelaying planes as the obvious targets.

W. F. Halsey

Copy to:
BuOrd
ComServRon Six, Pacific Fleet
Comairsopac
Comairsols

4th Endorsement
CinC Pacific Fleet
To: Opnav
Via: Cominch
1. Forwarded.

O. L. Thorne
By direction

COMMANDER-IN-CHIEF FLAG OFFICE RECEIVED
1944 APR 17 13 46

(2)

14

CONFIDENTIAL — COMAIRSOLS STRIKE COMMAND TBF INTELLIGENCE — CONFIDENTIAL

Struck 14 February, 1944

Target: Tobera, South Revetment Area. (secondary).
Mission: Bomb and strafe.
Flight Leader: Commander Brunton.
Squadrons: VC - 38 (6), VMTB - 233 (6).
Planes and Loadings: Ordered for mission 12 TBF's.
Actually bropped bombs 10 TBF's.
Loadings: 8x100 # plus
4x250 # inst. per plane.
Times: T.O. 0955
T.O.T.1140
A.T.A.1310
Other A/C Coordinating: 60 SBD's, 52 VF.
Enemy A/C: 6 Zeros at distance; 3 half-hearted passes were made, but none pressed home.
Damage to Own A/C: 1. Plane # 118, bullet hole in right wing and left elevator.
2. Plane # 203, shrapnel in hydraulic system.
3. Plane # 109, shrapnel hole in right wing.
Personnel Casualties: None.
Ammunition Expended: 30 calibre - 330 rounds
50 calibre - 595 rounds
Attack Tactics: When the primary target Vunakanau was found to be closed in, the secondary target Tobera was approached from the SW, high speed (240 K) 13000 ft; pushover at 6000', release at 1500' (280 knots), pullout at 1000' towards the NE. Rally 5 miles E. of mouth of Warangoi River.
Summary of Results: 8 unobserved and 2 estimated effective hits were registered in the revetment area S of the runway. Cloudy conditions, haze, and dust prevented close observation of the results. 3x250 # and 6x100# hung and were jettisoned. The area was strafed by fixed and free guns.
Weather: Route up: Excellent with a few low scattered clouds.
Over target: Primary target Vunakanau entirely closed in. Tobera was almost closed in by clouds to the N, NW and SE, bases at 2000', extending up to 5-6000'.
Route back: Same as route up.
Observations: 1. Enemy shipping: None.
2. Enemy ground activity: AA and convoy of 15 trucks on road 3 miles E of Tobera. Small arms fire from trucks was reported.
3. Condition of target before and after attack: Runway appeared serviceable before; dust was observed at NE end of strip rising to 1500', either as a result of a scramble or high altitude bombing. Two fires were started in the S revetment area, one near 2 parked planes. Smoke was observed at a distance of 50 miles on retirement.
4. Results of coordinated attack: SBD attack not observed.
5. Unusual circumstances: None.
6. Anti-Aircraft:
A. W of runway known heavy position, heavy, meagre and inaccurate fire (possibly 2 guns).
B. E of runway, known 2 auto position, meagre, inaccurate.
C. NE of runway, known 2 heavy position, meagre, inaccurate.
D. W end of runway, known light auto position, meagre, fairly accurate.
7. Miscellaneous:
1 Zero and 3 U/I planes were observed in revetments S of strip.
Search: TBF's spread out S of Cape St. George in order to search for missing planes. The results were negative. on route back to base.

James N. Truesdale, Lt. USNR.
A. C. I. O. VC - 38
INTELLIGENCE DUTY OFFICER.

Plane Number	Pilot	Passengers
110	Brunton	Wagner, Kemper
211	Scholfield	Ulrich, Dills
209	Giblin	Lee, Perkins
215	Draughon	Deal, Paul
201	Regan	Misner, Brandt
203	Leake	Boyle, O'Daniel
113	Takacs	Hall, Isom
218	Tulis	Crawford, Levine
125	Bauder	Kearns, Derouen
118	Phillips	Drolsbaugh, Hobbs
108	Morris, R. D.	McGee, Hundriches
109	Berdel	Enterline, Calvert

83

COMSOPAC FILE

SOUTH PACIFIC FORCE
OF THE UNITED STATES PACIFIC FLEET
HEADQUARTERS OF THE COMMANDER

Reg. No. 41588
R.S. No.

SECRET

WAR DIARY

OF

COMMANDER SOUTH PACIFIC AREA AND SOUTH PACIFIC FORCE

From: 1 February 1944 To: 29 February 1944

Original to:
Chief of Naval Operations
(Office of Records and Library)

Copies to:
Chief of Naval Operations
Commander-in-Chief, U.S. Pacific Fleet.

1

SECRET

At 1700 Blue forces on Nissan Island reported that work had been started on a 5000' air strip to the north and east of Tangalan jetty. It was estimated that the strip would be completed on March 8th. A parallel bomber strip 1000' farther to the east was reported feasible.

Approximately 900 natives were sent from Green Island to Guadalcanal by returning LSTs, and 200 others were retained as labor corps.

During the day a patrol from the 129th Infantry reconnoitered the Laruma River Valley to a distance of 5,600 yards north of the Torokina perimeter with negative results.

Reconnaissance troops of the 37th Division moved to House Kiape, northwest of Torokina, to secure the withdrawal of the two Fijian companies proceeding from Sisivei to the west coast of Bougainville.

It was reported that a patrol from the 132nd Infantry killed a Japanese approximately 900 yards northeast of the mouth of the Torokina River.

During the day the 54th Coast Artillery completed its occupation of field artillery positions and fired concentrations in the vicinity of Koiaris and in the area to the north of Mon; and the 3rd Marine Defense Battalion fired on the Tekessi and Reini River areas. During the night Blue artillery fired harassing missions into the areas west of the Torokina River forks, and east of the mouth of the same river.

At 0855, 47 SBDs and 18 TBFs armed with one-tonners, half-tonners, quarter-tonners and rockets hit the shipping in Keravia Bay, scoring 19 direct and 14 effective hits on 12 of 14 ships sighted. Fifteen hits were scored among approximately 20 barges on the south shore and a direct hit was made on the 4.7 inch naval guns southwest of Vulcan crater. A hit on an oiler resulted in a large fire, but a high explosive rocket hit on a tanker appeared to detonate outside the hull and no damage was observed. Photographs showed 1 medium and 3 small AKs, as plotted by the strike, to be missing; an AO (Kiyo Maru class) was observed to be deeper in the water after receiving further hits; two DDs were damaged with the stern of one awash; and a PC was seen spreading an oil slick. Moderate to intense AA of all types damaged 10 SBDs and 5 TBFs. Many small parachutes which were seen over Keravia were believed to have come possibly from AA fire. No interception was reported by the bombers although 15-20 Zekes were observed high above. The bombers also reported that the enemy employed a balloon barrage over three vessels to the north of Vulcan crater but south of the line of mines. Seventy-four Blue fighters which accompanied the strike encountered a minimum of 40 enemy VFs which made energetic overhead runs during the approach and attempted to harass our fighters during the retirement past Cape Gazelle. Seven Zekes and 1 Oscar plus 2 more VFs were shot down while our force lost 2 F4Us, one of which was shot down by AA fire.

During the morning two searching SBDs scored a number of effective hits on the Mibo River bridge in southern Bougainville, and strafed the buildings and a large barge in the same area.

February 17, 1944 Report

CONFIDENTIAL | COMAIRSOLS STRIKE COMMAND TBF INTELLIGENCE | CONFIDENTIAL

Struck 17 February, 1944

<u>Target</u>: Shipping in Keravia Bay.
<u>Mission</u>: Bomb and strafe.
<u>Flight Leader</u>: Commander C. E. Brunton.
<u>Squadrons</u>: VC - 38 (12), VMTB - 134 (6), VMTB - 143 (3), VMTB 233 (3).
<u>Planes:</u> Ordered for mission: 24 TBF's.
Actually dropped bombs; 22 TBF's. (1 plane did not take off, and 1 plane returned with hung bomb).
Loadings: 18 planes 1x2000 # 4-5 second delayed, 6 planes with 8 rockets and 2x500 # 4-5 second delayed fuze.
<u>Times</u>: T.O. 0705
T.O.T. 0855
A.T.A. 1025
<u>Other A/C coordinating</u>: 48 SBD's and 76 VF:
<u>Enemy A/C</u>: None encountered.
<u>Damage to own A/C</u>: <u>Plane # 101</u> - 20MM in starboard wing, M/G bullets in port wing, 50 calibre in fuselage 2 feet aft of turret, numerous shrapnel and bullet holes in fuselage.
<u>Plane # 232</u>: Hydraulic system knocked out by AA (probably shrapnel). 20 MM hole in cockpit next to pilot's seat. Shrapnel holes in port and starboard wings and center section of flaps.
<u>Plane # 313</u>: Bullet holes in starboard wing.
<u>Plane # 114</u>: Hit in engine by M/G.
<u>Personnel Casualties</u>: Commander C. E. Brunton in plane # 101 was hit by AA (probably 20 MM) from 240' DD just prior to releasing his bomb which scored a direct hit on it. He received a compound fracture of the right ulna with severance of the right ulnar nerve and multiple lacerations, lateral aspect of right thigh.
<u>Ammunition Expended</u>: 50 calibre - 2375 rounds.
30 calibre - 2200 rounds.
<u>Attack Tactics</u>: High speed approach at 13000' across Blanche Bay down to push over at 8,000' for attack at masthead level. The formation turned S. and approached Keravia Bay through the depression W. of Vulcan Crater released at mast head level and retired over the water towards Raluana Point. Rally 5 miles E. of Cape Gazelle, route back direct to base. Ships and barges were strafed by both fixed and free guns.

<u>Note</u> - Photos taken after the strike showed one medium and three small AK missing, and it is presumed that they were sunk. The results of the forward firing rockets are the subject of a separate report.

<u>Summary of Results</u>: 5 confirmed direct hits on the 475' Eiyo Maru N. Keravia Bay; photographic coverage showed that it had been damaged again and was seeping oil. Damage to shipping in NW Keravia Bay was reported as follows:

1. 2 confirmed direct hits and 1 u/o on a 300' AK which photograph showed to be missing from harbor subsequently.
2. 1 confirmed direct on 175' PC. Photograph showed damage and oil slick.
3. 1 confirmed direct hit on another 300' AK.
4. 2 near misses and 1 u/o on 265' AK.
5. 3 confirmed direct hits and 2 u/o on 400'AD.

In W Keravia Bay, 1 confirmed direct hit on a 240' DD. The stern was observed to be lifted high out of the water by the explosion of the bomb, and a later photograph showed it lying with its stern underwater.
In SW Keravia Bay, 1 near miss on 175' PC.
In SE KERAVIA Bay, 1 near miss and 1 u/o on 175 AK.

<u>Weather</u>: Route up: Squalls and scattered clouds 2000'-9000'.
O.T.: Clear, Ceiling 13000'.
Route Back: 8/10 clouds with base 1500' scattered squalls.

<u>Observations</u>: 1. Enemy shipping:
A. 1 AK (300') and 2 large SS N. of Vulcan Crater.
B. 20-30 large and small barges near shore S Keravia Bay.
C. One barge underway in Blanche Channel, thoroughly strafed by several planes.
D. Keravia Bay (See Summary of Results <u>supra</u>).

2. 2. Enemy ground activity:
AA, shipping and barrage bellons from 3 vessels N of Vulcan Crater.

3. Condition of targets before and after attack:
Smoke from damaged AK's and explosion at stern of DD after hits.
4. Results of coordinated attack: Not observed.
5. Unusual circumstances: Many small parachutes observed over Keravia Bay, possibly shot up or released for AA purposes.
6. [illegible]i-Aircraft :
[illegible] Vulcan Crater, known heavy (x4.7 naval [illegible]), [illegible]

6. Anti-Aircraft :

A. SW Vulcan Crater, known heavy (2x4.7 naval guns), moderate, inaccurate.

B. S Matupi Island, known heavy and light, moderate, inaccurate.

C. W of Matupi Crater, known auto, moderate, inaccurate.

D. W of Vulcan Crater, known auto (20 MM), intense, inaccurate.

E. W and S shore Koravia Bay, known light auto and M/G, moderate, inaccurate.

F. Cove S of Vulcan Crater, known light auto and M/G, moderate, inaccurate.

G. Lakunai: known light and heavy, intense, accurate.

H. From ships in Koravia Bay, (especially PC and DD), auto and M/G, intense, accurate.

I. Shore SW of Lakunai Airfield, known auto, moderate, inaccurate.

J. S of Raluana Point, M/G, intense, accurate.

7. Miscellaneous: 1 F4U was observed to crash in Simpson Harbor W of Matupi Island.

James N. Truesdale

James N. Truesdale, Lt. USNR.
A. C. I. O. VC - 38
DUTY INTELLIGENCE OFFICER

Plane No.	Pilot	Passengers	Remarks
101	Brunton	Wagner, Kemper	Hit on DD
103	Scholfield	Ulrich, Dills	Hit on AK
104	Giblin	Lee, Perkins	Hit on AK
105	Draughon	Deal, Paul	u/o on AO
108	Regan	Misner, Brandt	Hit on AK
109	Leake	Boyle, O'Daniel	Effective miss on PC
110	Bishop	Schramm, Barnes	Hit on PC
112	McDonald	Blank, Young	Hit on AO
~~[illegible]~~	~~Tahler~~	~~Blue, Brewer~~	~~Hit on AO~~
117	Bohn	Dill, Farber	Hit on AK
118	Leary	Greslie, Dale	Effective miss on AK
119	Gammage	Durham, Morrissey	Hit on AO
202	Glenn	Sticksel, Whiteanank	Effective miss on AK
206	Ranson	Fisher, Mac Adam	Did not strike
207	Philbin	Blazi, Williams	Hit on AK
209	Turner	Lochridge, Farris	Did not strike
213	Richardson	Wilson, Lane	Effective miss on AK
211	Wright	Adams, Brunson	Did not strike
230	Robertson	Dunelle, Ballard	Hit on AK
231	Bell	Bruzuskewicz, Hickman	u/o on AK
232	Lemmons	Sutton, Beecher	u/o on AK
235	May	Hull, McKenna	u/o on AK
236	Ball	Berryman, Kane	u/o on AK
5	Phillips F. G.	Drelsbaugh, Hobbs	Hit on AO
12	Berdel	Enterline, Calvert	u/o on AO
8	Takacs	Hull, Isam	Hit on AO
121	Tulis	Crawford, Levine	Did not attack
4	Bauder	Kearns, DeRouen	Did not attack
126	Morris R. D.	McGee, Hundrichs	Did not attack

Reg. No. OM 687
R.S. No.

STRIKE COMMAND, COMMANDER AIRCRAFT, SOLOMON ISLANDS

c/o Fleet Post Office, San Francisco, California.

3 March 1944

From: The Commanding Officer.
To : The Commander-In-Chief, United States Fleet.

Subject: War Diary, submission of.

Enclosure: (A) Strike Command, Aircraft Solomons War Diary for the period 20 November 1943 to 13 March 1944.

1. Enclosure (A) is forwarded herewith for information and in compliance with present instructions.

F.H. Schwable
F.H. SCHWABLE

Copy to: ComMarCorps (2)
CincPac (1)
ComSoPac (1)
ComAirPac (1)
ComAirSoPac (1)
ComAirSols (1)
ComAirSols Air Intell (1)
ComMarAirWingsPac (1)
ComMarAirWingsSoPac (2)
ComGen, FMAW (1)
ComGen, SMAW (1)
Director of Marine Aviation (2)
Bureau of Aeronautics (Lt.Cdr.H.H. Larsen) (1)
N.A.C.I.O.S., Quonset (Lt.J.B.H. Carter) (1)

COMMANDER-IN-CHIEF
FLAG OFFICE
RECEIVED
1944 APR 14 17 55

7245

85243

Targets for the SBDs were AA positions surrounding the field, on which 20 hits and near misses were scored, plus 25 in the area of various positions and two estimated effective hits on two Bettys parked in revetments. Two bombs dropped among buildings, one in the east revetment area, one was not dropped, and the remainder were misses.

The 10 hits on the concrete runway, plus five on the coral rendered it unserviceable, according to the TBF report. Six other TBF bombs were unobserved and three were not dropped.

Interception by 12-15 Zekes caused some trouble for the SBDs, even though only three or four attacks were pressed home. TBFs reported no interception, but both SBDs and TBFs reported 15-20 phosphorous bombs which while not effective, appeared to be more accurate than on preceding Strikes. No planes were lost to enemy VF.

AA of all types was intense and accurate from most positions against the SBD; moderate and accurate against the TBFs, several planes being damaged, but none shot down. The TBFs noted a definite slackening of fire during the SBD attack. The fire reopened, however, as the dive bombers retired. TBFs strafed gun positions along the ridge on the retirement course, fire from which was intense. One pilot, Lt. Harold R. Walker, was injured and his gunner, Sgt. Greydon H. Tabor, was killed by AA fire. The plane, an SBD, was badly damaged.

Enemy planes were sighted taking off from Tobera, Rapopo, Lakunai and fires in both the revetment areas and buildings were noted as the Strike retired. One Zeke which attacked an SBD was claimed as a smoker by the SBD gunner and two Bettys were burning off the southeast end of the runway. Six to twelve Zekes were seen in the west revetments and 15 to 20 Bettys in the east revetments, plus others in the trees southeast of the runway.

SEARCHES: A routine morning search by four SBDs dropped 4x1000# and 5x100# bombs, plus two 100# duds, on the various ground targets on Bougainville.

One SBD also acted as a spotter, dropping no bombs.

February 14 - STRIKES - At 1140 59 SBDs (1x1000), 10 TBFs (8x100) (4x250) attacked Tobera. TO 0955, TA 1310. All planes returned, three with minor damage. Interception by Zekes was slight, none pressed home. AA was generally moderate and inaccurate. TBFs scored two estimated effective hits and eight unobserved hits in south revetment area. 3x250 and 6x100 were hung up and jettisoned. SBDs dropped 56 bombs in area and destroyed 1 Betty and probably destroyed or damaged three more Bettys and 2 Zekes. Two fires, SW end of runway were visible for 50 miles. Weather enroute was excellent. Vunakanau, primary target was closed in, and Tobera nearly so.

Special Mining Operation - In early morning 25 TBFs in groups of 9, 7 and 9 loaded with 1xMk 12-1 mines, mined Simpson Harbor between Wesleyan Mission and Sulphur Creek. All mines dropped except for one hung up and 2 brought back. Searchlights and intense accurate AA were well co-ordinated. Six planes failed to return, of these four probably shot down, 2 in harbor and 2 on land side. Three were flamers. All crews missing.

SEARCHES: Three searches by TBFs for missing pilots were negative.

Seven SBDs on routine searches dropped 7x1000 and 14x100 on various targets on Bougainville.

WEATHER - The weather was generally good in the area with flying conditions until late afternoon above average.

February 15 - STRIKES - No Strikes went out this date.

Special Missions: Green Island landing. 16 TBFs, 23 SBDs and 2 PV1s flew 7 missions during the day acting on ground support, spotters for artillery and taking photos. No enemy interception except for 2 Vals chased by SBDs and 10-15 Vals attacking the shipping. No bombs were dropped. All planes returned without damage to our planes or personnel. 50 photos taken; no enemy shipping sighted.

SEARCHES: 4 SBDs loaded with 1x1000 and 2x100 both with 1/5 sec. delay fusing bombed targets on Bougainville. 2x100 hung up.

February 16 - STRIKES - No Strikes went out this date.

Special Missions - None.

Searches - Generally negative except as follows: 2 SBDs dropped 2x1000 and 3x100 with probable damage to bridge over Mibo River, Bougainville. Strafed barge and buildings on Mibo and dropped 1x100 miss on Aitara Mission.

9

February 17 - STRIKES - (1) 47 SBDs (1x1000 1/10 sec.) VMSB 244, VB 98 led by Major Reed, VMSB 244 and 18 TBFs (1x2000 4/5 sec.) and 5 TBFs (2x500 4/5 sec. x 8 rockets) led by Commander Brunton struck shipping in Keravia Bay.

All planes returned. 10 SBDs and 5 TBFs were damaged by AA. Three crew members were injured, none fatally. There was no interception, but 15-20 Zeros were seen.

AA was generally moderate to intense and inaccurate.

19 direct, 15 damaging hits on 12 ships. 15 hits among 15-20 barges, and one direct and one damaging hit on 4.7 SW of Vulcan Crater were scored.

Four rocket planes fired one hitting a ship's hull. Results were not observed.

Weather - Squally, .5 cumulus 2000-9000 feet, over target, clear -- 13,000 ceiling. Return route: squalls, .8 cumulus, bases 500 feet.

(2) 36 SBDs and 18 TBFs due to inclement weather failed to reach Radar Station on Cape St. George. All returned with bomb loads without injury or damage.

SEARCHES - 2 SBDs dropped 2x1000 4/5 sec. and 5x100 inst. and destroyed bridge on Lulua River. Two SBDs sighted possible DD, 2 barges and one AK, Moisuru Bay.

2 PV-1's dropped emergency rations, 62 dye markers to occupant in life raft at 04°-25 S, 152-30 E.

February 18 - STRIKES - No Strikes went out today.

Special Missions - 9 SBDs of VB 98 led by Lt. Lord loaded with 1x1000 1/10 sec. delay attacked Radar and Auto AA at Cape St. George. All planes and personnel returned without damage or injury. AA meagre, light and inaccurate.

Six hits were scored in close area of Radar screen and Auto AA with estimated destruction or serious damage to screen and some gun positions. Two bombs hung up - one hit water.

Routine Searches were negative except as follows -- 4 TBFs and 2 SBDs acted as spotter for artillery. Four at Green Island; two at Bougainville.

2 PV-1s covered Kavieng DD Mission, observed convoy 02-10S, 151-15 E under attack by Vals.

2 SBDs scored direct hits on bridges over Luluai to Araiona Rivers with 2x1000, 4x200. 2 SBDs strafed, one Jap between Mupeta and Jaba Rivers. Weather was generally good all day.

February 19 - At 1030 48 SBDs (1x1000 1/10 sec.delay) of VC-38, VMSB 241 and VB 98, and 17 TBFs (1x2000 4-5 sec.delay) and 6 TBFs of VMTB 143, (2x500 plus rockets) struck Lakunai airdrome, a secondary target Simpson Hbr. being closed in. All planes and personnel returned. One TBF had minor damage and 2 SBDs had holes in tail assemblies.

A small number of enemy ships were sighted in the harbor including two gunboats, an SS which submerged, 20-30 barges and small craft, 2 medium AK and a number of 4 motored flying boats and float planes.

5-20 Zeros were seen, but only 1 pressed home an attack and was shot down by TBF.

The AA generally was moderate and inaccurate showing a definite tapering off from previous missions.

SBD dropped 46 bombs and TBF dropped 24 bombs in area. Of 7 bombs not dropped 4 were jettisoned. The target in general was well covered with bombs and the runway, both concrete and mat, was rendered unserviceable. TBF scored 2 estimated and 5 confirmed direct hits, three estimated effective hits, one wild miss and 7 unobserved on runway. SBD scored 2 estimated direct hits, 14 estimated effective hits, 11 hits in area, 8 wild misses, 5 unobserved on various targets. Rockets scored estimated hits on 4.7.

Weather - Clouds over target .6, 3500-8000 feet; scattered cumulus .3, 3000-12,000 feet, on the way up. On the way back, same with thunder heads 50 miles East of New Ireland.

Searches - Routine searches were negative except as follows:

2 SBDs dropped (2x1000 x 4x100) on two bridges destroying NR-7 on ComAirSols chart.

6 TBFs (2x500 plus rockets) expended all on 8 hulks in Hat-

SECRET

30

CONFIDENTIAL — COMAIRSOLS STRIKE COMMAND TBF INTELLIGENCE — CONFIDENTIAL

Struck 20 February, 1944

Target: Bridges and AA installations, Monoitu Mission area. EXHIBIT T.
Mission: Bomb and strafe.
Flight Leaders: Lt. (jg) R. A. Marshall and Lt. Takacs.
Squadrons: VC - 38 (12), VMTB - 143 (6), VMTB - 233 (8).
Planes: Ordered for mission - 26 TBF's.
Actually dropped bombs - 23 TBF's.
Loadings - 12x2000 # 4-5 seconds delay.
14x2000 # 1/10 seconds delay.
Times: First flight - T.O. - 1040
T.O.T. - 1140
A.T.A. - 1215
Second flight - T.O. - 1110
T.O.T. - 1200
A.T.A. - 1235
Other A/C Coordinating: 39 SBD's.
Enemy A/C: None.
Damage to own A/C: Plane # 103 loaded with 1x2000 # 1/10 seconds delay, was seen to make steep dive from 3000' and to pull out (after release) at approximately 500 ft. Just after the plane levelled off with approximately speed of 200 k one half of the starboard wing came off, probably as a result of the bomb blast, and the plane flipped over on its back and crashed in the jungle in the Monoitu Mission area.
Personnel casualties: Lt. (jg) Herbert T. Leake, USNR, S Barcala ARM3/c and W. E. Dunton AOM1/c are missing in action as result of crash of plane # 103. J.H. Deal ARM3/c in plane # 126 received a cut on his arm as a result of the tail of the plane being shaken up by its own bomb blast.
Ammunition expended: 30 calibre - 3480 rounds
50 calibre - 1416 rounds
Attack Tactics: Due to cloud cover no concerted attack could be made and planes dived individually for the most part. High speed approach generally from the NW at 10000' pushover at 3000' with releases varying from 700' to 2000', pull out in general to SE.
Summary of results: Note: The assigned targets in the Monoitu Mission area could not be located by the majority of the pilots because of cloud cover and drops were made on bivouac areas of opportunity, as follows: 5 reported direct, 1 confirmed direct, 8 unobserved, 1 dud, and 1 not dropped. On the bridge over the Hongorai River, 1 confirmed direct was scored, and on the bridge over the Puriata River there was 1 confirmed direct with 5 misses in the area. Bivouac areas were thoroughly strafed by both fixed and free guns.
Weather: Monoitu Mission: 7/10 - 9/10 from 1000'-6000'.
Puriata River: 5/10 based at 2500'
Observations: 1. Enemy shipping: None.
2. Enemy ground activity: AA as described below.
3. Condition of targets before and after attack: Not observed, (two bridges probably knocked out).
4. Results of coordinated attack: Not observed.
5. Unusual circumstances: 4 large splashes observed in water 2 miles off mouth of Hongorai River.
6. Anti-Aircraft: Auto AA (with possibly some heavy) meagre inaccurate, bursts from 9000' - 6000' through clouds, positions not pinpointed. Moderate M/G fire from undetermined positions.
From target # 15 known auto AA, meagre, inaccurate.

James N. Truesdale
James N. Truesdale, Lt. USNR.
A. C. I. O. VC - 38
INTELLIGENCE DUTY OFFICER.

29

Plane No.	Pilot	Passengers	
102	Marshall	Lane, Tye	
210	McDonald	Bland, Young	
103	Leake	Dunton, Barcala	(did not return)
106	Tahler	Buie, Brewer	
105	Leary	Greslie, Dale	
107	Gammage	Durham, Morrissey	
113	Bishop	Schramm, Barnes	
118	Bohn	Dill, Farber	
111	Giblin	Lee, Perkins	(did not attack)
126	Draughon	Deal, Paul	
116	Hogan	Misner, Brandt	
119	Scholfield	Ulrich, Dills	(did not attack)
121	Takacs	Hall, Ison	
117	Tulis	Crawford, Levine	
10	Bruder	Kearns, DeRouen	
11	Phillips	Drolsbaugh, Hobbs	
5	Morris	McGee, Hendrichs	
216	Bordel	Enterline, Calvert	
8	Glenn	Sticksel, Whiteannack	
2	Stark	Winn, Johnson	
12	Philbin	Blazi, Williams	(did not attack)
202	Turner	Lochridge, Ferris	
205	Richardson	Wilson, Lane	
207	Wirht	Adams, Brunson	
Spares			
125	Radcliffe	Page, Mack	
1	Dowd	Brownfield, Butehorn	

CO[illegible]FIDE[illegible]TIAL

COMAIRSOLS
STRI[illegible] CO[illegible][illegible]D
T[illegible]F I[illegible]TELLIGE[illegible]

C[illegible]FIDE[illegible]TIAL

EXHIBIT V.

Struck 2[illegible] February, 1944

Target: [illegible]uraio Mission
[illegible]ission: Gr[illegible]und troop support - Bomb and strafe area ooutlined with smoke at request.
F[illegible] Leader: Lt. (jg) B[illegible]uce [illegible] Bishop [illegible]
[illegible]: (6) planes VC - 38, (6) planes V[illegible] - 143.
P[illegible]: Ordered for mission - 1[illegible] TB[illegible]'s.
Actually dropped bombs - 1[illegible] T[illegible]'s.
[illegible]: Loadings - 1[illegible]x12x100 [illegible] instantaneous.
Times: T.O. 1258
O.T. 1325
Landed 1414
Other A/C Coordinating: None.
P[illegible]rsonnel casualties: [illegible]one.
A[illegible]tion e[illegible]pended: 30 calibre - 560
50 calibre - [illegible]50
Attack Tactics: Approach[illegible] target from south at 60[illegible]' making left hand turns [illegible] gradually let down at [illegible]00 knots, crossing the target and dropping bombs from an eastern to western direction from [illegible]00' to 1000'. Rendezvous 2 miles north of target close to shore and made a second approach similar/first strafing area from an altitude of 50 feet.
Su[illegible]mary of results: Smoke bombs were fired by the artillery outlining a target roughly 1000 yads in depth extending from the beach to the [illegible]sinamutu River on the east and 250 yds in width in a north south direction. All planes got hits in this marked area and out of 144 bombs dropped, 8 were water misses close to the beach and one was hung and jettisoned. Reports from ground troops indicates, quote, "Target covered, well done". On ground orders the secondary strafing was made.
[illegible]eather: Good seaward with scattered clouds about [illegible]/10. Over land area scattered [illegible]/10. East of target closed.
Observations: No observations made except the presence of one blue Corvette and several barges [illegible] miles north of mouth of [illegible]uraio Riv[illegible]r and 1 mile off shore.

[signature]
Lewis P. [illegible]ilbourne, Lt. US[illegible]R.
A. C. I. O. [illegible] 233
I[illegible]TELLIGENCE [illegible] OFFICER.

Plane No.	Pilot	Passengers
105	Bishop	Schramm, Barnes
106	Behn	Dill, Farber
107	Tahler	Buis, Brewer
119	Draughon	Deal, Paul
3	Regan	[illegible]isner, Brandt
4	Scholfield	Ulrich, Dills
207	Morris	Duchesneau, [illegible]hitacre
208	Ferguson	Ayersman, Johnson
209	Venable	Rice, Caughlin
210	Hollis	Techenbrook, Haislip
5	Lackey	Dralle, Lauer
6	Wood	Howard, Merritt

CONFIDENTIAL — COMAIRSOLS STRIKE COMMAND TBF INTELLIGENCE — CONFIDENTIAL

Struck 26 February, 1944

Target: Vunapope (tertiary).
Mission: Bomb and strafe.
Flight Leader: Major Robertson.
Squadrons: VMTB - 134 (8), VC - 38 (9), VMTB - 233 (5).
Planes: Ordered for mission - 24 TBF's.
Actually dropped bombs - 22 TBF's.
Loadings - 1x2000 # 4-5 seconds delay each plane.
Times: T.O. - 0840
T.O.T. - 1030
A.T.A. - 1200
Other A/C Coordinating: 48 SBD's, 56 VF.
Enemy A/C: None.
Damage to own A/C: None.
Personnel casualties: None.
Ammunition Expended: 50 calibre - 6705 rounds.
30 calibre - 4585 rounds.

Attack Tactics: Due to cloud cover over Lakunai Airfield and Keravia Bay, Vunapope supply area, the tertiary target, was struck. High speed approach at 12,500' generally from SW, push over at 7000', release at 2000', pull out at 1500' towards NE. Rally 5 miles E of Cape Gazelle.

Summary of Results: Vunapope Supply Area - 3 confirmed direct hits, 1 reported and 3 confirmed damaging hits, and 11 unobserved.
Rapopo Area - 1 reported damaging hit and 1 unobserved.
Two bombs hung and were jettisoned.
The majority of the hits were in a concentrated area; hence it was impossible to ascertain individual results. The area was thoroughly strafed by fixed and free guns.

Weather: Enroute - 5/10 cumulus layers 2000-12000'.
O. T. - 8/10 cumulus 2000'-12000'.
Return - Same as enroute.
(Lakunai Airfield and Keravia Bay were completely closed in.)

Observations:
1. Enemy shipping.
None.
2. Enemy ground activity.
None, other than AA.
3. Condition of target before and after attack.
Explosions and smoke from TBF bombs observed.
4. Results of coordinated attack.
Several SBD hits observed in target area.
5. Unusual circumstances.
SBD made successful water landing 5 miles E of Cape Gazelle. Pilot and gunner were observed to get in raft and wave. They were later picked up by Dumbo.
6. Anti - Aircraft.
A. Over town and E and W of town, moderate heavy AA from 6000' to 9000', inaccurate. Position not pin-pointed.
B. From mound SE of Rapopo, moderate light (20 MM), inaccurate.
C. From Rapopo, Tobera, and Vunakanau through clouds at altitude of 4000' to 6000' meagre heavy, inaccurate.
D. Rapopo, both sides of R/W, meagre to moderate auto AA, inaccurate.
E. One 20 MM firing from Cape Gazelle, meagre, inaccurate.

James N. Truesdale, Lt. USNR.
A. C. I. O. VC - 38
INTELLIGENCE DUTY OFFICER.

19

Plane No.	Pilot	Passengers	
118	Robertson	Dumelle, Ballard	
104	Boll	Bruzuskewicz, Hickman	
121	Lemmons	Sutton, Beecher	
122	Anderson P. E.	Benjock, Zdrojowy	
124	May	Hull, McKenna	
125	Ball	Berryman, Kane	
213	Bishop	Schramm, Barnes	
7	Behn	Dill, Farber	(did not attack)
215	Tahler	Buis, Brewers	
209	Draughon	Deal, Paul	
204	Regan	Misner, Brandt	
217	Scholfield	Ulrich, Dills	
214	Marshall	Lane, Tye	
210	McDonald	Blank, Young	
211	Cole	Holmes, Mullen	
219	Hunt	Cleary, Burrow	
1	Leary	Greslie, Dale	
4	Gammage	Durham, Morrisey	
101	Voyles	Fitzgerald, Gilbert	
8	Radcliffe	Page, Mack	
10	Gonnerman	Benjavcic, Kazprazak	
11	Volbrecht	McCarty, Olevich	
13	Jaqua	Cannon, Cox	
107	Streiby	Richard, Gooding	(did not attack)
Spares			
105	Morris	Duchesneau	(did not attack)
106	Hollis W. L.	Techenbrock, Haislip	(did not attack)
212	Venable	Rice, Caughlin	(did not attack)
108	McLaughlin	Bandy, Smith	(did not attack)
108	Lackey	Dralle, Lauer	(did not attack)
111	Wood	Howard, Merritt	(did not attack)

20

TBF INTELLIGENCE

Struck 29 February, 1944

Targets: Jap concentrations in the following areas:
1. Mouth of Reini (Koiari) River.
2. Mouth of Jaba River.
3. Mawaraka.
4. Mouth of Mamaregu River.

Mission: Bomb and strafe.

Flight Leaders: Flight # 1 - Major Robertson.
Flight # 2 - Lt. (jg) Marshall.
Flight # 3 - Lt. (jg) Bishop.
Flight # 4 - Lt. Takacs.
Flight # 5 - Major Robertson.

Squadrons: VMTB - 134, (12), VC - 38, (11), VMTB - 143, (7), VMTB - 233, (6).

Planes: 1. Ordered for Reini River missions (2 flights of 9 planes) - 18 TBF's.
Actually dropped bombs - - - - - - - - - - - - - - - - - - - 18 TBF's.
Loadings - 4x250 # and 8x100 # alternato and instantaneous and 1/10, each plane.
2. Ordered for Mawaraka mission - 9 TBF's.
Actually dropped bombs - - - - 9 TBF's.
Loadings - 1x2000 # 1/10, each plane.
3. Ordered for Jaba River mission - 9 TBF's.
Actually dropped bombs - - - - - 9 TBF's.
Loadings - 1x2000 # 1/10, each plane.
4. Ordered for Mamaregu River mission - 9 TBF's.
Actually dropped bombs - - - - - - - 9 TBF's.
Loadings - 1x2000 # 1/10, each plane.

Times: 1. Reini River mission.

First Flight	Second Flight
T.O. - 1045	T.O. - 1330
T.O.T.- 1115	T.O.T.- 1355
A.T.A.- 1145	A.T.A.- 1415

2. Mawaraka mission.
T.O. - 1105
T.O.T.- 1125
A.T.A.- 1155

3. Jaba River mission.
T.O. - 1135
T.O.T.- 1200
A.T.A.- 1225

4. Mamaregu River mission.
T.O. - 1208
T.O.T.- 1245
A.T.A.- 1315

Other A/C Coordinating: 90 SBD's (6 flights of 15 each).
Enemy A/C: None.
Damage to own A/C: None.
Personnel casualties: None.
Ammunition Expended: 50 calibre - 12,599 rounds.
30 calibre - 12,400 rounds.

Attack Tactics: 1. Reini River area.
First flight approached target from NW in shallow dive from from 7000', released at 1500'-2000', and pulled out to SE. A second strafing run was made. Second flight approached target from W at 3000', released at 1200'-1500', and pulled out to E. Second strafing run was made.
2. Mawaraka area.
The flight approached from NE at 4000', released at 2000', and reteired to SW. A second run was made over the target area for strafing.
3. Jaba River area.
The flight approached from NE at 4000', released at 1500'-2000', and pulled out to SW. A second strafing run was made.
4. Mamaregu River area.
The flight approached from SW at 5000', released at 2000'-2500', and pulled out to NE. A second strafing run was made over the target area and adjacent beach.

Summary of Results: 1. Reini River area.
First flight - All of the bombs dropped hit in the assigned target area. Of 36x250 # bombs carried, 3 hung and were returned to base, and of 72x100 # carried, 1 hung and was returned to base.
Second flight - The target area was well covered by hits by hits. Of 36x250 # bombs carried, 3 hung and were jettisoned; and of 72x100 # bombs 5 hung (4 were jettisoned and 1 was returned to base).
2. Mawaraka area.
9x2000 # bombs were dropped in the assigned target area

3. Jaba River area.
The assigned target area was well covered by 9x2000 # bombs.

4. Mamaregu River area.
Of 9x2000' bombs dropped, 8 hit in the triangular target area, and 1 was in the water 30 yards off shore.

All target areas were thoroughly strafed by fixed and free guns in second runs.

Weather: 1. Reini River area.
First flight - clear over target.
Second flight - ceiling 3000' over target, a front moving in from NE.

2. Mawaraka area. - clear over target.

3. Jaba River area. - clear over target.

4. Mamaregu River. - good over target with light haze at 3000'.

Observations: 1. Enemy shipping.
Known damaged barges (2) south of Matupena Point.

2. Enemy ground activity.
1 burst M/G fire from beach near Mawaraka.

3. Condition of targets after attack.
Smoke from bomb explosions in all target areas.

4. Results of coordinated attacks.
Attacks were executed efficiently; many SBD hits observed in assigned areas.

5. Unusual circumstances.
Two parachutes (probably employed for dropping supplies) were observed in trees south of Mawarada and one east of Mawaraka. Dual tire truck tracks were observed on beach east of mouth of Reini River.

6. Anti-Aircraft.
One M/G, meagre, inaccurate, on beach near Mawaraka.

7. Miscellaneous.
The visibility in the Reini River target area was reported as greatly improved by the concentration of bomb hits. After the attacks the ground could be seen in many places which had been previously obscured by trees and foliage.

James N. Truesdale, Lt. USNR.
A. C. I. O. VC - 38
INTELLIGENCE DUTY OFFICER.

Plane No.	Pilot	Passengers
Flight # 1.		
110	Robertson	Dumelle-Ballard
112	Boll	Bruzuskowicz-Hickman
116	Lemmons	Sutton-Beecher
117	Anderson	Benjock-Zdrojowy
120	May	Hull-McKenna
123	Cole	Holmes-Mullens
205	Ball	Berryman-Kane
213	Kilgore	Dautel-Barzokas
4	Hunt	Cleary-Burow
Flight # 2.		
101	Marshall	Lane-Tye
102	McDonald	Blank-Young
103	Tahler	Buis-Brewer
104	Gammage	Durham-Morrisey
105	Leary	Greslie-Dale
106	Ransom	Fisher-Macadam
107	Patterson	Schmitt-Michaels
102	Cromwell	Batt-Wood
111	Warner	Campbell-Dunlap
Flight # 3.		
113	Bishop	Schramm-Barnes
115	Behn	Farber-Dill
121	Giblin	Lee-Perkins
122	Draughon	Deal-Paul
124	Regan	Misner-Brandt
125	Scholfield	Ulrich-Dills, P. J.
1	Nagoda	Hoelzel-Danaldson
2	Loyd	Selvey-Delcamp
3	Ferguson	Ayersman-Johnson
Flight # 4.		
203	Takacs	Hall-Ison
204	Radcliffe	Page-Mack
207	Gonnerman	Kasprzak-Benjavcic
209	Volbrecht	McCarty-Olevich
210	Jaqua	Cannan-Cox
215	Strieby	Rickard-Gooding
212	Paizis	Barrett-Satterlee
211	Belcher	McDonough-Cahoon
217	Bell	Burris-Drake
Flight # 5.		
110	Robertson	Dumelle-Ballard
112	Boll	Hickman-Bruzuskowicz
116	Lemmons	Sutton-Beecher
117	Anderson	Benjock-Zdrojowy
120	May	Hull-McKenna
123	Cole	Holmes-Mullen
205	Ball	Berryman-Kane
5	Kilgore	Dautel-Bartzokas
4	Hunt	Cleary-Burow

CONFIDENTIAL  COMAIRSOLS
STRIKE COMMAND
TBF INTELLIGENCE  CONFIDENTIAL

Struck 3 March, 1944

Target: Lakunai gun positions.
Mission: Bomb and strafe.
Flight Leader: Major Robertson.
Squadrons: VMTB 134 (12), VC 38 (6), VMTB 232 (6).
Planes: Ordered for mission - 24 TBF's.
Actually dropped bombs = 24 TBF's.
Loadings - 1x2000 w/ 1/10 second delay, each plane.
Times: T.O. - 0825
T.O.T. - 1025
A.T.A. - 1140
Other A/C coordinating: 48 SBD's, 36VF's.
Enemy A/C: None.
Damage to own A/C: None.
Personnel casualties: None.
Ammunition expended: 50 calibre - 215 rounds.
30 calibre - 125 rounds.
AttackTactics: Due to the fact that the target was closed in, the flight approached the area at 11000' from SE to NW on a line connecting Lakunai and Rabaul and racked off bombs through the overcast at 11000'.
Summary of Results: The results were unobserved, but it is felt that the drops were made in the vicinity of the target area. Of 24 bombs carried, 1 hung and was jettisoned over a plantation on New Ireland.
Weather: Enroute - 3/10 scattered clouds at 1500'-10000'.
O.T. - Completely overcast from Duke of York to the SW covering Matupi Island, Simpson Harbor, and the west shore of Simpson Harbor, 2500'-10000'.
Return - Same as enroute.
Observations:
1. Enemy shipping.
One small AK or hulls at pier E of Lesson Point.
2. Enemy activity.
None.
3. Condition of target before and after attack.
Unobserved.
4. Results of coordinated attack.
Unobserved.
5. Anti-Aircraft.
None encountered.
6. Miscellaneous.
The air strip on the Duke of York Islands was reported to show evidence of possible increased activity (nearing completion).

James N. Truesdale, Lt. USNR.
A. C. I. O. VC - 38
INTELLIGENCE DUTY OFFICER.

- -

Plane No.	Pilot	Passengers
101	Robertson	Dumello-Ballard
102	Boll	Bruzuskowicz-Hicman
105	Lemmons	Sutton-Beecher
106	Anderson	Benjock-Zdrojewy
107	May	Hull-McKenna
108	Ball	Berryman-Kane
124	Cole	Homes-Mullen
206	Kilgore	Deutel-Bartzokas
219	Hunt	Cleary-Burow
10	Patterson	Schmitt-Michaels
11	Cromwell	Batt-Wood
12	Warner	Campbell-Dunlap
109	Bishop	Schramm-Barnes
110	McDonell	Blank-Young
103	Marshall	Lane-Tye
113	Draughon	Deal-Paul
114	Regan	Misner-Brandt
13	Scholfield	Ulrich-Dills
115	White	Crumpton-Moon
122	Carter	McEnneny-Gruber
123	Burris	Lossie-Wagner
126	Laughlin	Akroyd-Spyghala
125	Lynch	Brown-Gerber
210	Humphrey	Martin-Norby

12

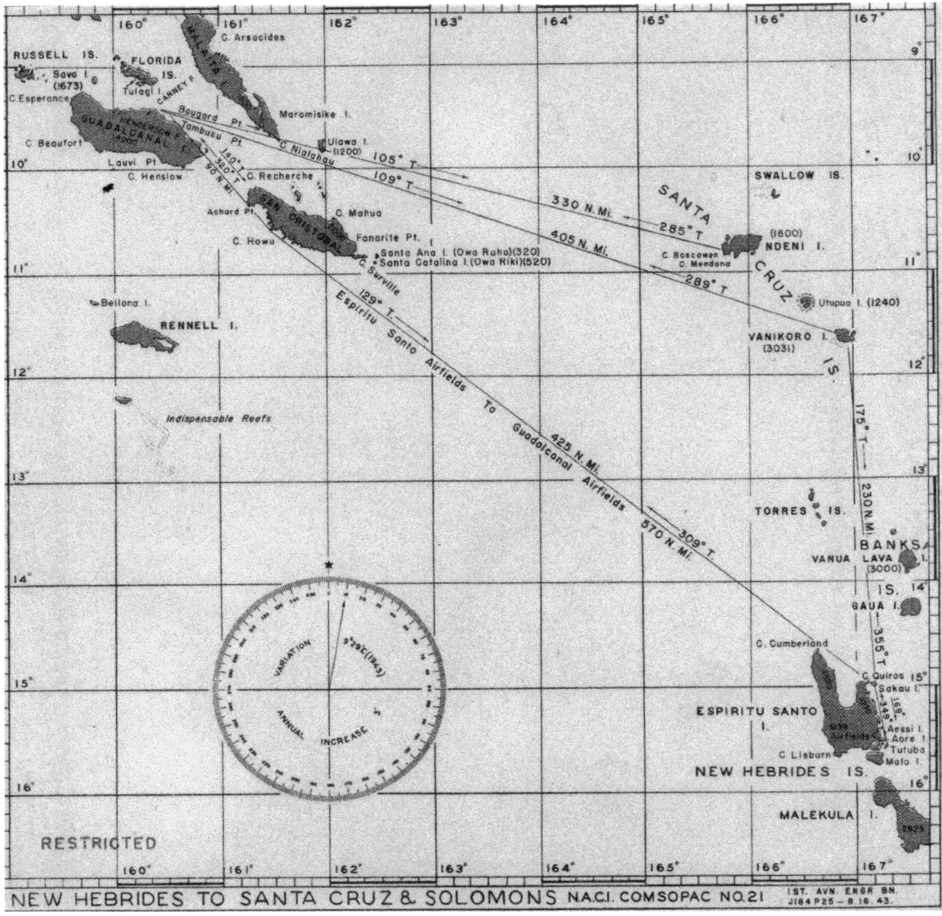

COMSOPAC Map of Carney Field (Guadalcanal) to Espiritu Santo Airfield (Source: Leary Family Collection)

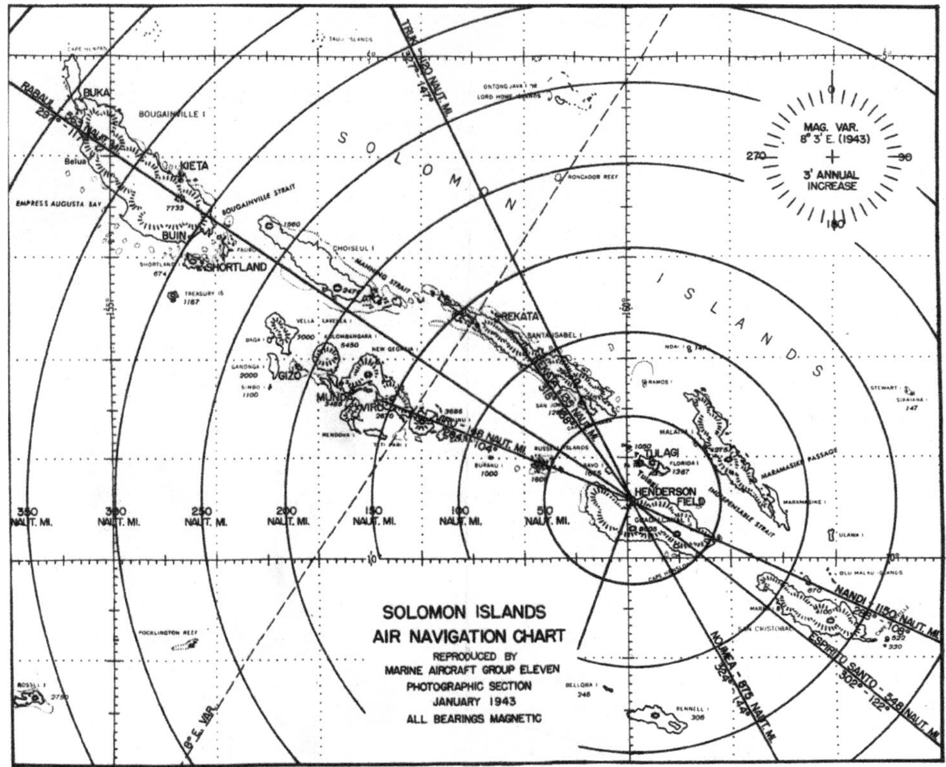

Henderson Field Air Navigation Chart of VC 38 Lt. John Leary (Source: Leary Family Collection)

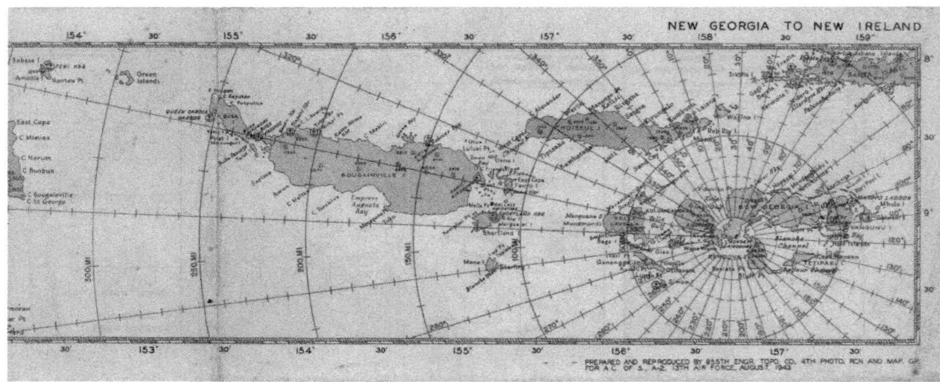

VC 38 Lt. John Leary's Pilot Reference Strip of Munda (New Georgia) to New Ireland (Source: Leary Family Collection)

Appendix F

Tribute to VC38

COMSOPAC Maps of VC 38 Lt.(jg) John Leary (Source: Leary Family Collection)

Composite Squadron 38 was commissioned June 12, 1943 under the command of Lieutenant Commander Charles E. Brunton. VC 38 trained with the Grumman TBF Avenger, a torpedo bomber plane, while at NAAS Otay Mesa Airfield (currently Brown Field airport) and NAS El Centro, California.

The squadron's flight training in the TBF-1 planes included torpedo bombing, gunnery, night torpedo tactics, catapult take-offs from carrier decks, carrier landings, anti-sub bombing, and night oxygen flying. The squadron spent over a month training at NAS El Centro practicing night illumination, mine laying, carrier rendezvous, and glide bombing maneuvers, all while flying at night.

VC 38 squadron shipped out from San Diego, California, on August 1, 1943, aboard the escort carrier, USS Long Island (CVE-1), for Espiritu Santo Island, New Hebrides (present day Vanuatu). VC 40 squadron (Red's Raiders) was also aboard ship.

USS Long Island (CVE-1) Source: National Archives photo no. 19-LCM-271 – February 14 1945

The ship crossed the equator on August 14, 1943 and arrived at Espiritu Santo on August 25, 1943. VC 38's torpedo bombing missions initially operated from Bomber #1 airfield, Espiritu Santo (code named "Buttons"). Training missions were conducted in early September 1943 from Espiritu Santo. VC 38 departed Buttons on September 13 to base operations from Hnderson Field (Code named "Cactus"). One of the first missions of VC 38 against the Japanese was on September 15, 1943, and was a bombing mission over Ballale airfield located a few miles southeast from the Island of Bougainville in the Solomon Islands. That mission is describe below:

INTELLIGENCE REPORT[1] - SEPTEMBER 15, 1943

S E C R E T TBF OPERATIONS - GUADALCANAL

DECLASSIFIED
Authority E.O. 13526
By: NDC NARA Date: Dec 31, 2012

Mission: Strike Ballale

Planes: 24 TBF' s (6- VC38, 6-VC40, 12-VMTB233)
30 SBD' s
72 VF

AA: Medium and heavy --- moderate to slight

SUMMARY

The 24 TBFs had joined the 30 SBD' s at the Russells after taking off from Henderson Field at 0912. At 1030 they made the rendezvous with the 72 fighters over Munda, and proceeded to the target over Vella Gulf, to the southwest tip of Faure before making the high-speed NS approach over Ballale, pushing over at 10,000 releasing at 2000 and pulling out at 1500 feet.

Of the 24 TBF' s dropped 24 x 2000 lb. bombs on various targets on Ballale. Nine of the one-tenth second delay bombs were strung down the runway. One two thousand pounder hit squarely in a revetment area SE of the runway, and one 2000 lb. bomb was dropped in a group of trucks at the SW end of the runway. The other bombs were dropped in target areas which consisted of gun positions and supply dumps. A large fire was started at the SW end of the runway, and a fire was seen on the E side of the island.

The TBF' s reported that the fighter cover[2] was excellent. Although several fighters jumped them, none of them made passes. A fire was seen on the N end of the runway at Kahili, and an AK about 200 feet long was seen in Tonolei Harbor. Three planes were seen to go into the water. It is certain that two of them were Zeros. Twenty-two TBFs landed at 1320 at Henderson Field. Two landed at Munda because one plane had a leak in his oil line. These two finally pancaked on

[1] Available declassified Air Command Solomons Intelligence Reports & War Diary of VC-24, VC-38, VC-40, VMTB-134, VMTB-143, VMTB-232, VMTB-233, VMTB-236, VMSB-235, VMSB-243, and VMF-213 are included in Appendix E. These were declassified on December 31, 2012.

[2] Air Group 38 flew with a team of Hellcat F6F fighters (VF-38 & VF-33) & F4U-1A Corsair fighters (VMF-213), SBDs (VB-38) and TBFs (VC-38).

Henderson at 1728. **W.M. Burns, 1st Lt. USMCR, Intelligence Officer, VMTB-233**

PLANE BU.NO.	PILOT	RADIOMAN	TURRET	TAKE OFF	LAND
			VC - 38		
24244	Larson	Wagner	Wright	0906	1329
47502	Regan	Misner	Brandt	0906	1325
23959	Leary	Greslie	Dale	0907	1322
47553	Wilson	Haller	Wilson	0907	1323
24182	Bishop	Schramm	Barnes	0908	1323
47504	Behn	Dill	Buis	0909	1324
			VMTB - 233		
06474	Bright	Dearing	Horne	0858	1316
23873	Dowd	Brownfield	Rosenthal	0859	1317
06432	Cornelius	McCarthy	Slipkas	0859	1318
23871	Croker	Schroeder	Casper	0859	1317
06406	DeLancey	Kozakewich	Miller	0900	1318
06429	Fuller	Rosellie	Embry	0900	1319
06329	Morris	McGee	Hundrichs	0901	1320
06115	Takaos	Hall, E.J.	Ison, Rourke	0901	1725
06420	Harris	Henderick	McElhoos	0901	1728
06472	Bartholf	Benschneider	Shoulof	0902	1320
47501	Bauder	Fyock	DeRouen	0902	1320
			VC - 40		
24283	Jackson	Adams	Powell	0903	1324
23970	Collura	Ruiard	Pittman	0903	1327
47599	DeVeer	Schneider	Meglemre	0904	1327
06145	Frees	Tufenkjian	Wubbens	0904	1326
23910	Bennett	Whitworth	Brantingham	0905	1325
23987	Tracey	Joachim	Temple	0905	1326

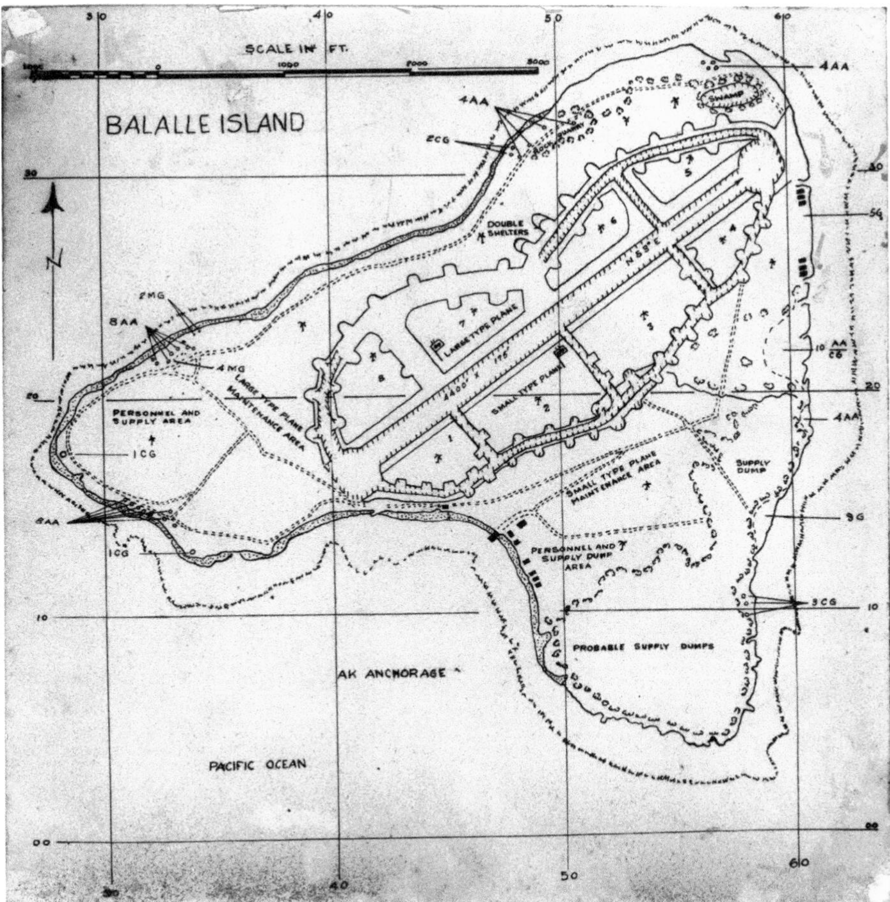

VC 38 Map of Ballale[3] Airfield (Source: Lt.(jg) John Leary's Map – Leary Family Collection)

[3] Unknown to US Forces at the time of this bombing, about 480 British prisoners of war captured in Singapore were brought to Ballale Island to build the airstrip. As they were not allowed to take cover, some were killed in air raids, those injured were left to die or were executed. When the construction of the airstrip ceased, all those remaining were executed and dumped into a mass grave. From this grave, 436 bodies were recovered after the war. As with all prisoners, the Japanese had removed all identification, so their names will never be known.

From September 18, 1943 to October 19, 1943 training operations were conducted from Espiritu Santo (Buttons) and on board the USS Breton and USS Saratoga. VC 38 Squadron were part of the Solomon Air Offensive that began after the Naval Battle of Guadalcanal of November 13, 1942. The VC 38 Squadron flew missions with other Naval squadrons and U.S. Marine Fighting Squadrons and Scout-Bombing Squadrons throughout September, October, November, and December 1943, mercilessly pounding the Japanese airfields of Kahili, Kara, Buka, and Ballale, including Japanese supply areas of Tarlena and Kieta, Bougainville. VC 38 flew missions with VC-24, VC-40, VMTB-134, VMTB-143, VMTB-232, VMTB-233, VMTB-236, VMSB-235, VMSB-243, and VMF-213.

The TBF attack of Kahili Airfield on October 26, 1943 is presented below:

INTELLIGENCE REPORT - 26 OCTOBER 1943

S E C R E T COMMMANDER AIRCRAFT SOLOMONS S E C R E T

STRIKE COMMAND

Squadrons: VMTB-232 (20 planes), VC-38 (7 planes), VC-40 (9 planes)

Type of Mission: Bomb Kahili Airfield

Planes: 36 TBF' s
Anti-Aircraft: Intense heavy, moderate light

Damage to Planes: Empennage of one plane damaged by AA; tail of another plane severely damaged by heavy AA; one plane shot down.

Observations: AA guns: 4 heavy guns on Kangu Hill and 4 auto- Southerly edge of Eberly' s base: one heavy gun at North side thereof. 2 heavy guns in Target #3; 2 guns to East thereof. 2 heavy guns in clearing South west of Malabita Hill. Heavy guns at North end of strip.

Ten barges along beach half way between Kahili and Moila Pt. Four ships off beach at Target #6. Two ships in Tonolei Harbor.

Lost Plane: First Lieutenant Philip Field, N.A., U.S.M.C., VMTB 232, pilot, Sergeant Edward R. Dzama, U.S.M.C., turret gunner, and Private Joseph D. Miller, U.S.M.C., radio gunner, flying in Plane Bu.No. 06416 were observed to pull out of glide at 1000 ft. The engine was on fire, and, after making a turn to the left, the plane dove into the water at a 20 degrees angle about half way between the beach and Erventa Island. Two men were seen to jump; one chute opened; the other did not and the man was seen to go into the water. No other information was obtainable.

. **Fredrick Frelinghuyson, Lt. USNR, VC-40, Intelligence Duty Officer.**

Plane Bu.No.	Pilot	Radioman	Turret Man	Out	In	
		VC-38				
24244	LARSON	Wagner	Wright	0717	1005	
23981	GAMMAGE	Morrissey		0717	1005	
47494	LEARY	Greslie	Dale	0717	1006	
24242	WILSON	Haller	Wilson	0717	1000	
24182	REGAN	Misner	Brant	0717	1006	
23975	LEAKE	Boyle	O' Daniel	0718	1006	
24265	PHILLIPPI	Bond	Tyler	0718	0839	DNA
24194	DRAUGHON	Deal	Paul	0720	1002	
		VMTB-232				
06406	Schrader	Seamonds	Jenkins	0729	1002	
06422	Goodman	Wood	Cardno	0729	1002	
24264	SMITH, Maj.	Waldvogel	Stanner	0721	0955	
47504	METZELAARS	Pollow	Eldridge	0721	0955	
06411	EVERETT	Ward	Norby	0723	0956	
06190	DAUGHERTY	Railey	Donovan	0724	0956	
06475	STAMETS	Severson	Brodeski	0722	0959	
24268	HUMPHREY	Martin	Adams	0722	0956	
47501	WHITE	Crumpton	Moon	0727	0957	
06118	McCOLE	Sears	Blackerby	0727	0958	
06341	BURRIS	Lossie	Wagner	0727	0958	

06416	FIELD	Miller	Dzama	0728	____
06432	EVERSON	Pell	Marker	0728	1001
06359	DEXHEIMER	Jackson	Nilsen	0729	0959
06125	SPARKS	Rader	Sauter	0729	1001
06489	THOMAS	Schleeter	Akey	0729	1001
24358	OLSON	Heke	Mitchell	0729	1001
47510	GARILLI	Schafer	Hall	0729	0959

Kahili Airfield Bombing (Source: Lt.(jg) John Leary's Photograph provided by the Leary Family Collection)

Initially these bombing missions were large scale assaults including up to 194 aircrafts, consisting of TBFs, SBDs, B-25s, P-39s, Kittyhawks, F4Us (Corsair) and F6F Hellcat fighter planes in a single attack. The TBF attack of Kara Airfield on October 31, 1943 was a combined effort of Navy, Marine, and Air Force power, and is presented below:

INTELLIGENCE REPORT - 31 OCTOBER 1943

S E C R E T COMMMANDER AIRCRAFT SOLOMONS S E C R E T

STRIKE COMMAND

Squadrons: VMTB-143 (7 pilot), VC-38 (9 pilots), VC-40 (8 pilots)

Type of Mission: Bombing of Kara Airstrip and AA, and strafing of area.

Planes: 24 TBF' s

Anti-Aircraft: 1. Heavy and light at point ¼ distance North of South end of strip and ½ way between Uquimo river and at a point a short distance NE of this.

2. AA puff noticed between 4000/5000 ft.

3. Light AA tracers seen ½ way between South end of strip and and Moila

Damage to Planes: 2 planes sustained minor damage by AA - one had starboard flipper shot away, and one hit in green house to rear of pilot' s head.

Attack: Rendezvous at 0814 at Baga at 12000 ft., on course 0820; high speed approach. Came from SW of Moila Pt. Attacked from M of strip, runs South and Southwest. Push overs 6000-9000 ft.; releases 1500-2500 ft. Pull outs 200-2000 ft. Made right turn going out. Area in vicinity of Kara airstrip strafed after bombing. Houses west of N 1/3 of strip strafed as was area to Moila Pt. A tower or wooden structure (one of three) was 40 ft. high strafed.

Observations: 1. 1 tug beached on reef NW of Shortlands
2. 2 barges of shore SE of Kahili.s

3. on rally long row of round, red and black buoys or floats extending clear across channel from Moila Pt. to Shortlands (possible sub net).
4. Heavies that hit target before the TBFs did a beautiful job along whole strip.
5. 2 SBDs hit guns west of S end of field.
6. SBD hit AA on Uquimo River.

Route: Between Moila Pt. and Treasury Is. And turned right to attack.

Route Back: Direct.

Myron Sulzberger, Jr.
Captain, U. S. M. C. R.,
Intelligence Duty Officer.

Plane Bu. No.	Pilot	Radioman	Turret Man	Out	In
		VC-38			
24406	LARSON	Wagner	Wright	0714	1023
06190	BISHOP		Barnes	0714	1023
23873	LEARY	Greslie	Dale	0715	1024
06432	GAMMAGE	Morissey		0715	1024
24358	REGAN	Misner	Brandt	0715	1024
06411	PHILLIPPI	Bond	Tyler	0715	1024
24242	MARSHALL	Lane	Tye	0715	1024
24265	TAHLER		Brewer	0719	1006
27595	DRAUGHEN	Deal	Paul	0720	1006
		VC-40			
24334	BEHL	Dunning	Drauden	0719	1004
23987	BENNETT	Brantingham	Whitworth	0717	1006
47494	KNOCHE	Crabtree	Camp	0717	1007
06341	COLLURA	Pittman	Accardi	0718	1006
47506	MORRISON	Loughridge	Joyce	0718	1005
24358	TRACY	Boyer	Rhodes	0720	1005
24403	COLLINS	Mocker	Rivard	0720	1008
06479	FREES	Wobbins	Tufenjian	0720	1004

06270	LOISELLE	Erby	McElmurray	0721	1008	
24282	HOLLIS	Teckenbrock	Haislip	0721	1008	
06455	LEIDECKER	Danielson	Hanson	0721	1008	
06452	WEBB	Visvardis	Miller		0722	1008
06420	TUNNELL	Black	Vorachek	0722	1009	
24268	DAVIS	West	Fisher	0722	1009	
06125	SMITH	Gates	Thomas	0722	1005	

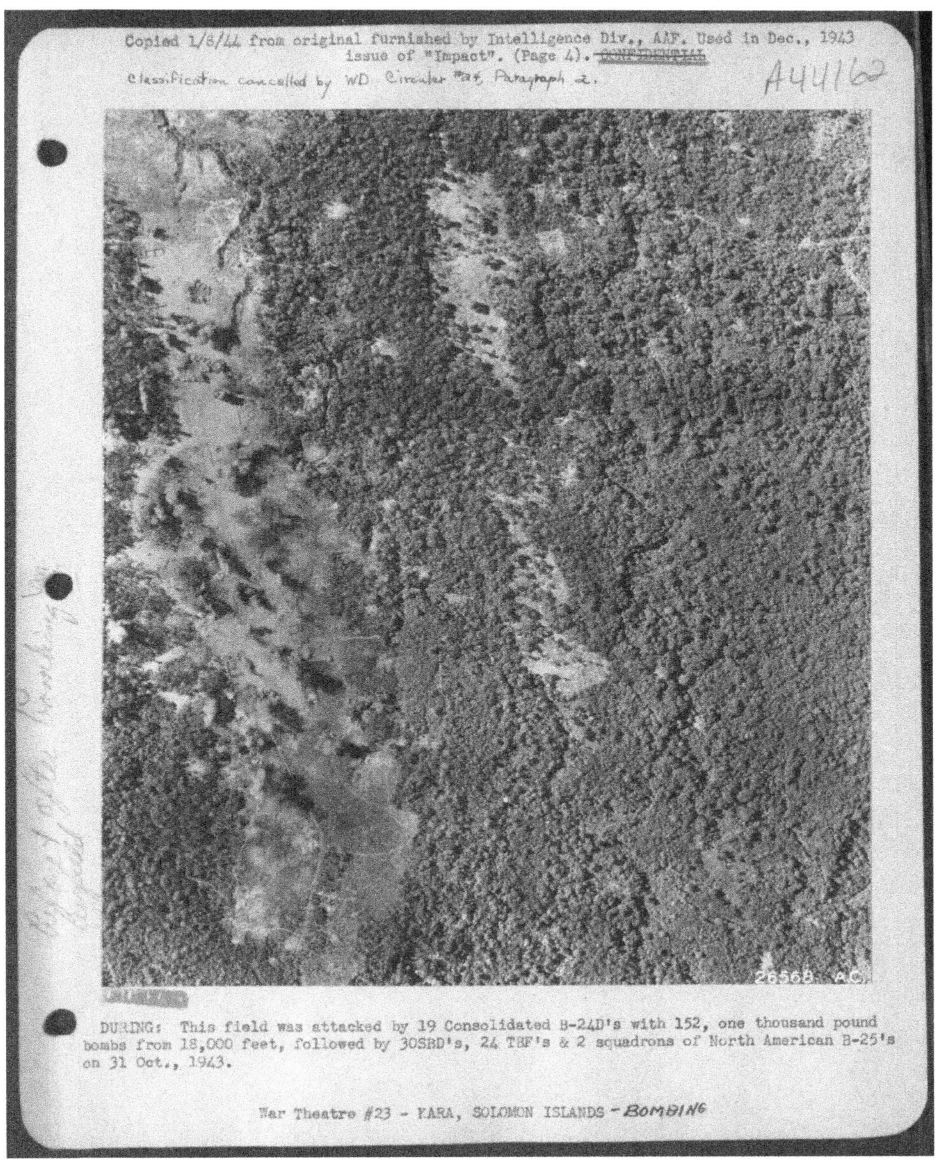

The 24 TBFs in the caption are from VC38, VC40, and VMTB-143. AAF Aerial Reconnaissance Photograph of Kara Airfield Bombing, October 13 1943 (Source: National Archives photo no. 342-FH-3A44162-26568AC)

The VC 38 Squadron was a ground based Navy squadron that island hopped from numerous air fields (Espiritu Santo, Guadalcanal, Munda, and Piva) during their combat tour in the South Pacific. Carrier-based training operations (USS Breton and USS Saratoga) were also conducted in late September 1943 to mid-October 1943. On October 17, 1943, VC 38 left Espiritu Santo to relocate land-based operations at Munda airfield, located on New Georgia Island of the Solomons Island chain. VC 38 was the first TBF squadron to be based at Munda (code named "Shag"). Strike Command Aircraft, Solomons (COMAIRSOLS) was based at Munda on November 20, 1943 under command of Colonel D.F. O'Neill.

TBF Planes at Munda Airfield, New Georgia – October 26 1943.
(Source: National Archives, photo no. 342-FH-3A44430-A80632AC)

The invasion of Bougainville (Bougainville Campaign) began on November 1, 1943 when the U.S. Marines (3d Marine Division and two attached Marine Raider battalions) landed on Cape Torokina, in central Bougainville's Empress Augusta Bay. VC 38 actually bombed the Japanese troops fighting the marines on November 14th and 20th, 1943 by dropping 100 pound bombs near the Japanese positions. Success at Bougainville setup the U.S. forces to finally reach the Japanese stronghold of Rabaul on the Island of New Britain.

INTELLIGENCE REPORT - 14 NOVEMBER 1943

S E C R E T TBF OPERATIONS MUNDA AIRFIELD S E C R E T

Squadrons:	VC-38 (12), VC-40 (8)
Type of Mission:	Bombing in support of ground troops.
Planes:	20 TBF' s Loadings: 12 x 100# fuse: nose 1/10
Damage to Planes:	Two planes received shrapnel and bullet holes in their tails, believed to be have resulted from our own bombs and strafing ricochetes.
Attack:	Course up direct. Upon arrival, contacted Bomb Base and Aircraft Liaison Party #21. Instructed by radio to orbit until 0830 over Cape Torokina; given coordinates of target area and instructed to bomb triangle area (approximately 500 yards to E side) north of base line upon smoke signals being given. ··· Released bombs at 600-1100 feet. After bombing run, planes circled and made strafing run over target area.

Fredrick Frelinghuysen, Lt. USNR VC-40 Intel O.

SQD. NO.	PLANE BU. NO.	PILOT	PASSENGERS	OUT	IN
1	24244	Brunton	Sunday, Kemper	0610	1033
2	23981	Scholfield	Ulrich, Dills	0601	1033
3	23959	Giblin	Lee, Perkins	0601	1033
4	24242	Tahler	Jeffery, Brewer	0601	1033
5	24182	Droughon	Deal, Paul	0609	1034
6	23975	Bishop	Schramm, Barnes	0603	1034
7	24265	Larson	Wagner, Wright	0608	1034
8	24194	Phillippi	Bond, Tyler	0608	1034
9	24208	Leake	Boyle, O' Daniel	0603	1035
21	24515	Leary	Greslie, Brandt	0603	1035
22	24490	Regan	Misner, Brandt	0609	1035
19	23970	Marshall	Lane, Tye	0605	1507

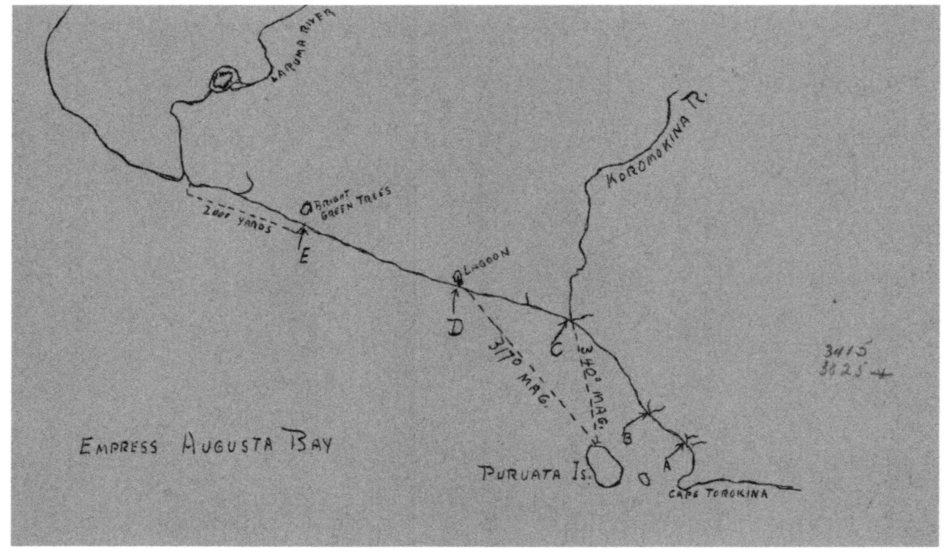

VC 38 Lt.(jg) John Leary's Map (Source: Leary Family Collection)

Rabaul was the Japanese fortress of military power, which included a harbor and five airfields. The march up the Solomons chain, starting at Guadalcanal to now Bougainville airfield (Piva airfield), allowed Allied fighter aircraft to finally reach Rabaul within their operational range. From December 27, 1943 to January 22, 1944, training operations were conducted out of Espiritu Santo. On January 23, 1944, VC 38 moved operations to Piva Airfield on the Island of Bougainville, Papau New Guinea. From Piva Uncle Airfield (Piva U), VC 38 flew missions on the Japanese airfields of Tobera, Lakunai, and Rapopo. All these airfields were located around Rabaul. Additional attacks included bombing Japanese concentrations at the Vunapope Roman Catholic Mission, the Kuraio Mission, and bombing Japanese shipping at Simpson Harbor and Keravia Bay, located at Rabaul, East New Britain Province, Papau New Guinea.

On January 25, 1944, headquarters of Strike Command (COMAIRSOLS) was moved to Piva, Bougainville. This command for varying periods of time directed operations and excercised tactical control of the following squardrons:

Attack Bomber Squadrons

1. SBD's
2. TBFs

The SBD squadrons included the following:

- VC 38 – Lt. A.R. Barber, USN and Lt. Ben Tappan, USNR;
- VC 40 – Lt. Cdr. John H. Pennoyer, USN;
- VB 98A – Lt. Cdr J.R. Little, Lt. (jg) W.G. Maerki, USNR, and Lt. R.T. Lord;
- VB 98B – Lt. Cdr. J.R. Little, USNR, and Lt. E.T. Penne, USMCR;
- VMSB 235 – Major E.E. Munn, USMCR;
- VMSB 236A – Major E.P. Paris, Jr., USMC;
- VMSB 236B – Major W.A. Cloman, Jr., USMC;
- VMSB 241 – Major James A. Feeley, Jr., USMC;
- VMSB 243 – Major Thomas J. Ahern, USMC;
- VMSB 244 – Major R.J. Johnson, USMC and Major Harry W. Reed, USMCR
- VMSB 341 – Major George J Waldie, USMCR, and Major James T. McDaniel, USMC.

The TBF squadrons included the following:

- VMTB 143 – Capt. G.U. Smith, USMCR, and Capt. H.W. Hise;
- VMTB 232 – Major R.W. Smith, USMCR;
- VC 40 – Lt. H.S. Jackson, USN
- VC 38 – Cdr. C.E. Brunton, USN, who also was Group Commander;
- VMTB 233 – Major R.W. Coln, USMC;
- VMTB 134 – Major A.C. Robertson, USMC.

Search and Reconnaissance squadrons included the following:

- RNZAF #1 (PV-1[4]) – Squardron Leader H.C. Walker;
- RNZAF #2 (PV-1) – Squadron Leader Greenway;
- VS 64 (SBD) – Lt. Cdr. Alfred D. Morgan, USNR;
- VB 139 (PV-1) – Lt. Cdr. Hanson, USN;
- VB 140 (PV-1) – Lt. Cdr. V. Williams.

Missions carried out by this Strike Command included bombing and strafing attacks against enemy installations, positions, airfields and shipping, support for our ground forces in the Bougainville campaign, reconnaissance, area searchs, patrols, artillery spotting, liaison with ground forces and direction of rescues.

[4] PV-1 Ventura was a bomber and patrol aircraft built by Vega Aircraft Company, a division of Lockheed.

VC 38 Squadron's heroic actions during the Bougainville and the New Britain campaign's from October 1943 to March of 1944 culminated in a Scorecard of 112 aerial missions, 3 night missions, and 37 aerial victories, with over 30 enemy ships sunk or damaged. VC 38's military war power in December of 1943 consisted of 12 Grumman F6F-3 Hellcat fighters, 17 Douglas SBD-5 Dauntless dive bombers, and 14 Grumman TBF-1 Avenger torpedo bombers.

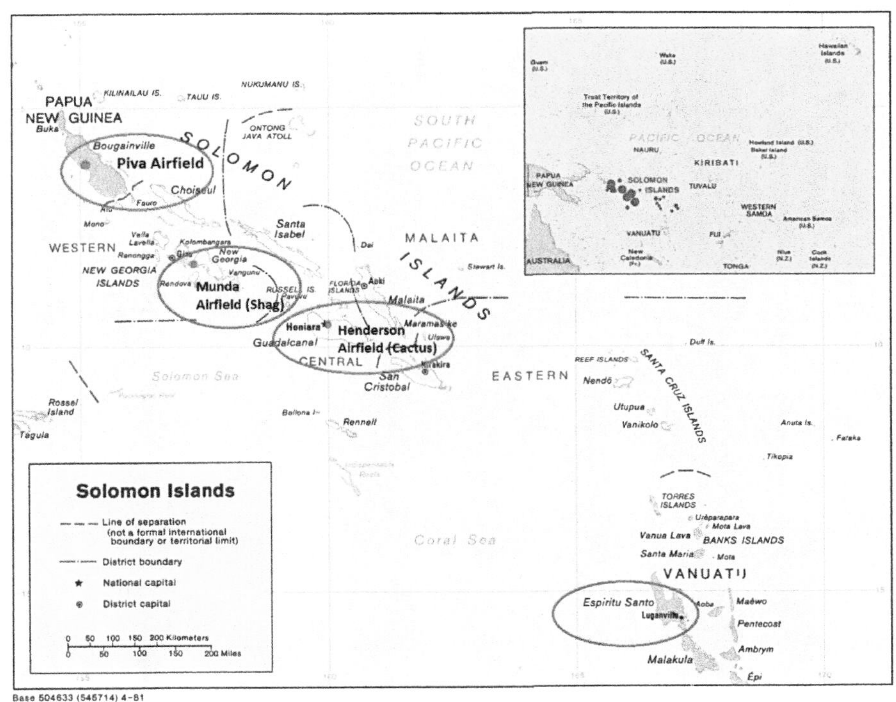

VC 38 operated from Espiritu Santo, Henderson, Munda, and Piva airfields

On February 12th, 1944, a secret dispatch from ComAirSoPac was received ordering TBF planes from VC 38, VMTB 134, and VMTB 233 to conduct mining operations in the north half of Simpson Harbor, near Rabaul (Operations Memorandum is included in Appendix E). The mining operation was to be conducted during the night with the intent of impeding Japanese shipping within the harbor. The attack would be in three groups of 9 TBF planes at one hour intervals. Each Avenger would be armed with one- 1,600 pound Mark 12-1 aerial mine.

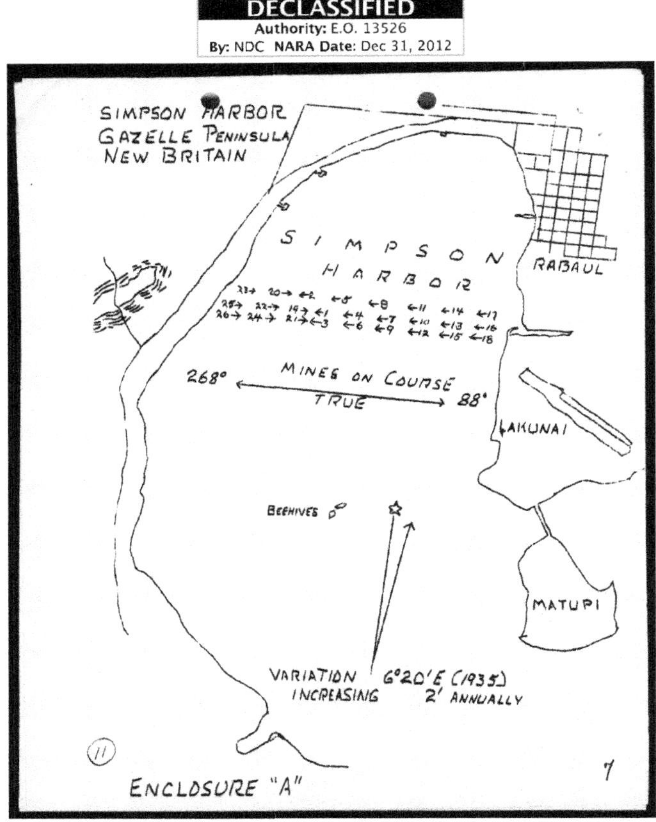

COMAIRSOPAC Operations Memorandum Map of Simpson Harbor Aerial Mining Mission (Source: www.fold3.com)

In the dark hours of February 14th, 1944, 25 TBF planes from VMTB 233 took off from Piva Uncle Airfield to conduct the mining operation. By some chance of fate, the pilots and crew members of VC 38 were redirected that morning to conduct other bombing operations at Tobera Airfield, located south of Rabaul. Over the Simpson Harbor target, each aircraft from VMTB 233 attacked from less than 800-feet altitude, flying at a slow speed or less than 180 knots to drop their parachute-mines weighting 1,600 pounds apiece. During the attack, the Avengers were targeted by searchlights and intense anti-aircraft fire. One plane was lost from Group A (attacking east to west), two planes were lost from Group B (attacking west to east), and three planes were lost from Group C (attacking east to west). As the first group headed back home to Piva, the flight leader of the first group, Major Royce W. Coln, tried to radio the other TBFs to warn them to turn back but he couldn't make radio contact. Plane after plane in the third group disintegrated in mid-air and fell in flames. A total of 18 personnel and six aircrafts from VMTB 233[5] were lost that night. Four of the TBF crew members were captured and subsequently executed by the Japanese. The VMTB 233 mission report of this tragic event[6] is included in Appendix E.

[5] Early morning on February 14, 1944, 26 TBF-1s (VMTB 233) loaded with MK 12-1 mines, took part in a night mining operation in Simpson Harbor, Rabaul. Mines were dropped by parachutes from TBFs. Japanese search lights picked up planes and intense accurate AA was encountered. Six planes and crew were missing, of these, 4 probably shot down, two in harbor and two on land side, three definitely flamers. Pilots missing include: Lt. Barthoff, Lt. Cornelius, Lt. Hathway, Lt. Fowler, Lt. Boyden, and Lt. Sherman – Strike Command Report by J.E. Butler, G-3, Strike Command

[6] The complete list of pilots and crew include the following: Lt. John F. Bartholft, Jr. (pilot of BN 06311), Raymond P Lagro (radio), Joseph A Sullivan (gunner); Lt. Hugh L. Cornelius (pilot of BN 47506), Edwin D. St. Germain (radio), Edward M Slipkas (gunner); Lt. Alonzo N. Hathway, Jr. (pilot of BN 25316), Willie Cleo Thompson (radio), John J. Edwards (gunner); Lt. James L. Fowler (pilot of BN 25327), John Joseph Pudil (radio), Cecil Marvin White (gunner); Lt. James W Boyden (pilot of BN 24264), Arthur J. Patrickus (radio), Bernard C. Pardun (gunner); Lt Robert William Sherman (pilot of BN 24240), William B. Cashman (radio), and James W Greene, Jr. (gunner).

By all accounts, the TBF attack on Keravia Bay - Rabaul, on February 17, 1944 was astonishing. Several of the TBF pilots of VC 38, under a curtain of anti-aircraft machine gun fire, flew low on the water to "skip bomb" several key targets. These heroic tactics resulted in several Japanese ships being damaged or sunk; including a battleship, transport ship, and patrol vessel. The COMAIRSOLS STRIKE COMMAND TBF INTELLIGENCE REPORT for February 17, 1944, vividly details this event (included below and in Appendix E).

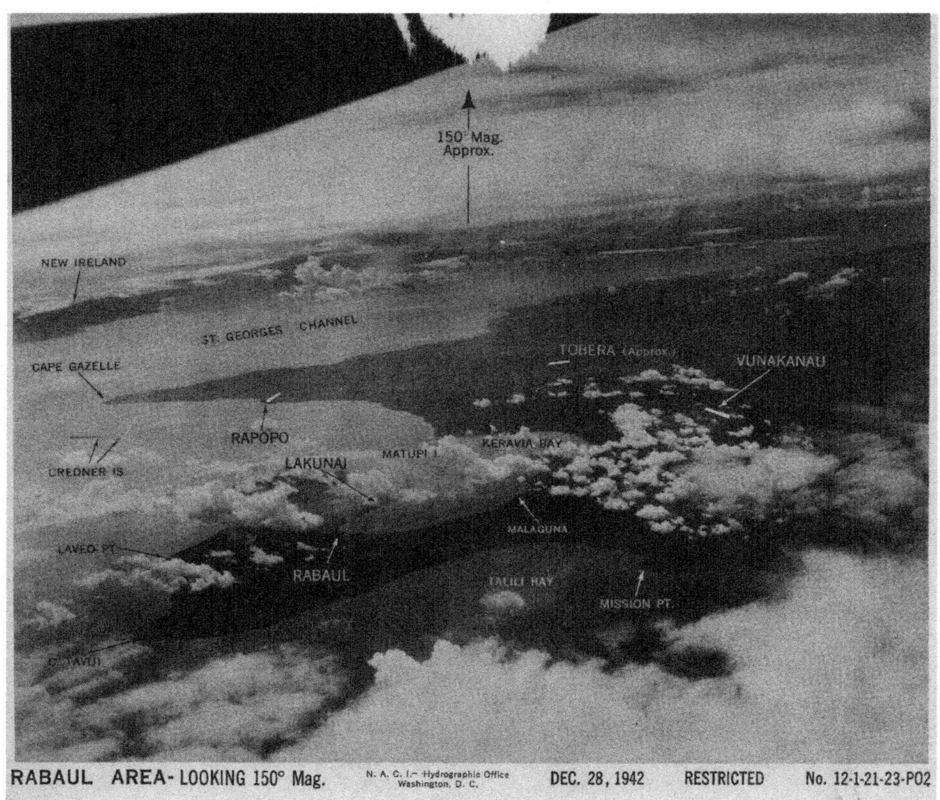

Aerial Photograph of Rabaul Area (Source: Leary Family Collection)

INTELLIGENCE REPORT - STRUCK 17 FEBRUARY, 1944

CONFIDENTIAL TBF INTELLIGENCE CONFIDENTIAL

Target: Shipping in Keravia Bay

Mission: Bomb and strafe.

Flight Leader: Commander C.E. Brunton

Squadrons: VC-38 (12), VMTB -134 (6), VMTB-143 (3), VMTB 233 (3)

Planes: Ordered for mission: 24 TBF' s

Actually dropped bombs: 22 TBF' s. (1 plane did not take off, and 1 plane returned with hung bomb).

Other A/Coordinating: 48 SBD' s and 76 VF

Damage to own A/C: Plane #101 - 20 MM in starboard wing, M/G bullets in port wing, 50 calibre in fuselage 2 feet aft of turret, numerous shrapnel and bullet holes in fuselage.

Plane #232: Hydraulic system knocked out by AA (probably shrapnel). 20 MM hole in cockpit next to pilot' s seat. Shrapnel holes in port and starboard wings and center section of flaps.

Plane #213: Bullet holes in starboard wing.

Plane #114: Hit in engine by M/G.

Personnel Casualties: Commander C.E. Brunton in plane #101 was hit by AA (probably 20MM) from 240' DD just prior to releasing his bomb which scored a direct hit on it. He received a compound fracture of the right ulna with severance of the right ulna nerve and multiple lacerations, lateral aspect of right thigh.

Ammunition Expended: 50 calibre - 2375 rounds

30 calibre - 2200 rounds

Attack Tactics: High speed approach at 13000' across Blancho Bay down to push over at 8,000' for attack at masthead level. The formation turned S. and approached Keravia Bay through the depression W. of Vulcan Crater released at mast head level and retired over the water toward Raluana Point. Rally 5 miles E. of Cape Gazelle, route back direct to base. Ships and barges were strafed by both fixed and free guns.

Note - Photos taken after the strike showed one medium and three small AK missing, and it is presumed that they were sunk. The results of the forward firing rockets are the subject of a separate report.

Summary of Results: 5 confirmed direct hits on the 475' Eiyo Maru N. Keravia Bay; photographic coverage showed that it has been damaged again and was seeping oil. Damage to shipping in NW Keravia Bay was reported as follows:

1. 2 confirmed direct hits and 1 u/o on a 300' AK which photograph showed to be missing from harbor subsequently.
2. 1 confirmed direct on 175' PC. Photograph showed damage and oil slick
3. 1 confirmed direct hit on another 300' AK.
4. 2 near misses and 1 u/o on 265 AK.
5. 3 confirmed direct hits and 2 u/o on 400' AO.

In W Keravia Bay, 1 confirmed direct hit on 240' DD. The stern was observed to be lifted high out of the water by the explosion of the bomb, and a later photograph showed it lying with its stern underwater.

In SW Keravia Bay, 1 near miss on 175' PC.

In SE Keravia Bay, 1 near miss and 1 u/o on 175' AK.

Weather: Route up: Squalls and scattered clouds 2000'-9000'

O.T.: Clear, Ceiling 13000'

Route Back: 8/10 clouds with base 1500' scattered squalls.

Observations: 1. Enemy Shipping:

A. 1 AK (300') and 2 large SS N. of Vulcan Crater.
B. 20-30 large and small barges near shore S. Keravia Bay.
C. One barge underway in Blanco Channel, thoroughly strafed by several planes.
D. Keravia Bay (See Summary of Results supra).

2. Enemy ground activity: AA, shipping and barrage balloons from 3 vessels N of Vulcan Crater

3. Condition of targets before and after attack: Smoke from damaged AK's and explosion at stern of DD after hits.

4. Results of coordinated attack: Not observed

5. Unusual circumstances: Many small parachutes observed over Keravia Bay, possibly shot up or released for AA purposes.

6. Anti-Aircraft:

A. SW/Vulcan Crater, known heavy (2x4.7 navel guns), moderate, inaccurate.
B. S Matupi Island, known heavy and light, moderate, inaccurate.
C. W of Matupi Crater, known auto, moderate, inaccurate.
D. W of Vulcan Crater, know auto (20MM), intense, inaccurate.
E. W and S shore Keravia Bay, know light auto and M/G, moderate, inaccurate.
F. Cove S of Vulcan Crater, known light auto and M/G, moderate, inaccurate.
G. Lakunni: known light and heavy, intense, accurate.
H. From ships in Keravia Bay, (especially PC and DD), auto and M/G, intense, accurate
I. Shore SW of Lakunai Airfield, known auto, moderate, inaccurate.
J. S of Raluana Point, M/G, intense, accurate.

7. Miscellaneous: 1 F4U was observed to crash in Simpson Harbor W of Matupi Island.

James N. Truesdale, Lt. USNR.
A. C. I. O. VC38,
DUTY INTELLIGENCE OFFICER

- -

Plane No.	Pilot	Passenger	Remarks
101	Brunton	Wagner, Kemp	Hit on DD[7]
103	Scholfield	Ulrich, Dills	Hit on AK
104	Giblin	Lee, Perkins	Hit on AK
105	Draughon	Deal, Paul	u/o on AO
108	Regan	Misner, Brandt	Hit on AK
109	Leake	Boyle, O' Daniel	Effective miss on PC
110	Bishop	Schramm, Barnes	Hit on PC
102	McDonald	Blank, Young	Hit on AO
114	Tahler	Buis, Brewer	Hit on AO
107	Behn	Dill, Farber	Hit on AK
118	Leary	Greslie, Dale	Effective miss on AK
119	Gammage	Durham, Morrissey	Hit on AO
202	Glenn	Sticksel, Whitcannank	Effective miss on AK
206	Ransom	Fisher, Mac Adam	Did not strike
207	Philbin	Blazie, Williams	Hit on AK
209	Turner	Lochridge, Farris	Did not strike
213	Richardson	Wilson, Lane	Effective miss on AK
211	Wright	Adams, Brunson	Did not strike

[7] Naval Abbreviations: DD = Destroyer AK = Cargo Ship/Barge AO = Oiler or Fuel Oil Tanker Ship PC = Patrol Vessel

230	Robertson[8]	Dumelle, Ballard	Hit on AK
231	Boll	Bruzuskewicz, Hickman	u/o on AK
232	Lemmons	Sutton, Boecher	u/o on AK
235	May	Hull, McKenna	u/o of AK
236	Ball	Berryman, Kane	u/o of AK

5	Phillips F.G.	Drolsbaugh, Hobbs	Hit on AO
12	Berdel	Enterline, Calvert	u/o on AO
8	Takacs	Hull, Isam	Hit on AO
121	Tulis	Crawford, Levino	Did not attack
4	Bauder	Kearns, DeRouch	Did not attack
126	Morris R.D.	McGee, Hundrichs	Did not attack

[8] Major Alben C. Robertson of VMTB 134, along with pilots Boll, Lemmons, May, Phillips, and Ball completed the first combat test of the forward firing rocket on a TBF during this attack – Rocket Plane Mission Report by 1st Lt. Charles L Jones, CCIO of VMTB 134.

Attack of Japanese warships at Simpson Harbor – Rabaul – November 5, 1943 (Source: Public Domain)

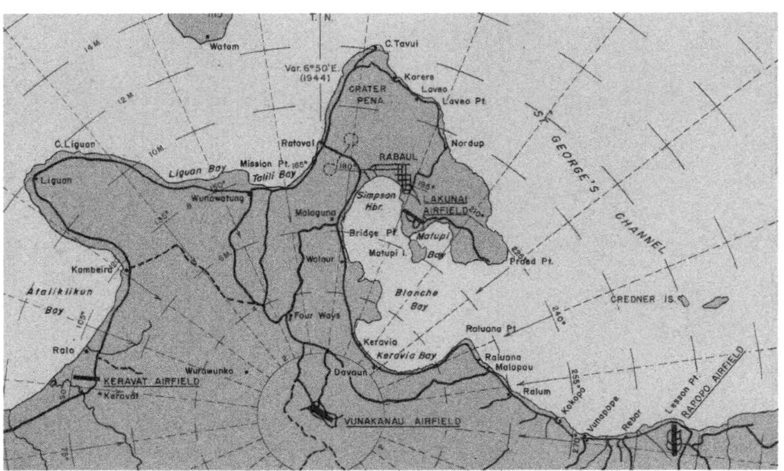

COMSOPAC Map of Rabaul Airfields (Source: Leary Family Collection)

I have been able to account for ten awards of the Distinguished Flying Cross (D.F.C.) to members of the VC 38 TBF squadron during this dive bombing attack, though there may be more. The list includes the following aviation officers:

- Cdr. Charles E. Brunton – D.F.C.
- Lt. (jg) Jack P. Scholfield – D.F.C
- Lt. (jg) Graham Tahler – D.F. C.
- Lt. (jg)Robert B. Giblin – D.F.C
- Lt. (jg) John A Leary – D.F.C.
- Lt. (jg) Robert F Regan – D.F.C.
- Lt. (jg) Arthur McDonald – D.F.C.
- Lt. (jg) Robert H. Behn – D.F.C.
- Lt. (jg) Bruce C. Bishop – D.F.C.
- Lt. (jg) Thomas M Gammage – D.F.C.

Following the return of VC 38 to the west coast, several members continued in the naval service and had distinguished careers. These include the following:

- Cdr. Charles E. Brunton – Rear Admiral
- Lt. Graham Tahler – Rear Admiral
- Lt. Robert B. Giblin – Commander of USS *Lexington*
- Captain Robert F. Regan – Command of NAS Corpus Christie (3 time D.F.C. recipient)
- Lt. Thomas Milton Gammage – D.F.C. as Section Leader of VT-47 (July 1945) at Honshu Island, Japan (2 time D.F.C. recipient)
- Cdr. Arthur McDonald – Commander of All Weather Fighter Squadron Four (VF[AW]-4

Several members of VC 38 also had distinguished legal careers, including the following:

- **Lt. John A Leary – Judge of New York State**
- **Lt. Jack P Scholfield – Judge of Washington State**

This list is likely incomplete, as my research was limited. Based on ARM 1/C Richard (Wag) Wagner's War Diary, VC 38 departed the Pacific Theater of War on March 20, 1944 aboard the USS Long Island, was disbanded in May of 1944, and was commissioned VT-38. VC 38[9] was one unit and one tour that contributed to the end of World War II within the South West Pacific Theater of War. By all accounts, they performed tremendously.

---

[9] According to the National Archives, no War Diary of VC 38 exists in their holdings.

The Times Record (Troy, NY):
February 21, 1944

HUDSON FALLS BOY HELPS TO DELIVER BLOW AT RABAUL

Lt. (J.G.) Leary Drops 2,000-Pound Bomb on Japanese Cargo Ship

Advanced South Pacific Airbase (delayed) (AP) – Former college athletes teamed up in the air to help deliver a heavy blow at Japanese shipping in Rabaul's harbor Thursday.

Lieut (j.g.) John A. Leary, Hudson Falls, N.Y., coxswain of the 1941 Syracuse University crew, dropped a 2,000-pound bomb on a Japanese cargo ship with the same accuracy he showed in manning the tiller ropes.

Leary made his successful run at masthead level through anti-aircraft fire which failed to prevent the South Pacific flyers from hitting 12 ships in all. It was his first raid on the New Britain base.

Lieut. (j.g.) Robert L. Regan, Cambridge, Mass., catcher for the 1941 Harvard baseball team, scored a hit on another Japanese vessel from his torpedo bomber.

Lieut. (j.g.) Bruce C. Bishop, Lookout Mountain, Tenn., got a direct hit on a large patrol boat. He's a former University of Tennessee quarterback who played three bowl games against Oklahoma, Boston College and Southern California.

Sergt. Gordon D. Marston, Stoneham, Mass., squadron chronicler, said Comdr. Charles E. Brunton, Pasadena, Cal., placed his bomb on a Japanese warship which was left severely damaged.

Liet. (j.g.) H. T. Leake, New York, saw the hit and said it lifted the warship's stern clean out of the water. Brunton's ship was badly shot up but managed to get home.

A 2,000-pound bomb from a plane piloted by Ensign Tom M. Gammage, Miami, Fla., smashed into the side of a Jap freighter. Among Gammage's crew members was Harold A Morrissey, Garnder, Mass.

"The explosion seemed to tear away the side of the ship," Gammage said.

HUDSON FALLS BOY HELPS TO DELIVER BLOW AT RABAUL

Lt. (J. G.) Leary Drops 2,000-Pound Bomb on Japanese Cargo Ship

Advanced South Pacific Airbase (delayed) (AP)—Former college athletes teamed up in the air to help deliver a heavy blow at Japanese shipping in Rabaul's harbor Thursday.

Lieut (j.g.) John A. Leahy, Hudson Falls, N. Y., coxswain of the 1941 Syracuse University crew, dropped a 2,000-pound bomb on a Japanese cargo ship with the same accuracy he showed in manning the tiller ropes.

Leary made his successful run at masthead level through anti-aircraft fire which failed to prevent the South Pacific flyers from hitting 12 ships in all. It was his first raid on the New Britain base.

Lieut. (j.g.) Robert L. Regan, Cambridge, Mass., catcher for the 1941 Harvard baseball team, scored a hit on another Japanese vessel from his torpedo bomber.

Lieut. (j.g.) Bruce C. Bishop, Lookout Mountain, Tenn., got a direct hit on a large patrol boat. He's a former University of Tennessee quarterback who played three bowl games against Oklahoma, Boston College and Southern California.

Sergt. Gordon D. Marston, Stoneham, Mass., squadran chronicler, said Comdr. Charles E. Brunton, Pasadena, Cal., placed his bomb on a Japanese warship which was left severely damaged.

Lieut. (j.g.) H. T. Leake, New York City, saw the hit and said it lifted the warship's stern clear out of the water. Brunton's ship was badly shot up but managed to get home.

A 2,000-pound bomb from a plane piloted by Ensign Tom M. Gammage, Miami, Fla., smashed into the side of a Jap freighter. Among Gammage's crew members was Harold A. Morrissey, Gardner, Mass.

"The explosion seemed to tear away the side of the ship," Gammage said.

CHAPTER PLANS EVENT AT MASONIC .EMPLE

Bethlehem Star Chapter, O. E. S., will conduct a dessert bridge luncheon at the Troy Masonic Temple tomorrow at 1 p.m. Mrs. Gertrude Woods is chairman of the arrangements committee.

Wednesday at 8 p.m., the chapter will conduct its business meeting in the temple with Mrs. Edna Willetts, worthy matron, and Oliver E. Anderson, worthy patron, presiding. A George Washington party will be conducted with Mrs. Sarah Stewart and Mrs. Helen Jones as the cochairmen.

VC 38 aboard the U.S.S. Long Island, August 1943

(1) Lt.(jg) Robert Regan; (2) Lt.(jg) Larry E. Englade ; (3) Ens. Thomas M. Gammage; (4) Lt.(jg) Jack Scholfield; (5) Commander Charles E. Brunton; (6) Lt.(jg) Graham Tahler; (7) Lt. William R. Larson (Lucky); (8) Lt.(jg) Robert B. Giblin; (9) Ens. Arthur McDonald; (10) Lt.(jg) Grant Phillippi; (11) Lt. James N. Truesdale; (12) Lt.(jg) John Leary

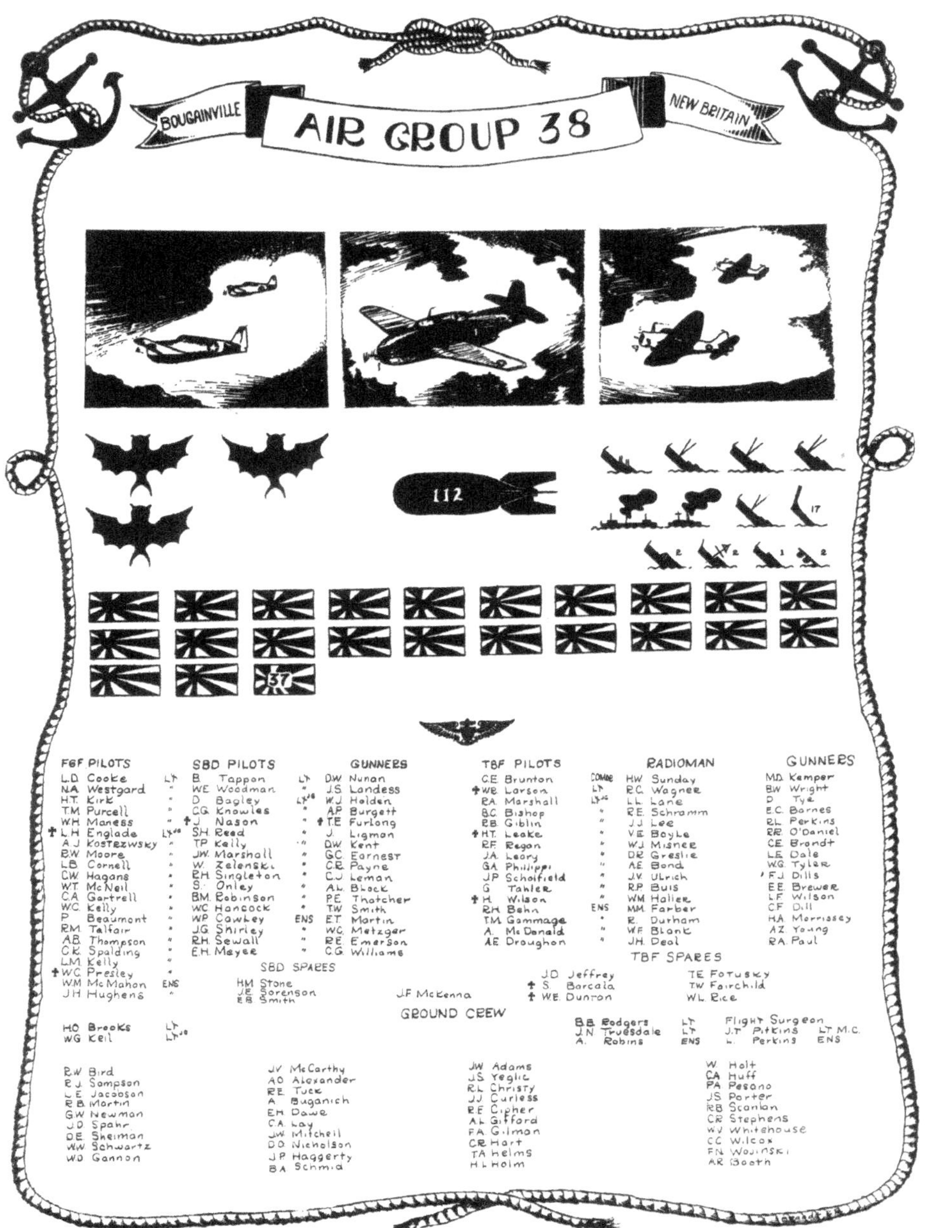

VC 38's Scorecard: 112 aerial missions, 3 night missions, 37 aerial victories with over 30 enemy ships sunk or damaged.

Air Group 38 – Bougainville-New Britain (June 1943 until April 1944)

3 night missions

112 missions

37 aerial victories

1 Japanese Destroyer sunk

4 transport/merchantmen ships sunk

17 landing barges sunk

2 damaged fuel oil tanker ships

5 other merchantmen vessels sunk

2 floating dry docks sunk

<u>VF-38</u>

F6F pilots

Lt. L.D. Cooke
Lt. N.A. Westgard
Lt. H. T. Kirk
Lt. T. M. Purcell
Lt. W. H. Maness
Lt.(jg) L. H. Englade+
Lt.(jg) A. J. Kostrzwsky
Lt.(jg) R. W. Moore
Lt.(jg) L. B. Cornell
Lt.(jg) C. W. Hagans
Lt.(jg) W. T. McNeil
Lt.(jg) C. A. Gartrell
Lt.(jg) W. C. Kelly
Lt.(jg) P. Beaumont
Lt.(jg) A. B. Thompson
Lt.(jg) C.K. Spaulding
Lt.(jg) L.M. Kelly
Lt.(jg) W.C. Presley+
Lt.(jg) R.M. Telfair
Ens. J.H. Hughens
Ens W.M. McMahon

F6F Fighter Crew Photograph aboard the USS Long Island, August 1943

From Front, Rows 1 and 2: Ground Crew - unidentified

Row 3 left to right: Theodore S. Condo[10] (died 2003), Larry Henry Englade* (KIA[11] Feb 29, 1944 over Namatanai, New Ireland, Papau New Guinea), Lt. Cdr. John Howard Anderson, Walter Thomas McNeil* (KIA Jan 5, 1945), H.O. Brooks (IO[12]), Oscar Ivan Chenoweth Jr.(Executive Officer).

Row 4 left to right: Robert M. Telfair (died 2001), Alex J. Kostrzwsky, David V. Senft (living), Allen B. Thompson (died 1994), Wilson Calvert Kelly*, Wayne C Presley* (KIA September 16, 1943 over Ballale Island, Solomon Islands).

Row 5 left to right: Clifford Arthur Gartrell* (died 1968), Leland Baucom Cornell* (living), Paul Beaumont (died 2002), Richard Wesley Moore* (died 1978), Charles William Hagans* (died 2001) , Walter G. Keil (IO – died 1980).

(Source: Names of VF 38 pilots by Mark Sheppard of Oxfordshire, England. Photograph source: W. Wagner)

---

10 *= Awarded Air Medal

11 KIA = Killed In Action

12 IO = Intelligence Officer

<u>VB-38</u>

SBD pilots / gunners

Lt. B. Tappan / gunner D. W. Nunan

Lt. W. E. Woodman / gunner J. S. Landess

Lt.(jg) D. Bagley / gunner W. J. Holden

Lt.(jg) C. G. Knowles / gunner A. P. Burgett

Lt.(jg) J. Nason+/ gunner T. E. Furlong+ ***(Nason was P.O.W. - survived)***

Lt.(jg) S. H. Reed / gunner J. Ligman

Lt.(jg) T. P. Kelly / gunner D. W. Kent

Lt.(jg) J. W. Marshall / gunner G. C. Earnest

Lt.(jg) W. Zelenski / gunner C. R. Payne

Lt.(jg) R. H. Singleton / gunner C. J. Leman

Lt(jg) S. Onley / gunner A. L. Block

Lt.(jg) B. M. Robinson / gunner P. E. Thatcher

Lt.(jg) W. C. Hancock / gunner T. W. Smith

Ens W. P. Cawley / gunner E. T. Martin

Ens J. G. Shirley / gunner W. G. Metzger

Ens R. H. Sewell / gunner R. E. Emerson

Ens E. H. Meyer / gunner C. G. Williams

<u>SBD Spare</u>

H. M. Stone

J. E. Sorenson

E. B. Smith

J. F. McKenna

VC-38/VT-38

TBF pilot / radioman / gunner

Cdr. C. E. Brunton / radioman H. W. Sunday / gunner M. D. Kemper
Lt. W. R. Larson+ / radioman R. C. Wagner / gunner B. W. Wright
Lt.(jg) R. A. Marshall / radioman L. A. Lane / gunner D. Tye
Lt.(jg) B. C. Bishop / radioman R. E. Schramm / gunner E. C. Barnes
Lt.(jg) R. B. Giblin / radioman J. T. Lee / gunner R. L. Perkins
Lt.(jg) H. T. Leake+ / radioman V. E. Boyle / gunner R. R. O'Daniel
Lt.(jg) R. F. Regan / radioman W. J. Misner / gunner C. E. Brandt
Lt.(jg) J. A. Leary / radioman D. R. Greslie / gunner L. E. Dale
Lt.(jg) G. A. Phillippi / radioman A E. Bond / gunner W. G. Tyler
Lt.(jg) J. P. Scholfield / radioman J. V. Ulrich / gunner F. J. Dills
Lt.(jg) G. Tahler / radioman R. P. Buis / gunner E. E. Brewer
Lt.(jg) H. Wilson+ / radioman W. M. Haller / gunner L. F. Wilson
Ens R. H. Behn / radioman M. M. Farber / gunner C. F. Dill
Ens T. M. Gammage / radioman R. Durham / gunner H. A. Morrissey
Ens A. McDonald / radioman W. F. Blank / gunner A. Z. Young
Ens A. E. Draughon / radioman J. H. Deal / gunner R. A. Paul

TBF Spares

J. D. Jeffreys
S. Barcala+
W. E. Dunton+
T. E. Fotusky
T. W. Fairchild
W. L Rice

Intelligence

Lt. H.O. Brooks
Lt.(jg) W.G. Keil
Lt. J.N. Truesdale
Lt. Ben B. Rogers
Ens. LeRoy Perkins

Medical

Lt. John T. Pitkin– Flight Surgeon

Ens. A Robins

Ground Crew

R. W. Bird
R. J. Sampson
L. E. Jacobson
R. B. Martin
G. W. Newman
J. D. Spahr
D. E. Sheiman
W. W. Schwartz
W. D. Gannon
J. V. McCarthy
A. O. Alexander
R. E. Tuck
A. Buganich
E. H. Dawe
C. A. Lay
J. W. Mitchell
D. D. Nicholson
J. P. Haggerty
B. A. Schmid
J. W. Adams
J. S. Yeglic
R. E. Cipher
A. L. Gifford
R.L. Christy
J.J. Curless
F. A. Gilman
C. R. Hart
T. A. Helms
H. L. Holm
W. Holt
C. A. Huff
P. A. Pesano
J. S. Porter
R. B. Scanlan
C. R. Stephens
W. V. Whitehouse
C. C. Wilcox
F. N. Wojinski
A. R. Booth

(+) Indicates missing or killed

Source: *http://forum.12oclockhigh.net/showthread.php?t=20083, corrections by author.*

A total of nine men of Air Group 38 are listed on their Scorecard as missing or killed. Their stories include the following:

Lt.(jg)Wayne C. Presley (VF-38)

On September 16, 1943, Presley took off from Munda Airfield in his F6F-3 Hellcat fighter, as part of the escort for 24 TBFs and 31 SBDs attacking Ballale Island. The escort consisted of 13 Hellcats from VF-38 and 11 Hellcats from VF-40, in addition to other F6F, F4U, P-40, and P-38's making up a total of 71 escorting fighters. Over the target, 40-50 intercepting Zeros and Tonys were met, and heavy anti-aircraft cover was encountered over the target. Presley and his Hellcat (Bureau Number 25940) was observed to crash into the sea and is listed as MIA. Lt.(jg) Presley was declared dead on January 9, 1946. Lt.(jg) Presley was awarded the Distinguished Flying Cross, Air Medal with Gold Star, and Purple Heart (posthumously).

VC 38 Radioman Richard Wagner's War Diary:

Today I went on my first strike against the Japs. It was the Island of Ballale just a few miles from Bougainville. Ballale is a small island with a bomb strip covering almost the entire island. There was lots of heavy AA[13] and zeros. One Zero started a move on us but a P39 shot him down before he got a good start. During the three day attack on Ballale **we lost two TBFs and three F6Fs**. Two of the fighter pilots were picked up but the others were not. We shot down 5 zeros. – September 15, 1943 entry

[13] AA stands for anti-aircraft fire

Lt.(jg) Joseph G. Nason & gunner Thomas E. Furlong (VC-38 SBD plane)

On October 23, 1943, pilot Joseph Nason and gunner Thomas Furlong, Jr., took off from Munda Airfield on a diving bomb mission to Bougainville. While dive bombing an anti-aircraft position near Kara Airfield, the plane was hit by anti-aircraft fire and caught fire. Nason bailed out virtually over Kara Airfield. His gunner Furlong was not seen to escape the stricken SBD aircraft and was presumed to have been killed when it crashed.

Lt. (jg) Nason was captured by the Japanese and became a POW. Nason survived the war and was one of only a handful of POWs that were liberated by Australians when Japan surrendered in September 1945. Nason passed away on October 12, 2012. He wrote a book about his history as a POW, Horio You Next Die! by Joseph Nason. The story of Joe Nason is available for view at http://vimeo.com/65439421

Thomas E. Furlong, Jr., Aviation Radioman, Third Class, was from Worcester, Massachusetts. His memorial marker is located at the Tablets of the Missing at the Manila American Cemetery.

VC 38 Radioman Richard Wagner's War Diary:

Strike Kahili – one SBD shot down. **Nason & Furlong – parachute both dead**. – October 1943 note entry in Aviator's Flight Log Book.

Lt. (jg) Harry W. Wilson (TBF pilot VC-38)

Lt. (jg) Harry Wilson (right) and Lt. (jg) John Leary (left) - assumed to be Munda or Guadalcanal Airfield (Source: Leary Family Collection)

On October 28, 1943, Lt.(jg) Wilson[14] crashed on take off from Munda airfield at 0619 and was killed. Minor injuries were sustained by Walter Martin Haller (Radioman) and L.E. Wilson (Turret Man). The Bureau Number for Wilson's TBF plane was 06118. 19 TBFs were on a bombing and strafing mission of Kara Airfield and anti-aircraft positions on that day. He was posthumously awarded the Air Medal. He is buried at Richmond Cemetery, Kentucky.

VC 38 Radioman Richard Wagner's War Diary:
Attack Kara on Bougainville. It was a bad day from the start. **Lt. Wilson was killed** on the takeoff. Jeffrey got hit in the back by a 20mm. Very little heavy AA but a lot of small stuff. – October 28, 1943 entry.

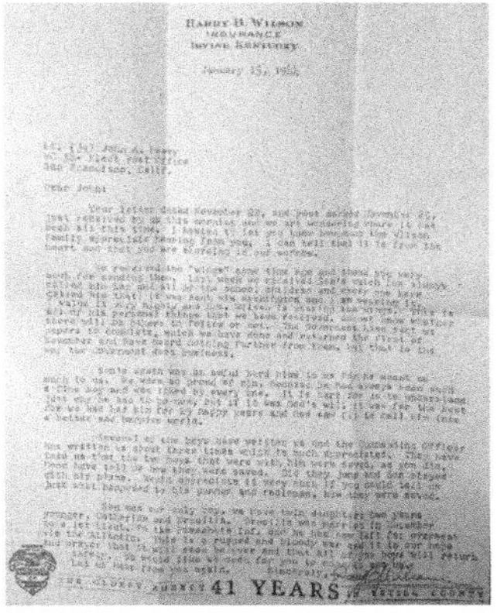

Harry B. Wilson
Insurance
Irvine, Kentucky

San Francisco, Calif.

Dear John:

41 YEARS

"Dear John [Lt. John A Leary], Your letter dated November 22, and post marked November 23, just received by us this morning and we are wondering where it has been all this time. I hasten to let you know how much the Wilson family appreciate hearing from you. I can tell that it is from the heart and that you are sharing in our sorrow.

We received the "wings" some time ago and thank you very much for sending them. Last week we received Son's watch (we always called him Son and all of the school children and every one here called him that) it was sent via Washington and I am wearing it. I value it very highly and Mrs. Wilson is wearing the wings. ...

---

[14] Confidential Commander Aircraft Solomons Strike Command Intelligence Section Report, dated October 28, 1943 by Captain Myron Sulzberger, USMCR, VMTB-143, Intelligence Duty Officer.

Son's death was an awful hard blow to us for he meant so much to us. We were so proud of him, because he had always been such a fine boy and liked by every one. It is hard for us to understand just why he had to go now, but if it was God's will it was for the best for we had had him for 25 happy years and God saw fit to call him into a better and happier world.

Several of the boys have written us and the Commanding Officer has written us about three times which is much appreciated. The have told us that the two boys that were with him were saved, as you did. None have told us how they were saved. Did they jump and Son stayed with his plane? Would appreciate it very much if you could tell us just what happened to his gunner and radioman, how they were saved. ... This is a rugged and bloody war and it is our hope and prayer that it will soon be over and that all of you boys will return safely. ... Sincerely, Harry B. Wilson." **January 15 1944 – father Harry Wilson - Irvine, Kentucky (Source: Leary Family Collection)**

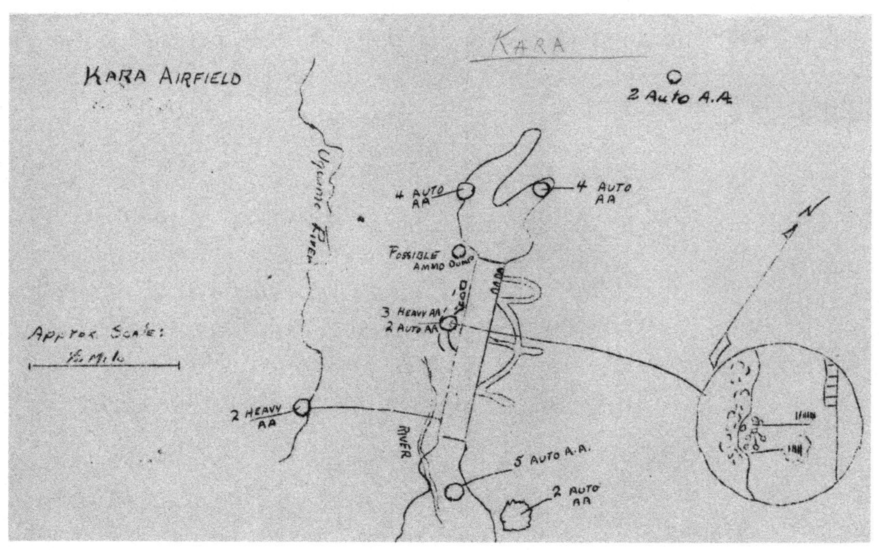

VC 38 John Leary's Map of Kara Airfield (Source: Leary Family Collection)

Lt. William R. Larson (VC-38)

On December 27, 1943, Lt. Larson was reported missing following the crash of a transport plane (R4D-5 airplane, Bureau #12432) coming from Tontouta, New Caledonia, enroute to Espiritu Santo, New Hebrides. The plane wreckage was spotted a few miles south of Ouvea Island in the Loyalty Group, northwest of New Caledonia (now Vanuatu). William was returning to the combat zone following rehabilitation leave at Sydney, Australia. William, along with six pilots and twelve gunners of another squadron (Bombing Squadron 98 – VB 98), along with the 5 person flight crew of VMJ 153, died in this transport plane crash. No bodies were recovered.

Lt. Larson piloted 22 TBF combat missions with VC 38 over the Solomon Islands area, and recorded 1,860 total flight hours with the USNR. William was the senior operations officer in VC 38. Lt. Larson grew up on the family farm in Sioux Trail Township, Divide County, North Dakota, and was 28 years old. William previously served on the USS Nashville as a SOC pilot from July 1940 to September 1942. While aboard the *Nashville*, he participated in escorting US Marines to Wake Island and Iceland, the Doolittle Raid on Japan, and defending the Aleutians in the attack on Kiska. He was posthumously awarded the Air Medal.

VC 38 Radioman Richard Wagner's War Diary:

Mr. Larson was killed returning from Sydney. The DC he was in crashed after leaving New Caledonia – December 27, 1943 entry.

Lt.(jg) Herbert Tucker Leake (VC-38), Santiago Barcala (VC-38), & Willard Earl Dunton (VC-38)

Lt.(jg) H.T. Leake (Source: Daniel Phillippi)

On February 20, 1944, Lt. Leake, Santiago Barcala (ARM3/c), and Willard Earl Dunton (AOM1/C) are missing in action as result of crash of plane #103 (Bureau No. 24495) during a bomb and strafe mission on bridges and AA installations at the Monoitu Mission area located on Bougainville. [15]Plane #103 was loaded with 1x2000# 1/10 second delay bomb and was seen to make steep dive from 3000-feet and to pull out (after release) at approximately 500-feet. Just after the plane levelled off with approximate speed of 200k one half of the starboard wing came off, probably as a result of the bomb blast, and the plane flipped over on its back and crashed in the jungle in the Monoitu Mission area. Leake was posthumously awarded the Air Medal. Barcala's memorial marker is located at Santa Clara Mission Cemetery, California and Dunton's memorial marker is combined with Herbert Leake's memorial marker located at Zachary Taylor National Cemetery, Kentucky.

ARM3 Santiago Barcala of Santa Clara, CA (Source: Pauline Winters)

<u>VC 38 Radioman Richard Wagner's War Diary</u>:

Attack ground positions just a few miles south of our camp. Our target was a bridge so the Japs couldn't move heavy art [artillery] up this way. We missed the bridge. **Leake went in** just as he was pulling out of his glide. Dunton was gunner, and Barcala[16] Radioman. – February 20, 1944 entry[17]

---

[15] Confidential COMAIRSOLS Strike Command TBF Intelligence report, dated February 20, 1944 by Lt. James N. Truesdale, VC38 Intelligence Duty Officer

[16] Santiago Barcala was born on November 23, 1922 to Spanish parents Juaquina and Eaustacio. The family included two brothers and three sisters. He attended high school in Gilroy, CA and he loved to read and work on cars. All the siblings and parents worked on ranches as laborers. Santiago entered the Navy right out of high school and was just 21 years old at the time of the plane crash. Source: Pauline Winters

[17] Based on VC38's Intelligence Reports, this mission was the first combat flight Dunton and Barcala flew (TBF spares)

Lt.(jg) Larry Henry Englade (VF-38 F6F Hellcat Pilot)

Lt.(jg) Englade, USNR Service Number 117107, was lost February 29, 1944, during a mission over Namatanai, New Ireland, Papua New Guinea.

As a fighter plane pilot during the occupation of Attu Island, Territory of Alaska, during May 1943, he repeately executed strafing and glide bombing missions at extremely low altitudes while being subjected to heavy anti-aircraft fire. He was operating off the USS Nassau and flying a F4F-4 fighter plane with VF-21. Lt.(jg) Englade was awarded the Air Medal.

Prior to missing in action, Lt.(jg) Englade[18] survived ditching his Hellcat fighter in the ocean on November 3, 1943. Pour weather prevailed all day that day with the regularly scheduled patrols to Bougainville. Lt.(jg) L.H. Englade of VF 38, got lost over Treasury Island was still missing at the end of the day, last having been heard from when he radioed that he was out of gasoline and was preparing to make a water landing at 1800. On November 6, 1943, Lt.(jg) Englade was picked up by natives on Ugi Island after making a forced water landing, and was subsequently rescued by Lt. Carten of VS68, and returned to USNB Segi (Segi Airfield, New Georgia Island).

Lt.(jg) Englade's memorial marker is located at St. Peter Catholic Church Cemetery, Louisiana.

---

[18] Declassified United States Naval Base – Segi – War Diary, 1 November 1943 – 7 November 1943.

Grumman TBF-1 (Source: National Archives photo no. 80-G-80154 – May 7 1943)

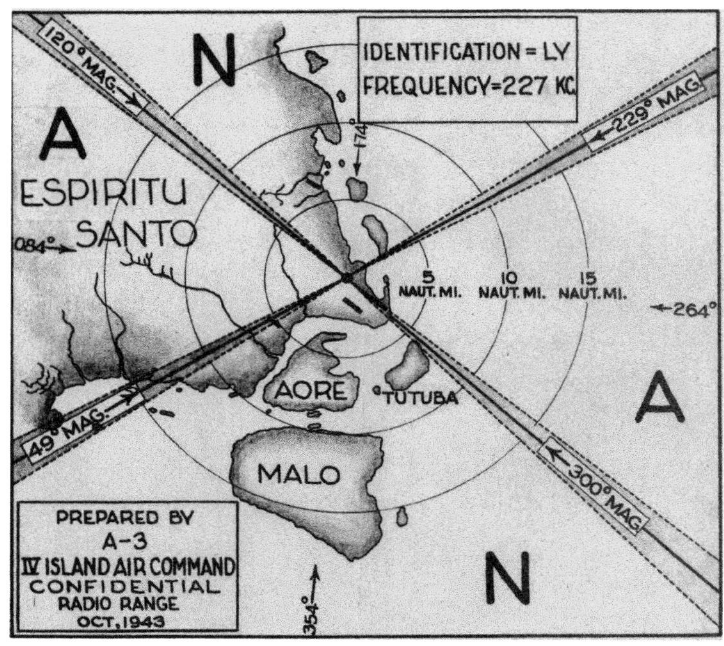

Radio Range of Espiritu Santo - October 1943 (Source: Leary Family Collection)

TBF Planes at Munda Airfield – October 26 1943, left to right: Plane #101, #104, #115, & #05 (Source: National Archives photo no. 342-FH-3A44429-80632A)

The above listed plane numbers had US Navy and US Marine Corps Aircraft Bureau Numbers (BuNos) assigned to each plane. Marine Corps aircraft were procured by the Navy, so they used Navy Bureau Numbers. By cross-referencing declassified Mission Reports[19] from 1943, a list of pilots who flew these actual TBF planes was generated.

Squadron Plane # / Bureau Plane # / Pilot name / Date of Flight / Squadron

#101 06190 Daugherty 10/26/43 VMTB-232, **McDonald 11/7/43 VC 38**, Leidecker 11/10/43 VMTB-143

#104 47504 Metzelaars 10/30/43 VMTB-232, **Gammage 10/31/43 VC 38**, Harris 11/10/43 VMTB -143

#115 47501 White 10/26/43 VMTB-232, Glenn 11/20/43 VMTB-143, Bauder 9/15/43 VMTB-233

#05 24182 **Leake 9/14/43 VC 38, Regan 10/26/43 VC38, Draughon 11/14 & 24/43 VC 38, Giblin 11/10/43 VC 38**, Boyden 11/20/43 VMTB-233, **Larson 10/2, 8, 9, & 10/43 VC 38**

[19] Mission Reports included in Appendix E.

TBF Planes at Munda Airfield – October 26 1943, right to left: Plane #118, #131, #108, #130, & #106 (Source: National Archives photo no. 342-FH-3A44430-A80632AC)

#118	06118	McCole 10/26/43 VMTB-232 and **Lt. (jg) Harry Wilson 10/28/43 VC 38** (killed on take-off at Munda and plane damaged beyond repair)
#131	47506	Morrison 10/31/43 VC 40 and **Leake 11/10/43 VC 38**
#108	06472	Bartholf 9/15/43 VMTB-233, **Larson 10/28/43 VC 38**, Webb 11/10 & 20/43 VMTB-143, Damiani 11/24/43 VMTB-233
#130	06341	Burris 10/26/43 VMTB-232, Collura 10/31/43 VC40, **Phillippi 11/10/43 VC 38**, Ranson 11/20/43 VMTB-143, **McDonald 11/24/43 VC 38**

Plane #108 (circled in red) was flown by Lt. William R. Larson of Hanks, North Dakota on October 28, 1943 while VC38, VC40, and VMTB-143 bombed and strafed Kara Airfield. These TBFs were a mix of TBF, TBF-1, and TBF-1c planes. The planes were all interchangeable between Naval and Marine squadrons based on Larson's Aviators Flight Log Book and the available Mission Reports. Other pilots of VC 38 are in **bold**.

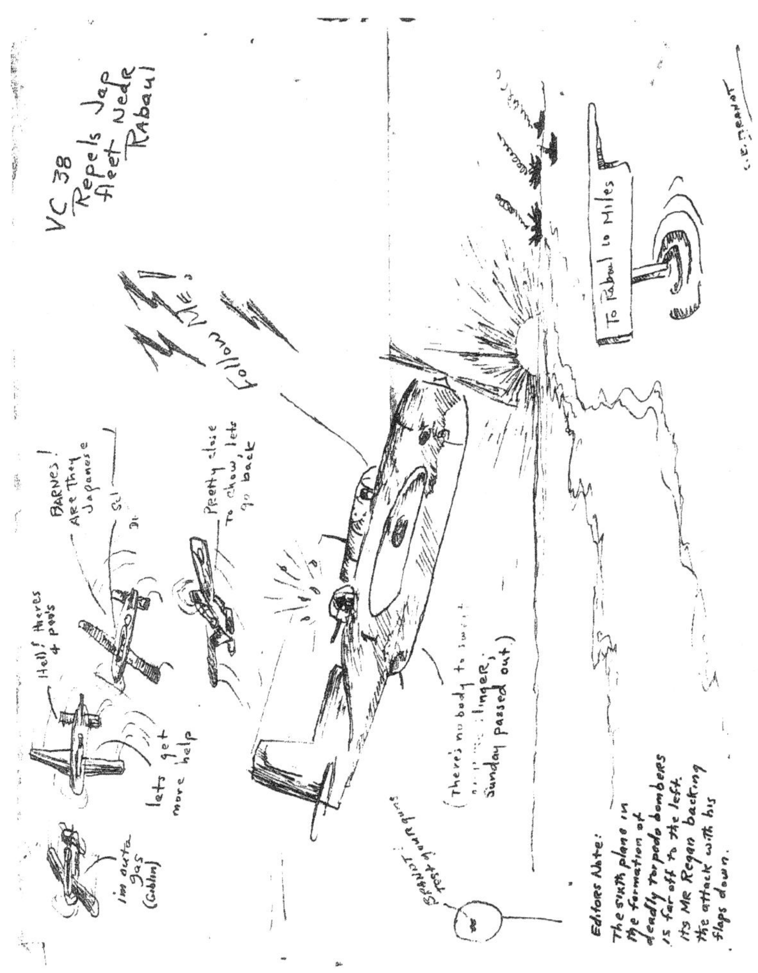

VC 38 Cartoon by Gunner C.E. Brandt

Source: W. Wagner

VC 38 at Luganville Airfield, Espiritu Santo Island – January 19 1944
(Source: W. Wagner)

Luganville Airfield – Bomber 3, Espiritu Santo Island – March 9 1944 (Source: National Archives photo no. 80-G-224013)

Close-Up View of VC 38 at Luganville Airfield, Espiritu Santo Island – January 19 1944

Front Row left to right: Robert M. Telfair, Jack P. Scholfield, Paul Beaumont, Larry H. Englade (KIA Feb 29, 1944), Dr. John T. Pitkin, Arthur McDonald, Steven H. Reed, James N. Truesdale, Herbert T. Leake (KIA Feb 20, 1944).

Row 2 L to R: Graham Tahler, Bud Kelley, Homer O Brooks, Clifford K. Spaulding, A.E. Droughon, Leland B. Cornell, Charles W. Hagans, Raymond A. Marshall, John A. Leary, Ben B. Rogers

Row 3 L to R: Thomas M. Gammage, David Bagley, Carl G. Knowles, Bruce C. Bishop, William E. Woodman, William P. Cawley

Row 4 Standing L to R: Alex J. Kostrzwsky, Walter G. Keil, Al Barbee, Lt. Cdr. Charles E. Brunton, Walter T. McNeil, Richard H. Sewell, Walter C. Hancock, Wilfred Zelenski, Elwood H. Meyer

Row 5 Standing L to R: Ben Tappan, John G. Shirley, L.D. Cooke, Richard W. Moore, Robert F. Regan, Joseph W. Marshall, Thomas P. Kelly, Grant A. Phillippi, Leroy Perkins, Robert B. Giblin, Sheldon Onley

(Source: Names of VC 38 pilots on back of photograph by Lt.(jg) John A. Leary. Photograph source: W. Wagner)

V.C. 38 OFFICERS' HOME ADDRESSES

NAME	STREET	CITY & STATE
J.P. SCHOLFIELD.	720 Main Street	Ft. Scott. Kansas.
J.A. LEARY	18 Wright St.	Hudson Falls, N.Y.
G. TAHLER	89-51 70 Rd.	Forest Hill, L.I.N
T.M. GAMMAGE	1334 S.W. 17th St.	Miami, Fla.
C.E. BRUNTON	465 E. Glenarm	Pasadena, Calif.
B.C. BISHOP	215 Richardson Av.	Lookout Mt. Tenn.
J.T. PITKIN	297 Linwood Ave.	Buffalo, N.Y.
R.A. MARSHALL		Leesburg, Va.
A. MCDONALD, JR.		Emmetsburg, Iowa.
A.E. DRAUGHON	1621 Irving	Muskogee, Okla.
R.B. GIBLIN	2137 Selby Ave.	St. Paul, Minn.
R.H. BEHN	92 Poplar St.	Floral Park, N.Y.
R.F. REGAN	110 Walden St.	Cambridge, Mass.
J.G. SHIRLEY, JR.	31 Overlook Terrace	N. Adams, Mass.
S.H. REED	Brook Lane	Corvallis, Oregon.
E.H. MEYER	1065 Gaylord St.	Denver, Colo.
R.H.SEWALL	291 Bacon St.	Waltham, Mass.
W.P. CAWLEY	556 Norton Ave.	Pittsburgh, Pa.
W.C. HANCOCK	%Mrs. Blake Ratliff.	Wadesboro, N.C.
J.W. MARSHALL		Fort. Summer, N.Mex.
R.H. SINGLETON	725 S. Skinlsen Blvd.	St.Louis, Mo.
C.G. KNOWLES	5014 Capitol Ave.	Omaha, Nebr.
W. ZELENSKI	6618 - 31st. Ave.	Kenosha, Wisc.
L. PERKINS	1401 E. 4th St.	N. Platte, Nebr.
B.M. ROBINSON	52 Glenwood Drive.	El Paso, Texas.
D. BAGLEY	361 Hillside Ave.	Hartford, Conn.
S. OLNEY	Box 301 Canyon.	Contra Costa,Co, Calif.
T.P. KELLEY	293 N. Broadway	Yonkers, N.Y.
W.E. WOODMAN	40 Burnet St.	Maplewood, N.J.
B. TAPMAN	9306 Rivershore Drive.	Niagara Falls, N.Y.
B.B. ROGERS	617 Grand St.	Machanicville, N.Y.
J.N. TRUESDALE	1244 Westover Terrace.	Greensboro, N.C.
A. ROBINS.	212 S. Grand Oaks, Av.	Pasadena, Calif.

List of VC 38 Officers' Home Addresses (Source: Leary Family Collection)

The Story of Commander Charles E. Brunton – VC 38

Charles was the Commander of VC 38. He was awarded the Distinguished Flying Cross (D.F.C) for action at Rabaul Harbor. On 17 February 1944, while leading a combined Navy and Marine mast-head bombing attack against enemy shipping in Rabaul Harbor, New Britain, he picked for his target an un-engaged enemy destroyer. In his approach to the target through heavy and intense anti-aircraft fire he was seriously wounded. Disregarding his own pain and personal safety he pressed home his attack with courage and determination securing a direct hit on the destroyer. This destroyer was later photographed close ashore with its stern awash. With the same courage and determination shown above, he flew his plane to its home base returning the other members of his crew to safety

Charles also served in Korea and became a Rear Admiral. Richard Wagner, Lucky's radioman, immediately flew with Commander Brunton following William's death and accompanied Cdr. Brunton during the Rabaul Harbor dive attack on February 17, 1944.

Distinguished Flying Cross

The President of the United States of America takes pleasure in presenting the Distinguished Flying Cross to Commander Charles E. Brunton (NSN: 0-62610), United States Navy, for heroism, distinguished service and outstanding leadership as Group Commander of Navy Composite Squadron THIRTY-EIGHT (VC-38), in the conduct of numerous missions against heavily defended enemy land positions and enemy shipping. On 17 February 1944, while leading a combined Navy and Marine mast-head bombing attack against enemy shipping in Rabaul Harbor, New Britain, he picked for his target an un-engaged enemy

destroyer. In his approach to the target through heavy and intense anti-aircraft fire he was seriously wounded. Disregarding his own pain and personal safety he pressed home his attack with courage and determination securing a direct hit on the destroyer. This destroyer was later photographed close ashore with its stern awash. With the same courage and determination shown above, he flew his plane to its home base returning the other members of his crew to safety. The conduct of this officer has at all times been in keeping with the highest traditions of the United States Naval Service.

Action Date: February 17, 1944

Service: Navy

Rank: Commander

Company: Composite Squadron 38 (VC-38)

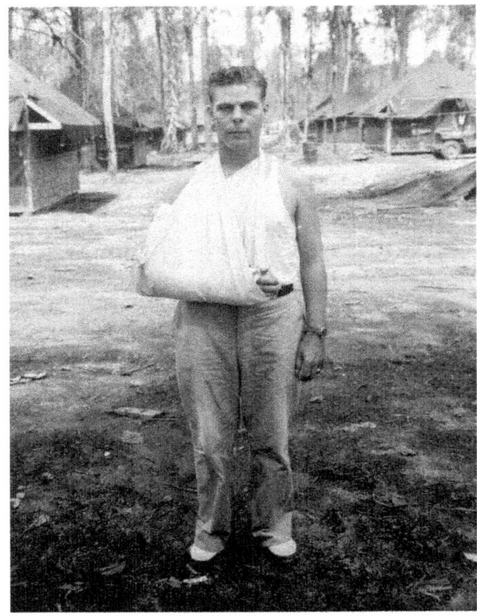

Cdr. Brunton wounded after Rabaul Attack – Bougainville Airfield (Source: Gregory Pons Collection)

Charles E Brunton

Birth: Apr. 29, 1906
Death: Jan. 7, 1993

Inscription:

RADM
US NAVY
WORLD WAR II
KOREA

Burial:
Golden Gate National Cemetery
San Bruno
San Mateo County
California, USA
Plot: 2A, 1426-A

The story of Lt.(jg) Joseph Nason and Thomas Furlong

SBD-3 Dauntless Bureau Number 06524

VC-38

On October 23, 1943, Pilot Lt (jg) Joseph G. Nason and gunner Thomas E. Furlong, Jr. took off from Munda Airfield, on a dive bombing mission to Bougainville. Nason and Furlong were on their first combat mission. The pair trained together as a crew. While dive bombing an anti-aircraft position near Kara Airfield, the plane was hit by anti-aircraft fire and caught fire. Nason bailed out virtually over Kara Airfield. His gunner Furlong was not seen to escape the stricken aircraft and was presumed to have been killed when it crashed.

Nason landed unhurt and managed to evade capture for a week. Captured, he was transported about a boat along the eastern coast of Bougainville to Buka. He was then taken aboard a Japanese destroyer to Rabaul. Nason was detained by the Japanese Army Kempei-tai (military police) in Rabaul, and later at Tunnel Hill POW camp. During his captivity, Nason was subject to harsh treatment and neglect. He was even used by the Japanese in a malaria medical experiment. Although sick, suffering from malnutrition and beriberi, Nason survived the war. He was one of only a handful of POWs that were liberated by Australians when Japan surrendered in September 1945.

Furlong was officially declared dead the day of the mission. He is memorialized on tablets of the missing at Manila American Cemetery.

Nason passed away at UMass Memorial Healthcare University Hospital, Worcester, MA, on October 12, 2012. He wrote a book about his history as a POW, Horio You Next Die!, by Joseph Nason. The story of Joe Nason is available for viewing at http://vimeo.com/65439421 .

Source: www.pacificwrecks.com/aircraft/sbd/03359.htm.

The Story of Lt.(jg) John A Leary

Source: Leary Family Collection

Judge John A. Leary was born on May 4th, 1919, the second of four children born to John and Adelia Leary. He graduated from St. Mary's Grammar School in 1932 and Hudson Falls High School in 1936. A graduate of Syracuse University with a BS degree, he went on to receive his LLB and JD from the Syracuse University College of Law. He began practicing law with the firm of Hart, Senior and Nichols of Utica, New York and subsequently returned to Hudson Falls where he practiced law for many years in an office over the present Evergreen Bank on Main Street.

From 1941 through 1945, Judge Leary was a carrier pilot in the United States Naval Air Force. During his tenure in the service, he was a two-time recipient of the Navy Cross and has shared his World War II experiences on a number of occasions with the students of Hudson Falls High School. From 1947 through 1949 he was a member of the Federal Bureau of Investigation. John married his wife, Maud, on September 13th, 1942.

John and Maud Leary (Source: Leary Family Collection

Judge Leary has served the community as a Justice of the Peace and as a member of the Kingsbury Town Board and he has been the recipient of the Liberty Bell award. During his career, he has also served as county attorney, district attorney and the administrator of the Assigned Counsel Plan. He has served as a judge in Washington County Court, Surrogate Court, Family Court and State Supreme Court as assigned. Judge Leary retired in December of 1989.

Judge Leary expressed tremendous pride in his Hudson Falls roots. The community was fortunate indeed to have another of its native sons return to the community that fostered his ideals. His interest in flying, originating during World War II, remained a constant - occasionally he could be seen taking off from Warren County Airport. He had three sons, two of whom are members of the area medical community and one who is an accomplished artist.

Judge Leary passed away on October 8, 2003.

John Leary- Torpedo Bomber Pilot

Midway was the turning point of the war. We had been at the [Battle of the] Coral Sea where we lost the USS Lexington. The USS Yorktown was badly damaged [at Coral Sea], but in any event the Japanese did not continue to invade New Guinea or Australia. Days later, after Coral Sea, when we arrived at Pearl Harbor we thought we were going home because the Yorktown was so badly damaged. But Admiral Nimitz had other ideas and he outranked most of us. They put on civilian workers to repair the damage and when the *Yorktown* sailed 72 hours later it still had quite a few civilian workers still aboard, repairing. They never mentioned their losses [of civilian workers] in the war.

Yorktown was hit again at Midway and they did abandon ship. But she stayed afloat and looked like she could make it, so about 200 men went back on board and unfortunately they were still on it when it was taken down by a submarine. But the battle was won principally, I think from our intelligence, because we outmaneuvered and outsmarted the Japanese.

From the island, the Marines were flying dive-bombers, which were outdated- the cockpit was made out of canvas, so they were a bit out of date. They had no diving flaps and they would dive beautifully, but there was no guarantee they would come back up.

There were only six Dive Bomb Fighter (DBF) torpedo planes involved, they were based on the island, only one returned and on that one, both crewmen were dead. These were the only DBFs they had; they had only torpedo planes, DBDs . There top speed was ...one hundred mph if they were doing well. They were no match for the Japanese. They launched fifty and had three come back. The carriers all together, that is all they had at the end of the day. George Gay was the only one (to survive) he had a ringside seat to the whole battle. He was in a life raft, so he was hanging on to them. George was the only survivor. He was a pilot and everyone else had been killed, everybody.

The Marines also had Brewster fighters, "Brewster Buffalos," they called them, I think they had 27. They lost all of those. They were just no comparison with the Japanese Zero. But with the help of God, the battle was won by the American carrier pilots, and we on *Yorktown* went over landed on USS Enterprise, some on USS Hornet. So we were holding our own. Later on we ended up at Guadalcanal, not too long after the Marines landed. They got into some open field and with one very short leave we went from Guadalcanal, I'm sure these gentlemen would know (points at Marines in room). The 1st Marines were at Guadalcanal and the 4th were at the north end on Bougainville and we ended up on Bougainville so we covered the Solomon Islands, all of them. And that cut the Japanese off because it destroyed their largest base at Rabaul Harbor, on New Britain. Rabaul had five Japanese airfields, a great harbor and we could hit it from Bougainville, and we did.

The correspondent that wrote this article - he was correspondent with the Chicago Tribune - two things about him: number one, he "demoted" me from Lieutenant Commander to Lieutenant Junior Grade, and then he wrote the article in a spirit of a party - he just wanted to have a good time.

Ex-athletes team up to sink twelve ships

Lt. (jg) John Leary and a TBF plane - assumed to be Otay Mesa, CA - July 16, 1943 (Source: Leary Family Collection)

Lieutenant Commander John Leary, Hudson Falls, was one of a group of former college athletes whose teamwork helped to knock out twelve Japanese ships in last Thursday's attack at Rabaul Harbor, the Navy disclosed today. The official account issued at a South Pacific airbase said that Leary, a coxswain of the 1941 Syracuse University crew, dropped a 2000 pound bomb with great accuracy on a Japanese cargo ship. He made the run over the ship at mast head height, braving heavy anti-aircraft fire from the vessel. In the same attack Lieutenant, Junior Grade, Robert F. Regan, 1941 catcher for the Harvard baseball team, demolished a Japanese vessel with a torpedo bomb and Lieutenant Junior Grade Bruce Bishop, star University of Tennessee quarterback, blew up an enemy patrol.

I took more fellas in with me than I brought home that day, unfortunately. It was 1944 because that's when they went in, on November 1st... [I was] about 23 or 24. It was the principal Japanese airbase. They had five Japanese airfields defending it. They had about 200 to 250 Japanese fighters there, which could have been interesting.

Hudson Falls man is aboard plane bombing Japanese cargo ship.

A short time ago, Mr. John Leary flew through a curtain of anti-aircraft machine gun fire to drop a 2,000-pound bomb on a Japanese cargo ship at Rabaul Harbor. Lieutenant Commander Leary, 24, of Wright Street, this village, a U.S. Navy torpedo bomber pilot and section leader in a hard-hitting squadron, flew in at masthead level to skip bomb the enemy ship.

All are second lieutenants. (Army Air Corps Photos)

Hudson Falls Marine Flier Bags Jap Ship Near Rabaul

BOUGAINVILLE (Delayed) — The little fellow who used to set the tempo as coxswain for the Syracuse university crew today flew through a curtain of anti-aircraft and machine-gun fire to drop a 2,000-pound bomb on a Japanese cargo ship in Keravia bay, a few miles south of Simpson Harbor, Rabaul.

He is Lt. (j. g.) John A. Leary, 24, Hudson Falls, N. Y., a U. S. Navy torpedo bomber pilot. A section leader in a hard-hitting squadron, Lieutenant Leary flew in at masthead level to skip-bomb the enemy ship.

It was his contribution to a morning raid that resulted in 12 ships, including one warship, being either sunk or damaged by Navy and Marine dive and torpedo bombers.

Lieutenant Leary, graduate of Syracuse in 1941, was seen to register a hit under the stern of the vessel. Other planes hit the same ship, rendering severe damage.

The former coxswain for the Orange crew has been on five Rabaul raids hitting shipping and airdromes. Before that he was among those who aided in knocking out the airfields at Kahili, Ballale, Kieta and other Jap stations in the south Bougainville and Shortland islands area.

He also participated in the bombing of Japanese shore positions shortly before U. S. Marines went ashore at Empress Augusta bay, Bougainville, November 1. Lieutenant Leary's fellow squadron members now fly off land taken away from the Japanese by the Leathernecks.

Dr. Belle Dodd To Talk Tuesday

Dr. Belle Dodd, Legislative representative, Teachers Union, will lecture on the "Equal Rights Amendment and Women in the War" at the Jewish Community Center, Washington avenue, on Tuesday at 8 p. m. The talk is sponsored by the education committee of the Knit for Victory club of Albany.

Those ships were reported by one of our submarines and they [the sub crew] couldn't do anything about it, because they had just finished up a patrol and were out of torpedoes. They [sub crew] followed these people with their naval escort into Rabaul harbor. They [sub crew] passed the word back to Pearl and they [radio control at Pearl] in turn got in contact with what they call "Com-air South", or "Command of the Air South." We were then called because we were the oldest outfit there [Bougainville]. We were briefed, then set out somewhere around midnight, we hit them around dawn. .. I was probably about 55 or 70 feet above the ship. We lost quite a few people, but the friends that I particularly had were in the troop transports.

We went up towards the Coral Sea on the U.S.S. Saratoga and two small carriers. One of the admirals came aboard, and he always wore a red cap. Well our carrier had duty that day, anti-sub duty. The Big DBF's that had four large depth charges and all the sonar buoys and all that. The sea on that day was as smooth as a tabletop, and they made only 17 knots on a good day. So the captain of our ship, the air officer and the air group commander, recommended "catapulting" off the ship. Just that, put on a catapult and shot off the ship. But the admiral said 'suppose the catapults are damaged?'. Still, he would have liked to see how they would work; well, none of us really wanted to do it. The first three planes went off, and they went down into the water and blew up, they never made it. The charges weren't set properly. A good friend of mine flew the last one off the ship, a man named Giblin. He was older than most of us and was a professor at the university of Minnesota. Well, Bob (Giblin) made it, he sunk below the bow, but eventually pulled up. He went on his patrol and when he got back, Giblin was called to the deck, the captain's deck and the admiral was going to question him. Now this was a three star admiral talking to a young lieutenant! Giblin didn't blink an eye, he (the admiral) asked him "what did you do that the others failed to do"? Giblin looked at the admiral and said, "I think that when they tried to climb, they pulled back on the stick." (That's the only way I ever heard of trying to climb was to pull back on the stick.) Giblin said, with a touch of sarcasm, "I just took the stick and held it off the water." Normally he would have been shot right there, but the admiral didn't say a damn word to him because he was in a bad bind. Giblin had the nerve to tell him he "held it off the water". So our people were thrilled with him.

The Marines and Navy pilots all went to the same flight school, although some had selected the Corps and some the Navy. But they all went through the same training. Joe Foss (leading ace of WWII, Joe Foss, the Marine pilot) and I, and Marion Carl, were in the same flight class. We've been friends over the years and Marion Carl ... was in charge of all investigations for the Marines until he retired, and he was murdered about a year ago. Someone broke into his house trying to rob them and attacked his wife, and he (Joe) tried to defend his wife, and he was killed. [I knew Joe Foss very well]...Joe sent me a story he wrote, an autobiography. He sent me a copy and I could hardly make out his signature. I called him and as it turned out that he had been in a little accident before that and had broken an arm and he was still trying to write with a broken arm. So Joe had let me know he had broken his arm. Joe was part Sioux - he was first president of the AFL, then governor of South Dakota.

When I came back finally, I had a couple of special projects. I was chief gunnery pilot for the Banshee, one of the first jets. One morning I went up for a test fire and a 20 millimeter shell exploded in the nose. The engines were in the back and when I pulled the trigger one of the 20's jumped the gun, it wasn't set right and blew the nose up. It was hard to tell who was screaming loudest, myself, or the Banshee! But it got down and landed all right. And they were very kind to me, the next morning they had a ceremony, I still have the medal. It's bigger than this, but it has more things on it I can't repeat here, but one of them was *"ENEMY PLANES DESTROYED: NONE, OURS: ONE".*

When I got out, I had a year in law school and I finished that up. Then being an Irish Catholic of my generation, you only had three options, to be a priest, a farmer, or a cop. So I went into the FBI.

Lt.(jg) John Leary - assumed to be Otay Mesa - July 16, 1943 (Source: Leary Family Collection)

I was banged up a bit but always made it back. I had two young fellas that were with me and I lost them both. My gunner was 18 years old, no 17, because it was his birthday the day he died. So, obviously he lied about his age to get in, and had a couple of bad days. There was a young man from around here, Randy Holmes, he hounded his parents to let him enlist because he was only 17. He went through apprentice seamen training, then he was ordered to the USS Oklahoma and he was in 2 weeks before Pearl Harbor. He was in it a couple days when it was bombed by the Japanese and capsized. [Editor's note: Randy Jones was on the *USS Oklahoma* on December 7, 1941, and had only been in Pearl Harbor 2 weeks prior to that. Randy Holmes was from Hudson Falls N.Y.]

Interviewer (Matthew Rozell): He didn't have much of a chance, did he?

John Leary: No, no- he didn't.

Judge John Leary passed away on October 8, 2003.

Interview originally recorded on 5/11/01

Source: http://www.hfcsd.org/district.cfm?subpage=439

The Story of Lt. Graham "Ham" Tahler

Lieutenant Graham Tahler, son of Mr. and Mrs. Abraham Tahler of Forest Hills, Long Island, was born on March 2nd, 1921. He attended the public schools of New York City, and studied at Queens College for 3 ½ years when he left to join the U.S. Navy. At Queens College he was captain of the baseball team, and a member of Alpha Lambda Kappa fraternity.

He received his wings in September of 1942 at Miami, Florida and reported to the West Coast. He was married on June 6, 1943 to Joan Margaret Wolf of Jamaica, New York, culminating a college romance. Best man at the wedding was Lt. John Leary of VC 38.

Graham and Joan Tahler – Wedding Day (Source: Leary Family Collection)

Lt. Tahler was a TBF pilot of Air Group 38. On his first tour of duty in the Pacific he was awarded the Distinguished Flying Cross for his part in the Solomon Islands and Rabaul campaigns.

He participated in combat missions at Okinawa and over Japan, and he led a major air strike on Tokyo from the aircraft carrier *Shangri-La*. He flew more than 140 aircraft carrier takeoffs.

After the war, he remained in the Navy and returned to college. He graduated from Columbia University. Other assignments included duty with the Navy's bureaus of personnel and operations, command of a Naval air training unit in Memphis and service on the staff of the chief of Naval air training, deputy to the president of the Naval War College and assistant chief for Naval reserve in the Bureau of Personnel.

He retired in 1974 after having served as commander of the 6th Naval district in Charleston, S.C. On his Navy retirement, Admiral Tahler moved to Pensacola, Florida. He returned to this area around 1980; at his death, he was living in Falls Church. He did volunteer deliveries for Meals on Wheels.

Graham Tahler, 77, died of leukemia October 31, 1998 at Bethesda Naval Medical Command.

His first wife, Joan Wolf Tahler, died in 1990.

Following is the citation with which the Distinguished Flying Cross was awarded to Lieutenant (junior grade) Graham Tahler, USNR:

Citation

"In the name of the President of the United States, the Commander South Pacific Area and South Pacfic Force takes pleasure in awarding the Distiguished Flying Cross:

"For extraordinary achievement while participating in aerial flight as pilot attached to a torpedo bombing squadron operating in the Solomon Islands area during the period from September 13, 1943 to March 5, 1944. In three tours of duy, Lieutenant TAHLER took part in forty-one strikes and special missions against heavily defended airfields and ground installations in this area. On most of these missions, he was subjected to intense anti-aircraft fire and enemy fighter plane opposition. On February 17, in a bombing attack against enemy shipping in Rabaul Harbor, he obtained a direct hit on an enemy transport. His outstanding skill and courageous devotion to duty contributed materially to the severe damage inflicted on the enemy and to the neutralization of Japanese airfields throughout the area. His conduct throughout was in keeping with the highest traditions of the United States Naval Service." – W.F. HALSEY, Admiral, U.S. Navy (Temporary Citation)

WWII Picture Collage of Lt. Tahler – assembled by wife Joan (Source: granddaughter Tamara Ashley)

The Story of Lt. Jack Prentice Scholfield

Source: Jim Scholfield

Jack P. Scholfield was born on January 4, 1920, and passed peacefully just shy of his 95th birthday, on December 11, 2014 at 2:00 pm in the presence of his immediate family.

Jack grew up and attended public schools, including high school and Junior College in Fort Scott, Kansas. He received a Bachelor of Science in Education from Kansas State Teachers College in Pittsburg, Kansas in 1941.

After working a short time for the Retail Credit Company in Kansas City and Joplin, Missouri, he enlisted in the Naval Flying Cadet program in November 1941, and reported for active duty on December 18, 1941 at Fairfax Field, Kansas City, Kansas. From there he went to Pensacola, FL for additional training and was certified a Naval Aviator on September 21, 1942.

Jack flew a Grumman Avenger (torpedo bomber) with Air Group VC 38 in the Solomon Islands campaigns and was awarded a Distinguished Flying Cross for skip bombing and sinking a Japanese freighter in Simpson Harbor, Rabaul on February 17, 1944. Jack joined VF(N) 91 in the fall of 1944, retrained as a Night Fighter pilot and flew an F6F5(n) while his squadron was attached to the aircraft carrier, *Bon Homme Richard*, flying numerous combat air patrols and strafing missions at night until the end of WWII.

Jack entered the University of Washington - School of Law on January 2, 1946 and graduated in June of 1948. He served as a Business Manager of the Washington Law Review for the academic year 1947-1948. Jack often spoke of his law school days and acquaintances made there as among his life's most enjoyable experiences. He commenced the practice of law with George Guttormsen and was later a partner in Guttormsen, Scholfield, Willits and Ager. The firm name was later changed to Scholfield and Stafford, and was until recently Stafford Frey Cooper.

Jack was appointed to the King County Superior Court by Gov. Dixie Lee Ray and was sworn in on September 30, 1977. He was elected to the State Court of Appeals and commenced service in that Court in 1982. He served two six-year terms, retiring in January 1995. While on the Superior Court he served as Presiding Judge for one year. He served a term of two years as Chief Judge of Division One of the Court of Appeals.

During his years of law practice, he became involved in Seattle-King County and State Bar activities, serving on numerous committees and was elected and served a term as President of the Seattle-King Co. Bar Association in 1971-1972. He was elected a Fellow in the American College of Trial Lawyers in 1972.

After retiring from the Court of Appeals in January 1995, Jack joined the Judicial Arbitration and Mediation Service, serving as a mediator and arbitrator until June 30, 2011.

Commencing in 2001, he served as volunteer attorney with the Eastside Legal Assistance Program (ELAP) conducting legal clinics designed to give legal advice and guidance to low income families, and in 2003 was named its Volunteer Attorney of the year. He was elected to the ELAP Board of Trustees in January 2004. Jack also served on the Washington State Bar Association Pro Bono and Legal Aid committee for two terms commencing on October 1, 2002.

Jack met his wife, Lucille Templeton, in El Centro, CA, while his squadron was stationed there in the summer of 1943 for experimental night flying work. They were married in the Memorial Presbyterian Church, West Palm Beach, FL on July 18, 1944. They had two sons, James and Donald. Donald died of cancer in September 1980, and James lives with his wife Margaret Booker in Los Gatos, CA where he is employed as an engineer with the Monterey Bay Aquarium Research Institute. Jack is also survived by a granddaughter, Samantha Scholfield, a graduate of UCLA. Jack was preceded in death by his sister, Ruth Bloodworth, his mother LuLynn Scholfield and his father John P. Scholfield. Jack is interred next to his son Donald and his wife of 70 years, Lucille, at Sunset Hills Memorial Park in Bellevue.

Source: The Seattle Times Obituary

During a telephone interview on September 27, 2013, Jack stated that Brunton [Charles] was the best commanding officer he ever had and he [Brunton] kept the unit in constant training. He also was most proud of his Distinguished Flying Cross and flew that mission right behind Commander Brunton. He flew with, "Bill Larson [Lt. William R Larson] on many missions and Bill Larson was very consciences and well liked."

Following is the citation with which the Distinguished Flying Cross was awarded to Lieutenant Jack Scholfield, USNR:

Citation

"The President of the United States takes pleasure in presenting the Distiguished Flying Cross:

"For heroism and extraordinary achievement in aerial flight as a Pilot of a Torpedo Bomber Plane in Composite Squadron THIRTY-EIGHT, during action against enemy Japanese forces in the Solomon Islands Area, September 13, 1943, to March 5, 1944. Participating in numerous successful strikes and special missions against heavily defended airfields and ground installations, many of which were carried out in the face of intense antiaircraft fire, Lieutenant (then Lieutenant, Junior Grade,) Scholfield pressed home an attack and scored a direct hit on a Japanese transport in Rabaul Harbor. His devotion to duty was in keeping with the highest traditions of the United States Naval Service." – For the President, James Forrestal, Secretary of the Navy

The Story of Lt. Robert B. Giblin

Lt. (jg) Robert Giblin in a F4F Wildcat - Luganville Airfield, Espiritu Santo January 19 1944 (Source: Leary Family Collection)

Lieutenant Robert B. Giblin, son of Mr. and Mrs. P.H. Giblin of St. Paul, Minnesota was born November 13th, 1917. He attended St. Mark's Parochial School, Maria Sanford Junior High and Central High School and graduated from the college of St. Thomas in June 1940, cum laude. All schools attended were in St. Paul. In high school and college, Lt. Giblin competed in tennis and played one year of hockey in college. He was Minnesota college doubles champion in tennis in 1938 and 1939. After graduation from college, he taught and coached in the public school at Falfurrias, Texas.

Robert enlisted in the Navy in August 1940 as apprentice seaman, V-7. On June 16, 1941 he was called to active duty to attend Naval Reserve Midshipman School at Northwestern University, Chicago, Illinois from which school he graduated and commissioned Ensign September 12, 1941. He earned his wings at NAS Miami, Florida on July 8, 1942.

Lt. Giblin took advanced operational training with Advanced Carrier Training Group, NAS Norfolk, Virginia. He then joined VGS-21 on the west coast. This squadron successively was designated VC-21 and then VC-38. With VC-38 he made a tour of duty in the Solomon Islands off land bases at Guadalcanal, Munda, and Empress August Bay, Bougainville. He flew 25 attacks and was awarded the Distinguished Flying Cross (D.F.C.) after returning to the USA. Robert was awarded two Gold Stars in lieu of 2nd D.F.C and Air Medal for action on July 24, 1945 near Kuse Naval Base, Japan and for aerial flight at Okinawa Jima and Kika Jima. Robert also served in Korea and Vietnam.

On December 27, 1944, he married Lt. (jg) Viola Turck of the Waves, a St. Paul girl. Robert passed away on July 2nd, 1984.

Following is the citation with which the Distinguished Flying Cross was first awarded to Lieutenant (junior grade) Robert B. Giblin, USNR:

Citation

"In the name of the President of the United States, the Commander South Pacific Area and South Pacfic Force takes pleasure in awarding the Distiguished Flying Cross:

"For extraordinary achievement while participating in aerial flight as pilot attached to a torpedo bombing squadron operating in the Solomon Islands area during the period from September 13, 1943 to March 5, 1944. In three tours of duy, Lieutenant GIBLIN took part in thirty-five strikes and special missions against heavily defended airfields and ground installations in this area. On most of these missions, he was subjected to intense anti-aircraft fire and enemy fighter plane opposition. On February 17, in a bombing attack against enemy shipping in Rabaul Harbor, he obtained a direct hit on an enemy transport. His outstanding skill and courageous devotion to duty contributed materially to the severe damage inflicted on the enemy and to the neutralization of Japanese airfields throughout the area. His conduct throughout was in keeping with the highest traditions of the United States Naval Service." – W.F. HALSEY, Admiral, U.S. Navy

Four Men Decorated at Air Station

Arlington Times – June 26, 1944

Three officers and an aircrewman received decorations for service in the combat zone at the Arlington Naval Auxilary Air Station on Monday, June 26th, when Rear Admiral Ralph Wood, USNR Commander Fleet Air, Seattle, presented the awards for Admiral W.F. Halsey.

The Distiguished Flying Cross was received by Robert H. Behn, of Floral Park, New York; Arthur McDonald, Jr., of Emmetsburg, Iowa, and Robert F. Regan, of Cambridge, Massachussetts, all naval aviators and Lieutenants, junior grade, USNR Richard C. Wagner, an Aviation Radioman first class, of Watertown, South Dakota, received the Purple Heart for wounds in combat. All four are members of the Fleet Air Detachment at the Station.

Following is the citation with which the Distinguished Flying Crosses were awarded:

Citation

"In the name of the President of the United States, the Commander South Pacific Area and South Pacfic Force takes pleasure in awarding the Distiguished Flying Cross for services as set forth in the following citation:

"For extraordinary achievement while participating in aerial flight as pilot attached to a torpedo bombing squadron operating in the Solomon Islands area during the period from September 13, 1943, to March 5, 1944. In three tours of duty, Ensign Behn took part in twenty-one strikes and special missions against heavily defended airfields and ground installations in this area. On most of these missions, he was subjected to intense anti-aircraft fire and enemy figher plane opposition. On February 17, in a bombing attack against enemy shipping in Rabaul Harbor, he

secured a direct hit on an enemy transport. His outstanding skill and courageous devotion to duty contributed to the severe damage inflicted on the enemy and to the neutralization of Japanese airfields throughout the area. His conduct throughout was in the highest traditions of the United States Naval Reserve." – W.F. HALSEY, Admiral, U.S. Navy.

All three citations were exactly the same, except for the number of strikes, or missions involved. Lieutenant Regan flew on 32, McDonald on 29, and Behn on 21. Admiral Wood congradulated the aviators, and wished them all another chance at the Japs. They are all in further training for return to the combat zone in the near future.

Showing Navy men after receiving decorations from Admiral Wood: Left to right—Lieut. (j. g.) Robert F. Regan; Lieut. (j. g.) Arthur McDonald; Lieut. (j. g.) Robert H. Behn; Richard C. Wagner, radioman 1st class.

Story of Radioman Richard C. Wagner and his War Diary

Richard (Wag) Clayton Wagner was Lt. William Larson's radioman and was born in Watertown, South Dakota on May 25, 1918. On June 26, 1944, he was awarded the Purple Heart for wounds in combat. Richard served until December 8, 1945. Wag settled in San Diego where he met his wife, graduated from college, and started a photography business. He is buried at the Fort Rosecrans National Cemetery overlooking the Pacific Ocean and the various U.S. Navy bases in San Diego Bay. His son, Walt, lives in Carlsbad, CA, and has been a great source of information on his father and the VC 38 Squadron for this book. His father's war photographs include two pictures of Lt. William Larson from Hanks, North Dakota. Wag passed away on September 24, 1982. (Photo Source: Walt Wagner)

War Diary of Richard Wagner

Service: US Navy
Enlisted: December 8, 1941
Discharged: December 8, 1945

1/6/42-1/18/42	Reported to Omaha for physical, stayed two weeks
1/19/42-3/2/42	Arrived at NTS Great Lakes for four weeks of boot training, shots every Friday (sick) 100% on Radio Test, ordered to Seattle for 16 weeks of radio school.
3/17/42-7/1/42	Radio School, NAS Seattle
7/2/42-9/15/42	Assigned to VGS-21 Squadron, Seattle
9/16/42-1/2/43	GS-21 to Alameda, CA to train (ARM 3c)
12/42	Log Book Entries Start with VGS-21, Three familiarizations flights
1/2/43-3/15/43	VT-38, Alameda
1/43	Three familiarization flights with three different pilots all later killed
2/43	First squadron to receive new TBF's, Field Carrier Landing Practice (FCLP)
3/16/43-5/20/43	VT-38, NAAS Brown Field, San Diego
3-7/43	Moved to Otay Mesa, Carrier ops on USS Pareton (?), landing accident
5/20/43-6/28/43	VT-38, NAS El Centro

6/28/43-8/1/43	VT-38, NAAS Brown Field
7/2/43	**Assigned to Pilot, Larson, from North Dakota, later killed returning from Sydney**
8/1/43-8/27/43	VT-38, *USS Long Island*
8/1/43	Left San Diego for South Pacific with VC-38 and VC-40 at about 4 pm aboard the USS Long Island, stopped in Hawaii for two days (8/8-10), crossed the equator (8/14).
8/17/43	Arrived in Pago Pago –Samoa at noon and I was on the beach by two. Johnson and I walked all over and bought some beads.
8/25/43	Today we arrived at our destination. Last night we had a raid. I saw my first search lights playing in the sky looking for the enemy.
8/27/43-10/17/43	Bomber #1, Espirito Santo (Buttons)
9/13/43	Ferry planes to Guadalcanal (Cactus)
9/15/43	Today I went on my first strike against the Japs. It was the Island of Ballale a few miles from Bougainville. Ballale is a small island with a bomber strip covering almost the entire island. There were lots of heavy AA and zeros. One zero started a run on us but a P39 shot him down before he got a good start. During the three day attack on Ballale we **lost two TBFs[20] and three F6Fs**. Two of the fighter pilots were picked up but the other was not[21]. We [Navy & Marine fighters] **shot down 5 zeros**.
9/17/43	Return to Santos and for a month operated off the *USS Breton.*
10/17/43-1/23/43	VT-38, Munda Point, New Georgia
10/17/43	Left Santos for Munda on the Island of New Georgia. We were the first TBF squadron to be based at Munda (Shag)
10/26/43	Attack Kahili on the Island of Bougainville. We encountered a great deal of heavy A.A. and also light A.A. I saw two Jap bombers on the ground.

---

[20] Pilot 1st Lt. Edward Albert Croker, O-014785, Gunner Cpl William Lloyd Casper, 383805 , and Radio PFC Henry W. Schroeder, 447659, of VMTB-233 were declared MIA after this attack. The crew took off from Fighter One on Guadalcanal. They were last seen on the bomb run over Ballale Island, but were missing thereafter. Ditched or bailed out in the vicinity. Croker was taken prisoner, the other crew did not make it out of the aircraft. Croker was transported aboard the Kokai Maru and transported to Rabaul (this ship was later sunk on February 21, 1944). Croker was imprisoned at the Navy's 81st Guards Unit. During January 1944, Gregory Boyington and he were cell mates.

Pilot Lt(jg) Rowland D. Hahn, O-121709, Gunner AMM2C William M. Ellis Jr., 2240025, Radio ARM2c Richard T. Dunn, 6142032, and Observer AMM1C Charles E. Wells, 3423028, of VC-40 were declared MIA on September 16, 1943. They took off from Fighter One on Guadalcanal on a bombing mission over Ballale Island. Armed with bombs fused with 4/10 second fuses. Over the target at 2,000' this aircraft released its bomb which exploded prematurely under the plane, blowing off one of the wings. The Avenger was observed to crash into the sea off the southeastern shore of the island.

[21] Lt. (jg) Wayne E. Presley of VC38 took off from Munda Airfield in his F6F-3 Hellcat fighter, as part of the escort for 24 TBFs and 31 SBDs attacking Ballale Island. Over the target, 40-50 intercepting Zeros and Tonys were met, and heavy anti-aircraft cover was encountered over the target. Presley and his Hellcat (Bureau Number 25940) was observed to crash into the sea and is listed as MIA.

	Everyone returned ok[22].
10/28/1943	Attack Kara on Bougainville. It was a bad day from the start. **Lt. Wilson was killed on the takeoff**. Jeffrey got hit in the back by a 20mm. Very little heavy AA but a lot of small stuff.
10/30/43	Attack Kara on Bougainville. About the same as the last attack. Not much heavy A.A. but a lot of 20 & 40 mm. Everyone returned ok.
10/31/43	Attack Kara on Bougainville. The heavy AA is about all gone and the small guns aren't firing as much as before. The B24s went in just about 30 secs before we did and it was a very good job. We dropped our usual 2000 lb bomb. I haven't seen a Zero since. Tomorrow there will be a landing on Bougainville by the Marine Raiders It is to take place in the Empress Augusta Bay area.
11/1/43	The Bougainville landing was quite successful. Just before the actual landing the ships shelled the beach quite heavily. The landing was met with some opposition but not too much. Our planes were covering the landing and spotting enemy guns for the ground unit.
11/2/43	Last night the Japs sent eight cans [destroyers] and four cruisers to get the landing party at Empress Augusta Bay. Our cruisers intercepted them and hit them quite hard. We were called out early loaded with torpedoes and tried to catch the ships before they reached Rabaul. We followed the oil slick left by the damaged Jap ships all the way to Rabaul but we didn't contact them before we were about out of gas and Rabaul was too hot at that time.
11/10/43	Attack Buka Airdrome on the Island of Buka. A great deal of heavy and light AA was encountered. The Marines lost two SBDs[23]. Our attack was very successful due to the fact that it was quite a surprise to them. We dropped our 2000 lb on the runway and I saw two ammunition dumps blow up.
11/14/43	Attack Jap ground troops in the Empress Augusta Bay Region. Our ground troops had too much to handle so we dropped one hundred lbs bombs on their direction. We killed about 300 Japs and those who were still alive were stunned so that our troops just stuck them with a knife.
11/20/43	Bombed Japanese troops on Bougainville. We flew very low and I got a good look at some of the encampments.
11/22/43	Attack Kahili Airdrome on Bougainville. A small amount of AA and light gunfire was encountered. The strip was full of holes and quite out of commission. Enemy air opposition here is all over.
11/24/43	Attack Tarlena. It looked like the Japs were going to build another strip near Buka so we nipped it in the bud. Quite a bit of heavy AA and small fire.
12/1/43	Attack Kara on Bougainville. Very little AA fire – Strip is out of

[22] First Lieutenant Philip Field, USMC VMTB 232 pilot, Sergeant Edward R Dzama, turrret gunner, and Private Joseph D Miller, radio gunner, flying in Plane Bu.No 6416 were observed to pull out of glide at 1000 feet. The engine was on fire, and after making a turn to the left, the plane dove into the water at a 20 degree angle about half way between the beach and Erventa Island. Two men were seen to jump; one chute opened; the other did not and the man was seen to go into the water. No other information was obtainable.

[23] Lt. Francis Bernard McIntyre, USNR VC-24 pilot and ARM2 William L Russel, gunner, flying in a SBD-5 Dauntless (Bu. No 35931) did not return from bombing mission against Buka and Bonis. In 2007, the wreckage and the remains of the two naval personnel were discovered by locals near Buka Airfield. Both crewmen were buried at Arlington National Cemetery in 2010.

	commission.
12/11/43	Attack Jakohina it is a Jap supply base near Kahili. We made a good hit on a house. Some small fire but no heavy A.A.
12/12/43	Attack Kieta Airdrome on the east side of Bougainville. No heavy AA but some small guns were firing.
12/13/43	Attach Chabai ground and coastal guns. We made a direct hit on a big coastal gun with a 2000 lb bomb.
12/15/43	Left Munda for our rehabilitation leave in Sydney Australia
12/27/43	**Mr. Larson was killed** returning from Sydney. The DC he was in crashed after leaving New Caledonia
1/7/44	I started flying with Comm. C.E. Burton our skipper.
1/23/44-3/20/44	VT-38, Empress Augusta Bay, Bougainville
1/23/44	Left Santos for Piva Airdrome on the Island of Bougainville, Empress Augusta Bay.

1/27/44 **Attack Tabera Airdrome on the Island of New Britain near Rabaul. We encountered a lot of AA and about 60 Zeros. I was hit by a 40 mm in the face and leg. Kemper, the gunner, came down out of the turret to give me first aid. I looked out and saw a zero making a run on us, so Kemper got back up and took a shot at him. I was plenty worried for a while because I was bleeding so much. Kemp came back down, and after I quit bleeding I laid down in the middle comp. The skipper made good time coming back from Rabaul. The meat wagon met us as soon as we landed, taking me to the hosp. The doctors took three pieces of shrapnel out of my eye. I still have a few pieces in me but feel ok. (27 zeros)**

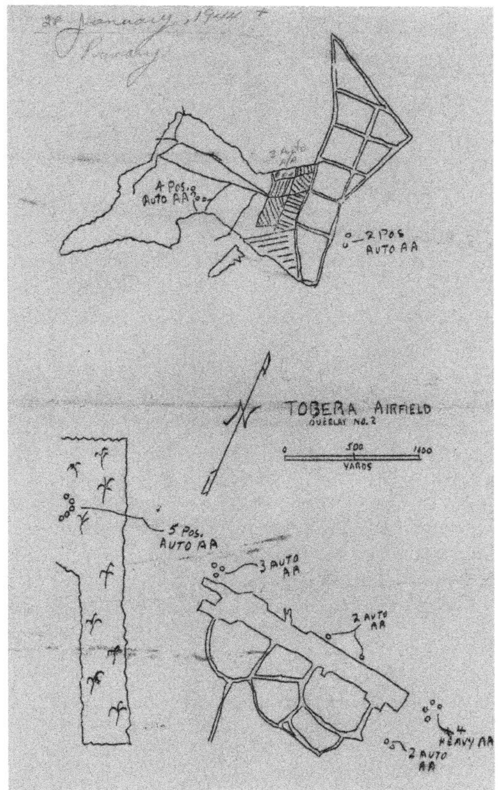

VC 38 John Leary's Map of Tobera Airfield (Source: Leary Family Collection)

2/5/44 Attack Lakauni Airdrome near Rabaul. AA was quite heavy, also small guns were firing at us. There were a few zeros in the vicinity, but none took a pass at us. This was my first raid since I was hit and I was sweating it out plenty. I saw a P40[24] and a F4U spin-in, also saw a few zeros go in. One TBF[25] didn't come back.

2/10/44 Attack Lakuni (night). After returning from the toughest strike I have ever made, I can say it is great to be alive. Last night six TBF's hit three strips at Rabaul. We were over the target about 15 minutes before dawn, and I believe we surprised them. However surprised they were in just about 30 secs after we started our glide they had their lights on us and we never once lost them. They fired every gun near the strip at us but failed to get any hits. We were under fire for about three minutes and it was heavy and light both concentrating on just two planes. There was at least one zero, but we didn't get a shot at him, nor he at us, however, he did drop a phosphorus bomb on us.

2/11/44 Spare for Tobera strike. We were spare and turned back before we got to the target. Our planes met approximately 25 zeros. Lost one F4U[26].

2/14/44 Attack Tobera Airdrome. Heavy AA was more accurate today, although it wasn't as heavy as before. Our plane had two very near misses, but no holes. We dropped 6-100's and 6-250's in the revetments making very good hits. We started three fires that were visible for almost a hundred miles. Last night the Marines lost six TBF's[27] and on the way back we were searching for some of the crews, but no luck. I saw a few zeros but none of them got through the fighter defense.

2/17/44 Shipping strike – Keravia Bay. Today was another bad day. The skipper was hit by machine gun fire breaking his arm and a flesh wound in the leg. He made a direct hit on a DD and was hit about the same time. There was plenty of AA both heavy and light, also saw a few zeros. I saw at least twenty float type airplanes in the bay near the ships. The skipper did a wonderful job flying the plane back in his condition. Both Kemper and I were afraid he was going to pass out from loss of blood and spin in all the way back.

2/20/44 Attack ground positions just a few miles south of our camp. Our target was a bridge so the Japs couldn't move any more heavy art.

---

[24] Flying Officer Ronald Bremner (422361) of the RNZAF flying a P-40N-1-CU Kittyhawk (Serial #NZ3120), took off from Torokina Airfield on an escort mission for 48 SBDs and 18 TBFs attacking Lakunai Airfield near Rabaul. After the bombing raid, the formation was intercepted by enemy fighters that followed them southward. This P-40 failed to return from the mission.

[25] Following a bombing raid on Lakunai Airfield, Rabaul on February 5, 1944, pilot First Lt. Stephen W Painter, Jr, turret gunner Harold Edward Dey, and radio gunner Charles S Brewer did not return in Plane #204 to Piva Airfield. Painter was captured and held as a POW until his death at Rabaul. No information is available on Dey and Brewer, but they are both listed as death 1/17/1946 at Manila American Cemetery

[26] Pilot 1st Lt. Allan S Harrison, 0-21213, of VMF-212, flying a F4U-1A Corsair (Bureau #55908) was lost on a mission to Rabaul, due to enemy action on February 11, 1944.

[27] Early morning on February 14, 1944, 26 TBF-1s (VMTB 134 & 233, VC38) loaded with MK 12-1 mines, took part in a night mining operation in Simpson Harbor, Rabaul. Mines were dropped by parachutes from TBFs. Japanese search lights picked up planes and intense accurate AA was encountered. Six planes and crew were missing, of these, 4 probably shot down, two in harbor and two on land side, three definitely flamers. Pilots missing include: Lt. Barthoff, Lt. Cornelius, Lt. Hathway, Lt. Fowler, Lt. Boyden, and Lt. Sherman – Strike Command Report by J.E. Butler, G-3, Strike Command

	Up this way. We missed the bridge. **Leake went in just as he was pulling out of his glide. Dunton was gunner, and Barcalla Radioman**[28].
3/4/44	DC-3 Bougainville to Cactus
3/5/44	DC-3 Cactus to Segi
3/10/44	DC-3 Segi to Cactus
3/20/44-4/22/44	VT-38, *USS Long Island*, Pacific Ocean
4/44	No Entries
5/20/44-6/21/44	VT-38, NAS Seattle
5/26/44	Seattle
6/21/44	Seattle, Seattle to Arlington
1/44-8/21/44	T-38, NAAS, Arlington, WA
7/44	Arlington
8/44	Arlington
8/24/44-10/23/44	VT-38, NAAS Ream Field, San Diego Met NB in 1944
10/23/44-11/2/44	VT-38, NAAS Holtville, CA
10/44	Holtville
11/2/44-1/2/45	VT-38, NAS Livermore, CA
11/45	Livermore
1/2/45-3/1/45	VT-38, NAS Klamath Falls, OR
1/45	Livermore
2/45	Livermore
3/3/45 – 6/9/45	VT-38, NAAS Brown Field, San Diego
3/45	Brown
4/45	Brown
5/45	Brown
6/9/45-10/18/45	VT-80, NAAS Ream Field, San Diego
6/45	Brown, Transferred to VT-80, Ream
7/45	Ream
8/45	Ream, 8/10 VJ Day
11/45	Ream
12/8/45	Discharged at San Diego

Source: Walt Wagner of Carlsbad, California – September 16, 2013

[28] On February 20, 1944, Lt. Herbert Tucker Leake, Santiago Barcala (ARM3/c), and Willard Earl Dunton (AOM1/C) are missing in action as result of crash of plane #103 during a bomb and strafe mission on bridges and AA installations at the Monoitu Mission area located on Bougainville. Plane #103 was loaded with 1x2000# 1/10 second delay bomb and was seen to make steep dive from 3000-feet and to pull out (after release) at approximately 500-feet. Just after the plane levelled off with approximate speed of 200k one half of the starboard wing came off, probably as a result of the bomb blast, and the plane flipped over on its back and crashed in the jungle in the Monoitu Mission area.

Released official Navy Photograph Date 6-27-1944
Admiral Wood congratulates Richard C.Wagner ARM 1/c
of Watertown, S.Dakota on the Purple Heart
Unit: U.S.Naval Air Station, Seattle, Washington

The Story of Lt.(jg) Steve H. Reed - SBD Pilot of VC38

May 11, 1920 — Jan. 26, 2012

Stephen Hartwell Reed died Jan. 26, 2012, at his home in Corvallis. He died in the same room in which he was born on May 11, 1920, to Edwin Thomas Reed and Katherine Hartwell Reed.

He graduated from Corvallis High School in 1938, and attended Oregon State College until enlisting in the U.S. Navy in 1941 to begin flight training.

Ensign Reed earned his wings in August 1942, and was first assigned to the aircraft carrier USS Long Island for training in carrier operations. Before being assigned to combat in the South Pacific, Stephen married Mary J. Kollins on Valentine's Day, 1943.

Shortly after his wedding, Stephen joined the Air Group VC38 Dive Bomber Squadron, which was assigned to combat operations in the New Hebrides in the South Pacific. He flew numerous raids in his SBD-4 dive bomber. He also flew combat missions against Japanese forces from the island of Bougainville. He served nine months in the South Pacific.

Stephen left the Navy in the fall of 1945. He returned to Oregon State College in January 1946 to complete his business degree. In 1946, Stephen and Mary purchased the soda fountain in the Memorial Union building on the OSC campus, and named it the O'Club. During the 13 years they operated the fountain, Steve and Mary thoroughly enjoyed their interactions with students and faculty. They became avid Beaver fans, and over the years attended hundreds of football and basketball games.

In 1960, Stephen returned to Oregon State University as a student in elementary education. He received his teaching certificate, and taught in the Corvallis School District for 15 years. When he retired, Stephen enjoyed salmon fishing, OSU athletics and time at Triangle Lake. In 1991, Stephen's wife, Mary, died after 48 years of marriage.

In September 1992, Stephen married Lucille (Lucy) Rogers. They spent recent years enjoying time with family and friends both at their home on Southwest Brooklane Drive and at Triangle Lake, traveling in their motor home and on ocean cruises, and sharing happy hour with friends.

Source: www.findagrave.com

Gunner Benjamin Wright • Pilot William R. Larson "Lucky" • Radioman Richard (Wag) Wagner – Bomber Strip at Munda Airfield, November 12, 1943 (bottom photos source: Donna Mattson [Greslie] and W. Wagner)

Lt. William Rudolf Larson of VC 38

Gunner W.L. Rice • Radioman Alton Earl Bond • Pilot Lt. Grant A Phillippi – Bomber Strip at Munda Airfield, November 1943 (Source: Lt. Col. Daniel Phillippi)

Gunner Lester E. Dale • Pilot Lt. John A. Leary • Radioman Donald R. Greslie – Bomber Strip at Munda Airfield, November 1943 (Source: Leary Family Collection)

Gunner R.R. O'Daniel • Radioman Vincent Eugene Boyle • Pilot Lt. (jg) Herbert Tucker Leake (KIA Feb 20, 1944) – Bomber Strip at Munda Airfield, November 1943 (Source: James Boyle)

Gunner Frank J. Dills • Pilot Lt. Jack P. Scholfield • Radioman Joe V Ulrich – Bomber Strip at Munda Airfield, November 1943 (Source: Jim Scholfield)

Douglas SBD Dauntless of VC 38 over ocean (Source: W. Wagner)

TBF crashed in landing – Bougainville
February 1944 (Source: W.Wagner)

TBF over ocean – Pilot Lt. (jg) Jack P. Scholfield flying (Source: W.Wagner)

TBFs Lined Up at Munda Airfield December 6 1943 (Source: National Archives photo no. 80-G-57251)

Side view of TBF plane (Source: Public Domain)

DIRECTIONS FOR APPLYING DECALCOMANIAS

1. Clean surface to which transfer will be applied of all greasy or oily substances.
2. Submerge decal in water for 30 seconds.
3. After paint film loosens from the paper backing slide it off on to desired location.
4. Remove all air or water bubbles.
5. Wash face of sign thoroughly to remove all excess adhesive. This will prevent breaking or curling of sign.

Graphic Arts Dept.
N.A.S. S.D.

These "score cards" are furnished by

THE ASSEMBLY AND REPAIR DEPARTMENT
U.S. NAVAL AIR STATION
SEATTLE, WASHINGTON

BEST OF LUCK

Stock replenished upon request.

Manufactured by A&R Dept.
N.A.S. San Diego, Calif.

Decalcomanias (Source: W. Wagner)

Shellback Initiation: Dunk tank (center of photo) and Beating Line (upper right). VC 38 aboard the USS Long Island, August 14, 1943, crossing of the Equator.

Shellback Initiation: King Neptune & his court - USS Long Island August 14, 1943 crossing of the Equator. (Source of both photos: W Wagner)

TBF over the bow - assumed to be USS Breton (Source: W.Wagner)

Tent in Munda - Signpost: *Munda Biltmore* – November 19, 1943
Front Row L to R: Alton Earl Bond, Robert E. Tuck
Back Row L to R: Walter Martin Haller, J.F. McKenna, R.E. Schramm
(Source: W. Wagner)

Biltmore Annex (bomb shelter), Munda – November 19, 1943
Radioman Vincent Eugene Boyle of VC 38 (Source: James Boyle)

Munda – November 8, 1943
L to R: Radiomen of VC 38: Leo Ambrose Lane, W.J. Misner, Robert Petry Buis, Richard Clayton Wagner, Donald R. Greslie (Source: W. Wagner)

Hotel Del Fubar – Piva – March 3, 1944
Front Row L to R: radioman Richard Wagner, Pain, turret gunner R.R. O'Daniel
Standing Row L to R: turret gunner E.C. Barnes, turret gunner E.E. Brewer, C.E. Brandt, gunner C.R. Payne (Source: W. Wagner)

Left to Right – W.L. Rice, "Wag" Wagner, "Bitter" Payne, "Agitator" Kemper, and "Zoot Suite" Brewer - Radiomen & Gunners of VC 38 – Piva - March 3, 1944 (Source: W. Wagner)

Munda – November 8, 1943
Front Row L to R: turret gunner Lester E. Dale, turret gunner E.E. Brewer, turret gunner Willard Earl Dunton (KIA February 20, 1944 over Bougainville)
Standing Row L to R: turret gunner R.A. Paul, Pain, turret gunner Benjamin W. Wright
(Source: Donna Mattson [Greslie])

TBF-1 at Munda with damaged wing as a result of Jap AA fire – October 1943 (Source: National Archives photo no. 80-G-295284)

Bomb train passes by TBF (Plane #19 – Bureau #23970) at Munda – October 28 1943 (Source: National Archives photo no. 80-G-56476)

Dive bomb attack of TBFs on Jap radar station on Short Island, Solomons – December 6 1944 (Source: National Archives photo no. 80-G-57283)

A strike force of Douglas SBD-5 Dauntless aircraft approach Rabaul, New Britain on March 22 1944. Rapopo airfield is in the center, just off the foreground plane's left wing tip; Rabaul harbor can be seen in the left background (Source: National Archives photo no. 80-G-57283)

Group of Solomon Islanders at Munda August – November 1943 (Source: National Archives photo no. 80-G-205885)

Natives work for the malaria control unit on Bougainville. Their pay is the food provided by the service mess (Source: National Archives photo no. 80-G-409051

Operations Tower at Piva Fighter Strip, Bougainville, with Mt Bagano trailing a heavy plume from its volcanic crater. Marston matting, articulated metal strips hinged together and laid over the coral surface levelled by Seabrees, gives a waffle iron effect (Source: National Archives photo no. 80-G-409046)

TBFs take off from Bougainville for the February 19 1944 strike on Rabaul. Plane #126 on right (Source: National Archives photo no. 80-G-409048)

Pilot briefing conducted at ready hut at Piva Yoke, Bougainville, prior to strike on Rabaul (Source: National Archives photo no. 80-G-409032)

1,000 pound bombs on dollies ready to be wheeled out of revetment at Bougainville and loaded in the bellies of Avenger torpedo bombers (Source: National Archives photo no. 80-G-409037)

Munda – December 12, 1943
Front Row L to R: J.F. McKenna and radioman Vincent Eugene Boyle
Standing Row L to R: radioman Walter Martin Haller, radioman R.E. Schramm, radioman Alton Earl Bond, R.E. Tuck (Source: Donna Mattson [Greslie])

Piva – March 1, 1944 – Gunners of VC 38
Front Row L to R: Frank J. Dills, Benjamin W. Wright, R. A. Paul
Standing Row L to R: R.L. Perkins, D. Tye, W.G. Tyler, Lester E. Dale
(Source: Donna Mattson [Greslie])

"Follow Me" Inn - Piva – March 1, 1944
Front Row L to R: radioman Leo Ambrose Lane, radioman Leonard T. Lee, radioman W.J. Misner
Standing Row L to R: radioman Vincent Eugene Boyle, radioman Robert Petry Buis, radioman A.E. Bond, radioman Donald R Greslie (Source: Donna Mattson [Greslie])

Lt.(jg) John Leary (left) & Lt.(jg) Harry Wilson (Source: Leary Family Collection)

Lt. (jg) David Bagley –VC 38 SDB Pilot (left) and 1st Lt. Clarence O. Pylant[29] – VMTB -233 TBF Pilot (right) in front of pilot mess hall at Munda airfield – November 30 1943 (Source: Gregory Pons Collection)

Note: Maudie's Mansion was named after Lt.(jg) John Leary's wife, Maud Leary

[29] On December 3 1943, Lt. C.O. Pylant, crashed in the target area at Monoitu Mission [Bougainville]. The port wing folded while the plane was in the dive. The plane exploded and burned when it crashed. Source: VMTB 233 War Diary

Air Combat Intelligence (ACI) Tent at Piva Airfield, Bougainville 1943 (Source: Carolyn Truesdale)

Pilot's mess hall sign at Munda. Navy censored photo on right – stamped "Not to be published under any circumstance Navy Department" October 28 1943 (Source: National Archives photo no. 80-G-205946)

Mark XIII Torpedo loading into bomb bay of an Avenger
(Source: Public Domain)

2,000 pound aerial bomb loading into bomb bay of an Avenger
at Munda (Source: National Archives photo no. 80-G-56475)

Fueling TBF Planes at Munda Airfield – October 26 1943 (Source: National Archives photo no. 342-FH-3A44430-A80632AC)

Squadron Plane #101 (Bureau #06190), piloted by 1st Lt. John Bryden DeLancey and crew of Kozakewich (radioman) and Butehorn (gunner) of VMTB-233, was ditched in the water 30 miles northeast of Treasury Island on November 16 1943. Crew was picked up and returned safely to Munda Airfield.[30] (Source: National Archives photo no. 342-FH-3A44429-80632A, Munda Airfield - dated October 26 1943)

[30] Confidential TBF Operations Report, Munda Airfield, dated November 16 1943 by Captain Myron Sulzberger, USMRC, VMTB 143, Intelligence Duty Officer.

William R Larson's Aviators Flight Log Book 1943

In reply address not the signer of this letter, but Bureau of Naval Personnel, Navy Department, Washington, D. C.
Refer to No.

NAVY DEPARTMENT
BUREAU OF NAVAL PERSONNEL
WASHINGTON 25, D. C.

83169
Pers-5353a-jlr

27 September 1944

Mr. Olaf M. Larson
Hanks, North Dakota

Dear Mr. Larson:

This Bureau has received the "Aviator's Flight Log Book" containing the official record of the flights of your son, Lieutenant William R. Larson, United States Naval Reserve.

The Bureau feels sure that you will value the book and is pleased to forward it to you under separate cover, by parcel post. Please acknowledge receipt by signing copy of this letter and returning it to the Bureau in the pre-addressed envelope which is enclosed. No postage is needed.

The Navy Department joins you in respect for the memory of your son, who died in the performance of his duty and in the service of his country.

By direction of the Chief of Bureau of Personnel.

Sincerely yours,

A. C. Jacobs

A. C. JACOBS
Commander, U.S.N.R.
Director of the Dependents Welfare Division

Encls:

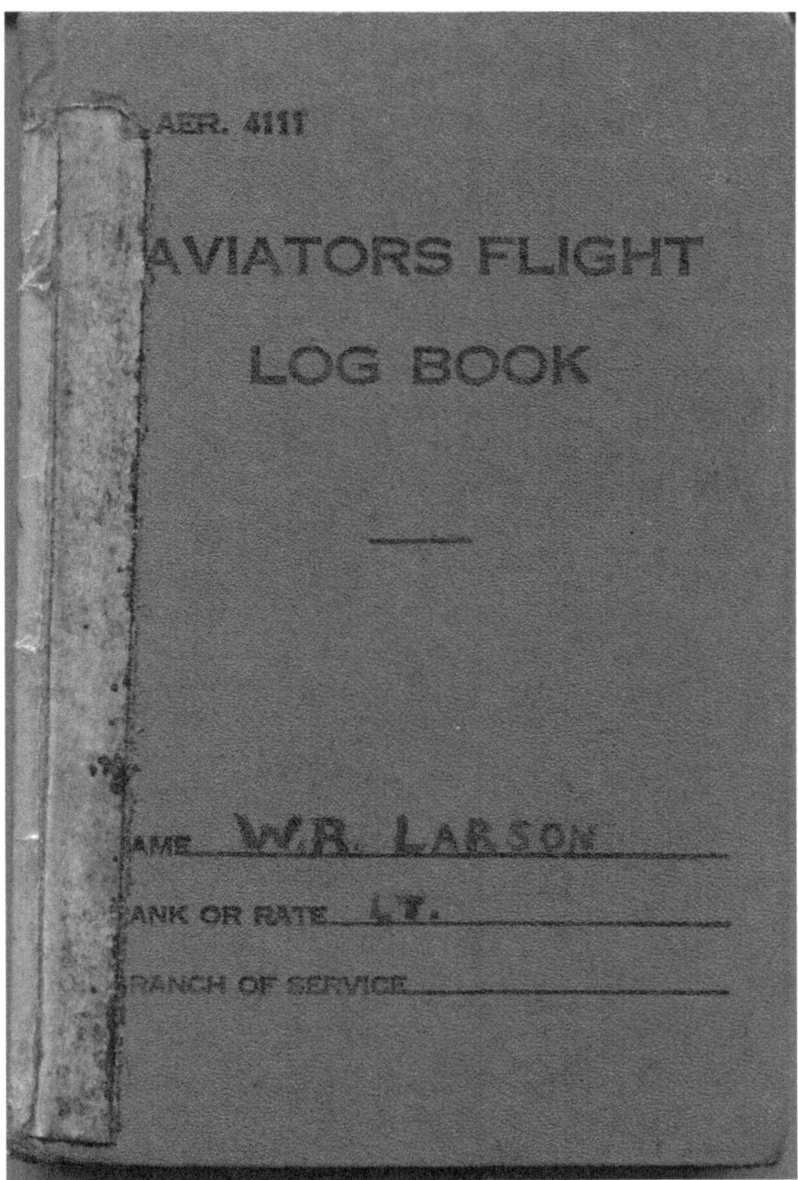

Character of Flight Codes: E = Familiarization, F = Gunnery, G = Bombing, H = Torpedo Run, J = Scouting/Anti-Sub Patrol, K = Tactical, L = Navigation, N = Ferrying, O = Utility,

JUN 1943

VGS-21 USS

	Pilot	Pass.	Total
Brt. Fwd.			1646.2
This Month			26.9
Total To Date			1673.1

I CERTIFY THAT THE FOREGOING FLIGHT RECORD IS CORRECT.

W. R. Larson Lt.

SIGNATURE RANK

Time brought forward from old log for June.

June 1943

Date	Type of Machine	Number of Machine	Duration of Flight	Character of Flight	Pilot	Passengers	Remarks
6-13-43	TBF-1	26514	.7	H.S. & Return	Larson	Lt. Marshall	North Island & Return
6-14-43	TBF-1	23959	1.2	Low Alt. G	"	[illegible]	Low Alt. Bombing
"	"	23975	1.4	K	"	[illegible]	Tactics
"	"	23958	1.4	GL G	"	[illegible]	Glide Bombing
6-15-43	"	06050	2.0	CV Rendez	"	[illegible]	Carrier Rendezvous
6-16-43	"	23937	1.2	GL G	"	[illegible]	Glide Bombing
6-18-43	"	06050	1.5	F	"	[illegible]	Gunnery
6-17-43	SNJ	6797	1.0	N	"	Lt. Marshall	El Centro to North Island
6-18-43	"	01882	1.0	N	Marshall	Lt. Larson	North Island to El Centro
6-19-43	T.B.F.1	23975	1.4	F	Larson	Jeffery, Stoney	Gunnery & Torpedo
6-21-43	T.B.F.1	23959	.7	N	"	Field members	El Centro to Otay
6-30-43	TBF	11564	1.3	F	"		T.O.W.

Total time to date,

JUN 1943

VGS-21 USS

	Pilot	Pass.	Total
Brt. Fwd.			1673.1
This Month			14.8
Total To Date			1687.9

I CERTIFY THAT THE FOREGOING FLIGHT RECORD IS CORRECT.

W. R. Larson Lt.

SIGNATURE RANK

16—15616 GPO

July 1943

Date	Type of Machine	Number of Machine	Duration of Flight	Character of Flight	Pilot	Passengers	Remarks
7-2-43	TBF1	23937	3.0	L	Larson	Tonlouse Wagner Hollingsfeld	Navigation
"	"	23959	1.3	F	"	Wagner Hollingsfeld	Gunnery
7-4-43	"	"	.9	F	"	Brando Wagner	" "
"	"	"	1.0	"	"	"	" "
7-6-43	F4F	12318	1.4	E	"	"	F.A.M. Lake Quamaca
7-6-43	TBF	23927	1.0	F	"	Tonlouse Perkins Paul	Gunnery
7-7-43	"	"	1.5	R	"	Wagner	Gunnery.
"	"	23981	1.0	K	"	Root Wagner	Tactics.
"	SNJ-3	05070	1.0	K	"	Regan	Tactics
7-8-43	TBF1	23981	1.2	R	"	Wagner Wright	S.B.A.E.
7-9-43	"	06082	.7	R	"	"	F.O.F.L.
7-10-43	"	23970	2.7	K	"	Wagner Lawrence	Tactics
"	"	"	.6	K	"	Wagner	"
7-12-43	"	23927	1.0	"	"	Mitchell Wagner	"
"	"	"	1.0	F	"	Wright Lawrence	Gunnery
7-13-43	"	58951	.2	N	"	Wagner Wright Webb	Ferry to North Island
"	"	"	1.4	H-D	"	"	Hyside Dhow
7-14-43	"	23981	1.0	K	"	Schinger Wagner	Tactics
7-15-43	"	06082	1.5	L	"	Wagner Cantrell	F.C.L.P.
7-16-43	"	24182	.6	"	"	"	" "
	Total time to date,		23	4			

July 1943

Date	Type of Machine	Number of Machine	Duration of Flight	Character of Flight	Pilot	Passengers	Remarks
7-16-43	TBF	23959	.6	L	Larson		F.C.L.P.
7-18-43	SBD	23937	.7	B	"	Wagner Cauthorne	Bombing
"	TBF	06080	1.3	"	"	Carts, Wagner	F.C.L.P.
7-19-43	"	06082	.5	O	"	Wagner Cauthorne	Utility-Towing
7-20-43	"	23937	1.2	O	"	Kent Wagner	Utility-Towing
"	"	06082	.6	O	"	Wagner Wagner Fyle	Utility Towing
"	"	06080	.7	FCL	"		Field Carrier Landing
7-21-43	"	23937	1.5	K	"	Wagner	Tactics
"	"	23959	.3	FCL	"		Field Carrier Landing
7-22-43	SBD-5	25769	1.5	E	"		Familiarization
"	TBF-1	23981	.5	FCL	"		Field Carrier Landing
7-23-43	"	23915	1.4	K	"	Wright Wagner	Coord. Attack
7-24-43	"	24180	1.5	N	"		Ferry to USS Copahee
"	"	"	.7	CL	"		& Carrier Landing USS Copahee
"	"	"	1.0	N	"		from Ship to Otay
7-26-43	SNJ-4	26952	.7	N	Marshall	H. Larson	Ferry to North Island
7-27-43	TBF1	23976	.4	N	Larson.		Ferry
7-29-43	Taylor Cub		.3	Fam	Larson		Cub Familiarization Otay Mesa, Calif.
			15	5			
	Total time to date,						

August 1943

Date	Type of Machine	Number of Machine	Duration of Flight	Character of Flight	Pilot	Passengers	Remarks
8-30-43	TBF-1	47553	.5	R	Larson	—	
8-31-43	TBF-1	47553	2.8	L	"	—	Tontouta to Espiritu Santo
					Total time to date,		

~~VCS-31~~ VC-38 USS

	Pilot	Pass.	Total
Brt. Fwd.			1726.8
This Month	Aug. 1943		3.3
Total to Date			1730.1

I CERTIFY THAT THE FOREGOING FLIGHT RECORD IS CORRECT.

W. P. Larson, Lt.
SIGNATURE RANK

SEP 1943

Date	Type of Machine	Number of Machine	Duration of Flight	Character of Flight	Pilot	Passengers	Remarks
1	TBF	23808	1.7	L	Self	Wagner.	
2	TBF	24244	1.0	L	"	Wagner Wright.	
3	TBF	23959	1.0	L	"	Wagner Wright	
3	TBF	23959	1.1	L	"	Tucks McCarthy	
6	TBF	24244	1.8	L	"	Wagner Wright	Haggerty
6	TBF	24244	1.5	L	"	Same	
8	TBF	24244	1.7	L		Same Perkins.	
8	TBF	24182	1.5	F	"	Same Haggerty	
9	TBF	24244	1.0	G	"	Wagner Perkins. Kemper	
9	TBF	24244	1.0	F	"	Wagner, [illegible], Haggerty	
10	TBF	24244	1.0	F	"	Wagner Perkins.	
13	TBF	24182	4.5	N	"	" Wright	Buttons to Cactus
15	"	24244	4.5	G	"	" "	Attack Ballale
18	"	24182	5.0	N	"	" "	To Buttons.
21	"	24244	1.2	G	"	" "	Buganich
22	"	24244	1.3	F	"	" "	
24	"	24244	2.0	J	"	" "	Anti Sub. 1 CL
27	"	24182	4.3	J	"	" "	" " 1 CL
28	"	47555	1.0	N	"	" "	To Buttons from Brenton
					Total time to date,		

OCT 1943

Date	Type of Machine	Number of Machine	Duration of Flight	Character of Flight	Pilot	Passengers	Remarks
2	TBF	24182	1.7	N	Larson	Wagner Wright	To Breton 1ck
2	"	"	2.0	K	"	" "	Att " 1ck
2	"	"	1.0	N	"	" "	To Buttons. 1 nt.
3	"	24244	1.7	N	"	" "	To Breton 1ck
3	"	23959	1.3	K	"	" "	Att. " 1ck.
3	"	"	.5	N	"	" "	To Buttons.
8	TBF	24182	3.1	N	"	" "	To Saratoga 1ck
8	"	"	.5	N	"	" "	To Breton 1ck
8	"	"	3.4	K	"	" "	Att Force 1ck
9	"	"	2.0	K	"	" "	" " 37 1ck
9	"	"	1.9	K	"	" "	" " 37-2 1ck
10	"	"	4.0	J	"	" "	Anti-sub Breton 1ck
10	"	"	.7	N	"	" "	To Buttons.
12	"	24244	2.0	K	"	" "	
13	"	29244	1.7	K	"	" "	
19	TBF-1c	24244	1.5	Ferry Bomb	"	Perkins "	Guadal to Munda
19	"	"	1.5	L	"	" "	Return to Guadal.
20	"	"	1.5	O	"	Wagner "	Ferry bombs to Munda
20	"	"	1.5	L	"	" "	Return Guadalcanal
25	TBF-1	29242	1.7	L	"	" "	Cactus to Munda
	Total time to date,		35.2				

October 1993 (cont.)

Date	Type of Machine	Number of Machine	Duration of Flight	Character of Flight	Pilot	Passengers	Remarks
10-26-93	24294	TBF-1c	3.0	Attack	Larson	Wagner - Wright	Bomb Kahili - 2000 1/10
28	TBF-1	06472	3.0	"	"	" "	Bomb Kara "
31	TBF-1c	29406	3.3	"	"	" "	Bomb Kara "
	Total time to date,						

~~VC38~~ Composite Squadron 38

	Pilot	Pass.	Total
Brt. Fwd.			1768.2
This Month			44.5
Total To Date			1812.7

November 1943

Date	Type of Machine	Number of Machine	Duration of Flight	Character of Flight	Pilot	Passengers	Remarks
11/2/43	TBF-1	06223	4.5	L	Larson	Wagner-Wright	Chasing Jap fleet with torpedo.
11/10/43	TBF/c	24265	4.0	Attack G	"	" "	Bomb Buka - 2000 inst
10	TBF-1c	24265	1.5	L	"	" "	Munda to Guadal.
11	TBF-1c	"	1.7	L	"	" "	Guadal to Munda.
14	"	"	4.5	G	"	" "	Bomb Troops Empress Augusta Bay - 12-100#s.
20	TBF-1	23981	3.5	G	"	" "	Troops in Emp. Aug. Bay - Rained out 12-100
22	TBF-1c	24334	3.1	G	"	" "	Bomb Kahili - 2000# 1/10
24	TBF-1	06455	3.8	G	"	" "	Bomb Supply Area, Tarlena, Boug. - 2000 inst

Total time to date,

~~USS~~ Composite Squadron 38

	Pilot	Pass.	Total
Brt. Fwd.			1812.7
This Month			26.6
Total To Date			1839.3

20.9

December 1943

Date	Type of Machine	Number of Machine	Duration of Flight	Character of Flight	Pilot	Passengers	Remarks
12/1/43	TBF-1	06474	3.8	G	Larson	Wagner-Wright	Bomb Kara via Chabai 4X500#
12/10/43	TBF-1c	24242	2.7	G	"	" "	Jokohina Supply & Personnel Area 2000#
12/12/43	TBF-1	23972	3.5	G	"	" "	Kieta Village (Pier) 4X500
12/13/43	TBF/c	24989	4.0	G	"	" "	Porton Gun Emplacement (Heavy) 2000#
14	F-6-F		1.2	E	"	———	"Hellcat" Familiarization. Munda Pt.
15	TBF-1	23975	1.4	O	"	Wagner-Wright	Ferry Aerial Mine, Munda to Guadalcanal
15	"	"	4.3	L	"	" "	Guadal to Espiritu Santos (Bomber #3)
			20.9				

Total time to date,

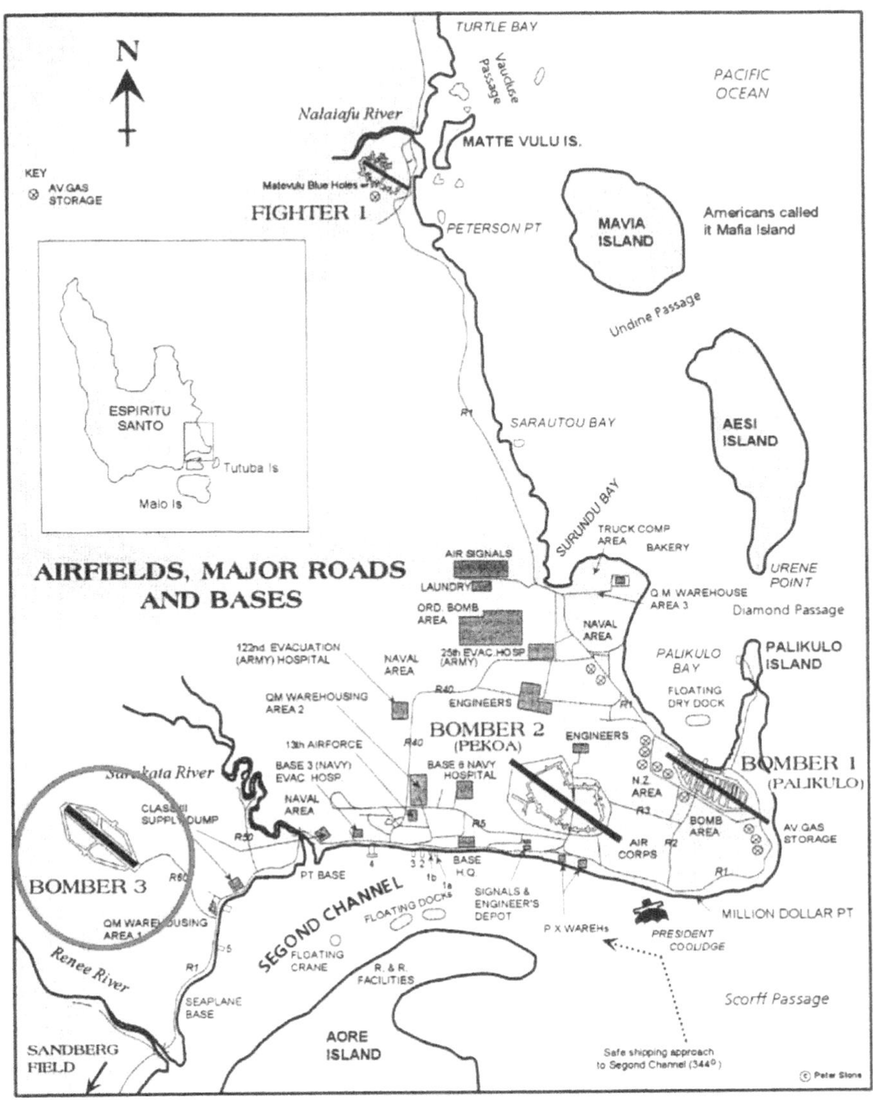

Bomber 3 Airfield - Where Lucky Landed on December 15 1943 on Rehabilitation Leave (Source: Public Domain)

Munda Airfield (Shag) 1943 (Source: Gregory Pons Collection, photo by Lt. David Bagley – VC 38 SDB pilot October thru November 1943)

Munda Airfield (Shag) October 26 1943, left to right: Squadron Plane #129, #101, #104, #116, #115, & #120 (Source: National Archives photo no. 80-G-205948)

COMSOPAC Strip Map of Bougainville – Solomon Islands (Source: Leary Family Collection)

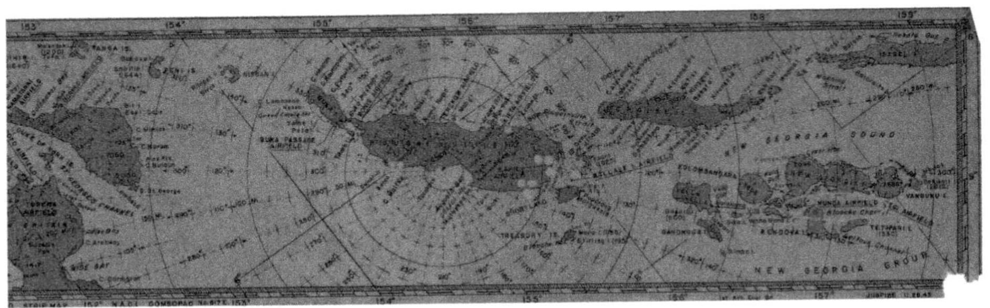

● **TBF Avenger Missions of Gunner Wright, Pilot Larson, and Radioman Wagner during September – December 1943**

APPENDIX G

The Making of *Lucky's Life*

Posting on www.pacificwrecks.com that began the discovery of my Uncle William R. Larson's full WWII story in the Pacific during 1943.

VC/VT-38 squadron

by **Wagarchgrp** » Fri Oct 28, 2011 10:56 pm

Looking for info on this squadron based at Munda and bougainville 43-44.

Wagarchgrp

Private

Posts: 3

Joined: Fri Oct 28, 2011 10:51 pm

Re: VC/VT-38 squadron

by **djltucker** » Tue Jul 16, 2013 10:31 pm

My uncle William Larson was a pilot of the TBF in Squadron VC 38 in June of 1943 who went on to fight in the Solomon Island campaign. what info are you looking for?

don Larson

Portland OREGON

USA

djltucker

Re: VC/VT-38 squadron

by **Wagarchgrp** » Sun Sep 08, 2013 11:50 pm

Don, thanks for the response, I haven't been on this site since I posted the note. My Dad was also in VT-38, and amazingly, was the radioman on your uncles plane. I have my Dad's log, and on December 15, 1943, he entered, "Left Munda for our rehabilitation in Sydney, Australia.". On December 27, his entry reads, "Mr. Larson was killed returning from Sydney. The DC he was flying in crashed after leaving New Caledonia." I have a lot of photos that he took, including one of you uncle. Would be happy to share anything I have that you might be interested in. Would be interested to know what you or your family may have that documents that unit and time, not much that I've been able to find. You can contact me at wagarchgrp@aol.com. Thanks again for the response.

Walt Wagner

Carlsbad, CA

The USS Midway in San Diego has a TBF on the hangar deck, alone with an SBD and F4.

Author and Walt Wagner, son of Lucky's radioman Richard Wagner, meeting in Portland, Oregon, November 16, 2013, to exchange photos and VC 38 information 69 years after William's disappearance.

Otay Mesa Airfield (now Brown Field Airport, San Diego CA) – June 17 1943 (above) and February 3 2014 (below)

In June of 2015, my oldest brother and namesake of Lucky, Bill Larson, Walt Wagner, and I toured to Honiara, Zipolo Habu Resort, Munda airfield, and Fatboys Resort in the Solomon Islands. We also traveled to Kokopo and Rabaul, Papua New Guinea and stayed at the Rapopo Plantation Resort, the former Japanese airfield of Rapopo. We scuba dived at all of these locations, a total of 38 dives including Japanese transport ship wrecks at Bonegi Beach (Hirokawa Maru and Kinugawa Maru), a B-17E plane wreck named "Bessie the Jap Basher", a Japanese I-1 submarine, an American P-39 Airacobra fighter, a Douglas SBD-4 Dauntless dive bomber, a Corsair fighter, a Grumman F6F-3 fighter plane of VC 38 which pilot, Lt. (jg) Richard "Dick" W. Moore, ditched at Blackett Strait, the 500 foot-long Japanese transport ship Toa Maru, a Japanese seaplane, and two Japanese Zero fighters.

The following photographs are some of the highlights from this adventure of following in the WWII footsteps of Lt. William R Larson and radioman 1st class Richard C Wagner from Henderson Field of Guadalcanal to Munda Airfield on New Georgia Island in the Solomon Islands.

Guadalcanal American Memorial - Honiara

Japanese Peace Memorial - Honiara

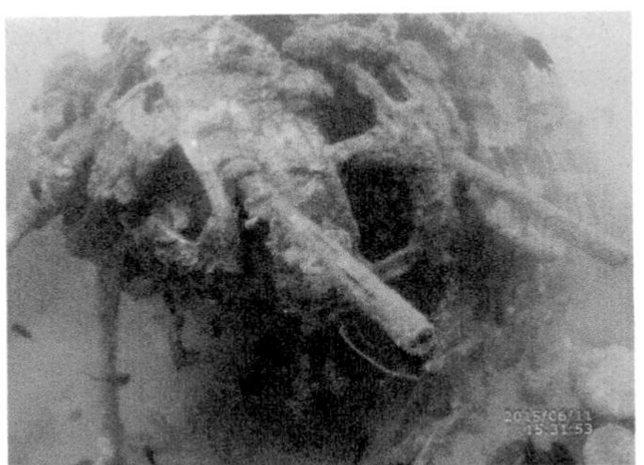

Turret Gun of B-17E "Bessie the Jap Basher"

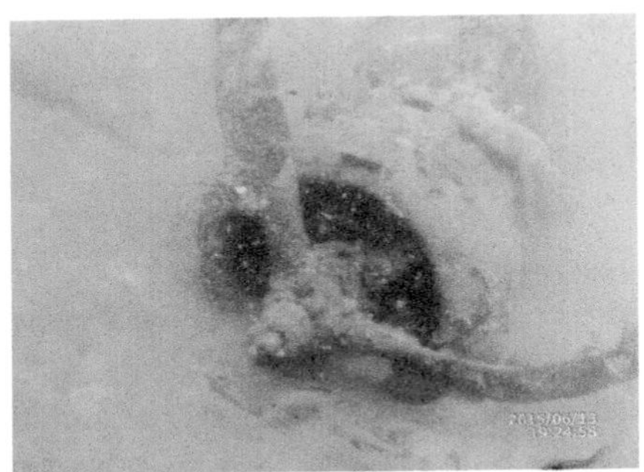

SBD-4 Dauntless Dive Bomber at Rendova Harbor

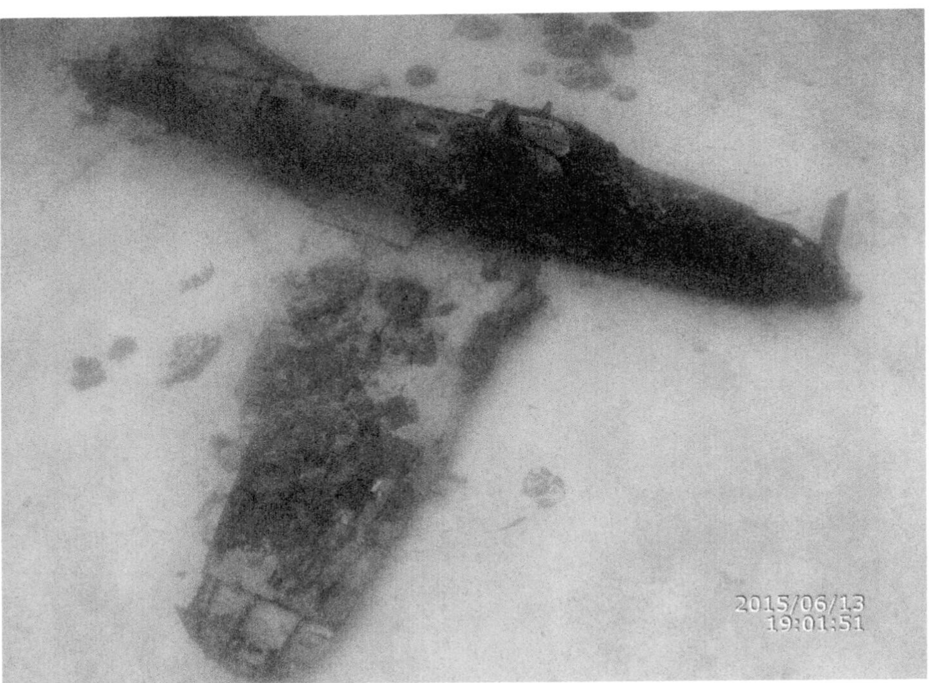

P-39 Airacobra at Munda

Airacobra Wreckage at Kohinggo Island

Solomon Island Boys at Kohinngo Island

Silent Japanese AA Guns north of Munda airfield

Corsair Fighter at Koviki Point – 170-ft Depth

Munda Airfield with Rendova Island in background

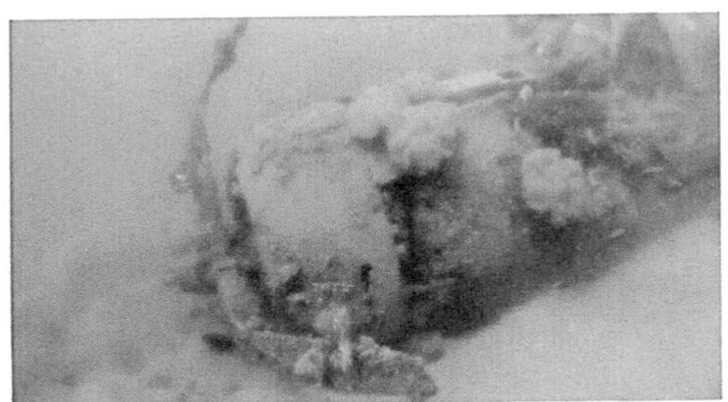
SBD-4 Dauntless (Bureau No. 10348)

Munda airfield

Stuart Tank at Kohinggo Island

Japanese Surface Gun at New Georgia Island

Don Larson, Walt Wagner, Bill Larson at Fatboys Resort - Gizo

Clown Fish at Gizo

Clown Fish at Gizo

Barney Paulsen - Proprietor, Dunde near Munda

F6F-3 Hellcat Fighter of VC 38. Pilot Lt. (jg) Richard W. Moore ditched this plane returning from a raid on Ballale Island on September 16th, 1943. Rediscovered by Danny Kennedy in 1986.

Sunrise at Fatboys Resort - Kolombangara Island in background

Soft Corals of Gizo

Bill Larson, Danny Kennedy of Dive Gizo, and author at PT109 Club

Rapopo Plantation Resort - Rabaul PNG

Japanese Barge Tunnels - Rabaul

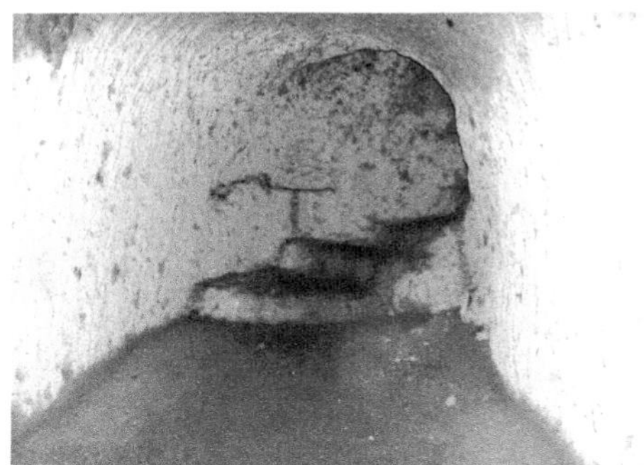

Nonga Underground Japanese Hospital - Rabaul

Japanese Zero Fighter (A6M) - Rabaul

Clown Fish at Rabaul

Simpson Harbor - Rabaul

Rabaul Sunset

Boiling River and Volcanoes of Rabaul

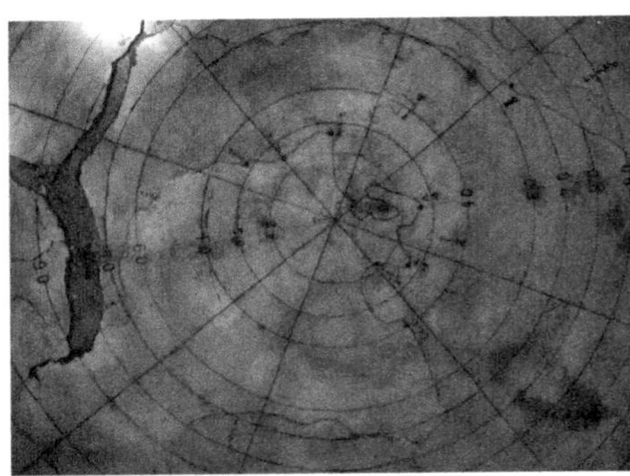

Japanese Marshal Admiral Isoroku Yamamoto's Bunker and Map Room - Rabaul. He planned the attack on Pearl Harbor from this location.

Japanese 3-man tank - Kokopo PNG

Exit of Japanese Underground Field Hospital on Kolombangara Island

Bill Larson, Walt Wagner, and author on the way home

Clown fish of Rabaul